ENGLISH WOMEN'S CLOTHING
IN THE NINETEENTH CENTURY

1874
Dinner dress of blue gros-grain and pink faille, trimmed with Valenciennes lace

ENGLISH WOMEN'S CLOTHING IN THE NINETEENTH CENTURY

A Comprehensive Guide with 1,117 Illustrations

by

C. WILLETT
CUNNINGTON

DOVER PUBLICATIONS, INC.
New York

This Dover edition, first published in 1990, is an unabridged republication of the
work originally published by Faber and Faber Ltd London, in 1937 with the title
English Women's Clothing in the Nineteenth Century (no subtitle). Ten illustrations, in
color in the original edition, are reproduced here in black and white. For reasons of
pagination two of the former color plates appear on pages other than in the original
edition.

Manufactured in the United States of America
Dover Publications, Inc., 31 East 2nd Street, Mineola, N.Y. 11501

Library of Congress Cataloging-in-Publication Data

Cunnington, C. Willett (Cecil Willett), 1878–1961.
    English women's clothing in the nineteenth century : a comprehensive guide with
1,117 illustrations / C. Willett Cunnington.
        p.   cm.
    "This Dover edition . . . is an unabridged republication of the work originally
published by Faber and Faber, Ltd., London, in 1937"—T.p. verso.
    Includes bibliographical references.
    ISBN 0-486-26323-1
    1. Costume—Great Britain—History—19th century.   I. Title.
GT737.C8   1990
391′.2′094209034—dc20   90-31248
                                                                                          CIP

PREFACE

IN a work of this nature the illustrations are necessarily an important feature. These are derived from various sources. Contemporary fashion-plates are informative, but should be accepted as being slightly diagrammatical and also as somewhat ahead of the current modes. During most of the century they were of French origin, so that they are not, by themselves, reliable guides to English fashions. I have tried to correct the balance by adding a certain number of contemporary portraits and photographs. These tend to be somewhat behind the fashions of the day and are often vague in their details. The colour-plates are from specimens in my collection which have been photographed in colour by Mr. P. Sansalvadore, to whom I am greatly indebted for the infinite trouble taken to obtain the results shown in them. *

I should like to express my best thanks to Miss Mary Gardiner for her accurate drawings from specimens in my collection, to illustrate technical details which are not usually shown in fashion-plates.

The illustrations of headgear have been drawn by my wife, basing her designs on contemporary plates. She is also responsible for the notes on that branch of the subject.

I am much obliged to the proprietors of 'The Queen', 'The Lady' and Messrs. Weldon for permission to use certain illustrations from their respective publications.

There are many others to whom my grateful thanks are due for help in preparing this book, in particular my secretary, Miss D. E. Coleman, by whose patient labours numerous imperfections have been removed and omissions repaired. By the courtesy of Messrs. Liberty & Co., Messrs. Burberry Ltd., and others, much useful information has been put at my disposal. The curators of museums throughout the country have been most kind in allowing me to examine the specimens in their charge, and many private individuals have likewise let me study their heirlooms.

But I am conscious that there is one whose claims to my gratitude are beyond all others. Characteristically she has preserved a ladylike anonymity; indeed to be publicly named would have shocked her nice standard of conduct; I will not therefore commit that outrage. But I must hint that it was she, my unnamed benefactress, who, in a material fashion, supplied not only the subject of this book, but also

*These plates are reproduced in black and white in the present edition.

the objects about which it deals. It was her personality they once adorned. They reflect not merely her impression of passing events, but in a subtle way they indicate her criticism. They are dumb witnesses against—God help him!—the man of her times, for they were moulded according to the standards he ordained. It is his ideals, therefore, which these cast clouts of hers reveal. How cunningly they display the nature of the man in concealing that of the woman! How precisely she always measured the length of his foot! It was by such weapons that the Unknown Warrior of the nineteenth century won countless victories. In admiration of her peculiar genius, then, it is surely proper to dedicate this book to the immortal memory of the Victorian Lady.

CONTENTS

———

1818
Evening dress of embroidered silk gauze; sarcenet slip

ILLUSTRATIONS

COLOURED ILLUSTRATIONS *

The photographs in colour are by Piero Sansalvadore from specimens in author's collection

COLLOTYPE ILLUSTRATIONS *

ABBREVIATIONS FOR THE COLLOTYPE ILLUSTRATIONS

G. of F.	*Gallery of Fashion*	L. Cab.	*Ladies' Cabinet*
L.P.	*Fashions of London & Paris* (Phillips)	L. & P.M.	*London & Paris Magazine of Fashions*
B.A.	*La Belle Assemblée*	J. des M.	*Journal des Modes*
C.	Author's Collection	L.T.	*Ladies' Treasury*
A.	*Akerman's Repository*	S.J.	*Sylvia's Journal*
Mus.	*Lady's Museum*	G.	*Gentlewoman*
L.M.	*Lady's Magazine*	B. & W.	*Black and White*
H.B.B.	*Heath's Book of Beauty*	H. & H.	*Hearth & Home*
W.	*World of Fashion*	L.R.	*Ladies' Realm*
N.B.M.	*Nouveau beau Monde*	Lady	*The Lady*
L.G.F.	*Ladies' Gazette of Fashion*	Gaz. of F.	*Gazette of Fashion*
Court.	*Court Magazine*	Cont. Phot.	Contemporary Photographs
	R.L.M. *Royal Ladies' Magazine*		

*All regular black-and-white halftones in the present edition.

xiii

xiv

xv

BLACK AND WHITE ILLUSTRATIONS IN THE TEXT

ABBREVIATIONS FOR THE BLACK AND WHITE ILLUSTRATIONS

C.   Drawings by Miss Mary Gardiner from the Author's Collection

H.   Drawings by Mrs. Cunnington from contemporary magazines (various)

W.   *World of Fashion*

P. & L.   From *Pictorial Times* and *Ladies' Newspaper*

L.   *Ladies' Newspaper*

L.M.I.   *La Mode Illustré*

L.T.   *Ladies' Treasury*

S.   Frontispiece of a contemporary song

Y.L.G.B. *Young Ladies of Great Britain*

E.D.M. *Englishwoman's Domestic Magazine*

V.   Various contemporary magazines

Q.   *The Queen*

G.F.   *Gazette of Fashion*

S.J.   *Sylvia's Journal*

Lady   *The Lady*

L.W.   *Lady's World*

Lib.   Catalogue of Messrs. Liberty & Co.

G.   *Gentlewoman*

Wel.   *Weldon's Home Dressmaker*

xviii

xix

CHAPTER I

INTRODUCTION

———

THE aim of this book is to describe and explain the clothing of the English Lady during the nineteenth century.

During that period the term 'lady' became progressively more and more generous in its embrace, so that ultimately it denoted not only an inheritance but an acquired status, even including some who earned their living. But always it implied a special attitude of mind, of which correct conduct was the outward expression. This was largely symbolised by her costume, the study of which, therefore, becomes for us a guide to her mentality.

It was a century in which this mental outlook changed more rapidly than in any other, but the rate of change was by no means uniform; the rate of change in fashions always corresponded. When, as in the '40's, feminine outlook seemed in a state of arrest the fashions followed suit; when, as in the '60's, the social horizon was first disturbed by the beginnings of feminine emancipation fashions changed with alarming rapidity. In fact, dissatisfaction with existing fashions has always implied a corresponding dissatisfaction with existing social conditions.

The nineteenth century affords us the best materials for the study of the theory of fashions, partly because of such changes and partly because ample material still exists. The social group comprising the 'Lady' was then, unlike previous centuries, a large one; while the group had not yet become, as to-day, unrecognisable as an entity.

It will be seen that during the greater part of the century, that is to say after the disturbing effects of the Napoleonic Wars had subsided, the design of woman's dress was governed by a principle which I have called 'Gothic'. Essentially it was the principle of disguising the shape of the body by clothing.

Art evolved new shapes for woman, or revived those which had been forgotten by the generation accustomed to the classical revelations seen during the first twenty years of the century, and gradually from having been a picture frame, the dress developed into a picture itself of which the human body was merely the invisible support. The dress and the wearer had, in a sense, exchanged functions.

This conception of dress survived, more or less, for the rest of the century and indeed after. It had this obvious merit: it gave the dress-designer limitless scope for

I

her imagination, seeing that she could assume her mannequin to have any shape she chose. When the body had almost no relation to the form of the dress physical imperfections were no great drawback. It was possible for a lady to buy as much beauty as she could afford, for she herself would be almost invisible.

She was free to adopt any form that art or fancy could suggest; at one time the Great Pyramid was her model; at another, a camel, or a wasp. The only shape that was forbidden her was that of a woman. In order to sustain the role of a Victorian Lady the art of dressing became an arduous business, extending far beyond the three or four hundred families which in the '40's comprised 'society'; the growing prosperity of the merchant class supplied an increasing number of women to whom 'dress' was a principal function in life. It became the outward symbol of social rank and the finer shades were closely observed. An elaborate ritual developed; a costume suitable for one moment of the day would be considered wholly unsuitable for another. The bonnet sufficiently gay for the Park would be flippant in church. Certain materials might be worn up to Easter, but not after; and at the close of the season there were special modes adapted for Cheltenham or Harrogate, for it seems one took the waters in subdued tones. On the other hand the sea-breezes of Brighton evoked a peculiar degree of exuberance. And always there was the haunting fear lest she should be slightly behind the fashion (and therefore dowdy) or in front of it (and therefore fast). An infinite sensitiveness was needed to preserve the balance.

Always the dress must conform to the feelings considered correct at the moment; the art of expressing grief for departed relatives was closely studied. The finer shades of mourning were a test of the Perfect Lady, the depth of whose sorrow was a matter of measurement in inches of crepe.[1]

We may marvel at the labour involved in the ceremony of dressing like a lady; we may criticise the expenditure of time, thought, and money, and perhaps shudder a little at the discomfort. But at least we must grant her the essential quality of genius: an infinite capacity for taking—and tolerating—pains.

The technical aspect of nineteenth century fashions has an interest of its own. There was, of course, the extraordinary progress made in manufactures with the advancing change from the hand-made to the ready-made article. As a result the lowering of price and the increasing output enabled women of only moderate means to follow the fashions of the day and become enmeshed by their fascination. The domination of fashion became thereby still more widespread, reaching its height in the '70's. During the last quarter of the century the march of democracy tended to make all fashions universal and therefore 'common', so that they at once lost their social significance.

The change from the hand-made to the machine-made article affected first the cotton industry in the '30's and then the woollen in the '40's. Australian wool began

---

[1] The word 'crape' was thus spelt until about 1840, when the French form 'crepe' came into general usage, the English form being reserved for the black 'crape' of mourning. Throughout this book the French form has been used, except where the English spelling appears in quoted passages.

to be imported in 1835 and the jute industry started in the '40's. Silk weaving retained its hold in Spitalfields, Macclesfield, and Coventry (famous for its ribbons), but foreign silks were increasingly used in this country, especially after the lowered duties in 1826. Eastern muslin fabrics found a serious rival in the French transparent textiles such as barège, and printed designs copied from Indian and Persian fabrics provided a cheap substitute for the original woven article. The shoe industry, on the other hand, was not disturbed by machinery until the second half of the century.

An influence which greatly affected feminine fashions from 1830 onwards was the development of railways, providing not only facilities for travel but also for the spread of new goods. The removal of the tax on papers in 1854 produced an ever-increasing number of fashion magazines at cheap prices bringing the latest modes to the knowledge of the multitude.

Fashions have never been slow in utilising new social conveniences, and the progressive improvement in domestic lighting by gas in the '40's and electric light in the '90's had their effect on the use of colours in dress. We find, too, how quickly India-rubber (in the form of 'elastic') became adopted for such articles as garters, corsets and goloshes.

The various innovations in textiles are described elsewhere in this book, together with such important inventions as chemical dyes and the sewing-machine.

A feature of dress which may more easily escape notice is the various methods of fastenings. These are, in the main, by strings, hooks and eyes, and buttons. The first was the principal method used in the first quarter of the century; from then until the middle of the century hooks and eyes were relied upon; while the '60's and '70's formed the great button era. It may be noted that the stud, as a fastening agent, was left in man's possession until the 'advanced woman' of the second half of the century started to loot the masculine wardrobe for novelties. (The enthusiastic Freudian must decide whether the theft had any symbolic significance.)

From the prices given in the annual summaries, even after allowing for the altered value of money, the impression is derived that throughout the century the average woman's wardrobe steadily increased in cost, until the economic depression of the '80's. It was almost necessary that this should have been so, for it was the distinguishing feature by which the Victorian Lady marked herself off from the social ranks beneath her. She practised the art of fine dressing with increasing difficulty until, finally, she became swamped by the rising tide of democracy.

The change is fundamental; the modern woman clothes herself; the Victorian Lady dressed.

The making of this book has entailed a good deal of research, revealing much conflicting evidence. Information has been obtained almost entirely from contemporary sources, a list of which is given; in particular from fashion magazines, books of the toilet, newspapers, illustrations and photographs, as well as memoirs and novels of the period; above all, of course, from examining actual specimens of contemporary clothing. I have been able to inspect over two thousand dresses, including some five hundred in my own collection, together with a large number of other articles of wearing apparel. It is unnecessary, perhaps, to say that the actual clothes reveal a mass of information which cannot be obtained from fashion books; especially is this the case with the early part of the century when such books were few and usually poorly illustrated. Moreover, fashion-plates, besides their exaggeration, have the disadvantage of portraying costumes in the flat; it is essential to compare them with the actual dresses which should, if possible, be seen worn. I have been able to do this with most of the specimens in my collection, learning thereby that many styles which appear grotesque in a drawing are by no means so on the living model. Flat illustrations also fail to give a sense of *texture* or 'hang'.

I have also derived a good deal of information from my collection of contemporary photographs, amounting to many hundreds. These, of course, only cover the second half of the century. They help to show how the dresses actually appeared when worn, and an analysis reveals which styles were the more popular and which were favoured by particular classes. They are invaluable as a means of checking the statements of the fashion article. Unfortunately we have nothing to rival the photograph in accuracy for the first half of the century; the portrait painter's habit of idealising and omitting inartistic details does not tend to accurate knowledge.

As regards information, the early magazines are sparing of details and omit much that we need to know. Moreover, they reveal, on careful scrutiny, a habit of borrowing from each other, sometimes with designs slightly modified so as to conceal the theft; and many of these 'fashion articles' were thinly disguised advertisements of particular dressmakers, while others were evidently supplied broadcast to English papers from a French source. The evidence of such witnesses therefore needs corroboration before it can be accepted as reliable, especially as many French fashions were by no means identical with English. A number, though advertised in the magazines, never, in fact, succeeded in crossing the Channel, while English variations certainly existed which do not appear in print.

As regards the coloured fashion-plates, it must be noted that many were crudely coloured by hand, often inaccurately and from a limited palette, so that they cannot be accepted as reliable. On the other hand the dresses themselves show remarkably little fading, especially those of the first half of the century when only vegetable dyes were used; these are therefore much more accurate indications of the colours employed.

It was not until the second half of the century that the magazines attempted to describe details of construction, such as can be learnt from the dresses themselves, or supply information as to underclothing. On the latter point, books of *The Toilet* prove useful. A certain number of dresses, etc., survive, of which the original date is known, and these are, of course, especially valuable, but curious tricks of memory may mislead the owners of ancestral costumes; even now there exist as cherished heirlooms more dresses said to have been worn at the Waterloo Ball than there were dancers on that historic occasion, and some are machine-sewn. Even museums are not infallible. . . .

We find that specimens made in provincial towns were often a couple of years behind the London fashions (especially in the days before railways), and home-made examples would carry on traditional features long after they had fallen into disuse by professional dressmakers.

This book is intended to meet the requirements of those who wish to know what was the correct costume for a given date, and also of those who wish to ascertain the date of a particular specimen. For the former the ordinary styles are described and illustrated in detail for each year; for the latter, all those small details of construction by which specimens can be dated are given whenever accurate information is obtainable. It would burden the text to give every reference for such points, but I have endeavoured to avoid making assumptions on insufficient evidence. It is not necessary to describe the mere freaks of fashion which had but a momentary vogue, or unimportant costumes such as 'Court dresses' which concerned only a very small section of the community.

The subject of women's clothing can be viewed from various aspects: the historic, the scientific, the aesthetic, and the technical. As mere 'things of beauty' antique costume has received ample attention; but with that aspect I am not greatly concerned, for a personal opinion is irrelevant to the purpose of this book. It is not very important, after all, that an author does—or does not—admire a particular style; it is unlikely that his opinion will govern the judgment of posterity. It is more important to note that almost every fashion has been admired, in its day, and that its primary object has always been not to be beautiful but 'attractive'; the mere fact that an obsolete fashion does not happen to attract the present generation would not have greatly disturbed the original wearers of it. It is well, too, to remember that the taste of to-day is always condemned to-morrow, and this is specially true of feminine fashions. Our instinctive contempt for our parents seems to extend even to their clothes, while those of our more remote ancestors, who are too far off to inspire dislike, may be allowed to possess the charm of distance.

It is more interesting to trace the *causes* of fashion, and in my book *Feminine Attitudes in the Nineteenth Century* I have discussed the psychology of the subject, giving reasons for regarding fashions in women's dress as an unconscious expression of the prevailing mental attitude. Hence changes of fashion are consequential and not vicarious. They should therefore be capable of scientific classification as are other phenomena produced by ascertainable causes.

That this is by no means a simple task is due to a variety of reasons. Contemporary descriptions lack precision; the fashion-writers with artistic—or at least commercial—enthusiasm, will invariably laud the oncoming and scorn the receding mode, than which nothing seems to them more contemptible. In their eagerness to proclaim the merits of a novelty they may overlook the fact that it is but a revival of some former vogue. Those writers of fashion articles in the nineteenth century invented a technical jargon—dressmaker's French—which was apt to change its terms and their meanings every few years, so that a standard phrase-book would rapidly become obsolete. But it is the business of one who attempts to explore those forgotten regions to acquire at least a smattering of the dressmaking dialects of the day, and to render them intelligible to modern readers. On the other hand certain obsolete terms have a flavour of their own. How much less convincing would 'long stays are entirely exploded' be in a translation! And there is no modern equivalent for 'fichu-robings', 'stomacher front' and 'imbecile sleeves'.

Dress-designers (at least in the nineteenth century) seemed to have lacked not only precision, but even perception, for they would give two names to one thing or one name to two things, and forget to describe some integral matters at all, so that the student flees from their loose verbiage to a study of the dresses themselves; they at least are not misinforming. It seems appropriate, however, that fashion articles instructing women in the technique of sex-attraction should be written in a spirit of deadly playfulness, ranging from the arch to the inane. An attempt to reduce, for the first time, this welter to order cannot hope to be completely successful. The needful elimination of 'sports' in order to elucidate the 'norm' may in one case be carried too far, and in another not far enough. Out of masses of models we have to decide which were, in fact, accepted at the time as fashionable, and this applies not only to illustrations, but to specimens in collections. And always we have to discriminate between fashions purely French and those which were accepted in this country.

To make the subject intelligible to the modern reader a good deal of simplification is required so that the types and not the individuals shall stand out. On the other hand the owner of a specimen which he is trying to date is concerned to find the type to which his example belongs; possibly there is none, for it may be a 'sport'. He needs, therefore, some information about the less usual forms which occasionally crop up. It must be admitted that certain types, much spoken of in contemporary fashion books, have apparently left no survivors; it is rare to see a specimen of the early '30's with 'fichu-robings'; there is not even an illustration existing of the 'divorce corset' of 1820. Where there are contemporary descriptions of such extinct monsters I have quoted them textually, but where our ignorance is complete I have thought it best to say so.

For those using the Annual Notes as a guide in identifying and dating specimens it may be well to emphasise that innumerable varieties of the conventional types abounded. After all, the taste of the wearer was an influencing factor, especially when every dress was made to measure. Thus, a specimen may appear to be a compromise between two nearly contemporary types as regards its details. The later of the two will give the approximate date. If the details differ by more than a year or two in their apparent date the specimen was probably home-made; if all the details seem exactly contemporary in style, the specimen may be considered to have been 'fashionable', in which case it should be possible to date it certainly within two years. At least in museums the label 'Early Victorian' (used to describe specimens from 1820 to 1860) might now be reconsidered.

The world of underclothing, in the first half of the century, is for us almost a *terra incognita*; a certain number of specimens, fortunately marked with a date by

6

their original owners, have come to light, and these in a measure help to fill the gaps. Our knowledge of these intimate matters may sometimes be enriched by the indiscretions of Gilray, Cruikshank, Heath and others, who drew in the days when artistic licence was a term liberally interpreted. And we owe a debt of gratitude to the advertisement columns of the ladies' papers, for they will betray curious secrets of the toilet. They also supply us with current prices; 'silk dresses from 30/-' is perhaps inconclusive, but 'corsets from 18 inches upwards' tells us a good deal.

The examples of prices included in the Annual Notes serve to illustrate not only the cost of clothes, but the materials in greatest demand. It should also be remembered that these trade advertisements were presumably used for articles with 'popular prices'. The most expensive are not usually proclaimed in such outspoken terms.

When considering the prices quoted in the Annual Notes it is necessary, of course, to bear in mind the current purchasing power of money. For this purpose the following figures may be taken as a guide:

The purchasing power of the £ sterling was equivalent, in terms of to-day's value—

in 1800 to £3 17s. 0d.,
in 1825 to £2 16s. 4d.,
in 1850 to £1 15s. 2d.,
in 1875 to £2 1s. 10d.,
in 1900 to £1 13s. 0d.

(For these figures I am indebted to the London School of Economics.)

It is mainly the first half of the century upon which information is scanty; during the second the enormous increase in the number of fashion magazines and papers (due, of course, to the removal of the paper duty), and the greater amount of detail given in them provides an abundance of information.

The first step in reducing the heterogeneous mass of material into order is to classify fashions. But what principle should we select for this purpose? If fashions were merely a series of accidental occurrences it would be impossible to do more than describe them *seriatim* as they chanced to appear, and any system of classification would be arbitrary and unreal. But inasmuch as fashions were symbolic expressions of the prevailing mentality of the nation (which in its turn was the outcome of ascertainable conditions, mainly economic) it is possible to subdivide the century into epochs, each characterised by a prevailing attitude of mind, and each expressing itself by a distinct mode of art.

Thus we find that the first twenty-one years were characterised by an unsentimental attitude of mind, and a taste for classical modes of art, and the fashions showed a marked emphasis on vertical lines. For our purpose we may call this the Vertical Epoch.

With a gradual return, from 1822 onwards, to the normal sentimentalism of the nation there was a return to Gothic forms of art, and in fashion an emphasis on angles and curves. From 1822 to 1864 the Gothic influence was undiluted, and angles prevailed; from 1865 until the end of the century the relation of the sexes was undergoing a profound readjustment, as women were being forced to discover other careers than marriage; the instinct of sex-attraction, being in a measure hampered by economic restrictions, showed itself unconsciously by a taste for curves in fashions.

We have, then, three epochs: the Vertical, the pure Gothic (with angles), and the debased Gothic (with curves). The table at the end of this chapter shows how each epoch can be subdivided, and indicates the mental attitude prevailing in each.

The psychological causes which I have discussed elsewhere may, of course, be disputed, but it can hardly be denied, as an historical fact, that fashions did fall into distinct epochs such as I have described and named. It cannot be disputed, for instance, that a vertical emphasis marked the fashions of the first twenty-one years, and that it then, as a universal style, vanished for nearly a century (until, in fact, after the next great war). It is impossible to suppose that this was due to chance or the vagaries of dress-designers. There have been, no doubt, minor waves of vertical taste when the 'Empire Style'—so called—had brief revivals in very much modified forms, sometimes associated with minor degrees of economic depression, sometimes—apparently—the result of political sympathy; but if we cannot with certainty discover the cause of these, we at least may note how superficial was their influence and how quickly the 'Empire' features were modified, and argue therefrom that the basic cause (whatever it may have been) could not have been a profound one. It cannot be a mere coincidence that whenever the nation grows prosperous there is always a revival of Gothic tastes in art generally and in women's dress in particular.

If it is correct that feminine fashions are unconscious reflections of the current mentality the study of the former becomes a scientific method of ascertaining the latter. Fashions, like fossils, reveal the habits of extinct beings.

One could picture an archaeologist examining, say, a dress of the '40's and deducing from its structure that the creature who once inhabited it must have been almost incapable of movement; that she could not have got in or out of it unaided, and that therefore a lady's maid was a necessity, in which case domestics must have been abundant. The shape of the dress would prove that breathing had become an atrophied function, whence he would conclude that health and circulation were poor and the extremities always cold. By logical deduction he would hypothecate the use of flannel petticoats, and arguing from these data he would assume the lower limbs to have become 'vestigial organs'. She would be classified—at least by the scientist—as a degenerate variant of the female *homo sapiens* with acquired affinities to the Crustaceae.

After all, he would not be more astray than the artist who, arguing on aesthetic grounds, exclaims that the being who wore such exquisite gowns, revealing a perfect knowledge of the laws of harmony in colour, must necessarily have possessed a polished mind, and have graced an epoch of high art.

Whereas the only safe deduction to be made from those obsolete fashions is that they must have appealed to the man of their day. They were not intended to be anything more than 'attractive'. It is, indeed, the word applied to every new mode. It is designed to *attract* the male. So-that we learn from past fashions what were the features that attracted the man of that time, and get insight into man's mentality from a study of women's clothes.

We discover, for example, that at one time he was allured by exhibitionism and at another repelled by it; that the doll-like and the dignified, the simple and the artificial, each have had their charm for him according to his scheme of life, for the average woman has always adapted herself to the standard demanded of her by man; we must suppose that a sex gifted with such elastic properties of mind and body can, in fact, have no absolute standard of taste. Even a definable shape is doubtful, and for that reason feminine fashions have always aroused man's speculative imagination. During most of the nineteenth century he was perpetually allured by the unknown. As an expert in the art of sex-attraction the woman of last century was without rival. It was a period when good dressing was the practice not of a small section of the community only, as in former centuries, but of a very large one; to the woman of the upper and middle class the subject was of vital importance; her future largely depended on her powers of sex-attraction, for during most of the century marriage was the only career available to her. It was natural, therefore, that she should have devoted all her intelligence and imagination to the task of rendering herself 'attractive'. Most of us to-day owe our existence to her success.

From the aesthetic point of view woman's dress presents three principal features, each of which in the hands of fashion can be made to dominate the picture. These are form, texture and colour.

FORM

The distinctive feature in a woman's shape is the disproportionate width of the hip-line, producing an inward slope to the legs, so that in the erect posture the outline of the body is wide at the middle and tapering towards the extremities. Such a shape imparts to the eye a sense of unbalance. Indeed, if the bias of sex-attraction could be set aside, such a shape would be unpleasing, because we have an instinctive dislike of objects that look top-heavy. Instinctively woman is conscious of this, and from the earliest times has attempted to conceal her hip-line. We are told that her first effort was by an apron of fig leaves, applied, no doubt, for that reason. Since then the main function of woman's dress has been to conceal the bad proportions of her body.

That such attempts are not merely a form of sexual protection is indicated by the methods used; in primitive states the apron-like covering is a disguise and not a protection; in civilisations where chastity has been despised, nevertheless, a garment was worn to conceal the breadth of the woman's hips. And when the skirt is worn too tight to conceal the obnoxious feature, attempts are made to reduce it by 'slimming'. From the same instinct a woman who is being photographed will un-

9

consciously slew her body sideways or stand with tilted pelvis to reduce its apparent width.

The broad hip has, of course, been admired by men, but only for its symbolism of the 'maternal' type of woman, at times when that particular type was 'attractive' to them.

In European culture the methods used to conceal or disguise the breadth of the hip have been two. Either the device of pretending that the 'waistline' is somewhere up on the thorax, so that the extra length of skirt, hanging in loose folds, entirely conceals the hips, which are therefore assumed by the spectator to be at the narrow line of the real waist; or else by widening the bottom of the skirt, which produces such a broad base-line that the hips seem by comparison narrow, especially if this optical illusion is assisted by tight-lacing to give the skirt a triangular shape. The former method is the essential feature of the 'Classical' style of dress, and the latter of the 'Gothic'.

Whereas the shape of a woman's body is composed entirely of curves, the form of her dress, from time immemorial, has been composed of a mixture of lines, angles and curves; and fashion has a way of picking out one or other of these three features and exaggerating it.

In the nineteenth century during the first twenty-one years, approximately, woman's dress was designed with a marked emphasis on *vertical* lines. This is, of course, the essential feature of the so-called 'classical style'. During the rest of the century her dress emphasised angles and curves. These are the features of the Gothic style.

These distinctive points were emphasised not only in the shape of the dress itself, but also in its accessories and the manner in which they were used.

As the Gothic period was approached a mixture of styles appeared, evolving, in the later '20's, into definite angularity of form.

At first the angular effect was indecisive and in a measure concealed by billowy materials; but essentially, the skirt was triangular; the wide shoulder line rendered the shape of the upper half of the body that of an inverted triangle; while the enormous width of the hat produced a similar result. In effect, in the dress of 1830, the outline, in spite of ballooned sleeves, was that of three superimposed triangles, the upper two being inverted.

As the Victorian Gothic movement rose to its height, the ever-growing skirt became more and more triangular, dominating the whole outline, with a pointed bodice shaped like an inverted church window of the 'Early English' period; presently the triangle shot upwards and seemed to swallow the bodice so that, from the apex of her spoon bonnet to the hem of her crinoline skirt, a woman of fashion in 1860-64 resembled a huge equilateral triangle. It would be difficult to select a geometrical figure less like that of a woman. It represented the climax of the Gothic impulse.

With its gradual decline, which can be dated from the middle '60's, the angulation of dress became steadily modified by the introduction of curves. It was a sort of 'decorated Gothic' period. Curves were, so to say, a refreshing change from the uncompromising rigidity of angles, and in the early '70's they ran riot. Every corner was smoothed over; new curves were added to a body already amply endowed with them; existing curves were exploited until a woman of fashion resembled an enormous bundle of balloons. And yet the angle was only disguised; if the outline were enclosed by straight lines the essential triangle with its wide base would have been found still present.

The singular interlude from 1876-1882, known as the 'Aesthetic Period', is discussed in the chapter on the '70's. It formed a minor and half-hearted return to the classical form without the psychological impulse needed to render it a complete expression of the vertical mode.

A more equal blend of angles and curves denoted the shape of the dress of the '80's, with, once more, a pointed bodice, and in the last decade of the century angles had recovered their charm, but instead of the old equilateral triangle a narrow isosceles was aimed at. The hips, which had become almost legendary after so long a submergence, now rose to the surface, in spite of all efforts to restrain them in stiff gored skirts.

The Gothic method of disguise, which had answered admirably in a more sedentary age, was no longer practicable. The more active woman became, the more urgent the problem of the hip-line. To the nineteenth century there seemed no solution.

Such were the changes of form of the dress which, it will be seen, always adapted itself to the artistic style in vogue at different periods throughout the century.

Although at first sight the number of types of dress seem innumerable, yet on analysis they can be reduced to a few.

1. The single garment.

The upper and lower half of the body was enclosed in a cylindrical garment from the neck to the feet. If of uniform material it was called a 'gown'. If the opening was at the back it was called a 'frock'. (It must be admitted that the exact meanings of these terms are now hopelessly confused, but during the greater part of last century there was still an effort to preserve their distinctive significance.)

2. The double garment.

Over the under-dress was worn a loose upper garment, reaching a certain length below the waist. If this upper garment was closed it was called a 'tunic'. If it was open in front and of a length to reach to the ground behind, it was called a 'robe'. (Obviously derived from a loose 'overcoat' worn originally as an outdoor covering above the dress.)

The robe admits of great elaboration; thus the upper part might be fastened across the bosom and the lower part cut away to reveal the petticoat or under-dress (a familiar form in the eighteenth century) or the front opening may be merely simulated by lines of trimming (a common form in the middle of the nineteenth century); or, again, the back of the tunic might be caught up to produce a 'bouffante' effect (such was the 'polonaise' of the '70's and '80's).

A further change in the tunic was popular in the period of curves; its upper portion above the waist disappeared and its lower portion developed into a short 'overskirt', applied separately, and open either in front or behind. The old name of 'tunic' still clung to it. We find that the simplest types of dress, namely the gown and the frock, were used equally all through the century, with trimming, etc., in keeping with the style of the day. The original tunic dress, being a 'classical' form, was confined mainly to the Vertical Epoch. The transformed 'tunic' of the '70's and '80's was only a tunic in name.

On the other hand, the robe was essentially a garment of the Gothic Epoch and the original form of it was a feature of the first or 'pure Gothic' phase. Its more fantastic form, the polonaise, belonged to the 'debased Gothic' period.

In this generalisation we are speaking only of fashions. At all times the individual might choose to wear unfashionable styles of dress, and such specimens may be found, or even seen in illustrations.

Owing to mechanical developments, and the increasing cost of labour, it was inevitable that ready-made dresses would presently be put on the market; even in the '50's there were advertised ready-made skirts 'with material for the bodice'. As long as the bodice had to be tight-fitting the ready-made article, which would fit no one exactly, was not favoured. But in the '80's the 'ready-made' for morning use, supplied the needs of the economical. It was an innovation bitterly opposed by the dressmaker, and it had but a limited range up to the end of the century. Drapers' advertisements, earlier in the century, offering dresses at so much 'the full dress' meant, of course, the dress length of material. The dresses of the first half of the century, being necessarily all hand-made, have the charm and interest inherent in hand work, and seem to possess some of the personality of the original wearers in a way that the 'ready-made' can never have, for they were made to fit the character as well as the frame. Many specimens which still survive were evidently 'home-made'; these show varying degrees of technical inability to master the intricacies of the more complicated modes. The cut of the huge sleeve of the early '30's may have been evaded altogether; in about 1850 basquins may have been attached as separate pieces instead of being cut in one piece with the bodice. Occasionally we see what was evidently an old dress of a former generation remodelled, in which case the nature of the material may be puzzling; a specimen in my collection, in the style of 1850, is of an eighteenth century figured silk, no doubt a grandmother's dress modernised. But even in the home-made article the amount of work put in is never scamped; concealed portions are as carefully sewn as the rest. There is never undue economy of material. Embroidery is laboriously perfect in its detail. The finer work began to disappear about the middle of the century when the custom of buying ready-made embroidery and trimmings was well established, but the art of the dressmaker showed no decline; indeed, the gored skirt of the '90's was, in a technical sense, a masterpiece.

The Victorian dress had of necessity to be a perfect fit, but the device of goring the material for this purpose was one never wholly congenial to the English spirit. It is true that it was introduced from time to time, as a novelty from France, but after being employed for a few years it was gladly abandoned in this country. The tendency to soften the outline of a gored bodice by added trimmings, or in the skirt to use gores at the sides only, and these concealed from view by additional drapery, as in the '80's, was doubtless instinctive. There was a Gallic touch about the definite precision which goring gave to the shape; the Englishwoman seemed to prefer a vaguer outline as more in harmony with her natural evasion of hard facts.

It is interesting to compare the three great periods of the gored skirt, the '20's, the later '60's, and the middle '90's. In each a powerful influence was dying out and a new one was seeking practical expression; the gored skirt served as a sort of stepping-stone between the old and the new. A foreign device was accepted tentatively, experimented with for a time and presently abandoned as soon as a more congenial style emerged. In the '20's the gored skirt was embarrassed by the load of heavy trimming round the bottom; when viewed on the living model in motion such a skirt tends to shackle the feet and destroy lightness of movement. In the later '60's goring enabled the bulk of the material to be shifted towards the back, thus freeing the feet in walking, but the mass behind dragged heavily until the crinolette and bustle came to the rescue. While in the '90's the gored skirt was ill-adapted to suit the growing taste for outdoor activity.

Nor was the Englishwoman ever quite successful in styles displaying solid masses of unbroken surface; it was the complaint of French critics during the Second Empire that no Englishwoman knew how to wear a crinoline; the dress always would look rumpled (as may be seen in contemporary photographs)! On the other hand we should expect, as a nation inherently romantic and sentimental, that Englishwomen would have found in the styles of the '30's and '40's modes exactly congenial to their nature, and, in fact, the dresses surviving from that time are almost all pleasing to English taste, while portraits of that period suggest a race of beauties.

TEXTURE

The texture of a dress is chiefly a matter of material, and the various materials used at different epochs will be described in the chapters dealing with them; here it is enough to remind the reader that all through the century there was a steady technical advance in the manufacture of textiles, especially in the mixing of two materials, such as cotton and wool, cotton and silk, wool and silk, and the giving of new surface values to them. We must note that the use of two different materials in one dress was an innovation of the '70's. It had, of course, been not unusual to use one material *over* another, as a trimming or separate garment.

The appearance of texture depends largely on whether a material absorbs or reflects light; until 1840 the interior of the English home, by night, depended for illumination on lamps and candles; gas was the usual form of lighting from then until the '90's; in both cases the illumination was much yellower and much dimmer than to-day. The effect was to require for evening dresses materials of the highest possible refractory power, these being silks and satins, and the colours could afford to be of a somewhat bluer tone to neutralise the yellow. The fashion for yellow, in evening dress, a feature of the '90's, may have been encouraged by the new electric light.

The pre-gas period was noted for a lavish use of metal ornaments by night; gold and silver lamé and cut steel, and, of course, precious stones as jewellery would have had their glitter considerably toned down by the poor quality of illumination. Similarly, some allowance must be made for the jewellery, feathers, etc., worn in the early years of gas lighting, permitting a degree of display which would seem intolerable in modern conditions.

A glossary of the principal materials used in the century is given at the end of the book, defining, so far as possible, their composition and appearance.

COLOUR

The general use of colours in nineteenth-century fashions is a subject of some importance.

It is not by any means easy, in all cases, to ascertain the precise tints employed; the surviving specimens may have undergone fading, while fashion-plates, especially in the earlier years, were apt to be crudely coloured, and therefore are unreliable guides. Moreover, the terms used in the fashion jargon of the day are frequently merely fantastic, or names of colours now given a somewhat different meaning. 'Terre d'Egypte', so popular in the '20's and '30's, appears to have been more red than brown, and the mid-Victorian 'Lavender' was much bluer than would be acceptable to-day; the modern eye might be puzzled to distinguish between 'London dust' and 'dust of ruins', while 'the flame of Mount Vesuvius' and 'the flame of burnt brandy' seem needlessly meticulous.

A table is appended giving a list of obsolete colour names used. Against each is given the modern equivalent as depicted in the *Dictionary of Colours* issued by the British Colour Council, with its official colour number. I gratefully acknowledge the help I have derived from that admirable work. By this means it will be easy for anyone faced by one of those obsolete colour terms to know what tint is meant.

In the fashions of last century colour was used in the following ways:

1. As an ornament, such as an intense contrasting colour applied in detail against a background of a neutral or subdued colour. This mode prevailed largely during the Vertical Epoch, when primary colours were extremely fashionable.

2. The equal distribution of two sympathetic colours; either by intricate patterns in detail (as in the '30's) or by 'shot' materials (as in the '40's); in both cases producing at a certain distance the effect of a blend of the two. This was the taste of the 'pure Gothic' period. We find in the '40's elaborate experiments with complementary colours applied as additional garments to the dress: a mixture permissible only when each forms a different layer, *e.g.* a mantle of rose-pink on a dress of apple-green, but the two would not be used on the same surface as in the dress itself.

14

3. An intense colour used as a background mass, with a subdued colour for ornament, a style gradually developing into the monochrome type of dress. Such was the principle employed during the second half of the 'pure Gothic' period from the end of the '40's till the middle of the '60's.

4. The use of two intense but harmonising colours. The rapidly increasing number of aniline dyes, following their invention in 1859, permitted a host of experiments in this direction during the later '60's and '70's.

5. The use of two or even of three intense colours, often contrasting, gave rise to the peculiar style of the '80's, being frequently employed in 'all over' masses.

In the '90's this system tended to be modified into separate masses for the upper and the lower half of the dress, and the use of a darker colour for the upper with a lighter colour for the lower. (When the wearing of a coloured spencer was in vogue, about the '20's, the skirt was white, which hardly ranked as a colour.)

Nothing in fashion changes so markedly as the popular taste in colour. A collection of specimens representing a century shows that the subject was regarded with intense interest at one period and almost with indifference at another; when exactitude of form is all-essential colour is often allowed to fend for itself; when form is elusive colour becomes the essential feature. It seems impossible for fashion to attend to both at the same time. We see how during the height of the crinoline period when form was all-important, the colours tended towards a monotonous monochrome, but in the '70's, when the billowy shape of the dress varied with every movement it was associated with an extraordinary riot of colours.

We find in the Vertical Epoch a marked taste for primary colours, which in the Gothic Epoch were considered somewhat vulgar. If we examine the books of etiquette and 'Guides to Good Taste in Dress' which appeared in such numbers all through the century, we learn from them how precise were the rules of colour in force during each epoch. We also learn that the good taste of one period was the bad taste of another. Without claiming that confident judgment which enables some writers to criticise the taste of our ancestors, we are content to draw attention to the remarkable colour sense displayed by the fashions of the '70's. A careful study of them shows that originality was shown far more in *colour* than in *form*.

In the use of colours for particular parts of the dress an intense colour would unconsciously be used for that region to which special attention was desired, either as an alternative to exaggeration of form, or even as an extra emphasis (*e.g.* sleeves of a different colour from the bodice, in order to make the latter stand out, a common practice in the '90's). Or, as a device of prudery, the intense colour may be used to emphasise some innocuous part, such as the arms; special attention drawn to an unimportant region suggests, of course, an over-consciousness of some other more vital part. In either case the localisation of intense colour to one region implies the wish, conscious or not, that the observer would kindly look this way.

It is notorious that there have been and are fashions in colours. That this is not due simply to chance is shown by the fact that a particular colour may go out of fashion for a generation and then return for no technical or economic reason. Yellow, for example, was popular during the first half of last century and then unpopular until the '90's. Its disapproval in the '70's may perhaps be gathered from a writer in that sex-ridden decade, who says: 'Red asserts a strong will and provokes observation, while green can only awaken amiable and gentle thoughts. Blue is an expression of purity and does not yet suit, or it no longer suits the time of Love.' Orange and the more aggressive yellows were regarded with disfavour; they seemed to imply a degree of animal passion which the pure ought not to possess. It may be noted that the richer tints of yellow (which suit brunettes) often figured in French fashions (*e.g.* in the '70's) without becoming popular in this country, the majority of whose women are blonde.

As a broad generalisation we may say that the colour sense of the century indicates a preference for harmony in the first two-thirds and for contrast in the last third. To say that this necessarily implies bad taste is to beg the question. We may argue with some show of reason that a taste for simple harmony in colour (or, indeed, in art generally) suggests an harmonious mental attitude; and that the growing sense of dissatisfaction evidenced by women during the last third of the century was, perhaps, responsible for the change; they were beginning to find themselves no longer in harmony with their mental environment, and they expressed mental conflict by a taste for discordant colours. To describe this as bad taste and to dismiss the art of that period as degenerate would be to misinterpret what was, in reality, a symptom of progress. Indeed, if a widespread taste for disharmonies in art is evidence of a widespread dissatisfaction with things as they are, then we may regard the periods of bad taste in our history with a certain feeling of gratitude.

THE USE OF WHITE

The use of white materials for women's clothing was remarkably prevalent all through the century, and may be attributed to various causes. As regards the dress and outer garments, that is to say the portion of the clothing intended to be seen, its widespread use in the Vertical Epoch has been noted elsewhere as inspired by the wish to produce the 'marble statue' effect of classical styles.

During the rest of the century, however, white served other purposes; it was considered specially suitable for summer-time and as a symbol of virginal purity. The preference for white dresses in hot weather might be attributed simply to a desire for coolness were it not that there have been seasons when, in spite of hot weather, white has not been fashionable. During the crinoline period, for example, an enormous surface of absolute white was felt to be too overwhelming, for white tends to increase the apparent size, just as black appears to diminish it. (Hence the use of black for mourning when the grief-stricken shrinks from observation.) The liking for white in summer is due, rather, to the wish to be conspicuous, but when enormous dresses are in vogue an apparent exaggeration in size might well be disadvantageous. The symbolic significance of white is well known and of great antiquity; we may note, however, that while a girl's first ball dress was generally white, the bridal dress was by no means invariably so. In the crinoline period, for example, a less glaring colour was not uncommon. In my collection wedding dresses of 1813, 1842, 1880, 1895 are cream-coloured; a specimen of 1871 is of grey silk, having been worn by a bride, aged 23, who was considered 'too old to wear white'. So hard was it, even in the '70's, to deserve at that mature age the white flower of a blameless life.

The use of white materials for underclothing has been described elsewhere; that its selection was symbolic rather than hygienic in origin is indicated by the fact that it was by no means accompanied by a high standard of bodily cleanliness; when the daily bath became the rule women began to adopt coloured underclothing. The excessive use of white implied that the wearer was of the leisured class who would have no occasion to exert herself, just as the masculine starched collar shows that the proud owner does not have to earn his living by the sweat of his neck.

White underclothing, therefore, indicated not only purity of the mind, but also that frequent ablutions were unnecessary. It was the growth of athleticism for women which eventually destroyed the illusion. The extreme visibility of white permitted the petticoat to be used discreetly as a provocative agent, which was abandoned only with reluctance in the present century.

THE USE OF BLACK

The use of black in women's dress calls for some comment. It served two distinct purposes, as a symbol of grief, and as a means of accentuating other colours.

For deep mourning the intensity of black is increased by giving the material a lustreless surface so that it reflects no light; this was admirably served by crape and similar fabrics. It may be mentioned that mourning dresses of the nineteenth century are now rare; it was, of course, unlucky to keep crape in the house. I have been able to find only one specimen of a widow's costume, and only one black dress of the Vertical Epoch. Half-mourning, of materials with a black pin-stripe or black and white, are fairly common.

All through the century black with a lustre surface (such as satin) was fashionable for visiting or evening toilette, except for a few years after the execution of the murderess Mrs. Manning, who was hanged in black satin. Black, as a background, tends, of course, to diminish the apparent size and helps to conceal a defective shape, so that its use would naturally appeal to the 'no longer young'. On the other hand, a black skirt with a light bodice would seem to accentuate the charms of the perfect figure, an effect equally obtained in a decolleté evening gown of black material. The fortunate possessor of pearls and diamonds was quite aware that there is no finer background for those gems than black velvet. In a word, black would be used in order to concentrate attention to some particular feature, while white would be used to emphasise the *tout ensemble*.

All through the Victorian era the 'black silk dress' was regarded as an invaluable standby, denoting respectability without undue pride, and was much used, therefore, on ceremonious occasions, in the presence of 'our betters', or death, or similar superior forces.

REVIVAL OF FASHIONS

The student of history discovers in the fashions of the nineteenth century a number of features reminiscent of former ages, and will sometimes assume that fashions repeat themselves. In reality they never do so. It should be impossible to mistake a typical costume of one period in history for that of another. But as the conditions, psychological and economic, of one period may have a resemblance to those occurring at another, so their fashions may present similar features, but each will have its distinctive marks. Even when, as in the mid-nineties, dress-designers proclaimed a revival of the 'leg-of-mutton sleeve of the '30's' they produced only a frozen commodity stiff with propriety.

Or, to go still further back, we find that after the devastating Wars of the Roses a style of costume, aptly called the 'conventual', with severe vertical lines, developed instinctively; we perceive that the spirit of that style was in many respects comparable to that of the Vertical Epoch in the nineteenth century, as we should expect; but the manner of expression in each case differed enormously. The theme was the same, but the treatment of it was in the hands of different composers.

Obviously experiences may be similar, but can never be identical, and the fashions symbolising them can therefore never be identical. For that reason it is misleading to name certain styles of dress after some former epoch, tracing them back to the limit of our historical knowledge. When we label a style as 'Tudor' it only betrays that we have not heard of the Middle Ages. The slashed sleeve, for example: are we to call it 'Spanish' as they did in the early nineteenth century, or 'German' or 'Swiss', depending on the extent of our researches? Yet it seems to have been used even in the fifteenth century. It is not so much on that account that I should prefer to call it Gothic, as that it has the spirit of the Gothic about it. It is simpler to recognise that certain features seem in keeping with classical and others with Gothic forms of art; that a feature which tends to reveal belongs to the former, and that one which tends to disguise belongs to the latter. For Gothic art is always reluctant to reveal the naked truth.

After all, it does not matter very much which nation first discovered that a woman's arm is more beautiful when it is made to resemble a leg of mutton; what does matter is that the classical age would not have believed it.

TECHNICAL INVENTIONS

From the purely technical standpoint past fashions have their interest, especially those of last century, the great age of technical improvements. Two in particular stand out, the introduction of the sewing machine, and the discovery of aniline dyes.

The sewing machine, though invented earlier, did not begin to be used by the public until early in the '50's; chain-stitch by machine may be found in dresses of 1854-55; lock-stitching some five or six years later, but for many years subsequent to that time hand-sewing was commonly employed. It is rare, however, to find a good class of dress hand-sewn after 1865.

About 1862 the first of the aniline dyes, solferino and magenta, came into use, and very rapidly from that year onwards a host of new chemical dyes were put on to the market, leading to a bewildering variety of new coloured materials. It may be noted that the dyed fabrics of that period have still retained their original hue without fading. In this relation it is interesting that Violetta Thurston, while advocating the wider use of vegetable dyes admits that 'a really fast chemical dye cannot be surpassed by any vegetable dye'. It was natural that shot textiles (woven of two differently coloured materials) became displaced by the cheaper printed fabrics, and also that a good many tints were tried which would offend the modern eye.

MATERIALS

A study of the materials used has a particular interest, hampered by the fact that numbers of fabrics are now obsolete or bore unrecognisable names. I have inserted a glossary defining as many as can be identified. The gradual decline of silk for day use marked the decline in prosperity of the leisured class, while its lavish use in the period 1840 to 1870 is significant of the rise. The most striking revolution in materials occurred in the '70's, and is discussed in the chapter on that decade. The economic condition of a class is always indicated by the cost of its clothing. We detect the insidious use of inferior materials in those parts of a dress which would be invisible to spectators, as a new device appearing in the late '70's when the *rentier* class was severely stricken; it became almost habitual in the '90's, when, in addition, scamped workmanship hidden by elaborate machine-made trimmings supplied a cheap substitute for the real thing. In the '70's began the practice of dressing silks with chemicals to increase their weight, a practice which was found at the time to produce splitting; it was not until the end of the century that the artificial dressing became so destructive that specimens only thirty years old now crumble like burnt paper. Fortunately the dresses of the early nineteenth century are more lasting.

UNDERCLOTHING

During most of the century the underclothing, although varying from epoch to epoch, displayed a persistent feature; it was curiously plain in design and material, even when immense pains were being taken over the dress. Only those portions of undergarments which were likely to be seen received any ornamentation. Thus the hem of the petticoat would be elaborately embroidered while the chemise would be entirely unadorned; and it was common for the stocking to be beautifully worked on the ankle with the rest quite plain, and silk feet with cotton tops was a subterfuge very popular in the '80's and '90's. It was not until the last

19

quarter of the century that 'artistic' underclothing was attempted in fashionable circles, a venture which gave rise to a good deal of misgiving in the bourgeois mind. As a magazine in the '90's informed its readers, 'No nice-minded lady would think of wearing expensive underclothing.' The modern notion that underclothes should be 'amusing' would have been regarded as a tactical error. They supplied an air of mystery essential to sex-attraction which the Victorian woman employed with skill.

Until the '80's it was the general rule that garments next the skin should be white, to conform with the purity of the mind; 'wool next the skin' was an old precept seldom practised by the fashionable until the end of the '70's, when woollen combinations (with, as an additional protection against chills, drawers of chamois leather) came into use. About the same time coloured vests and purple plush drawers struck a cheerful note. From the crinoline period onwards the red flannel petticoat was an outstanding landmark whenever visibility was good; the colour was not only patriotic, but an assured preventative of rheumatism.

Corsets were worn all through the century and tight lacing was the rule, except during the height of the crinoline period. It was perhaps most excessive in the '40's, the '70's and the '90's.

The bulk of underclothing considered necessary varied widely from period to period; from the thin chemise and single petticoat of the Vertical Epoch and the almost equally scanty Aesthetic Period, to the half-dozen petticoats (of which in winter two were of flannel) in the '40's; or to the less numerous but more ponderous garments of the '80's, when woollen combinations and a wadded petticoat formed a protection against winter draughts. It was natural, of course, that during the 'silk' period with expanded skirts ('40's to '60's) more underclothing was required than during the 'woollen' period following.

But all through the century there was no pretence that the underclothing worn was comfortable. The voluminous chemise, cramped into wrinkles by the tight corset: the multitude of layers surrounding the legs, with innumerable strings and buttons and hooks and tapes, were not meant for pleasure, and the cost of washing them was far from economical. Nor was that complexity of scaffolding even utilitarian in function; on the contrary; it must therefore have been adopted for some peculiar moral significance of its own. The burden of so much unprepossessing ballast was designed to check those hasty impulses which may assail the feminine mind; in that sense Victorian underclothing was admirably adapted for the purpose in view. It was not intended that such devices of a wholly private nature should be made public; men, it was hoped, would not suspect the existence of either the restraint or its need. The whole subject became a social taboo which must never be referred to lest it recalled anatomical facts, and those (as a Victorian lady so admirably expressed it) 'are not things, my dear, that we speak of; indeed we try not even to think of them'.

Underclothing was for the most part inherited from preceding centuries with the important addition of the drawers. Up to about 1800 these had been a purely masculine or children's garment, and the adoption of them by women was at first regarded as savouring of depravity, even abroad. 'Excepté les actrices les Parisiennes ne portent point de caleçon' (Mercier, 1783). The theft of masculine garments has always been considered at first fast, then fashionable, and finally common.

It is equally strange that on foundations of so dubious a nature there should have grown a veritable symbol of Victorian propriety; for such we may regard the Victorian drawers: an ever-present influence, unseen but potent, fortifying the restraint and rectitude of the epoch, and expressing in dumb show a Puritan fear of the flesh. To it we must attribute some, at least, of the moral qualities of the age, so that we may almost detect in its uncompromising features a religious force. . . . And if Victorian dress was a monument to Victorian morals, this humble garment formed, as it were, the very keystone of the arch.

Its moral progress may be gathered from a letter to her daughter by Lady Chesterfield, about 1850 (erased from subsequent editions): '. . . skirts that ended one inch above my ancles showing the vandyked or frilled edges of those comfortable garments which we have borrowed from the other sex, and which all of us wear but none of us talk about.'

That the English were pioneers of the fashion may be gathered from an unexpected source—a despatch from our ambassador in Paris on the visit of King Victor Emmanuel in 1855; Lord Cowley (vide *Memoirs*) reported that at a state reception a lady-in-waiting had the misfortune to trip over her crinoline skirt and tumble headlong in view of the Imperial party, whereupon the King exclaimed with enthusiasm to the Empress: 'I am delighted to see, Madame, that your ladies do not wear les caleçons, and that the gates of Paradise are always open.' The despatch revealing this 'secret d'Etat' was anxiously considered at a cabinet meeting in view of Il Re Galant' Uomo's approaching visit to Windsor, when Queen Victoria found his conversation 'startling in the extreme' and decorated him with —the Garter.

On the other hand, in 1859, the Hon. Eleanor Stanley, a lady-in-waiting to Queen Victoria, writes: 'I hear the last new "fast" ladies' fashion is said to be wearing "knickerbockers" ', and she describes how the Duchess of Manchester, in getting too hastily over a stile 'caught a hoop of her cage in it and went regularly head over heels lighting on her feet with her cage and whole petticoats remaining above, above her head. They say there was never such a thing seen—and the other ladies hardly knew whether to be thankful or not that a part of her underclothing consisted in a pair of scarlet tartan knickerbockers (the things Charlie shoots in)— which were revealed to the view of all the world in general and the Duc de Malakoff in particular'—whose subsequent description, 'ma chère, c'etait diabolique!' seems inadequate.

By the '60's drawers were accepted by the middle classes as a necessary adjunct to the crinoline, but they were not generally used by the lower orders until the '80's.

In a psychological sense the garment may be regarded as the most important of the Victorian wardrobe. Did it not express that Gothic instinct to conceal or at least disguise reality at all costs? Its place in the scheme of things seemed so in keeping with that guarded reticence which distinguished the Victorian lady.

Unfortunately the baser sex, perhaps in revenge for the theft from their wardrobe, discovered in it an endless source for ridicule and jest, so that the nice-minded woman would blush at the mere mention of the word. A vast literature was devoted to the subject (vide *Le Pantalon féminin*, Paris, 1906). It became a staple joke for comic papers and music-hall artists. Fashion papers shrank from exhibiting the garment except in a folded-up state. When at the close of the century the bicycle had compelled women to admit that they were to some extent bipeds, synonyms for the horrid thing were introduced, and even to-day the taboo exists, and euphemisms such as 'panties' and 'slip-ons' try to conceal the fact that a woman draws on a covering for her legs. May we ascribe her reluctance to the pricks of conscience?

ON THE USE OF GLOVES DURING THE NINETEENTH CENTURY

During most of the century gloves were almost as much an indoor accessory to the toilet as outdoor, at least among ladies of the leisured class. Out of doors, at any rate in a town, the etiquette was extremely strict. As late as the '90's a lady commented, as an extraordinary event, that 'she had seen a friend coming out of her house in London before she had finished buttoning up her gloves', and in the earlier part of the century such careless behaviour on the part of a lady would have been an act of gross indelicacy.

In the '50's, for example, we read of a young lady rebuked by her mother for having unbuttoned her gloves in church. 'But, Mama, what is one to do if one's hands perspire?' 'My love, the perfect lady does *not* perspire.' The question whether removal of the gloves in a sacred edifice was or was not quite respectful to the Almighty was still being discussed in the '70's. (See Annual Notes for 1876.)

Gloves were, of course, worn in the evening, being removed only at the table, but it is important to realise that they were also worn indoors during the day. At large house-parties ladies came down to breakfast in gloves, and we read of white kid gloves being worn during family prayers before that meal. At luncheon and tea parties, and in fact whenever there was much shaking of hands to be done, the ladies of the house usually wore gloves without bonnets or hats. A great Victorian nobleman was accustomed to go out shooting in his Blue Ribbon, and he required his housemaids to wear white kid gloves when they made his bed.

An etiquette book of the '40's states that 'gloves should always be worn out of doors and are always graceful for a lady in the house except at meals'; while a similar book some dozen years later states 'the fashion of wearing gloves indoors, or even mittens, has much died away lately'. Nevertheless, in the '60's and '70's girls were expected to do their lessons in gloves and old ladies were proud of their skill in crotcheting while wearing them.

There is, in fact, abundance of evidence that until the last twenty years of the century a lady of refinement regarded her hand as a part of her body which was not lightly to be displayed to members of the other sex. (I am indebted to a correspondent for a collection of evidence on these points.)

NOTE ON THE USE OF THE TERM 'GOTHIC'

Some explanation of the rather wide use, in this book, of the word 'Gothic' may perhaps anticipate and even disarm possible criticism. As an architectural term 'Gothic' is familiar enough, and in that limited sense Gothic architecture has been defined, by Francis Bond, as 'the art of constructing buttressed buildings'.

But, in a non-technical sense, there is an underlying spirit which may equally be found in other forms of art as well; we recognise, for example, in the period 1830 to 1850 a definite artistic movement, reaching far beyond the architecture of that time, which is called 'Victorian Gothic'. There was a certain attitude of mind which simultaneously influenced a writer like Dickens, a painter like Frith, a musician like Balfe, as well as an architect like Pugin. The spirit of the time was common to them all, and it is convenient that it should have a name, for it was also colouring the outlook of the general public as well as that of the artist. To describe this, simply, as 'romantic' is unpsychological, for while that epithet may properly be applied to the years 1822 to 1835, the period 1836 to 1849 would be more correctly described as 'sentimental'.

We need a term to denote both portions of the epoch and for this I have used the word Gothic, intending it to imply more than a mode of art (which, indeed, is but the reflection of a mental attitude). 'Gothic' denotes an ingrained habit of mind, possessed more by some races and by some individuals than others, which induces a person unconsciously to re-arrange phenomena at the expense of truth in order to produce an emotional reaction.

This habit of adjusting reality, by mental selection, entails either the drawing of a veil over some aspects or the magnification of other aspects of truth, and both imply a preference for illusion (a characteristic in which the English mind is specially rich). For that reason our nation, whenever circumstances are not too strong, is inspired to cultivate the Gothic attitude and Gothic forms of expression. We have a racial inclination to alter the appearance of reality by distortion, decoration or a discreet veiling.

The romantic mind uses its emotions to distort, and the sentimental mind uses its emotions to conceal reality. The former leans to flamboyant forms of expression, while the latter seeks shelter by 'turning all to favour and to prettiness'. The Gothic attitude may therefore be either romantic or sentimental, or indeed both.

The two are admirably illustrated by the costumes of 1830 and 1845: the former with its clamorous demand for attention at the cost of extraordinary distortion, the latter with its affectation of shrinking timidity. (Both are equally effective, of course, in alluring the male.)

During the whole of the Gothic Epoch women's fashions were largely concerned with sex-attraction, fascinating either by their audacious attack, or the apparent impregnability of defence.

It was characteristic that the romantic costume did not hesitate to take full advantage of such anatomical features as helped to exploit the dress, and it lavished its attention upon the bodice, producing a multitude of variations in design. The romantic mind has no horror of exhibitionism as such, but despises its cruder forms. The sentimental mind, however, shudders at bare facts and modestly conceals them; corsets become a virtue and ankles a sin.

Yet we find that in the ball-room the primitive urge could not be restrained, and the display of bare shoulders and bosoms was as generous in the '40's as in the '30's. Indeed, all through the Victorian era the high watermark of modesty would ebb after sunset some six inches, as though the instinctive feeling that we are then less visible still survived.

It will be observed in the ensuing chapters that various forms of ornamentation in dress design are attributed to 'Gothic' inspiration. The term is not reserved only for such ornamentations as have their origin in the Gothic architecture of the Middle Ages, but is also applied to any which serve no other purpose than to mislead the eye, distract attention from or draw undue attention to particular parts, creating thereby an illusory effect; such devices are the product of the Gothic mind, which regards it as a fundamental axiom that the body shall be subservient to the dress. It is the effect of the latter which is all-important, and such portions of the body as may be permitted to appear are but accessories. According to this notion it becomes not merely permissible but even desirable that the crude defects of Nature shall be remedied or concealed. It would be proper, therefore, to restore the bloom of the fading rose, but on no account to gild the lily. *Ars est celare artem* was the guiding principle.

It was characteristic of the Gothic Epoch in its most intense moment, at the end of the first half of the century, that the body almost entirely vanished from sight, at least by daylight. The face partly concealed by the hair, to say nothing of the bonnet and veil; the hands by the gloves which were worn even indoors; the shape of the trunk by the corsets, and the legs entirely by the long skirt: art had surpassed itself in its insistence that the shape of a Lady should have the least possible resemblance to that of a woman. It was the logical outcome of the Gothic mind.

And as we view pictures of the perfectly dressed Lady in the heyday of the Victorian era we perceive in a new light the accuracy of Francis Bond's definition—'the art of constructing buttressed buildings'.

FASHIONS AND SEX ATTRACTION

It will be observed that throughout this book I have regarded the instinct of sex-attraction as the principal motive force in feminine fashions. My reasons may be briefly stated.

Fashions are primarily designed to suit the youthful and would-be youthful woman of the day; her elders reluctantly follow her example. As soon as she has passed the age of attracting the opposite sex by her appearance fashion ignores her. It has always been the claim of a fashion that it is attractive. What, then, is the thing to be attracted but man?

A glance through any fashion article, ancient or modern, reveals the same perpetual note being struck, the insistence that a mode or device is bound to captivate or attract, fascinate, allure, provoke—or in modern jargon, excite or at least amuse. These active verbs demand an object to complete the sentence.

It is sometimes urged that women dress less to attract men than to outbid the rivals of their own sex: to display their social superiority or greater wealth or advantage in years. But are not such reasons disguised forms of sex-attraction whereby a woman seeks to prove (to her rivals) that she can attract or has attracted more successfully than they?

During most of last century the average woman depended on her powers of sex-attraction for a career; she would have been extraordinarily foolish, therefore, if she had not devoted her chief attention to the art. It is improbable that civilisation will destroy an instinct which is the chief source of human happiness, and therefore we may assume that feminine fashions will continue to provoke the susceptibilities of the male sex, while those who are too old to play will, as spectators, criticise the performers with approval or disapproval, as the case may be.

I cannot hope, of course, to convince those who regard the sex-instinct as a grave error of taste on the part of the Creator; but I am entitled to ask them to formulate an alternate hypothesis which will explain the phenomena better.

Epoch	Mode	Character	Period	Style	Social Theme	Sub-period	Sentiment
1800 to 1821	VERTICAL EPOCH	EXHIBITIONISM	1800 to 1807	PURE CLASSIC			Extreme Exhibitionism
			1808 to 1821	DEBASED CLASSIC			Modified Exhibitionism
1822 to 1899	GOTHIC EPOCH	CONCEALMENT	1822 to 1864	PURE GOTHIC ANGLES	Development of the 'Perfect Lady'	1822 to 1839	Romanticism
						1840 to 1864	Sentimentalism
			1865 to 1899	DEBASED GOTHIC CURVES	Sex Readjustment	1865 to 1881	Sex-attraction by 'dumb show'
						1882 to 1899	Prudery versus Emancipation

CHAPTER II
THE VERTICAL EPOCH

T HE preference for 'Classical' forms of art at the beginning of the nineteenth century produced in women's dress a distinctive feature lasting
some twenty-one years; namely, an exaggerated emphasis on vertical lines.
It survived, in a modified form, for some years after the classical wave had subsided in other art forms; so often is it the case that women's dress follows, rather
than leads a movement, and only reluctantly abandons the outward expression of it.
But the extreme forms of a fashion are revealed only at the height of such a movement; as soon as the mental attitude begins to change, the symbolic form at once
loses some of its energy and becomes modified.

Thus, the pure Classical form of dress distinguishes the years 1800 to 1803;
from 1804 it accepts fanciful additions; gradually the form itself becomes less
'classical', with increasing Gothic additions until at length the position is reversed;
the form becomes Gothic with Classical remnants attached.

The vertical line survives as a sort of symbol which is ceasing to have much
meaning; having sustained the nation through a period of strain its 'moral support'
is no longer required, and in the early '20's it vanishes for a century. The vertical
influence and the principles of anatomical display which govern the design of dress
all through this epoch tend to produce a superficial similarity confusing to the
modern student, who is prone to describe all specimens of this epoch as 'Empire
dresses', on account of the shape and the (relatively) high waist.

Actually the term 'Empire style' is unhistorical, at least as regards English
costume, as it appeared before and continued after the years of Napoleon's Empire
(1804-1814). It is also misleading, as it suggests a close imitation of the French
fashions, ignoring the fact that English fashions had their own distinctive features.
The extremes of nudity, the damping of the dress to produce a clinging effect, the
hair 'à la Titus', the whitened face 'à la Psyche', were but a few of the extravagances
which never crossed the Channel. The term 'Empire style', then, is better avoided
in describing English fashions of this epoch. 'Regency style' is at least historical,
though less descriptive than 'vertical'.

Our sources of information concerning Englishwomen's clothing at that time
are, unfortunately, few, inaccurate and sometimes contradictory; the 'fashion

articles' in the magazines are frequently imports from abroad, and their statements need careful scrutiny; however, by checking them with dated portraits of the period or with actual dresses of which the history is known, we can arrive at some degree of accuracy. It should be remembered that at a time when knowledge of new fashions must have travelled slowly, styles used in the provinces were probably obsolete in the capital. It is therefore not unusual to see a country dress, of which the date is known, some years behind the times in style. On the other hand, we read 'The Mail-coaches spread every kind of folly throughout Great Britain and a village Milliner and Mantua-maker regularly received the fashions from London, and dressed every creature they worked for, whatever might be their condition, exactly alike.' In trying to date a specimen the general impression is usually a safer guide than some isolated detail to which undue importance can be attached.

Particularly is this the case with the precise level of the waistline. 'Empire dresses have all high waists' is a very inaccurate summary of this epoch. Individual tastes, then as always, have to be reckoned with. It is correct to say that all through the Vertical Epoch the waistline of the dress was above the natural level, but even so it fluctuated considerably between 'very high' and a level only just above that of the true waist.

Between these limits we can distinguish three degrees which may conveniently be described as 'very high', 'medium high', and 'medium low'. In this sense 'very high' is to be understood as a level immediately below the breasts (which are usually pushed up by artificial means). 'Medium high' means a level showing a perceptible gap between it and the lower margin of the breasts (which are in the normal position). 'Medium low' is on the line of the lower ribs; it is still slightly above the true waist level.

Contemporary fashion articles are apt to mislead in using such expressions as 'waists are frightfully increased in length' (1809), when, in fact, they refer to a change from 'medium high' to 'medium low'. Still more bewildering to the reader are those confident items of news which prove later to have been only speculatory; when, for instance, we are told, in 1811, that 'the short Grecian waist is revived', we have to wait some three years before the change becomes really established. It appears that the anticipations of journalists are sometimes slow in fulfilment.

In attempting to classify this epoch into sub-divisions, it is convenient to distinguish between the form of the dress and its ornamentation. The following table affords a rough guide to the changes taking place during the epoch:

PURE CLASSICAL PERIOD

1800 to 1803. Classical Form. Greek Ornament.
1804 to 1807. Classical Form. Egyptian and Etruscan Ornament.

DEBASED CLASSICAL PERIOD

1808 to 1810. Classical Form. Spanish Ornament.
1811 to 1813. Debased Classical Form. Slight Gothic Ornament.
1814 to 1817. Debased Classical Form. Increasing Gothic Ornament.
1818 to 1821. Diminishing Classical Form. Increasing Gothic Form. Increasing Gothic Ornament.

One observes the gradual change from the Classical to the Gothic at first in ornament (the vandyking, gores, puffed hem, flounces, etc.) and later in form (the increasing width of the bottom of the skirt and the narrowing of the waist producing angulation).

In the middle years of the epoch the two irreconcilable modes of artistic expression are, somehow, reconciled, the Classical governing the essential shape, the Gothic its ornamentation; gradually the Classical loses its grip and the native Gothic more and more assumes command, until, as we shall see in a later chapter, the situation is reversed and we are presented (in the middle '20's) with a Gothic design having occasional Classical ornaments oddly inserted.

Throughout the epoch the vertical line is emphasised by the device of the high waist, producing a disproportionately long skirt which is narrow, either hanging in loose folds (1800-1803) or in stiff tubular form, while transverse lines are suppressed or at least minimised and angular effects are avoided. Accessories such as scarves are narrow and hang vertically, while sleeves, if present, are moulded to the arms.

Moreover, the Classical principle, that the dress should reveal the beauty of the body, is strictly sustained. Hence the paucity of underclothing and the taste for dress materials of a thin transparent nature.

'While expensive silks were worn they could not be attained by persons of small means, but when a few shillings could purchase a Muslin gown quite in the fashion every woman could command one. . . . Farmer's daughters came to market in white stockings and slippers, and sat on a sofa to receive company in silver turbans and elegant muslins. The lowest maidservant refused to wear *Pattens* and never went out without an umbrella. A pair of black worsted stockings was only to be found in—the Poor House.' (Written retrospectively in 1818.)

In addition there are efforts, especially at the beginning of the epoch, in the direction of nudity. ('When the first engravings of the Grecian costume—as nudity was called—were brought to England, they shocked every modest woman; and it was not thought proper to look at them in the presence of gentlemen; *how this delicacy wore away and how soon* is truly surprising, but certain it is that e'er many months had elapsed, originals exactly representing the Prints, were seen in every public place.') Sometimes a substantial area of the back is exposed, sometimes of the bosom, and always the shape of the breasts is emphasised, either by their being pushed up into prominence by mechanical means, or by the lightest of coverings. The arms, even in the day, are often bare to the shoulder. On the other hand, the legs are never exposed, but their outline indicated by the clinging material of the dress.

The 'classical statue' effect aimed at chiefly in the beginning of the epoch is accentuated by the preference for white muslins, to suggest a resemblance to marble. This (and the high cost of silks during the war) explains their relative abundance amongst those specimens of the Vertical Epoch which still survive. In my own collection out of some fifty dresses and pelisses of this epoch, half are pure white or have white grounds.

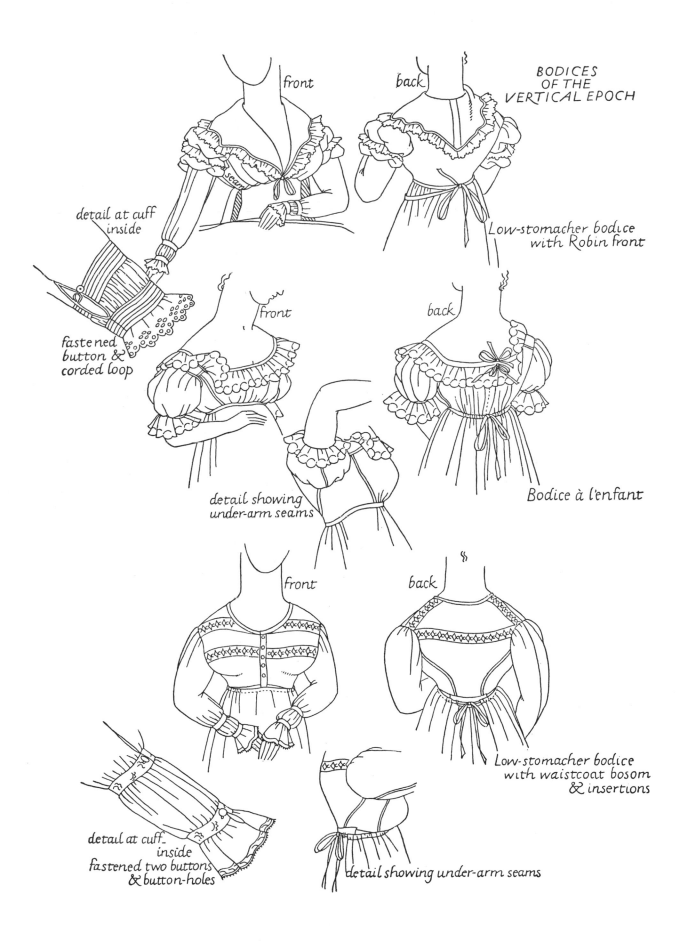

front back

BODICES
OF THE
VERTICAL EPOCH

detail at cuff
inside

Low-stomacher bodice
with Robin front

fastened
button &
corded loop

front back

detail showing
under-arm seams

Bodice à l'enfant

front back

Low-stomacher bodice
with waistcoat bosom
& insertions

detail at cuff
inside
fastened two buttons
& button-holes

detail showing under-arm seams

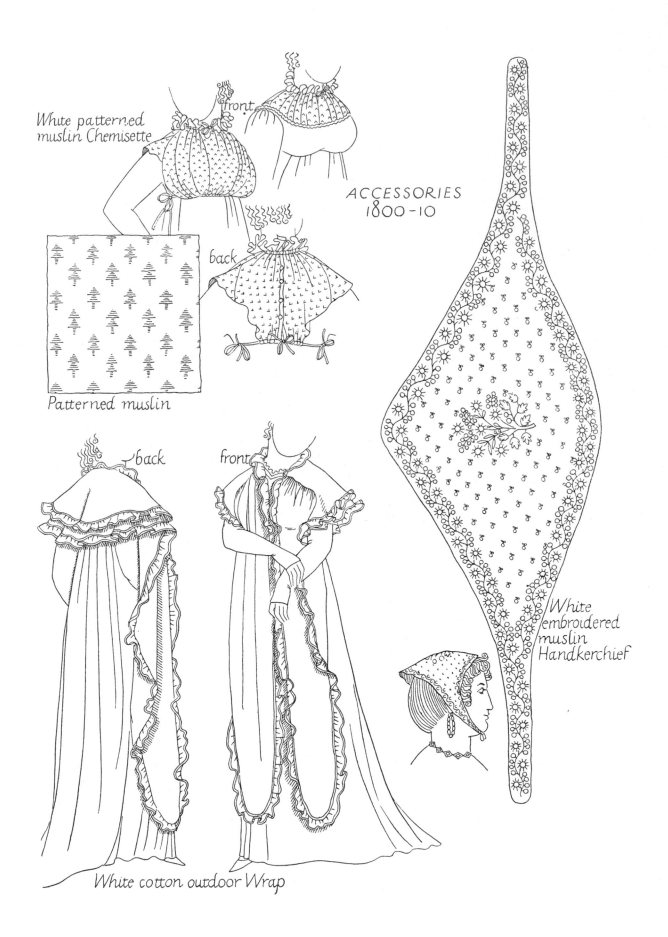

White patterned
muslin Chemisette

front

back

Patterned muslin

ACCESSORIES
1800-10

back

front

White cotton outdoor Wrap

White
embroidered
muslin
Handkerchief

The general effect of a woman's dress was one of studied simplicity. It aimed at drawing a transparent veil over the allurements of anatomy, and charmed by revealing everything it concealed.

The supposition that such a style was but a reaction from one more artificial and a praiseworthy approach to naturalism is belied by the fact that it was, in its way, highly artificial and unnatural. As though woman's dress has ever been otherwise!

As a contrast to the dress the headgear, all through the epoch, was arresting in shape and colour. Indeed, during the first ten years of the century when, as was said in 1806, 'a lady is not considered fashionable if she appears two successive days in the same bonnet', the variety of design was incredible. Almost every form of hat or bonnet subsequently worn by women had its prototype in that decade. They were of all sizes and shapes, and worn at all angles; they seem to betray every mood except, perhaps, the demure. It was a time when the face clamoured for attention.

Although the Napoleonic Wars lasted till 1814 (the subsequent Waterloo campaign being too brief to affect the mentality of the nation), we must not forget that the extreme nervous tension had been enormously relieved by the victory of Trafalgar (1805), and the advance in the Peninsular (1809-10); psychologically the sense of fear had passed and the innate Gothic impulses of our nation, apt to be suspended in times of profound anxiety, began to reassert themselves. Types of decoration dear to the Gothic mind became increasingly applied to a dress still classical in form. The skirt must needs be edged with narrow flounces engagingly pinked or scalloped. The narrow waistband becomes an ornamental sash; the marble white muslin is warmed by a coloured slip; its plain surface decorated by lines of rollio, coloured patterns, ornamental buttons, Brandeburgs, or by sleeves of a different material. The Gothic angle insinuated itself in the form of 'vandyking' almost from the beginning, a feature becoming more aggressive from 1807 onwards. In effect, instead of a marble statue we are given a coloured picture, in which the details matter more than the mass.

Towards the close of the epoch more and more is attention drawn to the bodice of the dress (always an indication of a reviving 'romantic' spirit). The shoulder line expands; the upper sleeve dilates; the waist is more constricted, while the width of the skirt increases. The Classical form is becoming Gothic. All through the epoch, in fact, there is a perceptible inspiration at work gradually effecting a transformation from one antithesis of style to another. It is unfortunate that we cannot avoid the use of such terms as 'epoch' and 'period', which convey the impression of a stationary phase, when in reality there is constant progression.

During this epoch the following types of dress were the usual ones worn:

1. The Tunic Dress: essentially for evening. It consisted of an under-dress, which was either round or trained, over which was worn a tunic, hanging loose from the shoulders and extending either to just below the waist or nearly to the ankles. The short tunic was rare after 1812; the long tunic rare before that date.

The tunic might be round or shaped, sloping away at the sides to a deeper

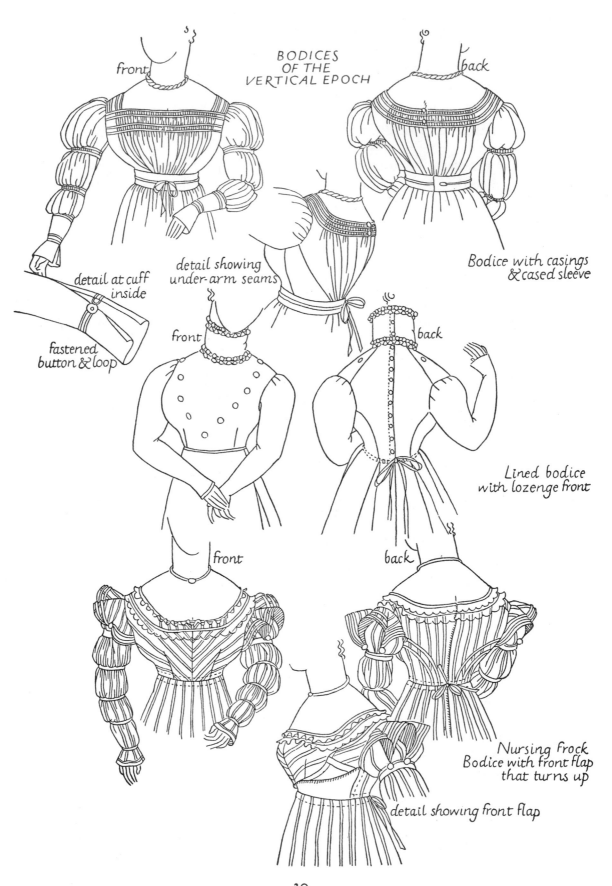

BODICES
OF THE
VERTICAL EPOCH

front

back

detail at cuff
inside

fastened
button & loop

detail showing
under-arm seams

Bodice with casings
& cased sleeve

front

back

Lined bodice
with lozenge front

front

back

Nursing frock
Bodice with front flap
that turns up

detail showing front flap

point at the back, or cut in points at the sides or at intervals round the body. Sometimes it was open in front with or without loose fastenings.

2. The Frock: that is to say, a dress with bodice and skirt in one, the bodice fastening behind by buttons or strings, or, at the close of the epoch, by hooks and eyes.

Of the frock there were various kinds:

(*a*) The plain high front with narrow or wide shoulder strap; the back being high or low, and with or without attached collar. For day use.

(*b*) The plain low front, worn with or without a tucker or a habit-shirt above its upper margin. The front may be shaped into a 'V' or square. For day or evening use.

(*c*) The ornamented bodice, *e.g.* with insertions or embroidery sometimes called 'French work' let into the front; or the 'lozenge-front' with strips of net and satin let in, slant-wise, forming a 'V' pattern. For day use.

(*d*) The bodice à l'enfant, the top of which is threaded with a string, en coulisse, which when drawn produces the effect of gathering. For day and evening use.

(*e*) The bodice en cœur.

(*f*) The 'cased body', or 'the body with casings'; a term denoting a series of transverse pleatings or gaugings running across the front.

White cotton buttons: white cotton button-holing & french-knots.

front

inside back showing padded bustle.

CONSTRUCTION OF HIGH STOMACHER DRESS 1803-4

front open

White hailstone muslin.

back

seam

3. The 'stomacher front': occurring in both the untrained round dress and also in the trained gown. This appears to have been the only method of front opening used in the Vertical Epoch until the separate bodice and skirt was introduced.

31

There are two types of stomacher front:

(*a*) The high stomacher, for day use. The upper third of the skirt is split down the sides to the placket holes, thus forming an inverted flap; to this flap is fastened the front of the bodice, which, after the dress is put on, is then pinned or buttoned up to the shoulder level. A drawstring threaded through the flap at the waist is tied behind. Frequently there are, in addition, side pieces to the bodice which pin across the bosom beneath the stomacher.

(*b*) The low stomacher. Here the flap does not include a portion of the bodice, but is tied round the waist by a string threaded en coulisse. With this type the bodice is closed across the bosom by various methods:

(i) The 'wrapping front', for day or evening. The sides of the bodice fasten in the cross-over fashion; if the front was cut to form a deep 'V' almost to the waist-line, with flat pleats or trimmings descending from the shoulders to meet at the waist, it was known as the 'robin front'.

(ii) The 'cottage front', for day use. Here the sides of the bodice do not meet, but are laced across the bosom over a habit-shirt.

(iii) The 'waistcoat bosom', for day use, the bodice being buttoned down the middle.

4. The Robe: a Gothic type of dress occasionally found in this epoch, when it denoted a trained evening dress open in front over a petticoat; a term frequently used to mean also any trained evening gown.

It may be added that the separate 'bodice and skirt' type of dress does not appear before 1818, when a front fastening bodice over a skirt fastening behind, and frequently of different materials and colours, begins to be used. It was a logical development from the use of a coloured spencer over a white dress.

The construction of these dresses of the Vertical Epoch calls for some further description. The skirt is drawn into the waist by small gathers all round; when the strength of the material permits the skirt is gathered direct on to the bodice or on to its lining; with flimsy materials a waistband, as narrow as possible, is used, except towards the end of the epoch when the band may be as wide as an inch. In the first two or three years of the epoch the skirt is often pleated on each side of the waist, the gathering being confined to the back.

From 1815 onwards the skirt is often gored at the sides, with the fullness carried to the back, where it is closely gathered. The skirt is always unlined; the hem narrow at the beginning and deeper at the end of the epoch.

In the stomacher front type of dress the back of the bodice has characteristic features. It is composed of a central piece, pentagonal in shape, with the corners squared off forming an octagon; it is often surprisingly narrow, the sleeves being set into its sides so as, in fact, to cover a portion of the back of the wearer. All through the epoch the bodice is frequently lined with a cotton material. The lining will be found to extend into the upper part of the sleeve.

Inside the dress, attached to the back of the waist, a small *bustle* may often be found, either a minute roll or pad some three inches wide, in specimens from the

1800. Morning dresses
Round Gown: yellow spotted muslin; epaulettes white muslin; union hat
Petticoat plain muslin, jacket of same: short sleeves, gauze veil fastened as mantle
Round Gown: fine muslin; bag bonnet, striped sarcenet
Round Gown of figured muslin; pink handkerchief across breast

1801. Evening dresses
Robe of Salisbury drugget, petticoat of white muslin trimmed with gold lace
Robe of black velvet, trimmed with gold lace, high tucker trimmed with lace;
petticoat of white muslin

beginning of the epoch; or a long sausage-shaped roll in specimens from 1813 onwards. With its increase in size the bustle after 1815 is no longer attached to the dress.

The usual form of button is of hand-made linen thread worked diagonally across a wire ring, a kind used as late as the early '30's. Sanders, of Birmingham, however, invented in 1802 the 'covered button', consisting of two discs of metal and one of millboard, the neck being japanned and the hollow between it and the shell filled with millboard. Later his son invented a button with a canvas tuft in place of the metal shank.

The alternative to the button was strings, en coulisse, the usual method of fastening the backs of silk or satin dresses (hence the term 'drawn back'), whereas buttons were used only for cotton or muslin.

Small brooches were frequently employed for attaching the flaps of a stomacher front, the shoulder points of a tunic, or the scarf, etc.

Hooks and eyes, hand-made of flattened copper sometimes tinned over, appeared about 1814.

Gilt barrel-snaps, for fastening cloaks and pelisses, appear about 1810, and were used for the next twenty years.

Pins with heads hammered round the shank were in use until about 1840.

NOTE: 'Nursing Dress.' A curious variation of the high stomacher front dress is occasionally found, in which the back of the bodice only is attached to the skirt, the side seams are left unjoined, and the front is tied down over the skirt by means of a drawstring. The flap thus formed could be easily turned up for nursing purposes. A specimen of this is in my collection. (See advertisement, 1814. 'New invented dress for Ladies who nurse their own children. It enables Ladies to nourish their infants in the most delicate manner possible, when full dressed.')

Table summarising fashions of the Vertical Epoch:

PURE CLASSICAL PERIOD 1800 to 1807

1800 to 1803. *Pure Classical form. Greek ornament*

1800 to 1802. Medium low waist. Trains. Loose skirts. Greek decorations. Colours white or monochrome, especially primary colours.

1803.   Waist medium high. Often tucks or single flounce. Colours white or two colours.

1804 to 1807. *Pure Classical form. Egyptian and Etruscan ornament.* *Bare backs and bosoms a marked feature*

1804. Waist medium high. Tubular skirt. Dresses plain.

1805. Waist medium high. Square necks. Trains.

1806. Waist medium high. High split collars. Embroidered hems.

1807. Waist medium high. Gored skirt, often vandyked. Very low evening dresses.

DEBASED CLASSICAL PERIOD 1808 to 1821

1808 to 1810. *Classical form. Spanish ornament*

1808. Waist medium high. Shaped bodice ('made with French gores'), cut very low.

1809. Waist medium high. Scalloped and vandyked hems.

1810. Waist medium low. 'Worked' bodice and sleeves.

1811 to 1813. *Debased Classical form. Slight Gothic ornament*

1811. Waist medium low. Shorter skirts. Still square necks. Fuller sleeves.

1812. Waist medium low. No trains. Tucks. Embroidery. Gothic decorations.

1813. Waist medium low. No square necks. Fuller sleeves. Vandyking.

1814 to 1817. *Debased Classical form with increasing Gothic ornament*

1814. Waist medium high. Short skirts. Several narrow flounces. Scalloping and vandyking. Coloured slips.

1815. Waist very high. Very short gored skirt. Two or three deep flounces. 'V' necks. Wider sleeves.

1816. Waist very high. Vandyked and scalloped hem, and festoons of flowers.

1817. Waist very high. Fuller shoulders. Puffing above the hem. One deep flounce. Mixture of colours.

1818 to 1821. *Classical form diminishing. Gothic form as well as ornament increasing*

1818. Waist very high. Fuller skirt. Satin rouleaux above hem; (evening) satin bodice with gauze skirt. Multiple flounces, scalloped or vandyked.

1819. Waist very high. Flounces or tucks up to the knees.

1820. Waist medium low. Puffed shoulders. Skirt elaborately trimmed with puffing, blonde lace, etc.

1821. Waist medium low. Round bodices. Capes. Excess of blonde lace. Skirt with two or three rouleaux. Mixed colours.

OUTER GARMENTS

The Pelisse

An outdoor garment, sleeved or with armholes only, of any material, to be worn over the dress. It differed from a coat in that it had no lapels. The name originally indicated a garment of fur (cp. pelt, a skin). It was sometimes without fastenings; sometimes made to button across the bosom; sometimes to button all down the front. Tapes were attached at the back inside, to tie round the waist. It was used all through the Vertical Epoch, developing in 1817 into the pelisse-robe.

Materials: kerseymere, shot silk, velvet, muslin (plain, printed or painted), satin, merino, cashmere, nankeen, twilled cotton, sarcenet, plush.

In the first ten years of the epoch the pelisse was generally short, demi or three-quarter length; in the later part of the epoch always ankle-length.

PELISSES

White spotted India muslin
c.1805

Pink China crêpe: cream coloured
cord trimming _ c.1816

White cotton _ 1820's

Pelisse Robe of
fine white piqué:
white muslin trimming
c.1826

open to
this button

35

Drab coloured Bath coating:
satin trimming to match
c.1805

Lilac satin c.1806

Princess Charlotte of Wales Body:
cream coloured satin & cord
to match — 1813

Rose & cream coloured satin:
cream coloured cord trimming
c.1815

Cream coloured striped satin
c.1815

Cream coloured broché silk.
satin piping & cord
trimming to match
c.1817

36

The summer pelisse was unlined; the winter pelisse lined (*e.g.* 'black velvet pelisse lined with pink plush', 1821).

Both in the early and later years it was sometimes cut away in front so as to slope off at the sides in the form of a robe; an odd variation was the Donnilette, in which the bodice was open revealing a fichu, while the skirt was buttoned down the front (1818). Another type was the wrapping pelisse, voluminous enough to wrap across the body (1809 to 1819).

In the main the pelisse followed the various changes shown in the dress in its cut and ornamentation. Eventually, by being closely buttoned down the front, it developed into a new type of dress, the 'pelisse-robe', and its later variation, the 'redingote'.

Various forms of pelisse are given in the Annual Notes.

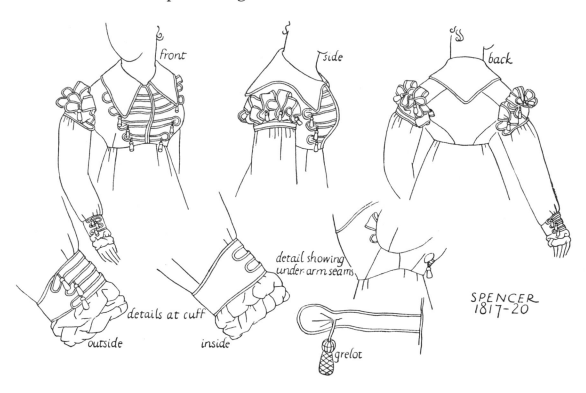

The Spencer

A short jacket worn over the dress, generally as an outdoor garment, especially in summer as a substitute for the pelisse; occasionally as an indoor ornamental garment for evening use. At the beginning of the epoch it was sometimes sleeveless. Until 1804 it descended below the waistline, but subsequently it terminated at the waistline and was cut round.

The spencer fastened up the front to the neck, which was sometimes made with an open 'V', sometimes with a closed high collar.

Like the pelisse it acquired the marks of passing fashions, and eventually in the early '20's it merged into the 'Fichu-Spencer' and then into the 'Canezou'.

It was essentially a garment to go with the high-waisted dress, and when the waist-line finally descended the spencer fell into disuse; its decorative effect was to emphasise the height of the waist-line.

Materials: muslin, lace, sarcenet, velvet, kerseymere, cloth, various silks and satin.

The Cloak

A sleeveless outer garment, loose fitting and usually of three-quarter or full length.

NOTE: The mantle is less full and slightly more shaped than the cloak, but the terms are used without much discrimination.

The Shawl

The shawls of this epoch were, approximately, one yard square.

ANNUAL SUMMARY OF FASHIONS

1800

DRESSES

Trained or round. Medium low waist.

Day
Types: wrapping front, stomacher front, dress à l'enfant or en cœur. Cord and tassel round waist. With high neck a chemise tucker (or habit-shirt), or neck handkerchief, passing round the shoulders, loosely crossing the bosom and tied round the waist at the back. Sleeves long, or elbow length with short over-sleeve, or long 'with full tops'.
Materials: muslin (white, sprigged or coloured), sarcenet, cambric.

Evening
Types: tunic dress, or robe, with 'V' or round neck. Often a 'velvet corset body'. Shoulder sleeves, puffed. 'Afternoon dresses' are of the semi-evening type, with hair full dressed, diamond necklace, fan, etc. Often a muslin apron descending below the knees and tied behind with silver cords and tassels. 'Queen Elizabeth' ruff of point lace round the neck.
Materials: generally muslins, white or yellow.

OUTDOOR GARMENTS

Spencer-Jackets coming below waist, with or without sleeves. 'Spencer of black lace, sleeveless, with open net work on the back seams.'

Pelisses
Three-quarter or full length. 'Pelisse of purple or shot silk, lined, trained and full length.'

Cloaks
Grecian cloaks fastened at left shoulder; in summer an embroidered veil fastened at the shoulders as a mantle. Three-quarter mantle with ruff collar. Black velvet cloaks trimmed with black lace, very low in front and short behind. Scarlet kerseymere cloaks. Short wadded *Coats* of sarcenet.

ACCESSORIES

Shoes
Day. Flat and pointed, of leather matching the colour of dress trimming. 'Half *Boots* up to the knee of cordovan leather which draw on by means of boot hooks are worn by many females of dashing ton.' 'The Comforts or double soled sandals' very general. Evening shoes of satin.

Stockings
of cotton or silk, generally white. 'The Obi stocking and slipper of a dark mulatto colour, much worn.'

Gloves
Long, worn well above the elbow. York tan or coloured to match the dress (blue, pink, yellow, etc.), white silk, net.

Lozenge-shaped *Ridicules*. *Fans* large. Much *Jewellery*: gold, coral, cornelians, as bracelets, necklaces and ear-rings.

Prices
'Full head-dresses, made of long hair, judiciously matched, 4 to 20 guineas. Real natural curl head-dresses; these cannot be described; they must be seen, 5 guineas. The Tresse à la

1802

Two evening dresses of sprigged muslin; buffonts of lace
over the bosom

Day dress of lilac silk with white satin sleeves,
edged with lace

Morning dress of cambric muslin with ruff

Walking dress of white muslin; white lace veil

1803. Full evening dresses
Short tunic of white crepe over white sarcenet
Patent net worked with gold; narrow lace tucker

1804. Promenade dresses
Morning dress of fine cambric, trained
Round dress of white muslin

grecque to be put over the short head-dress, half to five guineas.' Velvets for spencers, 7/- a yard. Gloves, 1/- a pair. Silk handkerchiefs, yard wide, 4/-.

1801

DRESSES

Morning

The bodice half-high and round at the neck, or en cœur with a lace edging, or with a shallow 'V' and an edging of ribbon. The skirt always trained. A coloured ribbon round the waist and tied in front. Sleeves short or long, with or without epaulettes.

Materials: muslin, plain or sprigged.

In her *Memoirs* Susan Sibbald describes her Curricle dress (1801-2) as 'a short open garment showing the petticoat in front, which was trimmed in the same way as the dress with short sleeves, the body open and low showing an embroidered French habit-shirt . . . worn in the forenoon; the afternoon or evening dress the same but of thin plain or figured muslin, the petticoat of silk or satin'.

Evening

Usually gowns or robes, *e.g.* a petticoat of white muslin trimmed with lace, over which is worn a sleeveless trained robe, with the bodice cut very low and lacing across the bosom over a high tucker. Short full sleeves. 'A round evening dress of pink silk, over the train a loose covering of black silk; full black lace sleeves.'

Materials: crepe, muslin (white or coloured), sarcenet, velvet, Salisbury drugget, 'Ploughman's gauze' with satin spots.

OUTDOOR GARMENTS

Spencers

of white muslin with long sleeves over coloured dresses. Spencer-jackets of velvet and coloured sarcenet.

Pelisses

'Half Pelisse trimmed with lace or fur.' 'Pelisse of scarlet kerseymere.' Cambric pelisses.

Cloaks

Hungarian cloaks of scarlet silk trimmed with black lace or fur. The Curricle cloak, half or three-quarter length, shaped in at the waist and sloping off at the sides from the front, edged with lace or fur. (This went on until 1806.)

Shawls

Large silk shawls with deep fringe. Square Scotch shawls of silk and cotton.

ACCESSORIES, ETC.

White and nankeen Day *Shoes*.

Gloves: white net (morning). *Parasols*: plain unfringed, often hinged, usually green. Black bear *Muffs*, and *Tippets* with long hanging ends for day. White swansdown muffs and tippets with evening dress. 'To rouge highly was all the rage and without your cheeks were the colour of a peony you were not à la mode' (Susan Sibbald).

1802

DRESSES

Day

Usually with wrapping fronts. Ruffs. Walking dresses round, untrained, with a coloured handkerchief worn as in 1800. Skirts may have narrow tucks at the hem, or trimming of narrow lace. Sleeves long, often of a different colour from the dress.

Colours: usually white.

Evening

Round or 'V' necks. Demi-trains. Full dresses with shoulder trains. Frequently coloured.

OUTDOOR GARMENTS

Spencers

with high open collar. 'Spencer of lead coloured silk, fur trimmed, with belt.' 'Spencer of white muslin with short sleeves and ruff.'

Pelisses

Three-quarter, with long loose sleeves tied in two places with ribbon. 'Pelisse, half length, sloping away over the hips.'

Cloaks

The 'Spanish cloak', short, fastened on the shoulders. The 'Hungarian cloak', of nacarat silk trimmed with fur. 'Cloak of black lace open on the left arm.' *Coats*: three-quarter length with lapels and stand-up collar. *Shawls*.

ACCESSORIES

Shoes of coloured velvet or leather.

Walking *Stockings* brown, grey or olive, of silk with yellow clocks.

Gloves: white silk, net, or tanned leather. *Para-*

sols: plain, often 'fan-parasols'. *Jewellery*: small watches worn on the bosom. 'Trinkets in the shape of harps fastened by gold chains round the neck; a diamond crescent is worn on the bosom, indicative, we imagine, of chastity; the horns of the lamp of Eve cannot be supposed to refer to the happy husbands of our modern belles.' Necklaces of pearl, amber and coral.

1803

'When I see a young lady displaying to every licentious eye her snow white bosom and panting breasts, with stays cut down before, the better to expose them to view—or when to shew a fine ankle the petticoat is shortened until half the leg is exposed—I blush for her indelicacy.'

DRESSES

Markedly plain. Waist medium high.

Morning
High neck with collar. Large neck handkerchiefs, and habit-shirts. Backs cut low. Sleeves long or short. Tucks round hem.

Walking
Often have one gathered flounce above the hem, the lower edge corresponding with the edge of the hem.

Evening
Cut low and round. Lace tuckers often used. Sleeves long or short. An upper robe of lace in the form of a long tunic is common.

OUTDOOR GARMENTS

'Military *Pelisses* and *Spencers* are the prevailing habiliments among the dashers of the haut ton.' 'Pelisse of white muslin, open on the side, trimmed with lace.'

Shawl cloaks and *shawl pelisses*, with armholes or sleeves, worn with a point behind. *Josephs* (Jewish long tunics with loose sleeves) worn as an outdoor garment. *Shawls*.

ACCESSORIES, ETC.
Shoes
of black jean, white kid and purple kid 'are extremely long quartered as to barely admit the toes'.

Large lozenge-shaped *Reticules*. Patent lace (*i.e.* machine-made) worn.

1804

DRESSES

Waist medium high.

Morning
Short, without trains. High collars. Handkerchief loosely tied round the neck. Sleeves long (except in walking dresses). Shoulders puffed. *Materials*: often muslin worn over coloured slips.

Evening
Plain. Very low in the bosom and back, with lace tucker for full dress, or habit-shirt for half dress. Skirt often short in front and trained behind. Under slip of white sarcenet or satin. *Materials*: white satin, sarcenet, crepe and muslin. 'The present style of dress is the most graceful that can be conceived.'

OUTDOOR GARMENTS

Spencers
Military spencer, with frogs, long sleeves, waist length.

Pelisses

Cloaks
of worked net, long narrow front pieces, short round shoulders; or with short elbow sleeves, the 'Spencer cloak'.
Large *Shawls* of embroidered white muslin. Small square shawls now replaced by long ones of plain muslin or linen, worked at the borders and ends, worn like tippets being looped down the back with a bow of ribbon.

ACCESSORIES
Shoes
Day. The colour of the dress or ribbons, the toes somewhat less pointed, ornamented with small bows. White satin shoes for evening.
Buff *Boots* (in winter) very pointed.

Buff *Gloves* sometimes worn with full dress instead of white.

Tippets (with long ends) and large *Muffs* of swansdown or silver bear. *Ridicules*. *Jewellery*: necklaces small, composed of flat stones or gold plates.

1805

DRESSES

The square neck, or 'chemise dress with full front', beginning to come in.

Day
Often trained. No ruffs or flounces, but instead a narrow edging of gathered muslin at neck and hem.

Evening
Bodices cut with a deep 'V' behind with close gathering at centre-back of waist. Full Dress. Occasionally with front panel of velvet.

OUTDOOR GARMENTS

Spencers
'Spencer of purple velvet with "V" front. Full long sleeves.'

Pelisses

Cloaks
Spencer cloaks are wider, the fronts reaching below the knee.

Shawls
Scarlet and Indian fringed. Sealskin. Imitation of Indian shawls 'recently made in this country'.

ACCESSORIES, ETC.

Shoes
of coloured kid, black jean and velvet. Buff *Boots.*

Gloves
Flesh-coloured picnic gloves. York tan.

New *Ribbons*
'"Velours epinglé", or made to resemble velvet.'

1806

DRESSES

Morning
Either with high upstanding collar split open in front, or ruff; or cut low and worn with a habit-shirt without a collar. The edge of collars with double trimming of muslin 'à la corkscrew'. Bodices laced or buttoned up the back. Sleeves long. No trains. Deep border of embroidery round hem. 'The most fashionable females consider no morning dress so truly elegant as the Chemise dress, of muslin or cambric, drawn close round the throat with a broad lace frill, and to set entirely plain in front so as to form the shape of the bosom, and fluted round the sleeves and the bottom of the dress.'

Walking
Trains, described as 'public dusters'.
Materials: hail-stone muslin, equal-striped muslin, corded cambric. 'A few of our haut ton have adopted the short frock of French cambric and cambric trowsers.'

Evening
Generally square neck, low back. 'Bosoms and arms much too much exposed.' Sleeves short and full. Greek and Etruscan decoration. Excess of lace going out.
Materials: gold and silver lamé, muslins. 'The Circassian Evening robe, of muslin, flowing loose from the shoulder shewing a chemisette and satin petticoat.' 'A lady with a well turned ankle should never wear her petticoats too short; cheap exhibitions soon sink into contempt; a thousand little natural opportunities occur to disclose this attraction without ostentatious display.'

OUTDOOR GARMENTS

Spencers

Pelisses
Pelisse of black velvet. Pelisse of sarcenet trimmed with mohair. Pelisse of nankeen. Pelisse à la Cardinal of silk, etc., with high collar, the back full, the front loose and tied down to the feet with loose ribbons.

Cloaks
Three-quarter length Spanish cloak of white lace with shoulder tippet. Mantles, with hoods, of silk, lace or muslin.

Shawls
Square shawls worn cornerwise, attached to the shoulder by a loop. Shawls of mohair.

ACCESSORIES, ETC.

Shoes
(Walking) made high and tied or laced up the instep. There is now a small, flat, wedge-shaped heel. Evening shoes always satin or kid, generally white with rosettes.

Stockings white or rose silk with narrow clocks.

Gloves
White kid, Limerick, or York tan for evening.
Fans circular, often with opera glass in the centre.

Lawn pullcat and printed pocket-handkerchiefs. Detachable *Pockets* frequently worn instead of ridicules. *Parasols*: fringed; green, purple and parti-coloured silk. *Jewellery*: large hoop ear-rings general.

Hair bracelets worn over the gloves. 'Diamonds now worn by unmarried belles; the fair nymph of 16 now blazes in them as brightly as the sober matron of 60 did formerly.'

New materials: shaded or 'mistake' ribbons, lavender ribbon.

Prices
Silk stockings with cotton feet, 7/6 a pair. Shoes, 4/6. India Muslin, 1/6 a yard; Terrendams, 3/6; Alliballies, 5/- a yard; cambric muslin, 1½ yd. wide at 2/9 a yard. French cambric, a piece 'large enough to make 10 pocket-handkerchiefs, 1½ to 2 guineas'; Scotch ditto, 12/- to 1 guinea; muslin worked robes at 2 guineas. 'Jacconets, very curious indeed, at 2/- a yard.' Long lace mits at 2/3. Long silk gloves, 3/6. 'Cotton drawers at 3/9, worth 5/-; worsted pantaloons from 14/-.' Toilet soap, 1/- a square.

1807
DRESSES

Day
1. 'Very high neck with triangle of let-in work on the bosom and three divisions above the hem.'
2. Plain high front with narrow shoulder-straps and low back.
3. Small puckered front and sleeves of coloured crepe.
4. White tiffany tunic over coloured sarcenet.
5. The lozenge front.
Habit-shirts with high necks, fastening down the front. Sleeves, either the surplice, gathered at the wrist into a deep cuff, or the double vandyked short sleeve.
Round dresses 'now made with the French gores so as to have no gathers at the bottom of the waist'. Hems often vandyked or scalloped, or with work let in. White dresses, except in summer, less common. 'The Roguelo dress (for morning) is much admired; it is made with a loose back and biassed front which, passing through a robin confines the dress to the shape and forms a sack, a low collar triangle cape completes the dress.' (Autumn) 'It is with satisfaction we remark the bosoms of our belles to be more shaded of late. The sated eye now keeps its proper bounds that, like the heart, tires with unlimited indulgence and on imagination loves to rest.'

Evening
Square necks, cut very low. Sleeves either long, or the short Spanish slashed sleeve, or short, full puckered sleeve, gathered into a narrow, tight band, or the plain short sleeve.
Evening aprons of lace or net.
Materials: black or coloured net with chenille edging over white satin slip. Often a central panel of embroidery in white cotton or muslin, carmine sarcenet.
Contrast of *colours*, *e.g.* blue and purple, primrose and lilac, pink and dove-brown.

OUTDOOR GARMENTS

Spencers, pelisses, cloaks and shawls.

ACCESSORIES, ETC.

Gloves
The Limerick, York tan, and white kid 'are those selected by the female of taste and propriety'.

Plaid *Ribbons* and *Scarves*, and scarves of elastic knitting introduced. *Fans*: circular, of ivory, painted. *Jewellery*: ear-rings. 'Though not insisted on in the morning costume, it is generally seen on the female of correct taste, in the form of an octagon or huge ring.'

Outside watches, garnets, pearls and cornelians fashionable. Three or four rings on the little finger. Gold elastic bracelets. Velvet *Ridicules*.

'It is so much the fashion to look pale that *first-rates* use a lotion to produce that interesting and sickly shade of lily.'

Prices
Muslin dresses, 'elegant patterns', 18/- each. Corded cambric at 2/6 a yard. Veils, thread, 15/-. 'Coloured and white dresses, 25/-; elegant dresses with lace, 2½ guineas.' 'Ell-wide lutestrings at 2/6; yard-wide Chambrays at 1/- a yard.' Printed cottons at 2/- a yard. Pelisses and mantles, 2½ guineas. Corsets, 1 guinea. Abdominal belts, 4 guineas. Cambric slips, 8/6 to 12/6.

1808
DRESSES

Waists beginning to lengthen. 'We hope that the good taste of our fair countrywomen will prevent so Gothic and barbarous a taste from becoming general.' By the end of the year 'the waist is fearfully increasing in length'.

1805. Three promenade dresses showing Tyrolese
cloak; lace borders

1805. Full evening dress
York tan gloves

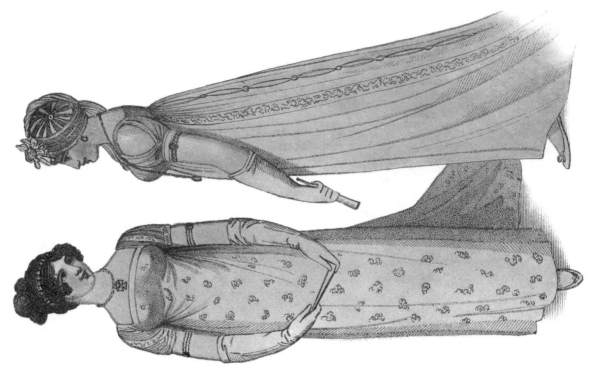

1807. Two evening dresses made as frocks; of muslin over coloured slips

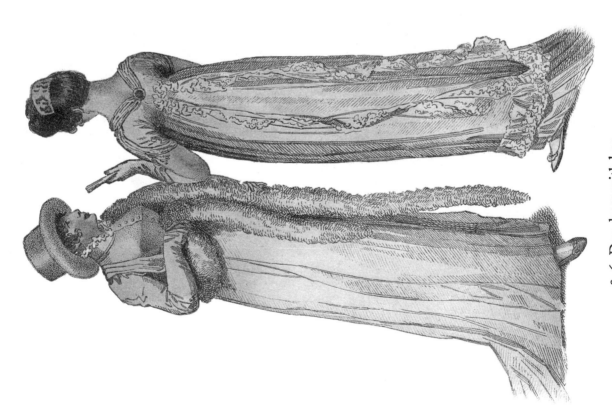

1806. Day dress with boa
Full evening dress with long tunic

Day
High gowns with lozenge front and long sleeves. Stomacher front; laced 'cottage front'; wrap front. Gored and round bosoms with short sash. Scalloped ruffs, or high Elizabethan ruffs. Sleeves full at the shoulder. Hems generally embroidered or vandyked. No trains.

Walking
with 'waistcoat bosoms' (*i.e.* bodice buttons in front).
(June) 'Some few striped trowsers we have seen worn but they are considered as only adapted for dirty weather—or the watering-place.'
White less common than coloured muslins.

Evening
with full 'robin front'; or shaped bodice. Also tunic dress attached to one shoulder only. Sleeves either short Spanish or of long transparent net.

Materials: white muslin over coloured slip; or coloured muslin over white slip. (Evening) Chinese silks, shaded and brocaded sarcenets fashionable.

OUTDOOR GARMENTS

Spencers
Spencer with slashed shoulders. Chinese Spencer with two long points in front.

Pelisse
of muslin, painted or printed.

Cloaks
Wrapping mantle, full length, trimmed with swansdown. Three-quarter length mantle, open over left arm, and cut into four points with tassels.

'A *Curricle Coat* of figured Chinese silk, with lapels, fastening at the bosom, sloping away to a long back; long sleeves.' *Shawls.*

ACCESSORIES, ETC.

Shoes
Day. Walking shoes of coloured kid, velvet or jean, cut high with strap or button. 'Half boots exploded.' Evening shoes of white satin, kid or silk, with chenille trimmings.

'*Parasols* are now worn of divers colours with deep shaded, fringed awnings.' *Ridicules* (containing fan, purse, scent-bottle, and card money) universal. Made of satin or sarcenet with tassels and strings. *Jewellery*: pebble necklaces and brooches.

Prices
Morning dresses, 12/- to 15/-. Dinner robes, 18/- to 25/-.

Circassian mantles and pelisses, $2\frac{1}{2}$ to $4\frac{1}{2}$ guineas.

1809
DRESSES
'Waists frightfully increased in length and the corset in stiffness; the cased hips, wasp-waists and trussed forms of many of our extravagantly fashionable fair.' (Actually waists not appreciably lengthened till next year.)
At the end of the year: 'The attempt to introduce the long waists has completely failed; they will never become fashionable; the Gothic taste which the introduction of the Spanish costume seemed likely to revive has now given place to the simple and more elegant form of Grecian antiquity; the long waist, that merciless destroyer of everything that is beautiful, must be no more known or thought of.'

Morning
High necks without collars. Front of bodices often made with small pleats from neck to waist. Bodices with front lacing, or 'worked body'. Sleeves long, plain and full at shoulder. Skirts short, with hem frequently scalloped or vandyked. Increase of white dresses. A few buttoned from the neck to the feet. The stomacher type becoming less common. At the end of the year the day dresses are high in the neck and buttoned all down the front.

Evening
Square necks, very low in front and high at the back. Shoulders much exposed. No shoulder straps. Sash brought round the waist and tied on left. Full melon sleeves. Quarter trains. Frequently coloured embroidery round the hem. Or a coloured robe, the 'chemise robe', fastened all down the front over a white slip. At the end of the year, evening dresses sloped to a point between the shoulders, wrapping front. Angles seem to have taken the place of squares in the formation of the dresses.

OUTDOOR GARMENTS

Spencers

Pelisses
made to fit tight to the figure, wrapping over the bosom and buttoning down the right side with small raised buttons. Band and buckle

round the waist. Armhole cut so as to exclude the shoulder cape, with a very shallow half sleeve over the long sleeve. Velvet pelisses with high collars. Pelisse-robe, 'the Hibernian vest', with waistband. Demi-robe pelisse wrapping round the body.

Cloaks

Scarlet gipsy cloak, with hood, of merino. Tyrolese cloak of sarcenet edged with lace, front hangs to knee level, rounded ends; covers shoulders. French cloak of coloured sarcenet, narrow front pieces edged with lace. Covers shoulders.

'*The Barouche Coat*', three-quarter length, tight to the shape with a round bosom and full sleeves, confined down the front with gold barrel-snaps, and round the waist by an elastic girdle and buckle. Spanish influence, *e.g.* Spanish short *Jacket* (of muslin) with slashed laced front.

Andalusian *Casaques*. (Tunics fastening down the centre with ribbons and sloping away to the level of the knees behind.)

Roman *Tunics* cut square just above the knees.

Shawls

Imitation India shawls of English make. Square shawls now exploded; instead large silk scarves with coloured borders and brocaded ends

ACCESSORIES, ETC.

'*Shoes* are much more trimmed and showy.' Cloth Half *Boots*. 'The Grecian Sandal', a half boot cut out on the sides to display the stockings. Pagoda *Parasols*. The 'Carthage Cymar', a fancy scarf of net with gold-embossed border, or of shot silk, worn attached to one shoulder and hanging down the back nearly to knee level. *Jewellery*: broad bracelets; combs of cut steel; hoop ear-rings: 'elastic ribbon bracelets' (elasticity from small brass springs). Watered *Ribbons*.

New Materials: corded and striped sarcenets, Imperial bombazine, Anglo-merino cloth, Scotia silks, Andalusian washing silks, crepe embroidered with chenille.

Rouge going out.

Prices

Merino crepe, 5/- a yard. Brazilian corded sarcenet, 7/6 a yard. Printed book muslin 4/- a yard. Double sarcenets, from 6/- to 6/6 a yard. Muslin dresses from 20/-. Corsets 18/- to 2 guineas (for

ready money only). 'Several hundreds of dresses ready made from 15/- to 4½ guineas, from the chamber to the drawingroom.'

1810
DRESSES

'An air of negligence should pervade every dress.'

Morning

High necks. Fluted ruffs. Bodices laced behind, or wrapping front, worked bosom and sleeves. The long loose sleeve tied with ribbon in three or four places coming in. Skirts wider.

Materials: jacconet, cambric with oblong spots, or sprigs of lace let in.

Mourning: day dresses of black bombazine.

Evening

High necks, moderately high backs in 'the frock style'. Long sleeves. Band for waist fastened with clasp. Full Dress usually a three-quarter tunic drapery, fastened either to one shoulder or hanging loose from both. With full dress 'small silk jackets are simply elegant'. (In winter, of velvet.) Short tippets often worn.

Materials: (Winter.) Stuff, cloth, velvet, sarcenet.

Mourning: evening dresses of black silk with crape and bugles.

OUTDOOR GARMENTS

Spencers

with tippets, and made with attached jackets. Spencer of blue satin laced with cord, full sleeve at shoulder, pointed waist.

Pelisses

Cloaks

Mantles (three cornered) with small hoods tied under the chin, made with buttoned armholes. Some with high plaited ruff.

Shawls

ACCESSORIES, ETC.

Shoes are now definitely rounded at the toe. Walking *Boots* with slight heels. 'Plain silk *Stockings* are preferred by our belles of fashion.' *Ridicules* of satin netted over with silk. *Muffs* of Angola and swansdown. *Watches* worn hanging from the waist. Lace *Scarves* worked in floss silk.

New Materials : brocaded ribbons, corded muslins, toilonette.

Prices
Advertisement: 'Novel and elegant Shawls of British manufacture.' Extra long corsets, 31/6. Black crape, 5/6, coloured 6/- a yard. Pelisses, 2-10 guineas.

1811

DRESSES

The waist tends to move up during the year.

Day
Ankle-length. Often a narrow tuck at the hem. or band of embroidery or tambour work, or coloured ribbon, or cambric frill. Bodice with antique frill or vandyked falling collar.

Morning
Sometimes white tunic of sarcenet or lutestring high in the neck with ruff, or in the pelisse or wrap form buttoning down the front with small raised buttons. Some round dresses button down the side.

'A *Walking* dress of muslin with "bishop's" sleeves tied with green ribbon.'

'*Chinese Robe*' *i.e.* morning wrapper.

Evening
Generally square, low necks. Short Spanish shoulder sleeve, or long sleeves. Skirts short with demi-trains. (Dancing dresses without trains.) Vandyking common. Often coloured crepe over satin slip. 'An evening dress of black velvet trimmed with gold cord.' 'An evening tippet of lace, or a handkerchief with pointed ends worn round the shoulders.'

OUTDOOR GARMENTS

Spencers, pelisses, cloaks and shawls.

ACCESSORIES, ETC.

Shoes
Day. Coloured shoes and half boots.
Evening. Roman sandals, or 'the more elegant little slipper with the heel entirely flat'.

Gloves
Shorter. Just below the elbow.
Day. York tan and Limerick.

Parasols of pagoda form, or with vandyked edge; sometimes with steel stick, and telescopic.

Ridicules of shot silk, or of the same material as the pelisse, but 'this article is considerably on the decline with females of a superior order'. Small *Aprons* with pockets sometimes worn instead of ridicules. Small Ermine *Tippets*. The large *Muff* has now gone out of fashion. Visiting Cards of vellum edged with gold. At the end of the year 'long stays fast losing ground'. *Jewellery*: pearls. *Fans* larger. 'Occasional *Scarves* of mohair or cashmere.'

Prices
Morning dresses 15/- to 21/-. Rich sarcenet full dress 52/6 to 5 guineas. Stockings : China silk, cotton feet, 6/6; fine India cotton, 2/6 to 3/6 a pair. Damask figured sarcenet, 6/-; twilled ditto 4/6; yard wide lustre, 3/6 a yard; cambric muslins, 1/8 a yard. Elastic petticoats, 3/6. Printed calicoes, 5/- to 10/6 the dress. Ginghams, 2/6 to 5/- the dress.

1812

DRESSES

Morning
High-laced up the front over a stomacher. Standing collar and square falling collar common. Military braiding across the bodice. Long loose sleeves. Embroidery on all dresses usual. Gowns fuller at the back. Tucks at the hem. 'The York Morning Dress', high neck and ruff; bodice with alternate strips of lace and muslin set en bias; buttoned up the back. Demi-train. 'Plain high dress of lutestring and bombazine, gored bodice.'
White muslin morning dresses worn even in winter.

Evening
Bodice cut low and square, or in a 'V' in front. Often no shoulder straps, the bodice being moulded tightly to the figure, neck of bodice often trimmed with puffing. Coloured velvet bodies over white satin and muslin dresses. Short sleeves with front button, or 'the short slashed bishop'. No trains except with full dress. Mother-of-pearl clasp at the waist. White lace aprons.
Full Dress. Square front, a mere strap over the shoulders so that the whole of the bust, shoulders and arms may be completely exposed. Small evening *Tippets*. 'Tippets, though much worn for dinner parties, are entirely exploded for the evening, and the back and shoulders are exposed in a manner that would have been

deemed extremely indecent some twenty years ago, and we will hope that this fashion cannot continue and that the bosom of beauty will again be shaded from the eye by those slight but delicate coverings which add to its attractions.'

(NOTE: 'Dinner' being an afternoon function at 5 p.m. or 6 p.m. was distinct from an 'evening party'.)

OUTDOOR GARMENTS

Spencers

Pelisses

Cloaks
'Short Cloak shaped behind like a Tippet and sloping to a point in front.' Wellington Mantle, a small Spanish cloak formed at the neck like a tippet with high collar vandyked round with lace.

Shawls

ACCESSORIES, ETC.

Shoes
Day. Half *Boots*, lacing behind. Slippers slashed across the front and square across the instep.

Gloves
'White kid gloves for full dress are once more universal, buff having entirely disappeared.'

Ridicules only worn in the evening. Circular *Fans* exploded. *Jewellery*: pearls.

New Materials: satin cloth, of silk and wool, light as sarcenet but warmer, veletine. Wellington mantle, Wellington coat, Wellington boots, Wellington bonnet, Wellington slippers, etc.

Prices
'Ladies wishing anything particularly beautiful in worked Tippets, Habit-shirts, Caps, Trimmings, etc., are respectfully invited to inspect W. & J. Evans extensive collection at No. 95 New Bond Street . . . (Moravian work) . . . is only to be had genuine at their house . . . Ladies may as usual have patterns drawn to meet their own ideas . . . real Moravian cotton for working Brussels, Honiton, sprigs. A quantity of worked dresses at 25/-, usually sold at 42/-.'
White satin, 5/- to 7/- a yard. Black crape, 4/6 a yard. Black bombazine, 2/6. White and coloured, 3/6 to 4/-. Silk velvet, 12/-. Pilgrim swansdown tippets, 31/6. English Poplins, (yard wide), 4/6.

'The Wellington mania has subsided and everything now takes its name from our beloved Regent.'

DRESSES

Walking
High necks, ruffs of triple lace. Bodices either with stomacher fronts, or buttoning or lacing behind. Long full sleeves, tied in three places with coloured ribbons. Some skirts have buttoned up pocket holes on each side. An occasional deep vandyked flounce. Frilling edging to hem.
'The Circassian Wrapper' shaped exactly like a night chemise trimmed with narrow flounce, and white brocaded ribbon at the waist. The body very low, and the front, composed entirely of lace, is shaped to the bosom. Sleeves of alternate strips of muslin and lace let in.
By the end of the year thin muslin dresses are no longer worn out of doors.
Materials: generally white, light yellow, or Pomona green. Muslin, figured muslins, bombazine, lutestring, merino cloth.

Evening
No square necks. Necks low, either round or 'V', with double fall of lace. 'We are sorry to say the bosom is exposed as much as possible.' 'That old fashioned article, a shoulder strap, is entirely exploded and the fullest style of dress is to be nearly naked.'
Shoulder sleeves fuller, sometimes of the melon form, or slashed. No shoulder straps. Hems occasionally with line of puffing, or embroidered with leaves. Lace aprons with dinner dresses. 'Lace dresses perfectly the rage.' 'Princess Charlotte of Wales body'—a bodice (*e.g.* of pink crepe) laced across the front.
The 'Corset frock' in coloured crepe, net or leno: in shape a short corset, the three gores in each side of the bosom in white satin, and lacing up the back. Short sleeve, edged with floss silk. The dress embroidered in spangles.
Some evening dresses with coloured tunics descending to ten inches above the bottom of the dress. 'Orange coloured Georgian cloth evening dress with pink satin bodice.'
Materials: white or coloured crepe over satin slip, satin bodice. Velvet, satin, satin cloth, sarcenet, jacconet muslin.
Cloth dresses in winter for morning and evening.

OUTDOOR GARMENTS

Spencers, pelisses, cloaks and shawls.

ACCESSORIES, ETC.

'Sandals are quite exploded.'
Evening *Slippers* are of white satin with silver rosettes.
White *Stockings*.

Gloves for walking dresses are generally of lemon, stone or lilac kid. *Jewellery*: pearls and pink cornelians fashionable. Small ivory *Fans* with painted borders of flowers.

1814

DRESSES

Waist medium high. Trimmings of floss silk and chenille are much used.

Walking
Stomacher fronts and wrapping bodices. Bodice and sleeves often 'cased'. High collars. Vandyke ruffs. Long sleeves gathered at armholes. Skirts ankle-length. Pleats of muslin or lace above the hem. Frequently three narrow flounces, or one full flounce. Sometimes a coloured scarf worn bracewise. Frequently coloured skirts and white bodices.
Materials: (Summer) Plain cambric, white French muslin figured with flowers or striped with colour. Chintz, French washing silks (or foulards) 'though of their possessing this economical quality we must be permitted to doubt'; and plaids. (Winter) Cloth, merino, kerseymere.

Evening
Necks cut low, generally round or 'V'. Square necks uncommon. The skirt 'affords too liberal a view of a well turned ankle'.

Types: 1. Crepe ornamented above the hem with silver lamé or cord; long crepe sleeves tied into divisions with ribbons.
2. Lace or crepe over coloured silk slip, full in the skirt and pleated at the waist, trimmed with scalloped lace or with festoons of flowers, or chenille.
3. Full drawn back, white sleeves and coloured dress.
4. The Corset frock: bodice lacing across the front like a corset, sleeves very short and full.
5. Dinner dresses with 'cased bodies'.
Colours: primrose, lilac, green.
Materials: white lace or crepe over satin slips. Sarcenet, poplin, satin, velvet.

'The *Bathing Preserver* is a most ingenious and useful novelty for ladies who frequent the sea-side; as it is intended to provide them with a dress for bathing far more adapted to such purposes than anything of the kind at present in use: and it will be found most necessary and desirable to those ladies who go to the sea-side unprovided with bathing dresses and will relieve them from the nauseous idea of wearing the bathing coverings furnished by the guides. Mrs. Bell's Bathing Preserver is made in quite a novel manner to which is attached a cap to be removed at pleasure, made of a delicate silk to keep the head dry. The Preserver is made of such light materials that a lady may carry it in a tasteful oiled silk bag of the same size as an ordinary lady's reticule.'

OUTDOOR GARMENTS

Spencers
with full sleeves, having five or six divisions. Sash with streamers and bow behind.

Pelisses
'now made cased in the back and sleeves if of sarcenet but if muslin they are cased all through the body; the casings are three together, as small as possible, and two inches between them.'

Cloaks

Shawls
India shawls of worsted, square, deep border on one side, narrow on the other, worn folded across. 'Our own imitations of India shawls have attained a perfection which we could hardly have expected; it must be a connoisseur who could detect the difference.'

ACCESSORIES, ETC.

Sandals and kid slippers for carriage.
Jean *Boots* for walking.

Ribbed *Stockings* with clocks.

Pagoda *Parasols*. Small *Fans* of frosted crepe or carved ivory.

Prices
India worsted shawls, 4 guineas. Cotton drawers, 4/-. Petticoat, 3/6. Silk velvets, 12/- to 16/- a yard. Sealskin and Vigonia cloth, for habits, 30/- to 60/- a yard (2 yards wide). Plain poplins, 4/6 to 5/-; figured tabbinets, 5/6 to 6/-; coloured bombazines, 3/- a yard. Silk stockings, 7/6 to 10/6 a pair. Cotton, 2/6 to 3/6.

DRESSES

Waists very high.

Walking

Bodices with cross-over or handkerchief fronts. High necks. Habit-shirts with lace ruffs universal. Loose coloured handkerchief round neck. ('The thunder-and-lightning handkerchief which is now suffered to sear our eyeballs.') Loose sleeves becoming wider. Skirts to level of top of boots, the fullness carried to the back of the waist by gores at the sides. Two or three deep flounces, or four lines of embroidery above hem. Sarcenet skirts with coloured bodices. Poplins with cloth bodices. 'Walking Dress of ruby merino over cambric petticoat of which only the double vandyked flounce is visible.'

Evening

'V' necks cut very low in front and behind. Sleeves either long, or the short melon sleeve. Very short gored skirts full at the back. Deep flounce of lace, and leaf pattern above hem, or line of puffing, or border of roses. Short sash tied in a bow behind. 'An evening dress of crimson satin with flowers above hem and over it a pink gauze slip.' 'An evening dress of beetroot coloured velvet.' 'An evening dress with pink satin stomacher made like a Swiss belt.'

Dinner

Tunic frock, tunic with two flounces at hem. Very short shell-shaped sleeves.
Materials: (Evening Dresses) gold and silver lamé on gauze, velvet and satin.
(Dinner Dresses) muslin over white sarcenet, India muslin, French spotted silk, or plain sarcenet. Or bodice of coloured satin with white silk skirt.

Colours: (Evening) primrose, celestial blue. 'The spring-tide of French fashions has set in upon us with a current that threatens to sweep away all the barriers of good taste.'

OUTDOOR GARMENTS

Spencers. Pelisses. Cloaks. Witzchoura, a German mantle with cape, side belts, and trimmed with fur. *Shawls*: French shawls.

ACCESSORIES, ETC.

Shoes
Day. Scarlet morocco slippers.
Wellington *Boots* and demi-boots. 'Invisible soles, of plaited horsehair, covered with velvet, worn inside boots.' Evening. Sandals of green kid, crossed ribbons.
Swansdown *Tippets* and *Muffs. Fans* smaller.

New Materials: levantine, angola 'the new invented lama cloth'; 'the Union', a mixture of silk and wool, shot; gros de Naples, 'a stuff resembling Irish poplin'; French washing silks, striped in shades; Japanese Batilla muslin; kluteen.

DRESSES

Waist very high.

Day

Necks high, or low with a fichu (broad full tucker of blonde lace), or with a triple fall of lace, or a ruff. 'The favourite form for white dresses is a chemise body which is let in all round the bosom with lace so as to form a tippet; alternate bands of muslin and lace down the arm.' Full sleeves. Skirts short, hem of coloured ribbon headed by a line of flowers or border of lace. White dresses with a full flounce of broad lace. Cloth dresses with a band of satin puffing cut on the cross, just above the hem, and sarcenet with two narrow flounces, the upper one headed. Morning white dresses with rows of narrow tucks above a worked flounce with a heading, or two vandyked flounces. 'A round muslin dress with the Ilchester braces of satin or coloured silk, crossing over the shoulders behind and forming a body in front.'
Materials: (Summer) cambric, white muslin, silk or sarcenet spotted or with vertical stripes. (Winter) cloth, poplin.

Evening

Round. Bodices very low over the shoulders. Necks round or square, or cut into a deep 'V'. Low at the back. No shoulder straps. Sleeves either long and full, or short and divided into compartments by satin rollio. Skirts ankle-length, and gored, with the fullness at the back. Hems deeply vandyked, or with border of scalloped lace, or festoons of flowers, or two deep scalloped flounces. Frequently coloured skirts with white satin bodice. Blonde and satin trimmings. In full evening dress the bodice and skirt are often of different colours, *e.g.* scarlet and green; blue and pink; purple and orange. Or (for dinner dress) worked muslin body, half-high, with a sarcenet skirt trimmed with patent net and ribbon disposed in draperies.
Materials: crepe, net and tulle over satin slips,

1808
White muslin walking dress with spencer of lilac sarcenet
Muslin dress over white cambric; waistcoat bosom
Cambric frock buttoned behind; Spanish vest of blue sarcenet

1809. Full evening dress of India muslin worked with gilt spangles; separate train from the shoulders (from author's collection)

velvet, silks, kerseymere, sarcenet, satin, lamé, shot sarcenet.

Colours: blue, green, violet, primrose.

NOTE: *Wedding Dresses* appear indistinguishable from evening dresses.

OUTDOOR GARMENTS

Spencers

Pelisses

'Walking Pelisse with high collar and three capes.' (The skirt gored and the fullness at the back; long full sleeve with epaulette.)

Cloaks

The Wellington mantle: of merino lined with sarcenet, resembling a Spanish cloak. There is no cape but a piece of honeycombed satin goes up each side of the back and across the shoulders and bosom.

Shawls

'Lyons shawl, 2½ yards square, of flowered silk with deep borders.'

NOTE: Great coats with multiple capes are fashionable in Paris and are there spoken of as 'Capotes'.

ACCESSORIES, ETC.

Walking half *Boots* of satin, lacing at the side. Silk half boots for carriage dress.

White satin *Slippers* for evening.

Evening *Gloves* of white kid.

China crepe *Scarves*, embroidered in colours at the ends. *Jewellery*: very little worn, except pearls and coral, but 'in full dress coloured stones of every description are worn'. Seldom ear-rings. Single eyeglass suspended from a long gold chain is very fashionable. 'The Armenian Divorce Corset.' 'Invisible petticoats, drawers and waistcoats of India cotton for summer.' 'Our English imitations of China crape and French silk.' Painted merino stuffs. The Roxburgh *Muff* of swansdown divided into compartments by bands of white satin. 'The terms Cap and Handkerchief are to be found no more in Fashion's vocabulary', being replaced by cornette and fichu.

1817

DRESSES

Waists very high.

Day

Bodices with round necks or en coeur. Triple vandyke ruffs and fichus, or habit-shirts with high frilled neck. Sleeves full at the shoulder, frilled at the wrist, often epaulettes. Skirts with vandyked, embroidered or scalloped hem, or headed by one or two lines of puffing; or a single flounce at knee level; or several bands of coloured ribbon; or rows of quilling.

Materials: (Winter) merino, poplin, bombazine, white with small coloured sprig. (Summer) cambric, dimity, muslin.

Evening

Bodices trimmed with satin rouleaux, corkscrew gauze, or frill of blonde lace. Sleeves short, held up by narrow satin bands. Skirts short and wide, trimmed with lines of puffing or festoons as in day dresses.

Materials: gauze, crepe (over satin slip). 'The new patriotic Spitalfields silk and sprigged poplins', poplin, Union silk, rep, sarcenet, book muslin. Dresses becoming more and more 'worked'.

Colours: azure blue, blush pink, green, purple, lilac.

OUTDOOR GARMENTS

Spencers

Coloured. Cord trimming. 'Spencer with Stewart neck.'

Pelisses

Coloured. Pelisse robes with or without capes. 'Pelisse with vandyked cuffs and rolled mancherons.'

Cloaks

Mantles with three capes. English Witzchoura, winter mantle of cloth with cape and attached hood.

Shawls

ACCESSORIES, ETC.

Half *Boots* of plum-coloured kid or blue, buttoned on one side, for walking. 'Every lady wears silk *Stockings* and fur caps; woe to the poor cats and rabbits!' Swansdown *Muffs*. Striped *Ribbons* of every colour on white. 'Wearing of *Pockets* entirely exploded.' Plaid *Scarves*: China crepe scarves, white with edge embroidered with flowers. *French* fashion—the wearing of an outside bustle known as a 'Frisk'. *Jewellery*: amber and gold ornaments. 'Ear pendants of a prodigious length.' 'Eyeglasses, we are sorry to say, are too much in vogue.'

Prices

Black bombazine, 4/6 a yard. Black shalloon, 2/6 a yard. Chip bonnet, 1 guinea. Servant's bonnet, 2/6. Silk gloves, 4/6. Kid gloves, 2/6. Fine India muslin, 13/- a yard. English muslin, 5/- a yard. Cost of making a gown, 2/6. 'Fine chip hats or bonnets, 18/-.'

1818

'Women have learnt to wear full petticoats but not to lengthen them. Pockets seem likely to return if it is found possible to hang them so low that they shall not spoil the beauty of the hips. The disgusting and frightful fashion of shewing the backbones is disappearing; but the bosom is still too much exposed and will continue so till the fathers and husbands interfere; it must ever be a matter of surprise that they should wish to expose women whom they love and esteem to derision. Have not many men declared that they are tired of looking at naked women?'

DRESSES

Waists very high.

Day
Bodices either high, fastening at the back, or low with a fichu tucker, or half high. Quilled ruff or one of Elizabethan type. Henrietta ruffs. Spanish ruffs. Sleeves full and long with epaulettes. Skirts short, with two satin rouleaux or foliage laid on, or two scalloped flounces. Bustles worn ('Nelsons'). 'A walking dress with open robe on nainsook, bodice half high, tight to the shape, sleeves open at the cuff with cambric engageants. Handkerchief with worked frill round neck.' 'The Cambridge breakfast dress, full skirt trimmed with fluted muslin, high body in chemisette form with falling collar; front fastens at the throat and wraps on the left side. Long loose sleeves with muslin strap.'
Materials: (Summer) printed or white muslin or cambric. (Winter) Tabbinet, figured sarcenet, levantine, rep, silk.

Evening
Necks round or occasionally square, very low. Short shoulder sleeve, puffed, and held up by narrow satin bands, with scalloped embroidery.

Dinner
Dresses with long sleeves finished at the wrist. Skirts ankle-length, two or three scalloped or vandyked flounces or festoons of roses often headed by corkscrew rolls or coloured muslin bouillons. Often coloured flounces on white skirts. 'Evening dress trimmed with puffings of reversed satin.' Ball dresses trimmed with wheatears or cockle-shells. Satin bodices, muslin or gauze skirts, one coloured, the other white.

Colours: Clarence blue, rose, lilac, amaranth, French grey.

OUTDOOR GARMENTS
Spencers. Pelisses
Cloaks
'Wrapping Cloak of moleskin or Bath coating with military cape and folding hood.'
Shawls

ACCESSORIES, ETC.

Long white *Gloves* for evening. *Ridicules* of green velvet; or cork, and blue satin. Very little *Jewellery* worn. Drop ear-rings.

1819
DRESSES

Waists very high, but with some inclination to lengthen.

Day
Bodices high, in frock style, fastening behind or with wrapping front. (Morning dress) ruffs double or triple quilled; muslin fichus. Sleeves full at the shoulder, often with mancherons; vandyked edging at wrist. Skirts ankle-length with three scalloped flounces and broad lace insertions between each, or with five broad tucks above a scalloped hem, or deep border of puckered muslin; or satin bands cut into straps. 'A day dress with front of bodice vertically pleated from shoulder down to the waist where it is drawn in.' Summer *Walking* dresses white, with loose handkerchief round the neck.
Materials: white muslin, cambric, corded cambric, sprigged India muslin, lutestring, poplin, sarcenet.

Evening
Half-high with line of bouillon round the bust. (Ball Dresses: bodices often of satin, vandyked trimming edged with cord; cut low round the bosom but less off the shoulders.) No square necks. Occasionally a small lace tucker. Sleeves short. Spanish slashing, the points attached to reversed points from the shoulder. Often short full sleeves of net over satin. Gored skirts ankle-length, with deep border of bias gauze or quilling, or festoons of flowers above

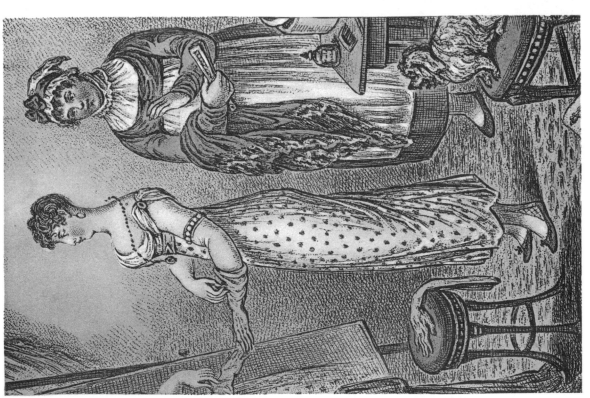

1810. Two prints by Gilray of fashionable lady dressing

1811. Morning carriage dress of
corded muslin; lilac satin
shawl

1811. Evening dress of sea-green
crepe vandyked round the
petticoat

a scalloped hem; or twisted rolls of embroidered ribbon or cord trimming.

Materials: satin, sarcenet, figured silk, coloured gauze, brocaded gauze, book muslin, Norwich bombazine, poplin, gros de Naples, white muslin over pink or blue satin slip.

OUTDOOR GARMENTS

Spencers
'Spencer with epaulettes or mancherons, high stiff collar open in front, occasionally Spanish slashing across the bosom.' Spencer of terry velvet.

Pelisses
'Pelisse with slashed mancherons and pointed straps for the cuffs.' 'Pelisse trimmed down the front with foliage or en languettes.' 'Pelisse with gored skirt and a pelerine.'

Cloaks

Shawls
'Shawl of English cashmere of rich pattern on sky blue ground.'
'Narrow cashmere Shawl with blue striped border and fringe.'

ACCESSORIES, ETC.

Variegated half *Boots* (Day). Evening *Shoes* with rosettes. Pale yellow *Gloves*. Pagoda *Parasols*. Large ermine *Muffs*. *Ridicules*. *Scarves* of barège crepe. Corset à la grecque. 'The Lucina belt for every lady expecting to be hailed by the endearing title of Mother.'

1820

DRESSES

Waists medium low. 'More than half way to the hip', but many still high.

Day
Bodices high, sometimes with lines of embroidery; a broad frilled collar or double vandyked ruff; or a semi-high neck with frilled habit-shirt. Sleeves puffed at the shoulder, epaulettes; loose sleeves with vandyked frill at the wrist.

'*Morning* gowns generally fastened behind; they are mostly laced, but a few are buttoned. The sleeve is so set on as to give breadth to the chest without falling off the shoulders.' Skirts somewhat longer, always elaborately trimmed, *e.g.* three gathered, scalloped flounces, deep puffing round hem; vandyked flounce between two lines of puffing; four narrow tucks above a scalloped flounce; flounces tabbed or headed by cord.

Materials: (Summer) muslin, white cambric, lutestring, jacconet. (Winter) bombazine, tabbinet, dark chintz, merino and cloth.

Evening
'It is sad to be condemned to the ball dress of to-day; I abhor the long waists, the miserable busks and the whalebone that carry us back to I know not what Gothic period.' Bodices with low, round, or square neck, with frill behind, or two rows of blonde lace round the bust. Occasionally folds of pleated crepe across the bosom, gathered at the centre; or bodice with blunt point; or with an attached triangular stomacher. Shoulder puffed sleeves trimmed with blonde lace. Skirts gored, just below ankle-length. No trains. Deep hem of puffing; or two lines of puffing; or rows of piping and festoons of blonde lace, or languettes up to the knee. Love ribbon tied round the waist with a small bow behind and long ends.

Materials: bodices of satin or velvet, coloured, with white muslin or gauze skirt over satin slip; gros de Naples (twilled, figured or plain); gauze with satin sprig; China crepe, terry velvet.

Colours: blue, mulberry, lavender, willow green, pink.

'I am surprised to see the British ladies making so ample a display of bare backs and capacious busts; by making these attractions cheap they cause them to lose half their value.' 'A certain great lady's pantaloons of fine cambric trimmed round the ankles with embroidered muslin.' 'The English lady of good taste just copies such of the French fashions only as suit her.'

OUTDOOR GARMENTS

Spencers
'Spencer with Gabrielle sleeves.' 'Fichu-Spencer of satin or velvet with long points in front hanging nearly to knee level.'

Pelisses
'Curricle Pelisse with three capes.' 'Pelisse with cocks comb trimming.' 'Pelisse with large pelerine cape.' 'Pelisse with broad bias band, or scalloping.'

Cloaks
Palatine tippet with front hanging to knee level. Turkish pelisse cloak (evening) with high collar of satin lined with chinchilla.

Shawls

'Long white scarf-shawl of real lace.' Shawls, made of wool imported from Van Diemen's Land, manufactured in Edinburgh.

ACCESSORIES, ETC.

Evening long *Gloves* with tops of puffed ribbon. Small *Fans*. *Ridicules*, urn-shaped, of kerseymere with steel clasp. *Jewellery*: pearls for ear-rings, necklaces and bracelets.

1821
DRESSES

Waists medium high. Skirts (day and evening) longer, nearly to the ground.

Day

Bodices mostly high and tight to the shape, with a double ruff at the neck. Some cut low with a slight 'V' back and front, filled in with a habit-shirt and a ruff. A few button down the front. Sleeves fuller, with mancherons or epaulettes, and vandyked at the wrist. Occasionally round robes or wrapping robe open on left side and tied at intervals with ribbon. In summer bodices half high, and short puffed sleeves with long net over sleeves. Skirts with one or two flounces headed by rouleaux of satin. Black silk aprons worn with morning dresses.
Materials: (Winter) poplin, sarcenet, bombazine, lutestring. (Summer) cambric, muslin, figured gauzes, chintzes with printed flounces, washing silks.

Evening

Bodices cut round and low, edged at the neck with blonde or puffing. Some with coloured antique stomacher, *i.e.* an extra piece, triangular, worn with point downwards over the front of the bodice. Short puffed sleeves, often slashed, or with buttoned points. Skirts with scalloped lace flounce at hem, surmounted by two or three rouleaux with decoration between. No trains. Waist ribbons broad, bow behind and long ends. The 'Corsage à la Sevigné' is a novelty.

Colours: pink, aethereal blue, lavender and spring green.

OUTDOOR GARMENTS

Spencers

Spencer 'pointed before like a cuirass and buttoned behind in the canezou style'.

Pelisses

Cloaks

Cashmere mantle with pine pattern border and scarlet hood.

Shawls

Square shawl of barège silk, white ground checked with colours.
Small *Capes* worn with walking dresses which, by the end of the year, become 'Pelerine Capes'. Similarly the Spencer becomes the 'Fichu-Spencer', or 'Canezou'.

ACCESSORIES, ETC.

Silk *Stockings* with coloured clocks, or richly embroidered, or open work.

Parasols of medium size, pagoda shaped, with long handles. *Ridicules* of red morocco and coloured beads. Mirror *Fans*, of mother-of pearl. *Jewellery*: ear-rings all of the drop variety. Barège silk begins to be used. Bustles hinted at.

HEADGEAR IN THE VERTICAL EPOCH

Specimens of caps, hats, bonnets, etc., can better be judged from illustrations than from descriptions, but a survey of the epoch reveals some general principles governing their design. The most noticeable is that while the classical spirit, to some extent, governed the design of indoor headgear for the first ten years, there was no evidence of it in the hats and bonnets throughout the epoch.

Some attempt was made to restrain them during the pure classical period (1800 to 1803) when they were at least small and insignificant, while from 1804 to 1807 they tended to be large but broad so as to preserve an appearance of proportion. As the classical spirit became debased (1808 to 1810) hats flattened in the crown, and as the Gothic taste grew, from 1812 onwards, they shot up into the air with extraordinary exuberance; after ascending, tall and narrow (1812 to

1816) they exploded like a rocket into a halo of brim and feathers (1817 to 1821).

Throughout the epoch they did not, as a rule, conceal the face, tending to be tilted back or to the side; but whatever their shape or position (and all were tried) they were never retiring. Whatever else you missed you could not miss the hat.

For the first ten years or so, small face-veils were applied, but, as rouge went out, the face demanded closer inspection and abandoned itself to the public gaze.

Caps modelled themselves, as best they could, on classical forms, at first Greek, then Etruscan and Egyptian, but the effort was gradually abandoned, and from the middle of the epoch young women, at least, cultivated once more the allurement of hair, with ringlets at the sides and coils piled on the crown.

One perceives in the headgear odd echoes of passing history; the Trafalgar hat, the military helmet, and souvenirs of our various allies, and occasional strange adventures—a Persian headdress, a hat composed of twelve thousand pieces of cork—but such are hardly examples of anything but the exhibitionist's art.

As regards the arrangement of the hair, it will be seen from the Annual Notes which follow that during the more classical phase of the Vertical Epoch some attempt was made to imitate the Greek style of hairdressing, while in 1805 and 1806 the Egyptian mode affected the hair as well as the ornamentation of the dress. As soon as the pure classical influence began to subside, the hair was closely cropped for a few years, followed by a fashion for ringlets at the sides and curls behind. With an increase of Gothic taste in the dress the hair was dressed to imitate the beauties of the reign of Charles II producing a notably unclassical effect. Indeed, all through the epoch the head never took kindly to the classical spirit.

At the very beginning of the century the French fashion for wearing a wig over cropped hair was imitated to some extent by the 'dashers of the haut ton'. 'Ladies would wear two different color'd wigs the same day, black in the morning, dressed in short curls, and in the evening and in full dress flaxen in a most elaborate style.' (Susan Sibbald.)

Before considering the headgear in further detail it is necessary to define certain terms now obsolete or having altered meanings.

INDOORS

Day

The Mob. A large cap of cambric or muslin fitting loosely over the whole of the head, and sometimes tied under the chin.

The Biggin. A large form of the mob, with a deep ornamented edging, and without strings.

Evening

The half handkerchief, pinned flat on the crown, with a corner hanging down behind or on one side.

The Cornette, used for both day and evening. A cap shaped with a cone-point behind and tied under the chin.

The Turban. Material folded round the head, often purchased made up in the shape.

The Toque. A close fitting hat without a brim for evening wear.

OUTDOORS

The Bonnet. A hat of which the brim is absent or much diminished at the back, and is tied under the chin.

The Capote. A loose-fitting bonnet, the crown made of soft material and shaped to the head, while the brim and sides are rigid (of straw, whalebone, etc.).

The Bag Bonnet. A name used at the beginning of the epoch for a capote, of which the soft crown loosely covers the back of the head.

The Slouch. A hat with the brim in front projecting so as to shield the face.

The Cottage Bonnet. A close fitting straw bonnet, of which the sides project beyond the cheeks.

The Calash. A hooped hood. A variation is the 'chapeau bras', which was small enough, when taken off and shut up, to be carried in a handbag.

In the Annual Notes it will be noted that hats were frequently worn at dinner; it must be remembered that this was almost an afternoon function (often at 5 o'clock).

Materials: It will be seen that a great number of textiles were employed as well as other materials. Of straws, the Leghorn was a constant rival of the Dunstable, while willow chip, which had been introduced into Bedfordshire in 1785, was frequently used. A certain number of specimens exist made of the fine straw which would now be called 'pedal'.

Ribbons were usually sewn on, but in some examples the original hand-made pins may be found fastening the ribbon in place.

The Turbans of this epoch are now practically extinct; we do not, therefore, know how they were made up into the shape seen in the fashion books. There is a turban-toque in the Victoria and Albert Museum.

Certain specimens of early straw bonnets exist with the ribbons threaded through slits in the straw; I am not convinced that these are necessarily of foreign origin on that account.

The day caps are usually enriched by embroidery and lace.

It should be noted that during the second half of the epoch caps were frequently worn under day bonnets, especially 'walking bonnets', but not under hats.

1800

1. *Morning Dress*. Chip hat ornamented with flowers.

2. *Morning Dress*. Bonnet of chip or mixed straw lined with pink and trimmed with pink ribbon.

3. *Morning Dress*. Black velvet bonnet with black feather and short veil of black lace, trimmed with pink ribbon and tied under the chin.

4. *Afternoon Dress*. Bandeau of gold and foil round the head with white and pink feathers.

5. *Afternoon Dress*. Scarlet velvet cap ornamented with rows of pearls and drooping ostrich feathers.

6. *Cap* smooth on the head with plain edging of lace in front and trimmed full behind, hiding all the hair.

1801

1. *Evening Dress*.

2. *Evening Dress*. Turban of crepe or muslin made in the form of a beehive and finished with a bow and end.

3. *Evening Dress*. Cap of white lace with a deep border on one side; band of white satin and bugles round the front; white ostrich eathers.

4. *Morning Dress*. Bonnet of pink silk trimmed round the front with black velvet and ornamented with pink and black; black feather in front.

5. *Morning Dress*. Straw hat turned up in front and trimmed with green ribbons.

6. *Bonnet* of white or buff muslin trimmed and tied under the chin with white ribbon.

1. *Walking Dress.* Bonnet of purple velvet covered with lace and trimmed with purple ribands; short lace veil.

2. *Curricle Dress.* A close bonnet made of green silk and trimmed with black.

3. *Morning Dress.* Bonnet of fine worked muslin, lined with pink, trimmed with small puffings of muslin.

4. *Full Dress.* A hat of brown muslin trimmed with silver to correspond with the dress (brown muslin), and ornamented with feathers.

5. *Travelling Dress.* Small jockey hat of dark silk or cambric muslin, trimmed with lilac.

6. *Evening Dress.* Cap of white lace, open at the top to admit the hair and confined with blue riband.

1803

1. *Promenade Dress.* Straw gipsy hat tied with blue.

2. *Afternoon Dress.* Dress hat of blue crepe ornamented with feathers.

3. *Promenade Dress.* A close bonnet of white muslin, the sides and top of crown trimmed with white lace.

4. *Promenade Dress.* Military or helmet hat made of willow or catgut, with military feather over the crown.

5. *Morning Dress.* Bonnet of straw or chip.

6. *Walking Dress.* Conversation hat of straw, lined and tied under the chin with purple or blue.

1804

1. *Full Dress.* Mameluke turban of white satin, white ostrich feathers in front.

2. *Evening Dress.* Hair dressed and ornamented with a gold comb.

3. *Promenade Dress.* Mistake hat of straw or chip.

4. *Evening or Promenade Dress.* Spanish hat of purple velvet turned up on one side and ornamented with a feather.

5. *Evening Dress.* Cap of muslin and lace ornamented with a wreath of roses.

6. *Promenade Dress.* Obi hat tied under the chin with pink riband.

1805

1. *Walking Dress.* Mob cap of worked muslin.

2. *Walking Dress.* Slouch straw hat.

3. *Morning Dress.* Biggin of plain muslin, lace border, trimmed with pale blue.

4. *Full Dress.* Hair dressed with diamonds set on velvet, with a profusion of white ostrich feathers.

5. *Full Dress.* Cap of apple blossom silk covered with lace and deep lace border; bunch of roses in front.

6. *Full Dress.* Handkerchief-cap of white crepe, finished with a bow on the left side.

57

1. *Evening Dress.* Trafalgar white satin (or blue crepe) turban.

2. *Full Dress.* Hair ornamented with a crepe handkerchief with painted border.

3. *Morning Dress.* Cantab hat.

4. *Walking Dress.* Straw hat trimmed with swansdown.

5. *Morning Dress.* Cap or cornette.

6. *Opera Dress.* Trencher-hat of crimson silk ornamented with pearls, the hair hanging in curls at the sides.

1807

1. *Walking Dress.* Gipsy hat of satin straw with edge à la cheveux de frise, tied with a handkerchief of Paris net or coloured sarcenet.

2. *Morning or Walking Dress.* Yeoman hat of purple velvet turned up in front in a triangular form, edge finished with border of shaded chenille; ornamented on crown with raised button and cord and tassel.

3. *Walking Dress.* Village hat of straw or chip, with silk crown and riband of coloured sarcenet.

4. *Walking Dress.* Small round cap of worked muslin with quilling of lace.

5. *Evening Dress.* Half-handkerchief of blue silk embroidered with silver pinned across the back of the head, the ends to fall over the bosom. Fancy sprig in front.

6. *Walking Dress.* Bonnet of velvet ornamented with black.

1808

1. *Full Dress.* Headdress with two ringlets before the ears, ornamented with a tiara of gold.

2. *Walking Dress.* Small bonnet of silk to correspond with the pelisse.

3. *Full Dress.* Cap of white crepe or net with lappets, ornamented with a red rose.

4. *Walking Dress.* Gipsy hat of straw lined with white satin and trimmed with white riband.

5. *Walking Dress.* Headdress of silk edged with fur.

6. *Walking Dress.* Bonnet of scarlet kerseymere to match the cloak.

1809

1. *Evening Dress.* Hair ornamented with beads.

2. *Walking Dress.* Yellow silk bonnet with straw flowers.

3. *Walking Dress.* Green silk headdress with short veil.

4. *Garden Promenade Dress.* Witch's hat in white chip with demi-wreath of fancy marigolds.

5. *Walking Dress.* Bonnet of green silk.

6. *Half Dress or Evening Dress.* Silver net dress cap lined with purple silk; silver cord and tassels.

1800

HAIR

Half is combed back and tied in a bunch on the top of the head, or in classical coils behind. The front hair is combed forward on to the forehead and parted in full ringlets, or worn dishevelled. Or cropped short; or 'highly frizzed in the front and turned up behind'.

For *Evening* 'the front and side hair slightly frizzed; the whole of the hind hair twisted round the back of the head in a double chignon and fastened in a diamond comb'. Or 'dressed in various forms and curls à l'antique'.

COIFFURE

Morning caps, of white muslin tied under the hair behind. Mobs and biggins.

Afternoon velvet caps, or bandeaux with ostrich feather in front.

Evening undress caps of white lace with small wreath of orange or poppy flowers. Dress caps of silk or muslin with red feather. Turbans. Evening hair nets.

OUTDOORS

Bonnets of chip or sarcenet. Bag bonnets.

Hats of straw or silk (morning).

1801

HAIR

'dressed in the Grecian taste, very full behind'. Light curls in front.

Evening. Hair dressed full in front, twisted round the head, and a bandeaux (of striped tiffany or silver) intermingled with it. The hair may be looped up with sliders.

COIFFURE

Evening. Turbans of crepe or muslin in the form of a beehive. Silver hair nets with tassels or spangles. Caps worn with full dress, sometimes with short veils in front.

OUTDOORS

Bonnets. Muslin bonnets. Poke bonnets hiding the face. Often a blonde lace veil thrown over the back of the bonnet.

Hats. Pilgrim and Obi hats of split straw and fine chip. Witching hat (or witches hat, also called a gipsy hat).

1802

HAIR

'The hair in general short on the forehead and parted', or 'worn very much over the face in small curls.'

COIFFURE

Day caps unchanged.

Evening. Half handkerchiefs worn on the head, or lace cap with the back hair projecting through an opening. Silk hair nets. Turbans of coloured sarcenet with lace veil behind. Or headdress of bandeau and feather.

OUTDOORS

Bonnets. Coloured velvet bonnets, some with feathers, some with veils. The gipsy and the cottage close bonnet coming in.
Hats. Spanish hats of satin, turned up in front and down on one side.

1803

HAIR

Unchanged.

COIFFURE

Evening. Half handkerchiefs, velvet caps; turbans (of Barcelona handkerchiefs); or silver net open at the top. In full dress, a tiara, gold comb, or wreath.

Hats. Straw hats with domed crowns; gipsy hats tied under the chin. Straw helmets. The 'Conversation Hat' (covering one ear and made of sarcenet, or muslin, with a wreath of flowers).

1804

HAIR

Unchanged

COIFFURE

Day. Morning caps. A cambric biggin or other form of mob.

Evening. Gold comb; half handkerchief; lace caps; Mameluke turban. Long veils reaching from the crown to below the knees common for full dress.

OUTDOORS

Hats. For walking, a cap of satin with small veil. Or Spanish hat, conversation hat or mistake hat. Gipsy or Obi hats of chip or straw. Occasionally a military helmet hat of beaver.

1805

HAIR

Unchanged.

COIFFURE

Day. Indoors, a handkerchief cap. Mob caps, often worn out of doors in the morning.

Evening. Plain Grecian or Egyptian headdress. Turbans. Bandeaux. Evening Cap. For ball dress, a wreath of grapes.

OUTDOORS

Bonnets of velvet.

Hats. Spanish hats. The slouch hat.

1806

HAIR

'parted on the forehead; the hind hair twisted into a cable or bow and fastened with a small comb; it is impossible to compress the hair into too small a compass for the present mode; steel, gold, or tortoiseshell comb with or without a brooch in front.' 'Hair in the Egyptian style.'

COIFFURE

Day. Caps, small and round, or *cornets*, for morning indoors.

Evening. Half handkerchiefs. Trencher hats of silk.

OUTDOORS

Bonnets. Conversation bonnets. Small velvet and straw poke bonnets.

Hats. Trencher and Yeoman Hats of kerseymere, velvet or sarcenet. Brown beavers. Jockey caps.

1807

HAIR

'in loose curls in front, or cropt behind with curls on the crown.'

COIFFURE

Day. Morning caps as before.

Evening. Small half handkerchief in embroidered net, placed at the back of the head, or in front with a central point à la Marie Stuart.

OUTDOORS

Bonnets. Close cottage bonnets.

Hats. Gipsy hats. Village hats. Yeoman hats.

1808

HAIR

'Cropt hair is becoming indiscriminatingly general.'

COIFFURE

Day. Morning caps of lace, muslin or needlework with lace beading.

Evening. The Minerva bonnet for dinner. Gold tiaras, lace or net caps. Turbans, bandeaux and half handkerchiefs going out.

OUTDOORS

Bonnets. Straw bonnets of mountain or cottage shape. Sarcenet poke bonnets.

Hats. Gipsy hats with Grecian mob cap beneath. Spanish hats. Yeoman and slouch hats.

1809

HAIR

'The hair cropt in full curls or partially in ringlets exposing the ear.'

COIFFURE

Day. Caps close to the head, raised rather more behind than in front. Or corded or gauze ribbon with lace edging and veils, ornamented with artificial flowers. Or the Brunswick mob cap.

Evening. Much jewellery worn in the hair without a cap. Steel or bronze combs. Occasionally a wimple (of gauze worn over the head). A few turbans.

OUTDOORS

Bonnets. Cottage bonnet with short white veil. Mountain bonnet of matted straw.

Hats. The patriotic helmet. Small gipsy. Wardle hat of straw with conical crown. 'It were an endless task to describe the various constructions which compose the velvet bonnets and hats. . . . They are generally formed of the same material as the pelisse or mantle and are either of the Spanish or helmet form, ornamented with lace, flowers or two short feathers.'

1810

HAIR

'Hair worn in thick, flat, irregular curls, braided behind and rolled round and sometimes brought across the face, twisted with pearls or silver.'

Evening. 'Hair in the Grecian style with hanging ringlet.'

COIFFURE

Day. 'Morning caps are very numerous but exhibit little novelty.'

Evening. Fillets of satin or crepe. Small combs. Wreaths with bandeaux. Evening lace caps close to the head.

OUTDOORS

Bonnets. Small poke bonnets.

Hats. 'For walking, white chip hats with rather high flat crowns and broad flat rims bound with ribbon and tied down with the same.' Slouch hats. Mountain hats. Jockey straws. 'Caps and veils, small fancy hats of silk or fancy chip decorated with flowers are in request.' 'Hats and bonnets worn very backward so as to discover the hair in full curls with plaitings of lace or small bunches of flowers in front of the forehead.'

1811

HAIR

'Hair generally worn parted on the forehead with round curls on one side of the face and a few long.'

Evening. For the ball, hair is twisted up behind and dressed in full curls in front, with a bandeau.

COIFFURE

Day. Unchanged.

Evening. 'White satin Grecian heads', or more usually bands or twists of beads terminating in large tassels; or a small lace handkerchief worn at the back of the head and pinned at the ear. A few turban caps.

OUTDOORS

Bonnets. For walking, cottage bonnets (over small lace caps or rosettes of lace or flowers).

Hats. For walking, Spanish hats, village hats, of white chip with a crown of crepe and sarcenet over a lace caul. Slouch hats. For the carriage, 'lace caps, flat on the head, and brought forward on the face, and projecting back in the form of a cone.' This is the *long Grecian* form, also used in the evening.

1812

HAIR

In the day, parted on the forehead with full curls on the temples.

Evening. 'Hair dressed in the antique Roman fashion with tresses brought together and confined at the back of the head ending either in ringlets or two light knots.'

COIFFURE

Day. Caps not much worn except by matrons. Morning cap close fitting with two rows of lace set on full and the strings crossed under the chin and tied in a bow on the crown.

Evening. Young women with flowers on one side of the hair. Gold and silver nets with a few ringlets on the left side of the neck. Bandeaux of jewels or polished steel. Moorish turbans for matrons. For full evening dress, small white satin hats turned up all round with three ostrich feathers in front. Spanish hats.

OUTDOORS

Bonnets. Walking bonnets, the crowns higher than formerly, some with long and broad strings crossing under the chin and tied in a bow on the top of the crown. Small cottage bonnets.

Hats. Spanish hats. Yeomans hat.

Veils. Black and white veils.

1813

HAIR

Flat on the sides, waved curls in front, and parted, with full curls behind and a hanging ringlet.

1812. Promenade dress of cambric
muslin with waggoner's sleeve;
cottage vest of green sarcenet
laced across the bosom

1813. Walking dress of jacconet
muslin embroidered up the
front; cottage mantle of grey
cloth, lined with pink silk

1814. Ball dress of French gauze,
open behind, over pink silk slip

1815. Walking dress of white cambric muslin, flounced; green
sarcenet pelisse

COIFFURE

Day. A close cap or a Brunswick mob.

Evening. Hair in irregular curls with flowers. No headdress. Or a small flat turban. For full dress, a Marie Stuart cap of cloth covered with beads, or cap à la russe. For half dress, a simple lace cap.

OUTDOORS

Bonnets. Walking. A cottage bonnet over a lace cap.

Hats. Walking. A small round straw hat tied under the chin by ribbon with a bunch of flowers in front. Small black beaver riding hat with short ostrich plume.

1814
HAIR

'Long hair is fast gaining an ascendancy over the short, and is now worn very low in the neck behind.'

Evening. 'Hair à la grecque, falling loosely and full on the temples, the forehead high, to turn up behind, and confined in a small cluster of ringlets.'

COIFFURE

Day. Lace mob cap tied under the chin.

Evening. Hair with flowers.

OUTDOORS

Bonnets. The Blucher bonnet. The Oldenburg bonnet. French bonnets, loaded with flowers. The Angoulême bonnet of straw with high crown and broad front, to tie on one side.

Hats. Sealskin hats. In general the crowns are getting high.

1815
HAIR

in full ringlets on each side of the face.

COIFFURE

Day. Mob caps.

Evening. Flowers or pearls in the hair, which is worn full on top with side ringlets. Turbans of embroidered crepe handkerchiefs, or gold or silver gauze, with ostrich feathers (for matrons).

OUTDOORS

Bonnets. Angoulême bonnet. French bonnet with plume: 'a chimney pot with the chimney sweeper's brush sticking out of the top.'

Hats. French hats, of straw with quilling of net round the rim and plume in front. Sometimes a white veil. Leghorns, and hats of straw and willow.

1816
HAIR

Day. Unchanged.

Evening. Hair in ringlets on the temples, braided behind in a circle.

COIFFURE

Day. Morning cap, close to the face, or lace with ribbon tied under the chin.

Evening. Cornettes for dinner, of gauze, lace or muslin, with oval crowns, very full, the front ornamented with a pleated ribbon, and tied on with a satin band. For full dress: toques with feather plumes; turbans of crepe, with aigrette; pearl tiara, or gold comb or wreath.

OUTDOORS

Bonnets. Silk or satin bonnets with ostrich plume in front. Leghorn bonnets profusely trimmed with ribbons and feathers. French bonnets. Leghorn bonnets of the Marie Stuart shape, over a lace cap. Or widely splayed pokes.

Hats of black straw or beaver with flowers, the brim turned up in front.

1817
HAIR

Unchanged.

COIFFURE

Day. For home and the morning, cornettes of coloured satin trimmed with blonde.

Evening. Turbans, toques, or French caps. In young women, the hair braided with pearls.

OUTDOORS

Bonnets and Hats. French bonnets and hats of moss silk, or plush or velvet, with feathers. The crown high and the brim turned up in front, with profusion of ribbons. Or Leghorn bonnet with a handkerchief tied over the crown. Or for walking dress, a plush cap with plume.

1818

HAIR

The hair is dressed high and full on the forehead; parted in front with light curls over the ears.

COIFFURE

Day. Morning caps, of lace, or cornettes without flowers.

Evening. Cornettes of tulle or satin with ribbons. Turbans. Velvet caps. Toque-turbans of tulle with plume.

OUTDOORS

Bonnets. Large Leghorn bonnets. For the carriage, toques.

1819

HAIR

Unchanged.

COIFFURE

Day. Plain cornettes for the morning.

Evening. For evening parties, toques with three points, one in the centre and one at each ear. 'The Marie Stuart toque.' Large dress hats with plumes. Full dress: young ladies with pearls or flowers; matrons with dress caps, turbans or toques. Madras turbans, of Madras handkerchiefs, blue and orange.

OUTDOORS

Bonnets. Mostly with low crowns and immensely broad brims; some cut short at the ears, others nearly meeting under the chin; in summer of semi-transparent materials. 'The bonnets for walking are still immensely large and have a kind of slouching appearance.' They are worn over a lace cornette.

Hats. For the carriage, hats of plush velvet and beaver, some turned up at the sides, others with moderate brims which are the same width all round. The Valois hat.

1820

HAIR

Day. The hair in loose curls in front, falling low at the sides.

Evening. The hind hair is brought up on to the crown where it is disposed in full bows and broad plaits; or with short curls on the neck.

COIFFURE

Day. Caps. Cornettes in the Marie Stuart shape, of net and lace, adorned in front with profusion of ribbons.

Evening. Semi-evening caps of simple form with low caul, either round or cornette-shaped. Turbans or small round hats of white silk and profusion of feathers. For young women, bandeaux of pearls with a plume.

OUTDOORS

Bonnets. Walking bonnets, in the Marie Stuart shape, of white satin and quilling edge. Or bonnets of satin or velvet with battlement edging and plume of feathers. Or bonnets of fluted materials.

Hats. Carriage hats of white satin, and small, 'the same shape as those worn by gentlemen,' ornamented with a good many feathers.

1821

HAIR

'in the Charles II style with two rows of curls; the forehead bare with corkscrew ringlets over the ears.'

COIFFURE

Day. Morning caps. Cornettes of coloured gauze with full trimming next the face.

Evening. Toques of white satin and polished steel beads. Dress hats with wide brims, often indented, of satin, with marabout plumes. Turbans of gauze, velvet or crepe, with pearls. With ball dress, a wreath of flowers.

OUTDOORS

Bonnets of Dunstable straw trimmed with coloured crepe and edged by a curtain of lace or blonde. Bonnets of plush silk, the crown low and the brim standing out from the face over the forehead, the brim profusely trimmed. Leghorn bonnets with high crowns, and pokes.

Hats. For the carriage, college caps of velvet with feathers of two colours. Or Caledonian caps.

1810

1. *Promenade Dress.* Woodland hat of lemon-coloured chip, with curled ostrich feather, lilac and white.

2. *Promenade Dress.* Cottage bonnet of white chip trimmed with ribbon.

3. *Evening Full Dress.* White satin head-dress with tiara of dead gold set with jewels.

4. *Morning Dress.* Helmet cap of alternate lace and stripes of embroidery, finished on crown with square of lace edged with ribbon, tied under the chin with ribbon. Bunch of roses in front.

5. *Evening Dress.* Cap· of satin and lace bound tight to the head and trimmed with apple blossom.

6. *Morning Walking Dress.* Bonnet of pink and white sarcenet.

1811

1. *Ball or Evening Dress.* Hair ornamented with fillet of twisted satin and pearls placed twice round the head; falling tassel finished with beads.

2. *Evening Full Dress.* Turban cap of white satin looped with pearls and edged with velvet; the hair combed over the face, in thick flat curls, divided on the forehead.

3. *Promenade Costume.* White satin Spanish hat with green rim (the colour of the mantle), ornamented with demi-wreath of cornflowers.

4. *Morning Dress.* French foundling cap of alternate stripes of lace and white satin, ornamented with blossom coloured ribbon and autumnal flowers.

5. *Morning Carriage Dress.* White chip hat tied round the crown with bow of lilac satin riband.

6. *Walking Dress.* Basket hat of straw ornamented with demi-wreath of half-blown roses.

1. *Evening Dress.* Hair in full curls and confined in demi-turban of very fine muslin tied with small bow.

2. *Morning Dress.* Peasant's cap with two rows of lace, confined under the chin by band of same material as cap, terminating in a bow on the crown.

3. *Morning Walking Dress.* Yeoman's hat of green finished in front with flat ostrich feather.

4. *Morning Walking Dress.* Cottage bonnet of yellow twilled sarcenet tied with large bow of yellow ribbon; small front which displays a lace cap. Bunch of cornflowers in front.

5. *Morning Walking Dress.* Lilac bonnet with helmet crown and small front, trimmed with wreath of laurel and two white feathers. Brand riband pinned plain under the chin.

6. *Evening Costume.* Spanish hat of pink sarcenet with three large ostrich feathers.

1813

1. *Morning Walking Dress.* Victoria hat of straw turned up round the front, lined with white satin; small ostrich feather on one side.

2. *Opera Dress.* Cap à la russe of celestial blue satin inlaid with silk lace to correspond with the robe, quartered on the top with pink satin; small ostrich feather. Hair full on the temples and plain on the sides, twisted up behind in a large full Grecian bow, or knot of curls with one or two stray ringlets.

3. *Morning Dress (Outdoor).* Small cottage cap of fawn coloured crepe, trimmed and tied under the chin with fawn coloured riband. Worn very much off the face to display a lace cap.

4. *Evening Dress.* Hair in a profusion of light loose curls in front, fastened up behind à la grecque by a small comb to match the necklace; the ends of the hind hair fall in luxurious ringlets in the neck.

5. *Morning Dress.* Brunswick mob cap of net and Brussels lace.

6. *Morning Dress (Outdoor).* Bonnet cap of jonquille satin and double borders of scalloped lace, confined on one side with ribands of the same colour.

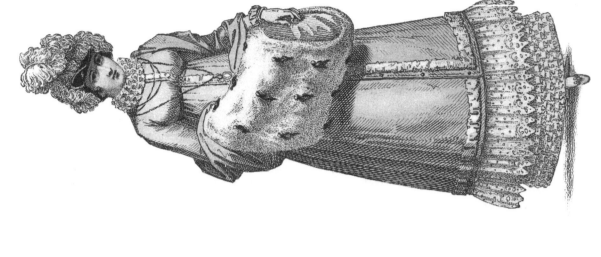

1817. Carriage dress of white poplin, deep blonde flounce; blue levantine pelisse edged with floss silk; blonde ruff; ermine muff

1816

Full evening dress of white gauze striped with blue; Austrian cap of satin and blonde

Walking or riding dress of jacconet muslin with deep flounce and ruff; lemon cloth pelisse

1819
Morning walking dress of white
muslin; white muslin pelisse

1820
Evening dress of patent net over white satin
Walking dress of jacconet muslin; three flounces;
purple gros de Naples spencer

1814

1. *Morning Dress.* Flushing mob cap of lace ornamented and tied with lemon coloured riband.

2. *Dinner Dress.* Small lace cap trimmed with pearls and tassels; fancy flowers in front. Hair in loose ringlets in front and twisted up à la grecque behind where it is fastened in a full knot.

3. *Walking Dress.* Satin straw hat tied with check or striped Barcelona handkerchief; small plume of ostrich feathers in front.

4. *Morning Walking Dress.* French hat of white and lilac satin; trimmed with tufts and bows of ribbon and large cluster of flowers.

5. *Walking Dress.* Huntley bonnet of twilled plaid sarcenet; ornamented with Prince's plume.

6. *Walking Dress.* The Oldenburg bonnet, which is immensely large, of the same colour as the petticoat.

1815

1. *Walking Dress.* O'Neil hat ornamented with feathers.

2. *Walking Dress.* French hat of satin straw with quilling of net round the rim; three rows of grey satin ribbon, plain or quilled, round the crown, and plume of white feathers edged to correspond.

3. *Morning Dress.* Round cap of white satin and quilled lace; white satin rose in front.

4. *Full Dress.* Hair divided on the forehead in light loose curls; simply braided round the head.

5. *Evening Dress.* Hat of white satin; narrow turban front with plume of ostrich feathers.

6. *Promenade Dress.* French bonnet of tulle fulled in and alternate folds of white satin laced with tulle; satin strings tied under the ear.

1. *Walking Dress*. White satin hat ornamented with flowers.

2. *Walking Dress*. Bonnet of black curled silk, lined, edged and trimmed with white satin.

3. *Evening Dress*. White crepe turban ornamented with silver and a long white feather.

4. *Evening or Bridal Dress*. Hair dressed low at the sides and parted so as to display the forehead entirely; ornamented with aigrette of pearls and sprig of French roses.

5. *Evening Dress*. Cap of white satin, band edged with pearls and plume of white feathers.

6. *Morning Dress*. Mob cornette of white lace ornamented with roses.

1817

1. *Walking Dress*. Caledonian cap of plush silk, with rich bands and foxtail feathers.

2. *Walking Dress*. Bonnet of moss silk ornamented with flowers and ribbon.

3. *Morning Dress*. Huntley cap of satin inlet with lace edge trimmed with three rows of lace and a rose on top; fastened under the chin with a diamond brooch.

4. *Evening Dress*. Hair dressed in the French manner, ornamented with coronet of flowers; the hind hair in a tuft.

5. *Evening Home Dress*. Opera hood with full garland of roses and lilies of the valley.

6. *Walking Dress*. Leghorn hat with bunch of roses.

68

1818

1. *Promenade Dress.* Toque of Ionian cork intermixed with fawn satin, finished with tassels and plume.

2. *Walking Dress.* 'Bonnet composed of about twelve thousand pieces of fine Ionian cork done in the same manner as mosaic gems', interspersed with pink satin and ornamented with flower to match.

3. *Evening Dress.* Cap of white satin, ornamented with blue satin and ostrich feathers.

4. *Dinner or Carriage Dress.* Bonnet of white gros de Naples, low crown and broad brim becoming narrower at the ears; trimmed with blond and flowers.

5. *Morning Dress.* Front hair in braids; hind hair in bows interspersed with rose coloured riband; rose coloured fillet round the head.

6. *Dinner Dress.* Parisian cornette of blond with branch of full-blown roses in front.

1819

1. *Promenade Dress.* Black Leghorn bonnet lined with white satin with quilling of blond round the edge; trimmed with black feathers and plain satin ribbon crossing the top.

2. *Summer Recess Walking Dress.* Bonnet of blush coloured satin with roses, myrtle blossoms or other small flowers.

3. *Walking Dress.* Round hat trimmed with tulle and roses.

4. *Evening Dress.* Hair dressed high with high coronet of hair.

5. *Evening Dress.* Turban of striped silver gauze with plume of white ostrich feathers; the hair in natural and irregular curls.

6. *Morning Dress.* Mob cap of lace.

UNDERCLOTHING IN THE VERTICAL EPOCH

Owing to the scanty information available from contemporary sources and the absence of dated specimens, our knowledge of the underclothing worn during this epoch is incomplete. We have to assume that in some instances there was not much difference in the first thirty years, and accept dated examples of the '20's as models.

The Chemise

Materials, cotton or linen. The shape was wide and almost oblong, the neck opening square and edged with a border of gathered muslin. The sleeves were short, with a gusset in the armpit. In length the chemise reached at least to the knees. That this garment was sometimes omitted is indicated by the following, dated 1811:

'Some of our fair dames appear, in summer and winter, with no other shelter from sun or frost than one single garment of muslin or silk over their chemise—*if they wear one!*—but that is often dubious. . . .' 'There are circumstances wherein the want of this decent garment might subject her to a shame never to be forgotten by herself or others.' 'The chemise, now too frequently banished.' 'The indelicacy of this mode need not be pointed out; and yet, O shame! it is most generally followed.'

The same writer informs us that there should be worn 'in warm weather, under the gown and slip, a light cotton petticoat, in cold weather a fine flannel petticoat'. 'Young women were killed by going from rooms excessively heated by Balls and Routs, into the open air while they wore only a *chemise* and one petticoat (under the dress).'

The Petticoat

Materials: cotton, cambric, or linen; in winter sometimes of fine flannel. It was made with a bodice attached, the latter being of a coarser quality than the skirt. The garment was made much like a low stomacher front type of dress, with narrow shoulder straps, the back being cut high except when a low-necked dress was worn. Towards the end of the epoch the bottom of the petticoat would have small flounces, in keeping with the dress, the hem being plain.

The Drawers

Before 1800 this was purely a man's garment, and, as is usual whenever women have adopted anything from the masculine wardrobe, the innovation is at first regarded as fast, later as fashionable, and ultimately as so commonplace that it is abandoned.

During the Vertical Epoch drawers were not worn by most women. Nevertheless there are occasional references to them in advertisements, *e.g.* in 1807 'the patent elastic Spanish lamb's wool invisible petticoats, drawers, waistcoats and dresses, all in one . . . very convenient for ladies on horseback'. 'Invisible Petticoats.' These were woven in the stocking loom, and drawn down very tight over the thighs 'so that when walking you were obliged to take short and mincing steps'. In 1811, 'Ladies' Hunting and Opera drawers in elastic India cotton'. In 1813, 'drawers with attached feet' were advertised, and in the following year, 'stockings or drawers made to any size or pattern'.

It is perhaps worth noting that French writers (vide *Le Pantalon Feminin*) have ascribed the introduction of this garment to the English as a mode originally for young girls. 'En 1807 nous arrive de Londres la mode des pantalons pour les petites filles. Les exercises du saut se pratiquent en Angleterre dans les ècoles de jeunes filles: c'est pour cela qu'on leur a donné des pantalons. Le gout français ayant fort embelli ce vêtement, quelques femmes, au printemps de 1809, tentèrent de se l'approprier. On les vit se promener en pantalon de perkale garni de mousseline.'

Detail at neck: white embroidered net & insertion of white moravian work in cambric.

hand-made button

GORED PETTICOAT WITH ATTACHED BODICE 1815-20

Detail at hem: rollios & white moravian work in cambric.

side · back · longcloth · seam · placket · pocket-role

The 'Pantaloon' seems to have been a garment with legs reaching nearly to the ankle (cp. 'their flimsy dresses and frilled trowsers,' 1817), but the fashion seems to have been but a momentary whim.

A specimen of drawers, apparently of this epoch, and now in my collection, is made with the legs separate except for a narrow waist band. They would reach just below the knee. A satirical etching by Gilray (1808) of 'a lady dressing' shows her wearing long corsets and a pair of fairly tight knickers. On the whole, however, it seems probable that most women did not wear any garment of this kind until the '30's.

The Stays

It is a common error to suppose that stays were not worn during the first half of this epoch; perhaps arising from the assumption that French fashions of the

71

Consulate period were identical with the English. It is possible that some English women did not wear any, but that the 'fashionables' did is clearly indicated. (The 'stayless' years were probably limited to those immediately preceding 1800.) There are numerous advertisements of corset-makers in contemporary papers, as well as frequent references to their use (and abuse). In 1809 we read 'stiff stays have been creeping in gradually till at length concealment is no longer affected'.

There were two types used:

Until 1810 or 1811 the long stay was in vogue. This, made of jean or buckram, with abundance of whalebone, reached below over the hips, and above to the breasts, pushing them up, while the back reached up to the shoulder-line with straps over the shoulders. The drawing by Gilray indicates no vandyking of the lower edge (as in the eighteenth century).

The following advertisement speaks for itself (1807): 'The long elastic cotton Stay obviates every objection complained of in Patent stays, not being subject to the disagreeable necessity of lacing under the arm, or having knitted gores . . . adapted to give the wearer the true Grecian form. Stays being in the present style of dress of great importance . . . long stays have now for a considerable time made part of the female costume. . . .' The advertised article 'will give an agreeable and graceful shape to the shoulders, reducing the bosom if too embonpoint or increasing its natural appearance if too diminutive'.

A maker of 'Stays-à-la-Diana' advertises that she makes 'fifteen patterns of stays, adapted to every size and age'.

A rival announces that her stays (costing three to four guineas, ready money) have succeeded, in five thousand cases, 'in removing with perfect ease the fulness of the stomach and bowels'. Under the circumstances we cannot be surprised to learn that in 1810 'long stays are wholly exploded', although there is still a delicate allusion to 'the present mode of bracing the digestive portion of the body in what is called Long Stays', and to 'the aid of padding to give shape where there is none', and to 'long stays to compass into form the chaos of flesh'.

In the following year we are given an instructive account: 'The Englishwoman must be at least embonpoint; the bosom must be pushed up by waddings and whalebone; the stays laced as tight as possible over the waist and hips; the excessive compression of those close long stays and iron busks produce diseases too frightful to name.'

From that date the new short stay came into general use by the fashionables. A mother is advised that to apply it correctly her daughter should lie face down so that her mother, by applying a foot into the small of the back can obtain the requisite purchase on the laces.

About the same time a variation called the 'Divorce Corset' came in; it consisted of a triangular piece of iron or steel, padded, and curved on the sides so that, when worn point upwards, it would fit in between the breasts, pushing them apart. It was claimed to produce a Grecian shape, and not being laced at the back, dispensed with the aid of a maid. (See advertisement, 1810: 'The newly invented patent Shield for the Bosom, displaying the most graceful form imaginable.') It survived well into the '20's.

In spite of these various improvements an indignant correspondent, in 1811, criticises the new fashion: 'By the newly invented corsets we see, in eight women out of ten, the hips squeezed into a circumference little more than the waist; and the bosom shoved up to the chin, making a sort of fleshy shelf disgusting to the beholders and certainly most incommodious to the wearer.' Evidently one of those hypercritical persons. . . .

In 1814 the exploits of our military hero are signalised by the 'Wellington corset' which 'represses that fulness which some ladies find rather troublesome in the present style of dress. Adieu to steel busks, long stays and all the torturing compression under which British beauty has so long laboured!'

The 'Pregnant Stay' is described (1811) as a corset of dimity, jean or silk, completely enveloping the body from the shoulders to below the hips. It is elaborately boned 'so as to compress and reduce to the shape desired the natural prominence of the female figure in a state of fruitfulness'.

The Bustle

Reference has already been made to the small bustles occasionally found in the dresses of the beginning of this epoch; after 1815 they increased in size, and doubtless helped to produce the forward stoop which was so fashionable for the next few years, when one saw 'the bent bodies of our damsels who appear like snails carrying their houses on their backs'.

In 1818 the bustle was popularly known by its wearers as 'the Nelson'.

Pockets

The dress itself having no pocket, it was not unusual to wear, under the petticoat, a pair of large pockets attached to each other by tape which tied round the waist. Specimens in my collection bear different dates; it became, later in the century, a form of under-pocket (when travelling) which was used well into the middle of the century or later.

'One of the very bad consequences of the scanty dress and the determination of shewing the shape of *all* the limbs was the necessity of giving up Pockets. The Grecian costume favoured us also with the *Ridicule* or bag to hold the Handkerchief. . . . After some years the Ridicules were given up and the Pocket Handkerchief was carried in the hand. . . . Some ladies had the indelicacy to give their Handkerchiefs to the care of the gentlemen and receive them from their hands when wanted, others threw them on a sofa when they got up to dance.'

In the Vertical Epoch the tied-on pocket was a useful but not a 'fashionable' arrangement, the women of fashion preferring to carry a small handbag or 'ridicule' (corruption of reticule), which was also known, in the early years of the epoch, as an 'Indispensable', *e.g.* 'A number of disputes having arisen in the Beau Monde respecting the exact position of ladies' indispensables (or new invented pockets)' (1801). And at Lord Melville's trial (1806) '. . . rows of pretty peeresses, who sat eating sandwiches from silk indispensables'.

73

CHAPTER III
THE DAWN OF ROMANCE 1822-1829

THIS period illustrates a transition from the remnants of a classical style, which had become merely traditional, to a full-blown Gothic, exuberantly romantic in spirit. The affection for classical details lingers on in a half-hearted fashion; the 'Gallo-Greek' bodice is a compromise between the opposing styles, specimens of which crop up occasionally as late as the early '30's.

The years '22 and '23 displayed a curious hesitation as though fashions were uncertain of their aim, but when, in 1824, the waist had finally taken the plunge downwards (it had been on the brink for two years), there was an immediate expansion of the skirt, and its triangular shape became conspicuous. The next year specimens of pointed bodices began to appear. The widening of the skirt required an increasing amount of goring until in 1828 pleating at the waist became necessary in order to cope with the mass of material, except in the lighter fabrics. The breadth of the shoulder line expanded gradually and persistently, the size of the upper sleeve becoming steadily fuller. Thus, in 1825, an occasional gigot sleeve was seen; next year the demi-gigot and gigot sleeves were quite common. In 1827 the gigot sleeve had expanded so that frequently it required whalebone supports to maintain its shape; and in 1829 the imbecile, Mameluke and Donna Maria sleeves presented veritable balloons, and the upper arm appeared to be quite double the size of the waist.

Tight-lacing, which was progressively more and more strenuous, served to exaggerate the contrast, increased by the expansion of the pelerine stretching across the shoulders.

By the end of the period the excessively wide hat suggested an inverted triangle balanced on a tiny neck, and the bodice another inverted triangle balanced on a tiny waist, itself the apex of a triangle formed by the skirt. This triple triangle effect was emphasised by horizontal lines of trimming across the shoulders and the lower part of the skirt. The purpose aimed at is indicated by a contemporary writer: 'As all objects when enlarged above and diminished below, have, like the inverted pyramid, an air of lightness and one of heaviness when oppositely constructed; the small headdress and enormous train characterise the more stately dame, while the large hat and bonnet and shorter dress distinguish the livelier girl.'

In addition, trimmings were themselves frankly Gothic in spirit and origin. By the summer of 1829 a woman of fashion was resembling a May Queen, her dress strewn with floral tributes, her hat giddy with coloured ribbons. She was the perfect picture of Gothic Romance. The transformation from the Classical had become absolute.

Like all transitional phases in art, this one displayed curious hesitations and still more curious experiments until at length the new mode found itself. While the inspiration was still lacking there was, as usual, a good deal of borrowing from French notions. The '20's was one of those moments in the century when English-women meekly accepted French fashions; the novelty, after the long years of war, of a trip to Paris was irresistible, and countless British matrons returned triumphant with their French spoils; their charm was not so much that they were becoming, as that they proved that their wearers had really crossed the Channel.

THE DRESS OF THE PERIOD

The bodice is almost always attached to the skirt, but occasionally in day dresses the two are separate (in which case the skirt is suspended by tapes over the shoulders). Day bodices are lined with cotton; occasionally with an attached cotton under-bodice having separate buttons and buttonholes. Silk and evening dresses are usually lined with sarcenet.

Day skirts are lined with silesia; evening skirts either unlined or with cotton muslin.

Walking pelisse-robes are lined with sarcenet except for side panels of silesia where the friction of the corsets would chafe.

The wadded hem is rare after 1828.

Occasional pocket openings occur in day dresses but no fixed pocket; probably a pair of detachable pockets were worn in such cases.

Fastenings: flat copper hooks and eyes, hand-made. Towards the end of the decade, occasionally copper wire, tinned. Pelisses and cloaks with gilt barrel-snaps. Hand-made cotton covered buttons; mother-of-pearl buttons. Evening dresses are sometimes laced behind. The large sleeves of the imbecile type often have inside tapes to which some kind of device, such as a crescent-shaped pad of down, was attached to keep the sleeve distended; or a lining of pleated book muslin.

DAY DRESSES

Two main types, the pelisse-robe and the round dress.

A. The Pelisse-Robe

Is derived from the outdoor garment, the Pelisse, which, by being worn closed evolved into a kind of dress. It was sometimes fastened down the centre by means of ornamental bows or by concealed hooks and eyes, or, later, with the opening only as far as the knee level; sometimes the fastening was on one side.

A variation, appearing towards the end of the '20's was the 'tunic-robe', either as an open tunic revealing the petticoat, or with trimmings outlining a tunic

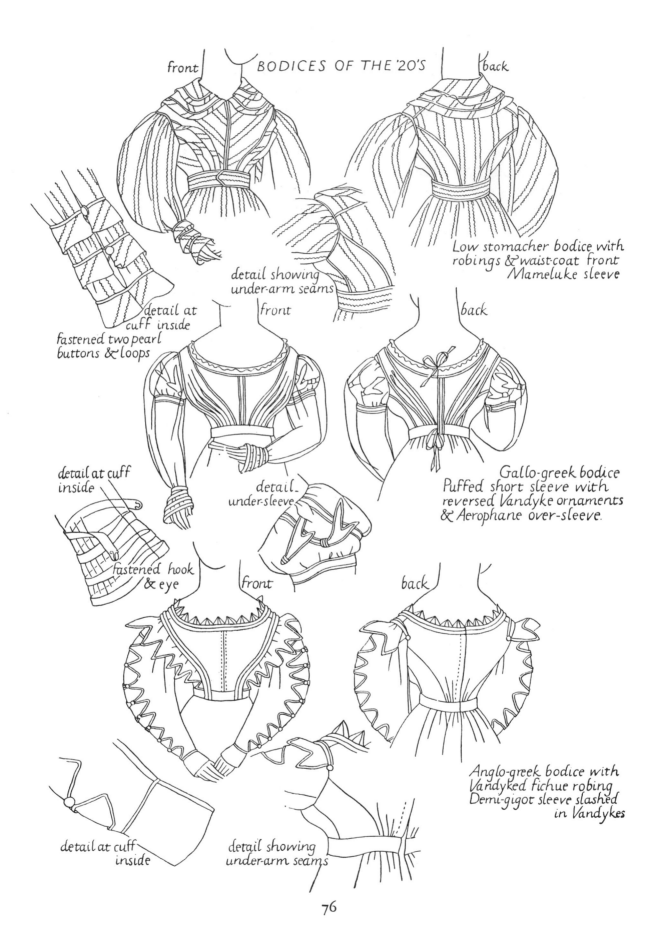

front

back

Low stomacher bodice with
robings & waist-coat front
Mameluke sleeve

detail showing
under-arm seams

front

detail at
cuff inside
fastened two pearl
buttons & loops

detail at cuff
inside
fastened hook
& eye

back

detail
under-sleeve

Gallo-greek bodice
Puffed short sleeve with
reversed Vandyke ornaments
& Aerophane over-sleeve.

front

back

Anglo-greek bodice with
Vandyked fichue robing
Demi-gigot sleeve slashed
in Vandykes

detail at cuff
inside

detail showing
under-arm seams

76

design on the surface. Another variation was the 'Bavarian pelisse-robe' with two lines of trimming descending from the shoulders to the bottom of the skirt, en tablier.

Another variation, the redingote, appearing in 1825, trimmed with three broad tucks up one side of the front and round the skirt, with a large embroidered pelerine similarly tucked; full sleeves with a band round the wrist. In place of the tucks there may be a line of puffing up the front.

B. The Round Dress

This can be classified by the design of the bodice, of which there were three main types, each producing variations:

1. A plain high or half-high bodice (gored and darted).
   - (*a*) The bodice en blouse (see Annual Notes for 1822).
   - (*b*) The bodice à l'enfant. Half-high and round, the neck gathered by a drawstring.
   - (*c*) The bodice en coeur, with a chemisette-tucker. (See 1828.)
   - (*d*) The front-buttoning bodice tight to the shape. (See 1826.)
   - (*e*) The bodice à la vierge. Half-high, or low and square cut, with gathers or narrow pleats descending to the waist. There is no drawstring.

2. A draped bodice.
   - (*a*) The bodice en gerbe (*gerbe* = a sheaf of corn.) The front is pleated fan-wise from the shoulders to the waist.
   - (*b*) The Circassiene bodice, with cross-over folds descending from the shoulders and crossing at the waist. (See 1829.)
   - (*c*) The bodice à la Sevigné; pleated folds covering the top of the bodice nearly horizontally and divided into two by a central bone which runs down to the waist.
   - (*d*) The bodice à la Roxalane, similar to above but the folds slant more decidedly downwards to the central bone. (See 1829.)
   - (*e*) Bodice à l'Edith, a compromise between the Roxalane and the Sevigné.
   - (*f*) The bodice à la Polonese, a variant of the cross-over, the folds crossing high up so that the right-hand fold forms most of the front seen. (See 1828.)

3. Bodice with flat trimmings descending from the shoulders inwards to the waist.
   - (*a*) The 'Gallo-Greek bodice'. The trimmings are narrow and flat and do not quite meet at the waist. From this developed
   - (*b*) The 'stomacher bodice'. A wide 'V' is formed by 'pelerine lappels' (*i.e.* revers) and the enclosed centre is filled with gauging or pleating, headed by a tucker.
   - (*c*) The 'Anglo-Greek' bodice with 'fichu-robings'; the lappels are broad and wide apart 'giving an unnatural breadth to the chest', and are often trimmed with lace, increasing their size. (See 1828.)

77

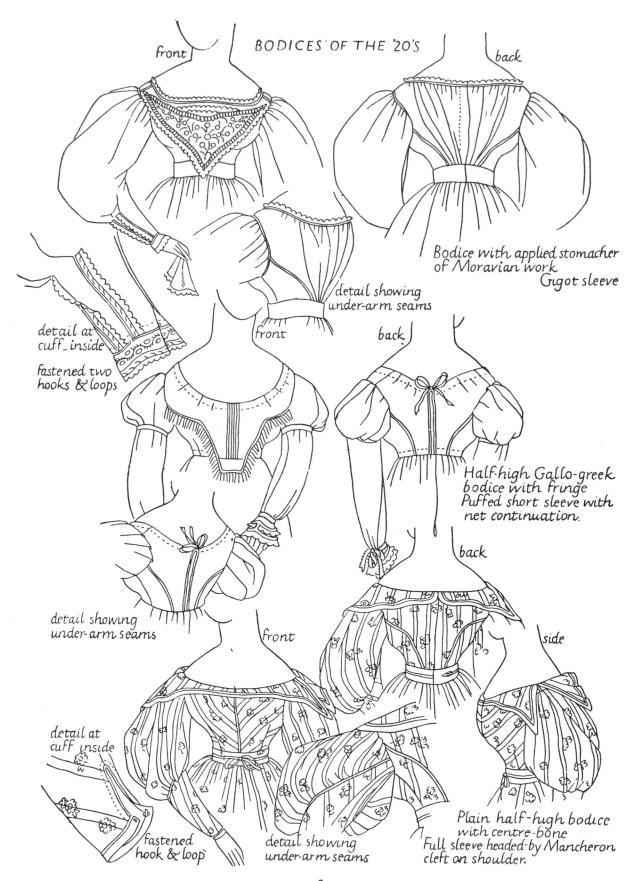

front

back

Bodice with applied stomacher
of Moravian work
Gigot sleeve

detail at
cuff inside

fastened two
hooks & loops

detail showing
under-arm seams

front

back

Half-high Gallo-greek
bodice with fringe
Puffed short sleeve with
net continuation.

detail showing
under-arm seams

front

back

side

detail at
cuff inside

fastened
hook & loop

detail showing
under-arm seams

Plain half-high bodice
with centre-bone
Full sleeve headed by Mancheron
cleft on shoulder.

78

1821. Summer carriage dress of India
muslin bordered with bouillon of
muslin; antique stomacher of
pink satin across the bust with
embroidered robings; double lace
ruff; village hat

1822
Ball dress of tulle over white satin
Promenade pelisse of blue gros de Naples ornamented with trefoils;
vandyked mancherons; triple ruff

The Sleeve

Various types tending steadily to increase in size.

(*a*) 'Full sleeve'; somewhat full at the shoulder and headed by a mancheron, often vandyked or slashed or puffed, and gradually tightening to the wrist, ending in rouleaux, or vandyking with an inside ruffle.

(*b*) The Marie sleeve. Full to the wrist but tied into compartments with ribbons. This type of sleeve was also used in the Vertical Epoch, and occurs occasionally later in the century.
NOTE: the name 'à la Marie' became, about 1827, also used as a refinement for 'gigot'.

(*c*) The 'demi-gigot'. The upper part is the shape of an inverted cone, the fullness terminating at the elbow; the forearm tight, usually with an 'Amadis' cuff (extending up the wrist like a gauntlet).

(*d*) The 'gigot'. Very full above, the fullness terminating just below the elbow.

(*e*) The Mameluke. Very full to the upper part of the wrist.

(*f*) The 'imbecile'. Fuller than the last, the fullness reaching the middle of the wrist, with a short cuff.
NOTE: The term 'imbecile' was not used as a term of derision, the sleeve so designated being simply copied from that of a 'straight waist-coat' used for lunatics.

(*g*) The Donna Maria. Similar to above, but the fullness on the forearm is confined by a loop on the inner side from the bend of the elbow to the wrist.

The Skirt

This is long, touching the shoe, until 1828 when it becomes ankle-length. It is gored until that year; after that, it is pleated.

The lower part is much ornamented, the depth of which increases gradually up to the knee level; at the close of the decade the lowest part is left plain, with a band of trimming or ornament at the knee level. The wadded hem is common at the beginning, especially about 1824, but rare at the end of the period.

Waist round with belt and buckle.

Colours tend to become more glaring with a preference for secondary tints.

EVENING DRESSES

Always with round or square necks, progressively cut more off the shoulders as the decade advances; but lower on the bosom in '22, '23, '24, than in '25, '26, '27, and lower again in '28 and '29.

The Bodice

The various styles are similar to those seen in day dresses, developing similar variations, but the *pointed bodice* appears occasionally from 1822 onwards.

79

A 'Swiss belt', or pointed ceinture, is sometimes worn in the second half of the decade.

NOTE: Bodices cut off the shoulders are kept up simply by their tight fit; neither yoke nor boned bodice was used.

The Sleeve

Always full at the shoulder, becoming fuller towards the end of the period. It may be worn short (as in ball dresses) or with a long transparent oversleeve of white tulle or muslin, having the shape of the fashionable day sleeve of the year. By '29 the short full sleeve for evening dress developed into the 'beret sleeve', in shape a widely distended circle imitating the beret headdress, and closed below by a band round the arm. The shape is sustained by a lining of book muslin with a close fitting inside sleeve. When a transparent oversleeve is worn this passes over the beret and is gathered into the armhole. Occasionally the beret is double, one above the other, and both fully puffed ('double bouffant').

The Skirt

The evening skirt shortens sooner than that of the day dress, and in fact new variants of style appear sooner in evening dresses than in day dresses.

The ornamentation above the hem is richer and fuller than in day dresses; *e.g.* a heavy line of puffing is common till 1827.

OUTDOOR GARMENTS

Pelisses

In winter these are made of cloth, velvet, wadded gros de Naples; all with fur trimming. In summer of silk, levantine, and muslin lined with cotton or sarcenet, with pelerine capes.

Mantles

These were not a prominent feature; references to a few appear in the annual summaries. Usually ankle-length with capes reaching to the waist, and worn in the evening or with carriage dress. Occasionally without armholes à l'assassin (*vide* 1825).

ADDITIONAL GARMENTS WORN ROUND THE NECK AND SHOULDERS

Chemisette

Worn to fill in the space when the front of the bodice descends in the centre (*e.g.* en coeur; variants of the 'folding-front'). Made of white muslin, cambric or tulle.

Tucker

Forming an edging to the front of a square-cut low bodice (evening). Usually narrow with a frilling. Made of white muslin, etc.

Falling Tucker

Similar but hangs down over the front of the bodice; towards the end of the period it becomes much deeper (3 or 4 inches). Made of white materials especially blonde lace. Edges often vandyked.

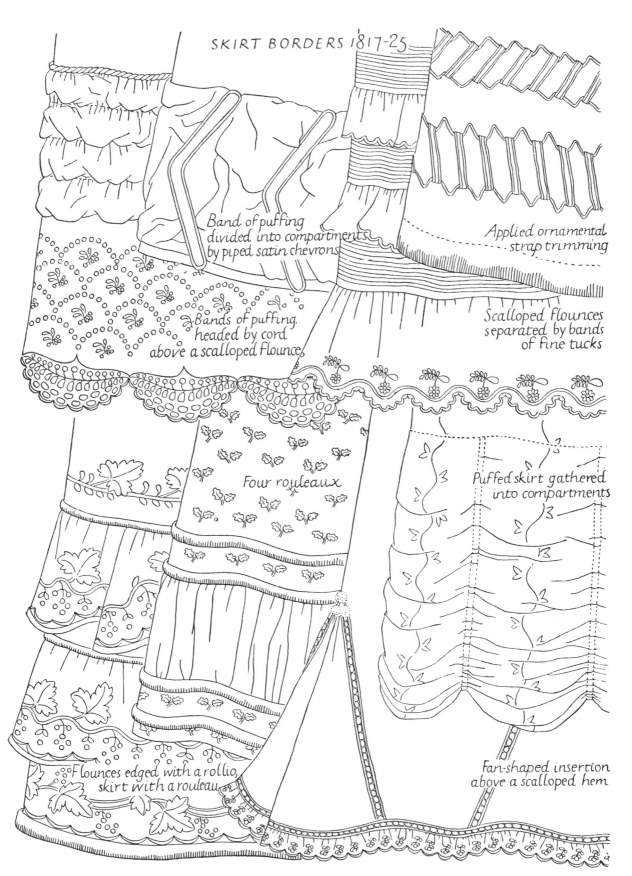

SKIRT BORDERS 1817-25

Band of puffing divided into compartments by piped satin chevrons

Bands of puffing, headed by cord above a scalloped flounce

Applied ornamental strap trimming

Scalloped flounces separated by bands of fine tucks

Four rouleaux

Puffed skirt gathered into compartments

Flounces edged with a rollio, skirt with a rouleau

Fan-shaped insertion above a scalloped hem

Ruffs

Worn round the neck, with day dresses. Single or double.

Falling Collar

Worn round the neck with or without a ruff, with day dresses. Edges often vandyked. Small and narrow at the beginning of the period but very wide towards the close. It develops into the

Pelerine

a collar extending as far as the top of the shoulders, and across the top of the bodice. By further expansion downwards (in 1825) it becomes a

Fichu-pelerine

the ends of which, in 1826, sometimes extend beneath the belt as far as halfway to the knee. The pelerine is usually of a white material but may be of the same stuff as the dress and have a double cape (1825). It is usually headed by a collarette. For winter a pelerine of velvet appears from 1827 on.

Canezou

A sleeveless spencer. Worn over a day dress (1824). Presently it loses the spencer shape and covers only the front and back, but not the sides of the bodice and functions as a 'fichu-canezou'. It is often worn with a ruff. Always made of a white material (muslin, lace, cambric, etc. and embroidered).

Sautoir

A coloured silk cravat often worn round the neck supporting the ruff in walking costume.

1822

DRESSES

Waist lengthens during the year, reaching the normal level by the end.

Day

The chief change is increasing ornamentation of the lower part of the skirt by rouleaux, scalloped flounces, embroidery, etc. 'Skirts much too long.' The gored skirt is common, the fullness being thrown behind, and moderately full in front, while over the hips it is plain without gathers. In summer the French 'blouse dresses' ('worn without stays which takes somewhat from their slammekin appearance; being somewhat short those who have not handsome legs generally wear pantaloons') lead to a modified form in this country, the *round dress* made *en blouse*. The front of the bodice is gathered in at the centre of the waist and over the shoulders so as to produce a pouching effect, the neck being round and half-high. The back, which is gathered in the middle, is fastened by strings. It may be added that, in muslin dresses, seams are sometimes *piped*, a feature not hitherto seen. The pelisse by being worn closed produces the *Pelisse-robe*. 'A walking dress, of light blue tulle, in two rows of figured pink trimming, and finished at the bottom with a large scallop. Skirt long and much gored so that body and skirt appear in one; red morocco girdle with gold buckle at the side. Sleeve with cape epaulette.' Day dresses sometimes gauged half-way down the front or with a band of embroidery en tablier. Round waist with belt and buckle. Summer day dresses white, worn with a pelisse; skirt with three flounces.

Evening

Gallo-Greek bodice. Short sleeves with Spanish slashing; with or without long white net over-sleeves. Skirt with flat wadded rouleaux, or notched and pinked, honeycombed or scalloped, or straps and buckles along the border. Occasional pointed bodices. Some high dresses to button in front and behind. Square cut bodices without tuckers, and very narrow shoulder strap. Some dresses used as high or low according to whether a small temporary spencer is worn; with them a short apron. 'Evening gowns no longer obtrude the broad Cleopatra back.' (July.) 'A round (evening) dress of pink shagreen.' Sashes worn with evening dresses, ends hanging in front.

Fashionable Colours: pink, violet, amaranth, olive green, jonquil, milk-chocolate, celestial blue, London smoke, Esterhazy, and various shades of blue.

OUTDOOR GARMENTS

Pelisses
Cloth. Plain silk lined with swansdown. (Summer) a pelisse with stand-up collar and satin facings.

Shawls
with broad net fringe. Cashmere shawl, white

ground bordered with palm leaves and blue flowers; or narrow embroidered ends. Norwich shawls introduced.

ACCESSORIES

Half *Boots*, or thin walking *Shoes* for day. White satin slippers for evening. 'Silk *Stockings* only when there is silk in the dress; otherwise open-work cotton.' Pagoda *Parasols*: some fringed. *Fans* of fine net with ornaments in polished steel; or of dark satin with gold edge; pierced ivory sticks, or mother-of-pearl. Plain silk *Reticules*. 'The new tortoise-shell reticules' with leather folds and cut steel clasps. *Jewellery*: necklaces of several rows of pearls twisted. Drop ear-rings of polished steel, of rubies and garnets. Cameo bracelets. 'Rings are worn on every finger.' Coral much worn with home costume. The King's visit to Scotland (August) makes Scotch tartan materials fashionable.

Prices
A dress of Urling's patent lace, 12 guineas, of French lace, 50 guineas.

1823

DRESSES

The chief change is a tendency to multiply the number of narrow flounces which now frequently reach the knee level.

Day
Morning dresses with bodice en blouse common. Occasionally en gerbe. Fashionable trimming for the bodice is rouleaux en serpentine. Sleeves fuller. Sleeves of walking dresses with strap at the wrist.

Evening
Occasionally two lines of embroidery from the waist down the skirt to suggest the style of an open robe. Skirts with borders of full rouleaux of satin round which are entwined leaves of the same material. A few demi-trains. Some bodices en gerbe, with short puffed sleeves with buttoned languettes. Spanish slashing of sleeves and sometimes of the sides of the bodice. Some lace dresses 'à la francaise', *i.e.* with the lace dress shorter than the slip underneath. Swansdown pelerine-tippet, with long ends reaching below the knee, worn round the shoulders.

Fashionable Colours: puce, drake's neck, geranium, Esterhazy, mignonette-green, lilac, marshmallow blossom, pink, celestial blue, amber, Indian red.

OUTDOOR GARMENTS

Carriage *Mantles*, partially fastening by invisible straps to receive the hands, and left open in front.

Cloaks now without hoods but with three large capes.

Shawls. Angola, raw silk, buff colour; China crepe.

Pelisses. Pelisse (Summer) of delicate spring colours, tied down the front with ribbon bows, and fastened by spring clasps; stand-up collar. Pelisse (Summer) of muslin with pelerine-cape but no mancherons. Pelisse (Winter): the wrapping type trimmed with fur à la Witzchoura.

ACCESSORIES

Black satin *Shoes* for dancing.

Gloves
Limerick, doeskin or lemon kid for day; long white kid for evening.

Jewellery: pearl necklaces. Eyeglass suspended on thin chain. Horsehair bracelets, dyed scarlet.

'Rainbow elastic *Scarves*' made of a chain of light texture, or coloured diamond work.

1824

DRESSES

'Waists moderately long.' (*i.e.* at natural level).

Day

Generally without collars but worn with a collarette of worked muslin or 'our imitation of foreign lace', or with a small kerchief, *e.g.* 'a morning dress with figured lace kerchief worn over the bodice and confined at the waist by a belt.' The sleeve en blouse, *i.e.* full and loose from just below the shoulder to below the elbow (precursor of the 'imbecile'). Mancherons on shoulders. Occasionally gigot or Marie sleeves. Sleeves become perceptibly fuller by the summer. Border of skirts trimmed with bias folds in waves, chevrons or chains. These are seldom, as formerly, quite plain, except in chintz and cambric dresses, where the folds overlap. Home dresses with front fastening, with Spanish bows or buttons. New type of home dress 'à la tunique'; the tunic long, appearing like a half-open pelisse with a false petticoat inserted. 'Pelisse robes of silk with petticoats of rich Moravian work' for home dresses (matrons). Common types of morning dresses—the pelisse-robe with small pelerine collar of same material, with or without falling collar; the half-high round dress, with or without fichu.

Materials: washing figured silks, chintzes with ground of two shades, muslins, barège, scarlet bombazine. Pelisse-robes of gros de Naples.

Evening

Bodices—Gallo-Greek, Circassiene, Sevigné, en gerbe (both front and back). Always with back fastening. Bodices tend to be plainer. Sleeves long, of white lace, tulle or lisse, with coloured silk dresses. Full mancherons. Short sleeves (full) declining. Skirts wider and more gored. Trimmed up to the knee with lines of embroidery, scalloped flounces cut en bias, puffing or corkscrew ornaments. Some tunic robes with demi-trains, the robe coloured over a white petticoat. Robes with Bavarian fronts.

Materials: shot silks, gauze with satin stripes.

Fashionable Colours: primrose, pink, Parma, poppy, ruby, Hortensia. The effect of 'the dazzling variety of colours displayed on one person' was said to be absurd. 'The general characteristic of youth should be meek dignity, chastened by sportiveness and gentle seriousness. Ladies are implored to maintain something of the ease and grace attached to the once dominant Grecian costume amongst us, against all the newly sprung up Goths and Vandals in the shape of stay-makers, etc., who have just armed themselves with whalebone, steel and buckram to the utter destruction of all native-born fine forms.'

OUTDOOR GARMENTS

Pelisses

with double cape cut square, worn with or without a ruff. Sleeves full, sometimes à la Marie, or tight to the elbow. Wrist closed by band and button 'in the French style'. (Winter.) Cloth pelisses buttoning down the right side with polished steel buttons. Pelisse with two wadded rouleaux on each side and round the hem; belt; no collar; full puckered mancherons.

The *Canezou* (a sleeveless spencer) appears.

Venetian *Mantle* (evening) trimmed with fur and having a hood.

ACCESSORIES

'Half *Boots* and gaiters of grey silk or of Turkey leather are much in vogue; the gaiters are buttoned, the boots laced.'

Gloves

Limerick, doeskin or lemon kid gloves for day; long white kid for evening.

Jewellery: bracelets very fashionable; always a pair, one on each wrist with carriage costume. With evening dress gold armlets above the elbow, as well. Necklaces of large pearls. Eyeglass suspended on gold chain. 'Not only children, but young ladies of 17 or 18 wear pantaloons of white cambric in the country. They are ornamented with four bias folds of muslin next the ankle. The short petticoat above belongs to a dress en blouse.'

NOTE: Early in the year the duty on imported silks and wool was much reduced. On foreign wool from 6d. to 1d. a lb. On East India silk

1826
Day dress of heavy silk with chiné satin stripe

from 4/- to 3d. On China and Italian silk from 5/6 to 6d. On Brazilian raw silk from 14/10 to 7/6. And foreign manufactured silks admitted at 30% ad valorem duty. As a result silks became too cheap to be fashionable and British chintz and muslins were patronised.

1825

DRESSES

Day

(1) Pelisse robe. (2) Round dress. (3) Redingote. (4) Bodice en blouse. Broad pelerine-cape and fichu-pelerine, or fichu-collar. Moderately full sleeves, sometimes gigot, with three bands at the wrist, or cuffs with reversed points. Occasionally the sleeve from the elbow to the wrist is divided by straps into puffed compartments. Some with short full sleeves to which long sleeves of white muslin are attached. Border of skirt ornamented with scallops, vandyking or foliage with rouleaux bands, or several wadded tucks, or four scalloped or pointed flounces. (Summer.) Open pelisses over petticoat of muslin, embroidered; often three or four pelerine-capes. Dresses of muslin, bodice en blouse, with wide sleeves confined at the wrist and up the arm by bracelets. Gauze striped handkerchief, fringed, often worn round the shoulders, as a pelerine, the pointed ends tucked into the waistband or sash in front.

Materials: white cambric, India corded muslin, printed muslins and chintzes, gros de Naples and striped ginghams, levantine, cashmere, striped barège.

Evening

Corsage en gerbe, Gallo-Greek, or à la vierge, or à la Sevigné, and usually plain. Round waist with sash in front; occasionally slightly pointed. Short puffed shoulder sleeve with or without over-sleeve. Skirt ankle-length, three or four scalloped flounces, or embroidery, or line of puffing nearly up to the knee. Often zig-zag trimmings headed by branches of flowers, or a deep border of satin leaves applied. Ball Dresses: short tunic robe over a petticoat of light material, slightly trimmed with flowers. 'Though we must ever admire the modest shielding of the bust yet we think it now carried rather to an extreme especially in full dress;

there is a confined awkwardness in the way the front part of the corsage is carried across the neck while the gown is made low in the back and rather falling off the shoulders.'

Materials: tulle, crepe-lisse, satin, gros de Naples; demi-evening dresses of striped materials.

New Materials: 'English Organdy, an improved form of Leno.' Scotch Madras with red and green stripes.

Fashionable Colours: Very bright colours fashionable. Terre d'Egypte, rose lavender, mignonette-green, blue, geranium.

OUTDOOR GARMENTS

Pelisses

Pelisse of muslin with three or four collar capes, trimmed with quilling of narrow tulle.

Carriage *Cloaks* with three capes and a hood. Mountain cloaks. 'Wrapped up in a solitary cloak à l'assassin, how can a lady either give or take an arm?'

Pelerine *Mantlet* of American grey squirrel and muff of same.

Shawls

Cashmere, white ground and narrow border; or yellow with fringed border of floral design; rich angolas; coloured China crepe.

ACCESSORIES

Parasols rather smaller. 'The newest are not lined; the handles are of ivory finished by a large oval ring.' *Jewellery*: pendant ear-rings and necklaces of pearl. *Handkerchief* carried in the hand. Cambric and lace *Ruffs* often worn with day dresses. The button of cloth with iron shank invented by Sanders.

1826

DRESSES

'Our fair countrywomen have resolved to make silk of the Spitalfields manufacture a considerable portion of their dress (to relieve a distressed industry). His

Majesty has given orders that the rooms of his palace at Windsor shall be hung round with silk of the Spitalfields manufacture.'

Day

Pelisse-robes or round dresses buttoning down the front; small pelerine-cape en suite. Bodices high, en gerbe, plain, or à l'enfant. Skirts with two moderate flounces, scalloped or bias, or flounces of pinked scallops, or three rouleaux at equal distances. Shawl dresses for morning (*i.e.* with border of skirt designed with shawl pattern). Carriage dresses decorated with rows of bands down the front in 'the Bavarian style'. Summer dresses. White muslin spencers worn with coloured skirts.

Materials as before, also tabinet and tartan silks.

Evening

Unchanged, except that many have a falling tucker of white lace, and the shoulder sleeves tend to be fuller, with epaulettes. The sash is often replaced by a plain band. Chevrons are a new form of trimming above the hem of the skirt. 'In gowns for full dress a great improvement has taken place; they are perfectly modest yet they do not utterly obscure the well-formed contour of a fine bust, but rather "double every charm they seem to hide".'

Materials: crepe, coloured gauzes with satin stripes, trimmed with satin ribbons. Taffeta.

Fashionable Colours. The fashion for bright colours is still marked (*e.g.* amaranth, pink, scarlet, canary yellow, geranium, and various shades of blue).

OUTDOOR GARMENTS

Pelisses

Made 'to fasten imperceptibly'. Pelisse with rouleaux, bust trimmed with chevrons; collar notched and half standing up. Pelisse trimmed with narrow fluted ornaments; collar of silk quilling; gigot sleeves.

Cloaks and pelerine *Capes* terminated in front by long points reaching to the hips.

ACCESSORIES

Gloves

Day, yellow Limerick. Evening, elbow length white kid.

Jewellery: numerous bracelets of chased gold, very broad and jointed. Brooches with shell cameos and mosaic.

'At Paris they recommend the corsets of Delacroix, fitted with paddings as may be required to fill up any deficiency. Young ladies may be seen with their breasts displaced by being pushed up too high and frightful wrinkles established between the bosom and shoulders . . . a ridiculous fashion by means of which the body resembles an ant with a slender tube uniting the bust to the haunches which are stuffed out beyond all proportion.'

Prices

'The new printed chintzes' at 7/- to 8/- a yard.

1827

DRESSES

Day

High bodice en gerbe, or plain with front buttoning, or pelisse-robe. The size of the upper part of the sleeve is increasing. Gigot sleeve sometimes stiffened at the top with whalebone, or held up by '8 or 10 drawstrings'; mancherons cleft at the shoulders or with double scallops. The wrist is frequently finished with 'antique' points, (*i.e.* reversed). Skirt trimmed with one deep or several narrow scalloped flounces. Fichu-pelerines, of same material as dress, with long ends worn under the belt. (Summer.) White embroidered muslin canezous—spencers with wide sleeves—worn with coloured silk skirt, or with coloured muslin dress; or coloured silk canezou with white skirt and sleeves.

Riding Habits of fine cloth with muslin falling collar and pink sautoir.

Evening

Bodice: à la Circassiene, à la Sevigné (with narrow vandyked tucker); Anglo-Greek; square with pelerine lapels with horizontal drapery; or bodice fitting tight to the shape. A few pointed front and back. Some with broad falling lace collar cleft on the shoulders en Paladin. The edges of the bodice trimmed with points, flutings, ruching or rouleaux. Sleeves 'larger than ever'. Short and full (full evening) or with long sleeves (demi-evening). Skirts with two scalloped flounces, en bias, headed by chenille chainwork cordon. Or with one deep bias flounce, headed. Or by two lines of bouffants. Sashes are replaced by belts with gold buckles. Pelerines of silk, with long pointed ends, worn

1823. Walking dress: pelisse of blue
gros de Naples trimmed with satin
rouleaux; patent lace ruff; Robinette hat
with cornette underneath

1824. Ball dress of tulle over pink gros de Naples,
the leaf ornaments in pink satin; the body of
pink gros de Naples ornamented with pearls

1825. Carriage dress: lavender gros de
Naples pelisse with pelerine-cape; India muslin cape; Lyonnese hat over
lace cornette

1826. Evening dress of patent lace over
white satin slip; satin corsage; blue
barège scarf

with high dresses (demi-evening). For an evening dress 10 to 12 yards of silk is required; with a flounced evening dress and its pointed pelerine, 25 yards may be needed. (Note: width of materials: heavy silks 18 to 22 inches; sarcenet 32 inches.)

Materials: poplin, satin, sarcenet, gros de Naples, black lace over white satin, tabinet trimmed with chenille, painted Indian taffeta, levantine, striped batiste, Japanese gauze with satin stripes, ball dresses of crepe, gauze or tulle, white or coloured with satin bodices.

New Materials: striped batiste, gros des Indes, gros de Naples with satin stripes, printed muslins and chintzes with yellow ground, British cashmere, cashmere 'shawl dresses', Palmyrene.

OUTDOOR GARMENTS

Pelisses

Worn with a white ruff, of black velvet, buttoning down the front, narrow collar, double mancherons, gigot sleeves. Pelisse of Pomona green gros de Naples with zig-zag trimmings of black velvet. Pelisse with pelerine-capes, mancherons and straps, requiring 30 yards of material. Pelisse with the front laid on in pleats. Pelisse with double mancherons à la Psyche. Pelisse of taffeta and gros de Naples. Pelisse with bias fold trimming and plain cape falling over the shoulders. Pelisse trimmed with a pinked ruche, wrists with long reversed points. Pelisse of silk with large round pelerine-capes of same materials.

Mantles

of swansdown, Zibeline fur, American squirrel, levantine lined with sarcenet (with a pelerine-cape and edging of velvet), satin, wadded; and tartan merino.

Shawls

Cashmere, white ground, palm leaf border, China crepe, fringed and embroidered in colours. 'Paraguay shawls of bright amber colour delicately figured over.' Gauze shawl half handkerchief, with patterns of satin-like brocade.

ACCESSORIES

Shoes

The toes now definitely square in shape.

Gloves

Evening gloves are shorter, just below the elbow.

Slate coloured *Gaiters* worn. '*Jewellery* of the most superb order; for bracelets there is a sort of mania.' 'Ladies now wear bouquets not merely in their bosoms but they carry them about in their hands as large as brooms, and when they sit down to dinner they stick their nosegays into the water glasses and the table looks like a bed of flowers.' (Croker.) 'Satin *Ribbons* stamped with black figures in imitation of the French ribbons à la giraffe.'

NOTE: In Paris 'petticoats are stuck out with whalebone', and pantaloons are worn with riding habits.

1828

DRESSES

Day

Bodice usually high, either en gerbe, en blouse, en coeur with chemisette tucker, Anglo-Greek without stomacher, and with fichu-robings; or pelisse-robes. Sleeves, gigot, à la Marie; with cuffs at the wrist or with reversed points. Some 'carriage dresses' with sleeves of white muslin or aerophane, à la Marie. Ribbon belt, or a 'zone belt' with slightly pointed centre. Skirt, less goring and more pleating, but 'those who have their skirts set equally full in pleats ought to have a fine shape, otherwise a single young lady is in appearance too full in size where she ought not to be.' Ankle-length. The line of puffing above the hem goes out by the end of the year. Trimming of one or two deep flounces, either cut on the cross and plain with or without a rouleaux heading, or cut in dents, or fluted; or a band of applied foliage, pointed, or embroidery at the knee level. Deep hem. Worn with pelerine-capes, single or double, made en suite; often cleft over the shoulders 'en Paladin'; or a pelerine with one to three falls of embroidered muslin. Sometimes a high French ruff and coloured sautoir; some with canezou-spencers buttoning behind. Pelisse-robes are plain with two narrow rouleaux down the sides in front. Sometimes a tunic pelisse-robe, the bodice with turned back lapels. (Summer) elaborate canezou-pelerines, of muslin trimmed with lace, with mancherons cut in points on the shoulders, are generally worn over outdoor summer dresses. A ruff is usual, either separate or attached to the canezou.

Materials: batiste, merino, bombazine, chintz.

Cachemire dresses: 'We do not mean the cloth so misnamed but a light kind of material something like the barège.'

Riding Habits
of cashmere or figured merino; sometimes a muslin canezou-spencer worn with wide sleeves and a cloth skirt.

Evening
Bodices usually square and cut off the shoulders; slight point at the waist in front; worn with or without a falling tucker, en Paladin, or narrow upright tucker with vandyked edge.

Types: à la Sevigné, à la Marie Stuart (*i.e.* a stiff bodice with long point below and a central bone). En gerbe, with central bone. À la grecque (*i.e.* a very wide front, the folds being brought together under the sash so as to form a wheatsheaf as they widen out towards each shoulder; the upper part of the corsage spreads out in an easy manner). By the end of the year the Roxalane bodice appears. Sleeves for demi-evening—gigot or à la Marie. For full evening, short and full with mancherons; and with or without tulle oversleeves to the wrist. Skirt ankle-length; pleated equally all round the waist. Trimming: one or two large separated flounces, headed by rouleaux; flounces scalloped or fluted or pointed; or a simple deep hem reaching nearly to knee level, embroidered in floss silk. Evening shawls of yellow cashmere flowered all over, narrow borders. (Summer) 'Muslin and tulle Canezou-Spencers are much worn in demi-toilette with a coloured silk petticoat' (skirt).

Materials: as formerly, but crepe-aerophane very fashionable.

During the year an increasing number of pointed bodices are worn. 'A certain chastened originality of English manner in dress is ob-servable', distinguishing English from French fashions. 'Not content with excessive tight-lacing our ladies pad themselves till they appear like bottle-spiders.'

OUTDOOR GARMENTS

Pelisses are simple; gigot sleeves; some of gros des Indes. A wadded pelerine-cape worn over it. Pelisse with wadded hem and rouleaux trimming; no collar.

Large *Cloaks* with black velvet capes. Opera cloaks trimmed with marabout.

Carriage *Scarf* of white Japanese gauze with satin stripes and brocaded with flowers; and cravat scarves of striped silk.

Pelerine fur *Tippet* with long rounded ends; large fur tippets of the Russian mantlet kind. Polish mantilla (evening) of levantine, fitting the waist and with loose drapery sleeves.

ACCESSORIES

Half *Boots* of kid, or of grey corded silk with kid tips, lacing on the inner side. Walking costume: kid boots with mother-of-pearl buttons, or lacing, on the inner side. *Shoes* tied 'en sandales'. 'The present new fashion of having shoes and stockings the same colour as the dress.' Silk *Stockings* with coloured clocks for ball dress. *Jewellery*: 'Gold chains with small essence bottles suspended from them are much admired.' Painted *Ribbons* much in fashion.

French. Bustles, of wadding between quilted sarcenet; some worn under the corset; some are a stuffing of wadding round the waist over the corset. 'Bouffants mechanique'—springs, fastened to the corset at the top, to distend the sleeve. 'Many ladies when riding wear silk drawers similar to what is worn when bathing.'

1829

DRESSES

The chief features of the year are the increasing width of the shoulder line with the increasing size of the upper sleeve, and the enormous size of the hats. 'Large sleeves are now so common that they are seen on females of the lower and vulgar class.'

Day
Bodices half-high, either en gerbe, à la Circassiene, à la Sevigné, or à la Roxalane. Or bodices with fichu-robings; or with horizontal pelerine, either à disposition or of muslin, extending widely over the shoulders where it is often cleft en Paladin. Sleeves: gigot, with Amadis cuff. Mameluke with close cuff, either with reversed points or with a reversed ruffle. Imbecile with a very short cuff. Donna Maria. 'We are happy to see the stiffening lately worn at the shoulders under long sleeves now entirely exploded; the

sleeve now falls down in all its amplitude.' Skirt short, and pleated round the waist, 'giving to the figure, especially if short, a Dutch doll-like appearance'. A new feature is a *trimming of fringe* at the knee level, or a line of ruching, quilled flounces, one very deep flounce headed by bouillon or a band of embroidery or chevrons. The hem is as high as the knee. Pelerines of muslin, cambric or net, enormously wide, worn. Pelisse-robes closed down the front with lines of bows or languettes; either high in the neck with a canezou-fichu, or open, with pelerine lapels turned back, and with a chemisette-tucker. Occasionally tunic robes over a muslin petticoat. 'Breakfast dress with muslin canezou and apron.' 'A summer dress of white organdy embroidered with crewel work.' (Winter) Merino dresses without pelisses as the sleeves are too big to draw a pelisse over them.

Materials: Norwich crepe, merino, printed muslins, chintz, gros de Naples, sarcenet.

Riding Habit

A buttoned bodice with falling collar and chemisette and frill of cambric; black stock; gigot sleeves; *cloth pantaloons*.

Evening

Bodices cut very low off the shoulders 'but are rendered perfectly decorous by a full broad tucker.' *Types*: (1) Plain and tight to the shape, with horizontal falling tucker of lace; (2) à la Roxalane; (3) à la Sevigné; (4) à la Marie Stuart. For demi-evening, a wrapping front with chemisette; or half-high bodice with narrow tippet or cape collar cleft on the shoulders. The corsage of ball dresses is often laced across the front. Waists generally round, with belt or sash with the floating ends in front; occasionally a slightly pointed bodice, or a 'pointed zone' girdle worn. Some 'Bavarian robes' worn. Sleeves short, very full, either simple or with double bouffant; some fluted, with a lace frill as heading. Occasionally long tulle oversleeves. Some beret sleeves over which are blonde ornaments à la Psyche, *i.e.* very full and hanging nearly over the sleeve. The skirt is short, especially for ball dresses, and trimmed with: (1) a deep headed flounce, often festooned; (2) a broad hem headed by a rouleaux; (3) a band of foliage or bows of material; (4) the hem covered with a deep ruching; (5) deep band of crepe puffing nearly up to knee level, confined at intervals with satin rouleaux; (5) broad flounces of blonde.

Materials: Full dress: Satin, velvet, poplin, crepe-aerophane, tulle, brocaded and painted silks, 'changeable' (*i.e.* 'shot') silks. Demi-evening: Norwich crepe, poplin, merino, gros de Naples.

Fashionable Colours: Azure blue, myrtle green, pink, amber, marshmallow, jonquil, stone-grey, straw, scarlet, yellow, Navarino-smoke, Egyptian earth, Hortensia, London smoke, plaids.

New French Materials: 'Crinoline', made of horsehair, for lining reticules and hats, and as a dress material. Egyptian muslin (printed with Egyptian patterns). 'Chaly' (or 'Challis') a textile of camel's hair.

OUTDOOR GARMENTS

Pelisses

with a deep hem to the knee level. Some fastened down the front with straps, crescent-shaped, with steel buckles; others fastened by languette straps; gigot sleeves and gauntlet cuffs. Pelisse of black gros de Naples with deep hem and deep Gothic points; pleated body tight to the shape; falling satin collar. Pelisse trimmed with fringe, and fringed pelerine cape. Pelisse fastening at the shoulders by concealed hooks to prevent the sleeves from being rumpled when it is put on. Pelisse of blue satin fastening down the front of the skirt with languette straps. Gigot sleeves separated from the body by a line of gathering. Gauntlet cuffs. Summer pelisse of white muslin, embroidered. Oriental sleeves (*i.e.* very full and not confined at wrist).

Carriage *Cloak* of satin with broad cape descending to waist level. 'Venetian cloak (evening) of black satin and collar cape; large Turkish sleeves.'

Shawls of painted crepe with white fringe. Openwork black shawls with fringed satin borders.

Large round *Tippets* (of swansdown, marten or chinchilla), 'called by the French "boas"'.

ACCESSORIES

Half *Boots* fringed round the top (for morning dress). Of coloured kid or morocco. White *Gloves* embroidered on the back of the hand (walking costume); or coloured kid. *Fans* small; usually carved ivory or mother-of-pearl. *Jewellery*: lockets suspended by gold chains. Girandole ear-rings. 'Never was seen such a display of crosses of every kind.' Chatelaines with chain attached. *Reticules* of silk net over white satin.

1. *Evening Dress*. Hair very high in profusion of full bows and plaits behind; front in full curls. Tiara of pearls and white crepe roses placed very far back on the head.

2. *Walking Dress*. Bonnet of white satin trimmed with green and white feathers; blonde or Valenciennes lace in front.

3. *Morning Dress*. Mob cap of rich lace trimmed with flowers.

4. *Walking Dress*. Bonnet of lavender coloured metallic gauze trimmed with draperies of plain gauze to correspond and a bunch of white flowers; tied with lavender coloured riband.

5. *Evening Dress*. Toque of lilac satin and white blonde confined with pearls. Pearl band round the crown and plume of white ostrich feathers.

6. *Walking Dress*. Black Leghorn bonnet lined with white satin ornamented with pink satin; brim finished by a full puffing of same material. Pink satin strings.

1821

1. *Morning Walking Dress*. Fancy hat ornamented with roses. Under it is worn a mob cap of fine lace.

2. *Evening Dress*. Headdress à la turque with bandeau of pearls, and marabout feathers on left side.

3. *Evening Dress*. Wreath of silver leaves round the forehead and one similar encircling the comb. Hair arranged à l'enfant with short ringlets in the neck.

4. *Evening Dress*. Hair in full but light curls on the temple; sprig of moss roses on one side.

5. *Morning Dress*. Lace mob cap ornamented with wreath and rosette of satin ribbon.

6. *Carriage Dress*. Bonnet of cerulean blue satin lined with white; full plume of ostrich feathers.

1827. Caricature by R. Cruikshank: 'Monstrosities of 1827'

1828

Evening dress of grey gros des Indes bordered with points en sabretache;
bodice à la vierge

Pelisse of fawn gros de Naples; satin lapels

Evening dress of celestial blue tabinet bordered with stiff satin scrolls. Sevigné
corsage; Marie sleeves of white aerophane

1822

1. *Ball Dress*. Sultana turban of geranium and white gauze with the Ottoman esprit plume in centre, of pure gold.

2. *Ball or Evening Full Dress*. Hair à la Gabrielle, with plume of white feathers.

3. *Walking Dress*. Bonnet of undressed crepe to match dress finished with satin pipings round brim and broad fan puffing on each side of crown.

4. *Evening Dress*. Full curls with small cluster of roses completed with negligée of blonde lace tied under the chin.

5. *Evening Dress*. White satin hat, 'rather inclining to the Anne Boleyn form', lined with fluted net; quilling of blonde at the edge and feathers in front. Hair in Vandyke style with cornet of fine lace with knots of satin riband.

6. *Morning Dress*. Cap of fine tulle and blonde trimmed with flowers to match the dress.

1823

1. *Walking Dress*. Arcadian bonnet to correspond with pelisse; lace cornet underneath, and white lace veil.

2. *Morning Dress*. French cornette of Urling's patent lace, with puffings of the same material; the caul has three drawings of riband crosswise.

3. *Opera or Evening Full Dress*. Turban of gold tissue with plume of white ostrich feathers. Hair braided on the forehead and in full curls on each side.

4. *Cottage (Country) Dress*. Village hat of fine Leghorn fastened with long strings à la negligée, and trimmed with straw coloured ribands.

5. *Walking Dress*. Bonnet of white satin with puffing round the edge and crown; top ornamented with small squares of satin and bunches of roses.

6. *Evening Dress*. Hair in full curls and bows with similar flowers confining each bow.

91

1. *Seaside Walking Dress.* Leghorn bonnet, village shape, trimmed with broad pink ribbon; lace cornette underneath.

2. *Ball Dress.* Hair arranged in the new Parisian fashion, short at the ears and elevated on the summit of the head; ringlets entwined with blue gauze and full blown roses, and separated from bows behind by a gold comb.

3. *Morning Dress.* Cap of French lace and flowers.

4. *Carriage Dress.* Lyonese hat of pink crepe with satin stripes under the brim a shade darker than the hat; quilling of blonde at the edge; crown ornamented with pink gauze and white roses. Lace cornette underneath.

5. *Bonnet* of gros de Naples, Pomona green to match pelisse, trimmed with bows of same material and roses; lined with pink.

6. *Private Concert Dress.* Armenian turban of Indian rose colour with three gold esprits and gold ornament.

1825

1. *Walking Dress.* Hat of morning primrose gros de Naples ornamented by bows of deep blue riband edged with pink, and broad strings left to suspend from the ear.

2. *Opera Dress.* Hair brought round the face in large Parisian curls; blue turban of crepe lisse with folds of amber of the same material; a plume of feathers confined with a diamond brooch.

3. *Carriage Dress.* Bonnet of lavender coloured gros de Naples (to match pelisse) with plaiting of white blonde at edge and a bouquet of full blown roses.

4. *Ball Dress.* Hair in full curls next the face with flowing ringlets behind, curls in front ornamented with gauze.

5. *Public Promenade Dress.* Black velvet bonnet with feathers, tied in a bow with lappets of white gauze edged with blonde. Lace cornette underneath.

6. *Morning Dress.* Cap of fine Urling's lace confined under the chin with a small brooch. Small moss rose on each side.

1826

1. *Promenade or Seaside Dress*. Hat of white gros de Naples trimmed with scrolls and large full blown Provence roses. Strings of broad variegated riband of chequers on a pink ground.

2. *Home Costume*. Fichu of Urling's lace disposed in front like a turban; half wreath of full blown roses on the hair; the caul has a row of roses across the centre; ends left loose.

3. *Evening Party Dress*. Hair in large curls with plume of white ostrich feathers.

4. *Walking Dress*. Cornette of lace with rose coloured riband under black satin bonnet ornamented with half blown damask roses and foliage; strings left loose.

5. *Evening Dress*. Hair in curls of moderate size with pearl bandeau placed obliquely across the forehead. A beret-turban of puffs of blue and rose coloured gauze with bird of Paradise plume.

6. *Morning Dress*. Cornette of thread tulle and lace with one full blown rose.

1827

1. *Walking Dress*. Hat of white chip with bows and long puffs of tartan ribbon, yellow on white ground.

2. *Carriage Dress* for paying carriage visits of ceremony. Fine Leghorn hat with white ostrich feathers and strings of tartan ribbon, dark and lively colours on white ground. Rosette of white ribbon on each side under the brim and bandeau of the same.

3. *Morning Dress*. Cap of blond with bow of cerulean blue ribbon lying on the hair; the other side slightly ornamented with same ribbon.

4. *Evening Dress*. Vienna toque of separate stiffened puffs of pink satin with short white curled feathers. One long loop of pink gauze ribbon depends over the left shoulder.

5. *Summer Evening Dress*. Transparent hat of white crepe ornamented with white ribbon chequered with green and straw colour, trimmed with 'branches of the tulip tree in blossom'.

6. *Evening Dress*. Beret of pink gauze decorated with pink satin ribbon.

93

1. *Morning Dress*. Hat of fine Leghorn trimmed with two different ribbons, one of the same colour as the sash, the other of plain cashmere yellow; the strings are also different from each other.

2. *Evening Dress*. Hat of pink gros de Naples, front of brim pointed 'en bateau' with point turned back and fastening to summit of crown. Trimmed with several pink feathers.

3. *Afternoon Costume*. Blonde cap à la Psyche, wings surrounded where they are stiffened by a rouleau of pink satin. Ornamented with bows of figured pink ribbon.

4. *Evening Dress*. Hair much elevated on the summit of the head, with a coronet ornament round the base of the Apollo knot, in pearls, and above, two birds of Paradise.

5. *Opera Dress*. Black velvet toque-turban, ornamented with strings of pearls and two pearl tassels.

6. *Morning Dress*. Bonnet of Pomona green gros de Naples with broad white blonde at edge of brim and ornamenting crown. The small bows trimming crown, and the strings, are of green and white ribbon.

1829

1. *Walking Dress*. Cottage bonnet of canary yellow satin trimmed with pink gros de Naples and ribbon.

2. *Morning Dress*. Bonnet of tourterelle coloured gros de Naples, crown trimmed with similar material and puffs of ribbon half pink, half white, the white painted with light green foliage. The same ribbon under the brim and composing the strings.

3. *Evening Dress*. Beret of celestial-blue spotted gauze ornamented with bows of blue and silver lamé ribbons and two white esprits.

4. *Back view of 3*

5. *Dinner Dress*. Hair arranged à la Naiad, adorned with bandeaux of gold and gold arrows.

6. *Morning Dress or Home Costume*. Blonde cap with three borders of a vandyke pattern, ornamented with bows of cornflower blue ribbon. Very long strings depending as low as the knees.

All through the decade there was a steady increase in the apparent size of the head, and especially in the breadth. The hair, instead of hanging in vertical ringlets by the side of the face was now puffed out in curls on the temples, causing the face to assume a round shape.

By 1824, in the evening, a new and remarkable form of arrangement began to appear, the *Apollo knot*. This was a single loop, or as many as three loops of plaited hair standing up on end on the summit of a pile of hair arranged in bows on the crown; in many cases these loops of hair were the owner's only by purchase, for specimens of such knots, attached to ribbon by which they were tied on the head, are to be found. One in my collection is some four inches long. They kept their erect shape by means of concealed wires.

The complicated hair-dressing required the use of high combs, the 'galleries', or horizontal portions, being elaborately decorated with gilt balls. Some of these combs were of tortoiseshell, but most seem to have been of gilt metal, the teeth often of copper.

Towards the end of the decade a coiffure 'à la chinoise' came in to fashion, in which the hair was tightly screwed up off the sides of the head and closely plaited on the crown into bows and knots, skewered into position by ornamental pins with large detachable heads ('Glauvina pins').

The day caps steadily expanded in breadth, and grew more and more decorative by the use of coloured linings, ribbons and artificial flowers, even in the day.

The bonnets, after a short phase of the 'Marie Stuart' shape, expanded in breadth and height, but always with an inclination to be tilted back off the face.

But the principal feature of the decade was the hats. About 1824 these, in the day, began to grow like a mushroom, and by the end of the decade they had acquired a size surpassing anything in the century. But it was not merely their size which was so extraordinary, as the riot of decoration on and under them; flowers, immensely wide ribbons, and huge feathers were heaped upon them, so that dogs barked and horses shied at them in the streets. The craving for size and polychromatic ornamentation seemed irresistible and hats of that description were worn not merely in the day but at dinner, and at the theatre.

It seemed to have been one of those phases of local megalomania which from time to time affects the female sex, comparable to the crinoline of the '50's or the bustle of the '70's, or the sleeves of the end of the decade now under review.

It was associated with an exuberant spirit of romanticism and certainly imparted to the wearer an air of supreme confidence in her powers to charm. After all, megalomania in any form is but a symptom of excessive self-confidence, and the young woman of the end of the '20's, brimming over with her gifts for romance, proclaimed the fact in the loudest possible fashion.

The usual materials of these large hats was either Leghorn or Dunstable straw. A specimen of the former in my collection measures 18 inches across and would not have been considered very large. Bonnets were of straw or satin or velvet; these materials were elaborately stiffened with iron wire to preserve their shape. A bonnet of white satin in my collection, is some 15 inches across, and the crown is built up on a wire frame. At the very end of the decade bonnets occasionally had a 'bavolet' or curtain hanging at the back.

The trimmings worn on these huge structures were remarkable for their mixed nature and colours. Ribbons, often four inches wide, and sometimes as much as fifty feet long, would be used to trim a hat; while flowers of every colour and shape, together with heads of corn or branches of shrubs seemed to shoot out at every angle. In the evening, birds of paradise, whole or in part, with daggers headed with Oriental figures, or drooping feathers and trailing vegetation advertised the heads of romantic young ladies. It was the age of reverberating headgear.

Capotes for day wear, were by comparison small and less decorated. The poke-brim in front was occasionally stiffened with whalebone.

1822

HAIR

Day. 'Hair parted from the forehead in moderate curls, and the hind hair gracefully wound round the head with a coronet-plait on the summit.'

Evening. Hair in curls and braids with a mixture of pearls and fancy flowers.

COIFFURE

Day. Morning caps, either mobs or fine lace or plain cornettes; for afternoon, cornettes of net or blonde with flowers.

Evening. Diadem combs of gold or polished steel. Glauvina pins of pearls or oblong ornaments of polished steel at each end (one of which is removable) for supporting the evening coiffure. The evening cap or 'handkerchief fichu' covers the forepart of the head only, and is tied under the chin. Evening dress hats with plume, small toques, turbans of gauze.

OUTDOORS

Bonnets. Walking bonnets, lined, the brim broad, often of the Marie Stuart type. Summer bonnets of net on wired frame.

Hats. Carriage, the Valois hat.

1823

HAIR

In a profusion of small curls. 'The hair is divided on the forehead with full curls on the temples; to give breadth to the face seems now the chief ambition.'

COIFFURE

Unchanged. Cornettes placed far back on the head.

OUTDOORS

Bonnets placed far back on the head. Some bonnets are very short at the ears; others almost meet under the chin; made of straw or Leghorn, with large plumes. The cottage bonnet type persists all through this decade.

Hats are bent in front over the face. The village hat, with strings down to the waist.

Veils. Long and white, with small bonnets; or black and white with carriage dress.

1824

HAIR

Evening. With curls and bows in front mixed with profusion of flowers; long tresses from behind are brought together in a close plait on to the top to form an Apollo knot.

COIFFURE

Day caps (cornettes) with the caul much flattened, often set out on a wire frame.

OUTDOORS

Bonnets. Close cottage and Marie Stuart bonnets.

Hats. Large Leghorn hats simply trimmed for walking; carriage hats loaded with flowers above and under the brim. A white cap worn beneath 'a hat of white gauze on which were laid stripes of lilac satin ribbon; the ribbons of

1829. Evening dress: blue crepe
over white satin embroidered with
floize silk; Anglo-Greek body and
falling tucker

1830
Carriage dress of violet silk; Donna Maria sleeves; black velvet pelerine, fringed
Dinner dress of crimson figured silk, en tablier; lapel robings;
Marino Faliéro sleeves
Promenade dress of pink gros de Naples, the body en gerbe; cloak of drab cachemire
embroidered in floss silk

the bonnet had a white ground bordered by two shades of bright green, and the other figures were small sprigs of the most glaring red that could be collected together; this ribbon was disposed in bows, puffs and rosettes, with bouquets of sweet peas, honeysuckle, red roses, musk and scarlet geranium'. The Valois hat is still fashionable.

1825

HAIR

Unchanged.

COIFFURE

Day. Morning cornettes of lace with small bows of coloured ribbons. Afternoon caps of blonde lace with floating lappets and coloured lining.

Evening. White dress hats, the brim narrower on one side than the other. 'The feathers worn on the toque hat are rather towering and are many in number; we cannot say we admire the very long drooping feathers now adopted in full dress, which descend as low as the elbow.' Dress hats instead of turbans for matrons, one side partly turned up, the other with battlement edging. Turbans with hanging lappet. The Bolivar hat.

OUTDOORS

Bonnets. Carriage bonnets of black velvet (winter) with wide brim and large plume of feathers, placed very backward. Capotes of coloured silk trimmed with broad full ruching at the edge, and bows of ribbon on the crown.

Hats. Hats with large velvet bows. The Austrian hat, with ostrich plumes, worn over a cornette.

1826

HAIR

Day. Parted on the forehead with clusters of curls on the temples; bows of hair on the crown with puffings of light gauze interspersed.

Evening. Hair with enormous curls on each side of the face with tiers of bows on the crown.

COIFFURE

Day. Morning cornettes on the front of the head without any caul.

Evening. The beret-turban, of white crepe and satin with a plume. Turbans of elastic material of brilliant colours, wound several times round the head, with tassels hanging over one shoulder, others of the beret style but immensely wide.

OUTDOORS

Bonnets of Leghorn and Dunstable straw, large and plain, with coloured ribbon and bow on one side, the strings long and floating. Black satin bonnets with ribbons of two colours.

Hats. 'Cotton hats are in high favour this summer; it is said they will actually bear washing with soap and water without injury.'

1827

HAIR

Afternoon. The hair with bows of ribbons and small flowers and puffs of gauze.

COIFFURE

Day caps with broad borders turned up and trimmed with ribbons; cornettes, some tied under the chin, some with loose lappets.

Evening. Large toques stiffened in loops. Dress hats worn on one side, the under-surface trimmed with blonde. Glauvina pins still worn.

OUTDOORS

Bonnets. 'Nothing could be more frightful and unbecoming than the size and form of the bonnets; immense puffings of gauze, sarcenet or ribbons of unusual breadth in profusion, with tulips, peonies or sunflowers; the last two nearly as large as Nature, the first larger.' Leghorn bonnets.

Hats of enormous size. 'The elderly matron in a large crape hat over which towers a packet of field flowers and shaking bunches of maize.'

1828

HAIR

Evening. The hair in plaited arcades, or 'it is the fashion to have the hair very high on the summit of the head and even to elevate the bows forming the Apollo knot by means of wires.'

COIFFURE

Day. Home caps of lace or blonde with large puffs of coloured ribbons and flowers. Morning cornettes with puffs of two coloured gauze. Puffs of gauze ribbon worn in the hair by young ladies at all times of the day.

Evening. Turbans very large with flat crowns, of brocaded gauze and esprit feathers. Turbans with aigrettes of bird of paradise. Young women wear diadem combs with high galleries; the Apollo knot is immensely elevated with birds of paradise attached. 'Papillotte combs' of tortoiseshell; a new invention three or four inches long, to raise the side hair. 'We are astonished that dress hats are allowed in the theatre; it is impossible for those behind to see the stage.'

OUTDOORS

Bonnets, fastened down by *mentonnières* of white tulle quilled on satin ribbon. 'We really grieve to see the ridiculous size of the gloomy black velvet bonnets, often increased by a deep blonde hanging over the face' (Winter). Bonnet strings hang down to the waist. Tuscan grass bonnets. Bonnets are so large that two ladies cannot walk arm in arm. 'A sportsman says his dog barks at the fashionable bonnets until he feels ashamed.'

Hats. Silk and transparent hats for carriage in summer. 'The hats and bonnets increase in size, with the exception of the straw and Dunstable, which being tied close down are not in appearance so enormous except when the straw is in the shape of the large pilgrim's hat, and then they are frightful.' 'A straw hat or bonnet cannot now be too coarse.'

1829
HAIR

Day. In curls and ringlets with puffs and flowers. Or with ringlets on one side and a full mass of curls on the other.

Evening. Hair with many ringlets on both sides and with high Apollo knot. Often à la chinoise; or with brilliants and rosettes and a high comb.

COIFFURE

Day. Caps with hanging lappets. 'Caps very wide and crazy looking.'

OUTDOORS

Bonnets in cottage shape, often with veils.

Hats much off the face, and the under surface highly ornamented.

1830

1. *Evening Dress.* Blue crepe hat, crown trimmed with blue gauze ribbon; drapery of same material inside brim terminated by white ostrich feather attached by an agraffe of silver.

2. *Back view of 1.*

3 and 4. *Evening headdress* of hair and ribbon. Requires 'a great deal of hair', and about 2½ yards of ribbon.

5. *Promenade Dress.* Bonnet of lavender coloured gros de Naples trimmed with three noeuds of gauze ribbon to correspond and one inside the brim. Mentonnières of white blonde net.

6. *Morning Dress.* Cap of tulle, the edges lightly embroidered in black, crown ornamented with 'entre deux' of embroidered tulle.

1831

1. *Full Evening Dress.* Hair full at the sides and arranged in large bow on the crown, round the base of which is a plaited band; ornamented with six golden arrows and a bouquet of white and rose coloured feathers.

2. *Morning Dress.* Hair in bands and ornamented with a ferronnière and two knots of Clarence blue ribbon.

3. *Walking Dress.* Bonnet of lilac gros des Indes; drawn, but lined and trimmed with ribbon only (Capote Modeste).

4. *Morning Dress.* Blue moiré cottage bonnet of the new French shape, trimmed inside the brim with a cockade of gauze ribbon to correspond and blond lace; knots of ribbon and bouquet of flowers on crown (Capote Roquet).

5. *Walking Dress.* Capote de paquebot of French grey crepe, shaped like a small sized English cottage bonnet with a square brim trimmed inside with blond and ribbon in the cap style; two long ostrich feathers.

6. *Walking Dress.* Satin hat with blond border mounted on rolls of satin.

NOTE: Nos. 3, 4, 5 and 6 are all known as Bibis by the end of the year.

1832

1. *Evening Dress*. A crepe hat ornamented with beads and feathers.

2. *Back view of 1.*

3. *Evening Dress*. Crepe turban à la Moabite ornamented with bird of Paradise and gold arrow.

4. *Front view of 3.*

5. *Walking Dress*. Hat of white satin lined with white or mauve crepe, surrounded by ruche of tulle and trimmed with satin edged with ruches of tulle and cut gauze ribands.

6. *Back view of 5.*

1833

1. *Ball Dress*. Hair in a mass of heavy curls on each side and large bows on the summit of the head; ornamented with gold bandeau and gold comb set with rubies, and bunches of grapes.

2. *Evening Dress*. Hair parted on the forehead and arranged in perpendicular bows on the summit; decorated with wreath of roses.

3. *Morning Dress*. Tulle cap with flat crown and front trimming en ruche; decorated with bows and bands of rose coloured gauze ribbon.

4. *Morning Dress*. Bonnet of rose coloured poult de soie trimmed with ribbons and flowers to correspond.

5. *Morning Dress*. Cap finished by a border of white blonde; bonnet of white tulle lined with grass green stripes, and one small bow under the brim; fanchons of ribbon on crown; black lace veil.

6. *Breakfast Dress*. Hair in pendant braids and a triple plait at the top of the head.

1834

1. *Walking Dress.* Hat of crepe, the front 'trés-evasée' trimmed with two bands of white gauze ribbon finished by a large bow, a rose 'unique' high at front of crown, and a wreath of small roses beneath the front; deep, full bavolet. Hair in smooth bandeaux.

2. *Back view of 1.*

3. *Coiffure de Soirée.* Cap of blonde with bows and ribbons of gauze and a small wreath of 'roses pompones' at the side.

4. *Back view of 3.*

5. *Walking Dress.* 'One of the new and curiously shaped Aragonese bonnets', of green silk adorned with roses and ribbon.

6. *Demi negligé.* Cap edged à l'enfant with ruche of tulle and wreath and sprig of flowers. Band of ribbon round the crown and small bow behind; brides of broad gauze ribbon.

1835

1. *Ball Dress.* Caleche of black gros de Tours lined with pink satin and trimmed with black lace.

2. *Morning Dress.* Cap of tulle blonde bordered with ruche 'en cornette'; caul trimmed with band of blue ribbon and full knots.

3. *Evening Dress.* Chapeau toque of black velvet trimmed with the foliage of a bird of Paradise dyed black.

4. *Back view of 3.*

5. *Carriage Dress.* Bonnet of finest plain Italian straw, brim lined with white crepe; tuft of red roses over right temple; crown ornamented with flat white ostrich feathers and white poult de soie ribbon.

6. *Evening Dress.* Italian turban of green crepe trimmed with pearls; tuft of hair which falls on right side intermingled with flowers.

1836

1. *Morning Dress.* White silk bonnet lined and trimmed with blue; lancer feather and demi lace veil sewn to the edge of the brim.

2. *Morning Dress.* Drawn pink silk bonnet tied closely down and trimmed en suite.

3. *Morning Dress.* Tulle cap trimmed with blonde; moderately high caul ornamented with band and knots of blue ribbon, light coques of which are intermixed with the single row of lace which forms the front; tulle brides edged with blonde.

4. *Ball Dress.* Garland of moss roses twined round the hair and formed into bouquets on each temple.

5. *Dinner Dress.* French mob cap, trimmed with lace; bands and brides of blue ribbon and a garland of forget-me-nots.

6. *Morning Dress.* Tulle cap of the Babet form decorated with band and coques of blue ribbon.

1837

1. *Dinner Dress.* Blue satin hat trimmed with blue and white shaded feathers.

2. *Public Promenade Dress.* Victoria bonnet of pink crepe, the interior of brim trimmed with flowers, the crown with ribbons edged with narrow blonde lace.

3. *Evening Dress.* Rice straw 'petit bord' trimmed with rose ribbon and bird of Paradise.

4. *Back view of 3.*

5. *Public Promenade Dress.* Rice straw half-gipsy hat, interior of brim trimmed with rosebuds, crown with white ribbons and bird of Paradise.

6. *Evening Dress.* Coiffure 'à la Levantine', decorated with a gerbe of early flowers.

1838

1. *Morning Dress.* Straw coloured satin capote Victoria ornamented with flowers.

2. *Morning Dress.* Back view of a wadded morning bonnet.

3. *Evening Dress.* A pouff of scarlet gauze striped and fringed with gold.

4. *Evening Dress.* Coiffure à la Fontanges ornamented with gold pins and blue ribbons.

5. *Evening Dress.* 'Bonnet Babet' of tulle, ornamented with pink ribbon.

6. *Home Dress.* Small round cap of tulle, trimmed with blonde lace, flowers and white ribbon.

1839

1. *Evening Dress.* Coiffure 'à l'Agnes Sorel'; hair in plain bands in front and a knot 'à la Chevalière', behind; decorated with Brussels lace lappets, velvet embroidered in gold, antique gold pins, and a demi circlet of gold.

2. *Evening Dress.* Turban front of white satin striped with gold and green velvet with an end falling on each side and bordered with gold fringe; white esprit on left side.

3. *Morning Dress.* White chip bonnet, French cottage shape, lined with pink crepe and trimmed with same material and roses.

4. *Dinner Dress.* Chapeau-capote of dark grey velours épinglé, brim lined with green ribbon and grey striped ribbon; bouquet of short shaded feathers on crown.

5. *Evening Dress.* Petit bord of violet velvet ornamented with velvet and a green bird of Paradise.

6. *Side and back view of 5.*

103

UNDERCLOTHING

Information on the underclothing worn in the '20's is mainly derived from specimens in my collection, especially those bearing a date, *e.g.*

A Chemise

dated 1825, of homespun linen, unshaped, one yard wide, with a low square neck edged with a narrow frill of cambric. Sleeves short, and gathered over the shoulder, set in with a large gusset under the arm.

A day Petticoat

of cotton, with attached bodice, made in the stomacher front style. No sleeves.

An evening petticoat of muslin, with attached bodice in the stomacher front style; short puffed sleeves. Above the hem, which is four feet wide, are seven narrow tucks.

An evening petticoat of cotton with attached bodice fastening down the back with hand-made buttons and a drawstring at the neck. The neck round and low, with an edging of embroidered insertion and lace. No sleeves. The skirt has a deep edging of scalloped and embroidered cambric, above which are sixteen lines of heavy piping up to the knee.

A Nightgown

dated 1825, of linen. Wide front opening with cambric frill edging; a shallow collar. The sleeves, set in with gussets, are long, finished with a gauged cuff edged with a frill and fastened with one button. The hem is four feet wide.

There is no reliable information about the shape of drawers or corsets, other than references to the occasional wearing of the former, and universal wearing of the latter.

A letter, dated 1820, however, suggests that drawers (often referred to as 'trowsers') were then a novelty and that they were made with the legs imperfectly attached to each other; the lady complains that: 'They are the ugliest things I ever saw: I will never put them on again. I dragged my dress in the dirt for fear someone would spy them; the blue and brown checked gingham I had in the house. My finest dimity pair with real Swiss lace is quite useless to me for I lost one leg and did not deem it proper to pick it up, and so walked off leaving it in the street behind me, and the lace had cost six shillings a yard. I saw that mean Mrs. Spring wearing it last week as a tucker. I told her that it was mine and showed her the mate, but she said that she hemmed and made it herself—the bold thing. I hope there will be a short wearing of these horrid pantalets, they are too trying. Of course I must wear them for I cannot hold up my dress and show my stockings, no one does.' (Quoted by Mrs. Earle. *Two Centuries of Costume in America*.)

A similar pair in my collection have the two legs only united by a narrow tape round the waist, which might conceivably give way and lead to the deplorable catastrophe such as the lady describes.

CHAPTER FOUR

FROM ROMANCE TO SENTIMENT
IN THE '30's

———————

THE fashions of this decade illustrate the transformation from a phase exuberantly romantic into one droopingly sentimental. The change occurred abruptly in the middle of 1836. The flood of romance which had risen to such a height by the end of the '20's reached a culmination, so far as fashions went, in the year 1830, when extraordinary attention was lavished (as always in romantic periods) on the upper half of the dress and the sleeves. Innumerable variations of the 'closed' and 'open' types of bodice appeared; in the Annual Summary for that year the principal ones are described. In addition there were at least a dozen different patterns of sleeve for day use; and when it is recalled that the hats were more startling in colour and size than the dresses it can easily be understood that the total effect was overwhelming, especially as the woman of fashion wore them all with an air of perfect assurance; the mode was not intended to be anything but ravishing and arresting; a spirit of conquest dominated the designs which burst upon the world in the year 1830.

But it was not possible to sustain that triumphant air for long; already by 1832 the modes were becoming slightly stereotyped, and the first fine careless rapture seemed to be passing. Attempts at mere novelty by widening the shoulder line yet more were uninspired and the increasing number of pointed bodices indicated the beginning of a return to purer Gothic forms; as inspiration faded in intensity the design became overloaded with details such as ribbon knots strewn over the surface and the copious use of lace.

At the same time the attention seems to have wandered from the bodice towards the skirt which increased in size and ornamental trimming; materials for the evening dress became even richer in design. All through 1834 and 1835 fashion was recovering its breath, slightly exhausted by the hectic experiences through which it had just passed. But we find, in other aspects of life besides costume, the same signs of a change towards a more subdued tone. The actively romantic mood was turning into a passively sentimental one. That this was not the outcome of a new reign

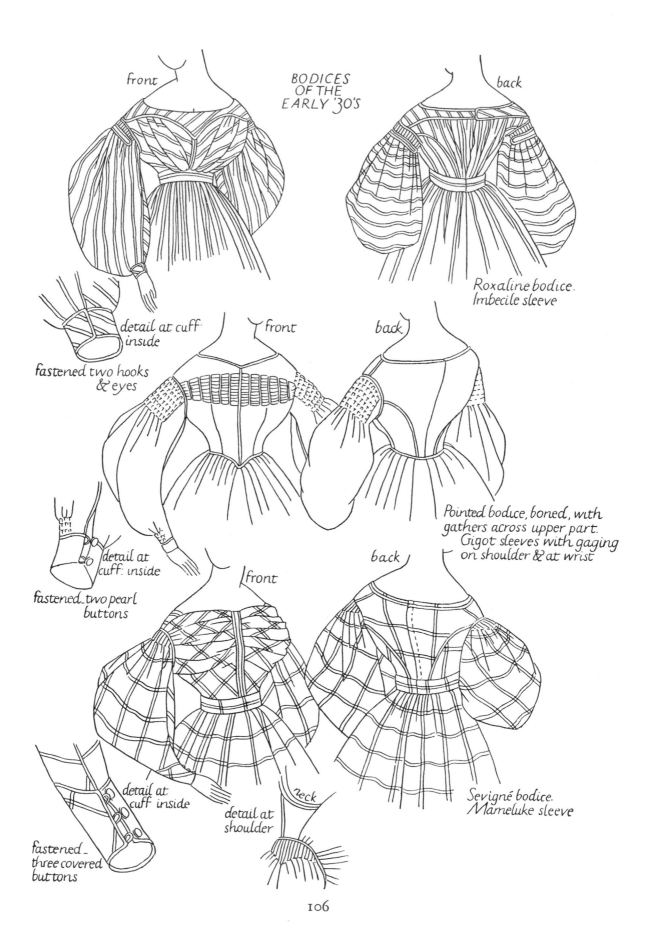

front

BODICES
OF THE
EARLY '30's

back

Roxaline bodice.
Imbecile sleeve

detail at cuff:
inside

fastened two hooks
& eyes

front

back

Pointed bodice, boned, with
gathers across upper part.
Gigot sleeves with gaging
on shoulder & at wrist

detail at
cuff: inside

fastened two pearl
buttons

back

front

neck

detail at
cuff inside

detail at
shoulder

Sevigné bodice.
Mameluke sleeve

fastened
three covered
buttons

with a girl as sovereign is shown by the fact that the change was symbolised by an abrupt alteration in the fashions of women's dress in the middle of 1836, a year before the beginning of the Victorian era. It began by the collapse of the sleeve and the shrinking of the upper half of the costume. Details of the change are given in the Annual Summary for the years 1836 and 1837, where it will be seen how the lines tend to droop and form themselves into long pointed angles, while the skirt increases in importance, presently to dominate the whole picture.

The structure of the dress of the '30's calls for a few comments. All bodices are lined with cotton, often glazed silesia, and also the day skirt, except in light summer materials. Pocket holes but not pockets are common in walking dresses. Flat brass hooks and eyes, hand-made, are the usual fastenings, but buttons of wood and mother-of-pearl are found. It should be noted that many dresses of, presumably, home manufacture, do not attempt to carry out in their details the full extravagance of contemporary fashions; the complicated designs in 1830, for example, must have been beyond the amateur's skill, and one finds therefore dresses certainly of that period with, for example, simple fairly close-fitting sleeves, or bodices in which 'fichu-robings' are only suggested in a crude form. It is in such home-made examples that details surviving from styles current in the '20's may crop up (*e.g.* the wadded hem or the 'Gallo-Greek' bodice). In this decade the use of India rubber, in the form of 'elastic' begins to appear for such articles as garters and stays.

A survey of the dresses of this decade creates the impression that in the earlier part fashion was more concerned with form, and in the later part with colour. When art is vigorously inspired it is apt to be indifferent to details and aims at creating its effects by bold strokes; as the wave of inspiration begins to subside attention is then lavished on detail. We see this well illustrated in the fashions of this decade. The striking varieties of form in the years 1830 to 1836 are not dependent on material; fashion was in the main content to use the fabrics already in use, and the incentive to create a host of new ones with fresh blends of colour only became marked as the next decade was approached. Technical improvements were the natural response to the new demands then made by fashion. Polychromatic printing on muslins, thin woollens and silks provided cheaper substitutes for textiles woven in patterns, and mixed fabrics of silk and wool, or cotton and wool, steadily increased in number and variety. It is interesting to find an artificial silk, made from wood, put on the French market in 1831, and called 'Sylvestrine'. The Jacquard loom (invented about 1801) was by this time capable of supplying endless varieties of patterns, but the designer of materials was subordinate to the designer of dress as long as form rather than colour dominated the fashionable taste. Towards the end of the decade there was an increasing tendency to revive styles established in the seventeenth and eighteenth centuries, suggesting that originality was giving place to 'reproductions from the antique'. In fact, whenever Dame Fashion is exhausted she puts on a series of revivals, and ransacks the wardrobes of a monarch's mistresses who, it is safe to assume, were experts in the art of sex-attraction. The amateur is ever ready to learn from the professional, and the Victorian Lady

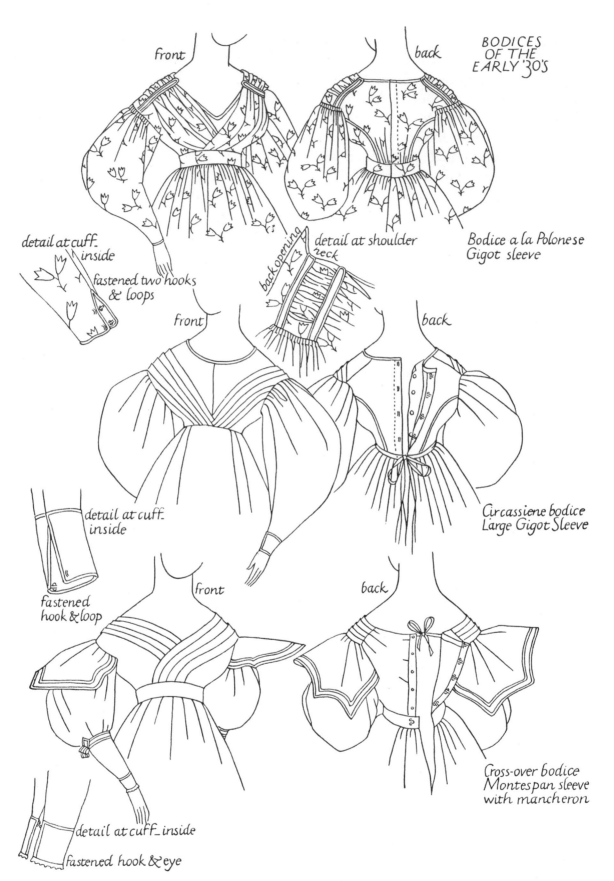

front

back

detail at cuff.
inside

fastened two hooks
& loops

detail at shoulder
neck

back opening

Bodice a la Polonese
Gigot sleeve

front

back

detail at cuff.
inside

fastened
hook & loop

Circassiene bodice
Large Gigot Sleeve

front

back

detail at cuff_inside

fastened hook & eye

Cross-over bodice
Montespan sleeve
with mancheron

108

1833
Day dress of flowered de laine

showed an unconscious hankering for the discarded modes of famous harlots, a compliment virtue is always eager to pay to vice. Styles which could whet the jaded appetites of Charles the Second and Louis Quinze must have irresistible qualities.

1830

DRESSES

Day

Low waist, always round, with belt and buckle, or occasionally a sash.

Types of bodice:

A. Closed and high.

(1) As a pelisse-gown with high collar, and fastening down the front.

(2) The 'corsage uni', *i.e.* the front plain and without seams; with such would be worn a white canezou-pelerine.

(3) The corsage uni with horizontal revers, similar to a falling tucker, but made of the same material as the dress, and cleft on the shoulders.

(4) With pelerine lapels, *i.e.* with revers set at an angle so as to leave a space, in the form of a stomacher, between.

(5) Front and back arranged in fan-shaped folds extending on to the shoulders.

(6) 'En chemisette' (Summer), with a band of embroidery round the neck and down the centre of the bodice.

B. Closed and half-high.

(1) En gerbe.

(2) Draped. (i) à la Sevigné. (ii) Cross-over. (iii) 'En eventail' (fan-wise). (iv) à l'enfant, with falling tucker. (v) With a white muslin or cambric canezou covering the front, or a canezou-pelerine.

C. Open Bodice.

(1) Cut into a 'V' with lapels turned back, and filled in with a chemisette, or if the 'V' is very deep with a habit-shirt. The lapels may be turned back so widely as to extend over the shoulders; they may be continued round the neck forming a cape (a type known as 'the bodice en schall', *i.e.* producing the draped effect of a shawl round the shoulders). The lapels may be cut down to the waist, front and back, and the space between filled in with a pleated chemisette. The lapels may be turned back with a square collar in the redingote style and a habit-shirt.

(2) The bodice 'en cœur', *i.e.* descending somewhat in the centre and having a number of narrow pleats along the upper edge.

Types of Sleeve:

Gigot; Imbecile; Donna Maria. The sleeve pleated from the elbow downwards in longitudinal folds.

'Montespan.' The upper half very full, with a band at the elbow; the lower part cut in points, with a ruffle hanging over the upper part of the forearm.

'Medici.' The upper part bouffante; closed at the elbow and continued tight to the wrist.

'Marino Faliéro.' Large hanging sleeves, caught up by a band at the elbow.

'Sultan.' Large hanging sleeves caught up in the middle of the upper arm and also in the middle of the forearm.

'Caroline.' Similar, but tight from the elbow to the wrist.

'Gabrielle.' Very full from the shoulder to the elbow; moderately full from the elbow to the middle of the forearm, thence a deep cuff, laced in the middle.

'Cavalier.' The upper half full; the lower half tight, being closed along the outer side by knots of ribbon.

The term 'Amadis sleeve', which is frequently used by contemporaries, refers only to the presence of a tight cuff-end at the wrist.

Skirt: ankle-length, trimming scanty and generally at the knee level; a line of fringe is especially common. 'That everlasting trimming worn on everything and by everybody.'

'Wrapping morning dresses for the breakfast table in the form of pelisses with large capes.'

Peignoirs (Summer) of white muslin and plain gingham.

'The redingote style is so decidedly in favour that it is adopted even in morning visiting dresses.'

Some muslin dresses (Summer) with the bodice separate from the skirt and forming a canezou.

Towards the end of the year flounces return, *e.g.* one deep bias flounce.

Aprons worn with morning dresses: of the same material as the dress, or of foulard, with braces and small round pockets.

Riding Habit

in the redingote style, gigot sleeves, chemisette, stock and frill.

Evening

The bodice is always cut low and off the shoulders.

109

Types of bodice:

A. Closed bodice.

(1) Corsage uni, tight to the shape, (*a*) with or without a fall of blonde or fringe; (*b*) with horizontal revers forming mancherons on the shoulders.

(2) The 'corsage carré,' *i.e.* square cut with narrow shoulder straps.

(3) The 'corsage à la Caroline,' *i.e.* with a narrow fall of lace and drapery forming a 'V' en pelerine.

(4) À l'enfant.

(5) En demi-cœur.

(6) With the centre slightly drawn down by a vertical rouleaux.

(7) Draped corsage: (*a*) à la Sevigné; (*b*) à la grecque, *i.e.* with horizontal folds and central bone; (*c*) with rouleaux arranged en eventail.

(8) Occasionally a corsage slightly pointed below, 'à la Marie Stuart'.

B. Open bodice.

(1) En redingote.

(2) En schall.

(3) With lapels open to the waist and a chemisette.

(4) With lapels turned back and the skirt open over an under-dress, *i.e.* the 'robe à la Roxalane'.

(5) With a bodice comprising lapels only, worn over a canezou.

Sleeves: short and very full.

Types of sleeves: beret; double beret; Marino Faliéro; 'Roxalane', the upper half bouffante, confined above the elbow by a fringed band, and very full to the wrist. These are worn with or without manchettes of white blonde.

Skirts: short, ankle-length, and round. Ornamentation mainly at the knee level, such as fringe, embroidery and foliage. Large flat pleats all round the waist.

'Evening dress of pale yellow gauze over white satin; corsage cut low and open front and back, with wide revers; white pleated chemisette; sleeves with double bouffantes; skirt plain with a deep scalloped and embroidered flounce.'

Materials: 'Painted and printed foulards now of English make.'

OUTDOOR GARMENTS

Cloaks

Large, with mantlet-cape, cleft on the shoulders, and with a smaller pelerine-cape and an upright collar.

Pelisses and Redingotes

with collars and capes. Vertical trimmings down the edges, or as a broken cone on the skirt.

The *Pelerine*,

of cambric or muslin, embroidered. Of two or three falls, usually pointed corners and extending widely over the shoulders.

The *Canezou*,

of same materials, may be pointed behind, with the front ends crossing under the belt, or crossing over the bosom, or may lie flat on the shoulders with a trimming round the bust.

The *Pelerine-fichu* is a pelerine with long hanging ends in front reaching nearly to the knees.

The *Canezou-pelerine* is a combination of the two first.

NOTE: The four last named are also worn as indoor garments.

ACCESSORIES

'*Shoes* cut into sandals and fastened with three bows on the instep' (Morning dress).

'Worked *Gloves*, white silk *Stockings*, and shoes the colour of the trimmings' (Carriage dress). Evening Gloves long, and finished with fringe or vandyking just below the elbow. *Fan* of white feathers, the stick with a small mirror attached. 'The most novel *Parasols* are in white gros de Naples, with a border but without a fringe. A large bouquet of flowers is embroidered in coloured silk in each compartment.'

New invention: 'Among the recent inventions at Paris an elastic stiffening of a vegetable substance has been invented, instead of that spiral brass wire now used for shoulder straps, glove tops, corset, etc.; it is valuable because it neither cuts the cloth that covers it nor corrodes with verdigris; it is said to be made of Indian rubber.'

1831

DRESSES

Day

as in previous year.

'Really a reform in the size of the sleeves is necessary.'

Waists round with belts and deep gilt buckles. Some summer dresses of jacconet are made en blouse, up to the throat, with a gusset on the shoulder. A few summer dresses have one or two scalloped flounces. For home dresses the pelisse gown, partly open on the bosom with high collar and broad lapels is usual.

Aprons, some black, with pockets and bib, very wide and long and the border ruched, are usual with home dresses.

'Cravat of flowered or shaded silk with pointed ends, fastened by a gold slide, is generally worn with a chemisette in Home dresses.'

Evening
Similar to previous year, but bodices tend to be less square across the bosom, being drawn down at the centre, or with crossed drapery, or en cœur. The lowness of cut is 'a fashion as unbecoming as it is indelicate'.

Sleeves usually of the beret or double bouffante shape. The short large sleeves are 'covered with a thin stiff gauze, rather than to have them supported by any undersleeve of buckram, which is apt to rub against the shoulders and indicates the presence of the females almost in the adjoining saloon'. 'A dinner dress of chaly or gros de Naples, half high, with crossed drapery in front and a plain tight back; gigot sleeve of transparent tulle, over short beret sleeve.'

Materials: Chiné silk mentioned as a dress material.

New Material: Sylvestrine, an artificial silk made from wood.

OUTDOOR GARMENTS

Mantles
with deep capes and fur collars (winter). 'A Mantle of green velvet lined with white silk; long cape, rounded at corners; long loose sleeves; black velvet collar.'
'A green velvet *Pelerine Cape*, fringed edge, worn over walking dress of fawn cashmere.'

'Canezous
Made en cœur and with collar, and scarf ends reaching half-way to knee; a broad ribbon gauze sautoir is an indispensable appendage.'

ACCESSORIES

Jewellery: Girandole ear-rings. Rather less jewellery worn than previously.
'Jackman's celebrated Health Preservers. Promenade and Carriage *Clogs* for Ladies and Gentlemen' (Advt.) Made of cork and leather, worn over the shoe.

Corsets. 'A recent discovery . . . substituting India rubber for elastic wires; the rubber is manufactured in strong but delicate fibres which possess all the elasticity of wire without being subject to snap or to corrode.'

1832

DRESSES

Day
The types of day dresses are unchanged, but the width of the shoulders is increased by the pelerine-cape and sleeves. Some of the gigot sleeves in summer day dresses are hooped.

'The skirts are longer and the hem is stiffened with flannel or stiffened muslin lining to preserve the form of the pleats.' Eight or nine breadths are needed for a skirt. They are wider with deep pleats and no gores.

Morning dresses in wrapper style with high neck and full back; the front of bodice and skirt wraps over to one side; skirt open and lined with sarcenet; no cape, but a deep collar. Or morning dresses with bodice close to the shape. 'Morning Dress of white jacconet, pleated corsage and dented hem under a lilac Pelisse with lappels forming a pelerine and mancherons' (Summer). 'Over a Pelisse dress an India muslin double canezou-pelerine, square and covering the whole bodice.' 'A carriage dress with sleeves pleated in at the shoulders.'

Materials: gingham, batiste de laine, washing foulards, chaly. 'There is a perfect rage for Chaly for morning, dinner and evening dresses.'

Evening
In full dress the bodice is cut very low and off the shoulders. A number of bodices are pointed in front, or front and back. The drapery forms are general (Sevigné, cross-over, à la grecque, etc.). Dinner dresses and half-dresses are either low or half-high; if the latter the open bodice with turned back lapels is usual.

The 'Corsage à la Regente' (pointed in front, plain square neck; boned) is sometimes seen for evening dresses.

The back and shoulders are trimmed with blonde, forming mancherons or jockeys. Frequently floating ribbons on the shoulders.

Sleeves are of the beret or bouffante or double bouffante kind, with or without oversleeves. The bouffante sleeve is often divided into compartments. Also the 'Soufflet sleeve', very short and full with separated puffs.

Skirts trimmed at the knee level with flowers or ribbons. A deep lace flounce is common. 'It is scarcely possible for the skirts to be too elaborately trimmed.'

Over dresses of black or white blonde over satin slips.

Materials: batiste de soie (embroidered with silk); organdy embroidered in worsted; gros de Naples printed in squares, colour on colour; moiré; and the transparent materials (crepe, tulle, etc.) over slips. For half dresses: Terry velvet, satin, moiré.

New Materials: Cameleon, Macabre, Buridan, Persian Thibet (for cloaks). Gauze sylphide, mousselaine velours, Ottoman satin (for dresses).

OUTDOOR GARMENTS

Mantles, with single or double deep capes. Mantles with shawl patterns; the pelerine-cape is deeper with two points in front and one behind; the over cape is smaller in the form of a falling collar. Witzchoura Mantles revived (Winter).

Shawls

Small square shawls; carriage shawls of black China crepe, the corners embroidered in gold. 'Hernani shawls'; of white silk net studded with a Grecian pattern.

ACCESSORIES

Shoes

Many with small rosettes or bows. *Boots* of aventurine cloth lined with sable (Winter). Circular *Fans* or 'hand-screens', ornamented with ostrich feathers. *Boas* (Winter). Palatine *Tippets* (with long ends hanging down in front).

Prices

Cashmere shawls with deep borders, 25/- to 60/-

1833

'In the days of our late Sovereign the style of beauty most esteemed was the embonpoint. Now, with much better taste, fashion bestows her favour upon the graceful sylph-like forms.'

'The skirts are now of the most extravagant and ungraceful width; the pleats doubled and often trebled, very hollow and add excessively to the size of the hips.'

DRESSES

Day

Fashion unchanged except that the pelisse-robe is very common; this is ornamented with ribbon knots down the front, and has a single or double pelerine, of the same material as the dress, which is round and deep behind but narrow in front. Or the bodice is plain and high (Winter) with plain back and the front gathered into compartments, and a single lapel.

Walking dresses (Summer) are half or three-quarters high, with round waist and large pelerine-fichu. A number of summer dresses have bodices open 'en schall' (known as shawl dresses), with open skirts. Shawl dresses: 'it requires an experienced eye to distinguish between a fifteen shilling dress and one of three guineas.' A few summer dresses of muslin have bodices with triple pointed waist; pointed bodices begin to come in, for day dresses, in the summer.

Sleeves of the Imbecile or gigot type, or the 'Amadis sleeve'.

Aprons of washing silk, three-quarter length, with pockets, worn with morning dresses.

Materials: gros de Naples, satin, cashmere, merino, chaley, sarcenet, foulard, poult de soie, chintzes, printed cottons, muslins, mousselaine de laine, batiste.

Evening

Pointed bodices with central bone for full dress during the first quarter of the year, subsequently also for dinner dresses. All cut very low and off the shoulders, either plain with falling tucker, or draped across, or cross-over, or en eventail, or à la vièrge.

The round waists have the front of the skirt decorated with flat ribbon bows. The waist ribbon is sometimes replaced by a cord and tassel. The pointed waist has a ribbon knot at the point. Sleeves: the double sabot the most usual; also single bouffante with lace manchette or long ornamental sleeves with knots of ribbon, *e.g.*, 'à la chevalière', gigot in shape with ribbon knots along the inner border.

Skirt very wide and pleated, often a deep single lace flounce.

'New fashion for making evening dresses; body cut low and square with a narrow line of blonde standing up round the bust; waist very low;

1831

Morning dress of lilac gros de Naples with pelerine en mantille; sleeves à la Chevalière
Capote anglaise
Riding dress of terre d'Egypte cloth with pelerine of black terry velvet; green veil
Morning visiting dress of citron foulard de laine; blonde cap

1832
Carriage dress: pink striped jacconet pelisse over jacconet
muslin dress
Carriage dress of green printed chaley with satin trimmings;
net pelerine

skirt disposed in triple pleats round the hips; bodice separate and with a long sharp point; short sleeves, divided by a band and bow of ribbon, very puffed out above, close at elbow; if of silk, sleeves trimmed at elbow with fall of black lace; if of white material the fall is of blonde.'

For dinner dresses the demi-redingote, half-high, with bust trimmed with lace, and long sleeves.

Materials: very heavy rich silks, heavily flowered; or crepe, organdi, etc. over satin slip; foulard, gros de Naples.

Fashionable Colours: green, yellow, rose.

OUTDOOR GARMENTS

Mantles
are very ample with sleeves falling over the hand; fur collar; and cape.

Witzchoura Mantles, single high collar and very large sleeves, no pelerine. Of satin and cashmere, often lined with grey squirrel.

Mantlets
A development from the pelerine, having a rounded shoulder cape with long wide ends in front, passing under the ceinture and descending to the knee. The cape has two falls and a collar, under which a cravat is worn. In winter the collar is of fur. 'A Mantlet of black blonde lined with green sarcenet, trimmed round the back with blonde, and long square front ends, worn over white promenade dress.'

A *Mante* is a smaller version of the mantlet.

Shawls
New, of French cashmere, 5 yards square, border 7 inches deep, of Oriental pattern, or with palm borders, the grounds black, white or blue.

ACCESSORIES

Gloves
'Knit Gloves are very much worn in the morning, of all shades and colours. Many prefer gloves of very fine Scotch thread. Leather gloves are only worn of very light colours (which) can only be worn for one day.'

Mittens recently revived for dinner parties; of black silk net worked on the back with gold, or 'the new mittens of white silk net or white kid worked in coloured silks.'

Shoes
Rather less square round the instep, but square toes: of silk or fancy leather. 'Prunella shoes are become so common that no lady wears them.' Evening shoes of satin (white for full dress, black or colour of dress for dinner). A passing fashion for shoes worked in carpet worsted.

Silk *Gaiters* much worn. *Stockings*, both plain and clocked, of extreme fineness, often with a faint tinge of pink. *Parasols* of moiré, gros de Naples and foulard, some with black lace borders. *Jewellery* less ornate. Pearl ear-rings. Wide gold bracelets with large clasp. Black silk *Mantillas* worn in the evening. 'Muffs and fur *Boas* are indispensable' (Winter). *New invention*: pins with conical heads made in one with the shafts. Fancy pins with cut ivory heads.

1834

DRESSES

Day
Bodice either high and close to the shape, with a central bone; or as a closed pelisse with turned back lapels (in winter these are of fur); the skirt being trimmed en tablier. The turned back lapels are frequently continued round the back 'en schall'. Or as a 'pelisse-robe', with open skirt. Waist usually round, occasionally pointed. Sleeves gigot or imbecile.

Skirts usually quite plain and very full.

Some morning dresses with high bodies and pelerines which are attached behind and before under the ceinture, and cut into points on the shoulders; such dresses always have pockets or pocket holes. Summer morning dresses of the peignoir shape, either fastening down the front with ribbons, or with mother-of-pearl buttons.

Short black mittens and black lace apron worn with a morning dress.

'An emerald green pelisse over an embroidered muslin dress; the body of the pelisse is high, close to the shape, and pointed; gigot sleeves and pelerine, en suite.'

'Summer silk dresses all of robe form with elaborate canezous and pelerines of embroidered muslin, and pelerine-mantlets which have very deep collars and very long ends in front.'

Chintz dresses. 'We must protest against those odious large glaring patterns that seem to be actually copied from the furniture calicoes of our grandmothers.'

A few muslin dresses with headed flounces.

Evening
Bodices either plain and close to the shape; or draped; or cross-over; or open with lapels. For

full dress all bodices are pointed and cut very low off the shoulders. For demi-evening, half-high; often pointed. Pointed bodices have a central bone and usually a line of ribbon knots down the centre.

Sleeves: for full dress, double bouffante or beret. Demi-evening, imbecile.

Skirts very full; either an open robe with underskirt, or with robe trimmings to simulate an open skirt, or trimmed en tablier. The underskirt may be in the form of an apron attached to the sides of the open robe by ribbon knots or ornaments.

A trimming of ribbon bows en tablier is common. Some open robes are open in the centre, others at one side or at both.

Dresses of lace with lace flounce, in the robe form.

'An opera dress of terry velvet, en robe, over white satin; the robe with pointed bodice, low round bust; double sabot sleeves with ruffle of blonde.'

Ruched ribbon trimming common.

Materials: Terry, satin, velvet, embroidered organdy, lace, crepe, poult de soie, and 'new silks of the antique kind.'

New Materials: Satin de laine, rep silk revived, damask silks and painted and printed taffetas coming in.

OUTDOOR GARMENTS

Mantles
Some without sleeves and with pockets in the lining; others with enormous sleeves and a band at the back of the waist; moderate sized cape.

Mantlets are fashionable; with fronts long and pointed, hanging outside the ceinture, the backs square and descending to the knee level; square collar which, with the edges of the mantlet, is bordered with velvet; made of same material as the dress. These are used with walking dresses. 'A summer mantlet of India book muslin with two falls (one very deep be-

hind) gathered at centre of back: open on the shoulders forming deep mancherons; the fronts reach below the knee.'

Materials: Terry velvet, satin and velvet (Winter). Chiné silk.

Canezous
of three falls, very wide and heart-shaped in front, pointed behind.

Cravats of rich ribbon worn with canezous and mantlets (Summer).

Carriage *Shawls* of thick twilled satin, generally black or brown with floral borders or bouquets in the corners.

ACCESSORIES

Boots
Walking boots of leather 'contrived so that the gaiter part is contained in a kind of shoe, not cut in two parts but encasing the foot in one entire piece of black kid'. Cloth boots only worn as wraps over a thin slipper (at the theatre, etc.). Carriage boots of velvet, trimmed and lined with fur, with a small tassel at the ankle. Black satin *Slippers* for evening. 'When will an Englishwoman learn that white shoes are unbecoming?'

'*Stockings* of the finest black silk are the most fashionable for morning,' without clocks, or with a stripe worked up the side.

Mittens. Long black silk net mittens for evening dress, with bouquet on the back in floss silk.

Jewellery: much fewer bracelets.

Parasols smaller.

'The long ribbon *Belts* should be worn twice round the waist, the second rather loosely with a rosette and ends hanging to the knee; $2\frac{1}{2}$ yards is the allowance for a nymph of slender proportions.'

Prices
Advertisement: 'French corsets producing a graceful and sylph-like tournure, 25/-.'

1835

DRESSES

Day
Bodices, either plain and high, close to the shape; or half or three-quarters high, en gerbe; or as pelisse-robes (redingotes), with cone trimming of ribbon knots. Pleated wrapping fronts for morning dresses. A few walking dresses with high bodies draped with folds

from the shoulders. Chemisettes, cut to fit the shape, are universally worn under high dresses. Sleeves, generally imbecile; frequently these are set in lower than formerly with narrow longitudinal pleats at the shoulder. Some gathered or pleated from the elbow to the wrist, with a cuff.

The 'du Barry' sleeve, very wide with two

bouffantes, one confined just above the elbow, the other just above the wrist.

Skirts plain and full, 'the front showing the ankle, behind just touching the ground'.

'A morning dress (Summer) of jacconet muslin, trimmed round back and shoulders with lace; square collar trimmed with lace; imbecile sleeves; front of skirt embroidered en tablier; line of coloured ribbon knots down the centre.' Satin aprons with chenille borders for morning negligé dress.

The Pelerines

Worn with day dresses, either of the same material as the dress, or of organdy or embroidered cambric, are round and double, with a deep hem edged with lace; others are round behind and cut in front to form a stomacher; others with scarf ends are deep and round behind, with a collar. The collars and edge of the pelerine are bordered with a very deep hem through which a coloured ribbon is run. Sometimes a small coloured collaret is worn round the neck over a white pelerine.

'The Pelerine continues an obstinate mode, though many ladies who are conscious of really fine figures dispense with a disguise invented to improve bad ones.' For summer walking dresses a *Mantlet-Pelerine* of cambric, round behind, with ends short and crossing in front, and having two falls. Some have sharp points in front, with one fall and a deep collar.

Materials: cashmere, merino, satin, organdy, silk and wool mixtures, foulards with satin stripes, silks with Eastern designs, cambric, batiste. Checks and plaids fashionable (Summer). Chaly. There is a marked taste for printed designs on all materials.

Riding Habits

of mazarine blue, brown or green. Tight pointed corsage with velvet collar en revers, showing a cravat and frilled chemisette. Short swallowtails. Gigot sleeves. Skirt in full pleats all round.

Evening

Bodices cut very low and off the shoulders. Generally pointed. Corsage close to the shape, either en cœur or round; draped, en gerbe or à la Sevigné. Often with ribbon bows down the front. An edging of blonde lace is common.

Sleeves: beret, double sabot, or Marino Faliéro. Blonde ruffles. Very wide mancherons extending from the bodice over the sleeves. 'The width of the skirt is very ample supported by stiffened muslin and frequently wire also', (but no specimen with wires is known to exist in any collection). 'The waist ribbons worn with evening dress unite every perfection of pattern and texture.'

Open robes, the underskirt of some striking colour, *e.g.* 'a maroon robe over a rose-coloured satin skirt with four flounces of blonde.' Occasionally the over-dress is looped up at the side, *e.g.* 'the underdress of rose-satin; the overdress of white gauze, its skirt looped up on one side.' Tablier trimming common. Often ribbon knots down the centre or down the sides of the tablier.

Dinner

Three-quarters high, of velvet or flowered silk with fichu (blonde or tulle) pointed behind and front points under the ceinture.

New Materials: for evening dresses: flowered brocades, Pompadour satins, tigrine.

OUTDOOR GARMENTS

Mantles

Winter mantles with hanging sleeves having alternate openings for the hands on the inner side. A mantle of lilac silk with mameluke sleeves and sable trimming. Velvet mantles with small capes. The short Polish mantle (or Polonaise), knee-length, with pelerine-cape, made of satin edged throughout with fur.

Mantlets

Black velvet mantlet, the pelerine and collar square with scarf ends very long and broad with wide lace edging.

Mantlet of black silk with attached caleche sometimes worn with ball dresses.

Shawls

New carriage Shawls of grenadine gauze, large plaid squares with a flower in each square. Square shawls of French cashmere with black grounds, flowered. Silk shawls with plaid pattern. Black satin shawls edged with lace.

Douillette

An outer dress, for *winter*, worn over cambric or silk walking dress which is almost completely concealed by it. The front made like a redingote; sleeves very full and long; pelerine-cape. Trimming of two narrow bias bands. Made of material with rich heavy colour (stamped satin, merino, cashmere) and lined with a bright coloured material.

ACCESSORIES

Shoes and Boots
Black kid boots with small rosette. Black velvet and satin brodequins, fringed at the top, with a tassel. Evening slippers of black satin. 'The toe is not so square as formerly.'

Day *Stockings*, white or grey, of Lisle thread or silk. Black silk with dark dresses. Ball dress silk stockings ornamented with rich blonde on the instep.

Gloves
Openwork silk gloves for 'promenade'. For negligé, suede or embroidered kid with elastic wire at the wrist. Evening gloves finished below the elbow with scalloping or ribbon ruching. Long *Mittens* for evening, short for day.

Jewellery: ear-rings of enormous length, imitating fruit and flowers. Short necklaces.

With white day dresses a 'Solitaire' or narrow, coloured *Scarf* is often worn round the neck and shoulders, loosely knotted in front and the ends hanging to the knee level. *Tippets*, *Boas* and *Fur Palatines*. Evening boas of Marabout. 'Muffs universal.' Sable and Kolinsky furs.

Cambric *Handkerchiefs* with three small tucks about an inch from the edge. Large *Parasols* of white silk, rosewood stick and gold head. Large *Fans* painted with flowers. Small *Bouquets* carried with both evening and day dresses.

Prices
'Dresses made up, plain, 5/6d; full-trimmed, 7/6d.' 'Corsets, 25/-. Patent caoutchouc instantaneous closing corsets; this novel application of India-rubber is by far the most extraordinary improvement that has ever been effected.'

1836

The chief change in this year is the shrinking of the sleeves which occurred abruptly in the early summer. 'The only absolute rule is to flatten the sleeve on the shoulder and banish for ever the memory of those enormous artificial balloons which gave to the delicate form of female beauty a breadth proportionate to Holbein's Dutch women.' So that in May it was said that 'Gigots and stiffness of sleeves are completely abolished'. At the same time the design of the dress became mildly sentimental and lost its exuberant romanticism. A demure prettiness took its place.

DRESSES

Day
For the first few months as in the previous year, the bodice half-high or high and close to the shape; sleeves of the gigot or imbecile type, but set in more off the shoulder, often with small, flat, longitudinal pleats above the bouffant.

From May onwards the bodice is plain and close, high in the neck behind but slightly open at the throat; occasionally with slight drapery folds from the shoulders down to the waist, which is round. The sleeve is now made with close pleating at the shoulder and from the middle of the forearm to an 'Amadis' cuff at the wrist, with a large bouffant occupying the middle of the arm; or there is a series of small bouffants or sabots extending all down the sleeve. The bodices become progressively much simpler and the turned-back large lapels disappear, together with the huge white pelerines. The skirt shows little change, 'the same ample fulness all round and the length just shows the foot'. The pelisse-robe, fastening down one side with a line of ribbon knots is the fashionable type of dress. Winter pelisse-robes of velvet or cashmere with deep pelerine-cape pointed behind, reversed collar and full sleeves ending in a cuff. Summer dresses as pelisse-robes with open skirts; one deep bias flounce or two small flounces becomes common.

'Aprons indispensable with morning dresses.'
Materials: mousselaine de laine, poult de soie, levantine glacé, plaid gingham, silk and wool mixtures, merino, figured and printed; figured satins and poplins, striped sarcenets. For summer: muslins, clear, chequered or striped; brilliantine, flowered cashmeres.

Evening
Bodices very low and off the shoulders, square, and close fitting; frequently a slight point at the waist. Generally boned. Draped either à la Sevigné, or with transverse deep fall of blonde,

or trimmed with ribbons from the shoulders enclosing a triangular 'stomacher', filled in with a chemisette. Often with ribbon knots down the front. A few with lapels en pelerine, edged with ruching or lace.

Sleeves: double bouffants or doubles abots, but smaller than formerly and headed by lace epaulettes. An increasing number with short sleeves close to the shoulder with several lace falls hanging from them. Dinner dresses with long tight sleeves, or with sleeves made of a series of small bouffants. 'As the sleeve diminishes the corsage fits more closely to the sylph-like forms of young aspirants to fashion.'

Skirts very full; either trimmed en tablier or en tunique, or open robes over an under-dress. Often with one deep bias flounce. Bows of ribbon or velvet common as trimming.

Sashes general, fastening to one side with long floats. 'What can be more unbecoming than to see the present tight apparel upon the person of a lath and plaster damsel, all skin and bone?'

Materials: Pekins, plain and striped, organdy, muslin over poult de soie, satin brocaded silks (for evening dresses). Moiré, glacé silk, foulards, poplins (plain figured or watered) for half dresses.

New Materials: Amy Robsart satin, grebe trimming for mantlets, reps imperials, brilliantine.

OUTDOOR GARMENTS

Mantles
Very ample with mameluke sleeves, and either a round cape or one with a point behind and scarf ends in front. Made of figured cashmere, trimmed with velvet. The *Casaweck* mantle: a short mantle with sleeves and close collar, of velvet, satin or silk, trimmed with fur, velvet or lace; always wadded.

Mantlets
Made up to the neck, with round pelerines, of black velvet. Mantlets of black silk bordered with deep lace, with long ends a foot wide. Winter mantlets, wadded, reaching to the knee, with large pelerines and collars.

Palatines worn with winter pelisse-robes.

Shawls
(Winter) large square velvet, embroidered round the edge with flowers and lace borders. Shawls of black gros grain, embroidered in raised pattern of coloured silks.
(Summer) mousselaine de laine damasked in satin stripes.

ACCESSORIES

Shoes
Black silk shoes, and silk or black velvet boots buttoned with gold buttons at the side for 'promenade dress'. Walking boots of stuff, the fronts very short and square, with a black tassel on the instep. Black satin shoes for evening.

Gloves
Day. Short, of coloured silk net confined at the wrist by coloured ribbon, or short with two buttons. Evening. Long black lace with ribbon edging.

Jewellery: mosaic and cameo pins for fastening scarves, etc. at the neck. Large oblong brooches. Eyeglass and watch hanging by chain from the waist. Jeannettes, of a narrow tress of hair or velvet, from which is suspended a heart or small cross of pearls, are fashionable. Bandeaux and ferronières worn in the evening. Velvet ribbon round the throat.

Reticules, lozenge-shaped, of coloured velvet. Carriage *Parasols*, very small, of white silk lined with pink, or light green and fawn; rosewood handles. *Boas and Muffs* fashionable. Furs of sable, ermine and grey squirrel. Grebe, as a new form of 'fancy fur' for boas and muffs. *Ribbons* of rich poult de soie, fringed or plain satin. Frequently ribbons are used for trimming dresses by passing them through the broad hems, in and out.

NEW ACCESSORY

Instead of a cravat a 'fraise' worn, with a scarf, for carriage dress, i.e. 'a piece of muslin half an ell long by one-eighth wide; embroidered and edged with a ruche; folded across the bosom and fastened by a large ornamental pin.' 'The long established custom of restricting silk materials to the winter and half-season is now abolished.'

The principal changes in the year are longer skirts and tighter sleeves.

DRESSES

Day

The pelisse-robe, with or without side fastening, trimmed down the front with ribbon knots, is the usual type. Or round dresses.

Bodices high or half-high, tight to the shape. Either plain, or with lapels en pelerine or drapery folds from the shoulders descending to the waist, which is round and slightly at a lower level than previously. Frequently the bosom is partly open showing a chemisette.

Sleeves long and tight to the wrist, with two or three mancherons round the upper arm. Some are bouffante just below the shoulder; others with fullness confined to the elbow. Amadis sleeve or short cuff, often with ornamental chicorées (*i.e.* material cut at the edge but not hemmed). Skirt plain or trimmed en tablier. Summer dresses with a deep flounce. 'Skirts continue their present ungraceful length.'

Cloth dresses for winter, with corsage buttoning up the front. With morning dresses a small pelerine of muslin, just covering the shoulders, with blunt point behind and front ends fastened with a brooch at the neck.

The 'Fichu Corday' of grenadine gauze bordered by a broad hem run through with a ribbon, the ends crossing on the bosom and tied behind, worn with morning dresses.

Collars, for day, small with points, fastened by a brooch.

'Our élégantes cannot be accused of slighting comfort for show, for out-door dresses at least offer a complete union of both.'

Materials: cloth, merino, plaid cashmere. (Summer) flowered foulards and quadrilled muslins fashionable, and especially organdy.

Evening

Bodices low, off the shoulders, and generally square; most are slightly pointed at the waist. Either close to the shape and plain, especially the 'corsage en corset', *i.e.* with the seams corresponding to the bones marked out by narrow rouleaux; or draped, à la Sevigné; or with transverse lace fall round the neck and shoulders; or with a double lapel forming a 'stomacher' or a 'heart-shape'. Some, instead of being square, descend slightly en cœur, either with wrapping fronts or drapery folds. 'Some corsages are cut so low as to be really indelicate.'

Sleeves short (half way down upper arm), and tight, 'but the trimming gives an appearance of fulness', *e.g.* covered by three falls of tulle or blonde, or ending in lace ruffles; or with small double bouillons at the shoulder over the sleeve; some, instead of a ruffle, end in a bouillon. Ribbon knots on the shoulders and sleeves are common.

Skirts long; a few with demi-trains. More dome-shaped. Very full. Often a deep flounce of lace, or of the dress material, headed.

The tunic dress: an over-dress of tulle, etc., shorter than the under-dress and looped up at the sides with ribbon bows or bouquets, or a tunic of gauze reaching just below the knee. This is very common. Or dresses trimmed en tablier. Or 'robes' with trimming simulating an open skirt.

Ruching much used as trimming.

Fichu-pelerine, of lace, just covering the shoulders, often worn with evening dresses.

Materials: rich silks, velvet, crepe, tulle. In summer, organdy or chiné silk.

Fashionable Colours: brown, violet, green, dark blue, for outdoor dresses. Violet, ponceau, rose, light green, and especially blue, for indoor dresses.

Summer Colours: white, light blue, rose, green, lilac, gorge de pigeon.

New Materials: Day dresses—Levantine folicé, poplin lactée. Evening—Ariel, satin velouté.

OUTDOOR GARMENTS

Mantles

Very voluminous, with a cape often pointed behind; some capes reach knee level in front and behind; open Venetian sleeves.

'A cashmere Mantle with deep fichu-pelerine with long pointed ends, and a small velvet pelerine-cape.'

'A satin Mantle lined with plush.'

Carriage mantle—the Witzchoura.

New form of evening mantle, the *Burnouse*, of satin, very loose, with sleeves.

Materials: damasked satin, satin Esmeralda.

Mantlets

very fashionable, largely displacing shawls. Some of the same material as the dress, others of satin, velvet (wadded in winter) or silk, in summer of embroidered muslins lined with silk

1833. Seaside dresses
Of jacconet muslin; mantlet of pink gros de Naples
Pelisse of green silk; double pelerine of white muslin worn over jacconet muslin dress

1834. Evening dress of figured muslin with bows of gauze
ribbon; blonde stomacher body; gigot sleeves

of grenadine. They are ample and round over the shoulders, often with a pointed hood, and long scarf ends in front reaching nearly to the feet. Many reach the waist behind and have a collar. No sleeves.

'There is really quite a rage of black silk mantlets.'

The Carmeillette or Capuchon, a short evening mantlet, waist length, with long close sleeves, and *hooped hood*.

Pelisse

The pelisse as an outdoor garment is going out; a few wadded.

Spencers

A few summer spencers of velvet, made up to the throat and close to the shape, fastening behind; long tight sleeves; worn over organdy walking dresses.

Shawls

Large square cashmere, with flowered borders; chenille shawls (Summer) of grenadine silk, two yards square, some with rounded corners.

ACCESSORIES

Gloves

short, white or coloured; for evening, with ruching at the top.

Scarves of embroidered silk with chenille edging.

Muffs of satin, the ends trimmed with swansdown.

Ribbons: white with very narrow coloured edge; satin figured in rings; the moss ribbon; satin stripes on plain ground, the stripes shaded.

Fancy silk *Buttons* with centred pattern, and enamel buttons in simple and compound tints, introduced.

1838

The chief change is an increasing preference for the open neck in day dresses, and the corsage en cœur in evening dresses, together with more flouncing, and trimming with ruching.

DRESSES

Day

Bodices half-high or high; plain or folding, or draped from the shoulders. Many with trimming to form a 'heart pelerine.'

Sleeves. The fullness at the middle is now cone-shaped, with either several volans above it, or lines of pleats repeated below it, or both.

The 'Victoria sleeve': two close volans above a larger one which is just above the fullness at the elbow; forearm tight with close cuff.

Skirts voluminous and pleated at the waist. Closed skirts with tabliers, or trimming or ruching in a broken cone; one deep headed flounce or several smaller bias flounces.

The pelisse-robe is very common. Round waist with or without ceinture and floats. The open pelisse-robes have ruched borders or are trimmed en tunic. Flounces of robes cut in large or small dents, or bias, or cockscomb.

The redingote style (flat back: front either with lapels or pleats from the shoulders to the waist; no belt) is revived.

Aprons with morning dresses, of velvet or black satin.

Fichus, replacing canezous, descending to the waist, with a collar behind, worn with day and demi-evening dresses. Or a flat collar with points in front.

Materials: cashmere, merino, satin, taffeta.

(Summer) printed muslins with small patterns, mousseline de laine, gros de Messine, foulards, and organdy are fashionable.

Riding Habit

of cloth; corsage buttoned with one row of buttons; velvet collar; tight sleeves; pantaloons of white coutil.

Evening

Bodices very low off the shoulders; some square, but most drawn down in the centre en cœur or demi-cœur. Pointed waist, some with very long points in front and short points behind. The corsage en corset, tight to the shape, is usual (often called the 'corsage en trois pièces'). A lace fall across the bosom; or drapery à la Sevigné; or pelerine trimmings.

Sleeves tight and short (half way to the elbow), with a lace ruffle. Multiple volans of lace at the shoulder, with a ribbon knot.

Skirts. The open robe is usual, with ruched border, over a flounced petticoat, the flounces being usually of lace. The closed skirt has a deep headed flounce or several small flounces, or a band of ruching at the knee.

Demi-evening dresses half-high, en gerbe, with long sleeves as in day dresses.

The tunic dress is also fashionable (*see* description in 1827).

119

Materials: crepe, grenadine gauze, satin-striped gauze, Pekins, rep velvet, black velvet, brocades, shot silk, terry velvet, organdy, grenadine, chiné silk.

OUTDOOR GARMENTS

Mantles

For carriage, full length and voluminous, with large hanging sleeves and pointed pelerine-cape. Other mantles are knee length, often cut with points in front and with a similar cape: edged with lace or fringe.

The *Pelisse Mantle*. Skirt short but very full; corsage full behind but made in front like a gentleman's coat, with hanging sleeves.

Mantlets

Very fashionable for day and evening.

Made with pelerine-cape and long wide scarf ends nearly to the ground, often edged with a bias flounce. Some with sleeves, others ('shawl mantles') with folds and generally hoods.

Materials: shot silk fashionable. Some of the same material as the dress.

Shawls

China crepe fashionable, especially those figured in the loom. Also of shot silk, glacé, white moiré, and white lace. Always square.

ACCESSORIES

Less *Jewellery* worn.

Mittens common with both day and evening dress.

'Victoria *Parasols*', for carriage, are of a very small size and with folding sticks; some trimmed with a fringe, others with embroidered border.

Advertisement: 'Worked hair sleeves and bustles, black and white, prepared whalebone covered.'

1839

The changes in the year are in the direction of increasing the sloping lines downwards so as to accentuate the appearance of drooping; thus, the bodice opens in front, the corsage is more often pointed at the waist, which is tight and longer; while the sleeves are set in below the shoulders and have the air of hanging limp; in fact, it is increasingly difficult to raise the arm. The skirt, even by day, is frequently open over an under-dress, with long descending lines of trimming, and materials with vertical stripes become very fashionable. The general effect is to produce long pointed Gothic angles, emphasised by the acute points of shawls and mantles.

DRESSES

Day

Types: the closed Round Dress; the Pelisse-Robe; the Robe Redingote.

The closed round dress calls for no comment, but the pelisse-robe is now developing new characteristics; the skirt is usually open over a petticoat and resembles the evening robes of previous years. The Robe Redingote is a term now used to denote a dress, the bodice of which has defined lapels; the skirt is trimmed to simulate a front opening. It is therefore similar to the 'pelisse dress' of former years.

Bodices are tight to the shape generally, and open at the neck, either en cœur or in a deep 'V' to the waist with draped folds at each side, filled in with a chemisette; or a shallow 'V' formed by crossed folds; or the 'corsage en schall.' The shallow open necks either show the edge of the chemisette or are trimmed with white ruching or a flat edging of white lace. A few have high necks with flat pointed collars.

The waist is very low; either round (with ceinture and buckle or ceinture of broad rich ribbon tied on one side); or pointed, especially in pelisse-robes; some even with 'antique bodice', *i.e.* with a long sharp point in front and the corsage descending all round below the waist line.

Sleeves: The Victoria sleeve, or modifications of it; either a fullness limited to the elbow with several small bouffants or volans on the upper arm and gauging at the wrist; or the 'bishop sleeve', full from the wrist (where it is finished by a tight cuff) to half way down the upper arm where the fullness is drawn into small vertical pleats extending to the shoulder and held in place by two or three narrow bands.

Skirts: The closed skirt, very full, pleated at the waist and cone-shaped, either plain or with one, two or three bias flounces headed by narrow rouleaux or ruching. Sometimes the flounces are made deeper behind than in front. Some are trimmed en tablier.

The open skirt, either trimmed with ruching,

velvet or narrow bias flounce of dress material. In the robe redingote the line of opening is marked out by ruching, pleating or ribbon knots. *Materials*: cashmere, shot silk, mousseline de laine, striped; foulards striped or plain. (Summer). Muslins, poult de soie, gros de Naples, gros des Indes.

Evening

Types: Semi-evening—round dresses.
Full evening—round dresses or open robes.
Bodices low off the shoulders and tight to the shape; some cut 'en corset'; a few with square necks, but the majority slightly or fully en cœur, and very low behind. Pointed waist; some with deep points 'in the antique style'. The neck line is sometimes draped with a fall of lace, usually three or four inches deep; this is now known as a *bertha*; in others the draping descends in folds from the shoulders to the waist; or the top may be draped across à la Sevigné, or with pleatings in the form of a bertha.
The 'corsage à la Maintenon' is close to the shape with ribbon knots down the centre, and the bottom of the corsage edged with a fall of lace.
Sleeves always short, *i.e.* half way down the upper arm, either tight, ending in a sloping ruffle or bouillon, or with small double bouffants or volans and a ruffle.
Skirts: Closed, with a deep bias flounce, or trimmed en tablier. Open, with trimmings en tunique, of velvet, ruching, lace or flouncing, revealing a petticoat of the same material, or satin.
Materials: damasked and flowered silks of the style of the seventeenth century; velvet, satin; Pekins; taffeta; shot silks; poult de soie; gros de Tours; rep velvet. (Summer) organdy, muslin and crepe.
Fashionable Colours: soft secondary and tertiary colours, and in summer, white.

OUTDOOR GARMENTS

Mantles

The mantle (winter use) is becoming less voluminous; it soon loses its hood which is replaced by a fur or velvet collar. The cape hangs below the waist and merges into large hanging sleeves with rounded corners. By wearing the upper part closed over the bodice it imperceptibly changes into a 'pelisse-mantle'. Its length is just clear of the ground. Chiefly worn in the carriage.
Materials: striped silks, levantine, satin, velvet.

For walking, a sleeveless mantle (*i.e.* cloak) somewhat shorter, with armholes, is worn.
The 'pelisse' as an outer garment has now become a mantle.

Cloaks

have long pointed scarf ends, with tassels, in front, reaching nearly to the ground; they are cut up at the sides to permit the arm to appear, and hang in a full point behind, with a small pointed cape or hood on the shoulders.
The Carriage Cloak comprises an under part like the skirt of a mantle, and a 'pelerine' in the form of a large shawl with front points, and hanging nearly to the ground behind, with a small cape covering the shoulders. The edges are bordered with fringe.

Mantlet

Chiefly for summer use, is rounded behind to the level of the waist with long rounded scarf ends hanging in front to below the knee, and is trimmed round the edges with ruching.
A new outdoor garment, the *Paletot* appears in the autumn. It hangs in stiff pleats from the shoulders, which are covered by a stiff short cape, and reaches to the top of the flounce of the dress. The armholes are guarded by flaps.

Spencers

of velvet. Open at the neck either en cœur or en schall, are worn occasionally with walking dresses.

Burnouse

Worn over evening dress. Of cashmere lined with satin. Reaches just below the knee, with rounded corners and fringed border, and fastens at the neck. A small 'capuchon' or serviceable hood is attached to the shoulders.

Shawls

The shawl is now becoming one of the important garments, tending to displace the mantle and the mantlet, especially in the summer; worn both for day and evening. Large and square; or with tasselled points which hang in front; or with scalloped edges. Most are lined with coloured silk or crepe, and fringed. The large shawl is worn with long corner point at the back.
Materials: silk plush, velvet, satin, damasked silk, shot silk, poult de soie, cashmere (with border embroidered in gold and silver thread), black gros grain; and for summer, muslin, organdy, and embroidered China crepe.

ACCESSORIES

'Fans are now made too large to be elegant.'
Fan Parasols.

By the beginning of this decade the headgear had already passed the climax of size. For the next five years attention was mainly devoted to inventing a host of variations on types already established in favour. Romance was now softening into sentiment. By about 1832 or 1833 the extravagant erections of hair in the evening coiffure began to subside; the Apollo knot no longer arrested the eye like a beacon and the modes of hairdressing associated with the names of Agnes Sorel and Madame de Sevigné introduced a more subdued effect. An air of demureness was thereby obtained and in the ball-room at least, flowers and ribbons woven into the tresses took the place of more aggressive devices. The use of huge combs was no longer required. The covering up of the ears by simple side loops of hair seemed to imply a desire to shut out sounds unsuited to virginal purity (a form of symbolism frequently adopted whenever that particular mentality is in vogue).

Day caps followed suit, becoming simpler in design and meeker in shape, with a growing tendency to conceal the ears by hanging lappets. By day the hat and the bonnet remained perpetual rivals; the latter pre-eminently for 'walking' and the former for 'carriage', while both disputed with each other for the 'promenade'. The bonnet tended, in fact, to shield the face while the hat seemed to invite inspection. Day hats soon acquired a shape not unlike that of the conventional bonnet, being worn further back on the head with the front tilted up to form a frame for the face. The novice may have some difficulty in distinguishing a hat from a bonnet as shown in contemporary fashion-plates, and may even be led to suppose that the terms were almost synonymous. In reality the distinction was carefully observed; the hat always had a brim of sorts at the back, even when it was concealed (as it often was towards the close of the decade) by a curtain or 'bavolet'.

We find, in 1831, the capote becoming extremely fashionable and dominating the next three years. It rapidly developed a number of variations, in particular the bibi. The different forms are described in the Annual Notes for that year and their various shapes are best appreciated from illustrations.

From the middle of the decade hats and bonnets gave an oval frame to the face, while from 1837 onwards the shape tended to become more and more circular, carefully guarding the wearer from impertinent observation. Just as the dress, from 1836 onwards, became less aggressive in form, so too the headgear, which no longer proclaimed the face but affected to conceal it. As a method of attracting attention this is a characteristically 'Gothic' manœuvre.

An important form of headgear in this decade was the 'drawn bonnet', the surface of which was made of gauged material; it possessed the practical drawback that its surface was a perpetual dust-trap and its use was reserved chiefly for special occasions. The 'cottage bonnet', with its simple but effective protection of the face against the weather, was a practical type of headgear always acceptable to the Englishwoman, and in the less fashionable circles was much used. But while protecting the face from the sun or even the rain it was awkward to control in a high wind; there was, in fact, all through this period a striking absence of 'sensible'

1836
Brown satin cloak and velvet cape; velvet undersleeves; satin oversleeves
Green cashmere morning dress

1837
Morning dress of black figured poult de soie
Promenade dress of white India muslin; mantlet of green gros de Naples
Carriage dress of pink satinet, en pelisse; fichu à la paysanne

headgear for rough weather, and we must assume that the fair wearers did not contemplate so perilous an adventure. While the cottage bonnet would at least shield the complexion from the sun the more fashionable shapes gave but slight protection, and veils of large dimensions in summer were usual and a parasol a necessity. The effect of the sun was especially dreaded; to be sunburnt was extremely unladylike, and the back of the bonnet or hat was curtained to preserve the skin of the neck.

In the evening caps, hats, toques and turbans were variously used to suit the importance of the occasion; young women preferred a coiffure of hair, but the married women wore something more impressive; the turban was pre-eminently the headdress of the mature matron. The beret disappeared early in the decade, and the toque became more and more of a hat which, in its turn, became more and more like a bonnet, with a backward tilt and the brim drawn down at the sides.

Materials used: Leghorn was the material best adapted for the huge hats and bonnets popular at the beginning of the period, but less suitable for the more complicated curves of the capote, and its cost was always great. The Dunstable straws supplied a somewhat cheaper substitute, but both materials found a rival, early in the '30's, in rice straw; the chip-bonnet on the other hand was eclipsed, as the material did not lend itself to the complexity of form fashionable. For winter use velvet was popular, especially in black, and drawn bonnets of silk and satin persisted all through the period. In the evening, dress hats were made of satin, velvet, terry and gauze. A growing tendency to use lace, especially English made, for caps was a noticeable feature. As the bonnet became smaller the custom of wearing a white cap beneath it was gradually abandoned in favour of flowers, ribbons, or occasionally a 'bonnet-front' of ruching, all these ornaments being now attached to the bonnet itself.

Specimens of the bonnets of this period as now seen in museums are generally without their inside lining. The brims of the huge Leghorns of the beginning of the period were unlined, but all bonnets and hats of smaller dimensions had, originally, linings of silk, terry, satin or gauze. The linings, however, did not extend into the crown itself, where the maker's label was affixed. Dress hats were, of course, always lined. Capotes and drawn bonnets were lined with materials such as velvet over a stiffening layer of book muslin.

It should be noted that while the headgear tended to become progressively smaller all through the decade, the bonnet took the lead and the hat lagged behind, so that during the middle years one finds small bonnets and large hats being worn side by side. It is a striking feature of this decade that profiles became unfashionable, and only the full face was displayed; even in the evening the mass of ringlets on the cheeks concealed, in a measure, the side view. It was the aim of the youthful belle of the time to be short and plump; as such the profile is perhaps not the most alluring aspect, and the type of face most in demand was the well-rounded, which should make its appeal only to the gentleman who was fortunate

123

enough to be *vis-à-vis*. Fashion did not encourage the fair charmer to look about her; or at least the obstacles to her so doing supplied a delicious thrill.

1830
HAIR

Day
Unchanged.

Evening
Hair often very tight and close to the head, with bows of ribbon in front of a comb with a high gallery; or the hair drawn up behind as tight as possible with three small combs at the back.

COIFFURE

Day
Caps 'built storey upon storey in wide and lofty edifices of blonde with floating strings'.

Evening
Dress hats of crepe and gauze, with low crown, partly turned up on one side. Evening berets and turbans, with cauls of openwork supported by rouleaux of satin, with flowers or aigrettes.

OUTDOORS

Bonnets. Bonnet brims closed and the crowns lower, being replaced by capotes.

Hats. Carriage hats low, with wide brims, and short at the ears. Of Leghorn or silk, or, in summer, of rice straw. The brims always trimmed on the underside, *e.g.*, with a band of ribbon twisted across it and ending in a bow. These hats are becoming more bonnet-shaped and less trimmed.

1831
HAIR

Evening
Lightly curled in front; the hind hair in bows or plaited braids with a knot of gauze; or in bows with two birds of paradise and a bandeau on the forehead, or a gold ferronnière.

COIFFURE
Unchanged.

OUTDOORS

Bonnets. Tuscan bonnets (made of English straw) with low slanting crowns, the brims square and rather wide.

The Capote Anglaise. Also known as 'bibi' or 'English cottage bonnet'. The crown, of drawn material, is round and placed rather far back; the brim, often of drawn material also, is of moderate size, cut square at the corners and low at the ears but open across the forehead; simply trimmed with a ribbon knot on the side of the crown and perhaps one feather. Lined with satin and often a curtain or 'bavolet' of blonde or silk.
Materials: Leghorn, rice straw or gauze on a frame.

The Capote Française. The crown is round, but not flat on the top, being either 'drawn in a spiral direction' or made to resemble the rind of a melon; the brim is larger and more open than the English variety. There are three chief types:
1. The Capote modeste, in which the crown is low and domed.
2. The Capote de paquebot, in which the crown is cylindrical and high, with a flat top, usually trimmed with bands of ribbon.
3. The Roquet ('pug-dog') bonnet in which the brim is shorter than the bibi, square at the corners, the crown of the same height all round and tilted very much backwards and rhomboidal in shape. Trimmed with gauze ribbons with a knot and bunch of flowers on the summit.
Materials: velvet, terry or satin.
During the year the Capote Anglaise developed a higher crown and became indistinguishable from the French form, and henceforth was spoken of as the 'capote' or 'bibi bonnet'. It was often worn over a white cap.

Hats. Carriage hats worn with mentonnières (attached to the strings and known in this country as 'chin stays').

1832
HAIR

Day
Parted in the middle with short curls on the temples.

Evening
Parted on the forehead and plaited behind in braids forming knots on the summit of the head, with a bow of ribbon inserted in each. Or hair à la Sevigné; curls at the sides of the face, with the rest of the hair drawn tightly back off the forehead and a low knot at the back, in front of which is a low pearl crescent.

Or coiffure Agnes Sorel: 'the hair is divided in soft folds on the forehead which it almost entirely covers; the braids descend very low on the cheeks and form a half-circle in turning back behind the ears.'

COIFFURE

Day
Morning caps with a low crown, very short at the ears and the front trimming narrower.

Evening
Hats in the style of Henri IV, with low crowns and small round brims. Berets and turbans smaller.

OUTDOORS

Bonnets. Bibi bonnets almost universal for 'promenade and carriage'; the brims smaller and more circular in shape, with less trimming. An extra small version of the bibi was the *Marmotte* bonnet. 'Drawn Bonnets, 20/- to 25/-.'

1833
HAIR

Day
Often parted in the middle without curls.

Evening
The hair 'in the style of the beauties of the court of Charles II'.

COIFFURE

Day
'Morning caps indispensable; made of tulle with a caul like a child's cap and the front trimmed with a double ruche; gauze ribbons.'
The Marmotte cap: a half-handkerchief put far back on the head and tied under the chin.

Evening
Hats of white satin trimmed with flowers; or chapeau-berets with wide brims rising on one side and very short on the other, with a long ostrich feather winding round; or blonde lace caps in the shape of a cockle shell. Small turbans, often divided in the middle into two lobes.

OUTDOORS

Bonnets with much smaller brims, the ears of which are longer.
Capote Bibi, the crown high and tapering; often no ornament inside the brim; one large ostrich feather or a single sprig of flowers or gauze ribbon.
Black blonde veil worn with it.

Veils. Black lace veils with walking dresses.

1834
HAIR

Day
The hair in flat braids low on the cheek, often with a good deal of false hair added.

Evening
Similar, or with side curls and a gold circlet. Or coiffure à la Sevigné.

COIFFURE

Day
Morning caps small, the crown round and simple, lined with coloured material; the front low. Or the Gothic cap, quite round to the face and trimmed with a double ruching; the crown very small.

Evening
Blonde caps worn very much off the face. Or dress hats, of rice straw with oval crown rather large and the brim evasé. Turbans of satin, covered with tulle, or simply a tulle or gauze scarf.

OUTDOORS

Bonnets. Aragon bonnets with pointed crowns. Capotes with pleated crowns and very small brims. Blonde fronts instead of caps worn under bonnets.

Hats. Of the capote shape, evasé in front but close to the cheeks; demi-veils in summer.

1835
HAIR

Unchanged.

COIFFURE

Day
Morning caps in the cornette shape.

Evening
Hats with turned up brims, placed far back on the head. Moabite turbans.

OUTDOORS

Bonnets with oval brims, long and deep and under lining of ribbon; perpendicular crown with blonde and ostrich feathers.
Hats. 'Curtains are now as frequently attached to hats as to bonnets.'

1836
HAIR

Evening
The hair with ringlets at the sides.

COIFFURE

Day
Morning caps, à la paysanne, or with high crown; or 'French cap'.

Evening
A white crepe hat with ostrich feather; or the Camargo hat, the brim raised in front and small. The Arab turban, without a tassel.

OUTDOORS

Bonnets close at the sides and evasé in the centre; blonde lace lining meeting under the chin.
Dunstable and Leghorn bonnets (Summer) with deep brims and very long at the sides; cone-shaped crowns.
Day capotes and drawn bonnets.

Hats. Carriage hats of velvet (Winter). Day hats with 'auriole brim', of a large size and perfectly round.

1837
HAIR

Unchanged.

COIFFURE

Day
Caps à la paysanne, à la babet; or à la fanchon; or of lace with lappets.

Evening
Caps, either à la paysanne, or silk lace; or the 'Italian cap' of embroidered tulle over white silk.

OUTDOORS

Bonnets: with deep brims, oval in shape, worn with a large white blonde veil. Drawn bonnets are either open shaped or bibi-shaped and small.

Note: the bonnets are much smaller than the hats.

Hats. Of white chip or Italian straw; the latter have the ribbons passed under the brim in order to prevent it from sitting close to the cheeks, and these are sometimes tied under the chin,

sometimes left loose. Pamela hats. Gipsy hats. Some hats have bavolets under which two ends of ribbon fall nearly to the shoulders and are called 'bishop's knot'. Hats and bonnets are trimmed under the brim with flowers or ribbons.

1838
HAIR

Evening
Either in soft braids over the ears with flowers, or with side ringlets and a knot at the back. For balls, the hair is dressed very low and quite at the back of the head; the hind hair mingled with feathers and jewellery; the front hair in tufts of ringlets with knots of ribbon.

COIFFURE

Day
Caps are small and worn at the back of the head, with ribbons.

Evening
Caps, the babet of the paysanne shape; dinner caps with long lappets. Evening hats with brims completely encircling the face 'en auriole'; the crown descending very low behind. Turbans of gauze with a bird of paradise.

OUTDOORS

Hats and bonnets are becoming smaller.
Bonnets. The Victoria bonnet, of satin, the crown without stiffening; the brim rather close and meeting under the chin; openings are cut at the sides through which the brides pass to tie under the chin; a long full bavolet at the back. Drawn bonnets of demi-bibi shape. The cottage bonnet is revived.

Hats of Italian or rice straw, with the brim turned up behind or cut away, are worn far back on the head. The brim encircles the face like a cap and is fully trimmed with flowers, blonde or ribbons.

1839
HAIR

Unchanged.

COIFFURE

Day
Morning caps of lace fitting close to the head, except the front, which is a little raised; narrow

cambric brides; a small rosette of satin ribbon on one side.

Evening
Turbans or turban-fronts, or *petit bords*.
Dinner hats of velvet; velvet toque-hats.

OUTDOORS

Bonnets of the cottage shape. Drawn bonnets of crepe lisse.

Hats. 'Rice straw hats are now made like those of Italian straw with the brim attached to the crown which prevents the seams that have a bad effect when the crown is made by the milliners.'
The summer hats are rounder in shape with auriole brim. Winter hats of cashmere, terry, velvet or satin.

UNDERCLOTHING

A contemporary (1837) informs us: 'Of all the articles of the toilet linen is the most important. . . . The softness and fineness of its texture produces no irritation of the skin and can be changed daily. . . . If the chemise be too large it forms creases under the stays which are troublesome and leave marks on the skin, and for this reason it should be made of very pliant and fine materials. A chemise of new linen should not be worn at first except in bed. The chemise should be made sufficiently low before and behind not to extend beyond the rest of the dress. The sleeves may have worked wristbands with an edging of net or lace.' Further information and authentic specimens of this decade are at present lacking.

On the subject of stays, the same author remarks: 'women who wear very tight stays complain that they cannot sit upright without them, nay, are compelled to wear night stays when in bed. A well-known effect of the use of stays is that the right shoulder frequently becomes larger than the left because the former, being stronger and more frequently in motion somewhat frees itself, and acquires by this means an increase of which the left side is deprived by being feebler and subjected to continuous pressure. When, indeed, corsets are employed to render the chest as small below and as broad above as possible, and greatly to increase the fulness and prominence of the bosom, when the young lady spends a quarter of an hour in lacing her stays as tight as possible and is sometimes seen by her female friends pulling hard for some minutes, next pausing to breathe, then resuming the task with might and main till after perhaps a third effort she at last succeeds and sits down covered with perspiration, then it is that the effect of stays is not only injurious to the shape but it is calculated to produce the most serious inconveniences . . .'

'Demi-corsets for the morning are made about eight or ten inches in height, furnished here and there with light whalebones. In other respects they are of the form of the upper part of the common corset; but the back edge ends in two long flaps which are fastened in front by means of a tape. The proper object of "The Complete Corset" should evidently be gently to support the figure, without diminishing the freedom of motion and to conceal the size of the abdomen when it becomes disproportionately large, either from corpulence or from accidents which naturally occur. The extension throughout the back should, for meagre persons, be produced by two pliant whalebones, or for plumper persons by two thin steels; for where the former are applied to a great variety of contour they are

127

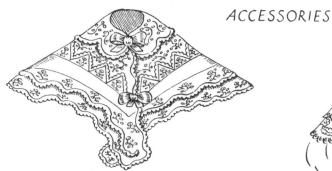

Half-dress Pelerine
of embroidered muslin _ 1835

Double Cape
with tulle ruche _ 1835

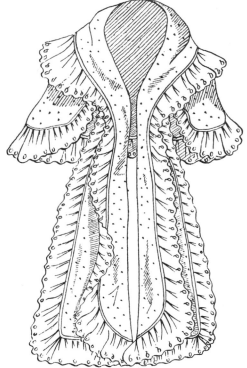

Tulle Pelerine-Mantelet _ 1837

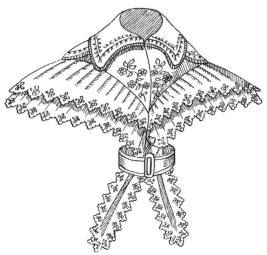

Pellerine with Lappets _ 1832

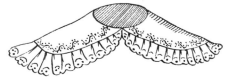

Embroidered muslin collar _ 1835

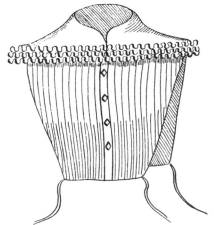

Chemisette of pleated muslin _ 1832

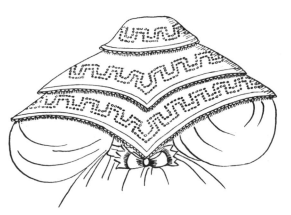

Canezou of embroidered muslin _ 1832

1838. (*circa*). Portrait of Baroness Le Despencer

1839
Carriage dress of grey gros de Naples with draped flounce; green velvet shawl
Evening dress of white satin trimmed with feather fringe
Morning dress of fawn silk, figured; bishop sleeves

apt to press painfully upon the skin. Under these circumstances, says a French writer, when the bones are not straight, wear the corset the wrong side outwards for a few days; that will suffice to put them straight! The extension throughout the part, and the pressure, if necessary, to repress any prominence inferiorly, should be produced by tempered steel of about 1½ inches wide, bent inward in a semicircular form and sufficiently long to extend over the prominence . . . below the arm in the middle may be a double whalebone to prevent disagreeable folds on the side. All shoulder straps should pass over the shoulders. . . .'

From the same source: 'Many persons endeavour to increase their size by aid of a considerable quantity of drapery. Size does, in effect, give a sort of dignity and majesty to the figure but this may be carried to an excess, as in the extreme enlargement of the hips by means of monstrous bustles, than which nothing can be more ridiculous, not to say indecent. When the bust is too long the defect is concealed by the fulness of the petticoats supported by a small bustle behind; nothing, however, can be in worse taste than the monstrous and ill-shaped bustles we commonly see, sometimes placed altogether on one side, and sometimes so irregular that they look as if some domestic utensil were fastened under the dress. French women have a much better contrivance which they call a Tournure. The tournure is a handkerchief drawn by the end through the stay-lace at the waistband. It raises up the folds of the dress, makes them fall with elegance, and diminishes in summer, the necessity of wearing a number of muslin petticoats. . . . Many persons under the sleeves of the dress wear skin-coloured sleeves, wadded or padded so as to render the arm of the necessary dimensions, and the padding is doubled to conceal the elbow if it be too sharp. . . . Trousers, rather light, supported by elastic bands buttoned to the corset, are suitable for women of a very delicate constitution who find a difficulty in walking and for those who are disposed to excessive plumpness. . . . Petticoats should not have shoulder straps because being placed over the straps of the corset, the pressure would be painful and the appearance ugly. Bodies, therefore, are now always attached to them. The bodies are made as plain as possible, and the skirts are not sloped but equally full above and below and equally filled in all round. The wide-flowing petticoat skirts are generally sufficient to conceal any slight deformities in the shape of the limbs. . . . Very fine white stockings and shoes made exactly to the shape ought to delineate perfectly the leg and the foot. If we wear thin stockings or prunella or kid shoes in winter we must expect that the natural state of the functions will be seriously disordered at particular times. It is absurd to imagine that worsted stockings or flannel socks are necessary in a state of health to prevent sore throats or catarrhs. Black stockings in winter, except in mourning, are in bad taste, unless the gown be black and then the stockings should, of course, be silk. If they are too narrow they fret the skin of the instep. . . . Garters of ribbon sit well but press too much and impede the circulation. Woollen garters with sliding knots irritate the skin. Garters which require tying ought to be loosely tied and if possible above the knee. If the calf of the leg is slender and the knee small two garters may be worn, one above and the other below. Elastic garters are greatly to be preferred. Some ladies attach two triangular pieces of elastic material to the straight edge of the gusset at the lower part of the corset; and from each of these descend two tapes which, passing through a loop of tape attached to each of the stockings, render garters unnecessary.'

In my collection is a bustle, dated 1833, a large crescent-shaped pad with long points to which tapes were attached for tying round the waist. It is stuffed with down. In a caricature by Heath (about 1830) is shown a bustle made of a series of gathered rows of stiffened material increasing in size from above. A petticoat with attached bodice, dated 1830, of linen, has short puffed sleeves gathered into a band; the neck is plain with a drawstring, and a tape is attached to the waist. The bodice has a back opening and a piped seam down the centre of the front. It is four feet wide at the bottom with six narrow tucks above the hem.

CHAPTER V
THE GOTHIC '40's

THE Englishwoman of this decade cultivated her feelings at the expense of her body. Physically she was less active than at any period in the century; she was absorbed in acquiring the art of expressing emotions by graceful attitudes rather than by movement. Her dress, therefore, was admirably designed for passive poses, and it was constructed to check anything approaching unlady-like activity. Needless to say, it was peculiarly unhygienic, but that was not a consideration which troubled her; it sufficed that it expressed exactly her frame of mind to which her body must submit to be moulded. Besides, an appearance of rude health was regarded as scarcely ladylike.

Sentimentalism in England finds a natural mode of expression in the Gothic, and it was the period when Victorian Gothic was at the height of its popularity. As we should expect, then, woman's dress showed a marked liking for Gothic forms, so that sometimes it almost suggested that it was built up of scraps looted from an Early English church. The general effect, all through the '40's, was a demure—or even a meek—passivity of mind and body. And just as the simplicity of 'Early English' gradually developed into the more elaborate style of 'Decorated' so, too, the simplicity of dress in the beginning of the decade presently acquired greater ornamentation, so that the fashions of the first half might be described as 'Early English' and those of the second half as 'Decorated', following the custom of all arts that the simpler style does not satisfy for long.

But the essential form remained unchanged because there was no change in the attitude of mind; the average Englishwoman underwent less development in this decade than in any other. It is also characteristic of her cloistered existence that passing historical events are less reflected in the dress of the '40's than in any other period of the century. The greater facilities for travelling provided by the new railways, the political upheavals, the economic distress, which were so disturbing the habits of the average man did not, as yet, affect the average woman. She did not travel and did not understand politics. It must have seemed to the contemporary man that the restless march of feminine fashions was arrested for ever and that the Fair Sex had at last arrived at the ultimate stage of elaborate perfection. Woman was acquiring, perhaps, an increasing consciousness of her social importance, but she was as yet afraid to assert herself by action. And so the fashions of her costume remained static except for an increase in the area occupied by the skirt, which steadily expanded with her growing sense of her importance.

Quite early in the decade the long waist, with its pointed bodice forming an acute angle emphasised by trimmings from the shoulders which met at a point at the waist, proclaimed a Gothic style. The preference for a bodice 'tight to the shape', over stays laced in to the utmost, indicated that physical activity was to be discountenanced. And the new device of setting in the sleeve (usually a tight one) below the shoulder made it impossible to raise the arm beyond a right angle. Such a dress, almost always with a back fastening of hooks and eyes, proclaimed that the services of a maid or sister would always be required. It symbolised a ladylike dependence on others.

The bodice was always lined and boned, with three bones placed fan-wise in the centre, and with side bones running up to the arm-pit. The lining was often strengthened by a broad tape sewn round the waist inside; sometimes, in addition, a pair of tapes were attached inside at the back and tied round the waist; and occasionally the lining had its own hooks and eyes under those fastening the dress; they were now of brass wire or black japanned iron. A number of these bodices will be found to have pads of wool attached in front to supplement the deficiencies of anatomy: a device specially common in the first half of the decade before the detachable 'Artificial Bust Improver' was invented to supply a long-felt want.

It was the fashion to be willowy, and young ladies assiduously practised slimming so that they might be able to display an eighteen inch waist; in consequence the natural figure too often needed the assistance of art. We also begin to find, early in the decade, the use of 'dress protectors', of india-rubber or chamois leather, sewn into the dress. A further novelty was the dress with two bodices, one for day and one for evening, either of which could be roughly tacked on to the skirt band as required. Apart from these few the bodice and skirt were always made in one.

The general effect of the upper half of the dress with its tight sleeves was restraint rather than allurement. The romantic spirit of the former period with its varieties of corsage designed to attract attention to the figure, had now given place to a guarded reticence. Even the ball dress, though cut low off the shoulders, preserved, with its long dagger-pointed corsage, a certain defensive air. The mechanical framework displayed marble shoulders and bosom—but they were immobile as marble, cold monuments of chastity.

It was the skirt to which fashion devoted its chief attention. The ingenious method (described in the Annual Notes for 1841) of gauging the material on to the waistband was a new and characteristic feature of the decade, and was used whenever the nature of the material permitted it. The effect was to throw out the skirt abruptly from the waist so as to give the skirt a dome shape. This was

1840

Public promenade dress: short silk pelisse-robe, ornamented en tablier
Riding costume (as worn by Her Majesty) of brown cloth; black silk cravat; black beaver hat; white veil
Morning visiting dress of dust-coloured silk en demi-redingote

1841 (*circa*). Portrait of Lady Elizabeth Villiers

1841 (*circa*). Portrait of Miss Dormer

further helped by the bustle underneath. During the first half of the decade, in skirts of heavy materials, there was frequently inserted a padding of wool between the dress and the lining just over the back of each hip, to increase the bustle effect. Towards the end of the decade when flat pleating tended to replace the gauging this padding was no longer needed.

The skirt (except with light summer materials) was invariably lined, either with silesia or, in evening dress, with book muslin. Towards the end of the decade the material 'crinoline' was occasionally used as a lining for the day skirt. Winter dresses were frequently lined with flannel in between the cotton and the dress material. In day dresses of heavy materials, the hem is braided, a device not hitherto used.

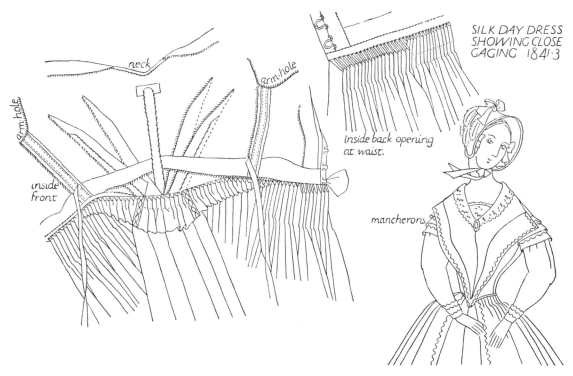

SILK DAY DRESS SHOWING CLOSE GAGING 1841-3

neck

arm.hole

arm.hole

inside back opening at waist.

inside front

mancherons

The outside watch-pocket hidden in the folds at the front of the waist was another innovation dating from the beginning of this decade. The large pocket in the skirt was in general use.

Towards the end of the period demi-trains were occasionally made for full evening dresses, but specimens are so rare as to suggest that this French fashion did not find much favour in this country. It is unfortunate that most of the English fashion magazines in the '40's were content to give their readers merely accounts of Parisian fashions; we may suppose these were largely drawn upon by English dressmakers, but not absolutely. It is significant, for instance, that the redingote style of day dress, so popular in France during the decade, is comparatively rare in existing collections; thus, of over thirty day dresses of this decade in my collection only three are redingotes. It seems probable that it was not so popular in England as the fashion articles would lead a reader of them to expect.

It is also noticeable that the tight-fitting corsage was, in this country, often modified by the addition of loose folds of material covering the front and descending to a blunt point at the waist; the number of such specimens in English collections implies that it was a style more used than the fashion articles would indicate.

The Annual Notes are of necessity derived from such fashion articles as exist, and it should be understood that in practice the more aggressive forms were often toned down by the average English dressmaker. It is always a characteristic English trait to soften an uncompromising outline. The more closely a specimen resembles a contemporary fashion-plate the more likely it is to have been a French model. (Dressmakers' labels were not attached to a dress until the end of the '70's, so that we can only assume the country of origin.) At the close of the decade a significant shortening of the front of the skirt, so that the foot was once more visible, indicated that women were once more beginning to walk.

If we were to consider only the form of the dress of this decade we might suppose that woman was almost indifferent to sex-attraction; the form, even with a flounced skirt, had a hard outline, at times almost Puritanical. But a glance through the advertisements of the period reveals a multitude of devices for enhancing the beauty or supplying gifts where Nature had been parsimonious: paint and powder and washes and unguents and dyes, together with artificial ringlets, bust-improvers, pads and bustles, to say nothing of eyebrow thickeners, lotions for rendering the eye more limpid or more sparkling, scents, breath-sweeteners, depilatories and dentifrices, hardly in keeping with Puritanism.

We have, in fact, only to glance at the dresses themselves to perceive wherein lay their power of sex-attraction. It was the colour. Primary colours were no longer considered good taste; indeed they were thought to be almost vulgar. The art of dyeing materials had reached a very high level; even to-day specimens a hundred years old show no fading. It is singular that vegetable dyes should at last have arrived at such a pitch of excellence only to be driven from the market in the '60's by the aniline dyes. Secondary and tertiary tints were mainly employed and materials shot in two, three or even four colours were fashionable. In addition colour on colour was worked out in endless variety of broché silks, damasks and printed materials.

· Colour printing had enormously improved; the French barège supplied a mass of ever-changing patterns. The merinos and cashmeres, both English and foreign, were now woven with technical perfection, and new mixed textiles, of which alpaca was one, were appearing in bewildering variety. By their use all sorts of delicate tones and depths of tint as well as texture could be obtained. It will be seen from actual prices given in the annual summaries that materials were, on the whole, cheap, and labour inordinately so.

A marked liking for harmonising tones in the dress, with contrasting tones in the outer garments worn over it, was usual. A lilac dress under a myrtle-green mantle with a lemon-yellow bonnet and gloves, formed a perfectly acceptable mixture. But, of course, it was essential that each should be of the precise tint.

There would be no blundering mixture of 'cold' with 'warm' colours. For example: 'A crimson opera-dress, worn with a light blue mantle and pale green velvet leaves in the hair.' 'A visiting dress of light green satin; mantle of shot pink and lilac silk; white silk capote trimmed with lilac.' 'Promenade costume: dress of drab silk; mantle of bright ruby velvet, bonnet of green velvet lined with rose-pink satin.'

Again it is necessary to remind the reader that the fashion-plates of that period are by no means exact reproductions of the colours of the materials used; it is only in the dresses themselves that we can perceive the subtle charm of those delicate colour blendings.

We may perhaps assume that the man of that day was more susceptible to colour than to form. Or perhaps there was something irresistibly piquant in the contrast between the rigidity of form and the softness of colour, suggesting that the demure Puritan might, after all, be a dainty rogue in porcelain.

In many respects it might be claimed that woman's dress of this decade was the most artistic of the century. In the sense that it most closely expressed the artistic taste of its day, this would be correct. It never verged from the spirit of Victorian Gothic, displaying both the admirable features of that period as well as its affectations; its fond efforts to revive an obsolete past from which the nation was not willing to part. In spite of Disraeli's advice, 'The age of ruins is past; have you seen Manchester?' the well-bred woman of the '40's declined to look; it was a last attempt to preserve a traditional pose. In her costume she assumed an air of sublime passivity, a standard so acceptable to masculine taste. It was her function to symbolise the domestic virtues, and she dressed up to the part.

1840

The principal changes in this year are in the direction of greater elaboration of the recent style with more variations in details. The day bodice is more frequently cut en cœur, and the opening is deeper and wider. Whereas in 1839 the back of the bodice was frequently gored with three seams showing, or with a centre piece, or with the material cut on the cross, in this year a single centre seam is the rule. The Victoria sleeve is varied by a return to greater fullness in the middle; the skirt is fuller and now completely domed; its trimmings are more impressive, the flounces being either more numerous or larger and the heading (such as a double line or bouillon) more evident, and the flounces are now often scalloped.

DRESSES

Day

Types: The Pelisse-Robe; the Redingote and the Round Dress.

The pelisse-robe: corsage open en cœur, or in a deep 'V' to the waist with side lapels (sometimes passing round the shoulders 'en schall'), or with draped folds from the shoulders to the waist. The skirt trimmed to simulate a front fastening, by lines of ruching, fancy buttons, etc.; or to simulate a tunic over-dress. In summer the pelisse-robe has an open skirt revealing a white petticoat.

The redingote: the corsage half-high and plain, with a simulated front opening, and the skirt similarly trimmed (buttons, etc.), or open (in summer).

The round dress (frequently described vaguely as 'a Robe'): the bodice half-high or en cœur, with drapery folds from the shoulders descend-

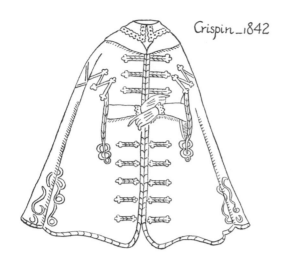

Crispin _ 1842

Camail _ 1842

Polonaise _ 1846

Pelisse Mantle _ 1846

Visite _ 1846

Cazaweck _ 1849

Outdoor Garments (1842-49)

ing to the waist, often in a 'heart-shape' (spoken of as forming a 'heart pelerine'); or the front of the bodice gathered to a blunt point at the waist ('en gerbe'); a few high to the neck with the front plain except for lines of buttons as in a riding habit (the corsage 'en Amazone'). With an open corsage a white chemisette is worn.

Sleeves: usually of the Victoria type, but frequently the fullness in the middle is larger than formerly, and the 'bishop sleeve' is common. By the summer the tight sleeve to the wrist (with very short upper sleeve) begins to appear. NOTE: During the year the loose and the tight sleeve rival each other in popularity for day dresses. The tight sleeve is fashionable for heavy materials, and is cut on the cross with one seam, and headed by a mancheron; with it the corsage is cut with three seams in front and excessively tight. The waist is usually round and a ceinture with long floats is common. Skirts fuller and domed; either plain or flounced (three, five or seven flounces), or trimmed en tablier. 'Brandebourgs' (transverse cording and tassels in the military style) are common.

Day Negligée. The peignoir is used as a morning dress, similar to a pelisse-robe but the corsage is full and without bones, and the sleeves of the 'bishop' shape.

Materials: quadrilled and plaided and chiné silks; mousselaine de laine; barège; organdy; foulards; barège-cashmere; batiste-barège; muslin; levantine.

Riding Habit

'A riding habit of blue, green or black cloth, the corsage trimmed with fancy buttons or Brandebourgs; sleeve tight or demi-large. Corsage open with cambric frilled chemisette fastened down the front with gold filigree buttons; deep cuff embroidered with lace; black cravat; half boots of kid or silk with kid tips; coutil pantaloons, strapped. Small round beaver hat, black or grey, or straw hat; veil; yellow kid gauntlet gloves.'

Advertised prices 3 to 5 guineas.

Evening

Bodices cut low off the shoulders, either square with a square lace bertha, or slightly en cœur surrounded with a fall of lace, or with flat drapery folds which sometimes descend to a point at the waist. The waist is pointed, the corsage being boned. A few with corsage 'en corset'.

Sleeves short and tight; being covered by the bertha there is no heading at the shoulder; the sleeve ends in two or three small bouillons or folds of dress material, or lace manchette.

Skirts: the open robe is rare but the skirt is often trimmed to simulate it. Flounces with headings are usual and increase in number nearly up to the knee; they are frequently laid on in waves. A single deep flounce of lace may be seen.

Semi-evening dresses half-high, or bodice en eventail, with long sleeve. Often in the form of a pelisse-robe.

Evening Negligée. A lace or organdy canezou, in the form of a jacket with sleeves is used as a bodice.

Materials: plain or embroidered organdy; satin; rep velvet; shot and figured silks rather than striped. Crepe or tulle over satin.

New Materials: Lavender poplin shot with cherry, Pekins chiné, barège-cashmere and batiste-barège, organdy printed in small patterns, cashmere Syrien, Pompadour chiné, Pekin point, broché moiré, resille de soie, marbled silk, Algerine. 'The new material, Tarlatan.'

OUTDOOR GARMENTS

Mantles and Cloaks

Except for evening and carriage these are largely displaced by shawls.

The burnouse-mantle, for carriage, long and full, with a pelerine-cape having long tasselled points below the knee, and a hood; easy sleeves. Opera cloak of brown rep velvet, lined with blue satin; shorter than the dress; no sleeves, but armholes; deep lapels, and a hood.

Mantlets

(Summer). Of embroidered muslin edged with lace, some lined; with a small shoulder cape attached, rounded behind and flat ends in front. Some are embroidered in flowers.

Paletots

as in former year.

Shawls

(Summer). Of glacé silk, trimmed with lace; figured silks; embroidered organdy with plain centre; white foulard, fringed. (Winter) Cashmere (French), velvet shot with orange.

ACCESSORIES

Shoes

much more pointed.

Gloves
Long gloves 'can now scarcely be called demi-long'. Buttoned or laced close to the arm.

Jewellery
Coral fashionable; also brooches and large ear-rings.
Fashionable winter *Furs*: Sable, chinchilla, grey squirrel and musk.

Porcelain *Buttons* invented by Prosser of Birmingham.
'Every article of the toilet seems at present to have reached its highest point of perfection for it would be difficult to imagine how any part of a lady's dress could be rendered more rich and elegant.'

1841

The principal changes in this year are the increasing use of the plain tight sleeve for day dresses, frequently without the heading of a volan at the shoulder; and consequently the narrower shoulder line, and in general a quieter tone; thus, flounces are less common, and the skirt, even in evening dress, is often plain. But the most important innovation, beginning to appear in the spring, is 'a new method of setting the skirt by gauging it round the top as far as the points of the hips; by this means the excessive fullness (which otherwise would be disposed in pleats or gathers) is formed exactly to the shape; but on the other hand this method lengthens the waist excessively and gives an air of stiffness to the figure'. The gauging is presently used all round the waist and is employed for all heavy materials, during the next five years, although pleated specimens are occasionally found. The practical effect is to emphasise the dome shape, which is increased by a bustle extending round the sides as well as the back. It is a method of construction which is entirely confined to the years 1841-1846, and is one of the few technical devices which were original to the nineteenth century; the gauging used in the eighteenth century was uneven and partial, whereas that of the '40's is distinguished by its remarkable evenness and its employment all round the waist. Its presence dates a specimen more certainly than any other feature.

The year is also notable for the introduction of the material *Alpaca*.

DRESSES

Day
Types: the Round dress; the Pelisse-Robe; the Redingote. Peignoirs (for morning negligée). Bodices half or three-quarters high, high at the back and open in front, often en cœur (with a chemisette). In round dresses either draped with folds from the shoulders forming a 'V', or with a flat fancy trimming enclosing the points of the shoulders and passing down to meet at the centre of the waist in front and behind, arranged in front in a heart-shaped curve; this type of trimming is very common and is known as 'trimmed with a heart pelerine', or 'with pelerine trimmings en cœur'. The term must not be confused with 'a pelerine', which is a separate garment worn over the dress, and this, of a narrow type, is sometimes used instead of a trimming. These trimmings are sometimes single bands, sometimes double, and bodices thus trimmed usually are pointed at the waist.

In pelisse-robes the bodice is trimmed either en pelerine or en schall; in redingotes the bodice is tight to the shape with turned back lapels. A chemisette is worn when the bodice opening is deep. Sleeves long and tight, with one or two small and close mancherons below the shoulder, or perfectly plain to the wrist with a small cuff with cambric edging.

Skirts: round dresses with one to three bias flounces, headed, or two deep separated tucks. but the plain skirt, or trimming en tablier, is more usual; pelisse-robes and redingotes have the skirt trimmed en tablier by a continuation of the bodice trimmings.

Summer dresses: the skirt of a pelisse-robe is open over a cambric petticoat; a cambric embroidered canezou (with sleeves) may replace

1841
Day dress of striped alpaca with Pompadour sprig

the bodice. In muslin dresses the bodice may be gathered 'en chemisette' or drawn in small folds. Peignoirs: for morning negligée, the bodice and skirt open except at the waist; in winter lined and wadded, pleated behind, without seams in front; trimmed en schall, with demi-large sleeves, often with tight under-sleeves.

Materials: rich plain silks, Saxony cloth, foulards, satin, shot silks, Pekins, organdy, barège chiné, broché and chiné silks, tarlatan. Negligée, of mousselaine de laine, cashmere and nankin.

Evening

Corsage low off the shoulders, drawn down in the centre, but the round low bodice becomes more fashionable. Trimmed with cross folds, or plain with falling tucker or bertha of lace or dress material. Always pointed at the waist. Some bodices made 'en corset' with long points. Sleeves short and tight, ending in a small bouillon or lace manchette.

Skirts either with one deep flounce of lace; or a flounced tablier; or two flounces en disposition. Ball dresses trimmed en tunique; or as an open robe; or with two skirts, the upper shorter than the lower.

Materials: velvet, satin, moiré, Pekins, shot taffeta, chiné taffeta, poplin broché, crepe and tulle over satin, tarlatan, grenadine figured, la Jardinière.

New Materials: Alpaca, Saxony, la Jardinière, poplin broché.

OUTDOOR GARMENTS

Mantles and Cloaks

These tend to be shorter; trimmings of black lace and fringe are common.

Mantlets

of black silk, with flounced edge and long scarf ends worn in summer.

Scarves

The long scarf, a foot wide, the ends fringed, often replaces the mantlet in summer; of silk with broad stripes, or muslin with a flounced border.

Shawls

Square, plain ground, rich border; or broché and damasked (fringed); or white cashmere, bordered. At the end of the year very large cashmere shawls with a point descending nearly to the ground behind, and very deep borders, come in. Borders of velvet shawls embroidered in coloured silks.

ACCESSORIES

Gloves

elaborately trimmed round the top, with tassels.

Mittens of black silk 'are indispensable for all social parties'.

Jewellery: gold smelling bottle suspended by a chain and hook from the ceinture.

The 'three fold' linen button introduced by John Ashton.

1842

The changes from the previous year are slight, but mainly a tendency to greater severity and plainness. Thus, for day dress, the redingote form is common, with sleeves plain but fuller in the upper part. In evening dresses the double skirt increases in favour.

DRESSES

Day

Redingotes with plain high corsage, long tight sleeve and skirt en tablier; in summer of nankin with pelerine trimmings en disposition. Some with full corsage, and skirt with buttons or brandebourgs down the front en tablier; or with corsage en Amazone, a plain high body tightly buttoned to the throat with small cambric collar and cuffs.

Pelisse-robes as previous years, but often trimmed with quilling.

Round dress, as before.

Some summer dresses of quadrilled gingham, the bodice en blouse with demi-large sleeves; and muslin dresses with gauged corsage en canezou. Peignoirs retain their popularity; in winter of cashmere or a twilled woollen levantine, and lined.

Materials: barège very fashionable, and passe-menterie trimming. 'The new barèges have given mousselaine de laine its death-blow.'

Evening

Demi-evening, three-quarters high and tight to the shape, the bodice opening with small lapels; demi-large sleeves; the skirt with two deep satin flounces, the upper one looped up at one side with a bouquet.

Full evening. Corsage very low and full, or in a deep 'V' with a chemisette or a bertha-pelerine; or low and round with a lace bertha. Pointed, some with scalloped point. Sleeves short and tight.

Skirts with two deep flounces en disposition; with satin dresses one deep lace flounce of tulle, crepe lisse, etc., over satin.

A new form is the tarlatan dress with double skirt; a deeply pointed bodice, the neck low and draped all round in full folds.

Ball dresses either en tunique, or with one side looped up and caught with a bouquet of flowers, or the overdress shorter than the under. Corsage very low and tight with drapery folds, or à la Sevigné, or with a lace bertha-pelerine (*i.e.* a bertha which opens on the bosom and descends down the centre to the waist). Short sleeves with double bouillons.

Materials: tarlatan very fashionable.
New Materials: Pekin Victoria.

OUTDOOR GARMENTS

Mantles and Cloaks
New Types: the Camail. A waist-length cloak, with armholes, rounded below, full round the neck with small falling collar. In summer of embroidered muslin, lined and lace trimmed, or of black silk, fringed. In winter wadded, of cashmere, satin or velvet.

The Crispin. A short mantle, occasionally with sleeves, cut on the cross; close round the shoulders and neck and with a small pelerine-cape. Of similar materials.

The Crispin-Cloché. A bell-shaped Crispin, knee-length.

The Cardinal (or Cardinal-Pelerine). A short collarless cape without sleeves, either just above or below waist level, rounded below. For morning, of barège or coutil; for evening, of lace.

Mantles
for carriage wear tend to be shorter than the full mantle of previous years.

Mantlets
large, and very low behind, with three lace flounces which terminate at the bend of the arm. Small cape and long scarf ends.

Pelerines
of cambric or muslin, for day or evening, are now cape-shaped, and merge into the mantlet form.

ACCESSORIES

Jewellery: brooches now much smaller. Bracelets containing a portrait fashionable.

1843

The changes of fashion during this year are but slight; in the bodice an increase of the point which is often rounded into a scallop, and in the skirt an increasing use of one or two deep flounces, which are often scalloped and pinked; these changes being seen in day dresses as well as in evening. Skirts tend to lengthen almost to the ground. But the principal developments are in the outdoor garments, the shawl being largely displaced by forms of cloak and mantle. The general effect is always towards a greater rigidity.

DRESSES

Day
Morning dresses of cloth, with high corsage, some closed, others open in front in the habit style; cambric collar and cuffs; waist either round or pointed. (By the middle of the year the point is usually rounded.) Plain sleeves either tight to the wrist, with a cuff, or short (halfway between the elbow and wrist) and halftight, with engageantes; often with two small rows of bouillonée round the upper arm. Some morning dresses have the bodice buttoned up to the throat so that by unbottoning the top, lapels are formed when used for 'half dress'.

Collars are small and square in form, trimmed with lace, and worn close round the neck.

The 'pelisse-robe' is largely worn for morning and afternoon dress.

The redingote, with skirt en tablier, for the 'promenade' and afternoon, is very common. The more formal or 'carriage' dress has the skirt with a series of tucks or two scalloped flounces, or one deep bias flounce of the same material, placed almost at knee-level and headed by pleated ribbon, or reaching from above the knee down half way to the ankle, simulating a double skirt.

Pockets concealed in the folds of the skirt be-

1841

Full length: Morning dress of striped silk trimmed with rows of reversed pleatings

Evening dress of straw-coloured silk, corsage à la grecque

Evening dress of pink striped silk, trimmed with tucks

Half length: Back of centre figure

Walking dress with sleeve puffed at the elbow

Evening dress, the corsage in folds

1843
Evening dress of blue and white Pekin silk, trimmed en tablier with passementerie
Ball dress of pink tulle over satin
Ball dress of satin broché with festooned lace flounces en tablier
Evening dress of white satin trimmed with lace en pelerine and lace flounces

come usual. Trimmings of flat braid and velvet and passementerie are much used.

Materials: plaid, shot and striped taffetas, pekins, poplin, satin striped foulards and varieties of barège.

Evening

Similar to previous year, but the point of the corsage is often scalloped. By the summer the corsage is cut less low and the double skirt becomes usual. A new type of corsage, the *Montespan*, with a deep peak front and back, is introduced, 'a kind of bodice, descending below the waist and taking in the hips; tight to the shape, cut square at the top and excessively low.' Ball dresses are made with two or three skirts in diminishing size, of transparent material over satin. The 'Cardinal-Pelerine' is a deep lace bertha, cleft in the centre, worn with evening dress.

Materials: shot and watered silks, chiné plaids, tarlatan, organdy.

New Material: Alpago.

OUTDOOR GARMENTS

Mantles and Cloaks

The Camail and the Crispin undergo modifications which render them almost indistinguishable, the latter preserving a certain close and rigid fit round the upper part.

Shoulder capes, under the name of Cardinals, are a development from the pelerine.

Paletot

The paletot, with three capes or 'pelerines' (two rounded in front and the third ending in a point at the waist) becomes a combination of a Camail and a Cardinal. Winter mantles are more voluminous, loose from the shoulders, very wide and nearly reaching to the ground, having loose sleeves and a velvet collar. They are made of satin, and lined with plush or silk.

Mantlet

The mantlet, or mantella, rounded and deep at the back with long scarf ends in front, is just beginning to acquire sleeves and will presently become yet a new garment with a new name. In its more primitive form, the wide scarf is still in use, draped round the shoulders with the long ends hanging down in front nearly to the ground. 'It is becoming as popular as during the summer of 1837, the period of its first introduction. In form it differs but slightly from those worn at that time, the chief alterations being that lace is no longer employed for trimming. Of black, puce or brown taffeta en negligé. Or light shot-colours for dress.'

Casaweck

The casaweck is similar to the mantle, but knee length.

Large square *Shawls* with black grounds thickly covered with flowers in full colours.

ACCESSORIES

Boots

Hall's patent elastic boots.

Ladies' Elastic *Gaiters* in silk, cashmere and woollens.

NOTE: Wire-drawn hooks and eyes, or brass or japanned iron, and pins with solid heads, are now in general use.

Prices

Fringed satin Cardinals, 12/6.

Musquash boas, 5/9. Squirrel boas, 9/6. French Sable boas, 28/6. Lynx muffs, 14/9. Sable muffs, 16/- to 31/6. Ermine muffs, 25/-. Chinchilla muffs, 21/-.

Merinos at 2/9 a yard. Spitalfields Ducapes from 1/4½. Satin Turcs from 1/7½. Striped silks from 1/3½.

Paisley Shawls, 21/6; with scarlet grounds, 31/6.

1844

'The time is past when great and sudden changes took place in fashions.' In spite of this contemporary opinion, expressed at the end of this year, we can detect a very decided move, after two years' immobility; the Gothic spirit is more noticeable; in day dresses the bodice is more open in front in a deep 'V' with lapels turned back; the close sleeve is expanding into a bell opening, and the skirt is apt to open over an under-skirt, so that long pointed angles are a feature. In evening dresses the same effect is got by a long pointed bodice above an open skirt. In addition materials are richer and trimmings more varied, and skirts tend to increase yet more in width so that for evening dresses the half-train is introduced.

141

The outdoor garments become so complex that their distinguishing names tend to be abandoned and they are described simply as 'pardessus'.

DRESSES

Day

The Round Dress, with high tight corsage trimmed with a pelerine or with lines of pass-menterie en cœur; round or pointed below; tight sleeves, and skirt plain or with a tablier.

The Pelisse-Robe with pointed bodice open down to the waist with lapels and chemisette; the sleeves often widening into a bell-shape with white undersleeves; the skirt open over a white petticoat. Or, as a variation very common this year, the front opening of the bodice and skirt laced across.

The Redingote, with closed tight corsage, tight sleeves, and skirt trimmed all down the middle.

The Peignoir (for summer) with corsage nearly high and en cœur, pointed over a wide-open skirt. Long wide sleeves.

'Aprons are in very great vogue' for home costume being made of black silk, or satin encircled with a stamped chicorée trimming; others in shot silk. (April) 'walking dresses are now commencing to be seriously thought of; the materials most in favour being rich satins, poplins, pekins and plaided cloths.'

The 'afternoon' or 'visiting' dress has the skirt usually trimmed either with a deep 'bias' composing the lower half of the skirt, or with two scalloped and pinked flounces, or tucks. In summer, with muslin dresses, the double skirt is sometimes used. The chemisette is beginning to develop into a blouse by the addition of sleeves which appear beyond the dress sleeves and serve as engageantes. During the summer skirts increase in width and 'flounces are quite the rage'.

Trimmings for day dresses largely braid, passementerie and velvet.

Materials: cloth and merinos fashionable, also alpaca; in summer, barège and organdy. For promenade dresses chameleon silk, florence and foulards.

Wedding Dresses

are now made more like a day dress, *e.g.* 'the corsage three-quarters high, round above and drawn in with a little fullness at the waist which is round; three-quarter sleeve of a series of small bouillons; double skirt.'

Evening

Corsage very low and tight with long tapering point; very short sleeves. Skirt either open with front facings of lace and velvet over a satin underskirt trimmed with three lace flounces, or an over-dress of transparent material with three skirts over a satin one.

Or the 'open robe', *i.e.* the corsage open with turned back lapels covering the shoulders and the very short sleeves, and finishing at the waist; the skirt open down to the knee over an under-dress. The open robe is very fashionable, and the bosom 'cut indelicately low', and round.

The 'corsage à la Norma', the front with a loose fold in the centre caught with a gold ornament. Demi-trains are introduced for full dress. Black velvet aprons worn in the evening.

Materials: The silks and satins are more elaborately designed and richer than in former years. Ball dresses (with double skirts) of organdy, tarlatan and crepe.

OUTDOOR GARMENTS

Pardessus. Crispins of wadded satin, with large sleeves and capuchin hood.

The Polonaise, of velvet or satin, close fitting corsage and sleeves; skirt half length and moderately full; a short square pelerine-cape.

The Caftan, between a paletot and a mantle.

The Polka, a short shaped mantle with sleeves.

The Camail, or Cardinal-Pelerine is large, while the Mantle is made in the form of a pelisse.

These outer garments tend to become more shaped at the waist and to approximate each other so that presently 'Pardessus' serves as a generic name for any outdoor garment of half or three-quarter length with sleeves, and shaped in at the waist. They have generally a short rounded cape or 'pelerine', and are trimmed with lace or velvet.

Paisley *Shawls* in winter.

ACCESSORIES

Gloves

Evening, short and plain, finishing just above the wrist.

Rubber *Galoshes* worn in muddy weather.

Jewellery: several bracelets worn on both arms. Large drop ear-rings. Barège *Scarves* with broad coloured stripes 'à la Bayadère' very fashionable in summer. *Parasols* smaller and often fringed. *Bouquets* and *Handkerchiefs* carried in the hand.

Prices
Cameleon silk, 1/10 a yard. Twilled cashmere, 8/9 'the full dress' (an expression meaning a full dress length of material).

Handkerchiefs, Irish cambric, 16/- a dozen. French ditto, 30/- to 70/- a dozen.
Polka Mantle, 25/-. 'The Pardessus Pelisse', 18/9.
Rich watered Peignoir, 38/6.
Squirrel Victorine, 5/9. Sable mink ditto, 8/9.

1845

During this year the interest is mainly concentrated on the skirt, which becomes more decorated; a fashion for rows of ornamental buttons running down the whole length in the centre of the dress contrasts with a taste for horizontal lines of trimming round the skirt in diminishing width as they pass upwards, the so-called 'pyramid style'. In addition the liking for flounces, especially scalloped, double skirts (now used for day dresses), and the skirt set with one deep bias, does not diminish. There are also further forms of the mantle.

As regards materials a host of variations of shot silk appear on the market. 'Velvet is employed for every possible article of dress' (winter).

'The days are past when fashions went from one extreme to another.'

DRESSES

Day
The previous types continue, but a new form of corsage appears in the summer, the *Caraco*, at first shaped like a jacket and later an actual jacket, open in front over a chemisette, and with the front longer than the back.
Sleeves, in cloth or silk dresses, remain tight, but of three-quarter length with a white under-sleeve to the wrist. In muslin dresses the sleeve is fuller and slightly bell-shaped at the opening. Skirts are plain or flounced, or double; in redingotes with lines of buttons descending en tablier. Many are trimmed with velvet or ribbon en pyramid.
The waist is either pointed or round (in which case a ribboned ceinture is worn).
Redingotes remain unaltered but round dresses are more frequently worn with two or three flounces. Visiting dresses are more elaborate, having more flounces, or double skirts.
Materials: (Winter) cloth. (Summer) balzarine, coutil, printed muslins, barèges, batiste, nankin (especially with the Caraco dress), mousselaine de soie, pyramid silks. 'Shot silks have become so common that plain silks are considered more elegant' (in the summer). There is a marked taste for materials with horizontal stripes, and trimmings of passementerie, braid and velvet.

Evening
Corsage always tight to the shape and deeply pointed; some round and off the shoulders with a bertha, others en demi-cœur, with a chemisette.
Sleeves very short and almost hidden by the bertha.
Skirts open as a robe, revealing a flounced under-dress; or trimmed en pyramid, or with multiple flounces. Some are trimmed en tunique or made as short open tunics. Ball dresses usually with double skirts of transparent material. 'Les Montants' or trimmings (of foliage or lace) placed on each side of the skirt.
Materials: shot silks, especially chameleon, chiné silks, velvets.
Fashionable Colours: shot colours and black are the most in vogue.

OUTDOOR GARMENTS

New forms are:
1. The Visite, close fitting, lined, and heavily trimmed with black lace or chenille. In shape between the camail and the scarf-mantlet; the pelerine is very large, and the scarf ends rounded and drawn in at each side of the waist so as to produce a kind of half-sleeve.
2. The Casaweck. A short mantle, lined and wadded, and quilted round the border.
Summer *Mantlets* of organdy lined with coloured silk and embroidered in feather-stitch.
The *Pelisse-Mantle*, of satin or silk, of three-quarter length, is a revival of the old-fashioned pelisse, but fitting the shape at the waist.

Mittens
still worn with day and evening dress.

Prices
Paisley Shawls, two yards square, 15/9 to 21/-.

Polkas, 16/9, Barège Shawls, 5/9.
Swiss muslin, the full dress, 3/9. Barège ditto, 4/9. Balzarine ditto, 10/9. Glacé silks, 1/6 to 2/6 a yard. Satins, 4/- to 6/9 a yard. French merinos, 3/- to 5/9 a yard.

1846

The chief feature of the year is the introduction of the 'waistcoat-corsage' and the jacket, while the varieties of the pardessus increase. The stiff effect is further diminished by abundance of trimmings, and the long pointed Gothic angles are broadening and curving into the ogee. The pure 'early English' period is changing imperceptibly into a 'decorated period'.

DRESSES

Day

The redingote form retains its popularity for morning and visiting dresses. It acquires the 'gilet corsage', open with lapels 'like a gentleman's waistcoat' (or the modern dress coat), closed at the waist by three buttons and sloping away a little in front and descending well below the hips. The round dress develops a 'jacket corsage'; *e.g.*, 'a morning dress of grey taffeta, the bodice being a jacket with basquins buttoning down the front and high in the neck; tight sleeves with reversed cuffs; five rows of frilling on the skirt as volans.' Or the jacket may be simulated by basquins (an extension of the corsage below the waist line). With the open corsage the revers extend down to the waist and are widely splayed apart revealing an embroidered chemisette; with a closed corsage an embroidered canezou of muslin or cambric descending in rounded points to the waist, front and back, is a common feature. Or, in place of a canezou, the 'corsage à basque' is 'encircled with a bias of black velvet forming a kind of round flat collar close up to the neck and descending down the centre of the front and round the sides'.

The waist is usually round with a ceinture with a knot and floating ribbons.

There is an increasing tendency to skirts without trimming 'for the extravagant width of skirts makes the addition of trimming very often ungraceful', but a number have five or six scalloped and pinked flounces; or plain tucks. Fringe is frequently used as trimming. Occasionally the skirt has, on the right side, half way up, a small slit enabling the skirt to be caught up through it in order to reveal a glimpse of the embroidered petticoat.

The peignoir (*e.g.*, with corsage widely open with revers of stamped velvet meeting those of the open skirt over a cambric under-dress, the sleeves loose with cambric undersleeves) retains its popularity for morning wear, especially in the summer.

In addition, the types of day dress seen in the former year are also worn.

'The gowns are still worn very full, that is seven breadths without and six with flounces, and these last and trimmings of all sorts, are much worn very high up; evening gowns made with rows of fringe up to the waist or tucks with ribbon through them up to the waist. Buttons are the rage and sleeves are not worn open or short so much as they were. Bodies are made straight or cross as one likes, and white collars are rather larger.' (Letter from the Hon. E. Stanley, Feb. 1846).

Materials: merino, satin-merino, cordelière, alpaca, cashmere. For afternoons, Pekins, striped and quadrilled taffetas, foulards, chiné silk, levantines, glacés, poplins, cloth, reps, cashmeres and velvet. (Summer) Wool grenadine, foulards especially quadrilled, silks with narrow white stripes on dark grounds, mousseline de soie, barège, printed tarlatans, glacés.

NOTE: reference is made to 'the striped silks or as they are called "Pekins".' This has become now a generic name for striped silks.

Evening

The long point of the corsage is even longer and the corsage descends still further over the hips with the skirt gauged on to it. It is cut very low, sleeves very short, and the skirt with numerous scalloped and pinked flounces, or lace or dress material. Or a double skirt, the hem of the under one fluted, the upper one looped up in three or four waves.

The open robe is less common.

1844

Promenade dress of dark striped Pekin silk; black satin pardessus with cape; gimp edging
Carriage dress of green satin under a Polish pelisse of black satin, ermine trimmed
Walking dress of plum-coloured satin with column of fancy trimming on each side

1845
Opera dress of white satin, with two broad lace flounces; dark velvet sortie de bal
Promenade dress of brown satin under a mantle of bright purple satin
Carriage dress of dark green velvet; palatine and muff of ermine

Ball dresses of crepe, tulle, etc., embroidered in colours.

Materials: damasks, velvet, satin broché, taffetas, and satin moiré. (Summer) Transparent materials, especially barège and organdy.

New Materials: reference is made to *Japanese* silks. Wool grenadine, rep-bluets.

Fashionable Colours: in country dresses or 'the morning walking costume' the conventional colour rules are deliberately broken, *e.g.*, a skirt of striped green and white barège and a jacket of violet silk; worn with a garden hat. Or a seaside dress, of light violet and white striped barège skirt and a jacket of sea-green cashmere.

OUTDOOR GARMENTS

Pardessus. 'Every day brings new forms of pardessus.'

The Polonaise is now 'with high corsage, buttoning half way down to the waist and then sloping away to reveal the dress; half-length and trimmed with black lace.'

The Marquise, a mantlet with short ends and short sleeves, the back with a deep flounce. These, with the Visite, now fit in closely at the waist.

The Casaweck is now a shaped jacket, like an 'Eton', and quilted, the revers forming a flat collar, the sleeves cleft at the end and hanging loose.

The Crispin is revived, of half-length, cut on the cross, wide below but close round the shoulders and neck, with a falling collar.

The Polish Jacket (for seaside and country) of cashmere, lined with quilted satin, with revers and collar similar to a man's dress coat; waist-length; the sleeves square and split open to the elbow on the inner side.

The Andalouse Cape, of silk, trimmed with broad volants of crepe lisse, fringed. The front ends are cut straight, and the arms are free.

The Polverino, a large wrapping cloak of silk, loose and unlined, with or without a hood.

The Caprice, an evening loose jacket with armholes but no sleeves; sloped away to a rounded point below the waist at the back; worn over evening dress.

There is an increasing use of taffeta for Pardessus.

Shawls

(Summer). Of embroidered China crepe, some black embroidered in colours. Crepe de Chine, red and embroidered; lace; muslin, lined; Italian silk.

ACCESSORIES

Gloves

extremely short (day and evening).

The 'La Sylphide' *Parasol*. The stick of metal (hinged below the handle) with ribs of whalebone and stays of iron. The cover of fringed taffeta. A carved ivory handle and point.

Furs: Siberian sable, chinchilla, grebe, Kolinsky, and grey squirrel.

Dress Clips, called *Pages*, formed in the shape of a negro's head, attached to the waist by a chain, and used to clip and hold up the skirt when walking. Mechlin *Lace* extremely fashionable, also Mr. Waterhouse's invention of machine-made 'Mechlin lace'. *Buttons* are worn very big; of amethyst, turquoise, marcassite, or cut steel.

1847

The attempt to introduce novelty in the upper half of the dress (by the gilet corsage and the jacket) has now subsided, and attention is once more devoted to the skirt and the outer garments (pardessus, etc.). It seems impossible for fashion to attend to more than one half of the costume at a time; the mood of 1847 expresses itself largely in trimmings; and for this purpose the skirt afforded a wide field. 'Skirts have now increased so that their fullness is enormous,' but fashion could not quite make up her mind what to do with this vast expanse. Flounces? 'Most of the silk dresses this season are made without lining to the skirt; in hot weather certainly a lined silk dress with seven breadths in the skirt and five flounces is no inconsiderable burden.' For muslins, in summer, or flimsy ball dresses, flounces by all means; but for heavy materials decorations of passementerie, gimp, lace, velvet and ribbons which would not appreciably add to the weight were an obvious solution of the difficulty. From a study of these and succeeding years we can see that there was an enormous urge to increase the size of the lower half of the costume, which was delayed simply by the practical difficulty, how to keep the skirt properly distended. The horsehair petticoat was beginning to collapse under its burden. The attempt to introduce, the previous year, half-trains in evening dresses was a French innovation which England was unwilling to accept; even in 1847 we read 'It appears doubtful whether this style will be generally adopted'— and in fact it was not. A few months later 'an attempt to introduce gored skirts has been received with disfavour due to its unbecoming appearance'—the side gores permitting the fullness to be thrown out behind into a train.

The former method of gauging the material at the waist could no longer take up the mass of material and for heavy stuffs pleating and gathering had to be employed. In *The Handbook of Dress-making* of this date we read: 'When the rise of the hips takes place then the pleats or gathers should thicken. Be particularly careful that your skirt rather drops than catches up at the back; the latter is extremely vulgar in its appearance. The graceful character of a dress is truly dependent on the easy fall of the skirt. Plain skirts are much admired by the Parisians and their method of supporting them from the figure is far more distingué than the plan adopted by our English ladies; with the former the crinoline or woven horsehair is introduced in wide strips into the hem of the skirt; should it be wished to make the skirt appear very full two pieces of the crinoline may be laid on in bands up the skirt enclosed in lining muslin. This quite supersedes the necessity of the stiff petticoat.' The average Englishwoman preferred her horsehair petticoat. A dress in my collection, possibly a French model, has crinoline lining.

The need for trimmings suitable for so vast an expanse led to a host of varieties of passementerie, etc., and in particular to an extensive use of lace. 'Lace was never so universally worn as at the present time. It may be said to form an integral part of almost every article of female dress.' (Honiton lace, being specially patronised by the Queen, was in great favour.) But mere varieties of trimming could not satisfy the urge to expand; true the average woman was as yet a sedentary creature who spent most of her time indoors; she seemed to be waiting, as it were, until some genius would invent an artificial crinoline, in which she could walk with ease and comfort, but for that she had to wait till the next decade. There is ample evidence that nothing of the sort was worn by Englishwomen in the '40's.

DRESSES

Day

The Peignoir, for early morning and in the house, of cashmere or cashmere-cloth, wadded and lined with satin, worn over a cambric under-dress with a corsage up to the throat and finished with either a cambric frill (in which case the corsage is pleated) or with lace (in which case the corsage is embroidered); large round cape down to the waist; full sleeves. In summer, of white or printed muslin, taffeta or foulard; open in front.

The Pelisse-Robe, *e.g.* 'of printed cashmere, lined with red silk, open in front; a tight corsage with pelerine lapels ending in a point at the waist; a muslin chemisette high in the neck; loose hanging sleeves and undersleeves.' The corsage is frequently made with revers which are continued down the front of the skirt.

A summer Pelisse-Robe 'of printed jacconet,

146

Pelerine with necktie of coloured ribbon. 1847

Lace Mantlet. 1847

Net Pelerine. 1847

Lace Bertha. 1847

cerise on a white ground; an open robe trimmed with a double frill set on in a quilling and the edge scalloped, and running up the front of the corsage which is high to the throat, and down the front of the skirt which is slightly open; sleeves of an easy fullness finished with a frill.'

With open muslin dresses a ribbon ceinture with floats fastened by a rosette or a buckle.

Or, the Pelisse-Robe, made with a closed skirt, becoming nearly indistinguishable from the redingote form, e.g., 'A Pelisse-Robe with corsage high and close, the front decorated with passementerie of silk and chenille en cœur, and similar trimmings down the front of the skirt; three-quarter tight sleeves.' Or with 'corsage open with revers and trimming on skirt en tablier'.

Compared with 'a Redingote, the corsage high and close to the shape, trimmed with a heart-pelerine of passementerie which is continued down the skirt en tablier. Three-quarter sleeves open at the ends.' In fact, the Pelisse-Robe when it is made open approaches the Peignoir with the addition of more formal trimming; when it is closed it approaches the redingote, which, however, has always a tight-fitting corsage with trimmings descending vertically to simulate a front opening. When the dress-designer speaks of a 'demi-redingote', it must be owned that it appears to be a distinction without a difference. 'The corsages of redingotes and pelisses are either plain or full, according to the figure or taste of the wearer, the tight body suiting a full and well-defined bust and waist which does not require the aid of art; but for those of a more fragile figure nothing can be more advantageous than those graceful folds brought from the shoulders and descending into the narrow waist which is straight and forming a kind of fan-body.' A cravat of silk or velvet is frequently worn with a high close bodice.

The round dress, which is now frequently spoken of simply as 'a Robe'. In this far more variations are possible. The corsage generally high, tight to the shape and closed. Some are high at the back, but 'en gilet' in front, or with revers passing round the shoulders 'en schall' and descending to the waist; others open only sufficiently to show the edge of the chemisette. In the summer muslin dresses often made 'en blouse' or en gerbe.

Basquins are now out of fashion. The waist slightly pointed or round. 'The front part of the waist is but slightly pointed to allow of a ceinture being worn but as the band could not be formed into the point of the back it is cut and attached separately to each side of the waist.'

Sleeves. 'The reign of long tight sleeves seems to be gradually declining; in all thin and transparent materials the sleeves are invariably made in easy fullness and without lining at the lower part of the arm.' In silks the sleeve is often cut with a horseshoe opening revealing the under-sleeve. But for winter materials the sleeve is still usually long and tight with perhaps two mancherons below the shoulder and an under-sleeve of small bouillons of cambric or muslin emerging at the wrist.

Skirts. 'The width of skirts is now so enormous that only in evening dresses are they trimmed round the border'—in the heavier materials. For these, trimmings of passementerie, gimp, fancy buttons and tassels, and 'velvet in infinite variety' especially in the form of foliage, are used. Trimming en tablier is a favourite form. In intermediate materials such as cashmere, 'rows of the material, cut bias, and with scalloped edge and velvet trimming' are laid on. Silk skirts are either plain or flounced, three or more flounces being scalloped or dented or festooned and headed by ruched ribbon; or fringe serving as flounces, or three rows of bouillon. Light materials, in summer, either with multiple diminishing flounces or two skirts, the upper considerably shorter than the lower. In plaided materials the flounces are cut bias.

Occasionally a jacket, in the dress material, with cleft tabs behind, is worn.

'Never was there a greater rage than for aprons' (of satin and shot silk) for morning or afternoon.

Materials: cashmere, merino, cloth, cashmere with arabesque designs, shot, striped and checked silks (*e.g.* a ground of green or apricot striped with puce, dark green or blue), terry velvet and ottoman silk (for winter). Mousseline de laine, balzarine, foulards, taffetas plaided and broché and chiné, poult de soie, plain and glacé pekins, barège, organdy and tarlatan (for summer).

Riding Habit

Of dark habit cloth, tight to the shape either buttoning down the front with small turn-over linen collar, or open with lapels showing a habit-shirt, collar and cravat. Sleeve not too tight. Full skirt. 'A veil is indispensable.' Beaver or Spanish hat with feather.

1846
Walking dress of grey silk with double revers in festoons
Dinner dress of grey silk trimmed en tablier with black lace
Young lady's dress of tarlatan; the skirt trimmed with rows of puffing
Dinner dress of glacé silk; the skirt en tablier

1847
Ball dress: petticoat of green satin under a lace dress à trois jupes
Evening dress of pink satin with lace flounce
Ball dress of pale yellow satin, the skirt trimmed with tulle fullings

Mourning

A high dress of merino-cashmere, trimmed with crepe or barpour; plain tight sleeve; the front trimmed with jet or passementerie.

'Atramental and all other lugubrious Attire consistent with every gradation of mourning' (Advt.).

Evening

Corsage low off the shoulders; the bodice 'en corset', with a deep point; the back cut all in one without side pieces.

(1) Cut round with a bertha of lace. The bertha may be large, forming a demi-pelerine behind; or smaller and open in front with rounded corners; or open on the shoulders with a knot of ribbon. Or it may consist of two falls of the dress material.

(2) Cut to descend slightly in the centre with drapery across in pleats.

(3) The Clarissa Harlowe: 'rather off the shoulders from which are folds confined to the waist by a ribbon.'

Sleeves. Always short and nearly invisible, but some with two or three lace falls, or with some fullness confined to the arm by a band.

Skirts. 'Flounces are indispensable' with less heavy stuffs, *e.g.* nine scalloped flounces set in groups of three. For plain evening dress four or five bias tucks. In heavy materials lace flounces or trimmings of passementerie, fringe, ribbon knots or lace.

Ball Dresses: (1) Of satiné gauze, two skirts both trimmed with blonde lace; the short upper one looped up at one or both sides.

(2) Of satin or crepe trimmed with passementerie fringe.

(3) Of organdy, with single skirt and one deep flounce looped up with ribbons, or two skirts, the upper one an open tunic. Corsage en cœur opening over satin.

Materials: satin with velvet stripes, pekins, damask, velvet. Ball dresses of crepe, gauze, tulle, organdy, over satin, or satin crepe.

OUTDOOR GARMENTS

An immense variety is introduced; thus 'a variety of names, Casaweck, Varens, Polkas, all merely variations of the same type; a short jacket with loose sleeves, made of cashmere or velvet and lined with silk.' Larger Pardessus, of three-quarter length, shaped in to the waist with sleeves long and hanging open, of velvet or silk, with lace edges, *e.g.*, 'The Montpensier Mantle' of black velvet trimmed with sable,

with large pelisse descending low at the back, slit up on each shoulder and forming a point in front. Visites 'of every colour, black, puce,

Pink glacé Pardessus. 1847

garnet, blue, green, etc'. Some with invisible sleeves.

Mantlets

(1) Pointed behind like a shawl and trimmed with frills of pinked silk or black lace.

(2) Straight or slightly drooping behind, and much gathered at the bend of the elbow. Lilac, blue, pink.

(3) The Scarf Mantlet, not very deep, almost straight behind and the front ends rather long.

(4) The Shawl Mantlet, deep behind and the front ends short.

The 'Marquise', longer and wider than a visite, always of taffeta and trimmed with flounces or lace.

The 'Andalouse', to knee level, with a pelerine cape instead of sleeves.

'The Mantlets and Crispins for winter are very small, made of wadded velvet, and trimmed with lace or gimp and sometimes with two rows of lace.'

Mantles

There are also full length mantles, *e.g.*, the

'Mousquetaire', of black velvet, edged with black braid, loose three-quarter sleeves, and outside pockets; lined with quilted satin.

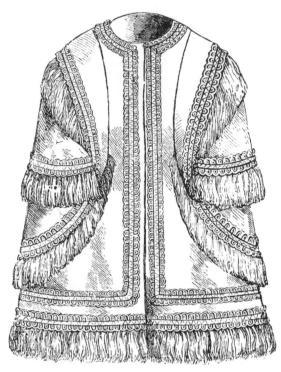

Cloak of garnet velvet lined with quilted sarcenet. 1847

The 'Armenian', of velvet or satin, open all down each side, the openings fastened by silk facings and tassels, and trimmed with lace.
Winter trimmings of sable, ermine, mink and kolinsky.

ACCESSORIES

Boots
Evening boots of white silk tipped with black satin. Elastic sided boots. Morning *Slippers* of dark velvet lined with red flannel. Patent India-rubber Goloshes. 'Godfrey's Improved Over-shoe; a sock or slipper to wear over a lady's boot or shoe in wet weather; of waterproof material.'

Gloves
Day, of pale yellow kid. Evening, short, of white or pale straw kid. *Mittens* still worn. *Pocket Handkerchiefs*, for full dress, with rounded corners, richly embroidered. *Jewellery*: broad and massive bracelets. Very little other jewellery. Large *Bouquets* carried: 'the haystacks which ladies now carry about with them, done

up in filagree paper.' The *Frileuse*, shaped like a pelerine, of quilted satin or velvet, fitting close to the waist behind, and with long loose sleeves, for wearing over the shoulders 'by the fireside or at the theatre'.

'*Lace* was never so universally worn as at the present time. It may be said to form an integral part of almost every article of female dress.'
'Our imitation lace is now carried to such a degree of perfection that only a connoisseur can distinguish the imitation from the real.'
Front fastening *Stays* with patent clips.
'Ladies Patent Chest Protectors of impermeable Piline.'
Dress protectors of patent Micaceous lining (made of talc); also for bonnet-linings, chest protectors and shoe-socks.

Prices
Shetland Shawls from 8/- to 10/-; Paisley cashmere, 10/9; wove Paisley, 15/9 to 30/-. Barège long shawl, 1½ to 2 guineas; short, 7/9. Paris wove corsets, 18 to 19½ inch, 16/9; 20 to 21 inch, 17/6.
'Entire headdress, £1 10 0; a beautiful front, 5/-; also ringlets and curls in combs.'
Ladies merino vests, 3/6 and 4/6.
Grenadines from 13/- the full dress. French satins, 2/10 a yard. Printed muslins, 12 yards, 5/9. Print dress, 1/6½. French muslins, 3/11½ the full dress. Barège wool dress, one guinea. Balzarines, 4¾d and 6¾d a yard. Glacé silk, 1/6½ a yard; French glacé, 3/11. French foulards, 1/10½. Best French merinos, 2/11. Angola plaids, 3/9. Cobden's best de laines, 4¾d a yard. Satinet, 26/6 the dress.
NOTE: 15 yards needed for full silk dress; 12 yards for a muslin.
Mourning. Bonnet, 12/6. Mantle of silk and crape, two guineas.
Bustles, of silver hair, from 1/0½.
Petticoats, 7/11.
Ribbons. French sarcenet, 7¾d a yard.
Fine Irish cambric handkerchiefs, 12/6 a dozen.
Common lawn, 2/6 to 4/6 a dozen.
Russia sable boas, Victorines and muffs, 35/- to 40/-.
Real Honiton guipure collars, 5/9.
Visites, satin checked Ottoman silk, 16/9; of rich moiré, 21/-.
Satin shoes, 5/6; cashmere, 6/6; Morocco, 4/6.
Ladies' elegant gold watches, 8 guineas.
Making a satin or silk dress, flounced and trimmed, 7/6. With plain skirt, 6/-. Making a visite, 3/6.

The flow of inspiration which this country had been accustomed to expect, in recent years, from across the Channel was in this year sadly interrupted by the Revolution of 1848; we could not hope for new fashions from France and the English fashions therefore did little more than repeat the old forms with trifling variations. There was, however, some inclination to introduce in day dresses the funnel-shaped opening to the sleeve; and by the summer the front of the skirt was decidedly shorter, so that for walking the foot became once more visible. As a novelty the Robe Princesse makes a tentative appearance.

The Basquin trimming to the corsage of day dresses returns to favour; varieties of the Pardessus multiply in number and name if not in form, and old names are now applied to new forms; the caraco, for example, now worn over a high morning dress, is described as 'fitting the shape, and reaching just below the hips, and rounded in front below, with the upper part open to display the corsage; the sleeves are half long and rather wide; it is made of satin or velvet.' While a casaweck is now 'a short jacket, very open on the bosom, with a deep basquin rounded in front, and funnel-shaped sleeves, made of velvet and lined with satin, to be worn over a home dress.'

DRESSES

Day

The Redingote form is very fashionable. ('Pelisse-robes, or as we now call them, "Redingotes".') The corsage is either tight to the shape and closed up to the neck, trimmed either en cœur with ribbon which is continued down the front of the skirt en tablier, or with two lines of velvet and a line of buttons in the centre. Or the corsage may be entirely open with revers of dress material, scalloped, or of black lace. The sleeves are long and tight with small reversed cuffs; or tight to the elbow and then expanding over an undersleeve of muslin or tarlatan. The bodice and skirt are sometimes made separate.

The skirt is sometimes open over a cambric under-dress, but more usually closed with a front trimming consisting of an extension of the corsage trimming.

The Redingote with double Corsage—an autumn innovation. 'Corsage tight to the shape, buttoned quite up to the throat and trimmed with two large lapels descending below the waist and remaining open; they are sewed in the arm-hole with the sleeves of the robe so as to have actually the appearance of a second corsage placed upon the first. Double sleeves, the upper ones tight above and widening as they descend in the funnel form, ending below the elbow.'

The Round Dress, or as it is now generally described, 'a Robe', shows no material change from the former year, except that the front of the skirt is slightly shorter. Occasionally the corsage is made with double points, and the basquin is again in favour. When made to resemble a jacket it is described as 'a corsage à caraco'. Five yards of material are needed for a morning dress.

As a novelty in sleeves a form is introduced with slashing along the outer side of a tight sleeve to reveal a white undersleeve.

The 'Coin de feu', a short coat, made high and closed at the top, with very wide sleeves, and made of velvet, cashmere or silk, is often worn with a 'home dress'.

NOTE: Muslin canezous, for morning dresses, are of the round form; for evening the canezou, if worn, is cleft in the centre.

Princess Robe: 'Corsage and skirt in one, the latter excessively gored so that it sits very closely round the hips, more so, indeed, than is generally becoming; the corsage and skirt in front trimmed with descending lines of ribbon and the central seam with a line of buttons; sleeves three-quarter and open at the ends.'

'No doubt our present long waists and immense wide skirts may appear very puzzling to a future generation that will invent fashions of their own; but they must nevertheless agree that much grace, coquetry and elegance mark our present century.'

Materials: cloth (always in the redingote form); merino quadrilled in satin, beche-cachemire, percaline, terry velvet, silk, striped gingham.

Evening
No change.
Materials as in former year; broché silks, checquered satins and moiré fashionable.
New Materials: satin-foulard, beche-cachemire, percaline.

OUTDOOR GARMENTS

The *Duchesse Pardessus*, for carriage dress, of coloured velvet lined with white satin, ample and rather more than three-quarter length; large sleeves bordered with ermine; small straight ermine collar; ermine down the front en tablier, turning back at the bottom in a broad band; large fancy buttons.

Summer Pardessus, trimmings of lace, fringe or material; some with one deep flounce, others with five or six flounces.

Prices
Poult de soie glacé, ¾ wide, £1 9 6 the dress length. Black Lyons silk velvet, 1½ yards wide, £7 10/- the full dress length. Rich Lyons velvet, 17/6 a yard. Rich Genoa velvet, 21/6 a yard. Satin castor, 4/11 a yard.
Alpaca umbrellas, 10/6.
Invisible curls on combs, 3/- a pair; magnificent skin-parting fronts made on an entirely new plan to avoid that formal look so much disliked, from 3/6. Long French cashmere shawls, 3 to 6 guineas.
New invented stays with elastic thread woven into the material.

1849

The wave of Republicanism in France led to some attempts in that country to revive modes of the first Revolution; these naturally did not cross the Channel. Here the fashions, still without French inspiration, were content, in the main, to mark time. In day dresses the French liking for the redingote form was more noticeable than the English; its smart cut lines gave an air of uncompromising assertion which did not seem to express the Englishwoman's taste. It seemed to her to convey almost a suggestion of boldness. Her instinct was for the more clinging femininity of the round dress with its soft flounces and slightly helpless undulating curves. However, we find the redingote a good deal worn in this country at the end of this decade, but we must accept the assertions of the fashion articles in the English magazines of this period with caution; most of them were written up from French sources, and did not necessarily indicate the real tastes of Englishwomen.

DRESSES

Day
Redingotes, either plain with rows of buttons down the front and with perhaps three lines of velvet ribbon on each side of them; or as a 'more dressy form' with the front of the corsage and skirt richly embroidered with passementerie or twisted floss silk. The sleeves tight except for a slight fullness of the shoulders and perhaps small jockeys, and mousquetaire cuffs.
Robes, either untrimmed or with flounces or velvet ribbons mounted nearly to the waist. Three, five or seven flounces, the uppermost with a ruched heading. The corsage half-high and opening en revers (in which case a canezou is worn); or closed, descending to a rounded point, the front trimmed with passementerie in the shape of a stomacher which descends down the front of the skirt en tablier. Summer dresses 'of barège or cashmere'; open corsage with 'a chemisette which is often fixed within the corsage to prevent its slipping up and down'. 'A carriage dress of grey silk, trimmed with ribbon flounces in three sets of four; corsage high behind and on shoulders, and open in front down to the waist over a poitrine of ribbon fluting; sleeves half length and full at the ends with ribbon frills; undersleeves and chemisette of muslin.'
Some dresses are made with two bodices, one for day and one for evening, the bodice being lightly stitched to the waistband.

'Many high dresses made for the present autumn have corsages which may be worn either open satin; the corsage high behind and open in a "V" in front down to the middle of the breast: thence laced, as is also the front of the skirt over a muslin petticoat embroidered en tablier.

Undersleeve. 1849

Cuff for mourning. 1849

Down each side of the lacing and the small revers are lines of stamped velvet leaves.'
Many redingotes are trimmed with robings en tablier, of embroidery in narrow velvet ribbon

White crape collar. 1849

or closed at pleasure; they button up the front and when it is wished to wear the corsage open the fronts are turned back to form revers.' In several specimens in my collection of about this date, the front of the corsage unhooks down the middle so that the upper part of each side can be turned in.

Afternoon
Redingotes with corsage open en cœur with lapels or revers en schall; or the Dubarry corsage, with the front opening square, the lapels, high behind, are open in front down to the waist over a chemisette. Basquins, rounded in front and sloped out over the hips; wide sleeves with double fall of lace.
Or Robes with similar corsage and multiple small flounces or two deep flounces, *e.g.* 'eight festooned pinked flounces'.
Sleeves are frequently of three-quarter length, the opening in the horseshoe form and trimmed with lace; or full length with small funnel openings.
A variation of the afternoon redingote: 'Of

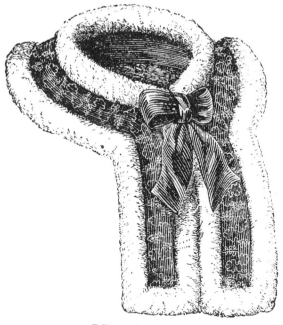

Victorine. 1849

which is continued on the front of the high corsage, or the trimming may be of black lace en echelle or in zig-zags.

Materials: cloth or cashmere for winter redingotes.

Muslin Pardessus. 1849

Riding Habit
of brown cloth; corsage with basquin tabs; open in front with revers; tight sleeves and long cambric cuffs; habit-shirt of muslin with turned down collar; black beaver hat with low crown and black veil: yellow gloves.

Evening
For semi-evening the Dubarry corsage, with sleeves half length, and skirt with flounces of dress material or lace.

For full evening dress, corsage low and deeply pointed en corset, with bertha. Sleeves very short and covered with a lace fall. Skirt with flounces (scalloped if of silk, and any number, from two deep flounces to a dozen narrow ones). In the summer, of transparent material over silk, with short pagoda sleeves and two or three skirts, flounced.

Dresses of rich materials, such as broché silk, made with corsage cut square and low in front or open en cœur to the waist with a chemisette, occasionally with revers; the skirt untrimmed.

Ball dresses: corsage very low; bertha with ruches which cover the short sleeve; either two or three skirts all trimmed with flounces headed by blonde lace or ribbon ruching, or small floral wreaths; or a single skirt with festooned flounces, the point of each marked by flowers; or a single skirt with two draped flounces open at one side.

Mourning Evening Dress
Of black Spitalfields radzimir; skirt with four graduated flounces, scalloped and edged with crape; corsage high and close to the shape; trimmed with folds of crepe and satin rouleaux; sleeves close as far as the elbow with shoulder epaulettes; the sleeve on the forearm slit open and laced.

Mourning materials: paramatta, Coburgs, barathea, radzimir.

OUTDOOR GARMENTS

Mantles
Pardessus: 'The variety of Pelisses, Mantles and Mantlets is greater than ever.' 'The variety of summer pardessus is so great that it is impossible to say what is most fashionable; perhaps the mantlet, or rather the family of mantlets since their number is considerable.'

The Casaweck for home dress; either loose like a paletot, lined and wadded, with wide sleeves; or 'the more dressy casaweck fits the shape and is cut bias, with wide basquins on the hips, and trimmed with lace.'

The Russian Mantle, with large pelerine-cape, small falling collar and wide sleeves.

Black Silk Visite. 1849

The Witzchoura Mantle, for the carriage, lined and trimmed with fur.

The 'Hortense Mantle'; three-quarter length; corsage en Amazone with falling collar and lapels; square pelerine below the waist, and fringed edge; a fringed flounce below it and the border of the mantle fringed, the fringe headed by rows of velvet.

The 'Armenian Mantle', a loose pelisse without cape; the front trimmed with passementerie.

Pelisse, three-quarter length, with large pelerine descending below the waist and falling over the arm, fastening at the neck, the fronts hanging square and loose.

Cloaks
Some Cloaks are made with detachable skirt.
Victorines: neck tippets, with flat ends, edged with swansdown.

etc.). With evening dress, a large hand *Bouquet*, in ornamental paper wrapping, is carried.
'Patent merino drawers and union dresses complete; ladies patent elastic invisible underclothing.' (Advt.).
'Crinoline and moreen slips in endless variety.'
'The registered bust improver, of an air-proof material; an improvement on the pads of wool and cotton hitherto used.'

Prices
'Ready made skirts, with three to five flounces, and material for corsage; of glacé silk, from 35/6; of balzarine, from 12/6; of barège, from

Muff in purple velvet, lined with quilted white silk. 1849

Palatines, similar, but with long ends reaching below the waist.

ACCESSORIES

Boots and Shoes
Dress boots of coloured silk, for evening; or silk or satin slippers with small buckle or rosette. For walking, cashmere boots, the colour of the dress. For promenade costume, shoes with a small rosette.

Jewellery
Ear-rings have gone out of fashion. 'Steel chatelaines; the greatest variety of this fashionable article.'

Parasols without fringe, with embroidered border; straight point and stick (of rosewood,

16/6.' French organdy, 9½d a yard; French printed barège shawls, 2 yards long, 9/11.
Longcloth chemises, 16/6 a dozen; nightgowns, 29/6 a dozen; drawers, 16/6 a dozen. Longcloth slips, 4 yards round, 2/3.
Barathea silk, 1/11 a yard, Coburgs, 1/0½ a yard, real Irish poplins, 2/6½; satinet, 1/9½; Welsh flannel, 9½d a yard.
French wove stays, 7/6; an immense assortment of petticoats and dress-improvers.
Wool barège dress of 12 yards, 2/11 the dress length.
Muffs: Squirrel, 6/11; American sable, 8/9; Minx, 15/9; Russian sable, 42/-.
'To ladies. The zone of beauty for 18/6, that much approved article of ladies' toilet which imparts of sylph-like roundness to the waist without restraint or pressure.'

An interesting feature of this decade was the gradual alteration in the apparent shape of the face and head. Starting as an elongated oval it ended as a rounded sphere. The change seemed to be in keeping with the mentality; from a pensive sentimental expression the face gradually acquired a more active animation which, in the succeeding decade, found a new outlet for feminine energy. The '40's was the epoch of ringlets, but in spite of their fascinations there was always an alternative pose permissible—the side loops of braided hair covering the ears. It was possible, therefore, to be roguish or meek, according to the taste of the wearer, and both were no doubt very effective. The former mood was perhaps in greater demand in the evening when ball-room ringlets were notoriously irresistible. Out of doors the bonnet and its partner the capote reigned supreme; the hat could do no more than imitate them so closely as to be practically indistinguishable from them except on close examination.

The assertive little high crown of former days shrank out of sight and became merged in the horizontal line formed by the brim. The latter closely guarded the ears so that, in effect, the bonnet supplied more than a material protection; it supplied a moral check against those whispered nothings which were, of course, so dangerous. It was not until the close of the decade that the fair wearer could obtain a glimpse of aught but the straight and narrow path ahead. . . . It must be admitted that the exterior of the shield was always prettily decorated, and if the passer-by could see little of the face he was consoled by a vision of flowers, feathers, ribbons and lace trailing gracefully over its curves.

The dress hat, worn in the evening, drooped away into nothing; flowers or wreaths were more in keeping with the spirit of the time, but we must not overlook those curious little toque-hats called Petits Bords, nor the fashion for reviving, in the 'Coiffures historiques' all sorts of antique headdresses extracted from the history books. One saw a modest young thing in a flounced ball dress, with the head of Anne Boleyn or Marie Stuart, or indeed of any of the heroines round whom a halo of sentiment still clung, but especially those who had formerly lost their heads; as, indeed, she in the '40's would gladly do, too.

From a more technical aspect the headgear, especially the varieties worn out of doors, reveal interesting features. The construction of the bonnet showed improvement, and the brim was no longer sewn on as a separate piece to the crown. Inside, a head-lining of gauze protected the hair from the straw, and all close-fitting bonnets had the brims lined as well. The crown of the capote was frequently stiffened by an underlining of canvas or book muslin or even of stout paper.

Materials: Leghorn, always costly, was largely displaced by rice straw for occasions of ceremony, while every summer produced a host of 'fancy straws'. But the characteristic headgear of the decade was the capote, which permitted the use of a wide variety of fabrics in its construction. An increasing tendency to having the surface 'drawn' by lines of gauging is noticeable. In winter, velvet was the stock material, and a nice distinction of seasons was observed, so that a 'Spring

1848

Bridal dress of white satin trimmed with blonde and ribbons
Carriage dress: a pelisse-robe of figured satin, trimmed with black lace
Ball dress of pale blue crepe; overskirt of lace
Ball dress of white satin, the overskirt looped up with ribbons

1849
Carriage costume of pink mousseline de soie; white silk paletot
Promenade costume of green moiré; mantilla of pink silk
Carriage costume of pale blue glacé

bonnet' became an annual event at Easter, when velvet vanished. Similarly feathers and ribbons for winter, and flowers and ribbons for summer were appropriate trimming. Of the textiles used terry velvet had a prolonged vogue, with lighter materials such as silk, crepe and lace for summer months.

The veil, at least in hot weather, was in general use, but seldom as a protection for the face, being mainly an ornamental affair draping the sides and back of the head, especially in its diminutive form, the voilette.

The cap was universally worn by day, the shape being small and retiring, with a trimming of ribbons. The evening cap was distinguished by its more lavish decoration. For youthful belles the popular coiffure was the natural hair worn in ringlets and decorated with flowers or a wreath. The devastating ringlets, however, were often natural only in appearance, and specimens in my collection, still attached to invisible bands, betray the secrets of the dressing-room. In effect, at least, the evening headdress of the '40's was one of studied simplicity; an artless virginal charm was aimed at and secured, if necessary, by purchase.

Early in the period bonnets and hats settled down into a stereotyped shape which persisted for the rest of the decade, so that it is now impossible to date a specimen exactly. This fixity of form was more marked than at any other part of the century. The finer shades of variation are indicated in the Annual Notes, but even contemporaries were frequently forced to complain of the sameness of the current fashions. The timid creatures of the '40's retired from observation. Towards 1850 the face begins once more to emerge, in a spirit no longer aggressive but perhaps inquisitive.

1840

HAIR

Day
Hanging in soft loops in front of the ears, or with short ringlets at the sides, and a knot at the back.

Evening
Hair with side loops and ribbon knots; for ball dress, hair in side loops and 'a full cluster of braided hair behind decorated with a wreath of coloured flowers'.

COIFFURE

Day
Morning cap, of organdy trimmed with lace; worn off the forehead with a plain caul but full and low over the ears.

Evening
Caps of velvet worn far back on the head, with lace lappets.
Evening petits bords of velvet with pearls and aigrette. Small toque-hats or 'toquets', of satin or velvet, worn far back, with a shallow brim in front turned up and ornamented with ostrich feather.
Turbans or turban-toques, with the hair in side nets.
Dinner hats in the bonnet shape.
Gold and silver filagree pins passed through the cap both in morning and evening.

OUTDOORS

Bonnets, 'although of a small size have the brims remarkably open and the shape is peculiarly calculated to be worn with ringlets. The morning bonnets are closer than those for afternoon. The brim is small and rounded at the ears, the crown nearly horizontal; many completely an auriole.'
Materials: (Winter) velvet. (Summer) gauze and crepe. Also of Leghorn, rice straw and fancy straw, satin, silk and lace, terry.

Hats. The carriage hats are larger than the bonnets but similar in shape except that they are more pointed at the ears.

157

1840

1. *Evening Dress.* 'Coiffure historique', of ruby velvet and gold lace, ornamented with scarf of gold net.

2. *Ball Dress.* Hair in full clusters of ringlets at the sides and a low knot formed of soft bows behind; ornamented with gerbes of flowers, two white ostrich feathers and a gold ferronière.

3. *Public Promenade Dress.* Italian straw bonnet, the interior trimmed with puffs of tulle and flowers, exterior with pink ribbon and bouquet of white ostrich feathers.

4. *Equestrian Costume.* Small black beaver hat, white veil.

5. *Back view of 3.*

6. *Morning Dress.* Small round cap of Brussels lace, ornamented with rose ribbon.

1841

1. *Evening Dress.* Demi coiffure, formed of a gold net enclosing the hair and a green velvet scarf fringed with gold disposed in front in the cap style.

2. *Ball Dress.* Headdress of hair decorated with feathers and gold ornaments.

3. *Morning Dress.* Bonnet of velours épinglé decorated with plaided ribbon of cherry and white. A full ruche of lace under the brim interspersed with noeuds of ribbon.

4. *Morning Dress.* Lace cap trimmed with coques of ribbon; short ends of lace descend on the throat.

5. *Dinner Dress.* Bonnet à demi-barbes of blonde lace, ornamented with wreath of red roses without foliage.

6. *Morning Walking Dress.* Drawn bonnet of straw coloured poult de soie, the interior trimmed with marguerites and violets; wreath of both flowers ornaments the exterior.

1842

1. *Evening Dress.* Bonnet à barbes of Brussels point lace; formed of a lappet disposed on the hair in the style of a cap front; ornamented with blue flowers and ribbon.

2. *Public Promenade Dress.* Rose coloured satin chapeau; interior trimmed with half wreaths of Indian roses; exterior with black and rose coloured striped ribbon and an extremely long rose coloured ostrich feather shaded at the tips with black.

3. *Morning Dress.* Organdy cap, the caul a little higher than usual; front of two rows of Valenciennes lace set on plain; trimmed with rosettes of ribbon with fringed ends.

4. *Evening Dress* for a Social Party. Hair in full clusters of ringlets at the sides and a round knot behind; the only ornament à peigne Josephine.

5. *London Public Promenade Dress.* Oiseau crepe chapeau, the material laid on in perpendicular folds over poult de soie of the same colour and passing over the brim borders the inside; exterior of brim and crown embroidered with silk to correspond; trimmed with half wreath of yellow cock's feathers attached by a knot formed of coques and ends of yellow ribbon; bavolet and brides to correspond.

6. *Evening Dress.* Embroidered tulle cap trimmed at each side with a single rose from which small flowers descend en gerbe; band and coques of rose ribbon.

1843

1. *Morning Dress.* Capote of plain bands of green and full ones of white ribbon, trimmed round the crown with white ruches.

2. *Public Promenade Dress.* Blue poult de soie chapeau; interior of brim trimmed with small flowers; exterior with a wreath of field flowers terminated at each ear by a full blown rose; white tulle veil.

3. *Evening Dress.* Demi coiffure; a lace lappet somewhat in the fanchon style upon the hair, the back of which is left exposed; band of rose ribbon with tuft of foliage on back fall of lace, similar band with wreath of full blown roses without foliage on the other.

4. *Evening Dress.* Turban of white and oiseau striped velvet; full bias ends trimmed with fringe fall upon the shoulders.

5. *Opera Dress.* Pink velours épinglé chapeau; interior of brim trimmed on one side with tuft of blue and yellow flowers without foliage and on the other with a noeud of crimson velvet; pink satin ribbon and a bouquet of pink ostrich feathers adorn the exterior.

6. *Morning Dress.* Organdy cap, the front embroidered, the back trimmed with a bavolet surmounted by a wreath of coques of ribbon and a tuft of white roses at each ear.

1844

1. *Walking Dress.* Bonnet of pale violet satin, trimmed with a band of the same edged with blond terminating at the back with a noeud and long ends of ribbon to correspond; a bunch of yellow roses in the centre.

2. *Evening Dress.* Coiffure composed of a Norma wreath of leaves and red berries.

3. *Morning Dress.* Cap of tulle 'à la Paysanne' trimmed by a bow of ribbon.

4. *Evening Dress.* Hair arranged in long ringlets, à l'anglaise, and beautiful shaded pink roses.

5. *Promenade Dress.* Bonnet of white satin with deep full curtain; crown with two full feathers fastened by a small bird; small satin bows; interior ornamented by pale roses without foliage.

6. *Evening Dress.* Cap à la paysanne, of double row of lace headed with small half wreath of yellow daisies; trimmed with large bow and ends of blue shot ribbon.

1845

1. *Morning Visiting Dress.* Pink crepe chapeau entirely covered with veil of point d'Angleterre confined round bottom of crown with band of pink ribbon; coques and ends.

2. *Morning Visiting Dress.* Chapeau of pink satin trimmed with one of the new autumnal ribbons, a sprig of white exotics and a tuft of foliage.

3. *Evening Dress.* Small hat of black velvet; inside of brim with rosettes of black lace and ends of velvet edged with lace; small plume of marabout feathers on crown.

4. *Ball Dress.* Wreath of flowers shaded pink and white and composed of velvet.

5. *Evening Dress.* Turban of green and white satin worked with gold thread, front and ends of white satin, crown of green, vandyked, each vandyke finished by small gold ball.

6. *Public Promenade Dress.* Pink and white shaded poult de soie chapeau, edge of brim bordered with plaiting of tulle à la vieille and interior trimmed with pink brides and flowers; the exterior with pink ribbon a white rose and a cluster of foliage.

1846

1. *Public Promenade Dress*. Chapeau Pamela of rose coloured velours épinglé; interior and exterior trimmed with coques, and ends of velvet ribbon to correspond.

2. *Evening Dress*. Green velvet turban trimmed with silver guimpe, fringe and ornaments.

3. *Morning Dress*. Cap composed of alternate rows of lace and crepe lisse, a rosette of the same materials on each side.

4. *Seaside Dress*. Hat à la jardinière, of straw lined with pink and trimmed with green and white ribbon.

5. *Walking Dress*. Drawn capote of pink satin trimmed with a satin ribbon.

6. *Evening Dress*. Round cap of white tulle, trimmed with lace, wreath of green leaves, and pink shaded roses.

1847

1. *Ball Dress*. Hair simply braided and decorated with a cluster of passion flowers.

2. *Dinner Dress*. Hat of dark crimson velvet 'à la Reine d'Espagne'; edged with gold cord; trimmed with small puffings of satin ribbon and full ostrich feather.

3. *Afternoon Dress*. Hat of white chip, the brim decorated with curled white ostrich feather.

4. *Evening Dress*. Coiffure of pale green velvet ornamented with strings of large pearls.

5. *Morning Dress*. Cap of white lace, decorated with pretty noeuds of pink ribbon.

6. *Carriage or Promenade Dress*. Bonnet of crepe, couleur de rose.

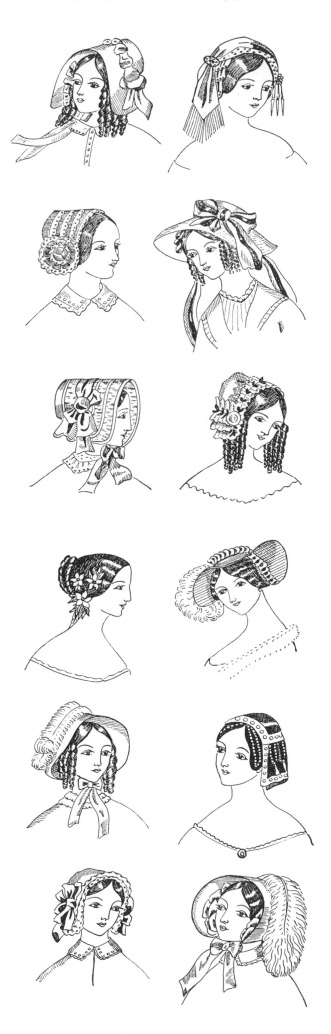

1848

1. *Ball Dress.* Headdress of white embroidered crepe encircled with folds of amber crepe intermixed with white, each edged with narrow gold trimming; long gold tassel behind.

2. *Evening Dress.* Simple garland of pink roses over the front, with blonde lace depending behind.

3. *Home Costume.* Hair arranged with a scarlet striped ribbon forming loops at the back.

4. *Carriage Costume.* Bonnet of pale primrose silk, with deep curtain.

5. *Afternoon Dress.* Hat of Italian straw decorated with a wreath of red roses and their foliage; strings of black velvet.

6. *Morning Costume.* Cap of tarlatan with large rosettes of rose coloured ribbon.

1849

1. *Evening Dress.* Bord à la Marie Stuart, of white tulle with white ostrich feather; lappets of white lace at either side of the back, arranged in loops and ends.

2. *Evening Dress.* Headdress of white lace attached to the head with a rose.

3. *Visiting Costume.* Capote of pink crepe; exterior trimmed with narrow tulle ruches; demi voile of white tulle vandyked at the edge; interior with noeuds of pink ribbon.

4. *Afternoon Dress.* Hat à la Marie Stuart, of Italian straw with long white ostrich feather.

5. *Evening Dress.* Hair in the Anne Boleyn style with ornament of diamonds and gold and branch of blue and white tiny feathers sprinkled with diamonds.

6. *Home Costume.* Cap of fine white muslin trimmed with white lace and round leaves of verdant green poult de soie. Hair arranged in bands.

1841
HAIR
Unchanged.

COIFFURE
Evening
A fashion for wearing 'coiffures historiques', *i.e.* à la Marie Stuart, Anne Boleyn, etc.

OUTDOORS
Bonnets
The crown and brim in one, the crown being flat on the head; brims of various shapes, round or square, but all descend low at the sides. Bavolets short or absent. Brims lined and trimmed with flowers or feathers. Drawn bonnets are close to the face, with a short crown; the bavolet is short and double, and partly concealed by knots of ribbon. Bonnet brims no longer meet under the chin. Crepe bonnets, the material laid on in folds, or bouillonee in close compartments. Trimming of hanging feather, or wreath of flowers. Marabout trimming very popular.

1842
HAIR
Day
Unchanged.

Evening
The hair worn with a comb at the back, *e.g.*, the 'peigne Josephine'. Or with long corkscrew ringlets at the side.

COIFFURE
Evening
Caps with long lappets.

OUTDOORS
Capotes retain their close form.

Hats. The sides of hats are now vertical and are not drawn in under the chin. Pamela hats of coarse straw trimmed with ribbon.

1843
HAIR
Day
Unchanged.

Evening
With long ringlets hanging on the shoulders.

COIFFURE
Day
Morning caps of muslin with small round caul, à la paysanne or babet.

Evening
The Montespan hat, of velvet, a small round brim turned up in front and trimmed with a plume.

OUTDOORS
'*Bonnets* shew little change from the forms of last year but the brim is somewhat shorter at the sides and the crown does not descend quite so low at the back.'

Hats. 'Morning hats with long brim, square at the ears but very open below; the crown large and made of material in the capote style.'

Prices
Bonnets: Leghorns, 20/-, Paris chips, 14/6, Tuscans, 6/- to 16/-, Dunstables, 1/6 to 10/-.

1844
'There seems to be a perfect mania for covering the head in every costume.'

HAIR
Day
Unchanged.

Evening
Long ringlets on to the shoulders are now general for evening.

COIFFURE
Day
Morning caps often have a fichu hanging down at the back, but most are very simple, round and small and without strings.

Evening
Flowers and wreaths worn in the hair. A few turbans, small and worn far back on the head, or a simple tulle scarf across the crown.
'Caps are most worn at soirées, concerts and the theatre, those with a small crown and blonde lappets, or those in fulled tulle trimmed with coloured ribbon and a knot at the side with floating ends.'

OUTDOORS
Bonnets low at the ears and the crown short; they are now tied under the centre of the chin and no longer at one side.
Carriage bonnets with large veils (summer).

1845

HAIR

Day

A centre parting and side loops over the ears; or ringlets.

Evening

'Long ringlets are now universal, drooping as low as the bust; sometimes only one is seen, worn with tufts of flowers; also with crowns of ivy, or the Norma wreath. Two long ringlets "à l'anglaise", touching the shoulder, the back hair in a plaited knot.'

COIFFURE

Day

Caps small, round and very short at the ears.

Evening

Dress hats 'of the demi-Pamela form'. Headdress of black chenille or net with bugles, placed on one side; the coiffure historique is going out of fashion.

OUTDOORS

Day

Bonnets are shorter and wider in the brim than hats. The bavolet is frequently replaced by a ribbon knot and loose ends.

(Summer) 'Voilettes are now attached to rice straw bonnets'—hitherto only to silk bonnets. The Pamela bonnet; the sides slope somewhat backwards revealing the ringlets, the brim being open.

'Rice straw, or as we call it, Chip.'

Hats. The Pamela hat, 'a kind of half gipsy hat of very coarse straw.'

1846

HAIR

Evening

Coiffure à la Agnes Sorel; or the coiffure Montespan. Or with side loops placed very low, with flowers and a back comb.

COIFFURE

Evening

Caps of lace, with a small caul bordered with lace which is full at the sides and forms a bavolet behind, trimmed with a wreath. Or a lace fanchon without any caul.

Capotes of velvet, satin and terry for 'half dress'.

OUTDOORS

Bonnets. If the shape is close the brim is untrimmed underneath; if of the Pamela shape it is trimmed with flowers. The outside always with a feather, either flat or willow shaped.

The Pamela shape is gradually being replaced by capotes with bavolets.

(Summer). Horsehair bonnets; fancy straws; and hats of crepe, silk, tulle and lace, as well as straw; short in the ears, with or without bavolets.

Rice straw bonnets trimmed with puffed tulle and ribbons; open shape with no trimming under the brims. Bonnets or crepe bouillonnée.

1847

HAIR

With centre parting and simply braided over the ears is the mode for day and evening, varied —in the latter—by the ringlets à l'anglaise, with a low comb behind.

COIFFURE

Day

Caps small and round; of tulle and ribbons.

Evening

Unchanged.

OUTDOORS

Bonnets during the year tend to shorten in depth both in the brim, which is round and now reveals the cheek, and in the crown which hardly projects beyond the neck. Bavolets are short. The edges of bonnets and capotes usually trimmed with a line of puffing. Bonnets are now made of a great variety of materials including crinoline.

The Capote is the general type, while the hat becomes somewhat rare.

Prices

Bonnets. Velvet, one guinea; Dunstables, 2/6; Tuscans, 3/6; Leghorns, 12/6; Paris chips, 12/6. Trimming a bonnet, 2/-.

1848

HAIR

as in previous year; the long ringlets à l'anglaise become less common.

COIFFURE

Day

Caps of more fanciful materials; a coloured rosette over the ear is a favourite style.

Evening

Caps of lace with flowers and coloured ribbons intermingled.

Evening dress hats very small, of tulle, crepe or velvet; petits bords worn placed on one side. A certain number of small turbans are seen.

Ball coiffure of wreaths, *e.g.* the 'Undine wreath of leaves or reeds veined with small diamonds'.

OUTDOORS

Bonnets

Assume more fanciful shapes and are made of a great variety of materials; besides the usual kinds of straw, silk, terry, lace, crinoline, velvet, crepe, moiré, satin, etc. are used. The brims are either round or oval, and the inside decorated with ruching of blonde; the outside often with lace, blonde, taffeta, ribbons, etc., as well as flowers and feathers.

NOTE: Feathers in winter, flowers in summer; the artificial flowers used always being of kinds actually in season.

Towards the end of the year 'a great change is now observable in the form of bonnets; the front being perfectly round, encircling the face, and sufficiently open on each side just at the ears so as to allow the whole countenance to be seen.'

The Marie Stuart shape for day bonnets, evening coiffures and evening caps is a noticeable feature.

Hats have larger brims than bonnets.

1849

The styles of the preceding year continue with very little change. There is perhaps some increase in the general *roundness* of shape both in the hair and the headgear, so that the face appears to be altering in form. Instead of an oval it is rapidly assuming a circular outline. Bonnets, etc. are more decorated than ever, and a wider variation in shape is permitted. The Marie Stuart with its slightly flattened brim is in keeping with the new form of face. The same effect is sustained by the side loops of hair now steadily displacing the ringlets. Breadth of feature seems to be in keeping with the width of the dress.

Prices

Bonnets. Genoa silk, 9/-; Terry velvet, 9/-; drawn silk, 7/-; drawn satin, 8/-.

UNDERCLOTHING

Underclothing consisted of the chemise, the petticoats, drawers and stays, and in addition the camisole, as a novelty, and the vest.

The Chemise

For day use this was usually plain and showed no essential difference from former periods. A specimen in my collection dated 1849 is of longcloth, the front square with a falling flap, the sleeves short and full and gathered into a band, with a gusset in the armpit. The skirt would reach to the knee, is unshaped, and the bottom is some four feet wide. Another specimen for evening is dated 1847 and is of cambric; the front square with a narrow frill edged with lace, and having a drawstring at the neck. The back is cut considerably lower and square. Short full sleeves gathered into a band edged with narrow lace. The front of the bodice has small gussets let in for the figure; the skirt is slightly shaped, and reaches to the knee with a four foot wide hem.

The Petticoat

It was usual to wear a number, depending on the season; the undermost was short and of some stiff material. Of the latter three kinds of material were used. Thus, one example in my collection is of horsehair warp and wool weft, pleated on to a waistband, the hem being six feet wide. Round the lower half of the skirt five lines of cord (resembling blindcord) are piped into the material to stiffen it. Another specimen is of stiffened wool, coarsely woven and open down the front, where tapes are attached by which it can be closed. It is heavily pleated at the back so as to throw out the skirt behind. There was an imitation of this material made of corded cotton, stiffened, used both for petticoats and dress-linings; specimens in my collection are stamped with the name 'crinoline'. We may assume that the material of horsehair was the original of the name 'crin' (derived from the Greek word for 'hair'), and that the word became used for the imitation, just as in the '50's it became used for the wire cage which took its place. Over this was worn one or more flannel petticoats, in winter, and above them a plain and above that an embroidered petticoat. Or in place of the crinoline petticoat a longcloth one heavily trimmed with cording up to the knees, the cording often extended up the back to the waist, would answer equally well to hold the shape of the skirt—at least in light materials. The outermost petticoat, of cambric, was elaborately embroidered and trimmed with embroidery, crochet or lace.

Yet another specimen in my collection is of longcloth with a bodice buttoning down the front (with buttons of metal covered with white cotton and without centre holes) and ending in a point at the waist; the back is cut in one and has a bone button in the centre at the waist line. The skirt is closely gathered and attached to the bodice with piping; round neck; short sleeves piped round the armhole. The neck, sleeves and skirt have a narrow crochet edging.

The Camisole

Introduced in the early '40's and worn over the stays to protect the tight-fitting dress. It is frequently spoken of as a 'waistcoat'. A specimen in my collection is of longcloth, shaped to the waist with gores and having basquins below.

Drawers

The use of this garment was by now becoming usual, at least in the upper classes. I have not, as yet, met with a specimen of this decade. Advertisements indicate that longcloth was the usual material, but flannel was also used.

The Vest

Merino vests are advertised and presumably sometimes worn, but the quotation given below seems to indicate that young ladies of that period were reluctant to spoil the excessive slenderness of their figures by wearing unnecessary under-clothing, at least on the upper half of the body.

The Stays

I have not seen an authentic specimen of this period but we can gather some information from the following quotation, from *The Handbook to the Toilet*, dated 1841

After warning his readers against the dangerous practice of wearing non-porous garments, for 'fever will be the result, as is frequent with those who wear leather waistcoats or have a rabbit-skin over their chest,' while 'the mackintosh requires in its use great caution' for the same reason, the author remarks: 'Flannel should always, during the day, in summer as well as in winter, be worn next the skin over the whole body and arms down to the middle of the thighs. Very few

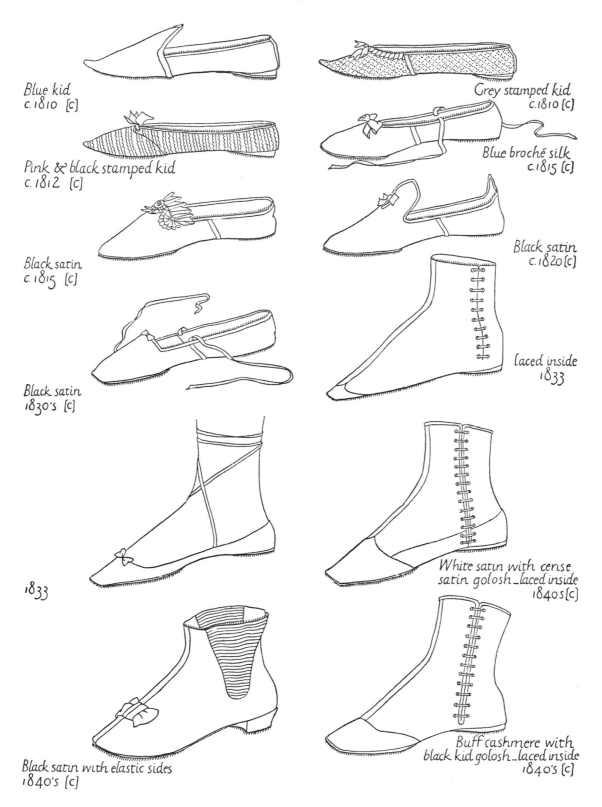

Blue kid
c.1810 [c]

Grey stamped kid
c.1810 [c]

Pink & black stamped kid
c.1812 [c]

Blue broché silk
c.1815 [c]

Black satin
c.1815 [c]

Black satin
c.1820 [c]

Black satin
1830's [c]

laced inside
1833

1833

White satin with cerise
satin golosh_laced inside
1840s [c]

Black satin with elastic sides
1840's [c]

Buff cashmere with
black kid golosh_laced inside
1840's [c]

ladies wear flannel next to the skin; many attacks of illness might be avoided if the vanity of having a small waist were overcome and the use of body-flannel adopted. It is the practice to make the flannel waistcoat, for both sexes, single-breasted; this is a mistake. There is an excellent material lately invented, from lamb's wool; waistcoats of this are called "angola waistcoats"; for the use of ladies a finer texture is made and little apprehension need be entertained of their thickening the waist. It need not be changed more than once a week. Ladies should not be sparing of flannel petticoats. . . Drawers are of incalculable advantage to women who expose themselves to a variety of diseases from the usual form of their garments. In France, drawers form a necessary part of female attire and many indispositions, to which British females are continually subject, are prevented by their use. According to our fastidious notions of propriety it is considered indelicate to allude in any way to the limbs of ladies yet I am obliged to break the ice of this foolish etiquette which is more revolting to modesty than favourable to it, by associating indelicate notions with what is in itself as pure and delicate as the lovely countenance of Eve before her fall. The drawers of ladies may be made of flannel, angola, calico, or even cotton stocking-web; they should reach down the leg as far as it is possible to make them without their being seen.

'The modern stay extends not only over the bosom but also all over the abdomen and back down to the hips; besides being garnished with whalebone to say nothing of an immense wooden, metal, or whalebone busk, passing in front from the top of the stays to the bottom; they have been growing in length by degrees; the gait of an Englishwoman is generally stiff and awkward there being no bend nor elasticity of the body on account of the form of her stays; they have become longer and higher and "lemon bosoms" and many other means of creating fictitious charms and improving the work of nature were invented, so that the habit of lacing from the top to bottom was adopted as being easier, a practice followed by a host of evils . . . the slightest effort, if the stays are tightly laced, occasions rupture; many young females have brought this upon themselves; it has spoilt the prospects and fortune of many a girl; besides, the downward lacing causes the stays to press the bosom down giving to the youthful virgin the forms of advanced age, a defect more remarkable among Englishwomen than among the women of any other nation.

'Many ladies, who eschew flannel as the bitterest foe to small waists, and therefore go too scantily clad during the day, cover themselves, before they enter their bed, with a profusion of clothing. A lady thus clad during the night, rises feverish and heated, with a parched mouth and foul tongue. She retains this load of clothes for fear of catching cold, without daring to uncover and wash her skin, the application of water being limited to her face, her hands, and a portion of her neck. Sometimes, even, her face is dry-rubbed lest water should injure her complexion. A very short nightdress is quite sufficient.'

'There scarcely exists an Englishwoman whose toes are not folded one over the other, each of these crooked, and their nails almost destroyed. From childhood, the rage for tight shoes and small feet exists.'

CHAPTER VI
THE 50's

―――――――

THE progress of fashion in this decade was interrupted during the years 1854-5-6 by the Crimean War, the immediate effect of which is referred to in the Annual Notes of those years. We may regard it as having been a somewhat costly extravagance indulged in by a wealthy nation, producing a general rise in the cost of living but no marked moral depression. It coincided with the close of the 'pure Gothic' epoch and no doubt hastened the end, but it cannot be regarded as the principal factor. Like many wars it was immediately followed by an outburst of extravagant fashion both in colour and in form, but this did not readily abate; indeed, the colour taste of the nation underwent a change which lasted for the rest of the century, accompanied, a few years later, by an equally profound change in form. It was the first symptom of the coming epoch of curves, in which the Gothic taste of the nation was overlaid by sexual symbolism. Moreover, if we examine closely the years immediately preceding the Crimean War, 1850–1853, we can detect in their fashions some significant signs. It was obvious that the skirt intended to expand still further and was only held back by technical difficulties; while in the years '51 and '52 woman boldly annexed the masculine waistcoat and flaunted it in its owner's face.

I have indicated elsewhere the extraordinary progress made by women in this decade, showing how they had begun to emerge from a modest domesticity and to assert their presence in the outer world. They were acquiring all sorts of social privileges and were even talking of their rights. Already, in '51, an American lady, Mrs. Bloomer, had demanded that her sex should be allowed to wear trousers, an extreme measure which received no sympathy in this country; the waistcoat seemed a happy compromise. Half a century before woman had stolen man's most intimate undergarment, but at least that was invisible; now she laid hands on his waistcoat, and a few years later his collar and tie. Before the close of the century his knickerbockers were destined to go the same way, and to-day we see him forced to share his trousers with the modern young woman. And this form of 'Danegelt' has never appeased the foe for long; the theft of each masculine garment symbolised a further step in woman's progress.

In fact we can attribute the ransacking of the masculine wardrobe to an irrepressible exuberance on the part of woman; the waistcoat episode of '51–'52 was a sign of the times. In the same spirit the soft harmonious colours which satisfied the '40's gave way to 'the brilliancy obtained by contrasting primary colours', noted by an observer in 1850, a taste becoming more noticeable at the close of the decade. It seemed to express 'the want of harmony that pervades the age; the restless anxious desire to embody thought in actual life; the dissatisfaction that the actual falls short of the ideal, and the want of faith in truth' (1855). The new taste provoked bitter comment, a writer complaining: 'Too much importance cannot be paid to the harmony of colours; no nation in this respect offends so much as the English.'

Owing to the greater amount of material required for a dress and the rise in prices after the war, the expense of a lady's wardrobe was becoming a severe tax on the domestic exchequer. 'Crinoline fashions are ruinously expensive' was the cry of every husband, while the excessive use of costly lace added to the burden.

The decade was notable for the introduction of two important technical inventions; the chain-stitch sewing machine began to be used early in the decade and the lock-stitch just before its close; while in 1856 the artificial crinoline appeared, of which details are given in the section on Underclothing. By its use the wearer was able to reduce the number of petticoats so that the total weight of clothing was considerably lessened but its disadvantages were great. There was the risk of fire, especially with flimsy dresses, and the impossibility of putting out the flames by compression, to say nothing of the extraordinary inconvenience of size. A circumference of four or five yards was nothing unusual even for a day dress worn in the streets. Moreover it was a fashion which few Englishwomen could properly master; the dress *would* ride up in front or the cage wobble as they walked. It could only appear graceful if the wearer took very short and equal paces, and Englishwomen tend to stride. . . . They accepted it, nay, welcomed it, as it seemed to express in unmistakable fashion their growing sense of importance, as though they were determined to occupy a larger space in the world. And, at the same time, it served as a barrier against the aggression of the Lower Orders, who were kept at arm's length—until even the Lower Orders themselves adopted the fashion. When, by the end of the decade 'your lady's maid must now have her crinoline and it has even become essential to factory girls' it was no wonder that the complaint was uttered, 'in modern days the distinction in dress between the higher and the middle classes is in many respects nullified.'

The victorious march of democracy could not be held back by wire entanglements.

CONSTRUCTIONAL FEATURES

The bodice is lined with white cotton or glazed silesia, with or without pads for the figure. Pointed bodices are boned, with two bones extending half way up on either side of the mid-line, and a short bone in the side seams almost up to the armhole. Jacket bodices are unboned. Sleeves are cut with one seam on the inner side, and in order to make the wide opening of the pagoda face forwards, the inner seam is caught up at its centre; there is a short close sleeve lining. Hooks and eyes are of brass wire, but with front fastenings the era of ornamental buttons begins. Some are of metal, glass, or covered with material. A new device is the detachable button held in place by a split pin.

Muslins are unlined except for a narrow side lining. An attached cotton lining with its own fastenings is not uncommon, serving as a camisole.

The skirt is lined with glazed silesia, book muslin or crinoline material, except with muslins. Lined skirts have braided hems. There is generally a watch-pocket at the waist in day dresses, and a large inside pocket opening from one of the side seams. The methods of attaching the skirt to the band are described in the Annual Notes; briefly, gathering was used only for muslins. With heavy materials side pleats, with gathers only at the middle of the back, except at the very close of the decade when box-pleats at the back appear, and this only with exceptionally heavy materials.

Materials tend to run 24 inches in breadth for heavy and 18 for light. The amount turned in at the top of the skirt becomes progressively less as the shape gradually changes from the 'dome' to the 'fan'. A noticeable feature of this decade is the comparative absence of new materials introduced, and the extended use of silk.

ANNUAL NOTES

1850

The Louis XV styles which had recently been revived become, in this year, still more noticeable; these, with the fashions of Louis XIV, and an increasing use of lace and trimmings, are especially marked in day dresses, the materials of which are nearly as rich as those for evening wear. To dress well is becoming an expensive necessity for the well-bred lady. Emphasis is laid on 'the refined taste of the present day; no indelicately low bodies; no frightfully short sleeves; no tight clinging dresses.'

DRESSES

Day
The term 'redingote' no longer denotes a closed corsage with high neck; this is now described as a 'corsage en amazon', and 'redingote' is used for any pelisse-robe which has vertical rather than horizontal trimming.

1. Pelisse-robe
Corsage: (*a*) Redingote or corsage en amazon.
(*b*) à la Louis XIII. The corsage is closed at the neck and at the waist, with the centre open displaying a 'chemisette à jabot' of cambric pleats or embroidery.
(*c*) Open jacket-bodice with a tabbed 'skirt', *i.e.* descending below the waist over the hips.
Sleeves. Long or three-quarter length, and tight,

with reversed cuff edged with short lace ruffle; or with slight bell opening and a closed and puffed undersleeve. The jacket-bodice always has this latter type of sleeve.
Skirt. (*a*) Plain.
(*b*) With a tablier of lace, ribbon or ruching.
N.B. The pelisse-robe is essentially the costume for morning wear.

2. The Round Dress.
(*a*) Corsage en cœur, with facings (*i.e.* revers) or edgings of frilled ribbon or ruching.
Pagoda sleeve.
Skirt with three flounces festooned and embroidered at the edge.
(*b*) Plain corsage with basquins; graduated revers or a facing of lace.

171

Easy sleeve, elbow-length, finished with double sabot of lace. Closed undersleeve of net.

Plain skirt.

(c) Plain corsage, demi-basque. Open in the form of a lengthened heart nearly to the waist, with a narrow horizontal strap across the bust, the opening edged with soutache in a zigzag design, or with a pelerine trimming.

Sleeve rather short and gradually widening. Closed undersleeves of tulle, cambric or net.

Plain skirt.

(d) Corsage in jacket form, closed to the neck and having a short 'skirt' extending below the waist over the hips, which is cut into square tabs (the Hungarian jacket).

Sleeve gradually widening to a slight bell opening which is cut into tabs over a closed muslin oversleeve.

Plain skirt.

(e) Dress à la duchesse. A low square corsage edged with ruching of dress material; chemisette of alternate rows of lace and embroidery.

Square pagoda sleeves partly open up the sides, with deep lace weepers.

Skirt with broad flounces edged with embroidery or stamped ruches of dress material.

These dresses 'are mostly of chiné materials in the pastel style'.

NOTE: Flounced skirts. With light materials the flounces are narrow and numerous, as many as six or seven. With heavy materials flounces are wide and not more than two in number. The brocades, moirés and poplins are unflounced.

With medium materials 'they are mostly trimmed with three broad flounces cut on the straight way, slightly fulled, the edge being cut out or stamped in patterns; or with ruches of lace and ribbon. It does not follow that because the corsage opens and closes in the pelisse form that the skirts cannot be trimmed with flounces; on the contrary this style is much adopted.'

NOTE: Sleeves. The pagoda sleeve is formed to the elbow and cut sloping at the lower part; the Louis XIV sleeve gradually widens, becoming very wide below without any sloping; it is generally ornamented at the edge with several rows of trimming fluted regularly all round.

Both types are common in 'carriage' and visiting dresses.

With morning dresses collars and cuffs of frivolité lace are worn; with a closed neck, a collar of broderie anglaise and a ribbon knot.

'Dresses trimmed with flounces have the corsage edged with a pinked fontange' (i.e. a ribbon gathered through the centre as in ruching).

The corsages of day dresses usually have a slight point in front; those of light materials (Summer) with a jacket bodice frequently have a sash with long ends in front.

Summer dresses of muslin are occasionally made in the form of an open robe over a worked cambric petticoat.

Pelerine trimmings on the bodice are not unusual.

Dresses with day and evening bodices are quite common.

Materials: (Winter). Cloth, velvet, moiré, brocade, poult de soie, satin, mousseline de laine, levantines, cameleons, Pekins, glacés, alcyone rep, Pompadour duchesse.

(Summer). Foulards, shot silks, damasks, taffetas, muslins, gauzes, crepes, barège, chiné silks, grenadines, ducape, bellona, pomella.

'Check materials are not worn by the ladies, being entirely given up to the nether integuments of the sterner sex.'

Evening

Corsage long and pointed. Types:

(a) Plain.

(b) en corset.

(c) en chemisette, with ruching from the shoulders forming an enclosed stomacher, i.e. à la Louis XV, or more precisely, à la Dubarry.

(d) à la vièrge.

(e) With diagonal pleating front and back, with square neck and long pointed waist. A bertha en disposition is a frequent addition.

(f) à la grecque, i.e., low off the shoulders and square, the front being in vertical pleats down to a point.

Sleeves. Short and tight, with edging of lace; or elbow sleeves with lace ruffles. Undersleeves when used, are of lace, and always open over the wrist.

Skirt. Very large. No trains.

(a) Multiple flounces, of lace or dress material, scalloped or pinked.

(b) With double or treble skirt, which may be caught up at the side with ribbon. With tulle and similar materials as many as five skirts, the edges with a broad hem through which is passed a coloured ribbon ('fontange'). Ball dresses may have as many as ten flounces, sometimes with lace and dress material flounces alternating.

The Watteau open robe is fashionable for ball dresses (i.e. the corsage cut low, with high shoulder pieces and shaped like a chemisette with a lace inlet at the back).

Dinner dresses are made with corsage à la vièrge, or with a bertha which descends in front to a point. Funnel-shaped sleeves.

Materials: in addition to the usual silks and satins, brocatelle and druggett, (for Summer) organdy, tulle, etc.

New Materials: armure, cashmere de baize, Valencia, satin de chine, Pompadour duchesse, l'alcyone reps, camayeux silks, barège de Pyrénées, nainsook, gros de Tours.

OUTDOOR GARMENTS

The coin de feu jacket, of satin, terry, silk or velvet, with lace or grebe trimming; short loose sleeves with cuffs.

The Caraco, 'less dressy than the mantlet'; when made of lace can be worn with an afternoon toilet.

The Caraco basquiné, for wearing with a bodice à la duchesse.

'The various thousand pardessus that have been introduced this year', *e.g.*, a small Paletot, fitting the figure, trimmed with volants of the same material, or black lace, for morning use.

A Mantlet, trimmed with lace or deep fringe, short in front, ending in a point in front and behind.

The Faldetta, a small mantle of coloured taffeta, edged with deep lace round the waist and over the arms, with a small lace veil attached to the collar.

'How we contrived to exist before the Pardessus was invented seems now a difficult problem to solve; a lady of fashion needs at least five: (1) of cashmere or merino for the morning, (2) of velvet for calls, (3) of silk or satin trimmed with lace for dinners, (4) of lace, for full dress, (5) one lined with fur for going to a ball. For (1) the "Louis XV", stiff with rich facings; for (2) the "Mousquetaire", coquettish; (3) the Duchess, magnificent in ornament; (4) the Puritan, elegantly simple; (5) the Hungarian casaweck, richly trimmed with fur.'

'Pardessus of the Pompadour style, of coloured silk heavily fringed; demi-long sleeves; some open over the chest and fastening with two buttons, others hanging loose and only closed at the neck.' (Summer use.)

The common type of pardessus is a three-quarter pelisse, tight to the waist and square at the bottom, with three pelerines fringed and with chenille trimming.

The Talma cloak, round in form, raised on the arm like a shawl; of velvet or satin.

The Surtout, a paletot with a point behind.

The 'Shawl-Mantlet', the back half rounded, with three falls, the front rounded and descending to the knee.

'Worsted lace is the height of fashion for mantles.'

Shawls. Of crepe de chine.

'New shawl of worsted lace, black for morning, white or coloured for afternoon.'

Also of cashmere, white orange or rose, embroidered in arabesque with floss silk and heavily fringed.

ACCESSORIES

Shoes
with half high heels. Elastic sided boots.

Gloves
with tassels. The duty on French kid gloves produced over £30,000 per annum.

Jewellery: Parian bracelets, the front of Parian, the back of elastic hair. Two or more bracelets worn on one arm. Ribbon velvet bracelets. Hoop ear-rings. *Fans*: Cora fans of painted feathers. *Parasols* in the marquise style, or moiré silk with deep fringe.

Prices
Silk stockings, 1/10 a pair.
Wool shawls, 4½ by 2¼ yards, 12/-; Paisley, 5 feet long, £1. Pure cashmere, £7 10. French and Paisley square shawls, printed, 13/-.
Spitalfields glacé silk, 1/10 a yard. Foreign 2/10.
Spitalfields velvet, 7/- to 9/- a yard; Lyons ditto, 12/- to 15/-.
Organdy, 1/3 a yard, English organdy, 7d.
French de laine, 1/10.
Gold hair nets, 'the height of fashion', 10/6.
Silk hair nets, 1/6.
'Hair snake bracelets to coil twice round the arm, £1 1. 0.'
Elastic boots 8/6 a pair.

1851

The chief feature of the year was an increasing attention to the bodice, and in particular the adoption, for carriage dress, of the *waistcoat*. This was elaborately embroidered and made 'as magnificent as possible'. It may be noted that as soon as women started to borrow this—the last of man's ornamental garments he began to give up its use, and to fall back on the plain waistcoat. The feminine 'gilet' indicated a bold advance, and its use was regarded as a daring innovation. The term 'fast' was now introduced as a useful expression to denote the growing aggression of the female sex.

While fashionable magazines emphasise the new mode a more bourgeois paper states: 'We cannot say that waistcoats are much worn; they may be ranked in the class of eccentric novelties introduced in Paris which seldom become objects of general adoption.' In a word, it was confined to the 'carriage class'.

A single specimen of these waistcoats is in my collection; no doubt there are others existing which from their general resemblance to the masculine garment (except that they are shaped to the figure by darts) may have been mislabelled.

Another feature is the increasing use of embroidered lingerie. 'Muslin work (chain-stitch, satin-stitch, tambour work, etc.) has enormously increased of recent years. A lady cannot be well dressed unless her collar, chemisette, sleeves, etc., harmonise with the style of dress worn.'

DRESSES

Day

The Pelisse-robe or Redingote. The corsage high and close-fitting, or open to the waist over a chemisette. Corsage in the form of a jacket extending below the waist as a basque (the 'corsage Agnes Sorel'), the lower edge being plain or tabbed; worn closed to the neck or open over a waistcoat. The waistcoat may be closed to the neck, or open in the middle revealing the frill of the chemisette, or cut into a deep 'V' which displays a pleated chemisette. It extends below the waist with flaps containing side pockets.

The skirt is plain or trimmed with a tablier.

Sleeves, long and closed with a deep cuff; or three-quarter length and cut up at one side over engageantes; or plain and wide below with a lace edging.

Engageantes and chemisettes for morning are of cambric, muslin or broderie anglaise. 'The bare arm must never be exposed in the promenade.'

Afternoon

Bodice half-high with square opening, in the Louis XV style, or en cœur; pointed waist. The fronts frequently fulled from the shoulders. Sleeves funnel-shaped; or fulled in the middle of the arm and close above and below.

Skirt either plain or flounced (flounces for indoor or carriage use).

'The present sleeve is becoming to the hand taking from the apparent size of a large one.'

Waistcoats are only worn with costumes of broché or Chiné silk. A variation is the *waistcoat body*—à la Louis XIII. The corsage is itself shaped like a waistcoat with basquins, the border being either rounded, sloped or tabbed, and made separate from the skirt. It may be buttoned up to the neck 'à la corsage amazone', but is usually worn open to reveal an embroidered under-waistcoat. The skirt is very wide with large pleats all round the waist and rather long behind; sleeves with deep cuffs and lace manchettes.

NOTE: 'The length of a lady's dress in these times is more calculated to sweep the crossings than to promote elegance or comfort.'

Peignoirs (morning wrappers) of white muslin or printed jacconet, worn over a cambric embroidered petticoat.

A canezou of muslin is often worn in summer, as a bodice, with a coloured silk or barège skirt. For home dresses a casaweck is often worn over the bodice, or simply over the waistcoat.

NOTE: Chemisettes are worn with or without a collar; often the front has rows of narrow lace; if a collar is worn with this it should be of lace insertion.

Wedding

'Of white muslin, worked or plain, with lace trimming, three skirts, edged with quilling of white sarcenet ribbon. Corsage high behind and open in front edged with tulle ruching; open sleeves edged with lace; square tulle veil; lilies of the valley wreath.'

174

Riding Habits

Of cloth, close corsage buttoning up the front; habit-shirt collar of plain cambric; short basque; sleeves with cuffs; cambric undersleeves; skirt plain and long; 'black beaver hat and veil.'

Mourning

'The recent revival of the old fashion of employing jet trimmings adds greatly to the elegance of mourning,' e.g., 'A black crepe dress with seven flounces which, with the corsage and sleeves, are ornamented with jet.'

Evening

Unchanged except for an increased use of ribbon trimmings.

Ball dresses are all with multiple skirts; or with a short 'tunic' of glacé over a skirt of transparent material (lisse) above a silk slip.

As an eccentricity may be mentioned the fashion for embroidering tulle and tarlatan ball dresses with *straw* (worn with a headdress of grass, straw and poppies).

With evening dresses a velvet band round the neck and velvet bracelets.

Materials: The following examples indicate the richness of materials used even early in the day: 'Walking dress of fawn-coloured satin; morning dress of blue silk; morning dress of blue brocade; morning dress of pale green moiré; morning dress of taffeta chiné; a walking redingote of green velvet.'

In addition, cashmere for winter (morning); silks and poplins for afternoon.

For summer morning dresses, alpaca, taffeta and foulard (foulard with three flounces and undersleeves either bouillonée or pagoda, with black mittens. Alpaca with one deep flounce edged with several rows of velvet, or in the redingote style). Afternoon dresses of pekin, taffeta, Pompadour, grenadine or barège; with two bodices (day and evening).

OUTDOOR GARMENTS

Mantles

The Chambord mantle, similar to a Talma, but setting in deep and hollow folds at the back.

Mantles are a little more pointed behind, with longer ends.

Mantlet Matilde 'descends behind in the form of a shawl low over the skirt; is sloped square over the arms forming a small mantlet in front; with a deep border of taffeta festooned in dents; some fringed, others with rows of guipure.'

'Mantlets, mantillas and scarves, everything, in short, that forms the pardessus, is in the greatest vogue this year.'

Cloaks

For walking, the round cloak, of cloth, cashmere or vicunia, plain or trimmed with braid or plush, and lined with silk, and having a tasselled hood. For evening, a burnouse. The Matinée, of jacconet or muslin, resembling a hooded pardessus, worn over a morning dress.

Shawls

'The long cashmere shawl, folded into two to form a square, the corner of which is then folded over. Very broad borders; centre of red, green or orange.'

'We scarcely knew a truer test of a gentlewoman's taste in dress than her selection of a shawl, and her manner of wearing it; and yet it is the test from which few Englishwomen come with triumph.'

ACCESSORIES

Gloves

Evening gloves, very short, three buttons. Day gloves short; usually lemon yellow.

The Victorine, or Palatine Royal; in fur with quilted hood and narrow ends hanging down in front.

Prices

'Ready made flounced skirts, in silk, five flounces, £2 5 6, eleven flounces, £2 18 6, with material for bodice; seven widths in the skirt.'

Rich ducapes, 2/- to 2/11 a yard.

Three-quarter wide glacés, 2/9 to 4/6 a yard. Moiré antique, 5/6 to 6/6 a yard. Chintz chiné glacé, ¾ wide, 5/6. French moreens, 4/9. Plain French delaines, 1/4½. Rich brocades from £2 to £3 10 the full dress of 13 yards. Lyons silk velvet, 5/9 to 14/9 a yard. French merinos, 2/2 to 4/3.

Riding habits, skirt 58/-; jacket, 42/-.

Gloves, best English, 1/6. Long white, 1/8.

French cambric handkerchiefs, 10/6 a dozen.

Long barège shawls, 8/- to 22/-; long Paisleys, 18/6.

Walking parasols, 4/6 to 15/-; carriage ditto, 7/6 to 30/-; silk umbrellas, 6/- to 18/-.

Bonnets, drawn glacé, 6/- to 7/-; drawn satin, 7/- to 9/-; millinery bonnets, 10/6 to 30/-; velvet bonnets, 21/-.

Satin boots, 3/6 to 6/6. Bronze kid, 3/6. Coutil, 3/6.

The principal features of the year are (1) a further elaboration of the 'waist-coat' style, which is now used both for morning and evening, either with a body in jacket form over a lace or silk waistcoat, or for day use a combined jacket and waistcoat in one. (2) A marked fashion for 'flounces à disposition', *i.e.*, the flounces are woven with the dress so that they have their distinctive pattern. The dress is, if possible, more ornate. 'Jewellery is now more than ever worn and is allowed even with the simplest indoor toilet.' Towards the end of the year the basques of the bodice are dented or fringed.

Although the size of the skirt is not diminished its shape is no longer rigidly dome-shaped. 'The stiff jupon is still worn but very much diminished in all its dimensions'; consequently the skirt tends to flow outwards on all sides.

DRESSES

Day

Morning deshabille. A plain skirt with a casaque or caraco jacket, or a pardessus. A white canezou with a coloured skirt.

Morning Dress. (1) A plain high body, with full bishop's sleeves and frilled cuffs; round waist and broad (4 inch) ribbon ceinture with floating ends. With light materials (Summer) 'the corsage may be drawn in fullness at the waist', or pleats from the shoulders. With other materials there may be 'narrow capes' (hitherto described as 'pelerine trimmings') descending from the shoulders to the point of the waist.

Skirt. Plain; or with summer materials, seven flounces. Some with as many as fifteen narrow flounces; flounces often scalloped.

Or (2). The body more or less open, some down to the waist, with small square or dented basquines, and fringe trimming. Waist round or pointed. Those partly open have a habit-shirt; those fully open are worn with a waistcoat, or have a series of bands crossing the chest over a habit-shirt.

'The waistcoat now takes first place in a lady's toilet'; either simple or embroidered, with fancy buttons; generally with high neck or open en cœur with a fichu or frilled habit-shirt; some double-breasted. Made of white silk or satin, or of white piqué, with long sleeves serving as undersleeves. Some have waistcoats made of the same material as the jacket.

Skirt. Five graduated flounces with horizontal stripes woven in. Or skirt with six to eight bands of velvet, instead of flounces. The 'Albanian robes', with flounces having edgings of coloured stripes woven in. Taffeta dresses with three flounces; plain stuffs trimmed with velvet or one deep flounce, dented.

Sleeves. The pagoda sleeve, for all day dresses, is usual, but new forms of sleeve begin to appear; thus, 'a new sleeve having two seams, one on the inner side and one on the outer; the outer descending nearly to the wrist, allowing room for a small puffed undersleeve'; the 'Grecian sleeve', slit open on one side and closed with buttons and worn as an undersleeve; the Louis XIII undersleeve in three bouillonées divided by ribbons (worn with a pagoda sleeve) in the summer; the Amadis sleeve (tight from the elbow to the wrist and closed by a row of buttons) begins to return.

Engageantes either large bouillon with reversed vandyked cuff, or full sleeve with ruffle.

Materials: (Winter). Poplin, Valencia, Bayadère silks (thick silks with stripes of velvet woven in) brocatelle, brocades.

(Summer). Printed organdy and barège (printed with palm-leaf flounces), alpaca, barège-mousseline, barpure, valencia chiné or satiné, taffeta, nankin, piqué, foulard.

New Materials: batiste de laine; pente. 'Tom Pouce' ribbon (a very narrow figured gauze ribbon).

Evening

Corsage. (1). 'Of the form called the veste with gilet under it'; the body half-high and very open in the shape of a jacket edged with ruching, over a white silk or satin waistcoat cut en demi-cœur with a rolling collar; or a basquin body laced across a muslin waistcoat. Pagoda sleeves.

(2). Low neck with bertha which may be horizontal or descend to a point at the waist. Short sleeves with lace fall.

(3). Low neck with pelerine trimmings descending from the shoulders to a point at the waist. Full short sleeves.

(4). Occasionally, an open robe (with lapels)

over a flounced skirt. Short sleeves with lace fall.

Skirt. Heavy materials, plain; lighter silks, etc. with three flounces; muslins, etc., five flounces edged with satin ribbon.

Materials: velvet, silks, brocades, organdy, nainsook, mousseline de soie.

OUTDOOR GARMENTS

Mantles

The Talma mantle, either with a hood or with a collar having two tassels.

The Victoria mantle, knee length, with shoul-

Gloves

With ribbon ornament at the wrist.

Jewellery. Coral returning to fashion. Steel chatelaines worn. *Parasols* 'with the newly invented white enamel sticks, jointed, 10/6 to 16/-'. Ornamental hairpins with large heads and pendant ornaments. Metal haircombs in place of tortoiseshell. Advertisement of 'elastic bodices without bones, thus superseding stays'. Nightdress case. 'This is an article, rapidly gaining favour among ladies of rank.'

Prices

Rich Spitalfields gros de Naples, 1/6½ to 2/6 a

Three mantles. 1852

der cape cut square in front and descending below the waist behind. Sleeve openings with trimmed cuffs.

Balmoral cloak, short, sleeveless, and with a narrow hood. Jocelyn mantle, knee length with double skirt and three capes, each of which is fringed; armholes. Summer mantlets: the Chambord; the scarf-mantlet, and the plain mantlet.

ACCESSORIES

Slippers

Now made with heels.

yard. Irish poplin, 3/6 a yard, Chameleon silks, 2/3½, brilliant Baratheas, 2/2½. 'The new Bayadère silks, ¾ wide, 35/6 the dress', moiré antique, 3½ guineas. 'Elegant brocades and damasks, 2½ guineas, ditto very chaste, 3½ guineas' (the dress length of 12½ yards). French organdie 'at the literally absurd price of 2/11½ the dress' (8 yards).

Bonnets. French satin or silk, 12/9 to 16/9. Widows' with double crepe fall, 14/6 to 18/6. Aerophane crepe, 14/6 to 16/6. Leghorns, 15/- to 30/-, Fancy Tuscans, 4/- to 6/9.

1853

The chief changes in this year are (1) the waistcoat body is largely replaced by the caraco body and the open basquin body. (2) Flounces are almost always 'à disposition'; in ball dresses the 'tunic' (*i.e.* a looped-up overskirt) is revived. (3). The skirt increases steadily in size, so that as a new device, for heavy materials, 'skirts are no longer gathered but pleated in deep pleats at the waist.'

From Paris it is reported that 'skirts become wider and wider. There is a vague rumour of the revival of the paniers of former days. Crinoline petticoats have three or even four rolls at the bottom of the dress.' The English taste lags behind but even here coming events cast their shadow before and the skirt is now almost unmanageable. 'Some years ago women tried to make their hips extraordinarily large, and the petticoat diminished towards the bottom; now basques are worn and the skirts being very full below have an exceedingly graceful fan-shape.' Such, at least, was the theory; in practice it was a shape extremely difficult to sustain, especially with light materials such as muslin; such skirts might be lined with stiff muslin, and 'some dressmakers place very slight whalebones from distance to distance which gives the ample fan-like form which is so graceful and so rarely obtained.'

DRESSES

Day

Bodice. Always made separate from the skirt and frequently two bodices (day and evening) to one skirt.

Types of bodice. (1). High, three-quarter or half high (en demi-cœur); long pointed waist and pagoda sleeves.

(2). The Watteau body, with low square opening in the centre, the front down to the waist not quite closed being fastened over the chemisette by a series of ribbon bows, and a basquin open at the sides, with elbow sleeves having deep lace falls.

(3). The basquin body with revers either opening down to the waist, or en demi-cœur.

(4). The caraco body, in the form of a loose fitting jacket open to the waist over a chemisette or, occasionally, a waistcoat; the lower part closed by ribbon knots. Some caraco bodies have wide revers. The caraco body is frequently of a different material from the skirt, *e.g.*, a blue velvet caraco body, and skirt of figured taffeta; a garnet velvet caraco body, and lavender poplin skirt; or, in summer, a caraco body of embroidered muslin over a silk skirt. A variation of the caraco body is the bolero, with basquins cut in points and fringed.

(5). The 'Polish pelisse', of silk, in the form of a coin de feu, with a full skirt attached which reaches to the knee; buttons from the throat halfway down to the waist; wide pagoda sleeves.

All these forms of bodice may be trimmed with (*a*) revers, (*b*) 'capes', (*c*) 'braces', or flat trimmings ascending from the point of the waist to the shoulders gradually widening and coming down the back.

(6). For summer materials, the corsage à la vierge, a full body gathered at the waist and shoulders; or a corsage pleated down the front and gathered into a gerbe at the centre of the waist. Or a canezou of embroidered muslin, either open over a chemisette or closed over a camisole.

In all forms of bodice basques or basquins are usual. (The former are sewn on to the bodice; the latter are cut in one piece with it.)

Sleeves. The pagoda is the usual form, but the mousquetaire sleeve with deep cuff having immense reversed points, and the large bishop sleeve (full and loose to halfway below the elbow where it is gathered, continuing as a bell opening with lace undersleeves) are not uncommon. Pagoda sleeves are often slit up the front and fringe-trimming is common. Jockeys at the shoulder and wrist may be seen.

Skirt. Flounces (three to five) in silks, barège and muslin, woven à disposition; poplins are not flounced but trimmed up the front with rich silk trimmings. Figured heavy materials are plain. Occasionally in carriage dresses the front has a tablier with flounces at sides and back. When the flounces are numerous they are made to overlap so that the skirt itself is not visible. In place of flounces the material may have bands woven in the material to simulate them. The flounce à disposition is a noticeable feature and many are woven with a Scotch plaid pattern, or with one deep band of velvet. The economical device of sewing overlapping flounces on to a calico skirt is often employed. The flounces may be of alternate silk and black lace, or may be deeply dented.

Materials used for day dresses do not vary from the previous year.

Evening

Bodice. (1). Corsage en stomacher, with pointed waist. Three 'capes', narrowing from the point in front as they ascend over the shoulder to form a bertha behind.

(2). A low tight bodice with deep point and bertha.

(3). A basquin body, half-high or open to the waist, the front crossed by rows of fringe over a chemisette.

(4). Occasionally the waistcoat and jacket body of the previous year, but this is 'less worn than the body en stomacher'.

Sleeves. Short and double with lace fall.

Skirt. Three broad, or five to seven narrow flounces. Heavy figured materials are unflounced. Occasionally an open robe is used. For ball dresses especially, the tunic or double skirt (the upper one being rounded at the sides or looped up). The underskirt may have as many as five flounces.

Summer mantle of embroidered muslin. 1853

Trimming of flowers or feathers, with abundance of lace and ribbon knots.

Materials as in previous year. A gold lamé material introduced, for ball dresses.

OUTDOOR GARMENTS

Mantlets

Scarf-mantlets, deeply edged with lace, and fringe. The mantlet Imperatrice, shaped to the waist, with a deep fringe headed by insertion of guipure.

The mantlet Hortense, not shaped to the figure, ending in deep rounded dents and wide guipure trimming.

Small mantles worn low on the shoulders, edged with black lace.

Mantles

A plain piece cut to fit the shoulders into which the fullness is set, descending to the knee, with a deep lace and fringe edging. Armholes cut lengthwise and edged to form a narrow sleeve.

'Square *shawls* are now most worn, the patterns of round shape and large.'

ACCESSORIES

Day *Boots* of stuff with small heels and laced on one side; evening shoes of stuff or black taffeta with a bow, worn with or without strings.

Taffeta bertha. 1853

Gloves with embroidered lines on the back. Velvet bracelets or velvet cuffs are worn 'to protect the wrists from sunburning'.

'Little spotted veils are all the rage.'

Parasols of marquise lace.

'Bustles are now made with rolls of crinoline.'

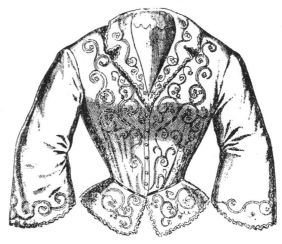

Jacket body of embroidered muslin. 1853

Prices

Sutherland silks, 3/11 a yard, Brocatelle robes, 5 guineas. Swiss cambric, 4/6 the dress. French poult de soie 1½ to 3 guineas the dress.

French kid gloves, 11/6 the dozen.

Bonnets, Dunstables, 2/11 to 4/6. Rice straws 3/6 to 5/6. White chips for brides, 10/6 to 16/6. Morning caps, 1/11 to 3/6.

The Crimean War, beginning in February of this year, influenced the current fashions in characteristic ways; there was a distinct liking for 'Oriental' effects and Turkish style in a host of details. The rich conglomeration of colours favoured in Eastern embroidery, with Turkish tassels, crescent brooches and ornaments, displayed our sympathy with our 'gallant ally'—of the moment. The dress-designers snatched the usual profit from patriotism by putting on the market an Alma mantle and an Inkerman cloak, but these were things of the passing hour. A survey of the year shows a definite arrest in fashions, as is generally the case at the beginning of a war. The old modes were refurbished with minor changes. Headgear showed practically no alteration, while the upper half of the dress clung to the jacket-effect under its various forms, basquin body, jacket body and caraco body.

But not even the onset of a war could arrest the inevitable growth of the skirt by which the modern woman of the day was unconsciously symbolising her increasing importance in the world. It was growing steadily more fan-shaped, for which purpose 'stiff petticoats are more worn than ever, not so much in the morning as in the evening when they are perfectly absurd.' The need for an artificial crinoline was becoming urgent.

Meanwhile the dress-designer fell back on trimmings to supply novelties for the season—always a sign that inspiration is flagging; ribbons and ruching and flowers and lace were, so to speak, strewn thickly over last year's models and satisfied the taste of the day.

DRESSES

Day

Bodice. Many are unboned, and back-fastening bodices begin to reappear.

Types: (1). Basquin body, with attached basques which are usually festooned or cut into vandykes. Closed to the neck with vandyked embroidered collar for morning; open nearly or quite to the waist over a chemisette, for afternoon.

(2). Jacket body with basquins which do not project beyond the hips. Closed to the neck, or open.

(3). Caraco body, with basquins which project beyond the hips. Closed or open.

(4). Plain body, closed by buttons up to the neck with bias 'capes' en revers passing over the shoulders. Some, with round waist, trimmed en tablier, from the neck to the bottom of the skirt.

(5). The Watteau body, nearly high behind and on the shoulders and half-high and square cut in front, with narrow revers passing up from the pointed waist over the shoulders.

Sleeves. (1). The pagoda, often slit up in front or at the side to the elbow,

(2). The full bishop sleeve, with velvet band above the wrist, and lace ruffle.

(3). The puffed sleeve, divided by bands into two to four puffs.

(4). Double sleeve, of same material.

Skirt. Plain or flounced. Flounces generally à disposition, or trimmed with braid, ruching, gimp or velvet. A Greek key pattern is not uncommon. As a novelty flounces are often of two different shades of the same colour. Skirts with jacket bodies have large flat pleats in front and at the sides; with basquin bodies the fullness of the skirt 'is set into a plain piece cut en bias'. Skirts of thick materials are pleated, and thin materials gathered. To sustain the fan-shape of the skirt 'crinoline and stiff petticoats are in great demand; under each flounce rather wide pieces of straw can be tacked.' Or they are lined with stiff muslin 'to make them stand out'. 'The excessive fullness of the petticoats has rendered flounces almost superfluous.' With a white caraco or canezou a ribbon cein-

1850
Visiting dress: green silk; three fringed flounces
Promenade dress: en redingote, of lavender taffeta
Dress of white barège; vandyked flounces; pink silk pardessus

1851
Morning dress: black satin; small jacket
Evening dress of pink silk barège
Evening dress of figured mousselaine de soie

ture is worn, or a 'Sultana scarf'—loosely tied below the waist with hanging ends, of Oriental colours.

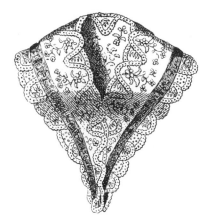

Lace canezou. 1854

Evening

The only material changes from the previous year are that the 'waistcoat body' had disappeared, and the open robe is becoming not infrequent.

Sometimes the skirt, instead of being open in front is open on each side over a breadth of white satin. The 'Watteau body' for evening dresses, is very fashionable.

Lace jacket with quillings of ribbon. 1854

Ball dresses are usually with tight pointed corsage, low off the shoulders, with a blunt point behind, and have a bertha, or tulle drapery. The bertha covers the short sleeves; with drapery the sleeves are short and puffed.

The skirt of ball dresses is either double, or with looped-up 'tunic', or with lines of puffing halfway up. Or there may be three to four skirts, especially of thin materials.

OUTDOOR GARMENTS

Pelisses

The Pelisse, knee length, of velvet or cloth, with guipure and deep fringe trimming. 'The body defines the figure, and the skirt is laid in large pleats on the hips and at the back; wide three-quarter sleeves.'

Mantles

The Talma is shorter and often called a 'Rotonde'.

Winter mantillas are cut deep behind, the front ends short and either square or rounded; trimming of broad black lace or fringe.

The 'Moldavian mantle', with a deep cape falling all the length and forming the sleeves called 'elephant sleeves'.

Summer mantillas, worn low off the shoulders, with deep lace fringe, the front ends reaching the knee. Plush is a good deal used, and a plush-like trimming of 'silk-moss'.

A double-faced plush, for winter mantlets, is a novelty.

ACCESSORIES

Evening *shoes* with heels.

Gloves

With two buttons. The variety of colours used for gloves can be gathered from an advertisement 'Garnet, pensée, Napoleon, groseille, olive, Adelaide, Rubis, Mazzogram, maroon, myrtle, Tracarad, coffee, Cuba 1/- a pair'.

Undersleeves

Very full bouillon with deep ruffle or a worked cuff, turned back and vandyked. Broderie anglaise much used.

Fans of coloured batiste, each fold being leaf-shaped. *Parasols* of black lace.

Evening hand bouquets now replaced by scent bottles.

Prices

Night-caps, 1/6 to 2/6. Dressing gowns, 8/6 to 18/6.
Ringlets on combs, 8/6.
Corset plastique, from 7/6.
Mourning silks, 25/6 the full dress; skirts trimmed with crape, 30/-.
Widows' caps, 3/6. Widows' silks, 2/10 and 3/6 a yard. Paramatta, 1/6 and 2/-.
French chintz muslin robes, 6/- the dress.

Riding hats, 12/6 and 14/-.
Lace. Brussels squares, 13 to 55 guineas.
Brussels flouncings, 14 to 100 guineas. Brussels and Honiton bridal scarf, 7 to 45 guineas. 'A beautiful imitation of the above at a very moderate price.'
Shoes. French kid, morocco, and white satin, 4/6, lace boots, 8/6 a pair. Enamelled overshoes, 6/6, Paris kid shoes with military heels, 10/6 a pair.
Shawls. Long barège, 15/9, rich woven Paisley, 21/-. Llama wool barèges and balzarines, 8¾d. to 12½d. a yard.
Silk dresses (12 yards), striped glacé, 18/9 to 30/-, brocades, 5 to 16 guineas, moiré, £3 15, satin de laine, 12/6, Lyons velvet, £5.
'The new elegant Turkish robes with oriental flounce, £3 15.'

'The Crimea cloak, 1 guinea.' Black cloth mantle, lined with alpaca and trimmed with velvet, 10/6.
Cloth riding habits, 5½ to 7 guineas. Ladies' riding trousers, of chamois leather and black feet, advertised.
'Evening dresses in silver and gold flounces, 18 yards in the robe for 5 to 12 guineas.'
Headdresses: chenille and velvet, mixed 3/4. Velvet in all colours, 3/9, velvet with pearl and gilt ornaments, 5/9.
'Frizz'd hair rollers for dressing the hair in the present beautiful style, 3/6.'
'The elastic bodice with front fastening, 10/6.'
Umbrellas, brown silk, 7/-. French myrtle green and Napoleon blue, 13/-.

1855

The influence of the Crimean War was still checking the natural development of fashions, but it must be remembered that a war at a remote distance was not vitally affecting the nation's morale so that while arresting, for the moment, the progress of fashion it was not powerful enough to deflect fashions towards a simpler, less Gothic form. The effort made in France, for purely political reasons, to revive the modes made famous under the first Napoleon completely failed under

Canezou for low dress. 1855

Muslin braces with ribbon quillings. 1855

the Second Empire. The necessary impulse was lacking. And England was steadily marching forward towards affluence with her Gothic tastes as strong as ever. During the year 1855 the megalomania of the skirt continued; by now the outline of the costume was that of an isosceles triangle, rapidly approaching the equilateral. Flounces no longer lay flat but stood out from the surface of the skirt, owing to their stiff backing; flounces grew down the sides of the sleeve and over the bodice so that the essential shape floated in a diaphanous halo—at least if the wearer was skilled in the management of her draperies; it must be admitted that while the fashion-plate suggests a bird of paradise many in reality suggested a domestic hen ruffling its feathers.

DRESSES

Day

The types of the previous year are mainly used, with some modifications; thus, for morning the basquin body often has 'bretelles' (braces) 'pointed both at the back and in front and open on the shoulders; with these a ceinture with long floating ends is worn'. The plain high body, buttoning down the front, is left open above the waist with two points like a man's waistcoat. A few bodices are now made to

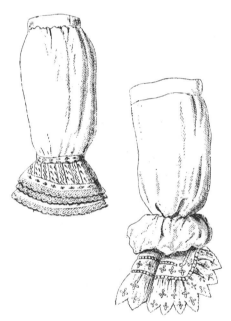

Morning sleeves. 1855

fasten behind. The caraco is now frequently made double-breasted, and cut rather deeper behind. The caraco, itself, develops into the *Casaque,* a form of jacket buttoned up to the neck and fitting close to the figure, having its basque extended downwards into a pronounced 'skirt' which lies flat over the hips; 'the skirt is now cut with the body but is of circular form.' Black velvet caracos are frequently worn with light coloured skirts.

Sleeves continue as before but the double bouffant sleeve, with deep ruffle, is increasingly fashionable; 'sleeves closed at the wrist are much more worn than in previous years.'

The Skirt. With heavy materials (poplin and moiré) this is attached to the waistband 'with

Morning fichu. 1855

pleats and plain pieces alternating except for six inches gathered at the back, so that the skirt falls in rich flutings'. Satins and poplins are

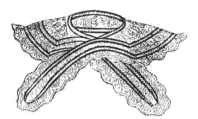

Morning fichu. 1855

either trimmed à la robe or en tablier; silks and light materials are flounces.

Flounces. Three to five, *e.g.,* three deep flounces

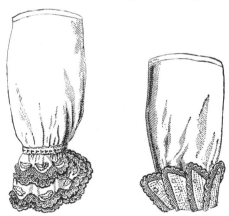

Two day sleeves. 1855

edged with velvet or ruching, or an edge of woven colour. Or flounces deeply vandyked, the spaces between being filled in with black

Muslin fichu for open dress. 1855

Sortie de bal. 1855

Muslin canezou. 1855

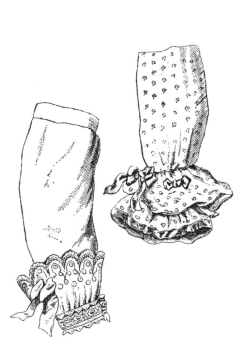

Evening sleeves. 1855

Lace sleeves. 1855

lace. Or flounces of two colours alternating (blue and white; green and lilac). Or a skirt with four flounces, the top one set into the waistband.

Occasionally a dress with high 'corsage mousquetaire', with a plastron ornamented with agrafes and basques; demi-large sleeves.

Evening

The usual type of corsage is low, with a point and a bertha of tulle or blonde folded and crossing in front; or with bretelles crossing the shoulders and meeting at a point behind and in front, crossing at the waist. Ribbon bows on the shoulders are common.

Short bouffant sleeves, or short sleeves concealed under the bertha.

Skirt. Flounces, three broad edged with ruching, or up to seven narrow, edged with ribbon. Or rows of puffed tulle and flounces alternating, or puffing up to the knee with an overskirt, plain, above. Some with three skirts, or with a tablier skirt and two over skirts open in front.

Lace flounces are common with ball dresses which are elaborately trimmed with wreaths of flowers.

OUTDOOR GARMENTS

Mantles

The Talma mantle. Winter mantles, knee length, trimmed with lace and fringe to form a deep cape and a collar.

The Victoria pelisse-mantle, double-breasted with buttons down the front, flat collar, short wide sleeves with reversed cuffs, side pockets. Made knee length.

Summer mantlets similar to those of previous year but guipure and fringe are elaborately used as trimming.

Materials: 'The new muslins strike the attention of every man; what effect they will have on ladies may be easily conceived.'

New Material: Barège de laine, 12/6 the dress. Marron is a new and fashionable colour.

ACCESSORIES

Parasols of coloured silk covered with white guipure or a deep fringe; sticks of carved ivory and coral.

Prices

Delhi Cashmere, 11/6 the dress (Peter Robinson)
Bayadère parasols, 7/11; moiré ditto, 4/11.
Elegant muslin and wool barège, 2/11 the dress.
Fashionable checks and stripes, silks, 27/6, brochés, 39/6 the dress.
Flounced silk robes, 18 yards, à disposition, 75/6.
French merino, 2/- to 4/- a yard.
French broché muslin sleeves, 1/9 a pair.
Embroidered habit-shirts, 1/11½.
Mousquetaire gauntlet gloves, 1/8 a pair. Kid gloves in 34 different colours.
'Hair frizettes, indispensable for the graceful rouleaux bandeaux, 2/6.'
The fashionable velvet headdress, 5/-.
Velvet mantles, 35/- to 5 guineas. Cloth ditto, 13/9 to 2 guineas.
Genoa velvet, 12/6 to 16/9; Lyons velvet, 6/6 to 15/9 a yard.
Crinoline skirts, 4/11 to 10/6.
Black silk aprons with coloured stripes, 2/9.

1856

'Notwithstanding the pressure of Income Tax (1/4 in the pound) and high prices, there seems no abatement in the richness and costliness of ladies' attire.' The explanation was not far to seek as regards the Upper Class. 'England is doing a roaring trade' was the expression of a contemporary; while another indicates not only the trend of fashion but also the significance. 'If the ladies' dresses continue to increase in breadth it will be absolutely necessary to widen all the public thoroughfares. Perhaps it is a spirit of exclusiveness which has induced the leaders of fashion to surround themselves with barriers of barège and other similar outworks to keep the common herd at arm's length—or rather, petticoats' breadth.'

While the increasing size of dresses was obvious to contemporaries they did not notice another change which was becoming perceptible—namely, an alteration in the popular taste in colours. Hitherto an harmonious blending of tones was the rule, but in this year a taste for strong contrasts began to show itself. For example, a dress of light green silk with dark green flounces worn with a talma of grey and purple check, and a purple and black bonnet; a dress of two shades of brown, a purple pelisse, green gloves and pale blue bonnet; a myrtle green dress with a claret casaque and light blue bonnet; a dress of light and dark rose coloured check, with lavender pelisse and ruby bonnet; a costume in which yellow, green and lavender, or green, brown and blue were conspicuous. While massive squares of two colours, three or four inches across, or stripes two and three inches wide, aggressively struck the eye. The pre-Raphaelite School no doubt regarded the tendency of the day as blatant and vulgar; we can regard it as indicating the growing demands of the nineteenth-century woman; it was, in a sense, a flag of war.

In a technical sense the year was important, historically, as having given birth to the *artificial crinoline*. We find, in October, the earliest advertisement in this country, of such: 'Whalebone skeleton skirts, 7/6'; and in December, 'The Parisian Eugènie Jupon Skeleton petticoat, 6/6 to 25/-.' While there is no doubt that the Empress Eugènie encouraged its use by her patronage from this date, it would be erroneous to assume that she 'introduced it'. The growth of the skirt in the preceding years, even before she became Empress, had made its appearance sooner or later inevitable; and her social position was, as yet, not sufficiently secure to permit her introducing so singular an innovation unless the time was ripe for it. For trade purposes it was convenient to attach her name to it. Even before its general use, while the stiff petticoat of crinoline material was still employed, the size of fashionable skirts was a subject for popular complaint. 'A drawing-room looks now like a camp. You see a number of bell tents of different colours, the poles sustaining them appearing at the summit. These are the signs of habitation. . . . Is there not power of repression under the Building Act?'

DRESSES

Day

Bodice. Basquin body with bretelles (especially for young ladies), short elbow sleeves and full undersleeves of three or four bouillons.

Jacket body, with a deep basque and generally bretelles trimmed with fringe or velvet. Sleeve close fitting to just below the elbow with bell opening or bias frill, and two or three flounces above the elbow. Bodices are more trimmed than formerly, generally having bretelles or 'capes' resembling them.

With summer materials a ceinture ribbon with floating ends is usual.

Occasionally a morning dress is in the form of a robe with a 'Watteau' pleat at the back.

Skirt. 'Flounces seem now to have attained the climax of fashionable favour.' Flounces may be pinked, ruched, or of lace or bouillon. While flounces à disposition retain their popularity. For winter, the flounces are often edged with velvet and brocade. Thin silks have three or four deep flounces or are entirely covered with narrow flounces nearly to the waist. Or there may be only one flounce, very deep, just above the knee level. Summer dresses, of barège and coloured muslin, have three or four flounces or double skirts. Rich silks with very broad vertical stripes 'the colours forming a strong contrast', and moirés are unflounced. A number of plain skirts with tablier trimming are seen.

Evening

Corsage. (Day and evening corsage common.) Pointed back and front. Cut low off the shoulders and the top elaborately trimmed with folds of lace or tulle brought from the shoulders to the centre of the waist en stomacher; ribbon bows on the shoulders and floating ceinture.

Or a bertha of lace, etc., descending slightly in the centre.

Short sleeves concealed by the trimming of the bodice.

Skirt. Two or three skirts, or innumerable flounces up to the waist. In ball dresses the skirt is still more elaborate, *e.g.* 'first skirt with four bouillons up to the knee, the second skirt

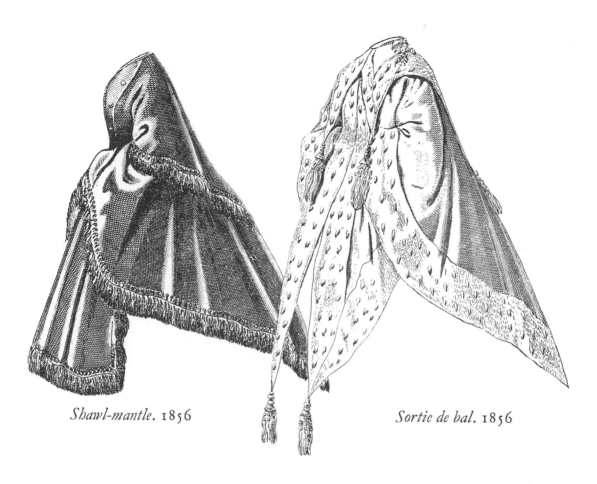

Shawl-mantle. 1856

Sortie de bal. 1856

Cashmere mantle. 1856

Velvet cloak. 1856

187

knee-length, with lines of descending bouillons.' 'Three tulle skirts looped up at the side with flowers, over a coloured silk skirt.' 'Skirt with four plain flounces; opening on a breadth of white satin which is flounced with white guipure.' 'Ball dress of blue satin with double skirt ("tunic skirt") the under one having a deep blonde flounce, and the upper—knee-length—trimmed with rows of blonde and roses.'

Evening dresses with Watteau body and tablier skirt are sometimes seen.

All are excessively trimmed with lace (guipure and blonde), flowers, ribbons and feathers, while bouillons or lines of puffing are increasingly used.

OUTDOOR GARMENTS

Pelisses

The Pelisse, knee-length, edged with fur or velvet, gored at the waist to fit over the expanse of skirt, and having velvet collar and lapels. Short pelisses have large pleats at the back and sides. The Paletot, often double-breasted, and trimmed with black silk ball fringe.

Cloaks

The Burnouse, for evening, of cashmere, of bright colours such as scarlet or blue, with a hood and a profusion of tassels. This Oriental garment was one of the Eastern tastes derived from the Crimean War, and its shape—or want of shape—was also used for day mantles, made of figured cashmere, broché woven or printed with Oriental designs.

The Sortie de Bal, shaped like a Talma with a hood, and made of cashmere with silk or satin quilted lining.

The Casaque, of velvet, deeply fringed, or with lace edging.

Sable boas. Small muffs.

Materials: There is a noticeable absence of new fabrics for dresses. Existing materials are, if possible, more richly decorated. Barèges are woven with brocaded edges for flounces à disposition; moiré flounces are applied to dresses of plain silks; fringe, galloon, and braid trimmings appear in greater variety, while, on the other hand, satins were less used. Yellows give way to mauves and purples, and brown becomes a fashionable colour. Chiné tones are too delicate for the modern taste which demands solid masses and strepitant checks.

ACCESSORIES

Fans with water-colour pictures; borders by Duvelleroy fashionable.

Bracelets and brooches with large cabochon stones.

Prices

Flounced silk dresses, 18 yards, 2 guineas; flounced and double skirt tweed dresses, trimmed velvet and plush, 18/6; ditto silk, 5 guineas. Velvet robes, double skirts 6½ guineas. Black moiré, 2 to 7 guineas. Ducape dresses, 14 yards, 24/- to 49/-. Flounced organdy, 10/6 the full dress. Muslin ball dress, flounced 13/9, ditto, double skirt, 21/-.

Finest jacconets, 5/-, organdys, 7/6, de laines, 8/9 a yard.

Black silk aprons with coloured satin stripes, 2/11.

Foulard washing silks, 21/6 the full dress.

Parisian bonnets, 21/-.

Long mantle-burnouse, 1 guinea.

Challis plaids, 1/1½ a yard.

Crinoline and moreen skirts, 5/- to 10/6.

NOTE: As a result of the Crimean War there is a perceptible increase in prices.

1857

Fashions, having in a great measure remained stationary for the last three years, now made a noticeable move forward; the most conspicuous feature being a still greater enlargement of the skirt. A silk dress now needed anything up to 18 yards of material. This might be attributed to the possibilities afforded by the new invention, the artificial crinoline, by means of which a colossal expanse of material could be sustained without difficulty. But we have seen how the skirt had been steadily increasing in size for some years; it had certainly reached the maximum possible over a horsehair petticoat, and the wire cage enabled the wearer to dispense with the weight of a multitude of petticoats. On the other hand the Crimean War undoubtedly checked the development of fashion generally during the years

1852
Promenade dress of figured barège; basquine bodice; pagoda sleeves
Day dress of white organdie edged with pink stripes
Morning dress of checked lilac silk; caraco body and waistcoat

1852

Carriage dress of taffeta; the four flounces with wreaths of stamped velvet;
white satin embroidered waistcoat

Ball dress of white satin; tulle bouillons above the hem

Carriage dress of satin with velvet bands; casaweck body; jean waistcoat

1854 to 1856, and as is commonly the case immediately after a war fashions seem to make up for lost time by a headlong rush. Apart from the size of the skirt, the general colour sense was changing. 'A few years back a pretty woman would not have dared to go out in the toilets of to-day; at present she actually wears, on either side of her skirt, mountings of a different colour from the dress itself and in the most glaring contrast to it.'

In addition the hat, at least for young women, was beginning to return to favour. Such changes were in keeping with the rapid change taking place in the feminine attitude of the day. Woman was no longer content to sustain the picturesque attitude of immobilised domesticity. The meek Gothic style was turning into a harsh challenge; there is nothing soft about an equilateral triangle, the new shape in which woman presented herself to a startled world. 'Bloomerism has ended in crinoline, the frilled trousers have expanded into willow bands or in petticoats and hoops. Short skirts have developed into trains half a yard long; spread out like fans, not bells. The bell shape is now absurd. All the tournure of the skirt is now in the forepart of the skirt in lieu of having it behind.'

DRESSES

Day

Bodice. (1). Basquin or jacket bodies closed to the throat, generally by front buttons, sometimes by back fastenings; either trimmed en stomacher with fringe of lace, or a cape à la bertha, or bretelles as capes, fringed. Some with basques 'so deep as to reach the middle of the skirt'.
(2). Plain high bodies without basques, and with a broad ribbon ceinture and floating ends worn on the left side; the waist nearly round.
(3). Jacket bodies, deep in front and behind, and sloped over the hips.
(4). Closing up the front in its whole length with the tablier trimming of the skirt continued up to the throat.
(5). The 'matinée'—for summer—a long casaque descending to the knee, buttoning down the front with mother-of-pearl buttons; flat collar; ribbon bow at the neck. Made of fine jacconet or quilting; plain skirt en suite.
In summer a white lace canezou may be worn as a bodice.
Sleeves. (1). The pagoda, slit up the front nearly the whole way, or made of three bias flounces.
(2). The 'double puff and bias frill', *i.e.* a plain piece at the top followed by a double puffing and a deep edging of material cut on the cross. Sometimes a single puff and a double frill. This style of sleeve is becoming more fashionable than the pagoda.
Large puffed engageants with cuffs.
Skirt. Five to six yards in circumference.
(1). Three deep flounces à disposition, often with several horizontal stripes of velvet or satin, or chiné pattern.
(2) Double skirts with very large pleats at the waist 'so that four or five go round the waist'. The upper skirt deeply fringed.

Fichu of spotted muslin edged with lace. 1857

(3). Triple skirts, the upper two fringed.
(4). Plain skirt with side quillings or panels, or with 'pyramids of velvet'. The front en tablier.
For walking, a device for raising the skirt so as to show the elaborately embroidered petticoat is sometimes used; a band of material about half

the length of the skirt is sewn inside the skirt on each side; it can be buttoned up to a button under the basquin, thus holding up the skirt at the sides.

White tulle canezou. 1857

For morning dress (summer) the 'fichu Antoinette', of fine muslin trimmed with black lace and narrow velvet, fastening behind with a small bow, the long ends floating at the back; it covers the shoulders like a shawl and crosses in front at the waist.

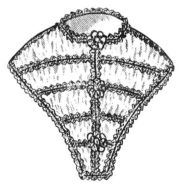

Evening canezou. 1857

The collars worn with day dresses are now very small.
Trimmings of dresses. Fringe, 'the most becoming of all'; bayadère trimmings (*i.e.* flat, either woven in or sewn on, of velvet, etc.); grelots (*i.e.* small drop buttons). Jet.
Materials: striped and checked silks; the stripes

very broad, of contrasting colours; checks of violet, green or sapphire blue.
(Winter). Reps, poplins, veloutines, druggets, cotelines, French merino, grey carmelite for country dresses, thick silks with horizontal stripes of velvet or satin. (Summer). White piqué, barège and muslins, always flounced, Tussore silk.

Morning sleeve. 1857

Many materials have broad vertical stripes.
Satin, which had fallen into disfavour since the murderess, Mrs. Manning, had been hanged in a black satin dress in 1849, now becomes fashionable again.
Fashionable Colours: lilac, green, brown and especially mauve.

Riding Habits of black or dark blue cloth, corsage without basques, sleeves wide at the ends;

Evening sleeve. 1857

cambric collar and turned back cuffs; black felt hat with plume.

Evening
Bodice: low off the shoulders and pointed behind as well as in front. Trimmed either with a bertha (covering the short sleeve), or with drapery (tulle, etc.) which covers the corsage, the sleeve being short. In addition flowers are used in abundance as trimming. The skirt is demi-

trained. Skirts with two or three deep flounces, often embroidered. Double or treble skirts, *e.g.* 'three skirts, the lower two each with a deep flounce; over the top flounce is the third skirt, of tulle, cut long enough to allow of the bottom edge being tacked to the top of the flounce so

Morning fichu. 1857

that it may fall over in a puff; it is looped at equal distances by black lace trimmings.' The puffed upper skirt (or 'tunic') is particularly fashionable for ball dresses; or there may be lines of puffing from the knee to the hem with two flounces or short skirts above them.

Ball dresses are trimmed with sprays of flowers, fruit and even grass.

OUTDOOR GARMENTS

Mantles

The Burnouse (the hood of which is now pointed), with Arab tassels.

The 'Basquin', of cashmere or Algerine, now denoting a mantle with deep basquins, with fringed trimming, a bertha and pagoda sleeves.

The Pelisse and the Casaque (of velvet, vicuna, satin, plush or moiré).

The single and double-breasted Paletot, of cloth or vicuna.

The Shawl-mantilla (Summer) trimmed with broad lace and two rows of fringe.

The 'sortie de ball', with hood, as an evening wrap.

ACCESSORIES

Fans. Painted and spangled, or of mother-of-pearl.

Parasols fringed and lace covered. Often fan-parasols.

Jewellery: hair bracelets and brooches, and *revolving* brooches.

Prices

New Spring silks, dresses, 12 to 18 yards, 35/6 to 55/6.

Chintz organdy, 6½d.; new barèges, 10½d.; balzarines, 6½d.; mohair carmelite, 7¾d. a yard.

Striped and checked tarlatans, 5/- the full dress; flounced ditto, 10/6.

Riding habits, 5½ to 8 guineas.

Patent railway safety pockets, 1/6.

Full size crinoline petticoats, 8/6 to 16/6.

Watch spring crinoline and muslin skirts, 15/- to 30/-. 'Patent spring petticoats, never crease or get out of order, 16/6.'

Quilted satin, satinette and glacé petticoats, 35/- to 60/-.

'Steel spring jupons, just introduced in Paris, 20/-.'

Lace canezou trimmed with pink ribbon.
1857

Velvet bonnets, 10/6. Felt hats, 6/6.

The new Pompeii ear-rings, 18/- to 3 guineas a pair.

Flannel dressing gowns, pink, sky blue, claret, cerise or scarlet, lined throughout, with a silk girdle, 30/-.

1858

'The hoop has reached its utmost extent unless our doors are to be made wider.' Having elected to transform her shape into that of the Great Pyramid, as a

191

lasting symbol of her social importance, it remained for woman to decorate the monolith appropriately. The problem was how to make a pyramid pretty. It was not surprising that multitudinous flounces did not suit those vast slopes, and so went out of fashion. The double and treble skirt did not break the line; vertical trimmings, broad below and narrow above, called very appropriately 'pyramids' were employed, and sometimes alternate panels of two colours, six in all (the dress 'à six lis'), so that she resembled a pyramid with six facets. As a slight balance the sleeves expanded below, the front being slit open nearly to the shoulder, or as a variation the 'full bishop'. 'The ordinary Pagoda is nearly extinct being replaced by the full bishop, with a jockey.' With so much attention paid to the skirt the bodice was by comparison insignificant, being usually front buttoned and conventionally trimmed; a small waist was no longer suitable for a costume that was monumental in its proportions and, in fact, tight-lacing was now forgotten. The measurements for cutting out a bodice are significant: 'waist, 24 inches, bust, 34; 16 inches across the shoulders; 14 across the back; side seams 8; length of back, $15\frac{1}{2}$.'

The colour schemes for decorating these vast surfaces were somewhat of the 'poster' style; a blue dress with pyramids of light green; a light purple with pyramids of light green; alternate stripes of pink and mauve; black chevrons, six inches deep, surrounding the hem of a light coloured skirt; and in ball dresses a coloured bodice rising out of a snowball of puffed tulle. In effect, the colours were laid on in flat masses of contrasting tones; and like a poster they made spectators stare. When happily chosen the general effect was dignified, at a certain distance; in any case it was never insignificant. Woman meant at all costs to be noticed.

The use of the sewing-machine begins to appear, and we read: 'The dressmakers of Paris are beginning to use the American sewing-machine; I am told it has for some time been silently in use at the principal dressmakers.' This probably refers to the chain-stitch machine, for the lock-stitch improvement only came into use at the end of this decade.

DRESSES

Day

Bodice. (1). The high, plain body, buttoning up the front to the throat; waist usually cut into two points in front. Either trimmed with bretelles-capes or fringed bertha, or untrimmed.
(2). Jacket body, with five points, two in front, one behind and one at each side.
(3). Basquin body, less usual.
(4). Occasionally, a pointed bodice lacing behind; in summer, the Watteau body, with ceinture, or a white canezou with a coloured skirt.
Sleeves. (1). The Venetian, very wide below and slit up the front nearly to the shoulder, over a large puffed engageante closed with a cuff.
(2). The 'full bishop', full from below the shoulder to the wrist, 'set into a plain piece at the top and a deep cuff at the wrist.' Muslin dresses may have a series of puffings all down the sleeve.
(3). Pagoda, less usual.
N.B. Most sleeves are now with a jockey at the shoulder.
Skirt. (1). Plain, for heavy materials.
(2). Double skirt, with quilles or pyramids at the sides. The quilles may be flat trimmings extending round the edges, or 'pleating à vieille', *i.e.* frills of hollow pleating closed at each end. The pyramids are breadths of material differing in colour and fabric from the dress. The lower skirt may be plain and the trimmings confined to the upper, which may be slit up at the sides.
(3). A single skirt with central pyramid extending up the bodice as a plastron.
(4). Two or three deep flounces heavily bordered with stripes or pattern à disposition.

1854
Day dress in lilac barège, the flounce bordered with quilled ribbons
Day dress of green barège with Pompadour pattern

1856. Evening dresses
Of pink satin with lace flounce
Of lilac taffeta, skirt trimmed with puffings
Of white moiré brocaded with blue; white cashmere sortie de bal

(5). Plain skirt with chevrons above the hem.
(6). The skirt 'à six lis'.

Materials: in addition to the usual fabrics, white piqué is very fashionable for summer négligée and mohair for country use. Tartans are much used.

Fashionable Colours: mauve, green, groseille and blue.

Evening

Bodice. Always pointed back and front and elaborately draped with trimmings, fichu or lace; some half-high, some à la vierge, with the fullness gathered to a point at the waist.

Sleeves generally more puffed than formerly—generally a bouillon of tulle with an epaulette of dress material.

Skirt. Double or triple skirts with broad quilles of same material down the sides, falling over all the skirts from the waist to the bottom of the lowest skirt.

Ball Dresses

The corsage is often of coloured silk with double or treble skirts of tulle, tarlatan, etc. The underskirt may be almost or entirely concealed by rows of puffed tulle. The bodice and skirt are elaborately festooned with wreaths of flowers.

OUTDOOR GARMENTS

Cloaks and Mantles

The Burnouse. The Algerian shawl-burnouse, of wool, with broad satin stripes.

The Shawl-mantlet, with two deep frills en suite.
The Pelisse (Winter) reaching below the knee with wide sleeves pleated into the armhole and deep mousquetaire cuffs.

The Casaque, similar, but with a small cape or cape trimming. Venetian sleeve.

The Mantle, of cloth, velvet, moiré and merino, either of the Talma shape or with deep lace edging and shaped in a curve at the back.
Spanish lace mantillas.
Sorties du bal.

New Materials: 'Velours de laine and ribbed velvet are the newest woollen materials.'
'A new form of brocaded silk called Matelassé.'

ACCESSORIES

Boots of kid, buttoned at the side.
Sable and ermine *Furs* for trimming cloaks.
Small *Muffs* of sable, grebe and ermine.
Square *Shawls* of black silk edged with black lace.
Chequered materials and bonnet ribbons.

Jewellery: coral, pearls, large brooches worn in the corsage; hair jewellery (with plain dresses). Fashionable lace, Chantilly.
'Fancy gilt, pearl, mosaic and stone buttons in great variety.'

Prices

French Merino dressing gowns, 24/6. Aberdeen Woolsey petticoats with patent steel springs and flounced, 10/9. Striped Linsey petticoats with elastic bands, 10/6 to 14/9.

Black silks 25% cheaper than last year (reduction of 50% on raw silk).

The new Bayadère bar glacé silks, 30/- the dress (rich raised satin Bayadère bars).

Mohairs: Norwich wove checks, 8/9; silk and mohair double skirt dresses 10/6.

Delhi cashmere, 15/-. Flounced challis robes à quille, 28/6.

White and buff marcella jackets, 12/6.

The new jasper plaid silks, 26/9; rich chiné Bayadère silk, 4½ guineas.

Norwich poplins, 18/6; Irish ditto, 27/6; moiré antiques, 58/6.

Velvet flounced robes, £5 10 0. Black velvet jacket as chosen by the Princess Royal, 2½ guineas; cloth jacket, 10/6.

Spanish lace mantillas, 3 guineas upwards.

The new Tussore cambric morning dresses, 15/-.
Ready made muslin dresses, 4/9; 9/9; 16/9.

Rich new chiné bayadère silk dresses, 4½ guineas.

Shepherds' plaid and Rob Roy silk dresses, 31/6.
The new Barathea cashmere dress, 25/6.

Embroidered Swiss muslin and tarlatan dresses, 5/6.

Flounced tarlatans and double skirts, 6/6. Light flounced barèges, 10/6. Light flounced and double skirt silks, 30/-.

Sealskin mantles, 1 guinea.

'The Highland cloak with capuchin hood for ladies, affords great comfort for excursions, measures 16 yards round the edge and falls in graceful folds, 2½ guineas.'

African monkey muffs, 6/11 to 10/9.

Telegram parasols, with deep fringe, 7/6.

'The new self-expanding jacket in white marcella, will fit any figure, 6/9.'

Elastic boots, evening, 8/6, of satin, 14/6, house boots, 6/6.

Lace breakfast caps, trimmed with sarcenet ribbons, 5/6.

French nainsook nightcaps, with pink runners and lace borders, 5/6.

Coloured undersleeves, very elegant and great comfort, 1/6½.

'There is a tendency to become somewhat more martial in appearance on the part of the divine portion of creation'; or in plainer phrase, woman was now becoming definitely the aggressor in the campaign against man. We perceive the first signs of a new weapon—or rather, the revival of an ancient one long disused—which in the coming years was destined to work havoc among the susceptible sex, to wit, the foot. We read of a 'decline in the amount of crinoline as well as the long dresses already shortening in front so that graceful figures and pretty feet (which have so long been masked by their ferruginous entourage) will be restored to their rightful dominion'.

The effect of this threatened manœuvre on a generation of males who for nearly twenty years had never caught sight of a woman's ankles, except by a fleeting accident, must have been overwhelming, like the first introduction of poison gas in war. To the more thoughtful it seemed a gross violation of all the rules of the game and a presage of terrible things to come—of females blatantly biped who would shrink from nothing to gain their ends; but, in fact, it was for the moment only an affair of outposts to test the efficacy of the new instrument of destruction: feminine generalship knows better than to wear out a weapon by overuse and ten years later the ankle was once more masked from sight by the dead ground of voluminous skirts while the attack proceeded on the other flank. The military spirit displayed in this year was emphasised by the introduction of the zouave jacket, borrowed, of course, from the Italian war.

The technical problem of constructing the enormous skirt was still puzzling the designer; a new form of dress with bodice and skirt in one without a seam at the waist and known as the 'robe Gabrielle' was a costly innovation as it required '18 to 20 yards of material; the bodies and skirts being all in one piece, the latter are, of course, very much gored; four large pleats are laid underneath at the waist, one on each hip and two at the back, for as skirts do not measure less at the bottom than $4\frac{1}{2}$ yards there must be some pleats as well as the gores'. Actually this was a French fashion which hardly began to be used in this country until the next decade. It was, of course, the forerunner of the gored skirt and indicates that the crinoline dress had reached its meridian. We also find a steady movement in the direction of the round waist in place of the pointed and the close 'Amadis' sleeve instead of the pagoda. The phase of the pure Gothic is drawing to its close.

DRESSES

Day

Bodice. (1). Slightly pointed front and back.

(2). A full body gathered in at the waist, with a belt and floating ends in front.

(3). A round waist, worn with a buckle or sash.

In all types the plain front buttoning up to the neck is common. A variant, the 'waistcoat body' pointed behind and buttoning up the front is sometimes seen. With these types a turn-down white collar is worn. For afternoon dress, pelerine trimmings on a bodice pointed front and back, or a low square bodice with revers and a plastron between them, or a bodice with deep basquines.

Sleeves. (1). The full bishop.

(2). 'Pagoda sleeves, or as they are now called "funnel sleeves"', expanding more uniformly from above. Often slit open in front nearly to the top, over puffed engageantes closed at the wrist.

1852-3
Summer dress of muslin printed en disposition

(3). The Amadis sleeve, set into the armhole in large pleats concealed by the epaulette, close-fitting and ending in a deep cuff, worn with a plain tight bodice.

(4). The Gabrielle sleeve, formed of a row of puffs from the shoulder to the wrist.

In all types an epaulette on the shoulder is general. Undersleeves closed at the wrist for day; for full dress very large and open and finished with lace and ribbons.

Skirt. (1). Plain, very full, and for afternoon, slightly trained.

(2). Plain with a tablier of velvet ribbons running across; sometimes the front panel is quilted.

(3). Two broad flounces trimmed with five or six narrow flounces.

(4). One deep flounce headed by numerous narrow flounces.

(5). Double skirt, the first plain, the second edged with quilles, velvet vandykes or key pattern, or lines of black guipure.

With heavy materials the skirt is very long and full, either plain or with a broad pleating à la vieille at the bottom, or the double skirt. The skirt is fastened to the waistband in large flat box-pleats with false pleats concealed beneath, the 'Montespan pleats'. With thin silks, etc., flounces à disposition, or numerous narrow flounces (ten to fifteen) reaching nearly to the waist. With muslins (Summer) one eight-inch flounce headed by a line of puffing through which a coloured ribbon is drawn; or a row of six to seven flounces; with cambrics and jacconets, tunic skirts; with mohair a single full skirt either untrimmed or with side trimmings (à la vieille or pyramids). The plain skirt is frequently trimmed with rosettes of lace with jet centres or butterfly bows of velvet up the sides (and up the front of the bodice), and black trimmings are fashionable.

Fashionable Materials: satins, brocades with large patterns, ribbed and plain taffetas and gros-grains; China silks figured with small bouquets; fabrics with vertical stripes; jacconet, barège, mohair and nankeen. Woollen materials trimmed with gimp placed across the body.

New Material: 'Pereale taffeta or cambric sarcenet.'

Fashionable Colours: Ophelia, violet, marigold, drab, emerald, chestnut, dark blue. Mixed colours such as a straw-coloured dress with mauve flounces; a bright green dress with plaided bands of poppy, yellow and white, worn with a pink bonnet.

NOTE: the robe Gabrielle, made without a seam at the waist, requiring eighteen to twenty yards of material, worn without a band, but two or three buttons are placed at the back of the waist and a row down the front.

The zouave jacket worn by young ladies. Of coloured silk made without a back seam, slit under the arms and rounded in front; edges trimmed with puffed muslin; fastened at the throat only and worn over a full chemisette with bishop sleeves.

Evening

The bodice cut off the shoulders, with a bertha of lace, or with bretelle-capes enclosing a stomacher which is covered with lace; short puffed sleeve, or double puffed.

The skirt, either double, with lines of puffing up to the knee, or the single skirt with three flounces heavily trimmed with lace. Sometimes an upper skirt open in front à la robe.

OUTDOOR GARMENTS

Cloaks and Mantles

Cloaks and mantles are very ample with long and wide sleeves, usually with a fringed pelerine-cape in place of the hood; trimming with ruches à la vieille are common.

The Victoria mantle, of grey cloth with a deep coloured border, cut round and nearly to the knees; a falling collar cut into dents each with a tassel; wide hanging sleeves.

Casaques, with large hanging 'Sultana' sleeves (slit open in front) and a cape, are fashionable, and also the Burnouse-mantle, in the shape of the Talma.

Shawls

Especially those of black lace, and 'large chessboard-looking black and white woollen shawls'; Glasgow shawls, 'when folded the lower point is rounded, the upper pointed and finished with a tassle; border and upper corner plaided'.

Summer shawls and scarves of the same material as the dress (organdy, grenadine, de laine, light silk).

NOTE: An attempt is made to render light materials non-inflammable by soaking them in a solution of zinc chloride.

ACCESSORIES

Gloves

Day, of yellow Swedish leather, lavender kid, Saxony, etc.

Shoes
Day. Elastic-sided boots. Evening shoes with or without small heels and rosettes.

The Watteau Port-jupe; to render the skirt, in walking, more manageable a new device was introduced: a ribbon-covered wire loop with a broad ribbon attached which hooks at the waist; a concealed buckle shortens the ribbon **at** will; a fold of skirt is passed into the loop to save having to hold it up in the hand.

Prices
French armures, 32/6; checked poult de soie, 35/3; new tartan flounced silks, 70/6; moiré, 58/6; broché double skirts, 75/6; all, the dress of 12 yards.

The Little Dorrit check silk, 29/6; mohairs, 10/6 to 18/6. The three flounced llama dress, trimmed with velvet, 10/9. The new rep mohairs, 8/9; the new striped winseys, 10/6; droguet plaids, 25/9 to 39/6 the dress.

Seaside dress of glacé linen, looking almost as glossy as silk, 14/9.
Satin reps, 32/6; brocaded silks, 39/6; moiré, 58/6.
The fashionable ten flounce silk dress, 3 guineas.
The new zouave jacket for evening wear, 21/-.
In Lyons velvet, 2–3 guineas.
The Solferino plush tie with rings, 2/6.
Jet trimmings, $\frac{1}{2}$ inch wide, $1\frac{3}{4}$d. a yard. Jet fringe, 1 inch wide, $3\frac{3}{4}$d. a yard.
'Linsey petticoats, scarlet, violet, and all fashionable colours.'
White alpaca jupons for ball dresses.
The Victoria crinoline lined with flannel, 25/-.
Watch-spring petticoats, 4/9 to 25/-.
White braid and tulle bonnets, 12/6.
Hair nets, chenille, 1/9 to 5/11. Gold and silver nets, 1/9; ditto with coloured beads, 2/6.

HEADGEAR IN THE '50's

1850

HAIR

Front parting with loops over the ears, or side ringlets. 'Now every style of coiffure is worn at once and the back hair plaited with a variety of forms that were formerly never thought of.'

COIFFURE

Day
Caps very small and worn far back, often with floating ribbons behind. Usually the fanchon shape, of lace with coloured ribbon bows on each side, fastened by large pins with coral heads.

Evening
Wreath or headdress of fruit and leaves descending on the shoulders. Comb at the back. Petit bords and ornamental hair nets often worn.

OUTDOORS

Bonnets with the brim meeting round the face and rather open, worn more horizontally. Inside, a fulling of tulle or flowers against the cheeks, and outside a feather or trailing flowers, etc. Short bavolet.
Materials: felt, velvet, terry, fancy and coloured straws.

1851

HAIR

Unchanged, except that ringlets are less usual; generally waved bandeaux with central parting.

COIFFURE

Day
Caps. 'The most fashionable shape for small blonde caps is the fanchon in the form of a half handkerchief with small bouquets of flowers on each side.'

Evening
Wreaths, etc., as before, and headdresses of the Marie Stuart shape. Petits bords, with open crown or net work, the front raised on one side, descending on the other, worn with a plume.

OUTDOORS

Bonnets. Fronts still large and open, the crowns round, low and small; capotes and drawn bonnets are common. The bavolet somewhat larger.

1852

HAIR

With centre parting and sides elaborately waved, or hair drawn back off the face. Ringlets have disappeared.

1857
Morning dress of green silk; Marie Antoinette fichu
Carriage dress of violet silk; double skirt; jacket body

1858
Robe of lilac taffeta trimmed with black velvet
Robe of green taffeta; double skirt

1850

1. *Young Lady's Country Costume.* Hat of Italian straw, à la paysanne, decorated with streamers of sapphire blue ribbon flowing below the waistline, and a cluster of white flowers placed on the right side of the low crown.

2. *Morning Dress.* Brussels net cap of a novel form, trimmed with rows of the same, festooned in lilac silk.

3. *Evening Dress.* Headdress of lappets and flowers.

4. *Promenade Costume.* Velvet bonnet of stone drab colour; quite plain with deep bavolet.

5. *Ball Dress.* Headdress of blue satin, trimmed with gold.

6. *Opera Costume.* Black velvet hat, edged with gold; feathers, shaded pink and white, droop on the right side.

1851

1. *Ball Dress.* Hair arranged with a wreath of small pink rose de motts, with a marabout feather at each end.

2. *Promenade Costume.* Capote of white lace lined with pale blue silk; brim large and open; bavolet or curtain of silk, edged with lace; interior ornamented with pale roses.

3. *Morning Dress.* Cap of white lace, trimmed round the back part with four rows of narrow white lace, finished on each side with a bow and ends of pink ribbon, with loops on each side of the face.

4. *Morning Costume.* Cap of lace 'à la Marie Stuart'.

5. *Morning Costume.* Headdress of hair.

6. *Promenade Dress.* Chapeau of white crepe, embroidered with straw round the edge of the front and in two rows on the bavolet, also round the fanchon over the crown; white and yellow roses on the side.

1. *Carriage Costume.* Bonnet of white satin, trimmed with black velvet; very low at each side are placed a white and black feather; the white feather turned up to lie on the front close to the edge, the black one droops; strings of broad pink satin.

2. *Front view of 1.* The interior edge of the brim lined with black velvet upon which is fluted a white satin lining; trimming consists of short loops of black velvet, below which are tufts of daisies and a narrow edging of blonde.

3. *Morning Dress.* Lace cap, trimmed with mulberry coloured ribbon, with a pink edge; loops of narrow pink velvet ornament the sides of the cheeks.

4. *Dinner Costume.*

5. *Evening and Dinner Costume.*

6. *Dinner and Evening Costume.* Cap of Chantilly lace ornamented with pearls and velvet.

1853

1. *Evening Dress.*

2. *Promenade Costume.* Bonnet of fancy straw trimmed with black velvet; on the left side forward on the front are placed three poppies and two more at the bottom of the crown above the curtain; inside is a cap of blonde with loops of black velvet and small poppies.

3. *Morning Costume.* Fanchon cap of lace, trimmed with blue ribbon.

4. *Carriage Costume.* Bonnet formed of rows of white blonde, each row headed by a piping of blue satin; a blue and white shaded feather is placed low at the left side; small blue flowers ornament the interior.

5. *Promenade Costume.* Transparent bonnet covered with blonde and trimmed with blue; low at each side are placed blue roses and bunches of fruit.

6. *Evening Costume.*

1854

1. *Carriage or Promenade Costume.* Drawn bonnet of green silk with curtain and double fanchon of black lace. On the front edge is white blonde and plaiting of green silk, with a very narrow ruche of black lace in the centre; blonde cap with small white flowers; broad strings edged with narrow lace.

2. *Promenade Costume.* Black velvet bonnet covered plain; broad pink ribbon striped with black velvet across the top and a full blown rose placed low at each side; front edge trimmed with narrow black blond; blond cap trimmed with loops of velvet and roses; broad pink satin strings.

3. *Promenade Dress.* Bonnet of lavender silk, covered plain and trimmed with narrow velvet and broad black lace; a large full blown rose at the edge of the front on the right side; blonde cap with rosebuds; strings of very broad pink ribbon.

4. *Evening Dress.*

5. *Carriage or Promenade Dress.* Bonnet of purple satin and black lace; roses and buds at edge of front on each side, below which is a broad lace sewn to the edge of front, forming a fall at each side; cap of white tulle and broad strings of white satin ribbon.

6. *Dinner Costume for Home.* Blonde cap trimmed with amber satin ribbon.

1855

1. *Ball or Opera Costume.*

2. *Costume for Home.*

3. *Carriage Costume.* Bonnet of paille de riz, à la Marie Stuart, with blue and white feathers; blonde cap with small blue flowers.

4. *Carriage Costume.* Bonnet of paille de riz, trimmed with pale blue satin; a shaded blue and white feather and flowers ornament the left side; edge of front finished by a blonde which is turned back at the top.

5. *Carriage Costume.* Bonnet of white chip, trimmed with lace and flowers. Blonde cap with small roses.

6. *Evening and Opera Costume.* Blonde headdress with feathers on the left side.

199

1. *Promenade Costume.* Bonnet of paille d'Italie, trimmed with black velvet, with roses at each side and cap of fullings of tulle.

2. *Morning Costume for Home.*

3. *Promenade Costume.* Bonnet of pink silk, trimmed with black lace and small pink feathers.

4. *Evening Costume.*

5. *Evening Costume.*

6. *Dinner Costume.*

1857

1. *Promenade Costume.* Hat of blue silk with black lace round the edge, trimmed in front with black velvet and on the right side with a blue and black feather; at each side under the brim are small blue flowers.

2. *Promenade Costume.* Bonnet of Napoleon blue velvet with deep curtain lined with very stiff net and with lace set on full at the edge; bonnet trimmed entirely round with blue feather trimming; blonde caps with loops of blue chenille.

3. *Morning Costume.* Cap of embroidered muslin trimmed with narrow velvet and pink ribbons.

4. *Carriage Costume.* White silk hat with broad blonde at the edge; at the left side a pink and white feather and roses; broad white strings with roses at the top.

5. *Evening Costume.* Headdress of pink ribbon forming fanchon, long ends left floating at the back; trimmed with a fringe and has a rose at each side.

6. *Morning Costume.* Cap of pink spotted tulle with deep double curtain.

1858

1. *Carriage Costume.* Bonnet of white and pink velours épinglé, ornamented with white blonde and feathers; tulle cap with tresse of roses; strings of white velvet with pink stripe at the edge.

2. *Ball Costume.*

3. *Carriage or Promenade Costume.* Mousquetaire hat of white plush lined with blue and edged with a narrow white lace; at the bottom of the crown is a band of blue velvet; across the front and on the left side of the hat are puffs of blue and white velvet ribbon; at the right side a long blue and white feather; rosettes and strings of blue and white velvet ribbon.

4. *Morning Costume.* Cache-peigne and lappets of black lace.

5. *Seaside Costume.* Capulet or hood of the finest cashmere, lined with silk and edged with a very narrow black velvet.

6. *Promenade Costume.* Bonnet of paille de riz, trimmed with black lace and pink and white shaded feathers; cap of full tulle with rose and buds; broad white strings edged with pink.

1859

1. *Promenade Costume.* Bonnet of white silk with deep fanchon of spotted net; tresse of mauve flowers.

2. *Seaside Costume.* Mousquetaire hat of brown straw with wreath of poppies and wild flowers; black lace falling round the edge.

3. *Country or Seaside Costume.* Hat of Italian straw called the 'Diana Vernon'; green feather; green rosettes under the brim and broad strings.

4. *Home Costume.* A cap of white tulle, the crown covered by black spotted tulle and surrounded by black lace; double border of white blonde very full at the sides with roses without foliage; a light green ribbon divides the black and white lace and forms floating strings; a large rose is placed low at the side of the crown on the left side; on the right are green bows.

5. *Dinner Costume.* Headdress a résille of cerise velvet and black lace ruche, long floating strings of cerise ribbon.

6. *Promenade Costume.* Bonnet of white chip with black velvet curtain; broad pink ribbon laid across the head terminated at the left side by a group of roses, and on the right by a rosette with rose in the centre; tulle cap with broad pink strings.

COIFFURE

Day

Caps smaller and worn still further back on the head.

Evening

Lace caps with long lappets, or ribbons or trailing flowers worn far back, at the sides.

OUTDOORS

Bonnets. The inside of the brim is more elaborately trimmed, often all round. Drawn bonnets and Leghorns are usual. The ribbon strings very broad; the size of the bonnets smaller and they are worn further back on the head. In the summer capuches, or sunbonnets, of muslin lined with coloured silk, are fashionable.

1853

HAIR

Centre parting, waved and somewhat puffed at the sides, being drawn back off the face. A twisted knot at the back.

COIFFURE

Day

Caps (of alternate rows of tulle and coloured ribbon) very small, and worn far back, with side rosettes.

Evening

Caps covered with flowers, with long bows at the sides; or a wreath with trailing flowers on the nape of the neck.

OUTDOORS

Bonnets with very low crowns, very open and short at the sides and worn far back. The inside of the brim excessively trimmed with blonde, flowers, velvet, or ribbon. Some without crown or bavolet.

'The bonnets are smaller than ever; they can scarcely be called bonnets; they are little coiffures of blonde, flowers and feathers, placed on the back of the head, and kept on, not by the strings but by great pins or by the springs lately invented.'

1854

HAIR

Centre parting and waved bandeaux, a twisted knot behind with a couple of short curls trailing on the neck. Hair in the Marie Stuart style is fashionable. 'Frizzed hair puffs fastened to side combs are placed under the natural hair.'

COIFFURE

Day

Caps unchanged.

Evening

Wreaths are small and worn far back with trailing ends on the neck.

OUTDOORS

Bonnets very flat on the crown and worn very far back; usually of the capote or drawn variety; trimmed lavishly under the brim, especially at the sides. Bonnets were compared to 'a horse's hoof'. 'They can hardly be called bonnets; they are made of a happy confusion of filmy gauze, blonde and tulle mingled with flowers and ribbons so delicately put together that it looks like fairies' handiwork.' We find the first reference to *Uglies*, an extra brim worn in front to protect the face from the sun (see drawing for 1862).

1855

HAIR

As before. The Marie Stuart style common. A few wear the hair in a chignon and hair net.

COIFFURE

Day

The day Cap, having become smaller and smaller, is now frequently omitted, and in its place a ribbon twisted into the hair, with floating ends on the neck, is used.

Evening

Trailing flowers, the ends hanging down behind.

OUTDOORS

Bonnets very small, the crowns sloping backwards, the front often in the Marie Stuart style; bavolets are deeper, and trimmings of flowers, lace and fruit are lavish. Materials are mainly flimsy.

A velvet bandeau is often worn in front of the bonnet to hold it in place.

An important innovation is the introduction of the *Straw Hat*, 'the size of a moderate sized umbrella, with strings attached to the front by which the brim can be drawn down. During the Queen's late visit to Paris several (English) young ladies made their appearance in this headdress; everybody turned to look, thunder-struck by the high-jinks of the costume.' And 'we lately saw two of them stuck fast in the narrow passage of Little Turnstile and impeded the thoroughfare for at least five minutes'.

1856

HAIR

With puffed bandeaux at the sides, and rolls at the back with trailing ends hanging on the neck as ringlets.

COIFFURE

Day
Caps when worn are very small and far back.
Evening
No wreath, but a narrow velvet band across the crown; flowers and lace hanging behind.

OUTDOORS

Bonnets very small and worn far back; always lined under the brim with a white frill, so that from in front this may resemble the edge of a cap, the bonnet being out of sight. The bavolet is lined with stiff muslin, pleated. The ribbon ends fall over the shoulders. The colours used in the trimmings of bonnets are strongly contrasting.
A fanchon of lace over the crown is common.
In place of an inside trimming of white, a tulle cap is often worn under the bonnet.
'Little spotted *Veils* are all the rage.'

1857

HAIR

Smoothly puffed at the sides with coiled knot behind, or coiled round the back of the head.

COIFFURE

Day
No caps. 'Young married ladies need not wear caps until they have acquired the endearing name of "Mother".'
Evening
Ornamental hair net worn far back, or narrow wreath with profusion of flowers at the back and lace fanchons or ribbons hanging on the neck. Small evening caps (dinner) worn far back.

OUTDOORS

Bonnets 'continue of very small size; the trimming is so profuse that the material composing the bonnet itself is entirely lost sight of.' Made of rice straw, lace, taffeta, crepe and tulle, with feathers, flowers and blonde. The ribbons wide, and often of chiné silk. Often of the Marie Stuart shape. The bavolet very deep and lined with stiff muslin, with a ribbon bow. A blonde or tulle cap with flowers at the sides worn under. During the year the bonnet makes a definite move forward and the front begins to rise. Often of two different colours and materials.
Hats become extremely fashionable, *e.g.* 'large round hats, covered with tussore silk, trimmed with a ribbon and bow on one side; the string fastened under the brim by ribbon rosettes' (for summer).
'A hat of blue silk with black lace hanging from the edge.'
'As hats are more adopted we shall expect to see our countrywomen assume their wonted beautiful complexions instead of the weather-beaten appearance they have had lately caused by exposure of the face to wind and sun.'

1858

HAIR

As before, or strained back and coiled above the nape of the neck, with a hanging curl.

COIFFURE

Day
A lace fanchon or ribbons are often worn at the back of the head, descending on to the neck.
Evening
Flowers, etc., as before.

OUTDOORS

Bonnets worn more forward; the bavolet moderately deep and set on in double pleats; a broad strip of velvet in one or two folds may be placed across the upper part of the crown, with short rounded ends hanging loosely on each side. A tulle cap with frilled edge is generally worn under the bonnet.
The Mousquetaire *Hat* remains in fashion.
For summer (seaside) use, the Capulet, or hood of cashmere with deep bavolet, and the garden hat, of white muslin with domed crown, are very fashionable.

1859

HAIR

Worn massed at the back, with the sides slightly puffed. Or in waved bandeaux at the sides, the back hair worn low. This fashion leads to the introduction of the Cachepeigne, or headdress containing the mass of hair at the back. It can be constructed, for example, of a piece of stiff black net, ribbon wire and three yards of ribbon; the latter is made into six or eight loops hanging down behind, attached to the net, which is held in place by the wire which curves over the crown of the head.

Bonnets, the front brought forward but open at the sides, the under side of brim fully trimmed; the bavolet short. Owing to the increase in size there is a return to straw as a material. In some the front of the bonnet is slightly pointed. The inside cap is generally omitted. Summer *Hats* remain in fashion.

UNDERCLOTHING

White underclothing in this decade did not materially alter from that of the preceding period, but there was a tendency to increase the trimming which in some quarters called for reproof. Thus we read: 'I am of opinion that the less trimming there is on underlinen the more ladylike it appears.' A chemise dated 1857, in my collection, is as severe as could be wished, and does not differ materially from the designs in use twenty or thirty years previously. It is instructive to learn that an industrious young lady could make for herself half a dozen each of good plain chemises, drawers, petticoats, and nightdresses for £1 18 0½. The chemise and petticoats should be 1¼ yards long, the drawers 1⅛, and the nightdress 1¼. If these *must* be trimmed a scalloped edging is best, and for chemises a crochet edging. 'They should be neatly marked in red cotton, not ink, which is an invention for the idle only.' 'One of the prevailing fashions for ornamental underskirts is the introduction of embroidered insertion between rows of tucks'; while guipure and frivolité lace are much used for collars, sleeves, etc.

Ready made prices. 1851. Longcloth nightdress, 2/6; chemises, 12/- to 16/- a dozen; drawers, 13/6 to 16/6 a dozen; nightcaps, 6/- to 10/- a dozen. In 1854 the prices had risen. Chemises (longcloth) plain, 2/9; richly trimmed, 3/9 each. Drawers (longcloth) plain, 2/-; richly trimmed, 3/6. Frilled nightdresses (longcloth) plain, 3/6; richly trimmed, 7/6. Irish guipure collars, 3/6 to 4/6; undersleeves, 9/9 to 10/9. Silk stockings (1852) 2/6 a pair; in 1854, 6/6. In 1859, after the reduction in the duty on foreign silks, 3/6 a pair. White cotton stockings, 6/9 to 10/6 a dozen; Balbriggan stockings (1854) 2/6 a pair.

Stockings

for morning were of fine cotton with clocks; for evening, silk or Lisle thread. Garters were of elastic with metal clasps.

Petticoats

The number of petticoats, before the introduction of the artificial crinoline, remained as in the previous decade, but the horsehair article was falling into disuse. 'The stiff jupon is still worn but very much diminished in all its dimensions' (1852). Sometimes it was enforced by three or four rolls at the bottom to hold out the dress, especially for evening dresses, while as an alternative the skirt of the dress itself might be lined in its lower part with crinoline. The quilted petticoat, for winter use, appeared early in the decade. This may be made of satin or alpaca and

1859
Home dress of grey silk; double skirt; mandarin sleeves
Dress of brown silk; trimmed with ruching
Dress of blue poplin cut en princesse

1853

1855

1856

1859

lined with wadding. Under petticoats were stiffly starched, while under the ball dress a stiff book muslin petticoat with a cambric one over it, was common. By such means an effort was being made to reduce the heat and burden of the day, and especially of the night devoted to dancing. We even read of 'gauze underclothing' for summer, while 'ladies' invisible underclothing' leaves much to the imagination. On the other hand, merino and lambs' wool vests and drawers are advertised for winter use (1856).

We find the bustle still advertised in 1854, but its use disappeared with the arrival of the hooped petticoat or artificial crinoline, first advertised in the autumn of 1856. 'Flannel lined crinoline skirts, 12/6; the Royal winsey scarlet petticoat 10/6 to 12/6.' And in December, the 'Parisian Eugénie Jupon Skeleton Petticoat, 6/6 to 25/-.' In the next year 'the new Paris watch-spring crinoline skirt, 25/- to 31/6' indicated a great advance on those made of whalebone and wire. 'Air tube skirts, 16/-', 'Lindsey woolsey flounced petticoats with steel springs', and 'the Victoria crinoline lined with flannel', 25/- were permissible alternatives.

We read, in 1857, 'it is impossible to make any dress sit well without the hoop petticoat. This should consist of four narrow steels; that nearest the waist should be four nails from it and be $1\frac{3}{4}$ yards long; the other three should be $2\frac{1}{2}$ yards long and placed—one at six nails from the upper steel, the other two each two nails from the second steel. None must meet in front by $\frac{1}{4}$ yard, except the one nearest the waist.' (1 nail—$2\frac{1}{4}$ inches). Already in 1859 there were rumours of the decline of the crinoline in fashionable quarters, at least as regards its front.

The use of the cage was by no means universal; for instance, we read, in 1858, 'many ladies of the highest taste and fashion wear four or five skirts of starched muslin, some with and some without flounces' in place of it. On the other hand a contemporary tells us: 'Your ladies' maid must now need have her crinoline and it has even become essential to factory girls.' The prevalence of the fashion can be gathered from the statement that in 1859 Sheffield was turning out enough crinoline wire a week for half a million crinolines.

Corsets

'The age of stiff stays has departed, and the modern élégante wears stays with very little whalebone in them, if they wear any at all' (1850). We are recommended 'the Corset Amazone' 'which by the aid of elastic lacings yields to every respiration, and by pulling a concealed cord can be shortened three inches, for riding.' Nursing corsets are provided 'for ladies fulfilling the dearest office of maternity', in which the withdrawal of two bones removes an entire gusset.

On the other hand, we are offered '100 patterns of Stays for Ladies and 50 for children, 7/- for eighteen inch waist, rising 6d an inch.' Stays with front fastenings were shown at the Great Exhibition of 1851, and towards the end of the decade had become usual. Thus in 1857 'stays with patent front fastenings, 8/6 to 15/6; family stays 8/6 to 21/-.' With the shortening waist towards the close of the decade the corset followed suit.

CHAPTER VII
THE '60's

———

THE prominent feature in this decade was unquestionably the skirt—and the remarkable sub-structures by which it was supported. Although the maximum size of the crinoline had already been reached by 1860, and in the main the decade marked a steady decline, there was no falling off of interest in that part of the costume. A brief phase of gored skirts was quickly succeeded by the development of the pannier-puff and the recrudescence of the crinoline under a new name and shape, the crinolette, while the puff required the revival of the bustle in 1868. Equally notable was the introduction of the 'double skirt' type of dress, affording opportunity for the use of two colours.

The decade actually provides three phases; at first the lingering influence of the former Gothic angularity of shape, followed by a short attempt to restore the 'Empire' mode, at least as regards the high waist. There was, however, no real desire to return to the classical principles and we may attribute this sham 'Empire' to the political influence of the French Court under Napoleon III. In spite of that attempt the natural course of change proved irresistible; the angle was destined to give place to the curve. By the end of the decade the epoch of curves was fully established.

All through these ten years the bulk of the skirt was steadily moving towards the rear, there to become more and more bulky and ballooned. Almost equally significant was the emergence of the feet and ankles from their concealment. Women were beginning to walk once more. The looped-up dresses with the singular display of many-coloured petticoats, calculated to draw attention to the ankles, proved to be extraordinarily fascinating to the male sex, and many a victory was won by neat footwork on the croquet lawns of England. The upper half of the dress lacked inspiration until, towards the close of the decade, the practice of tight-lacing revived the allurement of the 'figure'.

The change of taste in colours cannot be attributed merely to the introduction of aniline dyes. From the middle of the decade for the rest of the century the principle of contrasting colours, often violently so, was usual. In the second half of the '60's we find experiments with not only two colours but also with two materials.

The significance of this change has been discussed in *Feminine Attitudes in the Nineteenth Century*.

The prices given in the Annual Notes indicate a steady rise; and as the wardrobe of the average woman was also increasing, the economic effect was considerable. There was a growing complaint of 'feminine extravagance.' 'At the seaside most ladies change their costume four times a day.' The development of the 'walking dress' as distinct from the 'afternoon dress' was an additional expense. 'For the morning two or three silk dresses are quite enough, and among them should be a black silk,' is the advice given in 1868.

TECHNICAL FEATURES

Practically all dresses are machine-sewn (lock-stitch). The workmanship is usually good. The bodice is always lined, generally with white calico; many day skirts are unlined except for ten inches of book muslin at the bottom, but a number are lined throughout with crinoline or stiff muslin; perhaps those worn by women who did not succumb to the crinoline-cage vogue (of whom there were many). The usual large inside pocket and small watch pocket are the rule in day dresses.

Bodices have small bones extending a few inches up from the waist in front, and up to six inches at the sides. Pointed basques are specially boned. A basque is no longer cut in one piece with the bodice.

All day dresses have braided hems.

A remarkable variety of buttons are used; of glass, oxydised silver, and silk covered.

Hungarian cord trimming is a feature of about 1867. Other forms of trimming are described under the Annual Notes.

The use of shot silks and a wealth of new textiles from the middle of the decade onwards are noteworthy.

For the first time underclothing becomes an important part of the costume, at least to the spectator, and the notes on that subject will indicate the various forms, especially of the petticoat, crinoline,[1] etc. The quality of the material and trimmings used shows marked improvement, with, as a great innovation, the use of coloured fabrics for these garments.

As regards the head the extraordinary development of the chignon and the general use of hats in place of bonnets help to make this decade revolutionary, and the audacious appearance of 'the Girl of the Period' aroused a widespread alarm.

[1]Examination of a thousand contemporary photographs of this decade shows that only the ultra-fashionable wore the huge crinoline indicated in fashion-plates; actually the average crinoline was not so very unwieldy. An interesting photograph in the possession of Messrs. Bryant & May shows their women employees in crinolines while at work. My own collection also reveals that the 'bishop sleeve' was far more general, in the early '60's, than the fashion books indicate.

1860

'Crinoline no longer reigns supreme as it did last Spring' was the rumour at the beginning of this year, but it was certainly not yet dethroned. In fact, whatever may have been the mode of Empresses and their circle, for ordinary Englishwomen the crinoline continued unabated in size not merely this year but for at least two or three more. Nevertheless the first signs of a change can be detected, for in this year the skirt, both for day and evening, began to be slightly gored at the sides. 'One breadth on each side is sloped two inches at the bottom; five or six pleats are set in on each side of the front and three or four box pleats behind.' The effect would be, of course, to flatten the front of the skirt, so that the crinoline would have to be altered in shape to fit. This practical detail is of importance to those who try to fit one of these dresses over an earlier form of crinoline; it will not hang properly. The new modification led to the fashion for dresses with bodice and skirt in one, without a waist seam (the 'Isabeau style').

A still more important innovation this year was the general use of the two first aniline dyes, magenta and solferino; specimens of the latter tint, I find, match best with the 'fuschia' of the B.C.C. No. 199. The novelty was so much admired that magenta was used for dresses, petticoats, bonnets and stockings, as well as ribbons, etc.; it was described as 'the queen of colours'.

From now on an increasing number of dresses were made by lock-stitch machine sewing.

The Garibaldi jacket, of scarlet cashmere with military trimmings of gold braid, was hailed as 'the gem of the season', and the hero was still further rewarded by having his name attached to a biscuit. It is by such means that great men become immortal.

DRESSES

Day

1. Bodice high and buttoned in front; narrow falling collar of embroidery.

2. Bodice plain, or with a little fullness (for muslins, etc.); collar of one inch insertion made seven inches longer than the size of the neck so as to cross in front, and fastened with a brooch. Sometimes a narrow cravat worn.

3. Bodice en demi-cœur or open to the waist with revers, worn over a chemisette (Summer).

4. Bodice à la Raphael (high behind and low in front and square cut); a little fichu of tulle or dress material.

Sleeves

1. Plain tight sleeve with epaulette or small puff below the shoulder, or a single puffing down the outer side of the arm.

2. The small bishop sleeve, epaulette and cuff (for light materials).

3. The Gabrielle sleeve, a series of puffings all down to the wrist.

4. Open sleeve, especially the Isabeau sleeve, triangular in shape, the apex at the shoulder, and widely open below; made with an inner and outer seam.

Skirt. Plain or with tablier trimming, or a few narrow flounces at the bottom. Summer materials flounced with nine flounces in groups of three. Double skirts, the first with a deep pleated flounce, the second often open in front en tunic. With heavy materials the skirt is always gored at the sides and box-pleated behind. Occasionally there are two front pockets edged with ruching.

The Isabeau style: bodice and skirt in one without a seam at the waist, a line of buttons (often macarons) or rosettes all down the front. Occasionally a plastron trimming from the neck to the bottom of the skirt. Shaped to the figure by goring.

The robe à la soutane, similar but not shaped in at the waist.

A variation is the long casaque, of the same

1862

1861

1862

1864

1861. Ball dresses
Of sea-green glacé; a Greek pattern in pink taffeta above tulle puffing
Of apricot silk with lace bertha and flounce
Of white tarlatan; double skirts flounced with black lace

material as the dress, reaching below the knee, worn over a dress made with bodice and skirt in one.

The Manon robe: the fronts cut in one piece; the back with a seam at the waist and a broad double pleating commencing under the collar and flowing loosely to the bottom of the skirt in the style of a 'Watteau pleat'. One deep flounce at the bottom of the skirt.

Dresses without a seam at the waist are always of silks, and have a broad band of pleating, of a contrasting colour, round the bottom.

NOTE: With separate bodices the waist is short and round, and with light materials a ribbon ceinture with floating ends in front is worn, or a waistband and small buckle of steel, mosaic or aluminium. Some waistbands are of gilt leather. A definite 'seaside' costume begins to be differentiated from others by its material (piqué) and comparative ease; e.g., a deep jacket and plain piqué skirt, and sash with ribbon ends, worn with a puffed chemisette and high piqué collar, and cravat (of silk, one inch wide, edged with black lace); while the Garibaldi jacket can be worn over a muslin dress on such occasions. The zouave jacket, worn over a chemisette, with a light skirt, is also appropriate.

Evening

Bodice. Slightly pointed in front, either draped across with folds or with a bertha; cut low off the shoulders, or en demi-cœur and edged with ribbon ruching.

Sleeves. A short puffing, or double puff, with lace fall.

Skirt. As in the previous year, that is, either double with lines of puffing up to the knee, or a single skirt with three flounces, trimmed with lace; or a single skirt trimmed en tablier. Muslin dresses with seven to nine flounces.

Ball Dresses. Corsage with a long point, cut square and low off the shoulders, or à l'enfant; skirt double or treble, the upper two caught up with ribbon bows; or skirt with one deep flounce under an open tunic.

The satin underskirt, with tulle and muslin dresses, is a revival. Ball dresses of white moiré, with one deep lace flounce and a lace tunic above, are fashionable.

All the evening skirts are slightly gored at the sides.

Materials (Day). Poplin de laine in large plaids. Reps with wide vertical stripes, Nankin, piqué, Pekin velvets in broad stripes, spotted taffetas, foulard de laine, mousselaine de laine, as well as the usual fabrics.

New Materials: Turin velvet, velvet Impératrice.
Fashionable Colours: magenta, solferino, Azoff green, Havannah, Eugénie blue.

OUTDOOR GARMENTS

Cloaks

The cloak is now enormous in size, with wide sleeves; the 'Maintenon', of black velvet, with a broad flounce put on in broad pleats and embroidered in the form of a shawl, with a trimming of black guipure over the flounce; the casaque-mantlet, descending below the knee, fastening down the front and defining the figure, the sleeves of the Isabeau shape.

Mantles

Some mantlets are shaped round the shoulders with three large box-pleats set in which run down to the waist in front and behind. The burnouse, with hood, continues fashionable. Shorter garments are the zouave jacket (of velvet or cashmere with gold braid), and the Garibaldi.

Shawls

Shawls, especially of black maltese lace, and of black grenadine with lace edging. 'To meet the necessities of the mode vast cashmere shawls bordered with silk and edged with gimp and lace have been manufactured—colours, blue, black and white.'

NOTE: The duty on French silks and cambrics just removed.

Prices

The new striped, checked and chiné mohairs, 5/6 the dress of 12 yards.
Evening dresses in soie de fées (fire-proof) 10/6 to 60/-.
Broché double skirt silk dresses 3½ guineas.
French foulards, 17/6 the dress of 19 yards.
Swiss cambrics, 3/9; French ditto, 5/-, seven flounced muslins, 10/6—all the full dress.
Rich flounced challis robes, 20 yards, 16/9 to 27/6. Rich silk poplinettes, 29/6; best French barèges, 8/9; best British balzarines, 5/9; broché balzarines, 10/6; grenadines, 18/6; corded piqués, 7/6; flounced barège robes, evening, 20 to 22 yards, 18/9; broché Pompadour silks, 57/6; Pekin moirés, £5; richest moiré antiques, 4½ guineas; Scotch winseys, 9/- to 21/-; the new droguet dress, from 17/6; tartan droguet, 18/9 to 31/6; French merinos, 12/6; Poplin droguet, 40/-; the magenta poplin made-up dress, 1½ guineas. All the full dress (readymade skirt and material for bodice).
Rich Spitalfields silks, 4/4 a yard.

The Garibaldi striped silk, 2/6 a yard.

Seaside readymade muslin, mohair, Hollands, dresses at 6/6.

Seaside readymade embroidered piqué with jacket, remarkably ladylike, 18/9.

French organdies, the new fuschine, magenta and mauve colours.

Zouave jacket, half fitting in front, with a coquettish little basque at the back, 15/- to 21/-.

The guinea sealskin paletot. The new magenta camlet, trimmed with velvet, 21/-. Imitation sealskin paletots, 35/- to 65/-.

Thickest chenille hair nets, 2/11. Gilt clasps for waistband, 1/- to 2/6. Silk velvet waistbands with gilt clasp, 1/1½.

Chenille hair nets with stars, rings, coins, etc.— 5 dozen on each net, 4/11; cotton ditto, for bathing, 6½d.

Muffs, ermine, 10/6 to 25/-; sable, 1 to 5 guineas.

Frizettes on shell combs for raised bandeaux, 5/6 a pair.

Glacé silk mantles with large sleeves and full skirts, 2 guineas.

18 hoop watch-spring petticoat with silk band and tapes, 16/6; nine hoop jupon, 5/-.

'Rouge superseded by Oriental Schnouda which raises in a few minutes a beautiful and natural bloom on the cheeks, 2/6.'

The new 'Cage Empire' crinoline in all colours. Sewing-machines for Xmas presents, £4 10 0; the lock-stitch machine, £10.

French straw bonnets, 12/6 to 18/6. Full dress Paris chips, 21/-.

NOTE: As a result of the French treaty admitting foreign ribbons duty free an increase of 56,000 lbs. of foreign ribbons in four months was imported, producing a falling off of three quarters of the Coventry ribbon trade.

1861

The increasing activity displayed by women caused a growing simplicity in the day dress. 'Any trimming which conceals the figure or heightens or widens the shoulders is in execrable taste.' At the same time walking was made more possible, in spite of the crinoline, by further goring of the skirt. 'Skirts should be made with two whole breadths at the back; the gores formed by cutting one breadth slantwise are about three nails wide on the top.' (5 nails = 1 foot). And trimmings in the form of frillings, either pinked or hemmed, are preferred to flounces, the skirt being demi-trained.

'The rage for wearing long dresses often renders it necessary to raise the skirt as far as the ankle allowing the petticoat to be seen.' Hence the need for the elaborate petticoat, of all materials such as cashmere, taffeta, rep, alpaca, etc., embroidered or enriched with velvet. In summer the white petticoat for all but full dress 'has been discarded for one of alpaca made very full and gored with a band of velvet above the hem'. The walking skirt is caught up in order to reveal these charms; thus 'two loops of elastic on each side on the inner surface, with a small slit through which they can be drawn out and looped on to buttons attached just below the waist.' The crinoline itself is now frequently replaced by stiff muslin petticoats, flounced, 'which set out a dress (of thin material) in a more graceful manner than does a crinoline; a moderate sized steel petticoat and a muslin one, with, of course, a plain one over it, make a muslin dress look very nicely.' Or the alpaca petticoat with steel hoops sewn into it enabled the wearer to dispense with a separate crinoline.

Such changes, together with the growing fashion for wearing hats instead of bonnets for day use by the rising generation, coincided with a breaking away from passive domesticity. But it seems they were not yet prepared to sacrifice the dominating size of the skirt; 'in spite of the maledictions of husbands and fathers of families the dimensions of ladies' dresses are undergoing no diminution.' Nevertheless it seems that these changes were not recognised at the time for the wearers of fashions are hardly conscious of the first beginnings of a new mode. We find a contemporary remarking: 'dresses have not undergone the same modifications as bonnets, so that a robe of last year may still be worn without its wearer appearing behindhand in the march of elegance.'

DRESSES

Day

Bodice. High, buttoning down the front; the waist either round, with a ceinture, or pointed. Summer dresses, of thin materials, the bodice either high and full over a low plain one, or low with a fichu; white muslin bodice, full at the waist, worn with a Swiss corselet; or a low body without sleeves and gathered à la vierge worn with a chemisette with full bishop sleeves.

Some in the Agnes Sorel style, half-high, and cut square back and front, with full bishop sleeves. The high bodice is worn with a narrow scalloped falling collar, fastened with a large brooch. The 'corsage russe', of alternate bands of puffing and velvet, worn with a pointed velvet waistband; the sleeves puffed all the way up. NOTE: The white muslin bodice is frequently worn with a coloured skirt.

In place of a bodice the Garibaldi shirt, of bright scarlet merino braided in black with black buttons down the front, a narrow collar and black silk cravat, straps on the shoulders, and full sleeves gathered into a wristband, is fashionable with young women. It is worn with a Zouave jacket and a black silk skirt having a scarlet band at the bottom; the costume is completed by a black Tudor hat with scarlet feather and a scarlet hair net and scarlet stockings.

Sleeves. Either tight to the wrist with cuff, or bell-shaped and wide open if of rich materials. Full epaulettes on the shoulders.

Skirt. Much gored, *e.g.*, 'seven breadths joined nearly $\frac{2}{3}$rds of the seam down from the waist; in the lower third a gore of stiff muslin nearly $\frac{1}{2}$ yard wide at the widest is inserted on which is placed six flounces; a similar gore is inserted in the sleeves.' Often each breadth is piped with large pipings. The skirt is plain, with a band of velvet above the hem; some with pyramidal tablier or a row of buttons down the front.

Muslin dresses often with one deep goffred flounce headed by puffing, or a pleated heading, or several flounces.

The Isabeau style continues with, as a variation, the back of the dress cut in one piece but not the front.

Broad waistbands, some pointed above and below and laced in front, or closed by a buckle. With summer muslins a long duchesse sash ($2\frac{1}{2}$ yards × 9 ins.) with ends hanging at the side. Ceintures now of silk, velvet or gimp; the gilt and leather ones discarded.

A few 'promenade' dresses with open tunics.

Some summer dresses of nankeen with tight fitting caraco and waistcoat.

Evening

As in the previous year, but all have gored and demi-trained skirts.

The Swiss ceinture, of velvet, is common.

The waist is always pointed in front and often behind as well.

Ball dresses are 'of every form'; flounced and with or without double skirt; the waist either round, with a ceinture; pointed; or with a Swiss ceinture. They are profusely trimmed with lace and flowers.

Materials: Home and walking dresses. (Winter) Silks, droguets, linsey, satin. (Summer). Muslins, mohair, linen, grenadines, barège, foulard, nankeen, piqué.

Visiting dresses: Silks, poplins, merino, droguet, satin. (Evening). Silks, moirés, flowered taffeta, poplins, satins, barèges, muslins.

Fashionable Colours: Havannah, black and white, green, mauve, violet blue. Red for stockings, petticoats and gloves.

New Materials: Poil de chèvre, laine foulard. 'The new Coventry cambric frilling, with a gathering thread along one edge.'

OUTDOOR GARMENTS

Jackets

'The Zouave jacket is universally worn, in braided cloth or velvet.'

Outdoor jackets not quite fitting the waist; the redingote buttoning across from left to right. NOTE: Jackets are now called 'basquins'.

Cloaks

The Colleen Bawn cloak (of white grenadine, with a large cape caught up in the middle of the back with two rosettes).

Winter paletots and large sleeved cloaks, with large sleeves having revers on the shoulders and small capes. Summer paletots of linen, embroidered with coloured wool.

Pardessus, with large sleeves, either the Isabeau form, or the sultan (which is cut square, fulled into the armhole and left open the whole length). Tight fitting casaques with wide sleeves and a long skirt.

Mantles

Large Talma mantles. Mantles of velvet or drap velours, with passementerie on the shoulders.

Prices

Winter. Scotch linseys, 5/6; Scotch winseys, 8/6; honeycomb checks, 10/6; French merinos, 12/6; tartan droguets, 15/6; French reps, 17/6; brocaded droguets, 21/-; silks: checked poplinettes, 17/6; poult de soie, 35/6; brocaded silks, 42/-; pekin moirés, 63/-; satin reps, 29/6; bayadère bars, 27/6; rep mohairs, 10/6; richly printed silk challies, 23/6; gros de Suez, 45/-; laine foulard, 42/-; all the full dress.

Muslin dresses, jacconet, 2/11; organdy, 4/6; pompadour, 5/6; flounced muslin, 7/6 the dress. 'The fashionable morning dress of glacé linen, 12/9.'

Riding habits, 5½ to 8 guineas. Riding trousers, chamois leather with black feet, 21/-.

Mantle cloths, stout Melton, from 2/- a yard.

Colleen Bawn mantle, waterproof cloth, 21/-.

Shawls

Black Maltese lace, 10/6; black Spanish lace, 21/-; coloured silk, 18/6; cashmere embroidered, 21/-; llama, 10/6; mourning, quilted in crape, 18/9.

Gloves

Paris kid, two button, 1/6; one button, 1/- a pair; best 2/6.

Neckties, black, white, magenta, 3/6; Roman silk scarves, 1½ yards long by 6 inches wide, 4/6; velvet bonnet ribbons, 1/- to 2/- a yard.

Swiss belts, richly trimmed, 7/9; in Genoa velvet, 1/9½.

French sable muffs, 6/9 to 12/-; real sable, 1 to 5 guineas.

Invisible hair nets, 8½d. to 1/4½.

Petticoats, quilted silk, four yards wide, 20/-; quilted alpaca, 10/6.

Front fastening corsets, 3/6 to 4/6.

Quilted silk and cashmere chest-protectors, 6/6.

Garibaldi shirts, 6/6; brocaded silk tie to wear with same, 10d.

Hem-stitched handkerchiefs from 7/- to 22/6 a dozen.

Crinolines. 'The new Paris hair crinoline, light in weight, not easily broken, forms a bustle and is self-expansive, in white, 12/9; in magenta, 14/9.' Sansflectum, washable, 10/9 to 12/6. Watch-spring skeleton skirts at 6d a spring; 10/- for 20 springs. Horsehair crinolines, 8/6 to £2. Advertisements: 'Thomson's Crown Crinolines', and 'Belle of the Court' Crinoline in silk. 'The Cage Empire with upwards of 30 steel hoops increasing in width downwards.' 'Watchspring skeleton petticoats with 10 to 100 springs, 6/6 to 31/6.'

'Golden hair powder, now so fashionable.'

1862

The growing prosperity of the nation was encouraging the Englishwoman to develop styles of dress of her own, instead of meekly accepting the current French modes, which had been the custom of recent years. It is true that such borrowed plumes had generally been somewhat modified in detail to suit the English taste, but the crinoline dress had never been one in which the Englishwoman looked quite at home. She found it difficult to appear both enormous and chic; indeed, she was too apt to seem encumbered by its size. She accepted the goring as a necessary modification, but now she was devoting her attention, far more than the Frenchwoman, to the display of her petticoat. She may, indeed, claim to have introduced to her rival the delights of the scarlet flannel petticoat. We read that a State visit of the Empress enabled her ladies in waiting to ascertain the prevalence of this English mode. The coloured petticoat was far too ravishing to remain hid, so that the device of the hitched-up skirt became common. It is significant that the French fashion-plates of this year hardly give any of these dresses. Here, we learn, 'petti-

1861

1862

1863

1866

1866. Ball dresses
Of grey satin; tablier of pink satin with lace chevrons
Underskirt of white silk flounced with black lace; overskirt of blue silk
open on left side
Of white satin; green ribbon sash

coats are made of such varied hues that dresses looped over these have really an elegant and graceful appearance.' This will be readily understood by the statement 'bright colours are now being very much used for undergarments' (For the rest of the quotation see chapter on Underclothing).

Similarly, we find the English taste in bonnets was towards greater decoration, being so trimmed with flowers as to 'resemble a garden in full bloom' (a practice condemned by the French as bad taste), while their shape resembled 'porches covered with exotics'.

The English foot being in full view, at least in walking, brightly coloured shoes (blue, green, violet and scarlet) helped to draw attention in that direction. The growing liking for hats, when walking in summer, which had become 'indispensable for both married and single young ladies' also indicates that the Englishwoman had now definitely started on her long march towards freedom.

DRESSES

Day

Bodice. High and plain, buttoned down the front, worn either with a ceinture and clasp, or with a Swiss belt; or dress without waist-seam, usually trimmed en tablier. Pagoda or full bishop sleeve. With rich materials the sleeve is bell-shaped with mousquetaire cuff and engageantes. Towards the end of the year the

Tulle undersleeve. 1862

waistcoat body, with two points, and worn with a bolero jacket, is revived. Some bodices have a double point in front and a small postillion behind, and straight sides, with demi-closed sleeves shaped to the elbow.
Round waists are unusual until the summer.
Summer dresses have a low square-cut bodice with a chemisette.

White muslin dresses, for summer, are lined with coloured silk and worn with a sash knotted behind and arranged in a large flat bow. Also, in summer, pleated muslin bodice with insertion or lace inset, worn with a Medici band (made like a Swiss belt with narrow bands falling down the skirt on each side of the point, having

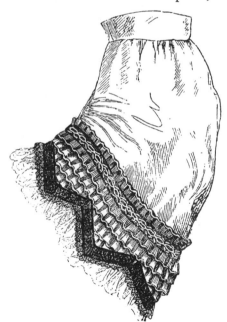

Tulle undersleeve with lace and insertion. 1862

small pockets inserted in the ends). Or the *chemise russe* (also called 'le veste'), resembling a tight-fitting waistcoat closed in front, of white or coloured cashmere, braided, often worn under a Zouave jacket. Also for summer use the caraco, or jacket with revers, closed at the top by three buttons, and shaped, with a basque; often of a different material from the skirt.

Summer Sleeves: for muslins, the full bishop, or the gigot trimmed up to the elbow with a quilling; for silks, a closed sleeve, slashed in a point below; for heavy materials, the open hanging sleeve. All these with undersleeves.
NOTE: The tight-fitting sleeve, closed at the wrist, is seldom seen.

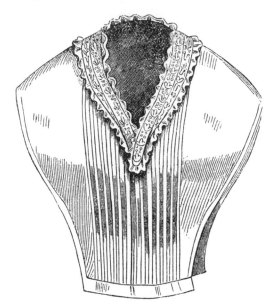

Chemisette with collar of lace and insertion. 1862

Skirt. Very full and slightly trained. For walking, the skirt is looped up by various methods, *e.g.* (1). A band round the waist having half a dozen looped cords hanging inside which can be attached to buttons sewn one on each seam about nine inches from the hem.
(2). The 'Watteau', a silk waistband with two ornamental loops hanging outside, one on each side, through which a part of the skirt can be drawn.
(3). An elastic waistband through which the skirt can be drawn up all round.
The length of even the walking dress provoked the remark: 'What can be more disagreeable than to see a lady's rich silk dress sweeping the streets as she walks?'
The skirt is either plain, or trimmed with a Greek pattern or one deep line of quilling above the hem. The trimming should be 'of a contrasting colour, *e.g.* brown with blue or mauve, or grey with blue, green or solferino trimming.'
Muslin dresses often with two lines of puffing above the hem; white piqué with dark velvet trimming.
The Robe Soutane (or dress without waist-

seam) usually buttons all down the front; at the back of the waist 'large box pleats are laid underneath to form the folds of the skirt and are hidden by two rich agraffes'.
Materials: (Summer). Notably alpaca, mohair, Holland and foulards (checked, spotted or sprigged). Chiné mohairs are now made to imitate silk.
Fashionable Colours: Grey, drab, brown, cerise. In the summer, black and white.
New Colours: Orphelian, Cuir.

Evening
The only conspicuous change is that the bertha is more pointed below front and back, and the short puffed sleeve has an epaulette. The skirt is usually double, or a tunic overskirt caught up. Elaborate trimmings of lace and flowers and frequently large velvet bows on the shoulders and at the front of the corsage. The Greek key pattern is commonly used.
Ball dresses have all double skirts, often with ostrich feather trimming.
The Medici ceinture and the Swiss belt are often seen in evening dresses.

Petticoats, etc.
With the looped up walking dress the petticoat 'of bright coloured French merino trimmed

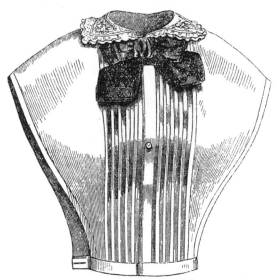

Habit-shirt of muslin and lace. 1862

with velvet or elaborate braiding, and two little fluted flounces', or of scarlet flannel in winter. For summer, a white petticoat trimmed with two fluted frills which are now more fashionable than open embroidery.
For ball dresses petticoats flounced to the waist, of tarlatan or nainsook.

214

The eiderdown quilted petticoat is worn in cold weather.

Crinolines
Now much reduced in size at the top, and trained. Often made with detachable flounces, buttoned on. To prevent the feet from catching

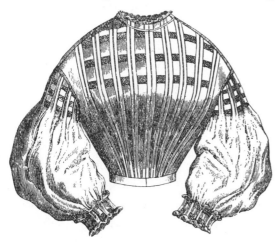

Blouse with bishop sleeves. 1862

in the hoops a jacconet casing is slipped over the lower part and buttoned in place.
Advertisement: 'Thomson's Crown Crinolines, Bustles and Skirt supporters.'

OUTDOOR GARMENTS

Cloaks
The short paletot, or 'yachting jacket', sometimes double-breasted, is specially fashionable; square cut below the hips, with large buttons down the front and capacious shaped sleeves. The long paletot, similar, but descending to below the knees.

Mantles
Mantles usually shaped to the shoulders with a pelerine design in guipure, soutache, or passementerie, pointed at the back.
The rotonde, a short circular mantle of the same material as the dress.
The Spanish jacket (worn over a chemisette) short, reaching the waist behind, the front fastened half-way down and then cut away towards the sides.

The Casaque, knee length, fitting the figure, wide open sleeves.

Shawls
Shawls are frequently made of the same material as the dress, for day wear.

ACCESSORIES

Coloured *Shoes*, 'blue, green, violet and scarlet, with high heels, worn with spotted stockings.'
Parasols, large, unfringed, sometimes with narrow lace edging; some pagoda shaped.

Gloves
Gauntlet gloves for wearing with 'yachting jackets'.

Prices
French organdy, 5/6; checked silks (12 yards,) 16/6; foulard, 25/-; moiré and pompadour silks, 63/-; washing mohairs, 9/9–11/6 the dress.
The International Exhibition of this year displayed: 'Wash-leather underclothing, strongly recommended in all cases of rheumatism, and

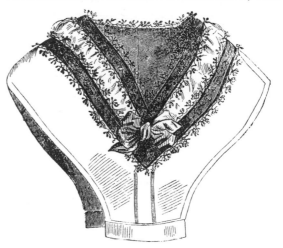

Chemisette trimmed with ribbon and insertion. 1862

chamois leather foot socks as supplied to Her Majesty and worn by the Royal Family.' Messrs. Wells's, of Nottingham, new patent stocking in which the seam and the stocking are woven simultaneously. Cork soles lined with wool.

1863

The trained skirt is now no longer universal but still the mode among the Best People. We read that 'the mode of wearing the dress drawn up, imitated from the English, is now becoming general in Paris. The cage americaine has proved to be the only substructure capable of supporting the drawn-up skirt gracefully.' It seemed impossible, for the moment, to devise any new developments in the lower half of the dress and more attention began to be paid to the upper. The Zouave jacket underwent modifications, more or less Spanish in form and resembling boleros, and the 'Alexandra' jacket expressed the popular enthusiasm over the Prince of Wales' marriage.

But we can detect a growing change in the colour sense for strong contrasts. The warning that 'glaring colours would be contrary to good taste, so important as the distinguishing feature in a true lady's costume', was becoming needed when such mixtures as 'a bronze-green dress with a drab paletot, ruby-red trimming and a white bonnet' were common objects. Coming events were casting strange shadows before and it is significant that for the first time in history an attempt is made to render the bathing costume an attractive object. Hitherto it had been a shapeless loose gown like a flannel chemise, in which the fair sex were adequately concealed from prying masculine eyes, but now inspection was positively invited. 'Very pretty costumes are made: trousers long and straight to the ankle in the shape of knickerbockers, and a long half-fitting casaque; or else a blouse-tunic with trousers; these are made in flannel or rep, black with blue or red worsted braid; white is to be avoided for obvious reasons.' It was a ladylike admission that, under certain circumstances, women were bipeds, but to betray more would be indelicate.

DRESSES

Day

Bodice cut square in front (with a chemisette 'worn over a vest of silk or flannel'). A fringed bertha trimming, with a bow in the centre, or pleatings laid on as a bertha, are common. Or plain high bodice, buttoning up the front, worn with a jacket or trimmed to imitate a jacket. In these the waist is either round, with a band, or sash tied behind, or the 'corsage postillion', having two points in front and short tails or a single point behind.

In summer materials the loose bodice (called either 'Garibaldi' or the 'Russian vest'), made very full and falling over the waistband or else tight with narrow pleats from neck to waist, is fashionable with young ladies. It may be worn with or without a jacket, and a coloured skirt. For summer, a bodice in the shape of a waistcoat with two points in front, often of white piqué, may be worn with a Figaro jacket.

Jackets for day use, both indoor and outdoor: The Alexandra: a jacket with postillions, the back made without a centre seam, the front opening with small revers and a collar; sleeve with epaulette and cuff.

The Figaro: close fitting and cut away in a curve at the sides, close sleeves with epaulettes.

Sleeves. Wide, made with an inner and outer seam and cut slightly round at the elbow.

Finished with a broad buttoned cuff. Some are open up the outer seam to the elbow. Small puffed undersleeves of cambric, or white buttoned cuffs attached to tight undersleeve. Epaulettes usual.

Skirt. 'Set in full gathers at the back and small pleats at the sides; every breadth gored; a gore of material a yard wide should be 25 inches at the bottom. The hem should be 6 yards round.' The effect is to give the skirt 'the shape of a bell'.

Many morning dresses are made with bodice and skirt in one without a seam at the waist (now called in England the 'Princess' style, and in France sometimes called the 'Agnes Sorel' style). 'The morning dress is more than ever simple and in the street a lady ought to appear, as it were, incognito.'

Trimmings. The Greek key pattern, or a narrow ruched frilling just above the hem which is often protected by Hungarian cord instead of the usual braid. Trimmings on the skirt to imitate Maltese lace; soutache patterns are going out of fashion. White piqué now trimmed with braid and not velvet. In summer materials there may be one or two narrow flounces.

Russian leather trimmings in stamped patterns for dresses are fashionable.

Materials: (Winter). Poplin reps and French merino, camlets, alpacas, winsey, linsey, for

Dress of brown moiré antique with Figaro jacket and Genoa velvet mantle. 1863
House dinner dress of green silk with semi-Figaro jacket. 1863

home wear; silks, satins, velvet, for visiting. (Summer). Muslins, barège, foulard, alpaca, mohair, percale, chiné taffeta, camlets (resembling alpaca, but slightly thicker and not so glossy).
'The new silk material faye.' (faille).
Fashionable Colours: The neutral tints, especially 'Russian leather'; also plaids. In summer white is very fashionable. 'The new colour Tourterelle is coming into fashion.'

Evening
No material change from previous year; all trained and gored with single box-pleat in front and double box-pleat behind: but a coloured pointed bodice worn with a white skirt (tarlatan, muslin, etc.) is common; and the 'Senorita jacket' (resembling a Figaro without sleeves), of velvet or silk is fashionable.
Satin striped gauze and black tulle are new materials for ball dresses, which are made with tunics knee length in front and sloping down behind.

Bridal
White, of satin, gros de Suez, glacé, poult de soie, moiré antique.

Petticoats

Are now gored.

'Petticoats are being trimmed almost as much as dresses, and as now every lady in the street shows more of the former than of the latter garment, it is absolutely necessary that they should be tastily got up; the inevitable flutings are even put round crinoline casings.'

'For wearing under crinolines we recommend the woven woollen petticoat to imitate knitting, made in all colours.'

The 'Alexandra petticoat', of poplin with broad plaid stripe above the hem.

Summer underpetticoats with three narrow flounces of frilling or piqué petticoats with printed borders.

Winter underpetticoats of quilted satin and silk trimmed with velvet or lace.

White petticoats worn with afternoon dresses.

'Under dresses of thin materials two petticoats (the first of cambric with a deep tuck, the second of muslin with a deep flounce) should be worn over the crinoline.'

A porte-jupe is necessary when walking.

Crinolines

Are bell-shaped, narrow above, and flounced for ball dresses.

OUTDOOR GARMENTS

Cloaks

The short paletot, now shaped at the waist.

The rotonde.

Garibaldis in summer.

Large round capes, knee length.

Close fitting casaques.

Talmas, burnouses, mantlet-echarpe.

The camail, or circular cloak, in silk, cashmere, or lace.

Capelines, or light hoods with cape attached, of cashmere or barège, for country use.

ACCESSORIES

Stockings

Coloured stockings, or with circular stripes, worn with coloured petticoats. Violet cashmere and plaid stockings for walking.

Sunshades on Fox's 'Paragon' frames. *Habit-Shirt* with stand-up collar and large bow, 'the cravate cocodès.' *Pocket Handkerchiefs.* Morning, with coloured hems or coloured vignettes in the corners Yak lace (first introduced at the Great Exhibition of '51 and made of the hair of the Yak ox) is now beginning to be used for shawls, cloaks, capes, etc.

Prices

The Alexandra jacket with lapel fronts and peg-top sleeves, 1 to 2 guineas.

Lyons velvet jackets, 2 to 5 guineas, zouave jackets, velvet, 2 guineas.

'Marguerite jackets in Lyons velvet, specially suited to the occasional requirements of married ladies, 42/-.'

Elastic kid boots, 8/6.

Llama, 7/6; jacconet muslin, 7/6; poplin de laine, 15/- the dress.

Best double mohairs, 8/9 to 13/6; Aberdeen winseys, 11/9 to 21/-; the Genappe cloth, 12/6 to 22/6; the full dress. Percale summer dress 12/-. Broché grenadines, 25/6 to 42/- the dress of 16 yards. French glacé silks, in thirty-three new shades of colour, £2 15 6 the dress of 14 yards. French foulards, 30 inches wide, 10 yards for 18/9. Gros de Suez, 2/11½ a yard. French cashmere burnouse in all colours, 15/6. Norwich Tamataves, 12 yards, 5/11.

Rich corded silk, 16 yards, 4 guineas the dress.

Real sealskin jackets, 14 to 25 guineas.

'The Ondina waved Crinoline, 15/6 to 25/6.'

Sansflectum Crinolines, the hoops covered with refined gutta percha, 10/6 to 25/-.

Thomson's watch-spring 'Crown' crinolines, from 2/- to 2 guineas.

Eiderdown petticoats, in rich quilted silk, four yards round, 50/- to 63/-.

The Staffordshire Potteries have forbidden the use of crinolines by their workwomen when at work as in one shop alone £200 worth of articles were swept down and broken by them in one year.

1864

The complaint that the dress-designers can no longer find anything new and are forced to offer old forms under new names is commonly uttered whenever a particular style is exhausted and a complete change is imminent. This year marks approximately the close of the epoch of angles; henceforth the Gothic style becomes concealed by curves. The change is, of course, a gradual one, and was

1864
Carriage dress of tartan glacé

entirely unrecognised by contemporaries. We, however, can see signs showing by the middle of this year of its approach. Perhaps the most significant is in the head-gear; abruptly in the summer the high 'spoon bonnet' collapses and becomes flat. 'Bonnets are now more like a cap than a bonnet: very different from the spoons and mussel shells which for the past three years have stood upright on every feminine head notwithstanding the ridicule of everybody.' Nothing is so contemptible as a fashion that has ceased to charm.

At the same time the upper part of the crinoline has shrunk in and 'all efforts tend to make the figure appear as slim as possible below the waist'. There was, in fact, a definite attempt on the part of the French Second Empire to revive, for political reasons, the fashions of the First Empire, 'improved by the addition of the crinoline'; it is interesting to note how they failed. No fashion has ever been adopted unless it chimes in with the prevailing mood of the day.

The psychology underlying the Epoch of Curves I have discussed elsewhere; here it is sufficient to add that in this year the bunched up 'double skirt' dress with curves instead of angles was already appearing in Paris in spite of the political move in the opposite direction. No doubt the influence of the French court under the Empress did something to delay the change which was approaching in spite of all efforts to enforce 'Empire' styles; but it will be noted how the new Epoch of Curves, its antithesis, came into being even before the collapse of the Second Empire in 1870.

The Englishwoman, never very happy in a huge crinoline, was now reluctant to adopt the so-called 'Empire' innovations; a contemporary explains, 'We are generally one year behind the French in adopting any new fashion.' But, in fact, she was ready enough to introduce the hitched-up skirt with its greater facilities for walking, and she was always more prone to detect immodest symbolism in new modes. Thus she exclaims characteristically 'What are called the new mantles are of the very fastest style imaginable; they are in fact men's coats in miniature; anything faster or in worse taste it is not easy to conceive'; while of the new hats, in the shape of jockey caps, these 'may be worn in the country but they are almost too fast for town'.

DRESSES

Day

Bodice. 1. Pointed in front with postillions behind (which may be cut as several square basques ['basque-habits'] and hang down to knee-level).

2. Round and short waist (Empire style) with deep waistband and four inch buckle, or a sash, the ends hanging behind. The sash may be made in one with the bodice, taking the place of basques.

3. Bodice cut low and square, with a chemisette and a Swiss belt (especially in summer).

4. Dress in the Princesse style.

5. Garibaldi bodice, either loose fitting 'now seldom made to bag over in front, and the skirt band is worn over it': or 'tight Garibaldis'.

6. Jacket, of the Spanish shape (Senorita, Figaro), over either a Garibaldi or a waistcoat.

New Garment: In place of a bodice, and for indoor use, the coat, with turned down collar and revers, buttoning down in front to the waist and sloping away behind in a long tail or basque, is a daring innovation. It is obviously stolen from the masculine wardrobe and therefore 'fast'. It may be made of silk or muslin.

Sleeves. Shaped to the arm, with epaulettes and reversed cuffs.

Skirt. Much gored and slightly trained except the hitched-up walking skirt. 'Why the dresses

219

should be worn so long is very obvious; if they were not so it would be positively indelicate for a lady to stoop or sit down.' The bottom of the skirt is often scalloped, and the hem often edged with velvet or cord.

The Fourreau skirt (so gored that it fits the figure without pleats at the waist) is common for morning dress.

'The skirt should measure at the top exactly half the width of the bottom.'

Towards the end of the year some morning dresses are made with the skirt open in front to show the petticoat or with a breadth of different material to simulate this.

Trimming. Day dresses are trimmed with braiding, fringe, chenille and grelots (ball fringe) mixed with jet 'round the hem, up the sleeves down the elbows, and on cuffs and epaulettes'. White bugle trimming for summer dresses. Trimmings of ruching and frilling put on the extreme edge of the skirt instead of just above; ruching on the bodice may simulate a jacket shape.

Dress buttons are often square, made of pearl, tortoiseshell or ivory.

Evening

The bodice cut very low off the shoulders, pointed front and back with pleats arranged in fan shape to a point in the centre (the Greek bodice); filled in with tulle puffing; or worn with a bertha.

'Basque-habits' are often worn.

Sleeves short and full.

Skirt. Trained. 'Owing to the diminishing size of the crinoline the double skirt for ball dresses (the overskirt being caught up at the sides) is returning to fashion.'

For ball dresses 'tulle puffings are still the favourite composition, arranged lengthwise on a gored skirt of stiff net, fitting round the waist without pleats; ten lines of puffing ascend from the hem, interspersed with sprays of flowers. Sometimes a tunic is worn over the skirt pointed behind and gradually shortening as it approaches the front.'

Wedding

These may now be made either with high or low bodice.

Materials: Morning dresses of serge are a novelty, while satin is restored to favour for evening.

Foulard is now greatly improved in quality being thicker and more silky, and the new glacé silks are heavier but less lustrous.

New Materials: poplin lama, Genappe cloth, plush velvet, linos, embroidered moirés, and moirés with satin patterns, muslins printed with imitation ruches and pleatings.

OUTDOOR GARMENTS

Cloaks

Cloaks trimmed with gimp ornaments and beads and bugles, with deep lace edging.

The rotonde, with three folds in the centre of the back from which hang loose ribbons.

The pelisse-cloak, with a deep cape pointed behind which forms sleeves.

Mantles

Mantles of burnouse shape, trimmed with gimp and tassels.

The short paletot, often made of the same material as the dress.

Woollen and cashmere capelines with hood in the Marie Stuart style worn out of doors.

ACCESSORIES

Boots and Shoes

For day, with high pegtop heels. The toes nearly square; large rosettes. Evening shoes and boots, white for white dresses, blue or pink with dresses of those colours. Heels 1 inch; large rosettes.

Stockings

Day stockings with plaid or circular stripes to match the petticoat, worn with boots; plain silk with clocks, worn with shoes.

Gloves

'Evening gloves are worn much longer than they have been for many years.'

Aprons with chenille tassels for morning use.

Muffs are now 10 to 11 inches across. *Parasols*, pagoda shape, with black lace pattern woven in.

Ear-rings large.

Narrow linen collars worn with morning dress. Corsets now shorter.

Prices

Poult de soie, in forty-five shades of colour, 55/6 the dress of 14 yards. Checked gros grains, 35/6; broché and checked gros de Suez, 55/6 the dress of 14 yards.

Two yard wide alpacas, 3/9 a yard. Waterproof foulards, 12 yards, 35/6. Lyons corded silk, both sides alike, 55/6 the dress of 14 yards.

Lyons silk velvet, 10/6 to 12/6 a yard.

Scarlet merino corsets, 10/6.

1863

1864

1865

1868

1867

Evening dress, upper skirt of green velvet en princesse; underskirt of white
satin with rows of puffing

Ball dress of pink silk; two skirts

Ball dress, upper skirt of blue silk cut with the body en princesse

The new lace hat falls, 4/6.
The new waistband ribbons, 2/- a yard. Steel buckles, 3/6.
Eiderdown petticoats, 4 yards round, 42 inches long, weight 25 oz. in black silk, 55/-.
Moiré antiques, 4½ guineas the dress of 9 yards.
Puffed horsehair jupons, 21/- to 33/-.

Genappe cloth, 12/6 to 23/6 the full dress (Peter Robinson).
Aberdeen winseys, 2/3 a yard (Peter Robinson).
Glacé silk (14 yards) the dress 55/6 (Peter Robinson).
Mozambique barège (14 yards the dress) 9/9 (Peter Robinson).

1865

If we recognise the essential significance of the crinoline, as a mechanical device to magnify the wearer and also to emphasise the triangularity of the skirt, we see that it was opposed to the democratic movement and belonged to the Gothic epoch of angles. We can therefore understand how reluctantly it was abandoned by the fashionable classes. Thus we read, 'At the beginning of the present season the news went about that the reign of crinoline was over; that the Empress Eugénie, its great creator, had at least reduced it within reasonable limits. The rumour, we regret to say, was a false one. Crinoline assumes proportions as huge as ever; not a year passes but in this country alone hundreds suffer death by burning through crinoline.' In the summer, however, 'many young ladies are brave enough to be seen without crinolines and to be remarked for their extremely forlorn appearance.'

We may conclude that the battle of the styles was hotly waged and that the reports from the war area were conflicting. Actually we may attribute the final defeat of the crinoline to three factors: its commonness, so that it no longer signified social rank: the increasing activity of ladies out of doors: and the impulse to express a sexual instinct symbolically by curves because of the growing obstacles to a more normal form of satisfaction. This too can be traced to democratic changes affecting the economic position of the upper classes. All those profound changes in our social system which began to be noticeable in the middle '60's, the decline of the aristocracy, the increasing difficulty in finding husbands for superfluous daughters, the higher education of women, the rivalry of the sexes in an economic sense, and the tension of unsatisfied sex instinct, can be traced to a basal cause—a disturbance in economic equilibrium. It would have been extraordinary if such a revolution had not produced an outward sign in women's fashions.

In this year, '65, we find two significant features: one, a growing attention to walking dresses, especially 'costumes' of a practical cut; and two, for the purpose, presumably, of sex attraction, a lavish use of artificial hair. It was observed that 'ninety-nine women out of a hundred do not know how to walk gracefully', and that 'the quantity of artificial hair which is worn at the present day is astonishing'. It was the head which charmed, or at least, the outside of it.

'The great problem just now is how to make a skirt, excessively long and ample, look very scant and narrow. This is done by goring every breadth of the skirt and arranging it in flat double pleats round the waist. Bodies are made with very short waists and look smaller still under the broad belts and sashes worn over them. . . .'

'There is a masculine influence shown and ladies wear coats, jackets, waistcoats, cravats and boots.'

DRESSES

Day

1. Plain close fitting bodice, with all round linen collar and velvet necktie: the 'coat' sleeve, wide waist-band. Gored skirt slightly trimmed; worn with serge or linsey petticoat (Morning).

2. Small Spanish jacket, rounded in front, with square basque behind, worn over a waistcoat; gored skirt trimmed up each seam with gimp, braid or jet. Worn with taffeta petticoat (Morning). Or the 'Russian jacket' (sleeveless) over a sleeved waistcoat.

3. Plain high bodice, with skirt open in front and behind, revealing a coloured petticoat which may be only simulated by a breadth of different material (Afternoon).

4. High bodice trimmed across with jet and

or coloured jacket and white skirt, with a silk sash hanging from beneath the jacket tail.

White chemisette with Swiss ceinture.

Garibaldis in coloured foulard, box-pleated in front.

'Garibaldi bodices can be worn with any skirt.'

Seaside dresses, with bands hanging from the girdle by which the skirt can be looped up.

Croquet dresses of muslin over coloured slip, sleeves, unlined, in a series of puffs and ribbons; a small pelerine, square in front and pointed behind; broad waistband.

A number of 'costumes' with casaque or paletot, bodice and skirt of same material.

Trimming. A fashion for steel trimmings tends to replace the ubiquitous jet.

Materials: (Winter—Morning). Silk and woollen

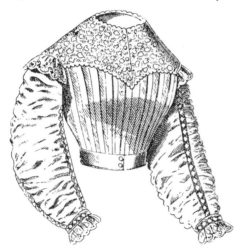

White muslin canezou over pink silk foundation. 1865

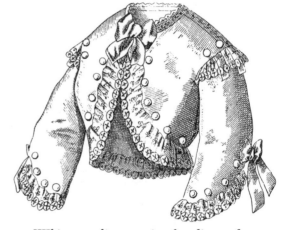

White muslin senorita for dinner dress.
1865

gimp, similar trimming composing epaulettes and cuffs; gored skirt edged with narrow box-pleated flounce, or cord.

5. With double skirts, the upper looped up by three or four velvet straps, called the 'Lyons loop', from the waist or a foot lower. The upper skirt often sloped away at the sides and long behind.

6. The Gabrielle dress, or dress en princesse, the bodice and front breadth of the skirt in one; three large box-pleats at the back, or one at each side and one behind; all the widths gored.

Often trimmed at the sides and front to simulate basques.

7. (Summer). 'The style of the Empire', the bodice cut very low, with shoulder straps, and an underbodice of muslin.

8. (Summer). White jacket and coloured skirt,

reps, serges, linseys, merinos, flannel. (Afternoon). Silk, gros grain, moiré, velvet, poplin. (Summer). Foulard, striped silks, the stripes running lengthwise. Shot silk, poplinette, piqué, percale, muslin, alpaca, mohair, grenadine.

Pompeian silk sashes, very wide, with black background and bright mythological subjects woven in.

Evening

The bodice is 'we regret to say, lower even if possible than last season', with embroidered insertion chemisette. The short sleeve is dispensed with and shoulder straps worn. In place of the bertha there are folds across the front descending slightly in the centre.

Or the bodice and 'tunic' (upper skirt) are cut in one piece with no pleats round the waist; the tunic measures about 18 feet round the hem and is usually made of tulle. This is known as the 'fourreau tunic'. As a variation the tunic may be open front and back, and much trimmed, over an underskirt, slightly trimmed with the hem corded or of gimp. A certain number retain the fringed bertha with a deep basque to the bodice at the back, or a round waist with long sash ends behind. Others have the bodice of the 'Swiss belt' shape, with muslin chemisette.

It will be seen, therefore, that the 'Empire' influence is responsible for the square cut, round

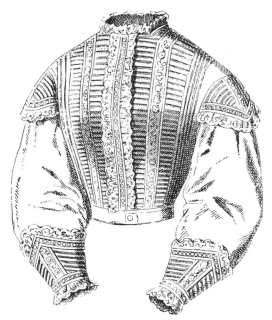

White muslin canezou trimmed with valenciennes and insertion. 1865

waist and shoulder straps on the one hand, while the bertha or folded drapery and sash sustain the Gothic principles. The tunic, if plain, belongs to the former style; but is amenable to modifications giving it, rather, a Gothic appearance.

Petticoats

'Gored petticoats of horsehair now worn in preference to crinolines', especially in evening dress, or still flounced net petticoats.

OUTDOOR GARMENTS
Cloaks
The short paletot (in summer especially made of the same material as the dress).
Burnouses, rotondes, shawls, of Yak lace.

The long paletot, fitting the figure, with the sides cut in deep scollops, and the back descending below the knees; edged with Maltese lace.
Casaques, fitting the figure, cut in scollops, and long at the back.
Jackets, loose-fitting and cut with straight sides, and having side pockets outside.

ACCESSORIES
Boots
Of grey coutil, with elastic sides, for day use. Croquet boots, in morocco kid or fancy toe-caps, with side springs and coloured ribbon lacings; peaked before and behind at the ankle, with a tassel.
Satin evening *Shoes*, pointed, with buckle.
Shoes with large square buckles and 'high heels', (*i.e.* 1½ inch).

Gloves
Day. Buff colour, with three to six buttons.
Evening, six to ten buttons, and elbow length.

Jewellery: large steel and oxidised silver buttons. Silver ornaments in fretwork. Dog collar necklaces of inch wide velvet with beads sewn on. 'An extraordinary taste for barbaric jewellery'; ear-rings of large gold plates with long pendants; gold chain with cross pendant; cameo necklaces and bracelets. Large coloured glass bead necklaces for both high and low dresses. Large headed pins with hanging balls and chains worn even in the day. Jet cameos, on caps, bonnets, jackets, dresses, etc.

Fans of painted sandalwood.

Stays of silk elastic, slightly boned, and quite short.

Prices
Yak lace rotondes, 21/-.
French piqué and percale robes with jackets, for the seaside, 12/9.
Aberdeen winseys, 1/6½ a yard.
'Patent velvet' (*i.e.* velveteen) with silk face and cotton back, from 8/- a yard.'
Irish poplins, 55/6 the dress of 14 yards.
Mexican cloths and poplinettes, 12/6 to 21/- the dress. Ottoman corded silk, both sides alike, 33/6 to 55/-. Mozambique, 12/6 the dress. Ginghams, 12/6 the dress.
Sealskin mantles, 33 inches deep, 6½ guineas; 36 inches deep, 12 guineas.

The struggle between the native Gothic and the foreign Classical styles was slowly moving towards the defeat of the invader. 'The Crinoline is now going out of fashion but it will be long before we have quite done with it. It alone preserves us from the ungraceful style of dress in vogue under the First Empire,' a remark suggestive of a wire entanglement as the last line of defence. As a new classical weapon the peplum is revived, but it is significant that this purely classical garment is immediately modified so as to become, in fact, a Gothic addition to the dress. The peplum is a short tunic hollowed in front and behind with points hanging down at the sides. A little more and these become glorified vandyking; further, by bunching out the back the garment easily becomes a polonaise, entirely destroying the classical appearance. We also read that 'peplums are so much covered with jet that it is nearly impossible to wear them on account of the weight'.

The principle of two colours in one dress is further developed. 'As three colours cannot be admitted in one toilet the overskirt must be either the same colour as the casaque or as the underskirt'; thus, a violet sleeveless casaque is worn over a short green dress which reveals a violet petticoat.

A further change in walking dresses is noticeable. 'Few looped-up dresses are seen now; they are replaced by dresses a little shorter than the petticoat which renders any porte-jupe unnecessary.'

The classical attack spends most of its energy on the trimmings, although at the time the invasion was causing positive alarm. 'The Empire fashion, with its ugly short waist, is becoming more and more the rage; some low bodies are not more than four inches deep.' These, supported merely by shoulder straps, evoked a cry of alarm. 'Those who adopt the fashion can no longer claim that inestimable quality—modesty.' The curious wave of exhibitionism occurring in these years has been described in *Feminine Attitudes in the Nineteenth Century*; it must be understood that it affected only a section of the fashionable world and that the excessively decolleté dress was by no means universally worn. Thus, a high chemisette was frequently employed to protect from slander the maiden's modesty.

DRESSES

Day

1. The short dress, '4 to 4½ yards round the bottom; three widths are gored, two of the slanting pieces joined down the centre of the back; the other widths are joined one slanting to one straight; the front width being cut apronwise. The underskirt, longer than the dress, is the same shape and size; neither has any pleats, not even at the back.' The short dress may be of 'the Princess shape now beginning to be called by an old name, the "fourreau", and buttoning all down the front'; frequently worn with a 'Peplum' fastened round the waist under the band.

2. The looped-up dress, *e.g.*, a grey dress looped up at each side with buttons or velvet straps over a scarlet petticoat with four bands of black braid above the hem; in summer, a white petticoat with insertion above the hem.

3. The plain skirt, the edge scalloped or dented or with cable cord, and 'much gored and set into the body or with large pleats, one in front, one behind and one on each side'.

4. The redingote. Of the Princess shape but long and open down the front and trained behind, being turned back and tied behind in two or three places with ribbon bows. Worn over a white silk petticoat.

With the above types the bodice is plain with round 'high waist' (in reality only slightly above the real waist line). Narrow waistband fastened at the left side with rosette.

Collar large and pointed in front, very narrow behind. Frequently loops and streamers of narrow ribbon hang down the back. Sleeves, often with epaulettes, are tight. 'It is impossible to wear undersleeves which are therefore replaced by deep cuffs.'

'Peplums which fit the figure, composed of a basque only, are added to dresses in the Empire style.'

'Jackets of every conceivable shape, with long basques behind are much worn.'

The fashion for 'suits' of one material is a feature, consisting of dress and casaque or paletot. The fashion for two colours is variously obtained: a low corselet and the upper skirt or peplum of one colour, with underskirt, upper part of bodice and sleeves of another; a redingote of one colour over a dress of another; a sleeveless casaque and underskirt of one colour and the looped-up overskirt and bodice of another; a short dress of one colour over a petticoat of another. Examples, green and violet; maize and purple.

Summer

The Watteau bodice, with deep square opening edged with lace. White bodice of muslin with high or 'V' neck; the front pleated or trimmed with insertion. Some open to the waist in front and behind over a chemisette.

Garibaldis with linen collars and narrow velvet cravats.

A variation of the Swiss belt is a corselet cut with tasselled points round the waist and bretelles with tasselled epaulettes, worn over a Princess dress. The skirt is frequently edged with a deep quilled flounce.

'Aprons are now in high repute and are indispensable to a recherché home toilette', nearly always black and square cut.

Evening

The bodice very low off the shoulders, with shoulder straps or bows of ribbon, sleeves 'apparently disappearing altogether'.

Or the 'Sicilian bodice', very low and square cut, laced up in front, and attached to a tunic which is without side breadths; the front and back, each divided in two, descend to below the knee as four 'sash ends'.

Or a corselet or Swiss body over a chemisette. The waist is generally round and 'high'.

Ball dress bodices are either square or with folds across the front, or attached to a peplum, or 'Empire'. The bertha is going out.

Skirts: multiple (two or more) except for heavy materials (when corded hem is common); or with short open tunic in the peplum shape; or trimmed (often with fringe) to simulate a tunic. Always trained. Frequently trimmed above the hem with a 'Greek border'.

Ball dresses with several underskirts of gauze worn over the silk or satin skirt; the upper gauze skirt is looped up and sprinkled with steel or gold beads. Often looped up with a small coloured bird, mounted flat 'which look remarkably well on gauze dresses'.

Fichus, for wearing over demi-evening dresses, of tulle on stiff net with blonde edging and black velvet ribbon threaded through. The fichu covers the front and back of the bodice with sash ends behind.

Bathing Dresses

The 'Zouave Marine Swimming costume, a body and trousers cut in one secures perfect liberty of action and does not expose the figure.' 'A picturesque costume so popular at Llandudno last season', of stout brown Holland or dark blue serge with scarlet braid trimming.

Materials: (Summer). Alpaca, leno, muslin, grenadine, jacconet. Trimmings of 'white guipure which is called Cluny lace' are fashionable. 'Velveteen for morning dresses (Winter) has superseded linseys, reps, poplins, serges and cashmeres.' Generally made with jacket en suite.

'Japanese silks are quite a novel introduction; they resemble foulards and are equally soft but the texture is stout and instead of hanging limp they stand out like a poplinette.'

Ball dresses of poult-de-soie, satin, tulle, tarlatan (striped or sprigged) and gauzes with gold or silver threads.

Wedding dresses of satin; bridesmaids', of white silk.

Afternoon dresses of chiné silks with wide stripes; striped materials very fashionable.

New Materials: Sultana, drap de Venise, Egyptian cloth, Japanese silk, crepon, Djedda.

Fashionable Colours: Bismarck (a plum colour), yellow, bright rose, purple, grey, light blue, buff.

New Colours: Bismarck, bois de rose, blue turc.

OUTDOOR GARMENTS

Cloaks

Paletots, half-fitting with large buttons, and narrow sleeves, often knee-length; of plush or flannel (Winter); others loose fitting in the 'sac shape', and short (some double breasted); the first with trained dresses, the latter with looped-up dresses.

Sortie de bal. 1866.   *Evening dress with Peplum.* 1866
Paletot with Peplum basque. 1866

Paletots are also made in the peplum form, with long points under the arms and short in front and behind.

The sleeveless paletot is a summer feature.

Casaques, generally of the same material as the dress, often worn with a belt. The casaque scarcely reaches below the waist.

Polonaises, of the shape of a redingote, made of moutonne, velvet or quilted silk.

Mantles
The Balmoral mantle, like an Inverness cape, in velvet, cashmere or cloth.

ACCESSORIES
Shoes
With 1½ inch heels and nearly square toes: rosette on instep. *Boots* of black morocco, buttoned, with tassel top; or laced, with tassel.

Gloves
With three or more buttons.

Muffs extremely small.

Jewellery: large buttons, of oxydised silver and jet with classic heads in relief or inlaid key-pattern are fashionable. Benoiton chains, of filigree silver, gold, jet or pearls, hang from the head on each side, or over the chignon or across the chest. Ear-rings and brooches of fantastic designs, 'ladders, saddles, bridles, birds, beetles, fish, flies and croquet mallets.' Large cameo brooches. Large gold bracelets worn high up the arm.

Shawls. Norwich shawls striped with silk in geometrical patterns on Cashmere grounds.
Fashionable *Furs*—grebe, sable, ermine, chinchilla, sealskin. Imitation fur trimmings. *Parasols* with short sticks and thick handles. *Cluny Lace* much worn for cuffs, collars, caps, capes, etc.

Prices
Waterproof mantle, 1 guinea.
Astrachan jackets, 8/9 to 14/9. Sealskin jackets, 5½ to 15 guineas. Scotch velveteen jackets, 1 guinea; Italian velveteen 3/4½ a yard.
Plain silk dresses of 14 yards, 3 to 5 guineas.
Riding habits of ribbed cloth, 5½ guineas.
Japanese silk dresses, £2.
Spitalfields moiré dress, 4 guineas.

1867

'What is to be said of the Fashions? Gentlemen ask each other "Where are all the pretty girls? Transformed into guys."' Such laments, uttered in this year, are generally to be heard whenever feminine fashions are undergoing a radical transformation. By '67 the new epoch of curves was becoming manifest but the tentative experiments with the new mode were still hampered by the older traditions, and it is difficult to combine angles and curves together. The result was to produce a phase which is usually condemned by a later generation as 'ugly'. Such phases are, in reality, extremely interesting, as they indicate the approach of some profound change of feminine outlook and are experimental in nature. We perceive, in this year, the different methods by which the curve is about to be exploited as a device of sexual attraction. The bulk of the dress moves further and further to the rear, taking on an undulating shape. The year was notable for the introduction of a new —or rather, a revived—garment, the *polonaise*, at first, tentatively, as an outdoor garment. 'Worth has produced an extremely pretty covering for outdoor use called "the Polonaise" or "Tallien Redingote"; it is a redingote opening heart-shaped in front, full at the back, with a sash tied behind in a simple bow. A sash-end of ribbon descends each side of the redingote and terminates in a bow; it is made of the same material as the dress or of black silk.' Presently it becomes more and more puffed out behind, and a garment intended to be a revival of a purely classical nature quickly becomes the principal device for producing exaggerated curves.

A similar spirit is seen in many of the dresses, the overskirts of which are hitched up behind into a bulging mass. No wonder a contemporary observes, 'It does not seem likely that the very ugly Empire shapes will, in the end, be generally adopted.' Finally their fate seemed settled when the Empress appeared, this year, in a dress with panniers on the hips, as though to indicate a definite return to the fashions of the *ancien régime*.

As a further innovation we read, 'In London a fashionable tailor and habit maker has recently set up dressmaking.'

DRESSES

Day
(a) Walking
1. The Empire shape. A gored skirt; either Princess or with a high waisted bodice attached, high neck, tight sleeves; trimming of velvet or soutache either to simulate a tunic, or down each seam.
2. Redingote shape, buttoning all down the front to a point just below the knee; long and rounded behind; cut up the side seams and buttoned; worn over a long trained underskirt of the same material or colour. Or the redingote (of silk or tussore) is gored at the waist and slightly full behind, being pulled back by an attached sash; worn over a coloured petticoat with a deep pleated flounce.

3. The short dress. 'The back breadth consists of two gores, the sloping sides joined together. On each side of this are three gores, similarly joined; thus there are eight gores and three or five plain breadths in front; a narrow box pleating round the bottom.' Ankle length. Usually in the Princess shape and worn in the morning.
4. The looped-up dress. Looped up at the sides over bright coloured petticoat (*e.g.* magenta, scarlet, striped, of merino, satin, poplin). The border, much trimmed with passmenterie, is cut into vandykes or battlements. 'Vandykes have succeeded scallops.' 'Long skirts for walking dresses and looped-up skirts are considered vulgar among the higher classes.' The looping-up is effected either by bands of the same material as the dress, two inches wide and

braided, or by loops descending three-quarters down each seam ending in a buttonhole which fastens to a button on the petticoat.

5. The Pelisse, combining a short dress and jacket in one; put on over the head as there is no opening in the gored skirt; sash at the waist; worn over a silk petticoat.

6. 'The Atlantic yachting suit' (a variety of the short dress); 'these are all the rage at Brighton; made of dark blue serge trimmed with white braid, the dress, petticoat and jacket alike; worn with a small round hat; round the neck a small half-handkerchief of muslin or coloured silk.'

7. 'Out of doors the long dress can be converted into a short dress by pulling the fullness of the skirt to the back and pinning the side breadths together behind; the rest of the fullness is drawn through the loop thus made; or a close fitting steel hoop is worn round the hips and the fullness of the skirt is pulled up through it, behind.' With the above types, when the bodice is separate it may be of white serge, rep, cashmere or velveteen, with or without basques, with a pointed turned down collar, and trimmed with jet beads or guipure. In summer, of muslin with bands of insertion. Tight sleeves.

Or a closed jacket, such as 'the Balmoral', with pointed fronts joined to form a waistcoat, fastening high up the throat and long pointed ends behind; or closed jackets with revers, over a chemisette.

(b) Afternoon

Bodice, either plain and high, with epaulettes and tight 'coat' sleeves, with or without a peplum-basque; with a fourreau, the bodice is cut low and square revealing the under-dress, or a chemisette, *e.g.* a 'fourreau of silver gauze with vandyked hem, cut low in the body front and back, with narrow shoulder straps, over a trained blue silk dress.'

Skirt trained, made 'of nine breadths, the front breadth entire; the next breadth is gored on both sides; the rest have each one straight side and one gored; there is no fullness round the waist, the skirt being sewn plain to a waistband with one box-pleat at the back.' Six yards round the bottom. 'It is now possible to cut a fashionable dress from 13 yards of material.' The skirt may be trimmed up the seams or to simulate a double skirt. Or a double skirt (of the same colour for town use and a different colour for country use), which is hitched up at the sides and long behind; or a fourreau (*i.e.* 'sheath') overdress, descending to the top of the deep pleated flounce off the underskirt; the bottom of the fourreau cut in deep vandykes.

With trained skirts 'a porte-jupe or metal clasp fastened to the waistband from which hangs a brooch which can be attached to small rings sewn to the skirt.'

'Sashes generally worn with every kind of toilette, the bows with fringed ends as large as possible'; or the 'cascade waistband' fringed with jet pendants arranged in vandykes, or the basque-waistband with five vandyked tabs. The ends of the sash behind may be looped under the upper part of the overskirt to puff it out.

Riding Habits

'Are shorter than ever; in a fast gallop it is almost impossible to help showing the feet, and when proper Wellington boots are not worn this is certainly not pretty; the habits are scantier with a large pleat in front and very little fullness on the hips. The bodies have a square tab at the back and a scarcely perceptible basque on the hips, and quite short and square at the waist in front. An all round collar is worn inside the neck of the bodice and fastened with a brooch.'

Wedding Dresses

'White book-muslins have in a measure superseded the heavy satins and silks. They are profusely trimmed with puffings divided by insertions of lace and are en tablier or simulating an open overskirt, the front panel being Cluny lace; sleeves small and tight with puffings of muslin separated by insertion.'

Materials: for walking 'suits': velveteen; 'shot silks are returning to fashion and striped materials are less fashionable than chiné or spotted.'

New Materials: Bengaline, bouracan, cretonnes, striped or chiné for summer morning dresses.

Colours: Bismarck brown, scabious, grey, green, bright blue.

Evening

1. The Empire style. Plain gored skirt with long train with deep box-pleated flounce; over it a tunic, either open in front or at the sides, the front reaching to the top of the flounce, and deeper behind. A low square bodice off the shoulders with a strap or short puffed sleeve, worn with a chemisette; the bodice may be in one with the tunic.

2. Double skirt dress, gored and trained. The overskirt may be caught up at the sides to produce a puffing behind 'in the Pompadour style'; or the upper skirt not looped up but

rather shorter than the underskirt. The underskirt with lines of puffing; the upper skirt of lace or with a deep lace flounce. The bodice often in the shape of a Swiss belt (*e.g.* of velvet) over a chemisette.

3. The upper skirt open in front as a robe, reaching to the top of the flounce; bodice very low off the shoulders and descending slightly in the centre. Narrow strap; sleeves off the shoulders. Broad sash of lace or ribbon with large bow behind, the ends of which may catch up the back of the overskirt.

Trimmings of plaits and pipings of coloured satin, ribbon bands and lace.

'Thus all evening dresses are double, *i.e.* the long skirt and the short skirt or tunic or peplum, besides the underskirt of silk or satin which is indispensable when the dress is made of tulle or tarlatan. It can be dispensed with when the dress itself is of silk or satin and the upper skirt is of light material. The under dress is always trimmed over the lower part with ruches, puffings or flounces, the upper skirt or tunic with trimmings put on plain, of satin rouleaux edged with beads or fringe or lace insertion. Young ladies frequently wear low white muslin bodices with evening dresses of silk, barège or grenadine.'

Ball dresses. Gored with long train.
1. As a tunic dress.
2. With double skirt; the underskirt with a deep pleating; the overskirt short in front and at the sides, with a long train caught up by the sash.

'Evening bodices are cut so low as to make it imperatively necessary to wear a border of pleated tulle or lace under the more curved-out part.'

A ball costume comprises:
1. A longcloth petticoat, gored and trained with three steels.
2. A white muslin petticoat, plain and gored.
3. White ditto, with deep pleated flounce.
4. A fourreau dress of silk or satin.
5. A double skirt or tunic of tarlatan.

Or, in place of a fourreau a corselet (a separate low bodice), often with basques, and worn over a low bodice of white muslin, with a separate skirt.

Materials: 'Thick materials such as velvet, satin and brocade, are again in fashion with the suppression of crinolines and the adoption of gored skirts.'

NOTE: Both with evening and day dresses a fichu may be worn, *e.g.* the Marie Antoinette fichu, of lace or dress material, round the shoulders the ends crossing in front under the waistband and hanging loose; the 'Raphael fichu', of white tulle or lace, cut square over the shoulders and the upper part of the bodice, worn over a high bodice 'to give a dressy effect'.

Petticoats
Under a short dress is worn one unstarched cambric petticoat; under a trained dress three or four muslin petticoats.

OUTDOOR GARMENTS

Cloaks
The paletot, a short loose jacket, richly trimmed with jet, bugles and fringe, with guides ('the inevitable reins' or hanging bands) at the back. It is frequently cut in vandykes or battlements, or peplum points.

The redingote paletot, cut like a Princess dress but opening at the top with revers and buttoning all the way down; some with circular capes.

Mantles
Long close-fitting mantles, with vandyked edge. Waterproof cloaks with small hood and pendant tassels.

Paletot-mantles with hanging 'Venetian' sleeves.

ACCESSORIES

Shoes
And *Boots* with rounded toes. High laced boots, with tassels at the top and bows at the toes; of every variety of colour. Kid walking boots with patent leather toes, buttoned. 'The elastic sided boot is not worn on dressy occasions.' Polish boots, high with pendant tassels and high coloured heels; 'what stony-hearted bachelor can resist charms like these?'

Parasols, 'the pagoda shape has entirely disappeared; handles are longer and tapered; parasols are made in self-colours, stripes and brocaded silks and satins.' *Buttons* on dresses, etc., large, of fancy gimp, cameos, open-work iron, pearls, carved ivory and enamel; olive-shaped of jet. *Jewellery*: with ball dresses, jewellery of artificial flowers in the cache-peigne, ear-rings, necklace, brooch and bracelets.

Morning *Collars*, small and high with cravat tied in a bow.

Prices
Janus cord mourning, two guineas the dress.
Black and white French silk dresses of 16 yards, 2½ guineas. Foulard alpaca, 11/9 the dress of 12 yards. Turco Poplinnes, 12/6 the dress of 12

yards. Gros de Suez, 3½ guineas the dress of 14 yards. Moiré antique, 4½ guineas; broche silk, 3 guineas. Figured silk, 2/6½ a yard; best velveteen, 5/9. Wool rep, 25/6; serge, 13/- the dress.

Polonaise skirts, from 17/6.

French leather trimming to apply to skirts, durable and cleaned with a wet sponge, 4/9.

Black Lyons velvet, 10/6 a yard. Atlantic serge dress, 12/9.

Muff-bags, lined with moiré, ormulu frame: astrachan, 28/6; Siberian fox, 28/6; black seal, 42/-.

Kid gloves, 4/4 a pair. Evening gloves, long white kid without buttons.

Flannel dressing gowns, in the Watteau shape, 25/-. Crinolines. The sansflectum, 17/6 to 21/-; the demisansflectum with no steels at the waist, 15/6; the fantail (evening) 21/-; the Pompadour, no steels, 25/6. Ebonite crinoline with scarlet flounce, 20/-.

Thomson's glove-fitting corset, 7/6 to 14/6, cut in three pieces, the centre one forming a Swiss bodice, the upper and lower pieces filled with narrow bones.

Made up Promenade suit, complete 25/-. Cambric morning dresses, 13/9.

Gored pleated skirts in bright colours, for croquet, 15/9.

Italian mohairs, 14 yards the dress, 8/9.

Cretonne cloth, 18/6½-29/6 the full dress.

20,000 chignons of hair exported from France to England in '66.

'A lady has given wholesale notice to quit to her tenants in Carmarthenshire and Pembrokeshire in consequence of their wives and daughters wearing crinolines, a practice to which she objects.'

1868

This year is notable for the recognition, after some years of hesitation, that owing to the greater activity of the modern woman her fashions for day must henceforth be distinguished into two categories: 'Day dresses may now be considered in two distinct classes; short skirts for morning wear, called *Walking dresses*, and dresses with long sweeping trains for carriage, flower shows, concerts and similar occasions, classified as Afternoon Costume. Dresses are not now made long and caught up by loops for walking; a distinct class of dress is required for each occasion.' As a result the wardrobe of the average woman became immensely increased.

In style the dress imitates more and more the modes of Louis XV period, and we have Regency, Pompadour and Watteau costumes. By the middle of the year the pannier dress, worn with a *bustle* and without a crinoline becomes a feature. For other dresses the crinoline is now small and hooped only behind and at the bottom, becoming, in fact, a *crinolette*. The elaborate fichu, of the Louis XVI period, is also noticeable. In a word, all traces of the classical style have vanished and curves especially at the back dominate the picture.

DRESSES

Day

1. *The Short Dress.* 3¼ yards wide. 'At last it seems that Fashion has made a step in the direction of common sense; it is said that the new fashion is not likely to become popular for the reason that many women have not got pretty feet. Short skirts, for outdoor wear, are really a necessity, as evidenced by the devices (cords, strings, etc.) for holding up the dress.' Always with a 'double skirt' (*i.e.* a body and upper skirt, and a jupon or underskirt which is generally of the same material or else strongly contrasted. The underskirt, with a deep pleated flounce, is generally striped and of silk or satin (or, to save material, of a cheaper material down to twelve inches from the bottom to which a silk band is attached); it should be just off the ground.

The upper skirt, twelve inches shorter than the under skirt, usually has the hem cut into tabs, scallops or vandykes, or edged with fringe or ruching. It is usually looped up at the sides, producing an apron-front and puffed out behind by means of the sash. The upper skirt may be in form a tunic, that is, made in one with the bodice, or both may be replaced by a casaque with skirt ends extending low enough to serve as an upper skirt. The bodice high and buttoning up to the neck; plain or trimmed to simulate a low square cut; tight sleeves. Narrow turned-down collar and cravat. The bodice may be replaced, in winter, by either a casaque or a tight jacket with a chemisette, or, in summer, by a muslin bodice, a Marie Antoinette fichu with or

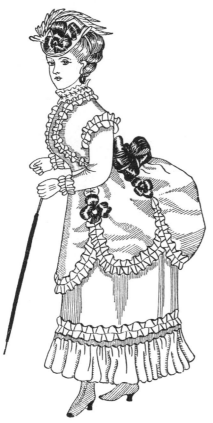

The Grecian bend. 1868

without an open tunic, or a polonaise (double-breasted and fastened slantwise down the front). The ends of the fichu are tied under the puff behind.

2. *The Trained Dress.* Six yards wide; the front and sides gored (two to three side gores), the back in small pleats all turned one way. The hem is bound with silk 'Hungarian cord' instead of braid.

(i) The single skirt, with plain or tablier front, the side and back breadths cut longer and fulled on to the tablier; these are bordered with a headed flounce cut on the cross.

(ii) Double skirts.

(*a*) The underskirt ankle length, plain or with a pleated flounce. The upper skirt knee length in front and longer behind. Often with a third skirt, very short and vandyked and looped up at the back with a broad bow.

(*b*). The pannier dress (worn usually without a crinoline). The upper skirt with a deep flounced border is looped up very high behind (the 'Camargo puff'); the underskirt with a very long train is short in front, the front breadth being flounced.

'To form a pannier puff, half a yard extra is added to the top of the back widths and gathered in to the side seams, the fullness extending some ten inches below the belt. A drawing string extended across the back widths draws them in to fit closely over the crinoline; the full material falls over the drawing string forming a puff.' A sash with wide ends has the bow at the back of the waist with a large loop below. Or the fullness at the back may be caught together by a ribbon band or strap or pieces of elastic sewn inside the seam on the side breadths and pulled through a gap in the seam and then hooked together behind, through which the fullness can be pulled. It will be observed that the puff may belong either to the underskirt, in which case the tunic is now worn apronwise with its fastening behind; or the puff may be part of the tunic, in which case it is open in front. 'The bunch at the back goes by an abundance of names, crinoline, panier, bustle or tournure.'

(*c*). The Watteau Costume. A round skirt edged with deep pleating; an over dress looped up at the sides, plain in front with a 'Watteau pleat' from the neck behind; the bodice open in front like a fichu.

(*d*). The Regency Costume. The upper skirt and paletot of velvet; the underskirt of satin.

It may be added that 'there is a great tendency to introduce flounces at the bottom of skirts, both with short and trained dresses'; and towards the end of the year 'the short double-skirted dresses are now used even for afternoon, the upper skirt being looped up en panier.'

The panier style was not entirely accepted in this country, a preference being for the single or double trained skirt of the simpler types; often worn with a tight-fitting polonaise.

The bodice of the trained dress is plain or trimmed to simulate a square low cut; the sleeves usually tight; waist short and round with a waistband. The Princess type of bodice and upper skirt in one is common.

Materials: shot silk, satin, foulard, poplin, moiré, cashmere, alpaca, and new mixtures of silk and wool; in summer, muslins, foulards, mohair, glacé. 'Sateen has been re-introduced this season.'

New Materials: alpaca de soie, Sultane, Ottoman velvet, satin Turc.

The rules for the use of two materials in one dress were as follows:

1. Two different figured materials must never be used. If one skirt is figured the other must be plain.

2. One of the skirts must be a quiet colour, two bright colours cannot be allied.

3. The mantle or paletot may be like either the upper or the under skirt.

4. If two striped materials are used one must have broad stripes, the other narrow, but both must be the same colour.

Fashionable Colours: Grenat, gas-green, Metternich green, Bismarck brown, Mexico blue, Ophelia, grey.

Evening

Always with long trains and double skirts. The underskirt (of satin) touching the ground with a deep pleated flounce; the overskirt trained. The overskirt may be flounced at the back with a tablier in front, or open in front, or as a tunic in the Princess shape, attached to the bodice. It is looped up behind as in the trained day dress.

Waist short and round. The over dress may be of lace, or, in ball dresses, of tulle. The underskirt may be bouillonnée up to the knee with a tunic or robings simulating one reaching that level. Bodice low with a pleating across the front, or cut low and square over a lace chemisette.

Wedding Dress

'It should be worn as often as possible in the early days of married life, without the orange blossom.' Usually of white satin; the skirt either untrimmed or with tulle puffing ¼ yard from the hem; a flounce of Brussels or Honiton lace round the skirt brought up the front as a tablier; trained skirt; high square cut bodice, very low, with a chemisette; elbow sleeves with ruffles.

Riding Habit

3½ yards wide; 50 inches long in front; 54 behind; left side 51; right 59. Front breadth much gored; 5 pleats at the back. Body plain and high in the neck with swallow-tailed point behind with two buttons. Buttons down the front; coat shaped sleeves; braided edge.

Bathing Costume

Of five yards of flannel or serge (32 in.) at 2/6 a yard, trimmed with black braid; a full bodice with attached tunic reaching to the knee, and buttoning down the front. Separate trousers reaching to the ankle. Short sleeves.

'The ugly loose blue gown like a bottomless sack is no longer considered the right thing for a bathing costume and a little more attention is paid by fair bathers to avoid looking downright frights.'

Additional Indoor Garments

The fichu, of lace or silk; the back rounded like a cape; the front like a sleeveless Spanish jacket; the ends, crossing at the waist in front, are tied behind in a bow with hanging ends. (Marie Antoinette form.) In the la Vallière fichu the fronts do not cross but just meet across the chest, being fastened by a button. These fichus are worn to give a dressy effect to an afternoon dress, with a low evening dress, or in summer as a substitute for a bodice.

The Bachlick, of cashmere edged with swansdown for winter, or of muslin for summer; in shape a fichu with a hood-like point behind with a tassel, and ends in front which are crossed. Worn with day dresses. The Capeline, of wool in winter or muslin in summer; a hood, cape and fichu in one, the ends hanging down in front. Worn indoors with morning dress, or over evening dress as an outdoor wrap.

Mantilla. Of lace, especially Maltese, often worked in coloured silks, worn over the head and descending over the bodice, fastening behind. Worn indoors both for day and evening.

Sashes. 'Dresses and paletots of all materials and shapes now made with sashes.' Either the 'baby sash', a plain bow with wide ribbon, or the fancy sash, the loop of which supports the puff of the overskirt with a bow half way down the skirt. Broad sashes worn on every occasion.

Crinolines

With the pannier style usually no crinoline was worn, but a crinolette and bustle; with other styles a small crinoline having four hoops at the bottom was usual.

OUTDOOR GARMENTS

Cloaks

The Casaque, tight-fitting at the waist with a band, and looped up at the sides.

The paletot, longer than formerly except for flounced dresses. (These may replace an upper skirt).

Mantles

1. The Carrick, with three or four capes of graduated size.
2. The Marie Antoinette, narrow behind with long ends in front.
3. The polonaise or redingote, buttoning slant-wise down the front with waistband and coat sleeves.
4. Mantles of Talma form but longer, and heavily fringed with jet. Generally with pelerine-capes.
5. Sealskin jackets.

ACCESSORIES

Shoes

The Cromwell shoe, with large buckle and tongue covering the instep 'is the favourite for croquet parties'. Button or elastic sided *Boots* with tassel or bow on the instep and broad square toes, or high laced boots of kid or satin. 'Much more attention is paid to boots and shoes since the introduction of short dresses.'

Jewellery. Brooches and ear-rings in the form of medallions with gold fringed pendants; ear-rings very large. Jet cameo brooches, ear-rings and combs, and necklaces with pendants.

Prices

Plain white Alpaca, 1/3½ a yard; Alpaca de soie, 12/6 the dress. Drap de Paris, 12/9 to 16/9; Japanese silk, 42/-; Koechlin freres' muslins, 5/6 to 10/6; Titus Salt Alpacas, 12/9; French satins, 40/- to 63/-; ready made mohairs, 19/-; foulards, 60/- to 75/-; all the made skirt with material for bodice. Galatea serge, 12/6 the costume. White piqué, 1/3½ a yard; Spitalfields moiré, 10/6 to 15/- a yard; grenadine, 1/0½; batiste, 1/4; gas-green poplins, 6/- to 7/6; Scotch gingham, 36 inches wide, 2/6; Scotch reps and camlets 2/6 and 3/- all per yard. Grouts Norwich crepe, 1/8 a yard.
Marie Antoinette fichu, 6/- to 10/-.
Yak lace shawls from 25/.
Sealskin jacket, £13; muff, 30/-.
French kid gloves, 2/6 a pair.
Silk tartan stockings, 7/6 a pair; ribbon merino ditto 1/3 a pair.
Nightdress with stand-up collar and made with yokes, 10/6 to 22/6.
Cashmere dressing gowns, 3½ guineas.
Petticoat, in scarlet cloth, the lower 12 inches kilted, 18/-.
Thomson's glove-fitting corset, 12/6.
'The fashionable long plait of three for forming the coiled chignon, from 21/-.' 'The sale of false hair has gone up 400% in the last dozen years.'

1869

'Fashion is now fairly upon that road of good taste which has been so ardently longed for by all sensible people.' This admirable sentiment (which tends to be applied by contemporaries to every new year) sounds especially odd when applied to 1869, the fashions of which were a frank revival of the modes of the Louis XV period. These, however appealing to the eye, were singularly inappropriate to the epoch of greater feminine activity now definitely started. The spirit implied by them is clear. The revival of tight-lacing with the prevalence of huge sash-bows at the back ('a very large bow has the advantage of making the waist appear much smaller'), the opulent undulations of puff and bustle behind, emphasised by high heels and 'the Grecian bend', were sensual appeals which the average woman found more important as means to gain her ends than attention to greater comfort and physical freedom. It was not liberty but the fetters of matrimony to which she aspired.

The noticeable changes of this year's fashions were towards further Gothic effects. The elaborate decoration with bows and fichus, the revival of small pelerine-capes, the deep 'V' of the bodice, and sleeves expanding into bell-openings are examples. We also have to notice the polonaise now becoming part of the dress and no longer merely an outdoor garment, and the crinolette as a definite substitute for the crinoline. The huge puff at the back is toned down and the panniers on the hips

233

merge into the general undulation. Greater attention is given to the display of 'the figure'; the bodice is more elaborately trimmed and revers attract the eye. Above all, every device is employed to emphasise the diminutive waist. It was determined, in short, that the new weapon for man's undoing should be the curve, of all weapons perhaps the least original but the most effective.

DRESSES

Day

'Bodices are of medium length, round at the waist. Shoulder seams are short and high defining the slope of the shoulders. The two darts in each front are short but taken very deep. Side seams are directly under the arm.' Generally cut (i) in a deep square; (ii) a deep curve; (iii) a deep 'V'; (iv) with revers; and worn with a chemisette which is frilled down the centre and trimmed with bands of insertion. Or a high bodice trimmed with fringed pelerine robings from the shoulders to meet a point at the waist in front and behind; or with an attached pelerine-cape, fringed; or with a separate fichu crossing in front.

In place of a bodice a tight-fitting casaque, cut up the sides and looped up and draped behind to form a bodice and upper skirt in one. Or the bodice may have attached basques at the sides, pointed and descending to the knee level. In place of the casaque a paletot cut as a jacket with pendant basques in front cut in the same piece, with postillions behind cut as separate pieces. Often a small pelerine or fichu is attached to the paletot.

In all cases a sash is worn with a large bow or jabot behind; sometimes the sash consists of a narrow waistband with fringed lappets attached and an elaborate bow sewn on.

Sleeves. Generally tight but sometimes with demi-wide openings, the cuff being marked by double pleating. A ribbon bow on the outside of the bend of the arm, known as a 'brassard' is common.

The skirt. 1. The looped-up double skirt. 'The looping is now by interior fastenings to form a puff; though the dress should always be full and ample at the back, the puff itself is not indispensable; the sash is far more so; it forms part of almost all toilets.' The upper skirt is usually open in front with corners turned back and edged with velvet; or as an apron-front with two gathered flounces and looped up at the sides. The underskirt with a series of gathered flounces or frizettes to the knee, or two or three lines of fluting.

2. A tunic, the bodice open to the waist edged with pleated flounce; the skirt closed at the waist and open below with one or two puffs at the back. 'Costumes just touching the ground; the upper skirt is rapidly absorbing the ungraceful puff.' (Autumn).

3. Single skirt buttoned all down the front (negligé).

4. The short round dress, or 'costume', with one skirt, usually trimmed en tablier with a headed flounce which extends round the sides and back.

5. The redingote dress, made en princesse, the back of the skirt being full but without a puff; a

New double skirt. 1869

double breasted bodice open in front with revers (of velvet). Or open and very low in front, kept into the waist by two buttons; under it a waistcoat buttoned high up to the neck.

6. A single flounced skirt worn with a sleeveless mantle which supplied the place of the overskirt.

'Nine-tenths of the costumes at Brighton consist in bright coloured silk petticoats with short black skirts very much bunched up, tight outdoor jackets and hats with cock's plumes.' (January.)

Trained Dress

Bodice plain and high with tight sleeve trimmed at the cuff; or as in the walking dress.

Skirts. 1. Double skirt, the underskirt edged

with fluted flounces; the overskirt short and puffed behind.

2. Single skirt, the puff being supplied by the basques of the bodice.

3. Single skirt with tunic casaque opening in front.

'Plain skirts may be worn trained, especially indoors.'

'The redingote, if raised behind on each side, may be worn over a trained skirt.'

4. The tunic dress, consisting of (*a*) a bodice with deep basques like a waistcoat. (*b*) tunic

Heavy silks lined for three-quarters of a yard with stiff foundation, with alpaca near the hem. French dresses are not bound with braid but hemmed up an inch deep.'

'The fashion of wearing low-necked dresses in daytime is becoming very common.'

Summer

Printed muslin with double skirts, the under with a deep flounce headed by a ruche, the upper with a ruche and looped up with ribbons; wide sash with large bow behind; bodice often

Pannier skirt—front. 1869

Pannier skirt—back. 1869

open in front and long behind, draped at the sides with velvet bows. It is, in fact, a casaque open in front. (*c*) trained skirt trimmed with narrow flat pleating with velvet heading.

5. Double skirts both trained, the under one plain, the upper somewhat shorter and edged with a gathered flounce. The puff is formed by looping up the basquine of the bodice with a ribbon sash above it. The upper skirt may be open in front as a robe and the under one en tablier.

'Trained skirts have a flat, gored front width, two narrow side gores and two full back widths. The fullness in pleats beneath the side seams; back breadths in French gathers. Five yards is the width of a moderate train worn over a small crinoline. Light silks lined with muslin.

cut à la Raphael or open to the waist; some sleeveless and worn over a sleeved chemisette. Sleeves often with a series of puffings ('Gabrielle sleeves') or flounces. Or in place of a bodice a short loose jacket with revers. Or a Garibaldi, usually of the cross-over type.

Materials: use of two different materials or two different shades of same material, *e.g.* mohair dress with black silk tunic. Walking dress, skirt blue, bodice and overskirt brown. Underskirt striped or tartan and overdress plain. Underdress of green grenadine, the overdress of black taffeta. Underskirt of striped woollen stuff and overdress plain but trimmed with flounces of the striped material. There are also complete 'costumes' of cashmere, serge, etc. Cloth (in which the flutings and flounces 'must be pleated very flat; in softer materials ruches and box-pleating are used'). Scotch plaid woollens ('tartan is the fashion and *must* be worn'). Cashmere, foulards, serge, linsey, velveteen, poplins. (Heavy silks do not lend themselves to being puffed and are therefore less used.)

(For Summer Dresses.) Muslin (especially printed with small pattern on white ground); grenadine; foulard; tussore; striped sultana; leno; alpaca; chaly. Striped materials fashionable. *New Materials*: Tussore; tussore foulard; alpine; crochet wool. Coloured fichus worn with white muslin dresses.

4. *Corselet bodices* (Summer), cut low and either square or with a deep 'V'.

5. Lace *jabots* worn with muslin bodices.

6. *Collars* of stiff net covered with lace, descending to a point, for wearing with open bodices. With high bodices a narrow upright collar edged with frilling or lace. Habit-shirts with turn down collars and narrow tatted cravats.

7. Muslin *jackets* with yokes, and trimmed with bands of insertion.

Ball dress. 1869

Ball dress. 1869

gros des Appennines; Byzantine granite; soyeux linsey; Bayadère.

Fashionable Colours: garnet, plum, ruby, marine blue, green, Vesuvian red, shot colours, golden pheasant, eau de Nil, caroubier.

ACCESSORY GARMENTS

1. *Sashes*. (*a*) Puff sash, with a puffed out basque behind and bretelles on the bodice. (*b*) Pannier sash, with three basques each forming a pannier, and bretelles. (*c*) Baby sash with plain large bow. (*d*) Roman sash, ten inches wide of Roman colours.

2. *Narrow waistbands* with fringed basques, short in front, long behind.

3. *Fichus*. The Marie Antoinette. Fichus of

8. *Shawls* are returning to fashion, especially Indian.

Evening

Dinner. Half-trained.

Full evening. Long train.

Ball. Either trained or short.

Bodice low off the shoulders, some square cut, others descending in the middle, edged with ruching or lace; trimmed with a bertha of satin piping and white blonde with ribbon bows in the centre and on the shoulders; short slightly puffed sleeves, or a chemisette with long sleeves. The skirts show no material change from the previous year. Ball dresses with two or three looped up skirts over a coloured silk slip, the underskirt with a series of narrow flounces or

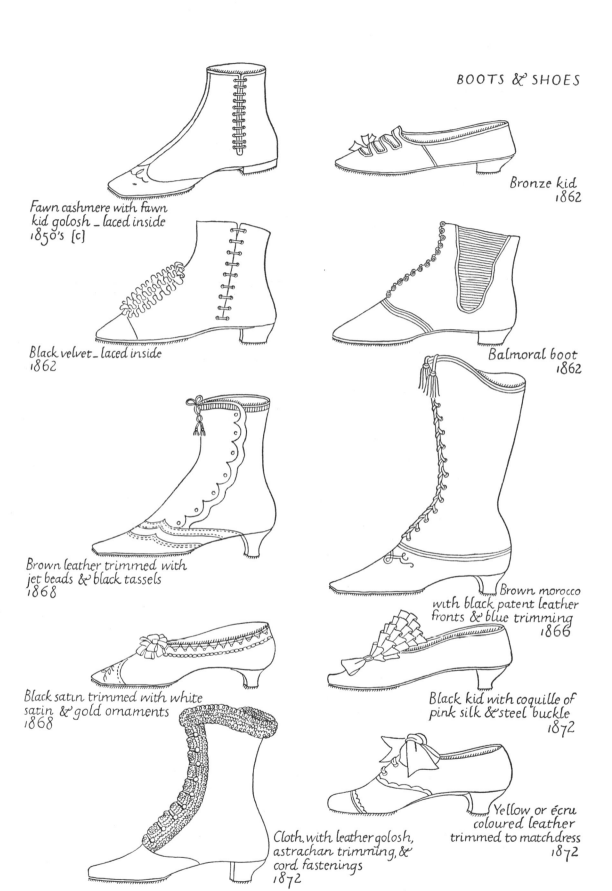

Fawn cashmere with fawn
kid golosh _ laced inside
1850's [c]

Bronze kid
1862

Black velvet _ laced inside
1862

Balmoral boot
1862

Brown leather trimmed with
jet beads & black tassels
1868

Brown morocco
with black patent leather
fronts & blue trimming
1866

Black satin trimmed with white
satin & gold ornaments
1868

Black kid with coquille of
pink silk & steel buckle
1872

Cloth, with leather golosh,
astrachan trimming, &
cord fastenings
1872

Yellow or écru
coloured leather
trimmed to match dress
1872

237

puffings, the second gathered up into pannier puffs; low bodice with round or pointed bertha; some with pointed waist.

The extensive use of satin ribbon bows as trimmings on the bodice and down the skirt, together with the inevitable sash and large bow behind may be noted. Crepe de Chine very fashionable.

OUTDOOR GARMENTS

Mantles

Are all with waistbands drawing them into the figure, many with large sash bow behind. They are richly trimmed with lace.

The rotonde is looped up behind at the waist round which it is fastened by a band passing through slits under the arms simulating sleeves; large bow behind. The Metternich, a very ample form of it has a seam in the middle of the back and one on each side; a detachable waistband passing through slits.

The polonaise, a mantle looped up behind, consisting of bodice and upper skirt in one, the latter knee length and looped up behind. No longer wholly an outdoor garment it is now frequently a portion of a costume, *e.g.* 'with a plain round skirt of broad green and black check a polonaise of smaller check with tight sleeves of the same material as the underskirt.'

Small mantlets, with pleats in the centre of the back, waistband, and front ends hanging loose. Tight fitting paletots with postillions.

ACCESSORIES

Shoes

Indoor, day and evening, of kid and satin, with large bows on the instep and 'high heels' (*i.e.* 1½ to 2 inches).

Long evening *Gloves* with six to eight buttons.

Jewellery: the Patti jets (a ball of polished jet pendant from ribbon necklace, with similar earrings) for morning wear. Sets of dark red gold, of barbaric designs; brooches of Moorish crescents. Jewellery enamelled in turquoise blue. Cut glass. Large square ear-rings.

Winter *Muffs* of velvet or plush edged with fur. *Fur Boas* coming in again.

Prices

Crepe de Chine 50 francs a yard in Paris.

Indian Shawls: Rampour Chuddar, made of camel's wool, without pattern, 2 to 6 guineas. Delhi shawls embroidered in raised silk (gold and coloured on plain grounds) 2 guineas upwards. Decca shawls, worked in bright coloured silks on black ground in larger patterns than the Delhi, 5 to 20 guineas. Cashmere shawls, of goat's hair, made in small pieces and imperceptibly joined, 10 to 200 guineas. Sealskin jackets from 8 guineas. Ditto mantles, 4½ to 20 guineas.

Norwich poplins, 2/6 a yard; Irish poplins, 5/- a yard. Velveteens, 1/9 to 6/9 a yard. Welsh flannel, 11d a yard. Spitalfields moiré, 8/- a yard. Superior four-fold crape, 5/6 to 10/6 a yard (Peter Robinson).

Broché silks the dress of 12 yards, 2 to 2½ guineas. Coloured quilted silk petticoats from 35/-; satin from 40/-; cashmere, 15/-, in all colours.

Danish silk finished alpaca, as worn by the Princess (32 in.) 10 yards 19/6.

Broché silk finished alpaca (32 in.) 10 yards 15/-. Mikado, silk cloth of Japan, great novelty, 12 yards 30/-. Balbriggan stockings, 21/- a dozen pairs.

The new patent stud, the back plate crescentic in shape to permit ease of insertion through a small buttonhole.

HEADGEAR

The decade is notable for the growth of the chignon at the back of the head, leading to a general use of false hair and—at the close of '64—to a complete change of style in bonnets. It is also notable for the growing use of the hat in place of the bonnet—a practice savouring, according to the elders, of a loosening of morals. The hat was not, of course, permissible in church, and was strictly forbidden for servants by careful mistresses who urged that a hat would presently lead to feathers and then 'to courting by young gentlemen'.

1860

1. *Ball Costume.* Headdress a torsade of white satin, ornamented with gold, gold résille; a group of roses at the right side.

2. *Home Costume.* Headdress of light blue chenille with a ruche of blue ribbon and bows and long ends at the left side, gold buckle in the centre of the bow.

3. *Promenade Costume* (also worn for riding). Black velvet hat ornamented by black feathers.

4. *Ball Costume.* Wreath of poppies and wheatears to correspond to the bouquets of poppies and wheatears on the shoulders and centre of corsage.

5. *Dinner Costume for Home.* Tulle cap trimmed with black lace, mauve ribbon and red and white marguerites.

6. *Promenade Costume.* Bonnet of Imperial blue feathers and black lace; tulle cap with tress of small roses, and broad blue strings.

1861

1. *Ball Dress.* Headdress composed of a ruche of black silk with large rose in the centre of forehead; at the back a deep black lace falls on to the neck. This dress is essentially for a very young lady.

2. *Ball Costume.*

3. *Promenade Costume.* Mandarin hat of black velvet with white and cerise feathers and aigrette of black and white feathers.

4. *Home Costume.* Morning cap of white lace trimmed with black and cerise velvet.

5. *A Dress Cap* of figured blonde, trimmed with black and white lace; at the top of front dark roses and rosettes of black silk; at the top are three roses, one light green, the centre one black, the other pink; bows of broad black ribbon at the back and long streamers of the same, edged round with blonde.

6. *A Dress Bonnet*, the front of white chip, the soft crown and curtain of white satin, the curtain covered with white lace; over the crown a network of very fine black chenille; entirely round the crown a black velvet ribbon which terminates in a bow at the back, the long ends falling over the curtain; ornamented by large pink roses, leaves and branches of rosebuds; tulle cap, the full tresse of tulle rosebuds and black velvet; broad white strings.

1862

1. *Carriage Costume.* Helmet hat of paille d'Italie, trimmed with black ostrich feathers; on the left side is a red plume.

2. *Home Costume.* Headdress of ruches of white lace ornamented with black velvet ribbon; black résille with ribbons.

3. *Home Costume.* Lace bow.

4. *Evening Dress.* Coiffure consisting of a torsade of black velvet and white silk tulle, with noeud of black velvet and a bunch of red roses placed in the centre front of head.

5. *Capote-écran* (screen), known as an Ugly, suitable for those with sensitive eyes, useful when driving, journeying or in the garden. It protects from the sun, and takes the place of a sunshade.

6. *Country Costume* or for travelling (chapeau batelière). Sailor hat in crinoline, trimmed with large black feather and small white feather.

1863

1. *Promenade Costume.* Hat of white chip with two rows of cerise velvet round the crown, and a large rosette in front to match in colour the trimming of the jacket (cerise).

2. *Promenade Costume.* Hat à la Reine of paille d'Italie; broad straw coloured ribbon round the bottom of crown, the long ends at the back trimmed with deep fringe; in the front poppies and wheatears.

3. *Ball Costume.*

4. *Carriage or Promenade Costume.* Bonnet of white chip edged with black lace with which the curtain is also covered. Blonde cap with roses and pink strings to match the dress (Bonnet Marie Stuart style).

5. *Seaside Costume.* Hood of white cashmere trimmed by a ruching of white and blue ribbon.

6. *Home Costume.* Cap of white Brussels net, spotted with black and trimmed with lilac ribbon edged with black lace.

1864

1. *Promenade Dress.* Bonnet of maroon velvet to match the dress.

2. *Home or Promenade Dress.* Ecossais hat of ruby velvet trimmed with black ribbon and a tuft of small black feathers.

3. *Ball Dress.* The ornaments of the head-dress consist of grapes, vine-leaves and pink ribbon.

4. *Promenade Costume.* Hat of white straw trimmed with black velvet and a large white feather.

5. *Promenade Costume.* Bonnet of black velvet trimmed with pink ribbon and roses; soft crown of black lace; in place of a curtain are frills of black lace of moderate depth.

6. *Home Dress.* Résille ornamented with poppy coloured velvet ribbon edged with lace. A black chenille fringe edged with crystal beads depends from the 'passe' and also from the chenille trimming down the centre of the back. Rose and corn are placed on the right side.

1865

1. *Morning Cap.* Made of muslin trimmed with strips of insertion edged with narrow stitched borders, which cross each other over the crown. In front, a quilling of scalloped out muslin, fuller at the top than the sides, with a few bows of coloured ribbon and long lappets. This cap is in the Empire style.

2. *Morning Cap.* More of the fanchon shape. Crown composed of strips of guipure lace insertion and narrow bouillons of muslin. The front quilling and the curtain are of muslin edged with guipure lace, the lappets of plain hemmed muslin.

3. *Ball Dress.* Headdress of white lace and flowers like those on the skirt.

4. *Day Dress.* Scotch cap composed of black velvet; trimmed with black velvet and a white aigrette. The hair is confined in a black velvet bag attached to the cap behind and ornamented on each side with a tiny blonde edging.

5. *Promenade Dress.* 'Pamela bonnet' of Leghorn trimmed with black velvet, black lace and branches of ivy leaves with berries.

6. *Promenade or Carriage Costume.* Leghorn bonnet without crown, blonde curtain to fall over the hair; broad strings of maize ribbon crossing the bonnet; at the top a group of violet flowers; blonde cap with flowers to correspond.

1866

1. *Promenade Costume.* 'Lamballe bonnet' of Leghorn trimmed with roses and lappets of white lace; narrow strings of white silk.

2. *Promenade Costume.* An Empire shaped bonnet; crown of white tulle with spots worked in golden brown silk; border, curtain and strings of green silk; long grasses and a large dragonfly at the back; leaves and grasses inside.

3. *Seaside Costume.* Three cornered hat of Leghorn straw trimmed with violet ribbon; in front a jet aigrette, a violet tuft and a white plume.

4. *Seaside Costume.* A fine Leghorn straw hat, bound with velvet the same colour as the dress; a small white bird in front.

5. *Morning or Breakfast Dress for Home Wear.* The headdress is an embroidered 'catalane' trimmed with Valenciennes lace.

6. *Ball Dress.* Hair arranged in long stiff curls which are pinned at the ends so as to keep them from falling as ringlets (Chignon à marteaux). A spray of briar and small dog roses mounted with gold leaves falls at the left side and a tuft of similar flowers behind the right ear.

1867

1. *Country Costume.* Japanese hat, made of white fancy straw and bordered with narrow black or any colour velvet; three fantastic ornaments of similar velvet on the top. Lined with similar coloured silk.

2. *Promenade Costume.* Black velvet bonnet in the Mary Stuart style; border forms a point in front; much raised at the sides and edged all round with a silver cord. Trimmed at the back with a wide border of black lace which simulates a curtain and is continued at the sides so as to form lappets. A bird with long spread out feathers is fastened in front.

3. *Visiting Toilet.* White terry velvet bonnet with small flat crown; front adorned with a feather; white satin strings and bandeaux under the front brim.

4. *Indoor Dress.* Cap for morning; tulle crown covered with three wide coloured ribbons placed across and edged with narrow Valenciennes lace. Border formed of a wide strip of insertion also ornamented with lace. Wide coloured ribbon strings.

5. *Morning Toilet.* Black velvet casquette with aigrette at the side; trimmings of stamped out black velvet with cerise edges.

6. *Ball Costume.* Headdress of blue ribbon and marguerites.

1868

1. *Morning Walking Costume.* Mantille bonnet consisting of black velvet with a long veil of black spotted net.

2. *Carriage Costume.* Bonnet, extremely small, of black lace edged by narrow band of mauve ribbon; deep fall of black lace at the back.

3. *Promenade Costume.* (Russian bonnet). Chapeau of scarlet velvet trimmed with black feathers; tuft of black feathers at the side.

4. *Morning Walking Costume.* Leghorn hat, the brim bound with scarlet velvet, turned up at the sides and fastened to the crown by three bands of velvet. Another band of the same velvet round the crown, with a bow in front and a large scarlet feather at the left side.

5. *Ball Costume.* The coiffure is a diadem of marguerites.

6. *Carriage Costume.* Bonnet of white crepe trimmed with mauve leaves and ribbon.

1869

1. *Walking Costume.* Tyrolese hat made of fine brown felt trimmed with a velvet band and a velvet cockade at the side, above which a brown feather forms a straight aigrette.

2. *Evening Toilet.* Coiffure ornamented with tea roses and foliage placed upon a puff of black lace.

3. *Promenade and Country Toilet.* Round hat in straw trimmed with black satin and wild flowers; lace fall.

4. *Promenade Costume.* Diadem bonnet in white lace and velvet with cluster of grapes on the side. (This is tied on with a ribbon passing below the chignon as is the case with all diadem bonnets.)

5. *Morning Toilet.* Coiffure composed of a muslin scarf edged with lace; the scarf tied at the back returns to cross on the bosom. A series of loops with a bow in the centre ornaments the front part.

6. *Visiting Toilet.* Puff Bonnet. Of fancy straw trimmed with two flutings of lace ornamented on the top with three large flowers and their foliage; lace barbe fastened at the side with a flower to correspond.

243

1860

HAIR

Central parting with side puffs and low chignon behind, frequently in a net. Sometimes side curls or plaits on either side above the ears, each plait looped down and back into the chignon.

COIFFURE

Day
Caps. Morning, small; the cache-peigne going out.

Evening
Small dinner caps. Ball: wreaths of flowers, ribbons, bandeaux with feather.

OUTDOORS

Bonnets rather large, slightly pointed in front and raised at the top. Of crepe, crinoline, silk, velvet, straw. 'Dress' bonnets of chip, or white blonde and embroidered tulle. Under-trimmings, flowers, feathers, fruit, ribbon, lace, gold ornaments, birds, butterflies.
Hats. Generally for seaside and country; in winter often of black velvet. Oval shape, the brims turned up at the sides and ornamented with feathers. An English fashion.

1861

HAIR

Generally curls at the sides; brushed off the forehead or waved. Sometimes the back hair is rolled over frisettes (*i.e.* pads) with a fulling behind. Often a comb is used. 'Marie Antoinette' style, waved in front, rolled back over frisettes with two long curls hanging behind.

COIFFURE

Day
Caps 'à la Paysanne', of embroidered muslin with ruching and quilling across the front. Chenille nets.

Evening
Young ladies. Velvet band across the centre in front, or wreath with cache-peigne of flowers behind. For matrons, diadems of flowers, feathers, gauze and gold cable cord twisted together. Dinner caps similar to day but more trimmed, and comb behind.

OUTDOORS

Bonnets. No change. Strings always wide. Many have straw brims and silk crowns.
Hats of straw for the country.

1862

HAIR

Centre parting with side puffs. 'Ladies are now wearing back and side combs (tortoiseshell) with balls on the top, some studded with steel.' 'Hair nets still worn under the fashionable hats.'

COIFFURE

Day
Nets, caps or fanchons indoors.

Evening
Scattered flowers, combs, or velvet coronets.

OUTDOORS

Bonnets high in front and fully trimmed over the forehead, with tulle or blonde 'cap' on the cheeks. Some have 'literally the appearance of a flower garden in full bloom'. Short veils sometimes worn.
Hats. 1. Oval with turned down brim and very low crown ('bergère').
2. The sailor, with higher crown and straighter brim.
3. Imperatrice hat.
(These three types are turned down).
4. Turned up or 'pork pie' hats.
5. The Scarborough hat, pointed behind, with deep turned up brim in front, but 'there is a certain amount of conspicuous vulgarity associated with them; therefore they should be shunned by all moderate people.' Hats now worn in the country by even the middle-aged.

1863

HAIR

As in 1862.

Evening
Coiffures slightly more elaborate; curls very popular and worn massed at the back.

COIFFURE

Day
Caps. Morning. Round, with a trimming of lace and blonde and a few ribbon bows.
Evening
Chiefly flowers worn.

244

OUTDOORS

Bonnets unchanged except for the Marie Stuart shape.

Hats. 1. High crown and narrow flat brim.
2. Marie Antoinette, lower crown, wider brim, slightly turned up at the sides and bent down in front and behind.

Capelines. Light hoods of soft material for country and seaside.

1864

HAIR

Centre parting, or brushed straight back; looped at the sides exposing the ears; large mass of hair behind set low on the neck. The chignon is plaited or tied low and turned up in a full puff, with invisible net.

Evening

A velvet fillet with tiers of puffs in front. 'False curls, plaits and bows, and false masses at the back are as necessary as crinoline is.'

COIFFURE

Day

Caps. Morning. Large and somewhat like the bonnets.

Evening

Caps worn rather high with a bunch of flowers in the centre. Ball. Toques and torsades (twisted coronets with long lappets of tulle). Large flowers held together with thick chenille.

OUTDOORS

Bonnets. A complete change occurs towards the end of the year when 'fashionable bonnets are very small; behind is neither crown nor curtain, simply the front of a bonnet like a small half-handkerchief and at the back a fall of lace.' Only to be worn by those having a mass of hair behind 'either natural or added'. Trimmed with lace, feathers, flowers, beads and fruit. The 'Passe' or bridge of flowers or trimming under the brim is not always attached to the bonnet.

Materials: poplin, moiré, terry, cloth, silk, chip, Leghorn, crinoline.

Hats. All varieties of the Casquette (a man's cap).

1865

HAIR

Very elaborate, especially for evening. Chignon worn higher and held in its place by 'two long pins with monster heads' (of gold, jet or filigree silver, and worn in the day). The hair is combed up over a large frisette. Hair nets, some of bright colours.

Evening

'What with rows of thick curls, plaits twisted and grouped in loops, short frizzed curls, numberless ringlets and false frizzes dotted all over the head the complications are infinite and bewildering.' False fronts with attached curls, mounted on wire, much used.

COIFFURE

Day

Caps always worn indoors. A plain muslin fanchon, pointed in front, edged with lace, and a large bow with hanging ends behind. Some are in the shape of a large net (for afternoon).

Evening

Caps. A square of Maltese insertion edged with lace and hanging over the chignon, with a velvet puff in front. Headdresses of detached flowers, etc., placed between the hair, and wreaths with crystal beads 'like dew drops'. The 'Greek headdress' consists of three bands of velvet placed in different spaces on the head with short frizzed curls between.

OUTDOORS

Bonnets. 1. The Fanchon, or half handkerchief, covered with crystal drops.
2. The Empire bonnet. (*a*) the Pamela. (*b*) the Lamballe; with very small curtain and large, perfectly round crown which comes up at the top higher than the front of the bonnet. Small in front.

Hats now worn with very large veils, ¾ yards long, of black lace, some hanging in front, some behind.

1866

HAIR

The chignon worn higher than ever and composed of (*a*) loose curls; (*b*) formal rows of curls ('marteaux') pinned down at each end. Worn without a net; (*c*) twists of hair or plaits; (*d*) hair combed over pads or frisettes.

'False hair is worn in incredible quantities and chignons are made of these marteaux all ready to be fastened on with a comb.'

Evening

Similar, but more elaborate.

COIFFURE

Day

Caps. For young ladies, silk net studded with crystal beads, or catalane of lace or embroidery. For matrons, white muslin or net caps either in the shape of an Empire bonnet or a fanchon.

Evening

On the crown is worn either a catalane (small square headdress) of flowers, or velvet bandeaux over which are fastened metal and crystal ornaments, or a veil at the back fastened to a diadem.

OUTDOORS

Bonnets. At first as in previous year, but gradually becoming flat without curtains or side facings, the strings tying under the chin. Dress bonnets (for theatre) have the strings fastened under the chignon, are made of tulle, and very small. Humming birds are immensely popular for trimming. Benoitons much used to ornament bonnets.

Hats mostly round or oval with shallow crowns (some with high), and small. Trimming of narrow velvet ribbon which hangs behind over the chignon in a loop. Frequently a flowing veil at the back.

Capelines worn for morning and evening.

1867

HAIR

Day

Chignon very large, now placed 'right on the crown of the head', sometimes enclosed in an invisible net. The front hair worn very much over the forehead, frizzed or in small curls. The chignon may be composed of large plaits or small curls or a coiled loop. 'The smaller the bonnet the larger the chignon.'

Evening

As in the previous year.

COIFFURE

Day

Caps very small in the Catalane or Marie Stuart shape. 'A mere puff of tulle or blonde with lappets.'

Evening

Plaited velvet bandeaux having ribbons hanging on each side. For dinner a small lace cap ornamented with flowers.

OUTDOORS

Bonnets of the fanchon type tied behind with narrow strings and in front a tulle scarf fastened below the chin. Trimming of metal berries of brilliant hues, and blonde lace.

Hats. 'Like the bonnets are diminishing in size and are worn perched over the forehead.' Crowns low and flat. Made of straw (maroon or black for morning).
The Toquet ('a more elegant phrasing for pork-pie') very fashionable.
N.B. Hats only worn with short dresses; trains imperatively require bonnets.

Veils both with hats and bonnets, fall just below the nose and are tied behind, hanging as lappets over the chignon.

1868

HAIR

'Chignons are increasing in size'; often weigh five or more ounces. Now tied at the crown of the head 'whence masses looking like rolls of hair are brushed over frisettes'; the whole encircled by a ribbon. The new American fashion of leaving the back hair to hang down loose is coming in.

COIFFURE

Day

Caps. Small fanchons worn.

Evening

A Spanish Mantilla, velvet bandeaux, or diadem worn.

OUTDOORS

Bonnets. 1. Fanchon shape slightly raised in front with lace falling over the chignon.
2. Puff bonnet, merely a small ornament on the front of the head, composed of a small wreath of flowers or fruit.
3. Mantille bonnet, 'composed of two wide scarves of blonde fastened in front by a bow and tied at the back of the waist,' draping the shoulders .
4. Chapeau russe. Quite round with slightly raised crown, trimmed round the brim with astrachan or feathers and an aigrette in front, and tied on with strings.
Hats. All small and tilted well forward.
Capelines ('A hood with a large curtain which may extend into a cape') popular as the small bonnets give no protection from the wind.

1869

HAIR

Chignon higher than ever, frequently composed of long curls (especially for evening) 'which is more graceful than the smooth round cushions of last year'.

COIFFURE

Day. Caps. Small fanchons.

Evening. Few ornaments, but placed high on the head.

OUTDOORS

Bonnets. 1. Diadem fanchon. 'A mere border an inch wide covered with tulle or lace ruching on which an aigrette of flowers or feathers is placed.' The ruching is continued in short lappets fastened in front under a satin bow.
2. Puff bonnet, as in 1868.
3. Chapeau russe, as in 1868.

Hats. All very small.
1. With flat crown in the Watteau style.
2. With high crown 'sloping off in front and behind and scarcely any trimming, the trimming put on upwards and not round the crown'.
3. Round hats with no crown, of the Japanese variety.
4. Large Leghorns with broad limp brims, for the garden.

Hoods. 1. Capeline, 'generally adopted by elderly ladies'.
(*a*) The Bachlick, a hood continued into a scarf wound round the neck; of cashmere or wool.
(*b*) The Donarière, a round hood with attached pelerine and sleeves, of quilted satin.
2. Capulet (fashionable for theatre toilette), consists of a velvet bandeau encircling the forehead to which is attached a veil or drapery covering the head, neck and shoulders, and brought forward on the bosom.

UNDERCLOTHING OF THE '60's

It is during this decade that underclothing began to emerge from its former obscurity, due perhaps to the indiscretions of the crinoline which was prone at unexpected moments to reveal the secrets of the underworld. Thus in 1862, we are told, 'Bright colours are now being very much used for under garments, knickerbockers, flannel petticoats and petticoat bodies, all of the most brilliant scarlet. The knickerbockers are confined just below the knee by elastic; those who are fond of gardening will find these most judicious things to wear.' And by '68 'underclothing is now frequently ornamented with embroidery worked on the material itself instead of being trimmed with it'. The growing taste for walking exercise and the beginning of outdoor games such as croquet led to a display of petticoats which immediately acquired a charm of their own by their colour and trimmings. 'They all attract the attention and criticism of both sexes' ('61). Underclothing was, in fact, simply obeying the rule governing the feminine toilet, that any garment which may be seen by man must be made attractive to him.

Chemise

The shape is unaltered, and nearly a yard wide at the hem. Scarlet cotton designs are used for trimming in '64, and by '68 the 'top is bordered with insertion and edging and on the front pleats embroidery is worked on the linen'. (In the same year we are told that for underclothing 'few people now use linen but prefer calico'). In '69 'a chemise with yoke of darned netting' implies further refinement. The use of broderie anglaise for trimming underclothing gradually ceases in this decade.

Camisole

Worn under dress with high bodice. In '67 it is described as being made of nainsook, the shoulder pieces and front being tucked and trimmed with embroidered frill. For evening dress a petticoat bodice, sometimes with attached chemisette was worn. By '69 with evening dress the camisole is edged with lace. It is no longer made with basques.

Chemisette and Habit-shirt

This began to return to fashion in '60 owing to the wearing of dresses with open bodies. They

247

soon became elaborate, *e.g.*, 'of muslin mixed with narrow insertions and very narrow black velvet' ('61). In the summer of that year a chemisette with full bishop sleeves is often worn with a low sleeveless day bodice. In '63 a 'habit-shirt with stand-up collar and large bow-cravat' (the 'cravate cocodès'). With the Swiss bodices of the middle of the decade a chemisette was frequently used. Towards the close of the period vertical bands of insertion and ribbon were the usual type of trimming. With low evening bodices the chemisette was of tulle or lace, often with coloured ribbon run through. The habit-shirt with front pleats and a frill.

Drawers

'If drawers are worn they should be trimmed with frills or insertion.' They were by no means universally worn, however. In winter the coloured flannel knickerbocker was often used. The drawers retained the shape worn in the previous decade. In '68 they appeared with five or six tucks at the knee and an edging of lace.

Vests

Merino vests, high in the neck with long or short sleeves are mentioned in '67, together with flannel undervests.

Petticoat

'For wearing under crinolines we recommend the woven woollen petticoat to imitate knitting, made in all colours' ('63). A short warm petticoat of wool or flannel, coloured or striped, was worn under the crinoline in cold weather. Over the crinoline two white petticoats or one coloured. The day petticoat (except with light summer dresses) was usually coloured, especially scarlet, *e.g.* 'We never remember seeing so great a number of red petticoats in the streets' ('67). The materials used were camlet, cashmere, flannel, taffeta, rep, quilted silk and alpaca, and black petticoats (for morning) of alpaca, llama, lutestring, glacé ('61). The bottom of the petticoat, now displayed by the looped-up dress, was elaborately ornamented, such as with rows of velvet each concealing a steel hoop, while in summer 'stiff muslin petticoats flounced set out the dress in a more graceful fashion than does a crinoline; a moderate-sized steel petticoat and a muslin one, with, of course, a plain one over it, make a muslin dress look very nice.' The white ones are usually trimmed with frills and the scarlet flannel ones usually scalloped and edged with white wool. Elaborate braiding and velvet bands decorate the merino variety. By '62 the white petticoat is usually flounced with frilling and often rows of insertion added. The next year striped and plaid petticoats appear and 'petticoats are being trimmed almost as much as dresses, and as now every lady in the street shows more of the former than of the latter garment it is absolutely necessary that they should be tastily got up; the inevitable flutings are even put round crinoline casings.' In '63 the petticoats are gored and sewn to a band 10 inches deep. In '66 a petticoat made of crinoline material was displacing the hooped article; in the same year the scarlet or pink flannel petticoat with four bands of wide black braid above the hem or white one with insertion above the hem are usual, while the Empress petticoat as a substitute for the cage has the top gored close and a deep flounce from above the knee to the hem. 'It measures 8 yards in circumference and trains nearly a yard on the ground' (for evening). The short dress now requires one unstarched cambric petticoat and the trimmed dress three or four starched and trained muslin petticoats, while coloured petticoats in stripes (black and violet, scarlet, orange, cerise or blue) are much worn by day. They are often made with an inside hem of fine black oilcloth (for cleaning purposes), while for afternoon dress a silk petticoat with pleated border is substituted. The walking petticoat (gored) may have three steels round the bottom, and measures three yards round. For the so-called Empire dress of '67 the 'Empire jupon', *i.e.* a gored petticoat with two or three steels round the bottom is worn, while under the ball dress and slip three petticoats, the first of longcloth, gored and trained, with three steels, the second of white muslin, plain and gored, and the third of white muslin gored and trimmed with a deep pleated flounce, are required.

In '68 'if white calico petticoats are worn under the crinoline they should be as simple as possible; if stiff muslin petticoats are worn between the crinoline and the outside petticoat corded muslin is the best material to use. The outside petticoat should be either like the dress or of bright silk. For morning white calico petticoats should have a pleating nine inches deep; for evening white calico petticoats with goffered flounces should be as long as the dress.' The coloured cloth petticoat is sometimes kilted 12 inches up. For winter day use 'white petticoats are now admissible; fancy alpaca, linseys, cashmeres, or quilted silks are more suitable' ('69). With the introduction of the bustle the white petticoat is frequently gathered just below the bustle and tied up with strings.

Crinoline

At the beginning of this decade the day crinoline would usually have some nine hoops and the evening some eighteen hoops of watch-spring, the former in coloured materials and the latter white. Those for ball dresses have a muslin flounce and it is announced that for day use 'crinoline no longer reigns supreme as it did last spring'. Next year the day crinoline is definitely flatter in front while for ball dresses 'the cage Empire, trained and with upwards of 30 steel hoops increasing in width downwards' is worn. 'The Sansflectum'—the hoops covered with guttapercha—is a washable variety, and Thomson's 'Crown Crinoline' has improved eyelet holes, and very narrow steels. In '62 the crinoline is much reduced in size at the top and often made with a detachable flounce. Some have jacconet casings to 'slip over the lower part and button on so as to save the foot from catching in the hoops'. The 'American cage', weighing half a pound, was a novelty in '62, its lower half encased.

In '63 the 'Ondina waved crinoline, so perfect are the wave-like bands that a lady may ascend a steep stair, throw herself into an arm-chair, etc., without inconvenience to herself or provoking the rude remarks of the observers, thus modifying in an important degree all those peculiarities tending to destroy the modesty of English women.' While the 'Crown' variety 'do not cause accidents, do not appear at inquests, are better than medicine for the health, are economical, graceful, modest, ladylike and queenly.'

Next year it is reported that 'crinolines are growing beautifully less', a rumour promptly contradicted: 'crinoline assumes proportions as huge as ever; not a year passes but in this country alone hundreds suffer death by burning through crinoline.' Actually the upper part of the cage was by now smaller while the bottom was still as wide, at least in the evening.

In '66 the fashionable world preferred using flounced muslin petticoats, while the crinoline, for those employing it, was made to fold inwards when in a sitting posture. This year a substitute is supplied in the 'peplum-jupon', a gored petticoat with three steels round the bottom and a deep pleated flounce, and in '67 horsehair petticoats gored and sewn into an elastic band, the lower part trimmed with three plaits of horsehair, appear.

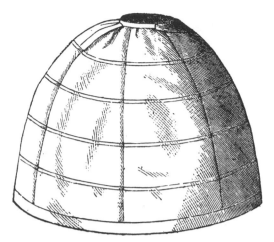

Crinoline. 1858

Crinoline. 1860

Crinoline. 1862

249

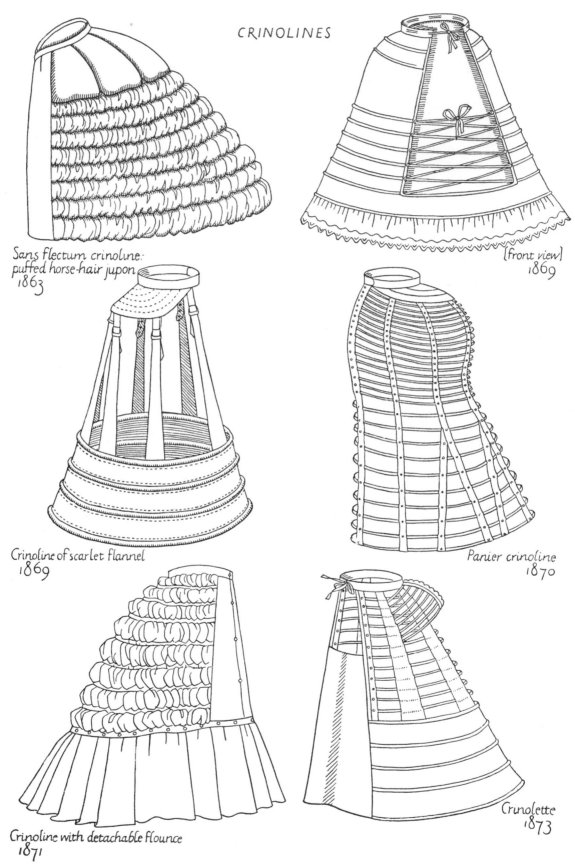

CRINOLINES

Sans flectum crinoline:
puffed horse-hair jupon
1863

[front view]
1869

Crinoline of scarlet flannel
1869

Panier crinoline
1870

Crinoline with detachable flounce
1871

Crinolette
1873

250

With the pannier dress the crinoline was discarded but with others it still survived, now in the form of three or four hoops suspended by bands from a broad waistband, and not more than 6 feet round at the bottom while to support the growing puff at the back of the dress the 'Zephyrine or winged crinoline', open in front with four or five steels either round or trained, appeared. The crinoline was, in fact, found to be as necessary as ever in its new form, as a support to the bustle, except for the short round dress.

In '69 the crinoline is hooped only at the back and the material buttons down the front, very often with a detachable flounce. In the same year appears the crinolette or half-crinoline, 'of steel half hoops with horsehair or crinoline flounces forming a bustle'; it retains, however, a front piece of material which buttons across.

As an alternative to the crinoline a horsehair gored petticoat, with flounces up the back headed by puffings forming an attached bustle, may be worn.

The Bustle

The revival of this device (the use of which had lapsed in the middle '50's) appears first in '68 as an arrangement of a few steels or whalebones inserted into the top of the petticoat to support the puff of the pannier skirt. This was immediately improved by wearing a separate bustle of horsehair or whalebone over the crinoline, and in '69 the bustle is often of steel hoops about the size of a melon, or of puffings of crinoline material, and may be permanently fixed to the crinoline or crinolette.

The Corset

'The taste for coloured corsets is rapidly increasing' ('62). As soon as the crinoline began to shrink in size tight-lacing returned, and by the end of the decade was a marked feature. 'All efforts tend to make the figure appear as small as possible below the waist' ('64). 'In Paris the favourite corsets are made of pieces of white silk elastic joined together by narrow strips of white tape forming an open network; very few bones are put in. The stays open in front and are fastened by small straps and buckles, and laced at the back' ('65). 'The old-fashioned stays, however, are still too generally worn.' Indeed, we find mention of red flannel stays at this time.

In '67 Thomson's 'glove-fitting corset', the front fastenings being kept together by a spring latch, and the French back-fastening corset with long steel busk down the front each had their admirers. The type with elastic strips between the bones was condemned by many as being 'positively dangerous to the figure', and from the lengthy correspondence in contemporary journals we gather that a waist measurement of 17 to 21 inches was the fashionable desideratum.

Stockings

'Coloured stockings or white ones embroidered with coloured silks are fashionable in harmony with the scarlet petticoats' ('61). Fashionable colours are scarlet, green, magenta, mauve, etc., according to the colour of the petticoat (day). Plaid or circular stripes ('64). While at the close of the decade vertical striped stockings and plaid stockings are conspicuous objects with the short dresses. With 'afternoon dresses' the stockings would be of the colour of the underskirt, worn with shoes the colour of the overskirt. White stockings are worn with white summer dresses.

Materials: woollen or cotton, but occasionally silk day stockings are mentioned. For evening, silk (white).

Nightdresses

'The hem of the nightdress should be $2\frac{1}{2}$ to 3 yards wide.' Usually of longcloth, the collar, cuffs and front trimmed with embroidery and fastened down by a strip of insertion. Some are made with stand-up collars and formed with a yoke ('67), the fronts being tucked.

Trousseau

A trousseau should comprise twelve or eighteen of each garment. The following are the items of a £20 trousseau ('68):

6 chemises at 4/9; 2 at 10/6.

4 nightdresses at 5/11; 2 at 9/6.

6 longcloth drawers, tucked, at 3/6; 3 trimmed with work at 5/6.

2 longcloth petticoats, tucked, at 8/6; 1 trimmed with work at 13/6.

3 camisoles, trimmed, at 4/9; 3 extra good at 6/6.

3 merino vests at 3/6.

3 flannel petticoats at 8/6.

1 printed cambric dressing gown at 21/-; 1 coloured flannel at 31/6.

12 pairs white cotton hose at 1/3; 6 pairs Lisle thread at 2/-.

12 cambric pocket handkerchiefs at 1/-; hemstitched at 2/-.

2 French corsets at 12/6.

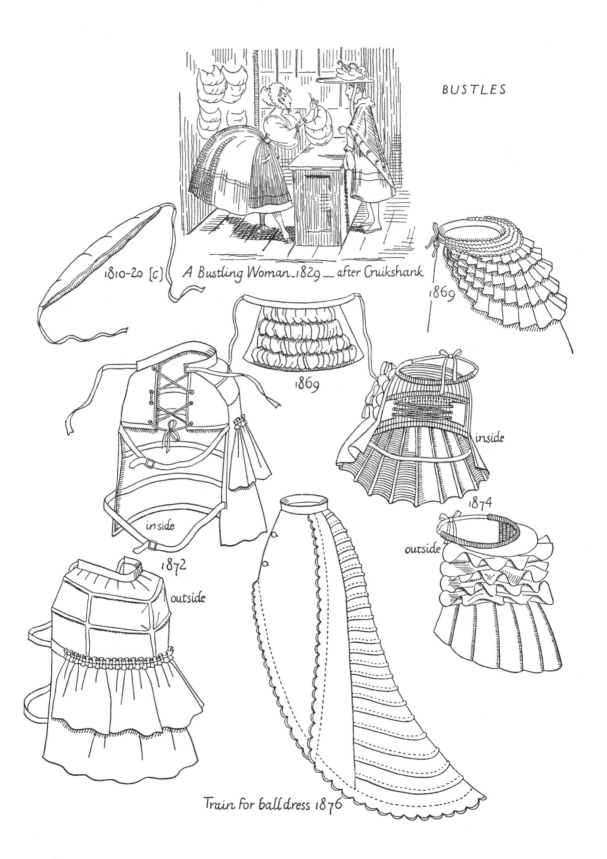

BUSTLES

1810-20 [c]   A Bustling Woman _ 1829 _ after Cruikshank

1869

1869

inside

1872

outside

inside

1874

outside

Train for ball dress 1876

252

2 crinolines at 12/6.

6 fine huckaback towels at 1/2.

(Such a trousseau as the above would be a minimum outfit for a modest income.)

The following are the items advertised in '67 for a trousseau costing £100, which may be taken as that suitable for a fashionable bride:

12 chemises trimmed with insertion and work, at 15/6; 6 with real lace at 18/6.

12 nightdresses at 22/6; 6 at 25/-.

12 longcloth drawers, trimmed with work, at 10/6; 6 with lace at 12/6.

4 longcloth petticoats, tucked and frilled, at 21/-; 3 cambric ditto, embroidered and frilled, at 27/6; 2 French pique, frilled, at 22/6.

1 dress petticoat, superbly embroidered, 63/-.

6 jacket bodies trimmed with work and insertion, at 10/6.

6 camisoles trimmed with lace, at 12/6.

6 patent merino vests, at 7/6; 6 ditto of India gauze, at 6/6.

4 flannel petticoats at 13/6.

1 white muslinette dressing gown at 35/6; 1 printed cambric at 25/-; 1 flannel ditto at 70/-.

2 muslinette dressing jackets at 27/6; 1 coloured flannel at 25/-.

12 pairs white cotton hose at 3/-; 12 ditto Lisle thread at 3/6; 6 ditto pearl silk at 12/6.

12 cambric handkerchiefs at 2/-; 12 hemstitched at 2/6.

2 pairs French corsets at 16/6.

2 crinolines at 15/-.

CHAPTER VIII
THE '70's

———————

THE clothing in this decade supplies many points of interest such as the marked change in form from the bouffante to the sheath with the intermediate 'tie-back'; the use of multiple colours, at first by contrasts and then by harmonies and the courageous use of three and even four in a dress; the decline in the use of silk and the widespread taste for woollens, together with the use of multiple materials are original features. At the close the artistic influence of the 'Aesthetic Movement' opened the eyes even of the fashionable world to a new conception—the idea that a woman's dress should harmonise with her surroundings; these became 'artistic' and the dress followed suit. It is perhaps in their colours that the dresses of the '70's are most striking to the eye; the monochrome has vanished and the blend of tones now produce the effect of a picture—sometimes even the appearance of stage costumes.

From the sociological aspect the decade supplies the beginning of utilitarian styles of dress which develop along their own lines. It is true that mere physical comfort was not—as yet—the primary consideration but the germ of the idea was present. A growing group of young women of gentle birth was now employed in work other than domestic and they began to use styles of dress distinct from the purely fashionable. Consequently specimens may be found so modified that they are now difficult to date. Although, for example, tight-lacing was the rule, there were many who resolutely refused to follow it and wore clothing which was 'sensible'. Similarly by no means all succumbed to the bustle, while at the end of the decade many cultured women had dresses composed to their individual taste with hardly any traces of current modes about their cut. Dresses designed by William Morris, for example, were veritable works of art.

It was becoming possible for a woman to be original without ceasing to be a lady. For the majority, however, the old rules were still strictly observed. A good example of this was displayed in the raiment considered essential in mourning, and it may be convenient to add here some indications of what was conventional in this respect. Thus, in '76, propriety demanded for a widow a dress of paramatta entirely covered with crape to within an inch or two of the waist; for the first nine months no tucks, then two tucks in the crape. The bodice entirely covered with crape; deep lawn cuffs and collar; cap of the Marie Stuart shape. Mantle of paramatta with crape; bonnet entirely of crape with a widow's cap inside; veil with a deep hem. This dress must be worn for a year and a day when the widow 'slighted her mourning' and adopted a black silk dress heavily trimmed with crape for six months, after which the crape was lessened and jet permissible. After eighteen months crape was omitted and after two years black, 'though it is in much better taste to wear half-mourning for at least six months more; many widows never put on colours again.'

Mourning for a parent or child—twelve months (six in paramatta with crape trimming; three in black; three in half-mourning).

For brother or sister—six months (three in crape; two in black; one in half-mourning).

For grandparents six months (three in crape: three in black).

For an uncle or aunt, three months black.

For first cousins, six weeks.

'A wife wears mourning for her husband's relations precisely as she would for her own; it is customary, when a man has married for a second time, for the second wife to wear slight mourning for three months on the death of a parent of the first wife.' A strict observer of these rules might easily find herself compelled to wear mourning of various grades for years together should she happen to lose her relations seriatim. It is in the '70's that the first signs of revolt against mourning appear.

The general complaint that a woman's wardrobe was becoming more and more expensive is a noticeable feature. It was not the materials so much as the trimmings and accessories which raised the cost. This decade was the great age of trimmings, which meant, of course, time and labour in the making and putting on. And tight dresses entailed good fit which meant using the professional dressmaker; who, alarmed at the growing taste for ready made costumes, no doubt did her utmost to encourage a style needing her skill.

This decade must be given the credit for originating several new types of dress and in particular the beginnings, at least, of the special dress for outdoor games. The bustle is, of course, only an exaggerated form of what had been used all through the first half of the century. The '70's can claim, too, to have introduced for the first time in history the shaped undergarment—that is, shaped to the outline of the body, and the close-fitting combinations marked a great advance. Chamois leather underclothing, though equally original, seems to have less merit.

Sex-attraction was provoked by various devices, new at least at the time, or rather, revivals of forgotten modes. The exaggeration of curves, especially those of the hips, marked the first years of the decade while later more dependence was placed on anatomical display by tight dresses. This was largely confined to the lower half of the body for the upper remained disguised by the corsets; here the curves could be as opulent as the corsetier chose. Indeed, the corset itself became an object of peculiar fascination and was exploited in the cuirass bodice, designed to suggest that the wearer had not completed her attire but was still in her bedroom. The symbolism of the corset, and of the corset-like bodice was never so marked as in these years. Another curious device to attract the male sex was the scarf swathed either round the knees to suggest that the woman was, as it were, 'tied up' and at his mercy, or in suggestive fashion round the sexual region. It is significant that the small ornamental aprons were called by the ladies themselves their 'fig leaves'. It is impossible to appreciate properly the fashions of the '70's without some knowledge of the current psychological forces at work. The influence of the sexual instinct can be detected more obviously in the fashions of this decade than in those of any preceding. Not that the instinct was stronger, but the normal forms of satisfaction were becoming blocked by economic conditions. Under these circumstances it found means of expression, as it always does when hampered, in unconscious symbolism.

In a technical sense the '70's are distinguished for their woollen textiles and fancy materials largely used as the overdress and gradually obliterating the underdress. These two layers gave the picture the quality of 'depth', which was further accentuated by the extraordinary use of trimmings. Workmanship was generally good, but democracy was beginning to demand cheap substitutes for the real thing; petty economies may be detected in places concealed from the eye. When a dress might comprise several layers it was a common form of economy to use up portions of an obsolete model, and a gorgeous polonaise would provide a new body to last year's chassis.

The '70's was notable for the 'Princess dress'—a type made fashionable by the Princess of Wales, although the name had been used for it in 1848, and for the return to trains even for walking dresses. The train, with its subtle suggestion that the wearer was socially above the rank of the 'walking classes' now swept the streets in spite of a thousand devices for holding it up. Any aristocratic significance became destroyed by its general use.

Owing to the multitude of layers and the substitution of woollens for silks, the total weight of the clothing was considerably increased during the first half of the decade, and then extraordinarily diminished towards the close.

1870

'All invention in the matter of ladies' dresses, especially ball dresses, seems to have ceased. The trains are a little longer, the hair is worn a little higher, the bows of the sash are a little more wing-like than ever; the last point of exaggeration has been reached.' This criticism expressed by a contemporary early in the spring needs, however, some qualification. During the year the shape tended to become less exuberant but the trimmings more elaborate, and the taste for using two materials and two colours for a dress developed. Thus, with two colours 'one should predominate; the secondary colour must harmonise with the first. Two contrasting colours in contiguity must not be equal in intensity; the darker colour

1. Trimming for coloured petticoat _ 1868

2. Trimming for dinner dress _ 1868

3. Trimming for Spring toilette _ 1870

4. Trimming for walking toilette _ 1871

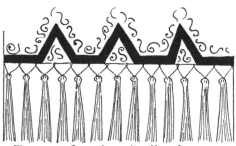

5. Trimming for toilette de ville _ 1871

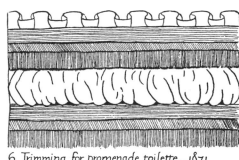

6. Trimming for promenade toilette _ 1871

7. Trimming for evening dress _ 1871

8. Trimming for ball toilette _ 1872

Skirt trimmings (1868-72)

should be used for the overdress and the brighter for the under-dress.' For example, a dress of grey taffeta under a tunic of black grenadine; a bodice and upper skirt of black satin with underskirt of black and white striped taffeta; an evening skirt of pink taffeta with a bodice and tunic of sky-blue faille. 'Fabrics, colours, and thick as well as thin stuffs are all allied in the composition of costumes.' In the same spirit we see black silk or velvet mantles over quite light coloured dresses, often of woollen materials. The darkness of the upper part is, of course, balanced by the large skirt when this is trained, but with round dresses the top-heavy effect is noticeable.

Although the monochrome dress with its surface broken by abundance of flounces and ruching, etc., still existed, the taste was for at least two shades of a colour, such as the dress of one tone with trimmings of a darker. Sometimes even three tones of a colour with three materials would be used, *e.g.*, merino skirt of light brown with medium brown silk flounces and dark brown velvet jacket. The prevalence of velvet as a trimming for woollens as well as silk stuffs is a notable feature.

The new fabrics introduced are mainly those having a strong refractory surface to resemble satin but made of wool or cotton, as substitutes for pure silk, indicating the importance attached to colour effects; while the rising prices of materials and the growing elaboration of the dress itself made these economies welcome.

The severely plain 'house dress', lacking the characteristic features of the period, was no doubt a necessity in the middle-class home and such examples may surprise those only familiar with more elaborate specimens of the same date.

During the year the round waist and the huge sash go out of fashion, and with them the 'short bunchy puff at the back', the bouffante effect being now obtained by the bustle itself over which the dress falls, especially with woollen materials. The pagoda sleeve gradually displaces the tight sleeve and the bodice open in front is generally substituted for the closed high-neck.

It is, on the whole, a year in which colour and texture, rather than form, supply the novelties. Once again we are told by a contemporary that 'our present fashions are far more graceful and becoming than they have been since the commencement of the century'.

DRESSES

Day

1. Plain single skirt, $4\frac{1}{2}$ yards wide, trimmed with ribbon velvet or bias silk bands; bodice either closed to the neck with square or pelerine trimming, or slightly open in front with or without revers; frilling round the neck; plain round waist; a short basque; coat sleeves. Or the skirt may be trimmed with a deep pleating headed by a velvet band. (Such are 'house dresses').

For walking, a slightly more elaborate single skirt, either plain in front and full pleats behind worn with a jacket bodice having basques, or a single skirt with one flounce in front and two behind laid on to simulate a trained overskirt and worn with a casaque.

2. Double skirt.

'Most of the dresses now worn consist of skirt, upper skirt, basque and paletot. The under-skirt measures $3\frac{1}{2}$ yards wide, having a very broad gore in front, a broad side gore and two straight breadths each $\frac{3}{4}$ yard wide behind. The

258

1870
Dress of amber satin with puffings; opera cape of cashmere
Evening dress of mauve gros grain and black blonde
Evening dress of blue poult de soie

1870

1876

1879

1879

front and side breadths are sewn to the waist-band without gathers. To flatten the front of the dress strings are sewn inside the side seams and tied back, in both the upper and under-skirts. Few skirts are lined; a facing of stiff cloth round the bottom with a braided hem. Over-skirts are elaborate and generally long with apron fronts, the back being caught up, some-times by tapes. Silk dresses have a full bouffante; cashmeres cling close to the figure but must be worn over a full bustle.'

Walking dresses of serge, cashmere, or poplin are made with jacket bodice with long pos-tillions behind and the front trimmed to simu-late an open jacket over a waistcoat: the under-skirt with one or two flounces, the upper skirt as a tunic open in front, or plain in front like an apron; cloth dresses have a deep pleated skirt, long half-fitting paletot and waistcoat with deep basques, the whole edged with narrow flutings and velvet bands. The basques of the jacket or paletot are deep enough to form an overskirt. The overskirt may be only simulated by a line of flouncing, especially in heavy stuffs. 'It is the exception to make a costume without an overskirt or casaque having the same effect; a last year's muslin dress with single skirt can now be used with a black silk walking skirt underneath, the muslin being caught up at the sides to resemble an overskirt' (Summer).

The trained walking dress is somewhat more dressy, e.g., 'underskirt with deep pleated flounce, a tunic open in front with revers be-low, bodice with square opening and basques'; or a single skirt with two scalloped flounces behind to simulate a trained overskirt, and a rounded flounce in front, with a casaque looped up behind; pagoda sleeves. 'The overskirt is now shorter than last year; it forms the pannier behind and remains open in front.' Summer. 'Some bodices have two sharp points in front and two behind, but most have jacket bodices with basques; these are sometimes long enough to form a double skirt; sometimes short when a tunic skirt is added. Sleeves are generally wide or half-wide with tight undersleeves for day. Bodices either square or heart-shaped in front with a plastron or waistcoat.' Mohair dresses have 'a short skirt, three yards wide, gored at the sides and trimmed to a depth of $\frac{1}{2}$ yard with a pleating, finished top and bottom with narrow box-pleated frill and a piping of silk; close-fitting overdress with bodice and bouffante skirt in one, the latter reaching to the top of the pleating on the underskirt. Bodice with revers;

white frilling at the neck and wrists; small bows up the bodice; wide sleeves.'

Two special types of day dress introduced this summer:

(a). The Shawl dress, 'taking their name from having been made, in the first instance, from shawls, borders, fringes and all being used,' especially Scotch shawls. Underskirt with three pleated flounces; overskirt, edged with fringe, 'is very long behind and open in points, these being looped up and crossed on the hips; a scarf of the material is draped from the left shoulder to the hip, the effect being that of a draped shawl; high bodice with short basque in front and behind. Coat sleeves, fluted collarette and cuffs.'

(b). The 'Frou-frou' dress. 'Light silk under-skirt trimmed with innumerable small pinked flounces, low corsage covered with short mus-lin tunic open to a point and having the skirts rounded off in front or else open at the sides; edging of lace.'

Visiting Dresses.
Underskirt: (a) deep pleated flounce, or
            (b) deep band of velvet, or
            (c) gathered deep flounce and fluted heading.
Upper skirt: (a) circular and edged with flut-ing, or
            (b) cut into four large points and fringed, or
            (c) slightly drawn up at the sides and edged with gathered flounces.

worn with a casaque which may be (a) tight with apron front, (b) tight with deep points at the sides, or (c) a bodice with open basques. All these have a waistband with small bow behind. The casaque has sleeves hanging or open (pagoda); pointed, square or rounded basques, often with deep basque behind forming the overskirt. A waistband and small bow behind. Fringe or lace edging. Bodices are either open in front en châle or with revers, square or en cœur. Sleeves either pagoda or duchesse with lace undersleeve.

Chemisettes are worn with open, square or heart-shaped bodices, and are covered with embroidery or lace with double frill for the neck; or else narrow tucks of fine cambric trimmed with lace.

Fichus are much worn 'of white muslin, lace or tulle, worn over high dresses whether open or not; with the former the fichu goes round the neck and meets halfway down the front and fastens into the waistband; a bow of muslin is at the back of the neck and another in front. With a closed bodice the fichu completely hides the front.' 'The plain linen collar is now obsolete.'

Trimmings

'A mere flounce is considered no trimming at all; it must itself be trimmed with flutings, pipings, bias bands, fringe, lace, etc; jet is quite out of fashion as trimming, but is only worn as ornament.'

'Camaieu' trimmings are piped round with satin of darker hue than the dress.

Materials: (Winter). velvet, velveteen, satin cloth, serge, merino, cashmere, poplin, faille, cloth, satin de laine; 'twills rather than reps.' German cloth is much used.

(Summer). Cambric, piqué, brown Holland, mohair, batiste écru, China crepe, jacconet, percale, foulard, alpaca.

New Materials: foulard, poil de chevre, carmeline, 'frou-frou', crepeline, Imperial velvet, satin jean, Japanese pongee, tripoline.

Colours: (Winter). Havannah brown, myrtle green, violet, mauve, grey, Mexican blue, eau de Nil, chestnut, plum.

Evening

Always trained, and with tunic overskirt. The underskirt with bands of fluting elaborately headed or puffing between flounces, or a plain tablier front trimmed up the sides and at the back. The tunic short and open in front and puffed out behind, often with a bow on each side; or a long tunic draped and looped up with bouquets. In front the tunic is often turned back with revers. Tunics of crepe de Chine are very fashionable.

Bodice: (*a*) Low and square, edged with flutings, bows on the shoulders, chemisette of lace.
(*b*) Half-low, en cœur, or square, with frilling edging.
(*c*) Low round bodice buttoning in front with bouquets on the shoulders.
(*d*) Jacket bodices with point in front and small basque behind which lies over the pannier.
(*e*) Bodice with basque, pointed in front with a narrow flounce round it; open and fluted behind.

The sleeve. Short and slightly puffed, or sabot sleeve descending to the elbow, with ruffles.

With evening dresses 'the train should be 65 inches long; the front and sides of the skirt are gored; two full breadths behind, each 27 inches wide, rounded off bluntly; width of skirt 5½ yards.'

Fichus are much worn over evening dresses.

Bathing Costume

'A basque bodice and drawers fastened below the knee with scarlet ribbon; some with short skirts; short puffed sleeve; bathing cap with net attached.'

OUTDOOR GARMENTS

Jackets

Tight fitting behind, loose and double-breasted in front; turned down collar with revers; open sleeve; fringe edging.

Paletot

Loose fitting, often with hanging open sleeve; some sleeveless with Watteau pleat behind and basques forming the overskirt.

Mantles

Usually with long points in front and one behind, the side pieces forming hanging sleeves; or draped like a shawl; fringe edging common. Others slashed in three places at the back; wide open sleeves. Trimming elaborate (cross bands of satin, edgings of fur, lace flounces, etc.).

However loose in front the mantle is drawn in behind at the waist to project over the bustle.

ACCESSORIES

Shoes

'Shoes are de rigeur for evening dress; generally of white satin or kid embroidered in gold, silver or coloured silk.' *Boots* of black satin, high heels; indoor shoes of bronze or coloured kid with rosette.

Coloured silk *Stockings*, or white with coloured clocks (evening).

Gloves

Five to seven buttons.

Ribbons are now of thick faille or gros grain, not taffeta.

New invention-studs with crescentic base.

Prices

Dress lengths. Spring sateens, 8/6 to 15/6; brilliants, 4/9 to 10/6; percales, 6/9 to 12/6; camlets, 10/6 to 25/-; Japanese silk, plain, striped and checks, corded figured and fancy, 25/- to 3 guineas. White silks for wedding, £2 to £3.

Muslins, black ground, chintz flowers, 8/9 to 10/6; Cable-cord pique, 15/6; satin de laine, 15/6; Irish poplins, 12 yards, 66/- to 72/6.

1871
Afternoon dress of striped Jap silk

Cheap silk dresses of 15 yards, 52/6. Satin costumes, 2 to 7 flounces, 40/- to 5 guineas. Moiré antiques, 4 to 5 guineas. Cashmeres, 15/-.
Black gros de Suez, 20 inches wide, 2/11 a yard; black gros grain 3/3 a yard. Satin faced brocades 3/6 a yard. Quadruple mourning crape, 10/6 a yard. Crepe de Chine, 30 inches wide, 6/3 a yard. Velveteens, 30 inches wide, 3/- to 4/- a yard.

Mohair dress (skirt, jacket and underskirt) 33/6. White Balbriggan stockings, 1/3 a pair.
French corsets, 12/6; riding ditto, 10/6; nursing ditto, 12/6.
Sansflectum jupons, 10/6. Bustles, 4/11 to 6/6.
Camlet petticoats, grey, fawn, etc., with 5 flounces, 10/6.
Lawn and cambric sunshades with coloured linings and white handles, 3/6 to 4/-.

1871

Parisian fashions were paralysed by the Franco-Prussian War from the middle of 1870 to the middle of 1871. Nevertheless new fashions continued to arise, in particular the polonaise, at first as an outdoor garment and then as an integral part of the dress; essentially it consisted of a bodice and tunic in one, the tunic being looped up at the sides, short in front and much looped up behind into a puff. It was, of course, only a revival of an eighteenth century garment but its acceptance may be fairly attributed to English rather than to French taste. In a special form, made with materials printed in chintz patterns, it was known as the 'Dolly Varden', appearing here in the summer and carried on, in winter materials. It arose as the result of the sale of Charles Dickens' property after his death, when the picture of his well-known heroine was included in the auction. The widespread affection felt for the deceased author no doubt gave the garment a special appeal to the multitude. It was not patronised by the 'best people'.

The other feature of the year was the decline of the puffing at the back of the waist. 'The enormously exaggerated form of the panier has gradually gone out of fashion.' While the use of different materials in one dress was common the colours were usually shades of one colour rather than contrasts. And we are assured that 'the present fashions are so elegant that it is not difficult to dress in artistic and graceful modes'.

'Suits, or as some call them "costumes" are very fashionable'; these, for morning or outdoor use, were sharply distinguished from the elaborate 'visiting dresses' of more than one material. For all purposes, however, the open bodice and pagoda sleeve was becoming general. It was now permissible to be picturesque even at breakfast; and when we read of a fashionable skating costume, 'over a gored flannel petticoat with a box-pleated horsehair flounce two feet deep is worn a claret coloured satin quilted skirt 1½ inches from the ground, with a velvet tunic edged with fur having large bell-sleeves and a bodice en cœur over a satin vest with tight sleeves, high button boots, a velvet hat with gold tassels,' we detect the same impulse striving to express itself under difficulties.

DRESSES

Day

1. Skirts just on the ground for outdoors; trained for indoors. Costumes made of one material (*e.g.* reps, poplins, plaids); basque-bodices with deep side basques, and trimmed 'en carré' (a simulated low square opening), or trimmed en pelerine. Sleeve either the pagoda or moderately wide at the wrist and left open at the back of the arm as far as the elbow ('en sabot'). Always two skirts.

2. The Jacket body. Open in front either square or en cœur. The jacket either short with two square basques behind projecting over the

bustle, loose in front with revers; wide open sleeves; worn with a tunic skirt not looped up; or in the form of a casaque with belt; or as a redingote, tight-fitting and long, with a short round pelerine attached. With these fichus are much worn.

3. The Polonaise. 'Seen everywhere. It is now a bodice with basques in front and short behind with a detached tunic which is long in front and short and puffed behind. The bodice is square in front and behind with muslin fichu and goffred frills.' The name is equally applied

Dolly Varden costume. 1871

to a bodice and tunic in one. The bodice is described as being 'in the Pompadour style' with square opening in front, sleeves tight to the elbow and finished with open frills.

4. The 'Dolly Varden', appearing in the summer of this year.

Further details of these four types

1. Costumes (of one material) preserve one colour but in various shades, *e.g.*, underskirt darkest, overskirt light, bodice dark, and light trimmings on dark and vice versa.

2. Jacket bodies with basques cut in short tabs or with postillions, or as a casaque with long

square basques at the sides. The tunic generally of the same colour as the dress but nearly always of different material; either apron-shaped or pointed in front and two points behind, and trimmed with fringe. With thick materials the tunic may be only simulated, the side and back widths of the skirt cut longer than the front, the side widths being gathered from about a third from the waist downwards and the gathers joined on to the sides of the front widths to give the fullness for the bustle behind.

3. The Polonaise. Always of a material and colour different from the dress. Either with apron front or with postillion basques. Worn with a skirt 3½ to 4 yards round the hem, flat and gored in front, and full behind. The polonaise may be made of any wool and silk or wool and cotton textile, or of black silk or muslin.

4. The Dolly Varden, of chintz or cretonne over bright silk petticoat, either plain, flounced or quilted. Later, for winter, the Dolly Varden may be of fine flannel or cashmere printed in chintz pattern, with black silk, satin or velveteen petticoat, often quilted or lined with eiderdown.

Single skirt dresses are permissible especially in summer with a casaque or polonaise which practically supplies the overskirt.

Trimmings of day dresses

Underskirt. The varieties are many. A deep flounce headed by quillings. Godet pleating. A deep 'Russian pleating' (kilting). Two pleated flounces headed by narrow pleating and fastened down by bands of velvet. Deep flounce and flat bands of velvet. One deep flounce with a tablier above formed by rows of flounces or rows of frillings. Ruchings frayed at both edges. Puffings of black grenadine; black lace over tulle, both pleated, and lace laid on flat (for visiting dresses).

Tunics trimmed with fringe or ruching or bias flounces.

Bodices with ruching and quilling.

Two different sorts of trimming on the same dress fashionable. Thus a visiting dress composed of 'a pink gros grain underskirt with seven bias bands edged on both sides with one inch double fringe; corsage en cœur, coat sleeves with deep pointed cuffs and lace ruffles; a casaque of white striped grenadine trimmed with lace, open at the seams, and having revers and large pink silk bows,' seems to savour of fancy dress. The lavish use of lace, often coffee-coloured, was a feature. 'Now that all dresses are edged with work at all the flounces 70 to 80 yards of trimming are employed on a skirt.'

Summer dresses are all cut low in the throat with net or folded tulle across the bosom; wide open sleeves with large undersleeves. 'To shew the neck and arms through the muslin is not ladylike.'

Evening

Bodice either square in front and low behind with a chemisette, or low off the shoulders, pointed in front and behind. Ribbon bows large and numerous; nearly always a large bow at the bosom. Sleeve elbow length with lace ruffle (dinner dress), or short and puffed (full dress).

Double skirt, the upper as a tunic (often of lace or tulle) which may be in the Princess shape with round tablier front and trained behind, with a panier effect. The skirt is elaborately trimmed with flounces and puffings; blonde lace, velvet bands, ruchings and quillings are much used.

The polonaise is also worn, either of the dress material or of sultane with gauze trimming.

For ball dresses multiple tunics, two or three, of diminishing length; floral sprays strewn over the bodice and skirts. The train of the dress is made to fasten up by a loop to a button at the waist.

Materials: Day (Winter). Cashmere, serge, merino, German twills, linsey, cloth, poplin, satin cloth, velveteen. (Summer). Foulard, muslin, chintz, cretonne, pique, cambric and linen (in two shades of the same colour).

('Foulards and poplins are appropriate for church service on account of the absence of rustling in those materials').

Scotch plaids (in compliment to the marriage of Princess Louise).

Evening. Silk, satin, tulle, tarlatan, grenadine, sultane, Pompadour silks.

New Materials: Gros de Rome, Drap de France, serge royale.

Colours: (Winter) violet, dark green, brown, turtle-dove. (Summer) grey, fawn and soft hues.

OUTDOOR GARMENTS

Jackets

Much worn, with basques often cut in tabs, or postillions; the front loose fitting and with revers; often double breasted. Coat sleeves with deep cuffs or pagoda shaped. Elaborately trimmed with fringe, passementerie, lace or pleating.

Paletots

Short and square cut, open up the sides and back; or in the casaque shape, tight to the figure, the front of the skirt being plain and square and the back moderately puffed.

Mantles

The Dolman. A mantle with sleeve cut out all in one with the side piece and hanging loose.

Mantles in the shape of ample tunic-casaques.

Waterproof

With pelerine cape pointed behind. The feature of all outdoor garments is that they fit the back of the waist and are often slit up behind and elaborately trimmed.

ACCESSORIES

Suede *Gloves*.

Jewellery. Massive gold bracelets with large oval in centre; large oval lockets with Etruscan border and star of pearls or diamonds in centre. Large ear-rings.

Prices

German tartans, reps and tweeds, 8/9 to 25/-; washing sateen (Koechlin frères) 32 inches wide, 15/- the dress of 9 yards; French batiste costumes, 12/9; German poplin, 3/9 a yard; German silk velvet, 2/11 to 9/11 a yard; Dolly Varden polonaise in chintz, cretonne, sateen, velveteen, 18/9 to 52/6; Dolly Varden cretonne (28 inches wide) 1/11½.

Norwich grenadine (28 inches) 11½d. a yard.

'Polonaise, comprising jacket and panier, in black silk, muslin, tussore, etc. 12/9 to 84/-.'

Dolly Varden caps, for morning, 2/6.

Clouds, of Shetland wool, 4 yards long, 2/11 to 3/11.

French chintzes, 1/- a yard; English, 4d and 6d.

Dolly Vardens for seaside wear, 18/6 to 29/6.

Serge royale, 1/6 a yard.

Best mourning crape, 5/6 to 9/- a yard. Making up a plain mourning dress, 9/6.

Kid gloves, 1/11½ a pair. 'With the open sleeve long kid gloves with 8 to 10 buttons have come in again.'

1872

The fashions of this year were marked by a change in the colour taste and a development of the polonaise. There were some who clung to the use of two approximate shades of one colour (the dress en camieu) while others boldly employed contrasts, but the general preference was for soft and 'autumn tints'. As a result one observer speaks of 'the exquisite combinations of blue grey and pink: salmon and grenat,' which another calls 'the weird mixture of colours now so fashionable'; and another, 'the dismal mixtures so much in vogue: deep violet and washed-out blue-grey'; 'sang de Prusse' and a weak tea-green; 'sickly pink and sulky blue'. Mixtures such as blue and green or sage green and eau de Nil are described as 'very sickly shades; the greens defy description'. Fashions played lovingly with bronze, olive brown and greenish grey (mignonette), using any two shades for a dress. One observer remarks 'yellow has been for many years greatly despised' and it is almost completely absent. It was thought to denote those animal passions incompatible with the ladylike habit. For evening dress faded hues were the mode. The hard metallic colours of the previous decade were regarded with contempt. There were, however, a number who demanded notice by startling contrasts and a lady on Brighton front no doubt attracted a good deal in 'a polonaise of orange colour worn over a bright blue skirt'.

The polonaise (or ' "petit casaque", as it is known in Paris') becomes this year so important, and to the modern reader is such a perplexing garment, that a clear account of it may be acceptable here. 'The Polonaise is but one modification of the Tunic and is itself subject to numberless changes. Generally speaking it is a sort of tight fitting casaque, a bodice to which is added a small skirt; this bodice is made with or without (additional) basques: open en châle or with revers; it may have postillions at the back of the waist like a jacket; the skirt may be made with a "tablier" or apron front which may be buttoned down the centre or open; the sides and back may be looped up in a hundred different ways, and untrimmed or ornamented with bows, lace or fringe.'

It is distinguished from the parent garment in that 'the Polonaise falls straight down in front and is draped at the back only; whereas the Tunic forms a drapery in front, the folds of which throw all the fullness at the back where it is draped rather higher than is the Polonaise.'

The origin of both garments is clear: 'The short puffed overskirt of last year has developed into a Polonaise and Tunic of this year.' (It is well to note that French contemporaries frequently speak of a 'tunic' which the English would call a 'polonaise', just as they called a 'Pompadour polonaise' what we called a 'Dolly Varden'). The polonaise must be distinguished from the casaque which by now has become a half-fitting jacket-bodice with long basques; when these are prolonged down the front, apron-wise, and at the back over the bustle the resemblance to a polonaise is close. But the back of the polonaise is always prolonged (in this year to the knee level) and the sides are always to some extent looped up, usually with a bow of ribbon at each hip.

It may be convenient to add here further particulars of the polonaise. The use of different materials for the polonaise and the skirt is more fashionable than the complete costume of one material. For the complete costume 25 yards are required; for a polonaise some 9 yards. The type with the front buttoned all the way down is less 'dressy' than the open front revealing the underskirt. It may be 'cut all in one at the back with a centre seam, open in front and worn with a waistband; or cut in one in front with a basque back; closed in front.'

Promenade dress. Francis I polonaise of black satin embossed
with velvet, trimmed ostrich feather. 1872

Materials: (Winter) cloth, cashmere, merino, velvet velveteen; (Summer) foulard, pique, muslin, grenadine, sicilienne—over a skirt of different colour and material (even a white polonaise with a black skirt).

Types with special names:

The Dolly Varden. 'Of every possible design; now with two large buttons at the back of the waist instead of a bow.' Of chintz patterns.

The Pompadour. Distinguished (in this country) from the former by being of black material (foulard) with large bouquets in bright colours (worn with a plain skirt).

Skating costume. Polonaise and skirt of waterproof tweed.
Military trimming. 1872

The Watteau. Made with a Watteau pleat from the neck and much looped up at the bottom of the back; usually of a white material strewn with small flowers.

The Blouse. (Sometimes called the 'Russian' or the 'French'). The bodice is loose and drawn in by a belt; the front reaches the knee, and the back, which is longer, is draped. It resembles somewhat the modern overall.

266

The Princess Polonaise. Made without a seam at the waist. Either buttoned all down the front to a blunt point at the knee level, or open in front over a deep waistcoat with basques. The sides are caught up and the back draped.

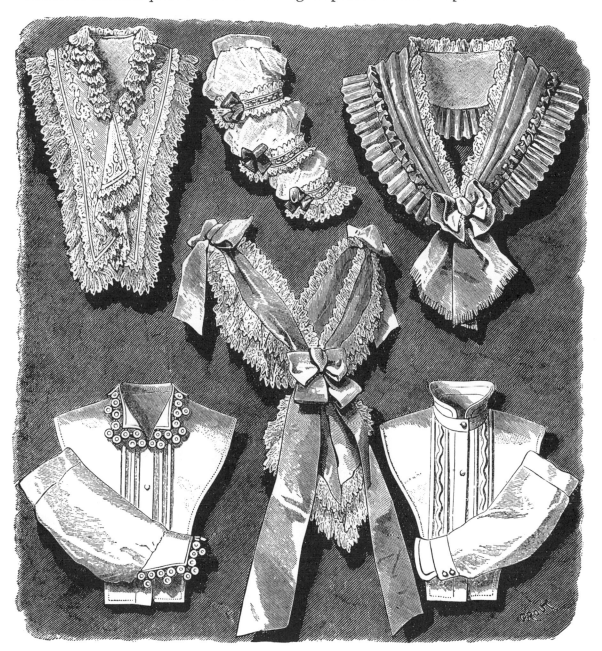

Lingerie fichus and berthas. 1872

The Polonaise Mantle. An outdoor garment reaching below the knee. Tight fitting and bouffante behind; often double-breasted. Length, 36 inches in front, 46 inches behind.

The sleeves of polonaises are, in winter, closed with deep cuffs; in summer, of the pagoda or Marie Antoinette shape.

267

DRESSES

Day

Skirts are generally trained but drawn up for walking.

In addition to the various types of polonaise dress there are:

described as a 'tunic'. This type of tunic is detachable at the waist. It may be much puffed behind and pointed at each side in front; or with rounded apron front and points behind, and often with square 'scarf ends' hanging at the sides. Large bows below the puff are com-

Widow's first mourning (Messrs. Jay). 1872

1. The single skirt with deep flat flounce or multiple flounces to the waist, and bodice with long basques. The basques may be long and square or pointed in front, often with long basques at the sides and the back with postillions or puffed basque over the bustle.

2. The double skirt, the upper now usually

mon. The looped up overskirt is now out of fashion.

3. The tablier front, either formed by the sloping sides of the tunic or simulated by trimming, the back of the skirt being trained. The bodice is of the jacket form with waistcoat front of a different material.

4. Costumes of one material. A basque bodice with or without postillions and having three seams down the back and two side seams 'making a most shapely waist'; or a jacket body with revers. 'Although the kilted flounce is much used for walking dresses very narrow flounces cut on the cross and put on flat are more fashionable.'

NOTE: The readymade dress (gallicé 'confection') has now become extremely popular and illustrated fashion books begin to be issued by large drapery establishments describing them (*e.g.* Debenhams).

Dresses are excessively trimmed, *e.g.* 'A deep flounce cut on the cross headed by ruching; a scalloped or vandyked flounce mounted in box-pleats, the heading sewn on with a rouleaux; a deep gathered flounce headed by a box-pleated flounce or an upright frill vandyked and corded with satin'; while every possible garment is covered with embroidery and trimmed with all kinds of lace, 'from simple Yak and guipure to the costliest old point'.

Evening

The bodice is low off the shoulders and usually round; sometimes square; short puffed sleeves. Waist with basques or round or pointed.
The skirts may be:
(1) a trained tunic en princesse.
(2) short tunic open in front.
(3) overskirt en tablier (square or rounded).
(4) multiple skirts, three to five.
(5) with a Pompadour polonaise.
All the above worn over a trained underskirt, and
(6) single skirt trimmed to simulate an open tunic.

As in the previous years the bottom of the skirt is trimmed with flounces, puffings, etc.; while the overskirt is of lace, gauze, etc. over a silk or satin underskirt. 'It is impossible to put too many flounces, puffings and flowers on the tarlatan, gauze, grenadine or tulle skirts of ball dresses.'

Fichus of lace with velvet ribbon, and of muslin, are much worn either with the low square bodice of evening dress or with the open bodice of day dress.

Example of a ball dress. 'A round skirt of pale green gauze (over a silk slip) with a deep flounce, which is striped with green satin cross-bands edged with white blonde and headed with scollops piped and edged with blonde. Bows of green velvet at intervals fasten down the flounce. A round tablier of gauze edged with blonde and draped at the sides under the tunic which is of green faille trimmed with blonde and satin cross-bands and made en princesse; the back of the tunic is tied up by ribbons into a puff.'

OUTDOOR GARMENTS

Mantles

The Dolman 'is nothing but a short paletot with wide hanging sleeves; only one is tired of the word paletot and a new one had to be found.'

Types: The Peplum dolman with points on the sides; the flat dolman, and the dolman with pleats in the middle of the back. All are more or less braided.

The Mantlet, round behind and slashed halfway up; short square ends in front; trimmed with wide black lace, bows, etc.

The Mantle, of cloth and velvet, with or without a cape, and heavily trimmed with black lace or fringe, often with a tassel at the back.

The Rigoletto Mantle, tight to the figure with large square puffed basque behind; a short embroidered lappet on each side and a short square basque in front. Sleeves open to the elbow.

Cloaks

Peplum Rotonde, a short circular cloak reaching to just below the waist and slashed halfway up the back; fringed edge.

The Carrick, a plain round mantle cut up the back, with a cape.

The long Casaque, the skirt of which forms a round tablier in front and is puffed at the back.

Small *Capes*, or Pelerines, are often worn over Polonaises.

Prices

French poplin, 1/4½; Shantung pongee (natural coloured silk) 1/-; Japanese silks (German made) 2/6½; Dieppe double twilled serges (28 in.), 1/11½; Maraposa (28 in.) 1/1½; Barathea, 1/11½; English sateen, 9¾d; French sateen, 1/2¾, all per yard. Flannel knickerbockers, 5/-; flannel petticoats, 5/11.
Dolly Varden aprons, 1/10.
Brussels gloves, 1 button, 2/6; 2 button, 3/6 a pair (brown, grey, lavender).
Quilted satin petticoats, 21/-.

'What will characterise the present epoch in the history of Fashion is certainly not the cut of our garments, for they are an odd assemblage of old fashions jumbled together without any regard for chronology. What will mark it, among others, is the amount of trimming with which we have found it possible to load every separate article, from the slipper to the monument we have agreed to call the bonnet.' This shrewd comment of a contemporary can hardly be improved on by the historian. The varieties of trimmings used were endless, with a tendency, this year, for the deep pleated flounces to be replaced by gathered flounces, puffings and ruchings, *e.g.*, the skirt of the day dress trimmed with two or three gathered flounces each headed with a band of puffing and narrow frill. The amount of material required is indicated by the description of a mourning dress advertised by Jay's of Regent Street. 'The present make of dress requires upwards of forty yards of the richest faille, so multitudinous are the folds, puffs, etc. in its composition. The secret of this is the French want to make as much money as they can and they are rendering these luxuries ultraluxurious. Skirts are more trimmed in themselves; that is, they are cut considerably longer than requisite but the extra length goes to form the puff and bouillons demanded by fashion. Some have as many as three tunics in front; these form folds which are all fastened down at the sides where the tunics stop; the back breadths are caught up to form . . . a series of inflations below the waist. Sashes are a prominent feature, very wide and long, sometimes holding up the pouf, sometimes draped round the waist.'

The 'bouillon' trimming is made as follows: 'The old-fashioned *Melon puffs* are revived for trimming in the handsomest dresses. They are made of straight widths of the silk joined at the selvedges and lined with foundation muslin. They are formed by tacking slight seams on the wrong side of the fabric at intervals of two or three inches, leaving the space between to form a puff on the right side; as there are no gathers in these smooth puffs the stiff muslin lining is necessary to keep them well rounded.'

The flounces themselves 'must be piped and edged and waved and headed with a score of more or less fanciful devices'; for the trimming of a lavender silk skirt, for example, we are offered 'a gathered flounce above which is another of white muslin with scalloped edge and worked in buttonhole stitch; above that is a much narrower flounce of embroidered muslin; then three narrow rouleaux of black satin with, above the top one, a heading of embroidered muslin and behind it a stand-up small flounce of scalloped muslin.'

'Bias folds of different shades of the same colour are much used for trimming; no longer the stiff stitched folds of last winter but soft folds put on one over the other without any stitching visible, *e.g.*, one slightly gathered flounce with three to seven bias folds of graduated shades above it. In striped materials the flounces are no longer cut on the cross and are pleated to shew only one colour on the pleats.'

Chicorée ruching is a fashionable trimming this year.

The approaching change in the shape of dresses is indicated by the remark:

1872. Evening dresses
Of blue satin with overskirt of blue gauze
Of pink poult de soie; tunic and bodice of straw-coloured faille

1875
Indoor costume of plain and striped materials; cuirasse bodice
Promenade dress of plain beige and check; cuirasse bodice

'Skirts are worn much closer to the figure and petticoats are cut so that there is not the least fullness about the hips. In order that the skirt may cling closely in front it is usual now to border them with a fringe or to lead them; the full round skirts looped up on either side are now a thing of the past; the Princess dress or the long tunic, draped but slightly and in the middle of the back only, are far more distinguished than the short retrousée skirts of last year; a slight figure is now considered the most graceful of any.'

A growing tendency to distinguish by trimmings the front breadth of the skirt which is made flat leads to the vogue for the *Tablier*, while the costume, for walking, has styles of its own. 'Since the blessed fashion of walking dresses was introduced women have taken at least twice as much outdoor exercise' is a significant comment.

The evening dresses are more than ever decorated with 'floral tributes' so that an observer exclaims that '73 will always be remembered as 'the year in which flowers were so much the fashion'. While another contemporary remarks with complacence: 'Good taste seems to reign supreme; we are arriving at an elegance perhaps surpassing anything that has gone before.'

DRESSES

Day

1. Plain morning dress; skirt with two gathered and one pleated flounce, the latter generally sewn down with broad cross bands. Tunic with rounded tablier draped high at the sides. Or in place of a tunic a casaque bodice with deep basque in front almost forming a second skirt; velvet collar and coat sleeves.

2. The robe de chambre, always en princesse, buttoned down the front.

3. The dress en princesse, trained, the front trimmed en tablier.

4. Morning dress with cashmere bodice, double-breasted with revers, and buttoning down the front, worn with a dark silk skirt.

5. The costume, with Princess polonaise. The front of the skirt, just touching the ground, trimmed en tablier either with pleating or narrow flounce; the sides and back with flounces having fluted headings or divided by ruches, puffings or cross-bands; these ascend half way up the back of the skirt; or they may reach the waist, in which case the polonaise is replaced by a basque to the bodice. The bodices are nearly all in jacket form having sleeves with mousquetaire cuffs. The front made to simulate a waistcoat of a darker colour, or a sleeveless jacket worn over the bodice gives this effect; the front of the waistcoat descending below the waist in the Louis XV style, sometimes long enough to form a tablier over the skirt. This jacket bodice, more or less coat-like, tends to displace the polonaise in demi-toilette. The neck opening either high or en cœur. 'Low bodices under transparent material are reserved for the evening and would be deemed intensely vulgar in the afternoon; last year they were all the fashion.' Those en cœur are finished at the neck with 'full Elizabethan frills', kept up by invisible wires.

The spotted polonaise is a feature of the year, and in the summer the light polonaise (worn outdoors without any mantle) over a dark skirt.

6. The 'mixed' or 'robe drapée'. Is more 'dressy' than the costume; double skirt, the underskirt of thick material and richly trimmed with ruches, puffings, lace, etc.; the upper of light material, plain and long and gathered up here and there in artistic folds. Or open in front, the edges turned back en revers. Or with a single skirt with a tablier with flat trimmings and the sides and trained back with flounces all the way up of material different from the dress.

NOTE: Sleeves of most day dresses have mousquetaire cuffs, in winter, and these or bell sleeves in summer.

Materials: 'All materials are fashionable this year as they were last' (especially spotted foulard). 'Nowadays cloths and woollens are made in such perfection that they are quite sufficient for both afternoon walking and visiting dresses.'

They may have several tones of colour which

must match; each should be a deeper or lighter tone of the original.

'18 yards is a very moderate allowance for a best dress; nine for a polonaise.'

Costumes: cloth, serge, velveteen, fancy woollens, foulard, écru batiste.

Princess and tunic dresses: plain silks, satins, moires, taffetas, poplins, faille, tussore.

Colours: Contrasting colours less used than shades of a colour. But we find exceptions, *e.g.*, a toilette of faille of cerise, maize and wood colour. A turquoise dress trimmed with dark green; a dark grenat dress with a pink tablier. While 'a black polonaise may be worn with any coloured skirt or any coloured polonaise with a black skirt'.

There is a complaint of 'the exaggerated mixtures of colours in which many people indulge just now'. The colours fashionable at Ascot this year were 'maize, light canary, or blue-green—trimmed with blue, olive, pink, grenat or brown'.

On the whole the trimmings tend to be lighter in colour than the dress. In mixed dresses 'the upper garment should be lighter in colour'.

Evening

The only notable change is the increasing use of the tablier front either formed by the front breadth of the skirt or by the front of the tunic, and the front is usually trimmed differently from the rest, *e.g.*, a tulle ball dress 'the front breadth with two pleated flounces, the sides and back with seven gathered flounces; tunic with tablier front, points at the sides and pouf behind; low silk pointed bodice with tulle fichu with epaulette or ribbon bow on the shoulder,' and elaborately decorated with sprays of flowers. A typical dinner dress: 'A blue satin trained skirt with two gathered flounces headed by pleatings; lace tunic looped up at the sides with garlands of flowers; square bodice edged with pleatings and lace; sleeves with puffings to the elbow ending in ruffles.'

'The round low bodice is especially reserved for the ball room; evening bodices are high at the back and en cœur or square in front, and worn with a ruffle.'

OUTDOOR GARMENTS

The Dolman, now with mantlet ends in front and full basque behind which is tied in to form a puff.

Paletots

Covered with braiding, the sleeve of dolman shape.

The double breasted *Jacket*, with turndown collar and revers, square pockets in front and coat sleeves; rather longer than the waist in front, and still longer behind, the basque at the back divided; no trimming.

Mantlets

Scarf-fashion, short and square in front, some with pointed hoods.

The *Cloud*, a long straight scarf worn as a capeline, of wool.

Immensely large buttons, of metal (steel, oxydised silver, etc.), are much used.

ACCESSORIES

Gloves

'We are told that several ladies have actually appeared in public without gloves; no gloves! Do not these two words imply a verdict of vulgarity?'

Chatelaines, of oxidised silver, steel or electroplate, containing purse, memo book, scent bottle, egg with pins, thimble, scissors, yard measure, penknife, etc. *Jewellery*. 'Never were ear-rings so much in fashion', in shape large round rings or small jewelled flies or beetles. Watteau lockets and ear-rings of enamelled porcelain. Crosses in onyx and jet. 'The rage for jet is revived.' Gigantic *Fans*.

Prices

Serge costumes (Debenham) £5 to £6.

Mignonette serge, 2/6 a yard. Sicilienne (28 in. wide) 2/11½. Aberdeen linseys, 9d to 1/4.

Poplin (24 in.) 5/6 to 6/6 a yard.

Silks. Black, 4/11 to 5/11; coloured gros grain, glacé, 4/11; Japanese, 1/11 to 2/9. Silk velvet, 4/11, Lyons velvet, 12/9.

Albert crepe, 1/9 to 4/6.

1874

The principle of distinguishing the front of the dress from the sides and back becomes steadily more noticeable, partly by the 'tablier' and partly by the device of tying back the skirt by inside strings. In addition the dress is made tighter round the hips; in effect, the wearer no longer stands, as in the previous decade, in the centre of a circle but at the very front of an ellipse. The same spirit is carried out above and by means of the 'cuirasse bodice' the figure is clearly defined. The ballooning effect of the pouf at the back steadily diminishes; indeed, we are told that 'bustles are quite dispensed with and not only the bust but the stomach must be well outlined; whenever tight dresses are the fashion the same whim is indulged in.' Anatomical charms obtrude from the framework and the well dressed lady drags her dressmaker at her heels.

The features of this year may be summarised as increasing use of the tablier, diminishing bustles, longer waists, tighter corsage, often with waistcoat effects, 'tie-back' skirts, trained, with a vogue for coarse woollen materials.

DRESSES

Day

Five types:

1. Costume 'rasterre' or walking dress just touching the ground, the front of the skirt trimmed (*e.g.* with narrow flutings and bias bands), the back plain. Frequently with flat bows at the sides. Worn with a tunic, polonaise or redingote. Those with tunics have either a semi-tight casaque or a jacket and waistcoat (the latter often only simulated by a 'plastron'). Alternatively the front of the skirt may be pleated from the waist and the back flounced. The jacket is frequently double-breasted with revers and basques.

'The complete costume of one material is now demodé; either two kinds of material, one self-coloured, the other striped or figured, or two different colours of the same material, are used.'

Materials: woollens, especially beige, cloth, velveteen.

2. Visiting dress, semi-trained. The skirt trimmed en tablier with pleatings or lace; the back either untrimmed or at least with different trimmings.

A short tunic, cut square, draped behind and open in front often with revers; or without a tunic, the front of the skirt demarked by side robings and the back flounced. Worn with a jacket-bodice, having square basques and revers. In place of a tunic there may be a long scarf-end hanging down in front and draped to one side where it is loosely knotted to a similar scarf-end descending from the back (the 'écharpe' dress). Or in place of the ordinary tunic there may be a long casaque reaching to the knee level. In place of the jacket bodice and tunic may be worn the *cuirasse* bodice and cuirasse tunic, a very long-waisted tight boned bodice and plain tight tablier-tunic in front, fastened behind by two long lapels and a bow of many coques. 'Long tight corsets are indispensable with the cuirasse bodice which moulds the figure to perfection.'

Some of these cuirasses are sleeveless. The cuirasse bodice is always of a different material from the dress, the sleeves matching the trimming. The jacket-bodice may be worn over a waistcoat or have a plastron.

3. The skirt is sometimes *perfectly plain*, the front and side breadths gored; at the back 'two widths are folded into one large double pleat and the side widths tied by tapes underneath the back'. ('tie-backs'). With these the tunic is not draped on the hips but is merely an apron hooked together behind under the folds of the back pleat.

4. The single skirt dress, now 'triumphantly sailing back into the height of fashion'; it may be plain but is usually 'so trimmed that it is more elaborate even than the double-skirt dress'.

5. The 'Fourreau dress' (en princesse), trained, long-waisted and gored in front which is quite plain, the back mounted in full pleats. The train is caught up with a wide sash and buckle at the side; with it a tunic is frequently worn, either put on as a tablier in front, or as a semi-train behind.

NOTE ON THE POLONAISE: Now generally tight and en princesse with buttons down the front. It is no longer so looped up at the sides. As it tends to conceal the figure it is regarded as less 'dressy' than the tablier dress, and it is frequently transformed into the redingote 'which is a short Princess dress with double-breasted bodice and double row of buttons all down the front; no bustle is worn but deep hollow pleats at the back fastened down under buttons at the waist and thence spreading out in the shape of an inverted fan'. The most fashionable polonaises are made with bodice and skirt apart but

of the same material, the bodice open for indoors and with a waistcoat for outdoor use.

The preference, shown by many, for the jacket
bodice is in harmony with the decline of the
'pouf' at the back; indeed, we read that 'the
bustle is fast disappearing; in several of the

Ball dress. 1874

most elegant dresses seen lately there is no puff
whatever but two or three double pleats in the
skirt at the back of the waist giving the requisite fullness to the train'. The pouf remains,
however, for thin materials.

A notable feature in the visiting dresses of the
year is the fashion for wearing 'high Elizabethan ruffs' at the neck, which is admitted to
have the disadvantage of catching in the ear-
rings and pulling down the hair. 'The fashion
for high ruches and ruffles has quite transformed modern lingerie; even linen collars are
made in the shape of pleated frills high at the
back and with small corners turned down in
front; sleeves have wide bands and fluted frills
falling over the hand for morning, or tulle and
lace for evening.' The prevailing type of sleeve
is the coat-shaped with wide mousquetaire cuffs.
As a curiosity of the year the *Violin bodice* (having a piece of darker material let in down the
back of the shape of a violin) perhaps deserves
mention.

Materials: 'The rage for homespuns, Scotch

cloth, vigogne and serge increases; all silks are
cheaper than they have been for the last ten
years.'

Summer costumes in washing materials trimmed
with broderie anglaise.

New Materials: bure, Oxford shirting, surah,
natte, matelassé, balernos, armurette, limousine,
knickerbocker, goaly, tamative.

Colours: 'The mixture of colours at Ascot are
more pleasing than last year. There are no less
than 1200 shades in new colours; the combinations of colours are eccentric and still artistic;
garnet trimmed with pink: bronze with blue:
salmon and Russian leather: sulphur and faded
rose; amethyst with écru. Two shades of one
colour are reserved for outdoor costumes and
morning dresses, the darker shade for the dress,
the lighter for the trimming.' There is, in a
word, an enthusiastic use of 'the delicate shades
of colour for which our age is and will be
celebrated'.

Feather trimming is fashionable on day dresses
(Winter).

Ball dress. 1874

Evening

'For the new style with plain trained-back skirt
14 to 15 yards are sufficient.'

Bodice high behind and square in front, or the
'marquise bodice', en cœur with a frill inside.
The decolletée bodice is only for full evening
dress. Often with sash basques at the sides.

Buttons down the front to a long point. Short puffed sleeves of tulle. The skirt with a tablier, of flounces or fringe nearly to the waist, marked off by side robings of satin rouleaux. The back trained with gathered flounces to the waist. Or the skirt with a long tunic, draped and looped up by a wide sash fastened by a large buckle. As in the day dress the tunic may be open in front with revers.

Ball Dresses

Either with a tunic covering the back only and a tablier, or without a tunic, the bodice having basques. Wide sash. With elaborate evening and ball dresses the side 'sash basques' are fashionable. Epaulettes and bows on the shoulders, trimmings of sprays of flowers and trimmings put on slantwise are features.

OUTDOOR GARMENTS

Winter. Rotonde with hood and fringed edge. Double-breasted waterproof.
Casaque-Dolman 'now losing its long sleeves and becoming a Pelisse slashed at the sides to simulate a sort of sleeve, covered with embroidery and edged with fringe or cocks' feathers'.
'As the pouf disappears the tight-fitting jacket for out of doors reappears, no longer slit up the back to make room for the exuberance of the tunic.'

Bathing Costume

'Should be made with a tunic and worn with a waistbelt and deep sailor collar not open at the throat if you wish to preserve the whiteness of your neck. Buttons down the front. The drawers should button on each side but a string should be added for safety, and they should be gathered just above the ankle.'

ACCESSORIES

Shoes

The colour of the dress (day) 'the fashion of shoes instead of boots is quite a revolution in female toilets'.

Gloves

Thread or suede, 4 to 6 buttons.

Jewellery: white jet beads and bugles, and black jet fashionable.

Prices

The new spring sateens, 6/9 to 12/6 the dress. Galateas, striped or plain, 8½d to 1/7 a yard. Imitation Jap silk, 6¾d a yard. Satin striped bamboo (28 in.) 2/6 a yard. Lyons gros grain (24 in.) 3/11 to 4/11; poult de soie, 6/11 to 7/11; gros de Suez, 4/11; Edinburgh camlet (28 in.) 2/1½; Tussores, 6¾d to 8¾d, stout Melton cloth (50 in.) 2/6½, Homespuns (30 in.) 3/3 a yard. Ready made homespun costume (polonaise and skirt) 29/6. Good black silks, 10/- to 12/6 a yard. Silk velvet, 14/- to 28/- a yard. Velveteen (27 in.) 4/9 to 5/9 (Debenham & Freebody).
'Coils of long hair with curl falling on the neck, 28 in. long, 21/-. Curls, 10/6.'

1875

'The reasons for the present extraordinary luxury in dress is that the surplus million of women are husband-hunting and resort to extra attractions to that end.' This acidulous suggestion of a contemporary was, of course, hotly denied by the husband-hunters; but all admitted that the new modes were very peculiar. 'Fashion is now going from the ridiculous to the shameful and the female form is presented swathed in a thin and narrow covering which, while presenting its outlines almost as distinctly as those of an uncovered statue, has the property also of burlesquing them.' The fashionable lady in a cuirasse body and 'tie-back' skirt, the train of which was popularly known as a 'mermaid's tail', appeared like an Odalisque in a pose plastique; to walk in such a costume was difficult and to sit down dangerous. It was now that 'the line of Beauty' became a current term. 'It is astonishing how *la ligne*, which one hears so much about, alters in shape and contour, now giving as the ideal of beauty a short waist and scant robe, now a long bodice and flowing skirt. La Ligne, as at present understood, requires a great deal of elongating and pinching in of the bodice and is very prononcé in slanting straight off from the

275

front of the skirt in an oblique direction to the point of the train.' Those who had fondly supposed that the function of a woman's dress was to shield her modesty were dismayed, exclaiming: 'Fashion had been for a time on the side of the doctors and patronised a loose fitting style of dress; now she has changed her whim and we are doomed to tight-fitting cuirasse and stiff whaleboned long-waisted bodice; all the supposed wisdom of the female community is melted away like snow and old errors are taken up with fresh eagerness. The cuirasse bodice reigns supreme.'

Woman seemed to have stepped out of her dress and to be standing in front of it, clothed in corset and petticoat. The device imparted to the ballroom the intimate charm of the bedroom, 'suggesting that the wearer has forgotten some portion of her toilet. Few husbands or fathers would allow their wives or daughters to appear in public thus undressed.' But of course it was not the husbands and fathers whom she was seeking to attract.

Technically the fashions of the year may be summarised in the quotation: 'Dresses must now be very flat at the back and very tight in front shewing the hips and figure as much as possible; puffs and bustles have disappeared. Were it not for the back-train dresses would look like a towel wrapped round. All bodies, high, low or square, day or evening, should be made long and tight over the hips; some descend halfway down to the knees; soon we shall have dresses all bodies!' Or, as another observer puts it, fashions consist in 'Long waists, long skirts, long tabliers, long ends at the back, deep basques and coat sleeves'. And 'the last vestige of the pouf is the large bow placed halfway down the back of the skirt'. But, as always happens when fashions go to extremes, many only used modified forms which to-day may be difficult to date exactly.

DRESSES

Day

'The short costume is still adopted for unpretending walking dresses; of coarse woollens or cashmere with velveteen skirt (winter), or fancy woollens (beige and mohair) and washing materials (linen and batiste) for summer,' but the more pretentious have the skirts touching the ground in front and trained at the back. For example, a 'Beach costume' composed 'of peacock blue faille and Madras fancy plaid; the skirt with a big flounce, piped and put on with a twice gathered heading above which is a deep plissé stitched down with narrow-piped frillings. Tunic of Madras with bias folds of faille forming a tablier draped at the sides and back and finished with two lapels joined together by bows of faille; cuirasse bodice of Madras piped with faille and trimmed with bias folds of the same, forming a plain collar and revers edged with frilling; sleeves of Madras with revers and finished with bows of faille.'

'For a walking tour you should wear a black alpaca underpetticoat with a large flat pocket on each side (judiciously packed with the requisites for a night or two), a costume of navy blue serge with five rows of narrow black braid on either side of a wide braid on the gored skirt; a plain polonaise buttoned down the front; linen collar and cuffs; white silk tie; felt hat pointed in front and behind with brim turned up at the sides with a silk band and a bird's wing; leather boots buttoned halfway up the leg; a light waterproof strapped to the waist, and a small umbrella.'

The typical day dress is made with some variation of the *Jacket-bodice* such as: 1. The cuirasse bodice resembling in shape a pair of stays. It may be made with deep plain basques, or with long side basques ('peplum-basques'), and especially in summer often sleeveless over an underdress. An extreme form, the 'Joan of Arc', descends as low as the hips, and when covered with jet or steel beads conveys the illusion of armour. The sleeves are either plain or much trimmed, sometimes with reeving down the outer side, and are made tight with frilled ruffs at the wrist. It is common for the cuirasse bodice to be made of two materials, the darker down the centre simulating a waist-coat or a plastron, and sometimes there is a similar plastron down the back.

2. The fancy jacket, tight-fitting, often double-breasted, with basques cut square, pointed or rounded.

3. The 'corsage habit', with coat lapels on which are large pockets.

'The poulter pigeon ruffs are seldom seen, though the ruff, generally of tulle, encircles the neck.'

The Tunic: This may be of various forms: (*a*) The Tablier-tunic. 'With thick materials it is made like a half-handkerchief, one corner reaching to two inches from the hem of the skirt and the other corners fastened under the basque of the jacket; when the material is not too heavy it is flounced up the back to the waist.' The long tablier 'stretched tightly across the front is a style very trying to a figure inclined to embonpoint'.

Or it may be draped across and looped up at one side with a bow; or long and pointed at one side; or simply as a square front. The tablier is edged with ruching or tassel fringe; it is commonly fastened behind under bows, single, double or en cascade.

The 'Scarf drapery' is a variant, originally consisting of a wide fold of some light material designed to fasten back the front of the skirt. 'It has now dwindled into a meaningless straight trimming sewn on the front breadth of the skirt and itself trimmed with rows of pleatings and frills and having no connection with the dress itself; it is now often made of a contrasting colour.'

(*b*) The 'Juive Tunic', must be distinguished from the 'Robe à la juive'. The Juive tunic is loose, Princess shaped, with wide armholes continued to a point as far as the hip, and open in a point in the upper part of both the front and back of the bodice; it is draped over an underdress and forms the train. It thus forms a costume and can be worn out of doors. It is made of cashmere or other plain woollen, striped with braid and the edge fringed.

The Robe à la juive is quite plain and falls down to the feet; it is made of soft material (*e.g.* crepe de chine) worn over a velvet or silk dress for 'reception' or evening. The sides are caught up under the back breadths at the waist. Both are forms of the 'Princess Polonaise'.

(*c*) The open tunic, the borders turned back in two large revers which are fastened together behind by two large bows forming an over-train, worn with a trained dress; being, in fact, a sort of redingote.

(*d*) The simulated tunic or 'Robe à quilles'. A trimming of frills 'arranged in large open pleat-ings' ascend the sides of the front breadth and join together across the back under large ribbon bows. Considered more stylish than the tablier dress.

Or 'when the dress is all of one colour a simu-lated tunic effect is obtained by making the front as long as the back and then gathering the front into the sides of the back widths, pro-ducing a series of folds all up the front. The sides of the front may be edged with a frill. The front widths are then tied well back over the train by large ribbon bows.'

The Skirt. Always trained. 'We regret to learn that all skirts are tied back, if possible, tighter than heretofore; with summer materials the fashion renders them indecorous.' The effect may be obtained by the back breadths being drawn and tied together at the back of the knee under a large bow; or by pleating at the back of the waist in a very broad and deep box-pleat, or four box-pleats on each side forming the '*Duchesse pleat*' 8 inches wide; or the *Bulgare pleat*, 4 inches wide, arranged in four folds, narrow at the top and widening towards the bottom. The tops of these pleats are often left open. The folds are kept in place by elastic sewn on at intervals on the wrong side.

The hem of the skirt is now edged on the inner surface (to protect it from wear) by a *Balayeuse* (a frilling of stiff white muslin). The skirt for walking may be caught up and passed through a loop at the waist. It is tied back (by inside tapes) 'so tightly that the wearers can with difficulty sit down. From beneath the box-pleating flows out a peacock's train spread upon the ground'.

Trimmings: The very close regular plissés called 'knife-pleating' is fashionable; also braid, fringe, and gathered puffing and flounces, and gathering mixed with pleating ('froncé' or 'shirring'), and narrow bias edging.

'We owe much of the over-trimming now pre-valent to the facilities afforded by the sewing-machine.'

Most day dresses are made of two materials.

Materials: 'The fashionable new material called "broché", a satin ground with velvet flowers.' Woollens, serges, matelassé, Japanese silks and their imitations, etc. Checks are fashionable. (Summer) Batiste especially with openwork designs.

Colours: dove grey, light brown, maroon, green and in summer checks and écru. Black is notably fashionable.

Evening

Cuirasse bodice cut low, generally quite plain, with a bertha of tulle or lace. 'The shape which left the shoulders covered is now exchanged for the corsage cut moderately low all round; the sleeves not quite so short and the waist longer.' Laced up the back and a long point in front; the opening above either a 'V' or square; some open nearly to the waist and filled in with net or tulle puffing. For dinner dresses the bodice is high at the back and with tight sleeves to the wrist.

Skirt trained and tied back. 'The three back breadths, cut 20 inches longer than the front, are pleated into a 4-inch box-pleat at the waist; bows of dress material placed on it.' Or the Duchesse or Bulgarian pleat is used. 'In wearing such a dress care must be exercised not to sit upon the back breadths; the train must be brought to the left before sitting down.' The front either en tablier or with spiral flounces, tunic (such as 'scarf drapery'), or trimmed as 'robe à quilles.'

'20 yards of wide silk should make a handsome dress with skirt 58 inches long, tablier and bodice and small fichu.'

The evening dress is often made en princesse with a separate train of velvet or silk added. An 'Aumônière' or ornamental handbag of silk or velvet is usually added.

Ball Dresses

Often covered with tinsel, etc. 'A modern ball-room looks like an assemblage of stage queens covered with paste and spangles.' Bodice, cuirasse, with shoulder straps. Or the Grecian bodice, with fluted pleats in front and laced behind.

Single or multiple skirts tied back by tulle scarves; the back supported by a train skirt (without a front) which is fastened to the dress itself. The custom of buying these skirts ready-made is now quite established.

A concealed clasp on the left side by which the train can be hooked up.

Materials: For matrons, brocaded velvets and silks richly trimmed in which everything should correspond ; 'the sum paid for some dinner toilets is larger than the annual stipend of many a curate'. For young people, tulle, net, etc. The tablier-tunic of lace, gauze, etc.

Trimming. The cuirasse may be plain or covered with jet; 'there are complaints from all sides of the excessive weight of these'.

The skirt always elaborately trimmed; lace trimmings are laid on flat.

OUTDOOR GARMENTS

'Now that the pouf is abolished more attention will be paid to outdoor garments.'

These are *Mantles*, such as the 'Visite', fitting the figure behind and loose in front with long ends; in winter fur-lined; the paletot with dolman sleeves; the dolman and tight-fitting jackets frogged and braided.

ACCESSORIES

Tussore *Sunshades*.

Jewellery. Dog-collars in chains and medallions fashionable.

'The rage for silver knick-knacks is on the increase; velvet bags, daggers with fans therein, are mounted in it, chains, collars and bracelets, etc., are made of it.'

Prices

'The price of silk is lower than it has been known since 1848.'

Matelassé, 15/6; poult de soie, 4/11; gros grain, 3/11½; Japanese silks in 86 shades of colour, 1/11½; Mikado (imitation Jap silk) 1/6½; Devonshire serges (27 in.) 2/3 to 2/9; Tussores (30 in.), 1/11½—all per yard.

Ribbed cashmere stockings, 4/- to 4/6 a pair.

Sable Muffs, 4 to 6 guineas.

Elegant cuirasse and large tablier entirely covered with jet, £2 19 6.

Brocade Lampas ribbon, of very thick silk embroidered with flowers, for evening dress sashes, 1 guinea a yard.

Readymade dresses in brown silk and velvet (Peter Robinson) from 4½ guineas.

'The rage for sealskins has well nigh exterminated the seal.'

A single consignment of 40,000 hummingbirds is common: to supply aigrettes 'the beauty of which tempts the most tender-hearted to condone the cruelty by which they are obtained'.

'It is now quite impossible to describe dresses with exactitude; the skirts are draped so mysteriously, the arrangement of trimmings is usually one-sided and the fastenings are so curiously contrived that after studying any particular toilette for even quarter of an hour the task of writing down how it is all made remains hopeless. Whether the bodice opens at the back, side or front is often a problem which no amount of study can master.' If this was the view of a contemporary expert the historian sixty years later cannot hope to be completely successful. However, another observer of the time sums up the year '76 thus: 'Fashion does not present any striking change of shape. The female outline is not sensibly modified; the body is still encased in a skirt so narrow as to render walking a somewhat difficult matter. Bodies are tighter-fitting than ever, with long waists and sleeves so narrow that it is impossible to lift the arm to any extent. The exaggerations of last year are still the order of the day, and yet there are far more ladies for whom such fashions are extremely trying than there are those to whom they are becoming. The result of this absurd custom is that each naively exhibits every one of her little defects firmly believing all the time that she is looking charming.'

There was, in fact, in a minor degree, a return to exhibitionism as a mode of sex-attraction and a revival of the directoire styles was prophesied. 'There are all sorts of inventions to make the drapery define clearly the limbs of the wearer; woe to the delicate woman who follows this indelicate fashion!' For example, the skirt being buttoned to a band attached to the stays so that no petticoat was needed, the latter being simulated by a deep muslin flounce sewn inside the bottom of the skirt, while in skating costumes instead of underclothing 'there are many who only wear chamois-leather tights'. 'The frightful scabbards in which ladies are imprisoned' is the stifled cry of one victim, while the trained skirts of walking dresses provokes Mr. Ruskin to exclaim: 'I have lost much of the faith I once had in the commonsense and even in the personal delicacy of the present race of average Englishwomen by seeing how they will allow their dresses to sweep the streets.'

Another observer remarks: 'Anything more absurd than to watch the wearer of a tightly tied-back skirt, and boots with high-pointed heels trying to enjoy a seaside ramble cannot well be imagined.' Equally unreasonable was the new fashion of this year of large ornate outside pockets placed far back on the skirt or polonaise. 'The outside pocket is now de rigeur both with polonaise and Princess dress, both being too tight to admit of an inside pocket and the polonaise too long to be raised as it used to be at the beginning of the fashion,' a mode proving a boon to the pickpocket. 'Who in the name of all that's amazing designed the present custom of a pocket worn at the back and outside? There could not be a more convenient arrangement for a pickpocket,' exclaimed an irate magistrate.

The discomfort of the fashionable dress led to a custom, which rapidly increased, of ladies appearing at the breakfast table in a loose dressing-gown. 'The dressing-gown mania is on the increase,' remarks a thoughtful writer who attributes to this unbecoming habit the growing indifference of the modern husband to his wife's charms; hence the relaxing of the marital bond and the ultimate decline of English morals. Such are the perils inherent in loose clothing. This new use of the dressing-gown was borrowed from France and was a sort of fore-runner of the tea-gown, a garment viewed at first with suspicion by the pure-minded. Do not loose clothes seem to symbolise loose conduct?

There is a return of the polonaise to favour which rivals the cuirasse bodice, sometimes the two forms being combined; while the 'tie-back' is considered so attractive that a proud mother boasts of her daughters' being 'the best tied-back girls in London'.

DRESSES

Day

Always of two materials, the skirt plain and dark in comparison with the upper garment (polonaise, cuirasse, tablier), which is lighter in colour and patterned.

1. 'The Polonaise, which for some time had been given up in favour of the tunic, has come back into fashion for negligée; it is very long and ample, buttoned all the way down in front and draped at the back under ribbon bows or in the Princess shape.' Some are double-breasted and long in front and short behind. The back may be raised into a slight puff at the knee level; the front may be trimmed with a series of long looped bows. An immense bow halfway down the back is common.

There are two important variations of the polonaise now introduced:

(i) The Cuirasse Polonaise. The front of the bodice is cut like a 'Joan of Arc' cuirasse descending below the hips from the side seams of which a polonaise extends with revers and train, over the back of the skirt.

(ii) 'The Blouse, as it is now called, in contra-distinction to the Polonaise, differs from it in so far that though cut in one with the tunic the bodice is made loose and confined round the waist by a band of the material' (for summer use).

'The outside pocket is now de rigueur both with Polonaise and Princess dress.'

2. The Cuirasse bodice (usually descending over the hips) worn with tunic and skirt. The bodice is now made with the back narrow, the shoulder seams cut far back and the neck high, often with two collars, one upright, the other turned down. A plastron may be inserted in front or behind. The sleeve is very tight with a cuff.

The *tunic* admits of a host of varieties.

(*a*) As a complete 'overdress' so long as almost to conceal the skirt.

(*b*) The 'laveuse' costume, the tunic being turned up in the same style as a fishwife's and buttoned behind where it is gathered together. There is an outside pocket on the turned-up border.

(*c*) A tunic draped across in horizontal folds turned upwards and reaching nearly to the knee level in front and looped up behind. Others are made of five broad pleats crossing the front slantwise.

(*d*) As 'scarf drapery' now worn as simply a width of some material quite straight and plain.

(*e*) Multiple tunics, *e.g.* 'four tunics of graduated lengths.'

In fact, the varieties of drapery are so many that a fashionable toilet was said to have four different aspects and one is described as presenting 'the right side in front is flat; the left side pleated horizontally; the right side of the back puffed and middle and left side of the back pleated perpendicularly'.

In all forms the neck opening is small. 'The fashion for "V" necks has had its day; dresses are now made quite up to the throat.'

Sleeves are tight and long in winter, with cuffs; in summer elbow-length and open at the end.

The Skirt. Eight yards of a 28 inch material needed. All demi-trained, the hem 3 to $3\frac{1}{2}$ yards. 'The three front breadths are gored without pleats at the waist; the two back breadths are sewn into the band in one large box-pleat with a drawing-string $\frac{1}{2}$ yard below the waist; the Bulgare pleat is less usual. Velvet is lined with silk, and silk with alpaca or linen, but many are unlined. There is no braid on the hem which is now stiffened by a deep border of crinoline over which the dress material is turned up. The front of the dress rests some three or four inches on the ground.

The tie-back effect is obtained by two sets of strings sewn to the second side seams placed quite low down; above them and half a yard below the belt is a drawing-string running across the back breadths. The train is sometimes made of a separate piece of material of a different colour attached at the back by a gathered frill.'

The front may be trimmed with vertical pleats to the waist or with a deep flounce of plissé or a 12 inch border of some other material contrasting in colour, and the back plain; or vice versa. Some have simulated tabliers of fringe or simulated polonaises. The dress itself may be made en princesse 'fastened back with cascades of ribbons', sometimes worn under a polonaise. Diagonal trimming and trimming different on each side are common features. Drapery is now lower down on the skirt than formerly; hence the need for long slender bustles.

Ball fringe and broderie anglaise are specially fashionable as trimmings, together with chenille, braids worked in classical designs, ruches, etc.

'As many as 15 rows of soutache or braid are often laid on round a cuirasse or tunic, forming a very chaste and elegant trimming.'

The fringe trimming may even be $\frac{3}{4}$ yard in depth.

NOTE: A writer, explaining that the term 'dress length' is now conventionally 12 yards says: 'Now, alas! we hapless females have to go through life carrying double and often treble that quantity in our outer garments.'

Materials: Always two materials used in a dress, the skirt plain and dark compared to the rest which is generally light and figured. The sleeves usually of the same material as the skirt.

Brocades, damasks, velvet, velveteen, cashmere, fancy woollens, *e.g.* 'snowstorm cloth' (a vigogne flecked with white wool), broché silk, foulard, batiste, linen with creole stripes, Sicilienne, Indian cashmere, alpaca, tussore, barège, Madras, China crepe. Plush again fashionable.

Colours: 'It is the exception to see a vulgar mixture of colours and violent contrasts. The seeds of refined taste sown by the "School of Art Needlework" are already bearing fruit. Never during the last 50 years have silks been so inexpensive; in the gradations of shade and varieties of colour they are really artistic.'

Fashionable Colours: red of every shade; sea green, ecru, grey, bronze.

Examples of two colours used in a dress:

'Moss green trimmed with pale blue, and green bronze with mastic, are both stylish mixtures.' Also almond-coloured poplin and chestnut cloth; ink-blue velvet and moss green cashmere; dark blue trimmed with 'Sultan red' (a bright crimson); bronze and cream; dark and light green; plum trimmed with cardinal red.

'The écru mania is as strong as ever; dead white is so completely out of fashion that even articles of underclothing assume what would at one time have been called a "bad colour".'

'Cream colour has become a disease.'

'The fashionable style is for a toilet to shew as many shades of the same colour as possible and two or three at least.'

Evening

Generally made with two bodices laced at the back. (1) Low, pointed in front with square basque behind, square cut at the neck and clusters of flowers on the left side. (2) High, with a plastron or lace stomacher.

'The high cuirasse and Joan of Arc bodices are formed of no less than 12 lengthwise pieces which fit the figure as though they were glued there.'

Often with velvet collars. Some bodices are even made of kid so as to fit perfectly. Short elbow sleeves with ruffles. The skirt, trained and tied back, is 'arranged to hang in a long narrow train or to spread on the ground like an open fan; to produce this a fan-shaped piece of crinoline 25 inches deep is pleated into the train, and an elastic band is fastened low down inside the skirt to keep the train in shape'.

The front has a square tablier or diagonal scarves; the tablier may be of net ornamented with fringe or tassels.

Or the dress may be en princesse with or without a Princess polonaise. Three or even four materials may be used, *e.g.* gros grain skirt; bodice and draperies of brocaded silk or velvet; bands of satin; pleatings of crepe lisse.

Trimmings of écru lace and 'large leaves of white chenille studded with pearls and blossoms of fruit trees'.

Ball Dresses

Are still more elaborate; the pointed bodice low en cœur or square and off the shoulders; very short sleeves of pleating and frill with ribbon bows. A bertha is usual. Some have a coloured bodice with a white skirt.

A Princess polonaise, the bodice en cuirasse and the skirt cut slantwise; or $2\frac{1}{2}$ yards of scarf drapery reaching nearly to the hem; or a plain cuirasse with or without basques and a draped tablier, are some varieties.

The trained skirt is usually with a plissé flounce and heading.

Colours: pale blue and peacock blue brocades; olive green velvet and cream lace; salmon pink silk and brown brocaded velvet; rich silks damasked in arabesques.

Fichus with single and double revers are frequently worn with evening dress.

OUTDOOR GARMENTS

These are usually long and cut to emphasise the slender lines now fashionable.

The Visite, scarf-shaped behind with long ends in front and short sleeves, is revived.

The Mantle is given a cuirasse back and long side points.

Long Paletots and Redingotes with revers, double-breasted and buttoned all down the front.

Materials: matelassé, armure and cashmere. Ball fringe a fashionable trimming; in winter, fur (sable, ermine, skunk, raccoon, marten, beaver and 'furs from the skins of rabbits and cats known by such extraordinary names as would make their owners very doubtful of their own identity').

ACCESSORIES

Gloves

Evening, to the elbow, with 15 buttons. Suede, with 3 to 4 buttons for day. 'The now common habit of girls taking off their gloves in church, although until comparatively lately this would have been considered a terrible breach of propriety; it was, I believe, Princess Louise who first set at nought this restriction as to remaining gloved through the service.'

Stockings. 'Day stockings should match the dress.'

Small *Muffs* with one band of fur as trimming.

Jewellery. Filigree silver bouquet holders. Earrings, an American fashion for these in the form of 'a most curious mixture of monkeys, saucepans, lizards, candelabra, cockroaches, birdcages, tortoises, and tongs and shovels'.

'A single firm in Birmingham turns out 10,000 gross of real pearl buttons per week.'

Nicholl's Patent Spring Hook and Eye, for hooking up the skirt to walking length advertised.

Dress holder, hooking on to the waist and from which two chains, six inches long, are suspended at the end of which various forms of clips are fastened to hold up a portion of the skirt.

Prices

The swan-bill corset for wearing under cuirasse bodice, 14/6.

Indian cashmere (48 inches) 3/3; French beige (24 in.) 1/4½; mediaeval linen (28 in.) 1/3½. Rich brocaded silks of the Early English period, 7/11; rich grisaille silk (Peter Robinson) 4/6; Tamise (32 in.) 2/6; all per yard.

Jay's black silk costumes, 6½ guineas. Lenten costumes in barathea and Sicilienne, 2 guineas. Rinking costume of grey stuff, Princess polonaise trimmed with ostrich feathers, small hat with ostrich feather (John Barker) 5 guineas.

Norfolk jackets in grey tweed from 1 guinea.

Rich velveteen costumes (Peter Robinson) 3½ guineas.

The rink dress suspender, 3/6.

Dagger fan in velvet sheath, 9/6.

1877

The movement towards exhibitionism encouraged (as it always does) a liking for vertical lines which now becomes marked. An enthusiast exclaims: 'Toilets have not been for years as elegant and becoming as they are just now because they are the very type of beauty, gracefulness and style; dress has become an art in which purity and beauty of outline are as much to be attended to as harmony of colour. The present style is a marvel of outline and design; it is downright sculpture.' (Anticipating, in fact, the arty jargon of modern days.) 'Fashion, Taste and Style but seldom agree. Fashion decrees the general shape; Taste often protests and endeavours to obtain improvements; Style puts the decrees in practice with a little exaggeration. This season Fashion decrees that dresses are to be narrower than ever; one gets into them how one can; Style consists in having the garment fit as closely as possible and to do so underclothing is reduced to almost nothing. The evening train is enormously long, rounded or pointed at the end. A lady appears as if she were tacked on to a heap of materials cleverly draped and looped up, of different colours. Taste permits the outline to be concealed by draperies and trimmings. The amount of discomfort an elegante will bear in order to preserve the encased swathed appearance which Fashion decrees her limbs should present is incredible. It would be impossible to make closer drapery; the limit has been reached. The modern gown shews the figure in a way which is certainly most unsuitable for the ordinary British matron.'

Existing modes are modified to increase the vertical effect and notions are borrowed from the directoire period, transformed by conspicuous corset and long waist. Social conditions, however, were lacking to produce a genuine 'Classical revival'; the Gothic spirit was shaken but not shattered, and as we shall see passed through the approaching 'Aesthetic Period' unscathed.

Two important forms of costume appear this year, the teagown and the tennis-dress (the fore-runner of a distinct style for outdoor games), while the tailor-made costume ('apt to follow the style of riding habits too closely') is firmly established. 'The fashion for dressing for five o'clock tea has now become very general in country houses; the teagown arose from the habit of ladies having tea in the hostess's boudoir and donning smart dressing gowns. Now that the gentlemen are admitted to the function 'peignoirs have developed into elegant toilettes of satin, silk, foulard, etc.' (NOTE: a lace and muslin mob cap is worn with the teagown.)

The growing use of other materials than silk is a feature, even in evening dress. A costume entirely of silk is uncommon; the preference for woollens and cambrics is ascribed to 'the frauds of silk dealers'. Silk is so adulterated and artificially weighted that '12 oz. are made to weigh 52 oz. and in a dress of 5 lbs, 2 lbs may be iron and other materials'. It was found, too, that such silk wore badly. A grave slump in the silk trade was the result; the makers discovered, too late, they had killed the goose with the golden eggs—or at least had driven her to other markets. The fashionable dress required so much material that the average woman could not afford to have it all in silk.

DRESSES

Day

The principal types were:

1. Basque bodice and tunic with underskirt. The cuirasse now extends well over the hips and the vertical lines are often accentuated by a plastron in front and often behind, or by vertical pleats. The front plastron may simulate a long square cut waistcoat; in the 'Breton costume' the square plastron begins at the bust level and reaches below the hips, the borders defined by embroidered galloons or rows of pearl buttons, which also edge the square basque of the bodice, giving the appearance of a jacket. Above the plastron is a habit-shirt with upright collar and tie. Worn with a trained skirt having a tablier similarly edged with embroidery. The bottom of the skirt has a plissé border. The Breton is essentially a walking dress. The long cuirasse is frequently laced or buttoned behind, and the tunic overskirt draped diagonally in front and very low at the back. So much of the underskirt is now hidden that for economy it may be made of petticoat material with simply an edging of velvet, cashmere, etc. or a deep plissé. The train may be made detachable (for walking) being buttoned on round the waist under the cuirasse.

The cuirasse is frequently made open in front with long basques behind, and called a 'habit bodice', worn with a waistcoat.

Or 'a long basque bodice in front with a Princess back falling low on the skirt; short shoulder seams and no stint of seams in the bodice' (in order to produce the glove-tight fit).

2. The Princess Polonaise 'in many forms now nearly touches the ground in front', *e.g.* closed halfway down the front and then open with revers; or the 'directoire' with high open collar and paletot-shaped back; 'some are shorter in front than behind or vice versa; some buttoned behind, others at the sides and others diagonally across the front; some open in front over a long plastron.' The back is seldom plain and is gathered very low down; the front is much trimmed with ribbon bows. The outside pocket is becoming merely ornamental.

3. The Princess Dress. A form so widely used that it is found in many varieties, all trained, *e.g.* the 'Medici' (with low square bodice, short sleeves and straight wide tablier), and the 'Sultane' with elaborate scarf fastened at one side, are dressy toilettes; many are cut with pleats down the back which spread out over the train, and trimmed in front with draperies, lace, braid and fringe.

At the other extreme is the *house dress*, untrimmed, with outside pockets, collar and cuffs, and often a Watteau pleat and train of different material. The form is also used for 'the breakfast dress, not to be confounded with the dressing gown proper, with semi-train and narrow pleating round the hem, either trimmed en tablier with velvet or with vertical pleats from the waist'.

In its more elaborate forms the Princess dress with scarves draped in endless varieties, or simulating a 'robe' open in front by means of trimmings (a form often used in the teagown) or merging into the habit with the front open over a waistcoat only, and the back en princesse, *e.g.* 'A teagown of muslin or barège, Princess in form, trimmed in front to the knee with embroidered flounces; plain flounce round the train, an embroidered flounce descends from each armhole and forms the train; a fichu forming an opening en cœur with a cascade of frilling.'

A common feature is a plastron continuous with a wide tablier of a ligher colour than the dress.

4. The Blouse bodice and skirt. This form, appearing during the summer, permits some relaxation of the corset and is used for the house (the blouse or yoke-bodice descending to the hips and worn with a belt; a chemisette fills in the square opening), worn with a kilted skirt. A modification of this blouse is the Norfolk jacket used for tennis. 'Very pretty fanciful costumes are worn to play this charming game in: the under-petticoat blue or pink, two inches from the ground, the skirt long and plain and looped up, when playing, by hooks and eyes to draw it up in a fold in front and elastic sewn inside to keep back the skirt behind; a closely fitting Norfolk jacket with three pleats down the front and back and a band round the waist; stand-up collar, black stockings and shoes; natty apron with bib and three pockets in front and long sash; straw hat with flowers or feathers.'

Equally picturesque are the *Bathing Costumes*, which 'are made more stylishly every season; pink, cream and even blue flannel are used but the most durable is bunting; loose full trousers to the ankle, and a short blouse fastened at the waist or a long jacket'.

With outdoor costumes *fichus* of great varieties and also mittens are worn.

Trimmings. Galloon, embroidered, is specially fashionable, and 'there are indications of a return to the old fashioned trimmings of drawn silk; "gauged" is, I believe, the modern technical term,' *e.g.* 'the front of a dress drawn or shirred'. Ribbon loops, two-faced, as shoulder knots, on the wrists and neck and down the front; chenille and fringe, and 'rainbow' and 'moonlight' beads. 'With their present braidings and cordings ladies represent the furniture of a drawing room instead of its ornaments.'

Materials: Two materials, as in the previous year, are general in a dress. Woollens are generally of the neigeuse type (*i.e.* speckled, or flecked with 'snow-flakes'), and edged with bands of velvet or galloon. *E.g.* 'walking costume, the underskirt of indigo blue cashmere, with deep fluting; long polonaise of blue neigeuse dotted with silver grey, draped down the back and trimmed with a band of dark blue velvet.' Also hairy cloths ('Thibet') of camel's hair, for walking costumes.

(Summer). Barège, coloured cambrics, prints, foulards, grenadine, India muslin, batiste 'the queen of summer materials'.

'There are 32 new names given to woollen materials this season.'

Colours: bronze, electric blue, and black and white, and tilleul (or Linden green) are fashionable. The use of two colours are exemplified in dresses seen at Hurlingham: 'Deep emerald dress with orange ribbons; black and white stripes with orange and black striped skirt; open dress of blue and green over a bronze green skirt; canary yellow trimmed with blue velvet; brown and pink; coral and green; blue and green; violet and mandarin; blue and scarlet; blue and pink.'

Yellow is now a dressy colour.

Evening

Dinner, with long plain trains, the front trimmed en tablier, the bodice square front and back and very low, filled in with lace or tulle. Elbow sleeves, either en princesse or with tunic open in front or looped up at the side over a flounced skirt; bodice of the long cuirasse (the back of four pieces ending in postillion loops) or open habit type.

'When the bodice and front breadth is of silk the train is of velvet; when the bodice is of velvet the train is of silk and velvet.'

The skirt is three to three and a half yards round the hem; gored except the two back breadths which are sewn into the waistband in one large box-pleat with a drawing-string half a yard below the waist; the skirt is unlined, but there is always a balayeuse.

The overskirt (tunic or polonaise) may be of transparent material draped as folds, scarves or pleats, but as flat as possible.

'A dinner dress, a plain skirt of tilleul faille with a gathered flounce headed by pleating; square cut train puffed at the top with sashes of caroubier velvet; basque bodice slashed behind to permit the puffing of the train to emerge; square opening at the throat, trimmed with white lisse and a velvet ruche with a small bow; marquise sleeves.'

Ball Dresses

Corsage low, long and square behind, pointed in front and cut high on the hips; ribbon loops on the left shoulder; some are entirely decolleté with a very long basque fastening behind. The sides of the skirt are trimmed differently, diagonal lines being the vogue. Many are made with cuirasse bodices ('as much like stays as can be') and Princess backs. Wreaths and flowers are laid over the surface.

Lace mittens becoming fashionable.

OUTDOOR GARMENTS

All designed to emphasise the long slender lines of the figure.

1. The short Paletot, half length, half-tight and straight, fastened down the front or at the side, or crossing over, by means of hooks and eyes or large mother-of-pearl buttons; pockets at the sides and a breast-pocket; coat sleeves; very little trimming. Made to match the dress or else of a light colour.

2. The long Paletot, fitting the figure like a loose Princess dress; sleeves somewhat wider; more trimmed (ruches, braid, etc.) and worn with long trained dresses. It often replaces the polonaise.

3. Scarf-mantlet, short behind with long straight ends in front, fastened with large bows; either with or without sleeves.

4. The long sleeveless Paletot.

5. The Visite, with wide square cut sleeves, profusely trimmed with embroidery and galloons, for dressy occasions.

6. The Dolman.

7. The Dust-cloak, similar in shape to the waterproof or 'Ulster', nearly reaching to the ground, often made with a cape, and severely plain. Some with triple capes and known as 'Carricks'.

8. The Jacket (also for indoor use), well fitting at the back with many seams, three-quarter length and close round the hips; no trimming but bands of silk or pearl buttons. Worn as an over-jacket in cloth, or as a paletot-jacket to complete a costume.

ACCESSORIES

Parasols are elaborately embroidered and trimmed with lace, with bows of embroidered ribbon on the handle and the top. *Muffs* are small; the Muffatee or wrist-muff, some five inches long, and made of silk, is a passing mode.

Prices

(From Peter Robinson). Rich brocaded silks, 10/- to 16/6; Pekin brocades, 4/11; Genoa velvet, 6/11 a yard. Promenade dresses, brown cashmere and velveteen, £3 18 6. Bronze cashmere and blue silk with cape, 4 guineas. Beige and matelassé costume, 38/6; prune snowflake and pink silk, £2 10 6. Mikado washing silk costume, 49/6.

Evening dresses. Pale blue silk, lace and gauze, £8 18 6. Pink and cream brocaded silk, £9 18 6. White tulle and silk with velvet leaves, £7 7 (from Dickins and Jones). Suede gloves, 2 button, 2/3; 4 button, 2/9; 6 button, 3/6 a pair.

'A great change has come over the style of English dressing within the last, say, five years. French fashions are no longer slavishly followed. The chief aim now is to look picturesque. We believe this change to have come through the furnishing mania, the idea of dressing in harmony with the surroundings,' is the remark of one contemporary; while another says: 'It is curious to note the decadence of the popularity of the purely Parisian importations. Englishwomen have become more original in their attire since they have taken up more independent action in other lines. The alteration of the position of the sexes has caused them to think for themselves.'

Whatever the cause may have been it is clear that English dress was now being governed by the English taste in art. A small section of the cultured class boldly proclaimed the superiority of the Pre-Raphaelite style which Mrs. Haweis described as being a revival of the forms and colours of the years 1327–1377—(natural waist, sleeves cut high on the shoulders, square neck, high or low, with a soft chemisette and 'indescribable tints'). This was the famous 'greenery-yallery, Grosvenor gallery' costume which had no counterpart in France. There the mode of Henri II was the equivalent of the Pre-Raphaelite costume; for example, 'a wide flowing skirt without flounces or tie-back, trimming of embroidery straight down the front and on the wide antique collar and deep cuffs ; bodice with square basques and panel pockets; the colours old gold and black, tawny brown and Morris green; and made of brocade, faille, grenadine and satin.'

The Aesthetic movement had its effect chiefly on domestic decoration which in its turn influenced the colour taste even of ordinary folk. Meanwhile two opposing schools of dress existed side by side; those who clung to tie-backs and trimmings, and those who employed the simple flowing folds—both effective in sex-attraction, while there are signs of a third group appearing who, disdaining allurements in dress, cultivate rational 'tailor-mades' and short skirts. Hence the conflicting remarks by contemporaries: 'The elaboration of trimmings is partly due to the fact that we have thoroughly studied the art; what we do well we like to do often.' 'Modern costume is made not to reveal beauty but to conceal defects' (Alma Tadema). 'The beautifully cut Princess clothing has revolutionised the entire system of cutting both under and outside clothing.'

The charms of classical dress are advocated by some and worn by a few while the ordinary male exclaims: 'It grates upon the common-sense of every thinking man when he sees a fashionable lady waddling along barely able to move her feet six inches at a time.' (But actually the hobbling of women, which has been repeatedly indulged in from time to time, however it may grate upon male commonsense, undoubtedly suggests a degree of enslavement which gratifies l'homme moyen sensuel.)

The general effect of these influences is seen in the colours of dress, from the 'School of Art dresses with neutral tint foundations and gorgeous needlework bands of net embroidered in filoselle flowers', to the combination of colours favoured by ordinary people. For example, fawn or beige with green (sage or olive) for day dresses, and for evening olive green and turquoise, pearl grey and pink, eau de Nil and black, bronze and old gold, claret and pink, claret and pale blue, while Liberty's Indian silks appeal to the artistic-minded.

Of actual innovations the year '78 sees the re-introduction of the short dress with a threatened return of the pannier; the use of the yoke in the structure of the day bodice which tends to become more blouse-like, and the admission into the fashionable world of the 'tailor-made'. We may also note the introduction of the 'Danish safety-pin', that is to say, the modern form with wide protecting sheath. More important is the introduction of 'Combinations' which, together with other subterranean advances, is described in the section on underclothing.

DRESSES

Day

The *Short Dress*, appearing in the summer.
Untrained and about two inches off the ground. Consists of skirt which may be kilted up to the knees and up to the top behind, or with trimmings of pleatings or flounces round the hem; a tunic in the form of a wide sash pleated across the front, either just below the hips or at the knees or a tunic hitched up in the washer-woman's style in front, and tied behind or bunched up; often the scarf is in reversed folds. The bodice with vertical pleats descending from a plain square yoke, and worn with a waistband; or a bodice in the form of a three-quarter pale-tot with a plastron of darker colour. The bodice buttons behind and has a large square collar and broad cuffs of linen with embroidered frill; long tight sleeves. An intermediate form, the 'Baby bodice' with square opening above and vertical pleats down the centre, and a basque extending some way below the waistband, is also used.

These short dresses are frequently tailor-made, as are those in which the jacket-bodice 'is shaped like a gentleman's coat with a waistcoat, actual or simulated' and prolonged down the back; a type known as the 'casaquin', 'buttoned straight down the front with added basques; the bodice is cut just across the hips and the basque resembles a long pocket; it remains apart at the back and the bodice is lengthened and pleated in the shape of a fan.' The neck of the jacket-bodice is open in a slight 'V' edged with frill, which may be repeated round the bottom.

Other forms of day dresses are based on existing modes. 'The Polonaise is now so long that no underskirt is worn but only a band covered with flounces or flutings which is tacked on inside the edge of the polonaise which is now simply a short Princess dress.' The Polonaise may be slashed in front, at the side, or twisted and turned up to show the underskirt, or if the toilet is of one material the polonaise may be made like a deep cuirasse in front, long and draped behind, over a tablier skirt, thus approaching the form of the robe.

The Princess dress, sometimes with a yoke, and often lacing behind, may have a blouse front and waistband; the plastron is a common feature.

It will be seen, therefore, that the rigid cuirasse bodice tends to loose its grip and become a shaped jacket, and the 'tie-back' skirt tends to shed its tail. This appendage, however, remains an ornament on dressy occasions and indoors.

The use of two materials in a dress is becoming modified; many are of one only, at least for informal use.

Trimmings are pipings, galloons and coloured beads; lace much used especially in cascades; and ribbon bows.

For morning dress, small linen collar and cuffs; for afternoon, lace collarettes resembling fichus.

Teagowns

Are generally in the form of an open robe with a plastron and tablier, and a Watteau pleat.

Bathing Dresses

Are in the form of combinations 'with short overskirt added to conceal the figure'.

Materials: Winter dresses of rough woollens (bourrette, serge, etc.), sateen, alpaca, tussore, foulard and grenadine, vicuna and cashmere. Summer dresses of India mousseline de laine, batiste, foulard and printed linen and fancy materials, and Pompadour chintz. (Linen dresses

287

either with double skirt and blouse bodice, or single skirt and long half-fitting paletot.) 'The speciality of this season is sateen, plain or figured.' Corduroy (ribbed velvet) is replacing matelassé.

The rules governing the use of two materials in day dresses are thus given: 'The bodice must be the same material as the underskirt, which must be of plain material (silk, velvet or wool); the tunic, open at the back, of fancy material.' The sleeves sometimes of the same material as the tunic, sometimes of the same as the bodice.

'It has lately become customary for brides to wear going-away dresses of rather a dark hue.'

Evening

Bodice high behind; low and square or 'V' or en cœur in front; often with lace collarette and jabot. Shaped as a cuirasse, or cuirasse in front and Princess behind, or with habit basque (or 'redingote') over a waistcoat; and as a new mode, a long pointed bodice (with an open tunic draped in panniers on the hips; the back of the bodice has coat-tails hanging over the train). The use of a single skirt is not uncommon when the front has a tablier or the front three breadths are of different material. Otherwise there is a tunic or scarf drapery. The train is square, often with a puff ornamented with bows. Sleeves elbow length with cuffs and frill. NOTE: 'Panniers are formed by cutting the side widths longer than the front and back seams; they are then pleated into these seams and lined with buckram to preserve their shape. The panniers almost meet at the back, the skirt being set into the body by flute pleatings, so that the panniers can be separated when sitting down and thus escape being crushed; the bodice is long, rounded over the hips and drawn to the back where the material is both puffed and falls as a train; the style is like a long tight dress over which is a kind of Dolly Varden pannier without the crinoline; the richness of material is more showy in the skirt than in the bodice and panniers; the skirt pleated and trimmed with lace; the bodice of brocade or foulard printed in flowers.' Dinner dresses are frequently Princess style with plastrons of shirred silk.

Examples. 'A simulated tablier of pleated rose-coloured faille with three fluted flounces and train of faille; the sides of the skirt of myrtle-green velvet; low velvet cuirasse bodice with deep basques edged with silk frilling; short puffed sleeves, of silk, with tulle ruching; the skirt looped up with satin bows.'

'An open robe of moss-green satin brocade, with pale blue faille underskirt.'

'A dinner dress, the front of pale blue satin, the train of ruby velvet with revers of blue velvet; the bottom of the train cut in vandykes under which is a pleating of blue satin and a lace balayeuse. A low bodice of velvet with blue embroidered satin plastron.'

Ball Dresses

1. Plain silk or satin Princess dress embroidered with gold or beads.
2. With a pointed bodice laced behind, and curved in at the hips, worn with a bertha, and very narrow sleeves.
3. Bodice high at the back with an Elizabethan collarette and very open in front.

The skirt, either Princess, plain or with scarf drapery.

Materials: satin and brocades specially fashionable.

OUTDOOR GARMENTS

The chief innovations are the Chesterfield coat; Dolmans with carrick capes and Talmas with coat sleeves. While the long Paletot and the Casaque (36 to 40 inches long) demi-fitting at the waist and the edges fringed, are usual.

Outdoor Jackets are out of fashion.

Fringe the usual trimming.

ACCESSORIES

Boas (of skunk, grey opossum, beaver, silver fox, sable). *Muffs*, very small, of cloth or velvet trimmed with fur.

Prices

(Peter Robinson.) Moss cretonnes, printed (32 in.), 9½d. Silk grenadines, 2/6 to 3/6. Cashmere de Paris, all wool (46 in.) 3/6; Sateens, 9d to 1/2 a yard. Duchesse satin (26 in.) 12/9. Black satins 5/9 to 10/9. Costumes in black satin, 10½ guineas.

Liberty's Indian silks (34 in.) 3/- to 3/6 a yard. Camel hair cloths (30 in.) 7/9 a yard. Fur paletots. Seal (36 in.) 14 guineas, Skunk (36 in.) 4 guineas. Sable, 20 guineas, Marten, 8 guineas.

The cleavage of taste, noted in the previous year, now becomes still more obvious. Ordinary folk, such as follow the fashions without much thought, develop a growing taste for the pannier. It is for them that the information is given: 'The pannier is replacing the sheath, that form of dress which in its indiscreet revealings would have been fit only for the jealous walls of a harem had it not been that the hard casings, the whalebone coffin worn inside it, deprived the visible surface of all vivid suggestion of the living and breathing body. Such as it was, it's day is done.' (A picturesque if exaggerated anticipation of coming modes.)

Meanwhile, in high-brow circles, the 'Artistic dress' is being exploited, composed, says one, 'of every textile hitherto in vogue for furniture coverings or curtains, such as cretonnes, and made up either as a draped polonaise of 1770 or with the gathered bodice, waistband and short flounced skirt of 1800; or in richer materials, blue, green, peacock-green, brick-red, brown and gold, with slashed and puffed sleeves and bodice full from the throat to the bust and then stay-like—these are the general notions.' Actually we detect a strong inclination to adapt the modes of the Pompadour epoch, with touches borrowed from 'Queen Anne' (a term very much employed to cover the first half of the eighteenth century).

The aesthetic world continues to clothe itself in dull greens, peacock blues and rich deep reds, and even adopts the Greek dress with a pallium attached to the shoulders and draped shawlwise over a Princess foundation buttoned down the front. To convey the impression created by aesthetic costumes on a contemporary I cannot do better than quote a description of an 'aesthetic At Home': 'All the women looked wan, untidy, picturesque, like figures of pre-Raphaelite pictures, with unkempt hair and

Ball dress. Princess robe in satin with overskirt of gauze. 1879

puffed sleeves. . . . They struck me as striving after some emotional expression. One lady was in red; red gloves and stockings; a serpent coiled round her neck; red tulips in her hair. What a fuzz it was! What a passionate tangle! . . . Two sad-eyed damsels with golden locks wore lank garments of white muslin, crumpled in a million creases; lilies in their hair and a long Annunciation lily carried in the hand. Another was dressed in a raiment of gold tissue with no vestige of waist or band; the two puffs on the shoulders gave the impression of being dilated by an immense sigh; the garment hung loosely about her long neck; tiger lilies were in her hair and crimson gloves reached midway up her arms.' In brief, the movement was towards individualism in dress design, using both Classical and Gothic devices: genuinely artistic with individuals of character, but degenerating into posturings with the herd of exhibitionists who swarm round such movements.

At the other extreme are those who patronise the 'tailor-made', which is much in evidence, it seems, on Brighton front where 'one of the chief objects of life among the young ladies is to appear as masculine as possible. The new paletot, with breast-pocket, cut away like a man's coat with tails: billy-cock hat over hair cut short: stand-up collar and scarf necktie with pin, and a coachman's ulster with multiple capes.'

It is significant that in those fashion magazines intended mainly for the middle-class there is no mention of the aesthetic styles, while in those for the smart folk it is equally ignored; indeed, any divergence from the purely conventional is disapproved of. It is obvious that Englishwomen are rapidly diverging into groups, each with their appropriate styles of dress and without much interest in the others. Consequently the threads of fashion, although at times entangled, tend to sustain distinct courses.

The general impulse of this year's fashions, however, is in the direction of emphasising the hips by panniers, toning down the vertical line by waistbands (with 'coat and skirt' effects), and borrowing artistic ideas from the domestic surroundings. This beautifying urge spreads even to bathing dresses ('people are much more particular about them than they were, the combination shape with braid edging and sailor collar being most popular'), and also to underclothing which, for the first time in history, is adapted to the configuration of the body; so that we read of 'the triumph of the shaped underclothing'.

There are also two dresses having some historical associations: the 'Pinafore dress' (recalling the opera of Gilbert and Sullivan), and the 'Jersey dress' recalling the name and figure of Mrs. Langtry.

DRESSES

Day

The varieties of these, which appear at first sight innumerable, can however be classified on general lines by distinguishing those made with the bodice part separate, and those which preserve the continuity of the Princess type.

It is the former which provides the varieties of the '*short* dress', now often clear of the instep and appearing with either a single or a double skirt. When the skirt is single it is usually kilted; when double the underskirt has a narrow flounce or a band of pleating, and the over-skirt (called indifferently 'tunic' or 'tablier') may be either:

1. folded across the front and draped behind.

alpaca lining

opening

pocket

back turned inside out
showing tie-backs

net frilling

AFTERNOON OR
DINNER DRESS
1879-80

gaging

gaging

silk buttons

BLUE GENOA VELVET,
PANNIERS & TRAIN
OF BLUE GROS-GRAIN &
EMBROIDERED NET TRIMMING

vandykes

ruching & pleats

2. shirred in front and falling in long lappets behind.

3. bridled with scarves across the front.

The bodice may be classified into the following types:

1. The tight basque bodice with obtuse point in front and with narrow lappets behind; buttoned all down the front with deep revers of a different material.

2. A blouse jacket, shirred at the shoulders and waist, with a waistband.

3. Coat jacket with revers and pointed basque in front.

4. The casaquin or tightly fitting bodice with square basques, revers and cuffs. Often of different material from the dress and worn over a long waistcoat.

5. A cuirasse deeply pleated in front and behind.

6. A plastron bodice with deep rounded basque; the plastron being buttoned on the outside of the bodice (distinguished from the waistcoat which is attached under the bodice.)

7. The jacket with panniers, the basques rounded off and draped into panniers on the hips; often called a 'Camargo', and worn over a waistcoat.

Of these varieties the first three usually supplied models for the 'tailor-made' dress of serge or cloth.

The Polonaise

'The polonaise, discarded for a time, is now in favour again'—but in new forms:

1. Tight fitting with long narrow revers in front made of fancy material; the draperies form deep facings at the bottom of the skirt in front and are draped behind with ribbon bows.

2. The jacket polonaise, made like a jacket in front with a pleated tablier and the back like a short Princess dress.

3. A polonaise simulating a jacket-bodice, and looped up over a skirt.

4. A blouse polonaise with waistband.

5. Given a more masculine cut it becomes a 'habit redingote' almost as long as the dress at the back, while the front is closed only down to the knee.

It will be observed that in all these forms the Polonaise preserves the Princess effect at least at the back; that is, there is no seam at the waist. When the front of the polonaise is so long as almost to conceal the underskirt it merges into the Princess dress; and, in fact, the latter is now frequently made with a false pleating sewn on under the front edge to simulate an underskirt

and the back draped on a full length lining; or a 'false underskirt' composed of lining material with an edging may be attached to the under side of the skirt at the knee level.

The Princess dress is trained or semi-trained, the train being square, and either applied to the back of the skirt halfway up or as a prolongation of the bodice (*i.e.* as a polonaise); the front of the dress is of some different material, usually a fancy fabric, and either shirred across or trimmed across with pleated scarves or with embroidery; above there is generally a plastron. The train may be detachable, or may be looped up for walking by means of two loops (fastened under the train) which can be attached to a button under the edge of the tablier.

Panniers

This fashion which comes in at the beginning of the year appears to be going out at the close. It is never used with woollens; when the bodice is separate the panniers are on the skirt, being composed of a short tunic open in front and draped over the hips; or of the side breadths being gauged at the top; when the upper part of the dress is in the form of a polonaise the panniers are made in the sides of it by inside tapes drawing them up.

It remains to describe certain named types of dress:

1. The Teagown

'Moralists would strive to teach us that they are a sign of the degeneracy of the age, and that this easy comfortable dress points to free and easy manners. Each season they become less like dressing-gowns and more elaborate and more like fancy dress.'

The simpler forms are en princesse with multi-coloured ribbon bows down the front; the more elaborate may imitate the Watteau sacque with high square bodice, elbow sleeves, fichu, panniers, and box-pleat from the neck, or indeed any fanciful historical costume. With teagowns, caps are always worn (*e.g.* of Pompadour satin with a flat crown like a sailor's hat), and mittens. 'Young ladies are not expected to wear teagowns as this apparel is reserved for the married.' They were made of Pompadour sateen, washing silks, black satin, velvet and brocade, and pekins.

2. The Jersey—or Guernsey—Costume

Introduced by Redfern's for the Princess of Wales and popularised by Mrs. Langtry. 'The latest eccentricity at Ryde is the blue or deep red jersey cut to the figure and worn over a serge or flannel skirt'—kilted. Made of finely knitted silk or wool with either an invisible fastening down the back, or with no opening but the neck. It is recommended only for those whose figures are perfect. Many of the jerseys are boned behind. A style sometimes worn for tennis.

3. *The Pinafore Costume*

Consists of a juive tunic shaped on the shoulders like a pinafore and worn with a waistband over a Princess-dress with kilted skirt; the tunic of light or fancy material, *e.g.* Pompadour sateen. A popular style for tennis.

4. *Tennis Costumes*

'A cream merino bodice with long sleeves, edged with embroidery; skirt with deep kilting; over it an old-gold silk blouse-tunic with short wide sleeves and square neck. The tunic looped up at one side with a ball-pocket sewn to it. Large straw hat of the coal-scuttle type.'

Or 'of blue cashmere with a light cretonne tunic bunched up at the hips, with a square bib.'

'Or an olive green woollen damask polonaise open below the waist and looped up to form panniers, over a white cashmere kilted skirt.'

Or 'a skirt of white corduroy, unpleated, with a wide scarf round the hips, round bodice with wide waistband.'

5. *Riding Costume*

The habit untrimmed, 44 in. in front, 57 in. behind. Double row of bone buttons down the front of the bodice which has a 7 in. basque behind. Long tight sleeves set in very high. Linen collar and cuffs. Bowler hat or top hat.

6. *Ascot Dresses*

'Mostly coat bodices distinct from the skirts. Velvet Louis XV coats over silks and satins, often of contrasting colours. Pinafore dresses such as blue sateen with Pompadour cotton pinafore tunic and bib; black velvet and white foulard pinafore tunic. Mrs. Langtry in a striped black and white muslin polonaise opening in front over a short kilted skirt of white tussore trimmed with lace and black velvet; bonnet of red poppies and black and white embroidery.'

7. *Various Dresses*

'Walking costume; short kilted skirt with a scarf in reversed folds above the knee, tied with a drapery behind; jacket bodice with yoke at the back and pleats.'

Seaside Dress: Silver grey sateen kilted skirt: Pompadour chintz overskirt draped en panier and turned back with revers; the opening in front filled in with hanging ribbon bows; sateen casaquin bodice with chintz waistcoat.

A morning toilet: 'Trained skirt of pale blue faille; overdress of brocade with long side panels tied back by ribbons to form panniers on the hips.'

Materials: Cloth, serge, oatmeal serge, gingham, velveteen, plush, shot woollens, cashmere for

Jersey tennis costume (Messrs. Jay). 1879

costumes; sateen with Pompadour patterns; Pekins ('the quantity sold is incredible'); Belgian linens and fancy silks for overdress. 'Art materials' (silk and wool damasks with conventional floral designs and Gothic brocades of rich silk imitating those of the eighteenth century); summer dresses of satinette, cretonne and Madras and cottons with Pompadour patterns. Foulards, surah and tussore washing silks, muslins. For all except plain costumes two to four materials.

'The production of cheap imitations of costly materials is a feature of the day.'

Colours: Varieties of blue, red, garnet, cerise, old gold, biscuit, terracotta, and grey-green ('moonbeam').

3. Corset basque like a corset with few seams; lacing behind or buttoned in front; low round neck with Grecian drapery of tulle caught in the centre; sleeves a mere frill.

4. The casaquin bodice, of different material and colour from the skirt, with satin bows down the front and on the elbow sleeves. High

Stylish mantles. 1879

Evening

Types of bodice:

1. With long points front and back, the sides being hollowed to define the waist line; generally of satin and laced behind.

2. The belted Josephine bodice, round with very low darts and a wide belt of silk or satin folds.

or low neck. It may be in the form of a silk jersey with square neck and lace sleeves.

5. A Princess polonaise dress looped up into panniers and falling as drapery over the train of the underskirt.

6. The peplum bodice, with long side panels forming panniers.

294

7. The waistcoat bodice; the waistcoat may be a separate garment with a back, or a front only or merely simulated. The effect is that of a casaquin, the centre of which is of satin with buttons down the middle and resembling a waistcoat, and bordered on each side with revers of another material (*e.g.* brocade), the rest of the bodice being made of a third material (*e.g.* a woollen stuff). Low square neck and elbow sleeves.

The Skirt

Trained, square or round, the train being stiffened by a lining of muslin. Some have a breadth of satin down the centre of the back and brocade at the sides, or vice versa. The back en princesse is common. The front of the skirt may also be en princesse but more usually is open over a tablier or a tunic which forms panniers at the sides, or with scarf drapery forming panniers. (2½ yards needed for a scarf.) The front is often trimmed with alternate flounces of lace and material such as foulard up to the waist.

Evening dresses are described as being 'of great variety and of art colours or startling mixtures; three to four materials may be used.'

Panniers may be single or even double and edged with lace. Mittens are commonly worn.

The neck openings are either square or in a deep oval with tulle edging or a lace fichu.

Examples:

'A bouillonnée tablier over a pleated skirt; bodice with panniers and plastron; low square opening with ruff edging; elbow sleeves.'

'A peplum bodice of claret velvet with short velvet sleeves; guipure round the bodice; trained skirt of pekin with satin pleatings; the front of the skirt with velvet bands and gathered satin.'

'A dinner dress of two shades of blue faille; pointed cuirasse bodice with satin bows down the front and on the sleeves, elbow length; the skirt with embroidered tablier; panniers; the back of the dress en princesse.'

'Dinner dress of black net embroidered with roses over black silk; low bodice with pointed basques laced behind; short sleeves. White pleating round the top of the bodice.'

Ball Dresses

The bodice is cut lower than formerly, some square front and back and very low, with shoulder straps; no sleeves but a lace frill, or elbow sleeves. Bodice is cut with many seams both in front and behind to ensure an absolute fit. Bead trimming is fashionable.

The skirt, which is 3¾ yards wide and shorter than formerly, may be made with panniers brought from beneath the point of the bodice or with panniers outside the bodice. The dress 'may be a simulated Princess or a shallow stay bodice pointed front and back and laced behind; no trimming but a lace edging.' The skirt is tied back, and the train a series of draped puffs. Others resemble ordinary evening dresses.

Examples:

'A plain tablier of white brocade; simulated open robe of white pekin trained with pink flounces; a waistcoat of brocade; low square neck; short puffed sleeves.'

'Low pointed bodice cut out in a deep oval at the top; tablier of alternate flowers and kilted gauze; panniers carried up to the bodice; plain train.'

It is common for the bodice to be coloured with a white skirt.

OUTDOOR GARMENTS

The Visite, with cape forming sleeves.

The half length Paletot.

Short Mantles heavily trimmed with fringe and ruching, often with ribbon flots at the back of the neck and a band of trimming down the centre of the back.

The India Cashmere shawl is revived as an outdoor garment.

ACCESSORIES

Jewellery: small ear-rings; no lockets; small brooches. 'Quaintness and oddity characterise the modern fashions', *e.g.* a gridiron with a ruby heart, for ear-rings (to suggest wasted affections); arrow and lizard pins; serpent bracelets. Cat's eyes and turquoises fashionable, in gold settings of Etruscan designs. Jet returning to fashion.

Stockings are all coloured with stripes or fancy patterns, of lisle thread or silk. *Muffs*, small; some of shirred satin with ribbon bows; others of fur.

'The Princess of Wales has set the fashion of wearing a flower on the dress just below the left ear.'

Prices

'The expense of dressing has nearly trebled in the last forty years.'

Liberty & Co. Shantung (19 in.) 15/- to 35/- for 20 yards. Tussore (34 in.) 21/- to 35/- for 10 yards.

Peter Robinson. Coloured silk costumes with 5 yards for bodice, 58/6. Embroidered tussore, 4½ guineas. Pompadour Surah, 4½ guineas. Brocade and velvet, 8½ guineas.

Cashmere costumes, 3 guineas. Lyons velvet evening dresses, 16 to 18 guineas.

Queen Anne chintzes (32 in.) 7d to 1/- a yard.

Scotch oatmeal cloth (27 in.) 9d.

Silk jersey costume, £3 10.

Rich Lyons silk velvet, black, 10/9; coloured, 13/6 to 21/- a yard. Corduroy velveteen, 3/4; Pekins, 8/11; Witney serge, 1/- a yard.

'In the present day the object of dress is no longer to conceal but to display the female form divine.'

HEADGEAR IN THE '70's

The headgear was more elaborate in this decade than in any other of the century. The wearing of false hair was general and the manner of so doing excessively complicated. The effect was to enlarge the apparent size of the head, especially the back. No doubt this balanced the forward tilt of the body due to the high heels, and harmonised with the pouf of the skirt. The hat or bonnet had, therefore, either to be tipped forward in front of the mass or to cling on to it behind as best it could. Such devices gave the face a small appearance which was much admired by the big whiskered male.

Nice distinctions between bonnets and hats were carefully observed; the former were more ceremonial and to wear a hat on Sunday was a social outrage. The nice-minded worshipped their Maker in bonnets strewn with dead birds, the slaughter of which provided a flourishing industry. Shiploads of human hair were imported to supply the fair tresses which man's imperial race ensnare, complicated with frisettes, scalpettes, nets, combs, pins, artificial flowers and insects.

1870

HAIR

Chignon larger, starting higher on the head and hanging lower on to the neck; formed either of loose curls or plaits forming a catagan tied above with a large ribbon; or the hair in rouleaux rolled smooth over a frisette.

COIFFURE

Day. Butterfly bows; fanchons, puff caps of muslin or lace; large caps with cache-peignes (morning).

Evening, as in 1869, or with drooping feathers and flowers, large butterfly bows, and ornaments of jewels, flowers, enamel insects (butterfly and grasshopper).

OUTDOORS

Bonnets and hats only distinguishable by the method of fastening; if tied under the chin it is a bonnet; if under the chignon a hat. Both frequently trimmed with veils, lappets or ribbons (known as 'follow me, lads') hanging over the chignon.

Bonnets larger and higher by means of the profuse trimming.

The Chapeau complet has crown, border and curtain of velvet with feathers and flowers above the crown; worn very far forward.

The boat-shaped bonnet, with high crown, the brim turned up in front and behind. Some like small hats bent down on either side.

Short veils are worn, tied behind and hanging down over the chignon

Hats 1. The Tyrolese, generally with long curled feather.

2. The Bergère, of leghorn or rice straw, bent down in front and behind; often turned up on one side.

3. Small round hat, as in '69.

Hats were kept in place by elastic under the chignon.

1871

HAIR

Hair in loose braids falling on the neck and scarcely tied up; front brushed off the forehead or waved in braids very low down. Nets worn, except in the evening.

1870

1. *Promenade Costume*. Rice straw bonnet, bound with black velvet; small lace scarf ornaments the top and falls over the chignon. A tuft and strap of lilac encircle the crown; lace strings.

2. *Seaside Toilet*. Hat of Italian straw edged with black blonde and trimmed with velvet flowing in long ends behind. A garland of field flowers is fastened in front and falls over the crown on to the chignon.

3. *Seaside or Country Toilet*. Mushroom Hat. Large straw hat trimmed with black velvet bows and tufts of field flowers.

4. *Morning Cap*. A square of muslin with a single hollow plait in the centre taken lengthwise. Bordered with rich Valenciennes lace gathered full and looped up at each side with a wide gros-grain bow.

5. *Visiting Toilet*. Brown straw bonnet with brim turned up in front. Two rows of lace cover the top of the bonnet. A tuft of purple flowerets surrounded with their leaves fastened above the lace. A large gros-grain bow of the same colour as the straw and falling with long ends over the chignon terminates the back of the bonnet. Embroidered tulle strings trimmed with lace and tied under the chin.

6. *Evening Toilet*. Coiffure composed of satin bows and diamond stars.

1871

1. *Ball Dress Coiffure*.

2. *Walking Costume*. Gipsy bonnet trimmed with lace and feather.

3. *Visiting Toilet*. Hat with brim turned up on one side and adorned with tassels, feathers and ribbon.

4. *Visiting Toilet*. Small Pamela fermé bonnet of English straw trimmed with satin ribbon and roses. Satin ribbon strings.

5. *Promenade Costume*. Straw hat trimmed by black lace ribbon and roses.

6. *Swiss Muslin Breakfast Cap*.

1872

1. *Ball Dress*. Headdress of full blown roses.

2. *Carriage or Promenade Costume*. Black velvet hat trimmed by mauve velvet and mauve ostrich feather.

3. *Morning Dress* (The Charlotte Corday Morning Cap). Small crown of muslin gathered all round under a green ribbon; front, of very wide Valenciennes lace slightly gathered, turned backwards at the side under a green bow also edged with lace. At the back small lace lappets and long green ends.

4. *Promenade Dress* (The Rabagas Bonnet). Small, high-crowned; brim turned up en auréole all round; covered with blue velvet. Top of crown on right side ornamented with garland of roses which forms a spray at the back. Other side and top of crown with row of loops of blue ribbon arranged downwards. Two ostrich feathers over both crown and chignon.

5. *Costume for a Flower Show*. Small round beret hat of rose coloured silk and white chip, trimmed by roses.

6. *Promenade Costume*. Black velvet hat, the sides turned up and lined by scarlet silk. Trimmed by bows of scarlet ribbon and scarlet feather.

1873

1. *Promenade Costume*. Grey felt hat trimmed with black velvet and a feather which is fastened by a small blue and black bird and descends en cascade at the back.

2. *Promenade Costume*. Velvet hat with low crown and turned up brim. Large bow with ends, of turquoise silk at left side; bandeau of the same across the forehead. Bunch of primroses to match turquoise silk at the top and long grasses fall at the back.

3. *Evening Dress*. Front hair arranged in four puffs above the forehead; combed up at the side from the temples over a coronet formed frisette. Back hair coiled and terminates with two ringlets. Two sprays of fern leaves across the coronet, and one falling at the back. Gilt comb at the top of the coils.

4. *Promenade Costume*. Marin anglais bonnet, of myrtle-green faille and velvet, ornamented with a garland of myrtle-green leaves and pale pink feather. Full rich bow at the back; strings tied under the chin.

5. *Visiting Costume and Promenade*. Panama grass hat with round brim lined with blue ribbon and feather trimming.

6. *Morning Dress*. Coiffure of embroidered muslin and ribbon.

1874

1. *Country Costume.* Shepherdess hat with velvet and wreath of flowers.

2. *Morning Dress.* Cap of white net wreathed with pink and brown foulard over lace edging. At the back, spray of roses, shaded from crimson to pale pink.

3. *Promenade Costume.* Bonnet of black felt with borders bound with faille; under the front a wreath of ribbon loops and bow. Feather fastened under a stylish bow.

4. *Evening or Ball Costume.* Catagan coiffure. Front of hair waved and brushed back from the face; back hair waved and placed in loops and torsades, terminating in a curled catagan with bow matching the dress; bands of velvet with stars of diamonds, steel or jet with star pins to match.

5. *Promenade Costume.* Page (or Charlotte Corday) bonnet of grey terry velvet; front ruched, crown soft; a velvet drapery divides the two parts and finishes at the back with a bow and falling ends.

6. *Seaside or Promenade Costume.* (Chapeau Couronne.) Bonnet formed of a wreath of cornflowers, lace ends forming a bow at the back and fastening under the chin.

1875

1. *Walking Dress.* Bonnet of rice straw trimmed with dove colour and lilac ribbons and bouquets of pink geranium.

2. *Walking Dress.* Shepherdess hat of Italian straw trimmed with bouquets of flowers and blue ribbon.

3. *Seaside Costume.* Hat of black straw, brim bound with white and turned up at the back with a plume of black feathers. Crown trimmed with scarf of blue surah with black edges tied in a bow behind.

4. *Walking Costume.* Bonnet of white rice straw; square crown and brim raised in front under which is a full wreath of cherry blossom. Crown also with the same flowers mixed with the fruit and bow of black faille.

5. *Dinner Dress.* Front and side hair slightly waved, the former turned back over a crepe and the latter with the back hair combed upwards and fastened on the top of the head, where the ends are arranged in curls.

6. *Morning Dress.* Cap of embroidered batiste edged with Mechlin lace; trimmed with bows and loops of pale lilac and deep claret gros-grain ribbon.

1. *Promenade Costume.* Capote, crown of navy blue faille, curtain of navy blue cloth. In front a shaded humming bird on a coquillé of cream worsted lace. A velvet string (the soldier's jugulière) under the chin and fastened at the left side under a bow and end of black velvet and cream lace.

2. *Walking Costume.* Toque in black velvet, soft crown (chapeau Bayard), narrow brim with ruching inside. White feather fastened in front with a silver ornament covers the crown, a similar one placed on the brim falls at the back.

3. *Walking Costume.* Chapeau Michel Ange in grey felt; steel braid round the crown and turned up brim. Turban of striped surah silk round the front, forming a bow at the side with a fringed end down the back. Grey feather behind.

4. *Ball Headdress.* Suitable to young married woman. Coronet of plaits, the hair in front in irregular waves. Portion of back hair also waved, the remainder falling in curls of unequal length. Gold braid crosses the top, with a gilt dagger on the left side. Spray of dark leaves with gold fruit falls at the back.

5. *Walking Costume.* Straw bonnet, with diadem front; small straw curtain at the back bound with yellow faille. Wreath of flowers across the front, and another round the crown fastening a tuft of blue feathers. Cream lace ties.

6. *Afternoon Dress.* Close fitting coiffure of white gazereselle with narrow pleating of tulle to rest on the hair; in front, cluster of oval berries, leaves and strawberry blossoms; at the back, a triangular veil-like fall of red crepe de chine, edged with waved silk fringe.

1877

1. *Walking Dress.* Felt toque, chestnut brown felt crown with beaver plush brim trimmed with chestnut brown velvet, pheasants wings and antennae of green feathers.

2. *Visiting Toilette.* Pifferaro bonnet in grey felt, the brim bordered with green and trimmed with crepe lisse, black aigrette and coque feather, fastened by loops of green cord; green and brown ribbon strings.

3. *Walking Dress.* Gold straw bonnet, trimmed with old gold silk; brim lined with crimson velvet and ornamented with a garland of double pink and red poppies.

4. *Fête Bonnet.* (Flower bonnet.) No crown, but the wide wreath composed of clove pinks and black currants; coronet front covered with wide band of cut jet beads; black tulle strings tied loosely at the side.

5. *Evening Headdress.* Front hair waved, forms a bandeau over the forehead; at the top of the head a gordian knot of hair. At the back a torsade low on the neck, and a blue aigrette at the side of the head.

6. *Morning Headdress.* Hair net of pale blue chenille; ribbon is pale plush on one side, and tilleul satin on the other.

1878

1. *Promenade Costume.* Yellow straw hat; brim lined with black velvet, with large bow of pale blue watered ribbon in front; crown with a garland of wild strawberries, and a spray of pink thorn and wild strawberries above the bow.

2. *Promenade Costume.* Beige straw bonnet, trimmed with feathers and satin ribbon; claret velvet lining.

3. *Promenade Costume.* White straw hat; border of brim, rouleau and bows at the side of black velvet; white feather spotted with black.

4. *Demi-Saison Bonnet.* Directoire bonnet in moss green felt, trimmed with satin ribbon and feathers of the same shade.

5. *Country or Seaside Costume.* The Ros-iki hat. White straw, trimmed with red braid and balls to match.

6. *Morning Cap.* Brim trimmed with a band of muslin edged with lace. Coquilles at the sides and falling over the hair at the back; front nearly plain and ornamented by a straw coloured satin bow.

1879

1. *Walking or Visiting Dress.* Trianon Poke Bonnet in black velvet, tied down over the ears by serge ribbon strings; bouillonné of old gold satin in the hollow brim and raised curtain; loose torsade round crown, and in front a tropical bird on a bed of brilliantly dyed feathers.

2. *Summer Bonnet* of white rice straw; spray of Persian lilac and mountain ash berries, in front and at the sides; brim lined with bronze velvet, with a silk and gold galon at the edge; cream ribbon strings.

3. *Promenade Costume.* Black long haired beaver hat; long black plume over the top, fastened on the left side with chased silver buckle; torsade of black velvet round the crown.

4. *Visiting Dress.* Niniche bonnet (or hat) of English straw, lined with blue faille and trimmed with roses and blue ribbon.

5. *Morning Hairdressing* for young lady. Hair arranged à la Chinoise in front; waved fringe falls over the forehead; back hair fastened as a loose torsade with a tortoiseshell comb, having balls on the top.

6. *Visiting Toilette* for a youthful married woman. Bonnet of claret net, embroidered with claret beads; edge bouillonné and trimmed with merveilleuse satin of the same shade; bouquet of tea roses on left side.

COIFFURE

Day. Unchanged. Breakfast caps larger than those for afternoon or evening.

Evening. Small lace caps the size of the palm of the hand, or as in '70.

OUTDOORS

Bonnets worn more off the forehead and tilted slightly back.

The Gipsy bonnet was very small; the Pamela like a small hat; also some much larger, tall in the crown, of terry and corded silk. 'No trimming can redeem their special ugliness.'

Hats. 1. With high crown and turned-up brim or flat brim.

2. Small toque hats.

3. Gipsy hats with wide brim, low crown, and known as 'Dolly Varden hats'.

1872

HAIR

At the end of the year chignons became much shorter, and only a few loose curls were worn on the neck, or none.

COIFFURE

Day. 'The fashion for wearing small caps at all hours of the day is decidedly on the increase.' 'More than 50 shapes of which the Charlotte Corday is the most popular.'

Evening. Small caps; flowers and leaves; white lace bows. 'The small Charlotte Corday caps are almost universally worn both at dinner and small evening parties.'

OUTDOORS

Bonnets larger and more tilted back.

1. The Rabagas bonnet, 'the border completely turned up and with moderately high crown'— extremely popular.

2. The Rubens bonnet, 'the brim turned up at one side with a bow and a feather or aigrette above.'

Hats. 'The hat is put on, sailor-fashion, at the back of the head.' Small round hats with high crowns; brims turned-up or straight. Beret hats resembling small mob caps.

Large Leghorns of the Dolly Varden or shepherdess styles.

Veils usually of plain white tulle without spots.

1873

HAIR

The chignon is smaller and not so low on the neck, but high enough to be seen in front. A high Spanish comb usually worn. In the 'Recamier' style the chignon is very high with curls on the neck.

Young girls often tie their hair at the top of the head, and then plait it in a single braid which hangs low on the back, tied at the end with ribbon.

COIFFURE

Day. Unchanged.

Evening. Combs, sprays of flowers, ribbon bows.

OUTDOORS

Bonnets. The tilt backwards very marked. Made very high and much trimmed with flowers, laces and feathers, and ribbon streamers behind. The popular 'Marin anglaise' bonnet or hat resembled a small boy's sailor hat turned up all round but much trimmed and perched at the back of the head. Variations of the Rabagas continue.

Hats. The 'Marin anglais' hat, slightly less trimmed than the bonnet, and tied behind, was sometimes worn with a separate bandeaux over the front hair to prevent its falling off. Generally of brown or black straw.

Large Leghorns for the country, with flat crowns. The Rubens hat with high crown and brim turned up on one side has many forms.

1874

HAIR

Short curls or ringlets ('generally artificial') falling over the forehead, and coques (*i.e.* thick short curls rolled up) built up on the head as high as possible. Small flat curls are frequently gummed to the forehead. The catagan is very fashionable, in which the chignon comes down once more to the nape of the neck.

COIFFURE

Day. Corday caps, with bows matching the dress, for young women.

OUTDOORS

Bonnets 'not only remain as high as ever but widen the brim to an alarming extent, with

wings and heads and whole birds, butterflies. . .'
1. Variations of the high-crowned.
2. Capotes, *i.e.* with soft crowns made of the dress material, of the Charlotte Corday shape or like a baby's bonnet (the 'capote bebé').
3. Coronet-shaped, hidden under a wreath of flowers.
Owing to the high tortoiseshell comb (the 'peigne giraffe') being too big for the bonnet it boldly protrudes; the high chignon on the top of the head is uncovered, being encircled by the so-called chapeau which is finished at the back with lace lappels, ribbons and trailing sprays of flowers.

Hats. The small hats and bonnets with high crowns are often indistinguishable.

1875

HAIR

The catagan is common. The front hair is brought down low over the forehead in frizzles.

COIFFURE

Day. No change; small lace caps with flowers worn in the afternoon.

Evening. Half coronets or wreaths, placed far back, with flowers fastening the catagan.

OUTDOORS

Bonnets. Small hats and bonnets indistinguishable; if worn well forward it is called a hat; if perched on the back, a bonnet. Strings frequently absent. 'Round-faced beauties can surmount their laughing eyes with a high and graceful arrangement of flowers, feathers, bows and jet with drooping strings which have the effect of adding apparent length to the face.'
The shapes are variations of the previous year's.
Hats. Shaped over the eyes with high crowns; often turned up behind. 'Large stuffed birds for trimming hats and bonnets—not the head and tail only but the whole bird; pigeons, doves and cockatoos are especial favourites.'

Veils. 'With summer bonnets white tulle veilettes have a softening effect and are very becoming to the complexion; for the seaside a gauze veil, long enough to be thrown round the neck as a scarf.'

1876

HAIR

As in previous year, but much less false hair worn; nets re-introduced. 'As many ladies have crimped and burnt away their front hair all manner of devices are resorted to in order to give the appearance of thick abundant hair; to the American is accorded the credit of introducing false fronts ("scalpettes"), made of invisible nets to which luxuriant tresses are attached.'

COIFFURE

Day. Catagan shorter and coiffure simpler. Corday caps.

Evening. As in previous year; usually long curls hang down behind.

OUTDOORS

Bonnets and Hats. 1. The Aureola brimmed, surrounding the head like a halo.
2. The Capote, with a high border, the space between it and the head filled in with trimming. Close over the ears, with a drooping ornament behind.
Many varieties of shape seen, the only uniform feature being the high front formed by either the crown or the raised brim.
Trimmings of flowers and feathers. 'In the new summer straw hats and bonnets feathered songsters are perched on the brim, resting on the hair. Humming-birds, redbreasts, longtails, tomtits, small parakeets and bronzed blackbirds are chiefly used.'

Veils. Of écru net with chenille spots. 'The new fancy is to put the middle of the veil smoothly over the face, cross the ends behind the head and bringing them forward again tie them under the chin in a mammoth bow.'

1877

HAIR

Day. A high chignon with or without a catagan. Nets fashionable. White chenille nets 'look frightful as they resemble nightcaps so closely'.

Evening. Hair arranged high, the front parted and waved; or the ends curved forward in crescent-shape on the forehead and gummed there in what are called 'Montague curls'. Scalpettes worn if the hair is thin.

COIFFURE

Day. Corday caps; little foulard fichus twisted round the head (for both morning and evening); these are edged with lace or blonde and fastened to the hair by gold pins. Sometimes a small spray of flowers 'put on coquettishly at the side, a style even the most youthful matrons adopt because they know it makes them look bewitching.' Young married women wear caps.

Evening. Sortie-de-bal of lace mantilla. 'The headdresses are so becoming that ladies prefer retaining them on their heads at the theatre instead of appearing in a bonnet.'

Bonnets

1. Bebé bonnets, the border turned up showing a cap-trimming of tulle with ribbons or flowers.
2. Capuchons, or floral bonnets. Composed entirely of flowers; even the strings. Only worn with a *silk* dress. The flowers are mounted on a very slight foundation, and only a very small portion of the head is covered by it; the flowers are scented au naturel; with this bonnet the hair is worn high.
'Fashion combines velvet and satin fruit (strawberries, greengages, currants, carrots, oranges) with flowers and small stuffed birds, ferns, grasses, moss, plantain, thistles and acorns.'
3. Gainsborough bonnets. Close clinging, fitting the sides of the head, high in front with broad crown sloping off abruptly behind. Of dark velvet with clusters of roses.

Hats

1. The toque, with high crown and much higher brim than formerly. Usually of felt trimmed with a bird's wing or a whole bird.
2. A very wide-brimmed sailor hat.
3. The pifferaro, a short chimney-pot with aigrette in front.
4. A flat round hat, the brim much turned back and worn at the back of the head, pinned with two long pins. Of straw.
5. Broad brimmed Leghorn. 'Only very youthful figures wear them.'

Veils. Scarf veils more than ever worn. Some entirely cover the face.

1878

HAIR

Artificial hair and padding much gone out of fashion.

Day. Either in waved bandeaux or perfectly smooth with a catagan behind, or in plaits and rouleaux in the antique style.

Evening. The front hair waved or frizzed and very low on the forehead. 'Light puffs superimposed are more elegant than plaits for the catagan.'

COIFFURE

Day caps are simple in the Corday style.

Evening lace caps worn by matrons; ornaments of detached sprays called 'piquets' with large tortoiseshell, gold or silver head-pins used 'unsparingly'. Flowers and butterflies of filigree.
Catagan nets still worn; those for travelling have added hair beneath the net and short curls on the top (see specimen in the Victoria and Albert Museum).

Bonnets

Small toques, capotes with diadem crowns, and the 'Directoire bonnet' with border broad and flaring at the top but close down over the ears with a square moderately high crown.

Hats

A great variety of shape; all with moderately small brims except the large Leghorns with flapping brims, for country use.
'When travelling tourists may even attend Divine service in hats.'

Trimmings for Hats and Bonnets: Large round beads threaded on wire. Ribbons, one to two inches wide, of watered silk and satin, fringed, shaded and striped; or of gauze with velvet pile. 'Green leaves are now made of oil-silk and green rubber tubing is used to hang like grasses or to thread pearl beads upon. Worm-eaten faded green leaves are among the most natural things in Spring millinery.'

Veils. Of black thread net speckled with tinsel; worn in mask style or as scarves.

1879

HAIR

'Very little artificial hair is now worn.' Much less voluminous. Both day and evening, in wavy bandeaux and a small chignon or a mass of wavy hair falling over the back and tied at the neck. Or the hair gathered to form a bow on the top of the head with a light fringe over the forehead.

For *Evening* it is more elaborate, the back hair being raised over a cushion at the top with

1878. Evening dresses
Of pink faille en princesse with simulated cuirasse; gauze drapery
Of eau de Nil silk, the back en princesse

1879. Costumes by Swan and Edgar
Dinner dress of grenat satin with gauged and puffed front; satin scarves and
drapery; sides of embroidered velvet; satin corsage; velvet waistcoat
Outdoor dress of blue pekin laine trimmed with striped satin and fringe;
laced waistcoat; ruby velvet collar and cuffs

curls in front of it. Or in classical style the plaited hair rolled round and round at the back.

COIFFURE

Day caps in the Corday style, worn in the mornings and with teagowns.

Evening caps of lace or silk, for matrons.

Pearls, diamonds or flowers in the hair; a single rose behind one ear is fashionable.

Bonnets

Generally larger and no longer perched on the back of the head.

1. The Directoire bonnet, for carriage and theatre.

2. Poke bonnet, the brim of an open evasé shape at the top and close at the sides; the border lined with shirred or pleated velvet or satin; no cap or interior trimming with it.

White chip bonnets of the caleche shape, with cluster of large flowers in front and white lace curtain and strings, for dressy use.

3. Small toque bonnets and sealskin capes.

4. The capote, matching the dress, for walking.

5. Cottage bonnets, the brim in front rolled upwards and covered with gathered satin; low behind the ears.

Variations of the larger bonnets, the Diana Vernon with low crown and wide brim; the Clarissa Harlowe, of Leghorn straw, the brim coming forward on the forehead and lined with dark velvet.

Bonnet Materials: Plush and beaver for winter; straw bonnets are frequently trimmed with plush; ribbon strings commonly cross over the top of the bonnet and form part of the trimming.

Hats

Much larger and fitting the head.

1. The Ninish, the brim slanted in front and turned up behind.

2. Gainsborough hat, brim turned up in front or on one side, and trimmed with feathers; for visits.

3. Toques.

4. Reed hats, which can be shaped into almost any form. For summer, with coloured braid over the top, they are much used by bathers. When trimmed with expensive flowers they are suitable for garden parties. 'They are peculiarly comfortable while playing tennis.' Often trimmed with coloured velvet.

UNDERCLOTHING OF THE '70's

Throughout the decade underclothing is affected by the growing sense of luxury and becomes even artistic; while during the second half the close-fitting dress necessitates a reformation beneath the surface. During the years 1870–73 the bustle reigned supreme, at first as an adjunct to the crinolette to produce the pannier effect and subsequently as a combination of the two. During this phase underclothing tends to remain as it was except for a growing taste for coloured materials in place of the old-fashioned 'white'.

With the arrival of the 'tie-back' dress and the steady tightening up of the front, underclothing shrinks, at first by goring and presently by discarding everything that is superfluous, leading at last to the shaped undergarment. But by a natural paradox the less the amount the more ornate it becomes. There is no longer space for flannel or even longcloth and thin washing silks become the only covering beneath the skin-tight dress of the fashionable lady—always excepting her stays.

The Chemise

Of longcloth, linen or cambric, trimmed down the front with insertion or with vertical pleats; the evening chemise cut very low with back fastening and trimmed with embroidered frill ('70), becoming slightly open at the neck to suit the open-neck dress of '71. In '76 'chemises are now made with breast seams shaped to the figure so as not to take up more room than possible beneath the stays', and in '77 a cambric pleated flounce edged with lace may be added so as to form a substitute for an underskirt. In the same year 'the new style of combining chemise and drawers' becomes the famous 'combinations' (said to have been invented by Mrs. Clark, 40 Conduit Street). We read that 'underclothing has reached a luxury unknown in any age. The most modest lady has now her chemise and drawers trimmed with flounces of real lace alternating with tucks, frills and insertion. A fashionable chemise looks like a baby's christening robe.' (It must be confessed that specimens in my collection are of a more homely description); we are indeed told that 'there is a disposition to diminish the dimensions of all underlinen but the majority of Englishwomen cling to the old styles'—or rather, the old styles clung to them. 'Chemises with pleated gussets on either side of the bust is a novelty' of '79, when four types of chemise are described: (1) like a Princess dress, (2) with three box-pleats in front and gored back, (3) with a front like a chemisette and much trimmed, (4) made like a cuirasse with one gore in the centre of the back.

Drawers

These and knickerbockers (of flannel) retain their old form until the tie-back era. In '76 'the new drawers are left open a finger's length up the outer side and the opening closed by three buttons'. Silk or flannel drawers reaching the knees are usual in '77, and 'ladies who do not wear foulard wear drawers of flannel under their cambric drawers'. Owing to the rival attractions of the combinations the use of drawers declined, to judge from the query of a correspondent in '78: 'Is it correct that caleçons are no longer worn? So many of my friends have discontinued this article of dress since crinolines were discarded.' In any case they 'should barely reach the knee and have a trimming of torchon or insertion with a frill'. Those who cultivate the svelte figure at all costs adopted drawers of chamois leather.

Combinations

This garment, originating in '77, is described in the following year as being composed of drawers and chemise in one with front or back fastening; some with high neck and long sleeves. Buttons are usually attached round the hips to which the petticoats are fastened. In addition to white materials, pink, white and cream washing silks are used. Enthusiasts employ 'chamois leather combinations worn over the other underclothing: not *on any account* next the skin'. While in hot weather gauze is substituted, and in cold, merino or thick lambswool.

Petticoats

Materials vary from eiderdown quilting, cloth, camlet, merino to alpaca and muslin, according to the weather, as well as silk and satin for evening. These have two flounces at least ('71). While the crinoline is still used a plain white petticoat is worn over it. In place of the crinolette a white horsehair or moreen petticoat with flounces at the back carried up to the waist was often used. In '72 petticoats with flounces edged with embroidery or lace reaching halfway up to the waist are 'sometimes worn over four or five plain white petticoats slightly starched or a small crinoline and over it a flounced petticoat and the embroidered one'. In '74 'indoor petticoats have a gore in front and one on each side, the back flounced to the waist and formed of stiff muslin starched, with tie-backs, and worn over a gored embroidered petticoat'. In '76 the petticoat was often omitted by substituting for it a muslin flounce on the inner side of the skirt 'so that the limbs are clearly defined'. The evening petticoat with a plain front and the back with a few steels and flounces at the waist is worn under a jacconet or longcloth petticoat with a treble box-pleat behind. More ornate examples are made 'of thin stiff muslin trimmed with lace and are almost pretty enough for dresses; a lace edged flounce half a yard deep, flat in front, and at the back it is cut with the peacock's fan of coarse muslin stiffened with wire; this is hidden by wide gathered flounces ascending to the waist, over which are finer flounces'. These are described as 'really works of art'. For ordinary day use an overpetticoat of cambric, etc., and an underpetticoat of pale blue or pink flannel were the rule.

The Princess petticoat appeared in '77 and in the same year 'the flannel petticoat is no longer fashionable'. It took up too much room. For day use one short petticoat would suffice, or with a Princess petticoat 'a second narrow skirt fastened to the edge of the stays reaches the knees and is edged with a deep kilting which descends to the ankles, bordered with torchon'. A walking petticoat is now $2\frac{1}{2}$ yards wide. For trained dresses the petticoat (4 yards wide) also is trained and has a drawing-string across the back breadth. The front and side breadths are gored, and many are made without a band, being buttoned on to the corset. The Princess petticoat buttons down behind to the knee level where there is a drawstring; and made of white material or coloured silk (serving as a slip). Short underpetticoats of knitted wool, chamois leather, felt, winsey, serge and bath coating were also used, by day.

Crinoline, Crinolette and Bustle

At the beginning of the decade small crinolines of wire were still being extensively used and Thomson's 'Pannier-crinoline' combined the bustle and the crinoline, the lower half being narrow and expanding above into a pannier. Or a full puffed bustle of white horsehair arranged in a number of puffs with a flounced edge would be worn over the crinoline. A detachable flounce was added to the latter when worn under trained dresses. A plain petticoat was worn over the crinoline.

A more fashionable article was the 'Eugénie petticoat', for wearing under short dresses. It consisted of a bustle of three or four horizontal and three vertical steels covered in material and buttoning round the waist; to it was attached four or five flounces and sloping side breadths. The front of the crinoline disappears or becomes merely a piece of material (*e.g.* scarlet camlet) buttoned across with some six half steels at the sides and back, carrying a deep stiff flounce buttoned on round the bottom. By '71 the bustle has expanded, often being made in three divisions and the sides extending more over the hips. 'It rises high above the waist and is of vast dimensions,' either of horsehair in three pleated flounces or of six half hoops of steel with a flounced edge. In '73 the bustle has become narrow and much longer, consisting of twelve steels encased in material and kept in place with elastic bands, under the tie-back skirt. Others are merely a series of puffings on a steel foundation. The crinolette is simply the intermediate form between the circular crinoline and the bustle.

By '74 'the bustle is fast disappearing' or at least diminishing, being driven out of the field by the long-waisted tight dresses. It remained, however, as an optional device and in fact with the pannier dress of '78 it even re-appears as a small flounced arrangement used by some to accentuate the hip effect.

Corsets

The corset remained unchanged in shape until '75 when 'the long corset and tight lacing to give the long slender figure fashionable' became a marked feature. 'Figures that are shapely—a small waist and a large bust—very often as they advance in years develop unduly and require a strong busk to keep them down', the busk being prolonged to an excessive degree. With the sheath dress of the succeeding years the overpetticoat was buttoned to the corset direct to save space; for the same reason corsets covered with black satin and trimmed at the top with a bertha enabled the camisole to be omitted. In spite of constant rebukes on the subject young ladies *would* tight-lace. 'The worst of it is that since attention has been drawn to tight-lacing the evil has increased greatly,' is a lament which suggests that current fashions are not to be controlled by reason.

Nightcaps

'Ladies are resuming the use of nightcaps in the shape of mobs' ('70).

The fashion goes out at the close of the decade.

Nightdresses

These become more ornamented; thus, in '70 they are tucked down the front with a yoke; by '76 they are 'as much trimmed about the back of the bodice as the front', and in the following year 'some are made with a Watteau pleat; the front with long tucks down each side of the centre pleat; buttons are no longer put on a flap but in the centre pleat; collars and deep cuffs are usual'.

The more fashionable ones are now of foulard with tucks, lace ruchings and frillings, and are described as being 'very thin'. Others are 'open down the whole of the front and trimmed with a frill'.

Petticoat Bodice

These are progressively more shaped to the figure and by '78 are made with a heart-shaped opening.

Vests

From '75 onwards these may be of washing silk, coloured, with long or short sleeves. It will be noted how with the advent of the tight dress undergarments tend to be scantier and made of thinner materials.

Garters

The conventional form of elastic with buckle attachment is still the usual. But in '78 the suspender, attached to the bottom of the stays and clipping on to the stocking makes its appearance.

Camisole

A word usually synonymous with petticoat-bodice, but frequently used to denote a short dressing-jacket.

CHAPTER IX
THE '80's

———————

THE fashions of the '80's were more remote than those of any other decade from modern standards of taste. But if, on that account, we are pleased to call them ugly we only beg the question—not very important—which is the better taste. Their interest to us lies in their significance for they display an unusual amount of symbolism. Economic depression forcing many women to seek other careers than marriage, coupled with increasing outdoor activities, produced fashions in which the ordinary devices of sex-attraction were absent. The tailormade costume, for example, seemed to the older school repellently masculine. It was the first move towards a style signifying (unconsciously) that the wearer was engaged in some other pursuit than the capture of man. Even the evening dress, majestically ornate, avoided the cruder methods of allurement; the high neck for dinner wear, the minimum display of physical charms until the close of the decade, and the preference for heavy materials, all were in keeping with the spirit of the period. The principle was strict, that beauty should make no passionate appeal. The epoch was, above all others, anti-anatomical.

We have to note, also, the growing divergence from the influence of Paris. The 'sports' costume, as a definite entity, as well as the tailor-made for practical work, were innovations for which England can claim the credit. This new conception of women's dress, the most important, historically, of the century, was a tacit recognition of woman's advance towards equality with man. She was showing that she no longer depended on her powers of charm. A contemporary remarks: 'Women whose minds are occupied with other things tend towards simplicity in costume while those who are empty-handed and empty-headed oftenest appear in fantastic and gaudy garments.'

An important feature was the Rational Dress Reform Movement which was now struggling to overcome the tradition of centuries. 'It is remarkable', observes a discerning writer, 'that the present movement in favour of dress reform is the first in all the history of fashion in which women have themselves taken an active part.' The Exhibition of 'reformed dress designs', held in '83, was a milestone on the road. The designs reveal the difficulty of escaping from tradition and the hostile criticisms were discouraging. 'The Exhibition has proved conclusively that it is impracticable to urge further reform unless there is beauty to recommend it. Whatever may be said of the harm (of modern dress) there is one important item, that of combining health and beauty.' It is difficult to detect this ideal in a forecast of 'the dress of the future' which is to comprise: 'a crimson and black satin shirt-body to which is attached a kilted skirt reaching a little above the knees; the legs are encased in striped satin trousers gathered above the ankles; a brocaded velvet sleeveless jacket with two tails and a colossal sash of black satin complete the costume.' (We observe the strange attraction which trousers had for the female sex). One contemporary critic suggested, despairingly, that when Macaulay's intelligent New Zealander 'comes to write the history of fashions of the Victorian Age he will wade through an ocean of articles and letters and books and, if he survives, proceed to his work with only an ulster to reward his search, for that is the only garment we can boast of as our own'. (Which shows how easily the significance of contemporary changes can be missed.)

The principal feature of the decade was, no doubt, the Bustle—or rather, the distinctive shape which that ancient accessory to the toilet then acquired. Its admirers declared that it helped to set off the carriage of the back and gave an artificial dignity; no one seemed to find it alluring. To us, envisaging the deserts yet to be crossed before emancipation was reached, this camel-like disguise seems almost appropriate. We are not surprised, however, to find that this and other fashions of the day evoked the fury of contemporary artists. G. F. Watts, in *The Nineteenth Century*, Jan. 1883, observed: 'The persistent tendency to suggest that the most beautiful half of humanity is furnished with tails can hardly be in good taste, yet amid the constant change of fashion this strange peculiarity is almost as constantly preserved,' and he adds: 'the expression "good taste" has come to be used seriously for much that is in the worst possible taste (pinched in waists, bloodless looking hands with pointed nails, distorted feet).'

William Morris laid down the law that: 'no dress can be beautiful that is stiff; drapery is essential. The period most worthy of reproduction is the ninth to the fourteenth century costume, perhaps those of 1250 being the most simple and elegant.' These expressions of taste indicate, at least, that artists were becoming interested in the design of women's dress, and the decade of the '80's, still greatly influenced by the Aesthetic Movement, showed an increasing tendency for women of taste to have their costumes designed for them by artists. The fabrics designed by Morris were, of course, noteworthy, while others such as Mrs. Nettleship were evolving original styles for individual clients.

In a technical sense the dresses of the '80's show a falling-off in quality of material and also in workmanship. For the average woman the ready made dress was, no doubt, a godsend; cheapness was now a desideratum to most, and appearance mattered more than quality. 'The present craze for cheapness is spoiling our manufactures' is a current cry. We can detect hidden little economies, cheap linings, scamped work and the like. The paw of democracy has left its mark on them. In-

1886
Dinner dress of satin; tablier of uncut velvet on satin, and pearls on net

ferior imitations of good materials flooded the cheaper markets, and the velvet, plush and satin of the prosperous soon found echoes in velveteen, plushette and sateen for the economically minded. Machine-made lace abounded and we may find it on quite expensive costumes. The best work was undoubtedly in the good class tailor-mades which carry their novel features with conviction, while the more gorgeous robes for evening were too often decorated with trivial ornaments as though inspiration had been lacking. For it was, on the whole, a practical age in which charm had the air of being forced.

Towards the close of the decade the 'Empire revival', remodelled by Gothic hands, affords a good example of how a foreign style becomes speedily changed to suit the prudish spirit of the nation. The colour sense reflected the economic depression prevalent during most of the decade. The Aesthetic Movement had toned down the violent colour mixtures of the '70's and the notion that her dress should harmonise with her surroundings was generally accepted by the woman of culture. But those surroundings with their mass of artificial ornaments and colour schemes ordered by authority were not easy to live up to when your dress must not match anything but must harmonise with everything, the plates on the wall, the draped piano and the chair covers and the plush overmantel . . . so that drab tones were safest and always ladylike. Above all, one must avoid looking like one of those vulgar coloured fashion-plates which a later generation accepts as portraits of the period.

1880

'At the present moment women go about hobbled after the fashion adopted by our forefathers to prevent the straying of their horses and asses when turned out to grass,' was the significant comment of a contemporary, implying that such a pose was gratifying to the male sex, now becoming anxious at the prospects of feminine emancipation. (It will be remembered that a similar fashion of 'hobble skirt' came as a counter-blast to the Suffragette movement thirty years later; the woman of fashion has always preferred to hug her chains.) Another remarks: 'We hear much about the exercise of private taste at the present time by educated women with regard to the fashion and colour of their dress, but this is only done by one here and there, and chiefly in London. The majority have no taste but that of their dress-maker; sometimes even no eye for colour to be shocked with harsh contrasts and jarring incompleteness of harmony. The attempts at dress reform have as yet met with but partial success. Perhaps it is their practical and sensible qualities which prevent their being more universally adopted. The influence of aesthetics on dress is still very potent. We shall never, thanks to it, be seen again in the crude and startling colours of some few years back.'

But the artistic movement seems to have had its detractors; one writes: 'The mania for high-art costumes is on the increase; it is really lamentable to see how some very pretty girls contrive to make themselves almost ugly and plain personages are often painful to look upon. Some of the low-toned colours make the wearers look positively ghastly.' Evidently there was a minority whose aim was to appear unpleasantly artistic. In the smarter world 'simplicity is out of fashion. Present modes are observable for glitter and glare, varied and intricate patterns and Oriental amalgamations of colour.' It is not easy to reconcile these criticisms with the more flattering assumption that: 'Fashion has now but one aim, to make every lady look her best,' unless we believe that one man's meat is another man's poison.

Actually the year 1880 was marked, on the one hand, by a steady growth of the 'tailor-made' style of day dress with its significant disdain of mere 'sex appeal', in keeping with the growing emancipation of the upper-middle class young woman who patronised that mode; while the 'appealing' type of costume relies more and more on Gothic devices and less on the vertical effects introduced by the Aesthetic movement. Long pointed angles adorn the surface which is broken up by beading, gauging and fancy trimmings. Capes and collars recall a similar Gothic return in the '20's; while the revival of the polonaise obliterates the revelations of the tight sheath skirt. The Princess dress is far less seen, although it may still serve as a sort of foundation on which to build. In evening dress the shoulder strap met with strong disapproval in Royal quarters as being 'scarcely decent'. The Englishwoman was entering the anti-anatomical era of the '80's, an era marked by sex antagonism and falling marriage rate with depression in most trades except drink and prostitution.

DRESSES

Day

The varieties are numerous but the principal types may be classified according to the kind of bodice; this is usually separate from the skirt, often of a different material; the skirt is always accompanied by a tunic of some kind which is of a different material. Walking dresses are 'short', *i.e.* untrained and just on the ground; afternoon dresses are trained, the train being of moderate length (sometimes detachable from the skirt) and slightly tied back with some puffing below the waist over a bustle which is now returning to fashion.

Types: 1. With pointed bodice; 2. Cuirass bodice; 3. Coat bodice; 4. The Polonaise.

These are similar to those of the previous year with a tendency to accentuate the 'Early English' angles (in such things as plastrons, bodice openings, etc.). The cuirass bodice is itself often made with a point in front and side jacket basques, or hollowed out in front with points at the sides, and in fact, tends to merge into a casaquin bodice over a waistcoat (real or simulated) in afternoon dress.

The coat bodices have very long basques made sometimes by added hip pieces, but more often cut in one length and pleated at the back like a man's frock coat with two buttons. These are generally tailor-made, with outside-pockets, are high at the throat, and fasten all down the front, sometimes double-breasted.

The polonaise, returning to fashion, is long, fastening in front or behind; usually a line of gathering, ten inches long, in front, draws it up into folds, or the front is drawn up at one side to produce a slanting line, or a plastron may be added all down the front. Some are loose in front and worn with a belt. They are occasionally embroidered with beads or jet. Plastrons and chemisettes are frequently gauged. The tunic is made of some different material from the dress, and is worn either as an overdress caught up at the side so as to form a slanting line down the front; or open in front and draped at the sides; or turned back; or as scarves, single or multiple.

The sleeve of day dresses is long and tight with a cuff and frilling; 'sloping shoulders are out of fashion' and the sleeve may be slightly puffed at the top, or padded.

The skirt is pleated often to the waist with box-pleats or double kilting, or with three kilted flounces. For dressy toilets 'fan-shaped pleatings are used, the front breadth being arranged as a fan, being gathered a few inches below the waist very closely for about ten inches, and again below the knee; the fan is edged with fringe and beneath it are two or three narrow pleated flounces edged with fringe', *e.g.* a fantablier of silver-grey satin with an upper dress of dark claret satin. Some skirts have single box-pleats two inches wide, often reaching to the knee, with a scarf-tunic above. Others have flounces only at the edge of the skirt, one all round and a second above it in front only. With thin materials there may be kilted flounces alternating with rows of gathered lace, extending to the knee. Kiltings are now secured only at the top and are allowed to fly out somewhat. For rough wear the hem of the skirt is protected by a strip of black mackintosh edged with rubber piping.

Walking dresses are 'short', *i.e.* untrained; indoor dresses are trained. The lower part of the train is lined with stiff muslin tacked in, some ten inches deep, which appears like a trained petticoat. The train can be looped up and buttoned at the hip.

A number of costumes have pelerine-capes, sometimes multiple, and neck ruffs of lace and frilling, or deep 'Cromwell collars' are a feature of dressy toilets. 'Many day dresses have large double collars, either both made of the material trimming the dress or the inner one made of the dress material; some of these collars are deeply pointed in front, others square front and back. On summer muslins large embroidered linen collars are worn by young ladies and fichu-collarettes by older women.'

The fashion for wearing a detachable hood, known as the 'Langtry hood' and resembling the academical form, displaying the lining of rich brocade or brightly coloured silk, is notable; the hood was attached by hooks or with short ends crossing in front and fastening behind.

The 'artistic dress' has its own features, *e.g.* 'Of grass green brocaded china silk, the bodice pointed front and back; double row of buttons up the back, slightly gathered in front, with leg-of-mutton sleeves. Large lace collar reaching the shoulders. Draped skirt.' Another: 'A loose short gown in tussore, cut low in the neck and fitted high to the throat by an under-bodice of pale copper-coloured satin much gauged. A pleating of the same above the ankles. Narrow tight sleeves with high puffings at the shoulders. A sash of soft silk with long ends.'

A feature of the year is the 'Handkerchief dress', composed of a number of pieces of spotted material with wide border, resembling large bandanna handkerchiefs. 'Two large handkerchiefs form the tunic, the point of the lower reaching nearly to the hem of the skirt (of which the front is plain and the back kilted); the point of the upper just shows beneath the deep basqued jacket; a straight drapery is puffed behind; the bodice is plain coat-shaped with waistcoat and revers.' Others have three pleated flounces one above the other with the tunic pointed at the sides. These dresses are made of cotton or soft woollen stuffs with red, brown, or black spots on white ground, and made up on a stiff muslin foundation.

The 'Pilgrim's dress', of brown or grey soft woollens, with plain skirt, tunic drawn in at the

Aesthetic dress (Liberty and Co.). 1880

waist by a cord and tassels, bodice with no pleats in front, deep cape and hood, close sleeves and cuffs, is also a passing mode.

The 'Veronese dress', of woollen material, is a long plain cut Princess tunic, knee-length, with deep points reaching nearly to the hem of the underskirt which has a deep box-pleating of silk. The Veronese cuirass is a jersey bodice lacing behind.

Examples of various dresses:

'*Afternoon Dress* of heliotrope silk. On the left are 17 narrow flounces reaching the hip; four of these are carried round the base of the skirt. Cashmere overdress draped in folds on the right side and at the back, open to shew the flounces on the left. Plain pointed corsage with short basque, cut square and open, with revers over a white muslin and lace chemisette; elbow sleeves.'

'Afternoon costume of blue surah and pale blue brocade. The front of the skirt with five flounces, each headed with gauging. Bodice of brocade with pointed plastron, gauged. Panniers at the sides. Draped tunic edged with pleating.'

'Trained afternoon dress, the tunic long and square in front, cut at the back as a cuirass with side points and habit basque; deep Cromwell collar edged with double ruching and a ruff of frilling.'

'*Garden Party Dress* of pale pink batiste; skirt with a dozen or more flounces edged with lace; a scarf tunic finished off behind with a cascade of batiste and lace and a pink satin bow; bodice gathered in front, plain behind; narrow satin band and buckle; lace jabot from the throat to the waist; elbow sleeves; lace mittens.'

'*Tennis Costume*, the skirt, of gold-coloured sateen, kilted very high in front; a tunic of pale blue open in front with deep rever on one side and a square pocket on the other; the tunic is caught up with a bow at the back; bodice, blue, with or without a sash.'

'*Tailor-made Costume* of stockingette draped with large scarves of spotted silk, the drapery forming two points in front; a small scarf round the shoulders and a hood.'

'The jersey has degenerated into an immodest garment of flesh pink, sky blue or cream, so thin and elastic as to show every line of the wearer's form.'

'*Bridal Dress* of white satin and lace, with deep box-pleats; a tunic in reversed pleats across the front, edged with lace. Bodice with pleated panniers and a long point; a simulated waistcoat and lace revers; ruff; elbow sleeves and ruffles. Veil on the head reaching the ground behind.'

'*Bathing Costumes* this season are very neat; a loose blouse of dark blue serge; elbow sleeves and collar; wide drawers a few inches above the ankle, all trimmed with wide braid; and a red woollen sash and coarse straw hat.'

'No artistic dresser would be without a *Smock*, cut exactly like a farm labourer's, with square turned-down collar and gatherings front and back, gathered full sleeves, worn over a habit shirt, and looped up over an underskirt with a belt at the waist.'

Materials: (Morning) Oatmeal cloth, Pompa-
dour sateens, foulards, percales, pekin, nankin, serges. 'The great novelty of the new Spring fabrics is their exquisite colourings, most of the materials being plain coloured wool and wool and silk mixtures; materials such as cashmere, French and German beige, vicuna, stockinette and Paisley and Pompadour fabrics; black and white small checks trimmed with velvet and Pekin.' 'There is a rage for plush', and for Japanese patterns. Summer dresses of soft figured cream Madras for drapery; batiste; cambric; printed satin foulards, printed corah silk, nun's veiling, muslin. 15 yards are required for a costume.

Fashionable Trimmings: Gimps, fringes, narrow flounces and pleatings. 'Fabulous sums are spent on real flowers worn on bonnets and parasols and on the left shoulder.'

Colours: Tailor-mades, of cloth or serge, bottle green, brown, claret, cardinal, spots and checks. Heliotrope, crushed raspberry, Etna brown (a rich red-brown), 'fiery reds and yellows.' Cardinal red (*e.g.* bonnet, parasol, gloves, stockings and dress all red, or red batiste skirt, box-pleated, with upper dress of cream, starch-blue, grey or rose-pink foulard or batiste). Heliotrope and light green; olive and blue; apricot and heliotrope. Pink (some pink dresses of one material; others a pink skirt with black satin casaquin). 'No colours seem too bright; the combinations of them are sometimes quite startling.' Coloured balayeuses are general.

Evening

Bodice in the form of a cuirasse, casaquin, or habit. Square or wide 'V' opening; sleeve to the elbow in a succession of puffs or short at the shoulder, or concealed under a bertha. Or a staylike bodice, of white or coloured satin or gold brocade, low and square in front and lacing behind; a coloured bodice being often worn with a white skirt and tunic. The low pointed bodice often with a pleated muslin underbodice. Some with gathered front en princesse but hanging loose like a smock with a Watteau pleat behind.

Trained skirt; the tablier in a series of narrow pleated flounces, or with lace flounces often slantwise, or gauging.

'Evening dresses are of endless variety and strong contrasts in colour; Worth uses lavender satin and yellow brocade; a white satin bodice, very pointed front and back, and blue and silver brocaded satin skirt; another of black velvet and red satin.' Another of 'garnet satin bodice and pink tunic trimmed with jet'.

'Old gold plush casaquin with cream satin dress; or deep crimson plush with pale pink silk dress.'

'A dinner dress of peacock blue cashmere trimmed with eau de Nil satin; Princess shaped with trained skirt and deep pleating; two cashmere scarves on the skirt, both knotted in front and fastened behind in large bows; the ends of the lower scarf forming an upper train. A plastron of puffed satin from the back of the neck descends all down the front to the kilting; the scarves are edged with knotted fringe. Tight elbow sleeves; the bodice is open in a "V" with a frill of lisse.'

'A trained skirt of brown silk with two kiltings of silk; next, a puffing of light brown satin edged with lace; again two kiltings and another band of puffing; a long jacket, fitting close to the figure, with a puffing of satin at the edge which is continued up the front and round the neck; a kilting of lace at the edge of the trimming; the jacket is open from the throat to shew an under-jacket of similar shape; tight sleeves with satin cuffs; large cravat of dark satin.'

'A Classical evening dress of white cashmere bordered with gold; the upper skirt draped as a peplum, the low bodice pleated and gathered in at the waist with a gold band.'

A singular variety is 'a Greek dress with the addition of a Watteau sacque'.

The Jersey is now used for evening dress, *e.g.*, 'A Jersey cuirasse with a long point; rose worn on the left shoulder; skirt with slantwise reversed pleatings across the front; edging of pleating; short sleeves.' Sleeveless 'coats of mail', composed of netted bugles are novelties; the effect of which 'over plain satin bodice is striking'.

The blend of colours used may be gathered from the examples quoted; 'a ruby satin train and bodice with a tablier of terra-cotta gauze and trimming of moss roses and primroses' is among the more striking.

Ball Dresses are generally with white tulle or tarlatan skirts, the front drawn in flat pleatings or puffed with scarves, the train with small pleated flounces; many are untrained. The bodice a pointed cuirasse, often of coloured satin. Others are en princesse. The short dresses have coloured casaquins fitting closely over the hips, in bright colours, of satin damask, brocades or plush, with skirt of white cashmere, muslin or Algerian.

OUTDOOR GARMENTS

Dolmans; paletots of jacket shape; the cassock mantle (very high in the neck, gathered on the shoulders and down the centre of the back, coming below the knees. Short sleeves. 'Nothing could be more peculiar or unbecoming.' Black or matching the dress). 'Dolmans are labyrinths of lace, ruching, fringe and jet.'

'Round cape-mantles, entirely composed of jet and covering to the elbow, for young ladies; for matrons, dolmans or scarf-mantles covered with jet.'

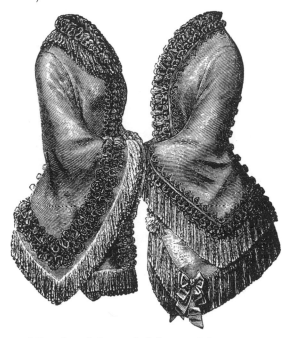

Mantlet visite and dolman visite. 1880

Winter Mantles, of brocaded and plain silk, velvet and satin, are long and gathered on the shoulders, with large loose sleeves, and are often called 'Pelisses'. Visites, resembling long tight coats, are worn by young ladies.

'At the Grosvenor gallery Mrs. Langtry wore a costume of black satin, the hood of the mantle lined with crimson and gold stuff, and trimmings of gold butterflies and green and blue bugles.'

'Beads are used on every conceivable kind of outdoor garment except coats.'

ACCESSORIES

Jewellery. Amber fashionable. Silver bracelets, necklets and brooches; coin brooches; small silver watches hung from chatelaines; enamelled brooches with mottoes and emblems.

(Peter Robinson) Mother Hubbard mantles, 2 to 14 guineas. Plush mantles from 8 guineas. Duchesse satin (23 in.) 5/3 a yard. Black satin merveilleuse, 5/6. Walking costumes: black silk or satin £3 18 6. Satin and brocade, 5 to 10 guineas. Satin foulard costumes trimmed with lace, 5½ guineas.

Louis velveteen from 3/11 to 6/11 a yard.

All wool French beige, 1/3. Pompadour cretonnes, 6¾d to 10¾d. Pompadour sateens, 10¾d to 1/4½. Coloured cashmere (46 in.) 2/3½ to 3/6.

'Greek Art brocat, a most artistic looking cloth, would suit the most aesthetic taste (24 in.) 2/11½.' Dolman, cashmere, £2 12 6; coloured silk, £3 13 6. Serge tailor-made braided dresses, 39/6. Oatmeal cloth, 1/6½. Fancy galateas, 8¾d. Black silk grenadine (23 in.) 1/2¾. Surah (24 in.) 3/6. Sealskin jacket 'a fair one can be bought for 20 guineas'. Seal cloth (2½ yards for a jacket) 21/9 to 29/6 a yard.

1881

The fashions of this year depended rather on changes in details than style, the principles being maintained. 'Never were fashions so erratic; no two persons dress alike.' This may be interpreted to mean that women were beginning to exercise far more individual taste than formerly simply because of the growing diversity of their lives. The 'tailor-made' young woman was discovering passionless fields of activity while emotional energy found an outlet in the Arts. Both types were far more marked in this country than in France where the early marriage remained the conventional and only career. 'Every year English and French fashions are drifting apart. Artistic gowns, as recognised in England, are unheard of in France,' and equally the severer forms of the tailor-made. The scorn shown by the average person towards those displaying artistic leanings was not so much inspired by the normal English contempt for art as by the contempt paid to those who have failed to attract the other sex. The humour of Lady Jane in 'Patience', produced this year, was characteristic of the period. Similarly we have the aesthetic costumes of the day described as: 'the saffron coloured dresses worn by sallow-faced maidens whose first youth has vanished, winding shaky mystically-suspended garments robing fleshless contours.' While the 'strong-minded women' who dared to suggest that female clothing might be made more practical (and less alluring) were equally criticised. 'The dual garment which so-called dress reformers are trying to introduce is not only ungraceful but most inconvenient.' Nobody in the present day need wear 'masses of petticoats round the figure. Knickerbockers made of swansdown, flannel or twilled cotton fastened under the knee, a knitted woollen petticoat and over this a silk, satin or even cashmere petticoat lined with a thin layer of eiderdown, and well gored, is not an ounce too heavy for walking purposes.' The average woman, belonging to neither of these extreme schools, found, however, that her fashions partook of features derived from both. For everyday use she accepted the tailor-made while for more dressy occasions 'the reign of plain bodices and tight sleeves is now over. They must be draped or gathered or puffed.'

The technical features of the year may be summed up in a line: gauging (smocking, gathering), flounces, bustles, crinolettes, metal beads, lace.

DRESSES

Day

'A season when princess dresses, demi-princess polonaises, bodices with waistbands, coats, bodices with basques of various shapes, pointed bodices, long sheathlike casaques, panniers cut with the bodice and draped or made separate as scarves, are all in fashion; loose trains, tabliers

over which are draped the most elaborate tunics and draperies of every description, many of which are trimmed or faced with shaded stripes in their turn, making dressmaking a most difficult art. Bodices are cut off at the waist, or with jacket basques or long basques like an ulster, or polonaise. The polonaise is trimmed as elaborately as the skirt; the underskirt is sometimes formed of one deep kiltpleating or trimmed with several pleated flounces, from three to five, the pleating either kilted or box-pleated. Sometimes the polonaise is open in front showing the whole of the underskirt; others are caught up at one side to the waist; the backs are pouffed. Some bodices are full and gathered into a point at the waist; some with round waists; some cross over and are fastened at one side.'
While the tailor-made short jacket buttoning

Indoor costume of olive green cashmere. 1881

of scarf draperies, tunics unequally raised, skirts opening at the sides to shew a pyramid of little flounces, overskirts open in front, turned back with large revers, draperies across the front and sides of the skirt ending behind under the long breadth that forms the back of the tunic.'

Short dresses, for walking, two to three inches off the ground.

'Walking costumes with short narrow skirts

House dress of bronze beige with satin kilting front and back. 1881

down the front, or cut away from the waist, with an edging of braid, was worn with a plain or kilted skirt, the yoke bodice with wide collar and 'the new surplice shape for bodice, in full gathers at the neck and shoulders and over the bust' was worn with a skirt trimmed with ruches at the hem headed by puffs and drapery. Gauging was introduced wherever possible, as on the sleeves, trimmings and collar, bodice and skirt, especially the honeycomb pattern; 'gauging is being run to death.'

Sleeves, set in very high on the shoulders, show puffings, slashings, gauging and modified leg-of-mutton forms. Very narrow cuffs.

The round skirt, $2\frac{1}{4}$ yards wide, has 'the front breadth sloped on each side; then a gore and the back breadth straight, the small gores cut off from the front being inserted on each side of the back breadth; if the skirt is completely covered with draperies it can be made of stiff muslin with 10 inches of material round the bottom. Drapery is now put on to increase the size of the hips, a pleated skirt having a tight lining to keep the pleats in place. At the back wide bows hang in loops attached to the centre of the back of the panniers; the front panniers are gathered into the waist or made in one with the polonaise. Pleated skirts of heavy materials have a deep box-pleat at the back with five kilted pleats on each side.'

The wide hip effect was aimed at in all dressy costumes, with greater fullness behind (over the bustle).

The re-established polonaise (which 'can be worn out of doors without a cloak') 'is raised by pleats or drawings or made narrower in the skirt, being merely left open part of the way up the front; this portion is lined and turned back and the points fastened behind with a large bow over the pouf which is made by draping the back breadths with strings.' (Three of these strings, or ribbons, are usually fastened across the back breadth inside.)

Worth 'is now making his skirts much fuller, with four widths: two straight ones for the back, two gored ones for the front; over the skirt is draped a straight flounce of five widths of satin or silk gathered into the belt with the skirt and reaching the knees where there is a cluster of gathers, and below this another flounce to the hem; all round the foundation is a pleating. His polonaises imitate long vests in front but the back is a pointed bodice of four pieces, two in the centre and one each side; each seam is whaleboned.'

The elaborate dress is now built up on a foundation which may be invisible and therefore of inferior material.

'The coloured balayeuse is going out.'

Three or four materials may be used; e.g. 'a velvet polonaise with bow drapery behind of moiré, a skirt of brocaded velvet with satin side panels and at the back plain velvet box-pleats'; or a cashmere skirt with satin scarves, etc. and plush bodice.

The plain black silk dress is going out, owing to poor quality of material and is now used only as a foundation.

Examples

'*Morning Dress* of sateen trimmed with cream lace; plain skirt with three box-pleated narrow flounces; a tunic of Pompadour chintz open at the left side to the hip to shew a series of narrow flounces.'

'*A Walking Dress*, en princesse, the full front gathered and smocked on the chest, at the waist and halfway down the skirt; upright folds also cross the front; puffed flounces round the bottom; sleeves full from the shoulder to the elbow where they are gathered and smocked, and thence tight to the wrist.'

'Costume of green cashmere, striped green and maize Surah, plain green silk and plain maize satin, all the greens being of different shades.'

'*Travelling Dress* of rough cheviot: a shooting jacket (made over a tight lining) with double box-pleat behind, the front double-breasted with a box-pleat on each side; two rows of buttons down the front; Byron collar; wide belt; skirt tucked, each tuck two inches wide and two inches apart, eight tucks in all; box-pleating at the bottom; tucked tunic forming a pointed apron drawn to one side.'

'*Garden Party Dress* of white brocaded satin open in front over a mauve silk skirt gathered in pleatings; bodice with profusion of lace laid on in spirals down the front. Another of pale mauve foulard trimmed with alternate flounces of satin and lace; high projecting panniers; long coat of violet plush trimmed with lace and open behind to the waist; waistcoat of embroidered cream muslin trimmed with lace.'

Goodwood Dresses: 'One of black brocade, very bouffante behind over a crinolette, the front covered with gold embroidery. A grey silk polonaise, looped and puffed behind, laced across the front with gold cord, over a black velvet skirt. Another of pale mauve crepe de

Chine, the front with flounces embroidered with pansies and chenille, the puffs at the back tied with large bows of violet velvet.'

'*A Teagown*: pale pink satin petticoat kilted from the waist, the lower part of the kilting left loose to form a flounce; an overdress of ruby plush with Watteau pleat fastened in at the waist with a band; lace and muslin fichu and cap.'

Bathing Dresses 'now without sleeves; tunic and trousers reaching to the ankle; they have the advantage that when wet they do now shew the figure with undue distinctness.'

Trimmings, etc. Fichus and cravats: the Steinkirk tie for full morning dress and large coloured silk ties in a large bow at the back, the ends carried down the front passing under two straps to the waist.
Collars of all shapes with large jabot at the neck, in front.
Spanish lace much used for trimmings.
Gauged plastrons. 'Owing to gauging the work of making a dress is doubled.'
Materials: 'Alpaca is unfashionable for its stiffness and stubborn refusal to be draped.' Cashmere, plush, beige, nun's veiling, sateens (some with large patterns and called 'Alsatian'), striped materials, woollens, foulards. In summer, cottons with dark colours (washing dresses are unfashionable), Japanese designs, floral and geometric, on printed goods. Japanese silk and moiré returning to fashion.
Colours: (Winter) brown, green, dark blue, claret, deep ruby. (Summer) heliotrope, art bronze, terracotta, peacock blue, grey, shades of orange, jonquil, dull green. Combinations of brown and green, pink and bright yellow, salmon and ruby, cardinal and dark blue.

Evening
Bodices low in front and rather higher behind; elbow sleeves with ruffles: garland of flowers on the left shoulder very fashionable. Many are deeply pointed; some round with waistband going round to the back and brought forward again to the front lower down where the ends are tied in a bow. Dinner dresses are all with high neck or Medici collars; elbow sleeves.
Skirts with long train descending from a triple box-pleat at the waist. The front of the skirt with scarves or flounces. Lace and tulle lavishly used for trimmings. Lace fichus and jabots.

Examples
'*Ball Dress*, a satin bodice cuirasse form cut out over the hips; black lace tunic and trimming.'

'Dress of olive green silk with brocade plastron of two shades of maize relief on pale olive ground; ribbons of two shades of carnation; chenille fringe.'
'Dress of cream nun's veiling, caroubier satin and cream lace. Trained skirt trimmed with

Spring pelisse of satin or cashmere. 1881

alternate flounces of veiling and lace. Two scarves, one satin and one veiling, slantwise. Pointed bodice with gauged plastron cut in a wide "V" above; very short tulle sleeves.'

'*Dinner Dress* of peacock blue satin and plush. Plush skirt cut in dents with pleatings of satin

319

intervening; satin tunic draped in reversed folds, with a point in front and puffed at the sides; plush drapery round the hips forming panniers. Pointed satin bodice with plush plastron; small straight collar; elbow sleeves of satin with plush revers; a thick ruche borders the train.'

'Semi-Evening Dress, a polonaise of cream nun's veiling open in front in a deep point on a plastron of blue foulard; embroidery outlines the opening; the polonaise is draped across the front over a skirt with alternate flounces of scalloped lace and kilting.'

Many evening dresses are of hand-painted materials. Bengaline is also used.

Trimming, etc. Gold and steel embroidery, steel fringes and laces and bugles much used; large Medici ruffs worked in steel, gold and silk, supported by wire, for dinner dress. Gauze scarves fringed with chenille worn over the head as theatre wrap.

OUTDOOR GARMENTS

Cloaks
Mother Hubbard Cloaks (in brocaded silk or velvet, or dress material, or plush, cashmere or sateen, lined) three-quarter length, fitting high round the throat with turn-up collar and gauging over the shoulders; loose sleeves; fastened with long strings at the throat.
Plush Mother Hubbards, lined with quilted satin, and trimmed with ostrich feathers, as opera cloaks.
Long Paletots buttoning down the front, with cape and bishop sleeves which are attached to the centre of the back by an ornament.

Coats and Mantles
Sealskin Coats and mantles, fuller at the back with broad flat bow over the bustle. 'A lady can now raise her arms above her head; last year she could scarcely blow her nose.'
Chenille Capes and Visites. Alpaca Dust cloaks. 'Ponderous Mantles loaded with trimmings.' Pelisses. Long tailor-made Coats with large plush directoire collars. Dolmans (with deep collars) bordered with plush, sealskin, etc.

ACCESSORIES

Walking *Boots* with low heels.

Gloves
Buttonless and very long, tucked under the sleeve even with elbow sleeves. Evening gloves above the elbow. Suede gloves have replaced mittens. Beaded gloves.

'*Muffs* most elaborate, sometimes matching the dress, sometimes made of feathers with a bird, wings outstretched; muffs of black satin painted with humming birds. Small muffs for balls.' Muffs with pocket for card case.

Parasols dome-shaped, lined, of bright colours and edged with lace. Large crystal or china ball handle.

Jewellery. 'A change has crept over jewellery in the past two years; artistic handiwork abounds and gems are not as popular as the chased metal trinkets scarcely one tithe their value. Whitened silver is affected by the fashionable world, in sets; chased flowers interspersed with birds and insects; motto inscriptions; small charms on bracelets and necklets representing the animal and insect mania from the elephant to the shrimp.'
Jet fashionable. Dog collars of filigree or plain gold. Snake bracelets. Bracelets worn over gloves and even above the elbow.

Prices
Broché velveteen, 1/9 to 2/6; Pompadour velveteens, 1/3½ to 1/11½. Corduroy velveteens, 1/3½ to 1/6½. (Redmayne & Co.) White satin duchesse for bridal dresses (27 in.) 10/3 a yard. Coloured satin merveilleux, 5/11; coloured surah, 3/4 to 4/6 a yard. Beige, fancy and striped, 1/6.
Jay's Lyons velvet costume (including 4 yards for bodice) 12½ guineas.
Handkerchief costumes, 48/6.
Swanbill corsets, 14/6 to 21/-.
Tan gloves, black, stitched backs, 4 buttons, 2/6 a pair. Stocking suspenders, cotton, 2/9; silk, 4/3. The British Woollen Association, started by Lady Bective, to encourage the use of English woollens.

1882

'Is it not possible that forty years hence the elaborate fringes, tight fitting jerseys and tie-back skirts of 1882 may in their turn be classified by our successors among the rococo absurdities of a bygone age?' But, after all, that was a forecast which may safely be made in any year for all obsolete fashions appear absurd when

1880
Handkerchief dress of moss-green batiste with red and pink border
Handkerchief dress of batiste; cuirasse bodice

1882
Evening dress (front and back) of blue satin trimmed with coloured
embroidery on lace; flounced lace tablier; crepe paniers

their primary function has passed away. 'Never was there a more marked difference between the fashions of Paris and London; while Englishwomen affect Newmarket coats and all the more rigid severity of tailor-made suits the French shew a decided preference for everything that is Watteau-like and dressy.' In fact the English-woman's aim now seemed to be to look either severe or striking, but never alluring. Actually the day fashions of '82 showed a distinct softening of the former; the hard surface of the skirt was tempered by more trimmings. But the most notable feature of the year was the steady growth of the bustle effects at the back, leading to the inevitable alterations in cut and trimmings. Hips expanded under panniers while the crinolette and bustle sustained bouffante effects, designed to give a majesty to the carriage. The device of putting steel hoops in the back of the skirt was not so successful. 'No one can maintain that the steels now inserted into the back breadths of the skirts can improve the set of them; on the contrary they wobble from side to side and have the most ludicrous effect. The tournure, on the other hand, sets off a dress to advantage.' For a moment fashion seemed to hesitate between a return to the crinoline or to the bustle, but as inasmuch as women were now beginning to walk the choice would be the bustle.

The decorative dresses, those for afternoon and evening functions, deserve notice on account of their mixture of colours as well as materials, designed to draw attention to the dress rather than to the person within. The armour-plating effect of the excessively long points, front and back, to the bodice, suggested a kind of chastity belt, while the panniers concealed the hips from impertinent scrutiny.

DRESSES

Day

While some of the tailor-mades preserve their masculine appearance (such as those in large checks, the skirt with deep box-pleated flounce and double-breasted jacket with basques, opening at the neck with revers, and showing 'a masculine made-up scarf necktie with a pin in the middle', or a double-breasted cloth coat coming only to the waist in front with two long square ends behind like a tail-coat), most of the day skirts have the front softened with trimmings, and always with afternoon or ceremonial dresses. (The French 'promenade dress' corresponded with the English 'garden party or flower show dress'.) The side breadths are no longer gored but have two pleats at the waist. The elaborately trimmed skirt is made with a foundation, the bottom of which is trimmed with several rows of pleating or ruching or 'anything to stand out' simulating an under-skirt over which the real skirt falls. Perpendicular pleatings broken by bands of gauging and puffing running across them, a 'skirt ruff' (a thick ruching of the dress material quilled in the centre) at the hem to make the bottom of the skirt stand out, are devices for breaking the surface of the day skirt which in the 'toilet' is further elaborated by a series of flounces (such as lace and dress material alternating, up to the waist, or a brocaded tablier with side panels of different material, or the bottom cut into 'battlements', scallops and vandykes.

The summer skirt has its surface relieved by rows of puffings with narrow lines of gauging between, or by three narrow kiltings headed by bands of puffings, or by three deep flounces headed by gathering. The hem edged with broad ruching.

Elastic bands have now superseded tapes inside the skirt to give the tie-back effect.

'The crinolette becomes larger every month and skirts all wobble more or less.'

The tunic is now shortened into mere panniers emerging from under the point of the bodice where it is slightly gathered, folded on the hips and forming a succession of puffs at the back; or its place may be taken by a broad scarf coming from beneath the point of the bodice in front and tied in wide loops behind ending at the back point.

The polonaise is much worn especially in summer. It may be pleated at the back and caught up to the waist on one side forming drapery in front. The bodice may have a plastron or be double-breasted, or have a lace cascade down the front.

NOTE: The English prefer, in summer, the polonaise to the French redingote. 'Worth detests the bunched up panniers at the back.'

Mourning costume. 1882

Bodices have long points front and back, and are cut up over the hips; the front relieved by frilling or a cascade of lace down the centre, or by guipure revers or bretelles of embroidery. The use of lace or muslin jabots and cascades is a feature. Or a jacket-bodice with revers and a waistcoat, the back often cut out 'into the fashionable leaf shape points'. The severe cut of the bodice is often modified by battlement

basques. Sleeves are tight but full on the shoulders. They tend to be high, often padded on the shoulders, a fashion started by the Princess of Wales. While the sleeve of the morning dress reaches the wrist and is plain or with a simple cuff, that of the afternoon dress is elbow length and has a ruffle.

The return of the troops from Egypt is marked by a fashion for Hussar jackets, military braidings and brandebourgs.

'A feature of this winter is ribbons worn everywhere, at the back of the neck, in front of the neck, at the shoulders, and waist, on tunics, and scattered all about the dress,' (except for morning dresses).

Examples

'*Morning Dress*: a casaquin bodice with turn-down collar, buttoning down the front to below the waist; deep rounded basque, coat shaped. The skirt kilted and with side panels.'

Summer Dress. 'The skirt of cream nun's veiling with two narrow pleated flounces and above them seven rows of puffing; a Pompadour tunic and panniers of Madras muslin edged with embroidery; tight pointed bodice of nun's veiling; loose scarf round the neck.'

'Pointed bodice with pleated muslin plastron and cascade of lace down the front; elbow sleeves with ruffles; Pompadour polonaise edged with lace, in full puffs at the back and panniers. Skirt with seven flounces, kilted, on each of which is a row of lace.'

Ascot Dresses. 'White satin skirt with long white brocaded velvet bodice, coat-shaped, trimmed with lace.' 'Of white sateen covered with small pink poppies: the skirt draped in three places over a pink sateen petticoat, the openings filled in with pyramid frills; bodice and panniers gauged and trimmed with Spanish lace. A pink silk sash, knotted on one side.'

'Brocaded skirt trimmed with vandykes and narrow pleats; the tunic turned back at the sides revealing the plush lining.'

'*Shooting Suit*: Norfolk jacket and box-pleated skirt, knee-length, in check homespun; knickerbockers; gaiters.'

'*Riding Habit*: skirt side seam 38 in. bodice cut open in front with a stand collar like a clerical dress waistcoat.'

'*Tennis Dress*, woollen, the skirt with three box-pleated flounces; full bodice pointed front and back, to which are attached pannier draperies with three rows of gauging just below the waist and a bow with long ends behind.'

'*Teagown*: a jacket bodice with cascade of lace down the front; large bow at the neck and wrists; kilted skirt and draped pannier tunic.'

Materials: (Winter) woollens, vicuna, plush, and small shepherd plaid checks for morning; shot velvets, moiré, satin and brocades for afternoon. (Summer) nun's veiling, beige, casimir, Umritza, sateen, printed cottons with dark grounds and large flowers and leaves, batiste, foulard, surah.

New Material: Ottoman silk. Music-striped faille. Brocades in four colours. 'Ottoman is really the old terry-velvet revived. There are two kinds of foulard, the India pongee silks which are white when received from India; these are printed in England; and there is the French foulard which is a thinner material resembling the old fashioned sarcenets.'

'The only dresses now made of one material are braided cashmeres and serges.'

NOTE: Duchesse satin made in Coventry and woven in Manchester; surah made in Macclesfield.

Colours: Copied from flowers and foliage, *e.g.* sycamore and lichen green; petunia and orchid purple-red; azalea red; sunflower yellow; maize; leaf brown. Electric blue; rifle green; dark blue and red 'in honour of the Household Brigade' (just returned from Egypt).

Many morning dresses have a plain bodice and skirt often in broad stripes of two colours (red and blue, écru and brown); otherwise morning dresses are of one colour but several materials may be used.

Evening

The dinner dress closely approximates to the afternoon 'reception dress', having a high neck and elbow sleeves; or a square neck and Medici collar; or cut low and rounded, often with a high ruff behind. These are draped across the top, the neck opening having an edging of ruching or lace. The principal feature of the bodice is the excessively long points front and back, and the absence of trimming except for the top, the back lacing and close fit giving the effect of armour. Large lace jabots and plastrons, however, soften the surface of dinner dress bodices. Elbow sleeves with ribbon bows.

Full evening dress, with low bodice, has a mere strap for a sleeve, and epaulettes of pearls or loops of chenille or flowers. Skirts with long trains, the fronts elaborately trimmed. Panniers are general and side panels frequent.

Ball dresses of tulle with birds in appliqué, or silk pompoms; bodices of plain satin and brocaded velvet, often with pompoms on one shoulder.

Evening dresses for young ladies are usually of white nun's veiling.

Examples of the principal types:

'*Dinner Dress*, the bodice and panniers of carnation satin; plastron and sleeves and tablier of broche silk.'

'*Evening Dress* with tablier of salmon brocade; long side panels of bronze velvet; velvet and brocade train with a full ruche; basque bodice with coat-tails which are lined with blue satin; lace jabot; full elbow sleeves gathered high on the shoulders, ending in lace and blue satin.' (Dress by Russell and Allen).

'Evening dresses have rarely been prettier or in better taste; for example, low blue satin bodice, pointed front and back, a blue net skirt with pleated flounces to the waist; a train drapery all covered with tiny silver drops; across the front a garland of shaded cardinal pompoms and bows or narrow ribbon.'

'Pointed bodice of geranium plush with gauged plastron; Medici lace collar; the long point of the bodice ending in a large bow; skirt, sleeves and train of lemon moiré, the skirt with a series of narrow pleatings to the waist; draped tunic, edged with lace, forming panniers.'

'*Ball Dress* of pale pink silk with deep lace flounce, headed by horizontal pleating of white satin; above this, a garland of plush roses and velvet leaves with puffings of crystal spangled tulle like dew drops.'

'Ball dress, a round skirt shrimp-pink moiré in front and satin behind, bordered with thick satin ruche; satin panniers with pearl fringe; large moiré bow behind; low pointed satin bodice trimmed with folds and pearl fringe across the top; no sleeves.'

'There is no limit to the number of colours or materials in evening dresses.' *E.g.* 'Orange velvet and blue crepe de Chine. Sapphire blue velvet, primrose silk broché, pink roses, lace. Turquoise blue faille, deep green plush, apple blossoms, silver embroidery.

Fuchsia satin, topaz gauze, deep red ribbons, gloire de Dijon roses.

Moonlight blue sicilienne, terracotta brocade, cream lace. Myrtle green and salmon pink. Claret velvet and pink satin. Copper and black.

Sky blue and bronze satin brocade, blue satin, Spanish lace and blush roses.

Fuchsia red plush bodice and amber silk skirt.

'There is no doubt that art in this country is entering upon a new renaissance.'

As a matter of historical interest reference may be made to the movement for 'rational dress' and Lady Harberton's 'divided skirt' dress resembling a 'close fitting short and deeply kilted skirt with drapery above; usually worn with a Zouave jacket with loose front'. At the same time Mrs. Pfeiffer's attempt to revive the Greek costume with dresses designed by herself, copied from classical statues, attracted some attention.

The degree of tight-lacing may be gathered from the statement that 'the fashionable dressmaker's waist measurement is 20 to 24 inches'.

OUTDOOR GARMENTS

Cloaks and Mantles

'The Mother Hubbard cloaks are now made with side seams ripped and the back slightly gathered up with ribbon bow across it' (to allow for the bustle).

Mantles with chenille trimming and ribbon bows on the shoulders and sleeves.

Dolmans loaded with trimmings; of Ottoman silk, velvet, plush, brocade or matelassé. Chenille fringe, pompoms, cord braiding, gimp and passmenterie. Some made out of old Paisley shawls. Slightly slit up the back, or with a wide box-pleat.

Deep fur capes (opossum, raccoon, marten). Musquash paletots. Visites (i.e. capes with long ends in front), the shoulder piece set in high and full.

Winter coats, long and short. Pelisses (long cloaks) completely covering the dress; with pleats at the back seam and sleeves starting from the elbow.

ACCESSORIES

Gloves

The popular long suede evening gloves, with 16 to 18 buttons, receive a snub from the highest quarters: 'Her Majesty has forbidden suede gloves to be worn in the Drawing rooms; these are therefore no longer admissible in dress circles.' Of day gloves 'there are numerous complaints of their bursting owing to their being worn so tight. A few years ago sizes were $6\frac{1}{2}$ to $8\frac{1}{2}$; the majority sold being $7\frac{1}{4}$ to $7\frac{1}{2}$; now these are $5\frac{1}{2}$ to $6\frac{3}{4}$.' Gauntlet gloves worn at the seaside, for driving and playing tennis. Tan chevrette kid gloves, reaching almost to the elbow, with 2 to 3 buttons at the wrist, for day.

Silk *Stockings* elaborately embroidered up the front; others of ribbed cashmere, but 'however shapely the limb or elegant the stocking they are better concealed'.

Parasols, very large, with ribbon bows, many painted; cotton parasols used. *Fans* with very large ostrich feathers and tortoiseshell sticks. Large flat *Boas*, $3\frac{1}{2}$ yards long, of fur or feathers for carriage; and of swansdown for evening.

'There is a rage for buckles and birds.'

We must note the fashion for machine made lace 'almost indistinguishable from real' and especially for lace of a string colour. *Jewellery*: small ear-rings and oblong brooches. Fancy pins are used instead of brooches to fasten the collar.

Prices

Liberty & Co. Umritza cashmere (26 in.) 9 yards 21/-. Lahore satin (26 in.) 7/6 a yard. Printed Mysore silks (34 in.) 5/- a yard. Indian corah silk (34 in.) 7 yards 17/6 to 25/-. India tussore (34 in.) $9\frac{1}{2}$ yards, 21/- to 42/-. Chinese shantung (19 in.) 19 yards 25/- to 42/-. Printed cottons (32 in.) 10 yards 12/6.

Nun's veiling $10\frac{3}{4}$d to $1/4\frac{1}{2}$ a yard. Bradford beiges, $8\frac{3}{4}$d to $10\frac{3}{4}$d a yard.

1883

During this year the steady growth of the bustle led to various secondary changes; the polonaise returned to general use with an elaboration of the overskirt. 'The short festooned tunic has gradually given place to the more fully draped polonaise—a revival of five years ago—which bids fair to be once more the fashionable style of overdress.' With double skirts it became possible to elaborate the thinner material of the upper one by puffings, etc., while the same influence affected the bodice so as to produce a blouse-like appearance. But instead of the opulent rotundities of the '70's, so alluring to the male, the new style concealed rather than exaggerated the normal curves; the horizontal bands of puffing across the front tended to form loose folds disguising any latent charms, while the massif formed by the bustle seemed more than adequate to protect the rear. In heavy materials the tailor-made dresses 'are however made in a simple, almost severe style, perfect fit being relied on to produce the—we must say it—"mannish" effect which is, unhappily, the prevailing taste.'

The pannier folds 'known in England as the Pompadour' and in America as the 'curtain drapery' (and by slangy young ladies as 'hip bags') gave an immense breadth to that region, supposed to emphasise the slenderness of the tightly corsetted waist above; they suggest, rather, some kind of fortification. In evening dresses a novelty was the 'ballet skirt' (or rather, multiple skirts).

A contemporary sums up the fashions as 'puffs, frills, ruches and all kinds of fussiness for light materials, and majestic plain skirts for heavy fabrics. These are the two styles in vogue.' And we are again reminded that 'in English Society dress is totally different from what it is in Paris'. It is significant that 'a large and increasing number of women are dissatisfied with dress as it is'.

DRESSES

Day

The tailor-made dress has a skirt with kiltings and scarf draperies and a bodice of various forms: 1. a braided Hussar jacket, frogged and worn with a waistcoat; 2. a close fitting jacket with short round basque and long tails behind; 3. a polonaise. Such dresses have flat trimmings and are of cloth, serge, vigogne, of a brown, navy, rifle green or copper colour. The ordinary day dress (morning or walking) has a skirt with box-pleating or kilting, often with strips of velvet between the pleats. Or the front may be panelled with tabbed edge. The back of the skirt frequently shows a new feature known as a 'waterfall back'; the middle breadth behind 'is set in deep pleats at the sides and caught at intervals with strings underneath the dress; the top at the back is set in fine pleats on each side of the centre where the pleats meet. Latterly the pleats were in a similar place; now that the crinolettes are worn the reverse is the mode and the pleats at the top can scarcely project too much. Near the edge of the dress the pleats are tacked here and there to keep the fullness in place. Thus with a projecting bustle the skirt seems to pour itself over a precipice.'

The scarf drapery in front forms the usual panniers and tends to hang lower in the shape of an apron, becoming a kind of polonaise.

By the autumn some morning dresses have 'a skirt with large triple box-pleats set in at the waist and over this a second skirt gathered full into the waist, being looped up afterwards with pins or ribbon bows; all those pleats and gathers form a tremendous fullness round the hips— quite a cushion in fact—and the waist looks all the more slender in consequence especially if the bodice be pointed.'

With a plain skirt and heavy materials tabbed bodices are frequent, in the shape of long jackets with collars, cuffs and side pockets, and generally open in front over a waistcoat of different material and colour. With thin materials the skirt may have the 'Zouave puff', a horizontal band of puffing which hangs almost in a pouch, sometimes single, sometimes double.

The day bodice either with a short basque or as a jacket with a long round basque, while in the summer a blouse bodice appears, the front of which sags and is often called a 'bag bodice' (worn with a waistband). The same effect is seen in waistcoats ('bag waistcoats').

NOTE: The bodice with basque cut into tabs is popularly known as a 'turret bodice'.

From four to six pounds is not an unusual weight in one dress.

Afternoon dresses are, of course, more elaborate, and some open robes over flounced petticoats appear.

'For making the skirts stand out insert three steels, the lowest 27 in. from the hem and 22 in. long; above it, one of 18 in. and above that one of 13 in. These are kept out by a small mattress, 8 in. long by 5 in. wide; or else by small crinolettes tied by strings on either side of the skirt so that they do not shake about independently.'

'The crinoline is steadily coming in again in

spite of the valiant opposition of our Royal leader of fashion the Princess of Wales.'
No balayeuse now used with walking dresses.

Examples

'*Indoor Dress*, a long pointed bodice; underskirt with narrow pleatings; plush overskirt cut in tabs; silk tablier-tunic; apron shaped in front and draped in puffs behind; silk panniers on the hips.'

'*Walking Dress*, the bodice pointed in front with coat-tails behind, skirt with the new accordion kilting, a fishwife tunic headed by broad silk scarf in flat folds over the hips and in loops behind.'

'*Summer Morning Dress*, deep kilted skirt of écru embroidery over red surah edged with red pleating; red surah tunic in folds, apronwise in front and puffed behind. Pompadour pink surah bodice with panniers; the bodice open to the waist with revers shewing a red surah guimpe.'

'*A Teagown*, a short Princess dress of grenat plush, opened up the back to shew cream lace on pink satin tied across in three places with wide pink faille; the front of gathered lace with large Pompadour bows of pink and a satin waistcoat with large lace jabot.'

'*Visiting Dress* of crushed raspberry faille pleated skirt ornamented in front with two ribbon bows; brocade side panels of a deeper shade; puffed tunic behind; brocaded bodice edged with the new fringe made of narrow ribbons.'

'Another, the skirt of red satin with deep lace flounce headed by satin puffing; the upper part of tablier in reversed folds; panniers and bodice of satin striped in red and gold; pointed plastron of red satin outlined with lace.'

'*Afternoon Costume*, broché velvet round skirt bordered with thick satin ruche and satin ribbon bows; polonaise of broché surah and jet passementerie and lace in cascade down the front.' (The use of three materials and three colours or shades is fashionable.)

'*Goodwood Costume*, tablier of fan-shaped pink satin kiltings and bands of brown satin surrounded with lace; long pointed bodice of brown satin with pink plastron outlined with lace and a lace cascade; high sleeves, puffed at the shoulders, draped at the elbows with lace. High lace collar. Back of the bodice in a long pleated basque; back of the skirt pleated with a drapery above.'

'On the front at Eastbourne, a skirt of lace over blue with a pale blue satin bodice with wide sash brocaded with velvet tulips in yellow and plum colour; rather elaborate but very pretty. The skirt was ornamented with satin bows and plum-coloured pompoms.'

'Another of spotted muslin trimmed with lace draped over a pale salmon satin skirt; the bodice of crimson velvet cut away from the neck with muslin chemisette and garnet buckles.'

'*Garden Party Dress* of cream mousseline de soie embroidered with cream spots; two van-dyked flounces headed by satin puffing with a satin kilting at the hem; blouse bodice forming panniers and draped behind with a flat bow of satin: pointed bodice ending with a satin puffing. high neck with upright collar; gathered elbow sleeves.'

'*Shooting Costume*; many ladies who go out with the shooters have regular shooting suits with gaiters, knickerbockers and short skirts.'

'*Tricycling Costume* of dark serge; Norfolk jacket or double-breasted jacket bodice; plain skirt with two kiltings, the lower one weighted; length to the instep.'

Tennis Costumes of flannel, nun's veiling, sateen or gingham; colours, crushed strawberry, yellow and cream stripes, cream and crimson checks. Banded bodice with long basques caught up into panniers. The skirt short and full, often embroidered in cross-stitch or with pompoms. Scarf drapery, or long pointed tunic; some with long side pocket convenient to carry the racket 'when partaking of refreshments or when holding a parasol'. Worn with black stockings, gauntlet gloves, patent leather pumps with silk bows; and sailor hat with silk handkerchief twisted round the crown.

Bathing Costumes: belted tunic and drawers loose below the knee; no sleeve but an epaulette.
Trimmings, etc. 'As many as 70 yards of fine lace are sometimes arranged on a teagown.'

'So much is fancy work used that Bulgarian and Turkish cloths, recently used as chairbacks and sideboard cloths, are now cut and adapted for trimmings.'

Materials: 'Lustrous materials such as mohair and alpaca are returning to fashion owing to the fuller skirts.' Soft materials (surah, foulard, etc.) much used for draping effects. Ottoman, gros de Suez and other silks are returning for the skirt, with woollens for the bodice (winter); with flowered sateens, ginghams, llamas printed with pine pattern and embroidered batiste for summer.'

Evening

The chief novelty is the 'ballet skirt'. 'The new ballet skirts, of tulle, are cut wide and free with a narrow single pleating of silk or tulle at the edge and over that some three or four skirts one above the other and all of the same length. They are gathered into a pointed band below the waist. The uppermost is spotted with stars, pearls or beetles wings, or embroidered in shaded wools.' These ballet skirts are mounted over a silk or satin foundation. The bodice worn with them is coloured, of velvet, plush or satin.

Evening trains are about ¾ yard long.

The balayeuse in evening dress is a series of internal flounces of muslin.

Ball dresses have low or square necks draped with folds of tulle, pointed or Princess bodices with berthas. Many are decorated with numerous pompoms sewn all over the skirt.

Other forms of evening dress may be gathered from examples:

'*Dinner Gown*, the square cut train of chestnut satin bordered with figured velvet on ottoman ground; the front of the skirt of ottoman brocade with satin scarf drapery fringed with silk, chenille and gold beads; this drapery ends on one side of the skirt in fan-shaped folds. Plain velvet bodice; a pointed panel of brocade on one side of the skirt' (Marshall & Snelgrove). 'Bodice of tan-coloured surah is full in front, secured by maroon velvet Swiss belt which begins only at the side seams; the back of the bodice is plain with velvet tails; skirt consists of the new accordion kilting (the pleats are secured underneath to soft elastic); draped tunic' (Debenham & Freebody).

'Dinner gown, the tablier of black embroidered net, falling over narrow kiltings of plain black satin; black lace flounce at the sides; black brocade bodice with beaded net fichu; panniers to correspond; tucker of folded tulle; elbow sleeves; train of black brocade.'

NOTE: In many the panniers merge into the train so that no tunic is apparent; in front the 'tablier' effect is increased by the use of separate materials and side panels or trimmings; the effect is to approach that of an open robe, the train being separate and of a different material.

'*Ball Dress*; a silver grey gauze skirt with several rows of goffred frills; the overdress of prune Dumas velvet with wide square side panels edged with chenille pompoms; bodice with deep point in front and square basque behind; tulle tucker; from beneath the basque behind hang two wide velvet loops.'

Colours. 'Bright colours are again used; in ballrooms lighted with the new electric light the aesthetic shades of colour lose their effect and something more pronounced is necessary.'

OUTDOOR GARMENTS

These are still further adapted to fit over the growing bustle, but with no special features distinguishing them from those of the previous year. They are all either very short or very long.

ACCESSORIES

Shoes

For dancing, of suede or black glazed kid with hand-painted toe, or bronze coloured. Pointed toes embroidered in fine beads; French heels. Day: 'Boots are scarcely ever seen in town on well-dressed people.'

Gloves

Evening gloves, of coloured silk, are often a yard long.

Jewellery: the growing taste for fancy jewellery, in silver and cut steel such as 'large silver spiders fastening fichus or on the shoulder of an evening bodice, bees, flies as pins and ear-rings, jet butterflies in the hair' is notable.

Muffs. These, of fur such as skunk, raccoon and marten, are often immense. Smaller muffs of velvet are decorated with owls' heads, birds, squirrels and even the entire body of a kitten.

Parasols. Eccentric forms abound of which an extreme instance may be quoted: 'a large pink silk sunshade bordered and crowned with ostrich feathers, the crown being decorated also with écru ribbons and a green bird perched on the top.' The handles are usually elaborate and it is the fashion to have a sunshade to match each costume.

1884

'It is difficult to say what style of dress prevails. Sometimes we seem to perceive some tendency to a return to simplicity; then again we are struck with the profusion of draperies, puffings and trimmings with which modern toilets are over-loaded.' Existing modes continued but we can detect an increase of the 'bagginess' of the front, especially in summer dresses; the blouse-bodice, the bag-plastron, together with baggy effects down the front of the skirt, while the puffed drapery behind tends to be replaced by a more solid looking bulge over the bustle, now a separate article. 'Panniers and draperies are slowly giving way to gathered and pleated skirts encircled with tucks. Nearly all skirts are now made with a few gathers at the waist, the foundation being made as closely fitting as possible, but the real skirt should fall easily without any apparent tightness. 2½ yards is the usual width and 4½ to 5 yards for the foundation to allow for the distension of the steels and the horsehair pad at the back of the waist.'

The year is notable for the revival of the silk dress. 'Gowns made entirely of silk are again to be in vogue. For nearly ten years the silk trade has been under a cloud' (owing to the widespread use of woollens).

Meanwhile the 'sports costume' (for tennis, archery, boating, shooting, fishing, tricycling and walking tours) begins to form a distinct class in itself and shows signs of becoming more practical. The fanciful tennis apron is abandoned but physical freedom is still checked by the horror of anatomy. In the tricycling costume, for example, there is an extra fold which when unbuttoned lengthens the front of the skirt some six inches 'thereby concealing the feet and ankles from view', so that the rider could use her legs while denying their existence.

DRESSES

Day

Types of bodice: 1. tight fitting with points front and back; often with edging of ruching; 2. The blouse bodice draped over the chest; 3. The jacket bodice opening over a waistcoat and fastened with one button at the top, the fronts slanting off, coming a good deal below the waist. In place of the waistcoat a bag-plastron is common; 4. The habit-bodice with postillions; 5. The short round basqued bodice, edged with a 'cock's comb' ruching or lace studded with ribbon loops; 6. The polonaise, usually with a plastron and full tunic in front which is draped behind, 'smartly bunched up and trimmed with ribbons.' With these varieties the overskirt may be pleated and fully draped over the hips front and back; or made clinging over the hips, being tightened inside by two rows of elastic fastened by safety pins instead of strings. In place of the puffing behind some overskirts fall in deep hollow pleats over the bustle down to the hem. The underskirt is round, fully gathered at the waist and edged with narrow pleating. A new feature on the skirt is tucks or rows of braid horizontally, or accordion-pleating. In summer, especially, the skirt may be flounced to the top, or with rows of embroidered material.

The Redingote, with tight bodice buttoning down the front and narrow turned-up collar, is, in effect, an open robe; its skirt has an extra width let in behind to form five double hollow pleats which form a waterfall back. The fronts are open to show the underskirt. The underskirt 'of light silk trimmed with scalloped flounces or accordion-pleated all down; these pleats form a pretty rustling at the least touch'. Many dresses still retain the scarves and panniers and drapery. The tailor-mades have a bodice with one short point, or a postillion basque of three pleats; a simulated waistcoat of rows of braiding, and a skirt in wide hollow pleats fastened underneath midway down and then left loose, with a tunic 'looped up in the old but very pretty fashion' in a wide drapery coming up to the hip. With heavy winter materials the underskirt may be false, merely an edging showing.

Some dresses are cut Princess fashion in the back with a waterfall in place of a puff.

'Shoulder puffs and pillows appear to die hard,' but diminish.

'Afternoon tea Aprons are most elaborate and

quite de rigueur.' Made with a small bib, *e.g.* 'of black satin with a tiger lily in gold thread worked on it.'

NOTE: 'Cravat bows are now discarded; the very narrow band which finishes off all high bodies is invariably fastened with some pretty little brooch; ruches are still worn round the neck and cuffs.'

Examples

'*Indoor Dress*, the check woollen skirt bordered with deep velvet band; plain woollen overskirt draped high on the left side to the waist; pointed bodice of plain woollen with deep added basque of velvet; velvet plastron; guipure collarette.'

'Plain skirt mounted in box-pleats; broché overskirt reaching to within a few inches of the bottom of the underskirt and its edge turned up inside to produce puffing. Plain bodice with long points.'

'*Summer Costume*, the pleated skirt of shot silk broché with chenille flowers; bodice and tunic of plain faille with a scarf from the right shoulder crossing the bodice to the left hip.'

'*Garden Party Dress* of striped terra cotta silk, the bodice with waistcoat points and extending behind in a waterfall; open in front on a vermilion satin plastron, lace collar and jabot. Three deep guipure flounces form a tablier each caught up at the side with a satin bow.'

Tennis Costumes with sailor collars.

Materials: the return of silk, especially shot, and mohair, are notable. Bengaline tends to replace ottoman as it shows no creasing. Faille is now much softer.

Evening

The bodice may be oval, round, slightly pointed or square; the edge trimmed with folds of tulle or lace. The square cut is often filled in with a chemisette, while the pointed may have a stiff ruff. Short puffed sleeve or epaulette for full evening dress; elbow sleeve for dinner, often slashed down the outside. The waist is long and pointed front and back, or with a short tabbed basque in front; generally laced behind; sometimes laced in front over a contrasting colour. The Princess robe, however, becomes fashionable again.

The skirt. 1. Tablier-tunic draped into panniers; 2. The front with flounces or folds of lace; black lace with beads in common; 3. The redingote form. Skirts are made round or trained.

'Evening dresses are literally loaded with lace.'

Ball dresses: the bodice, of satin, velvet or brocade, is round, or pointed with very little trimming except a bertha of flowers or beaded border. The skirt, of tulle, lace or gauze, is

Seaside costume. Skirt and plastron of cream serge trimmed with rows of blue mohair braid. Vest and tunic in blue serge. 1884

round, and made as a ballet skirt or with waterfall back. A ballet skirt is three yards wide and required 20 yards of material.

Evening dresses are said to display 'quiet good taste combined with rich materials', and as new trimmings a variety of dead animals are used, *e.g.* 'two small birds nestling up to each other, worn on one shoulder; moths as large as hedgebirds; a set of butterflies on wires across the

Carriage mantle trimmed with passementerie. 1884

front of the skirt,' while materials woven with a flight of swallows across the skirt, are also examples of quiet good taste.

'*Evening Dress*, the skirt of primrose satin cut in turrets, decorated with autumn foliage; bodice and train of broché silk in primrose and shell-pink with blush roses on the side and on the shoulder; a plastron of autumn colour.'
'Another, the skirt of salmon satin with narrow flounces; the train and bodice of sapphire velvet; the train with square-cut sides and end is lined with salmon satin with a border of ruching; the square cut bodice has a Medici collar and long pointed stomacher of beads; epaulette sleeves; a large bouquet of salmon coloured flowers on the left side.'
'Evening dress of pale pink satin and light blue brocade. The front of the skirt with five lace flounces to the waist; three satin kiltings above the hem. Side panels of brocade; draped train; pointed bodice cut low and round above, edged with lace fichu; lace elbow sleeves.'
'Evening dress of biscuit coloured faille with Zouave jacket, Swiss belt of brown velvet, bodice trimmed with passementerie, the belt edged with a ruching.'
'Dinner Gown, the tablier and waistcoat of Pompadour brocade; the Princess open robe of dark velvet with square train, and trimmed with black lace; long sleeves with ruffles.'

OUTDOOR GARMENTS

Mantles of the cape or visite shape, high necked with ruching, short behind with long scarf ends in front and lavishly trimmed with black lace, fringe, jet tassels and ribbon loops. The front and back comparatively narrow, the sleeves giving the necessary width. Often made of two colours and two materials.
Dolmans. Pelisses. Dust Cloaks pleated front and back with a cape forming sleeves.
The outer garments tend to be puffed out over the bustle and to have the high shoulder following the example of the dress, but the square shoulder comes in during the year.
Materials: a return to the use of terry is conspicuous.

ACCESSORIES

Jewellery: a fashion for Indian jewellery may be ascribed to the recent Calcutta Exhibition.

Prices
Gloves: kid gauntlet, 3/11; silk jersey, 6 button, 1/6; to 20 button, 2/11. Kid, 2 to 6 button, 1/10 to 3/9. Four button black taffeta, 10d.

To appreciate the Bustle Era of the '80's, now at its height, it is necessary to recognise that it was accepted as an alternative to the greater horror of the crinoline. The latter would have made the tailor-made walking dress an impossibility whereas with this excrescence behind progress forward was still possible. But just as the crinoline paralysed fashions by its very size so now the bustle tended to stereotype a style of dress which could not develop further, and the year '85 was almost sterile of invention except in minor details of tailor-mades and sports costumes. The struggle between the Practical and the Picturesque seemed at a deadlock. 'In many ways France is now losing its sovereign sway in the realm of dress' was one comment, while 'the absence of elegant drapery is the crying sin of modern dress' is equally suggestive. 'Whatever may have been the case (formerly) it is now altogether absurd to suppose that there is no such thing as purely English fashion in dress. English tailors alone can design the tailor-mades and English women alone can design the dresses in which English women appear at their best.' We were, in fact, trying to escape from Paris without a clear idea of where we did want to go. But it was the overskirt much more than the bustle which hindered progress.

DRESS

Day

Walking. It seemed impossible to face the world in a single skirt and compromises were tried. With woollens the tunic was either open in front in two points or draped across the upper part in folds, or caught up at one side to the waist, the drapery behind in circular folds being known as a 'spoonback', the underskirt being in box-pleats or stripes. A variation was the 'milkmaid skirt', made plain in stripes of two colours (e.g. red and blue, grey and pink), with overskirt fully gathered at the waist, turned up at one side to show the lining and drawn through a loop of cord; worn with a bodice laced across the front and a kerchief of the striped material round the neck, the ends coming under the lacing—a costume which elicited the comment, 'We aim much at being picturesque and we occasionally succeed.'

A popular, if simple, form of single skirt was, in fact, used this year—and slightly in '84, for homely occasions, known as the 'housemaid skirt'. This was a single skirt with five or six tucks round the lower part, usually worn, by younger women, with a velvet corselet and a full pleated blouse bodice. It was not, of course, suitable for the matron.

An alternative to the tunic was the polonaise and the redingote, the tunic being represented by their lower part.

A new device whereby the incumbrance of the overskirt could be eliminated was now introduced for figured materials, plush, etc. The two skirts were joined together, the under one forming a 'foundation'. Thus 'three breadths of brocade form the front and sides; the back is of plain silk or woollen; the brocade is smoothly attached to the foundation with merely a hem at the edge of the skirt and a box-pleated frill below. The back-breadths are in broad box-pleats or close gathered folds from the waistband. The sides of the front breadths are also sewn to the foundation and trimmed with revers of the brocade panelwise from the waist.' The effect is that of a tablier, while the foundation enables the 'limbs' to remain perdu in a ladylike way. Inside the foundation are sets of elastics or strings, and often three steels.

Skirt measurements: front 46 in. width, 14 in. at top, 25 in. at bottom. Gores 47 in. long (width, 10 in. top; 20 in. bottom); back length, 48 in. 25 in. wide, and straight. Fourteen yards of 27 in. material needed.

Examples

'Tailor-made gown of brown cloth with pleated panel of crimson; the draped tunic is short and in folds round the hips falling as drapery to below the knees behind. Bodice in habit form with a waistcoat of crimson cloth.' (It is owing to striped skirts being worn that the tunic drapery is shortened and tends to become a polonaise.)

'Tailor-made, the kilted skirt of red serge; tunic

and bodice of navy blue serge; the tunic looped up on both sides to the waist.'

'English tailor-mades generally made with a foundation of sateen or mohair, the skirt pleated in front and gathered behind.'

'*Indoor Costume*, the pleated skirt of broché grey woollen; the upper part of the bodice is gathered; black velvet corselet, cuffs and collar. Woollen tunic short and puffed in front and sides, pleated behind.'

'Indoor toilette of embroidered canvas, yak lace and dark green velvet. A velvet Spanish jacket; the tablier and lower part of bodice of canvas; open skirt; upper part of bodice of yak lace.'

NOTE: Toilettes are frequently made in the open robe style with Princess backs.

'*Jersey Costume*, olive green cashmere skirt tucked to the waist and tunic draped in front and behind. Pale blue silk stockingette jersey bodice ornamented in front with steel beads, front fastening.'

'*Afternoon Dress*, a silk foundation skirt bordered with satin kilting; a broché tablier crossed by a satin draped scarf; the right panel of satin; the left of velvet; the broché basque bodice fastens slantwise. Velvet upright collar. The satin overskirt falls behind in full folds.'

'*Garden Party Dress*, the skirt of écru lace; tunic and bodice of greyish-green Liberty silk with revers of moss-green velvet; the long tunic is open in front with revers; the bodice revers form a "V" to the waist; lace jabot and falling collar.'

'*Summer Costume* of cream canvas and red canvas embroidered in cream. The silk skirt is covered with cream canvas which is perfectly plain; embroidered canvas is used for the scarf (knotted in front of the waist and hanging in loose ends), panniers and tunic. The latter forms two side panels and a large pouf behind reaching nearly to the knee; the tight bodice with high collar, and sleeves just beyond the elbows, is of embroidered canvas with folds of cream canvas outlining a plastron.'

'*Boating Costume* of butcher-blue cotton made close-fitting with a belt, the bodice full front and back; skirt in box-pleats with straight tunic in front and behind; high throat band with lace turning down from it and linen collar within; white sailor hat.'

Tennis Costumes are of striped flannel; the skirt plain in front and in wide pleats behind,

measuring $2\frac{3}{4}$ yards round the hem. Tunic is either long on one side and turned up to the waist on the other in the 'milkmaid style' or short and drawn back ending in two long sash-ends. Or the skirt is in the 'peasant style', round and full with two or three tucks rather wide, and a fall of lace. The bodice is round-waisted with band and fancy buckle. The skirt has an alpaca foundation with one steel and a horse-hair bustle.

The collar and cuffs are frequently replaced by a loosely knotted handkerchief.

Trimming. Jabots and fichus are less used. Yak lace, often machine made, very fashionable.

Materials. Cloth or serge for tailor-mades; cashmere, velvet, faille and soft ribbed silks for afternoon. During the summer canvas had an extraordinary vogue. Also printed delaines.

Colours. Dark blue, red, Chartreuse green. 'The dim aesthetic colours are decidedly going out and we are reverting to the vivid blues, greens and pinks that characterised Berlin wools in days gone by.' Tailor-mades in drab, sage, fawn and Oxford and Cambridge mixture.

Evening

These show little in the way of novelty except for the corselet-bodice, and bodices of beaded lace (worn with soft silk or satin skirts). Bodices, often of velvet, are 'cut like stays, glove-fitting and lacing behind', generally with a 'V' opening. Skirts are, of course, trained, often the train being entirely separate from the skirt, and even detachable. Many are in the form of a Princess dress with a square train, and opening in front over silk blended with lace.

Figaro jackets, short and sleeveless, cut in scallops behind are sometimes worn over high or low evening bodices.

The use of ribbons in variegated colours down the front was a device much practised (both in evening and afternoon dresses), in the form of a graduated cascade of ribbon loops (red, blue and yellow) ending at the waist and known as the 'flow-flow' 'very useful for brightening up a dress'.

Ball dresses have three or four full balayeuses at the back of the skirt, which is some three yards round with one steel halfway down. A curved bustle, 9 inches long and 6 inches wide, is also worn. The bodice is either square, en cœur or quite low, and the sleeves are double straps of satin tied up with bows, or puffed up as short sleeves.

Examples

'Home *Dinner Dress* of grey nun's cloth spotted with green chenille and beads. The collar, demi-plastron and sash of dark green velvet; bodice folded en fichu with a velvet bow at the waist; a scarf is draped round the basque and arranged as a waterfall behind.'

'Dinner dress of dark red velvet broché with pink, white lace and Sicilienne. A broché skirt with pointed side panels of satin edged with lace; full draped tunic of Sicilienne; broché overskirt behind; broché pointed bodice open with revers to a point, filled in with lace; high collar; elbow sleeves.'

'Dinner dress, the bodice and train of black velvet; the front of the skirt of black satin; a ruching all round the hem; a tunic apron of alternate stripes of velvet and black and gold lace, with a long scarf of the lace draped at the back descending over the train. Bodice trimmed with jet and gold beads; network of lace forms the elbow sleeves and fills in the square opening of the bodice.'

'*Evening Dress* of white satin and tulle; round satin skirt edged with box-pleating; full tulle overskirt draped with satin bows; low bodice draped with tulle; elbow sleeves.'

'Evening dress of mother-of-pearl satin, skirt embroidered in arbutus leaves and berries in natural colours and poppies in bright orange silk; two rows of velvet flowers above the hem and on the right hip; low pointed bodice and train in prune velvet; the latter lined with satin and turned back in revers; folds of china crepe across the top of the bodice; beaded tulle shoulder straps.'

'Evening dress with corselet bodice, square train and side panel in bronze plush; overskirt and bodice trimming of lace; short skirt in amber satin merveilleux; long train of primroses and foliage from the left shoulder descending across the draped tunic.'

'Evening dress in tilleul Ottoman brocaded with velvet and chenille nasturtiums. Pointed bodice and draped tunic in shot nasturtium velvet; stomacher and bertha in guipure worked in gold; sleeves to correspond with ribbon bows on shoulders.'

'*Ball Dress* of Chartreuse green satin and white lace; underskirt (edged with a pleating) is of green silk covered with lace flounces at the back and lace draperies in front festooned with rosettes. Low satin bodice edged below with a ruching, the front open to a point nearly to the waist and filled in with a tulle plastron.'

Materials: two or more materials are used. Tulle, faille, lace brocades, velvet; embroidered patterns of birds, velvet flowers.

Colours: ruby velvet and pink satin; emerald velvet and salmon pink or amber; eau de Nil ottoman silk and myrtle green velvet; terracotta and moss green; pale blue and olive; salmon and apple green. Chartreuse green is especially fashionable.

OUTDOOR GARMENTS

Long coats (velvet); plush mantlettes; short glove-fitting tailor-made jackets with basques in full box-pleats round the hips; short braided jackets; ulsters with hoods and 'sling sleeves'. Hussar jackets with military braid were inspired by the Egyptian campaign.

'A dustcloak of grey silk waterproof, lined with red satin; the cape with sling sleeves is lined with satin and has a high collar. The cloak is full at the back below the waist where it falls in a succession of pleats. Buttons down the front.' Mantles 'a glittering mass of beads', especially *leaden* beads. The Zouave jacket (some of plush or fur) fitting the figure behind and loose and open in front, are sometimes worn over ordinary dress bodices. The fashion for bullet-shaped buttons is perhaps a compliment to the military.

ACCESSORIES

Shoes

(Day) 'Oxford' laced. Buttoned boots of patent leather (12 to 16 buttons) with kid or satin tops; plain or Louis heel. (Evening) Pointed toe; low heel; in silk, satin, bronze, glazed kid, a large bow on the instep.

Stockings (Day). Plain coloured with coloured clocks, or spotted on the instep. (Evening). Fancy silk openwork.

Prices

Mohair chiné, 2/3; chintz llama, 33 in. 6¾d; French zephyrs, 31 in. 10¾d.

(Jay's) Satin duchesse, 3/-.

(Liberty & Co.) Satin plush, 10/6. Arabian cloth (30 in.) 15 yards 21/-. Mysore silk (34 in.) 7 yards 35/-.

(Dickins & Jones) Cloth Hussar jacket, astrachan trimmed, 57/6.

(Peter Robinson) Tailor-made stockingette jackets 55/- to 4 guineas. Mantle in canvas cloth, trimmed with guipure and ribbons, 3½ guineas. Full length mantle in ottoman silk with pleated back, quilted with silk and edged with bear, 5 guineas; ditto in rich brown plush, 10 guineas. Day gloves, suede, 6 button, 2/11; 10 button mousquetaire, 3/11. Evening gloves, 16 to 20 button, silk, 3/6 to 4/9; kid, 7/6 to 8/6. Crinoline petticoat with two steels round the front and cushion bustle, 15/-. Merino combinations, the luxury of the age, 18/9. In silk, 33/6. Longcloth Princess chemise, lace trimmed, 12/6; ditto combinations, 10/6. Longcloth nightdress, 9/6 to 14/-. Flannel petticoat, 12/6. Stockings, cotton, 2/6; merino, 3/6; silk, 11/6.

1886

'The times have changed since we used to have a dozen frocks and gowns. Now we manage with four or five, or even less, and we get a great deal more wear out of them than we did.' Economic pressure was forcing an increasing number of 'young ladies' into earning a living, and all, except the plutocrats, were practising economies in dress. It is more than ever necessary, therefore, in studying the fashions of this period to distinguish between the elaborate 'fashion-plate' dresses and those actually worn by all except the rich. The coloured fashion plates were mainly of French origin and by no means represent accurately the clothes as worn by the average English Lady. We read, for example, that 'the much puffed hips which are liked in Paris are not popular here', nor do the gaudy supplements supplied with some magazines agree with the statement 'English tailors have quite changed Parisian outdoor fashions by introducing correct simplicity.'

The tendency of '86 was towards fuller and simpler skirts with fuller and more ornate bodices. The supports at the back of the waist began to shrink. 'No crinolettes are now worn and the steel cages are apparently to disappear until the next period of lunacy comes round.' That the change was slow in arriving may be gathered from a description at the seaside of 'the awful revelations produced by a high wind; every steel stood out in high relief under the most bouffante drapery; upper skirts broke away from the under and displayed the sorry fact that the latter were only shams of lining calico with patches of good material where the overskirt was cut open'. But for the most part steels were abandoned together with cage-bustles and tie-back arrangements of elastics, at least by day. Trains appeared only in full dress. The bodice front was fuller, and 'the inevitable waistcoat' was a feature of the year; indeed, 'more than one wife has borrowed her husband's washing ones, running a long perpendicular tuck down the back.' The corselet, the Zouave jacket, and the fuller sleeve all indicated a return to more romantic modes.

DRESSES

Day

The tailor-made and walking dress has usually a habit-bodice with postillion basques; the skirt is fuller, the folds falling straight from the waist; 'some skirts appear to be all tunic, the underskirt being invisible'; the fullness round the waist is in box-pleats, but during the year the loose blouse-bodice and open jacket become fashionable. The blouse-bodice develops from the waistcoat which in one form or another distinguishes the year. (Numerous waistcoats may be made for a bodice, whereby variety may be combined with economy.) Winter waistcoats are of plush or velvet, in summer of white piqué, cambric or embroidered fancy materials. The blouse-bodice, appearing in the summer, resembles the old 'Garibaldi' (e.g. of striped flannel) under a small sleeveless Zouave jacket, and is worn with a broad waist-belt, and a skirt of different material. By the winter the bodice, slightly fulled, is often made with a yoke or a straight band on the shoulder into which it is gathered, a turn-down collar,

DRESS WITH POLONAISE
AND PANNIERS
1886

RED SPOTTED SATEEN
WITH EMBROIDERED
NET TRIMMING
(Koechlin frères)

front opening
of polonaise

inside back
of polonaise

back of red sateen
underskirt

bustle stuffed
with straw

pocket

steels

white book muslin

335

cuffs and belt of velvet, or a petersham belt. In flannel, linen or foulard of all colours. The jacket is loose-fronted, fastened at the throat

Summer Tailor-mades (Messrs. Redfern). 1886

and waist with large buttons or clasp; the waistcoat may be replaced by a loose scarf extending below the waist round which it is fastened in a bow at the back, so that it is visible below the edge of the jacket all round.

The habit-bodice with high velvet collar round the throat has now no frilling edging.

The growing freedom of the bodice is accompanied by a looser sleeve which may be full to the wrist, with band and ruffle, or full above faintly suggesting a 'gigot sleeve'. Others have deep cuffs standing away from the arm like gauntlet gloves.

For visiting and afternoon dresses silk is more used; the tunic draped high at the hip reveals a panel on the underskirt, the rest of which may be invisible (and made of inferior material). Pyramid shaped panels or 'Pentes' (of silk and velvet in graduated stripes) are sold for this purpose. The bodice preserves the long 'V' opening (often with a 'violin back'). Drapery is arranged in long folds and points in order to

slighten the figure and give the effect of height. The tie-back effect is reduced. Two materials are always used. There are always two skirts, the under one (with narrow kilting) which may be (1) almost unseen; (2) as a tunic draped high on the hip; (3) open in front to the waist. Occasionally a polonaise is seen; the Princess dress is rare. Loops of ribbon adorn the shoulders and down the front of the skirt. 'The ordinary skirt seldom weighs less than 4 lbs', and is 2½ yards wide.

NOTE: 'It is the fashion to use the word "gown" instead of "costume" or "dress".'

Teagowns, of plush or velvet and surah, *e.g.* olive plush and shrimp-pink surah. The surah front forming a continuous waistcoat and apron with a bag-plastron of lace over it. 3½ yards of surah for the front, 10 yards of plush for the outer gown; 4 yards of muslin lining and balayeuse; 4 yards of piece lace.

Examples

'*Teagown* of plush striped with moss-green on old gold; pink satin, and white lace. Pink satin

Dressy polonaise of cashmere with velvet skirt. 1886
Teagown in foulard with pleated muslin front. 1886

skirt bordered with a kilting and covered with white lace; open robe of plush with a plastron corresponding to the skirt; mauve velvet sash.'

'*Morning Dress* of brown fancy canvas with panels of brown Sicilienne striped in brown and gold, and orange satin. In front a pointed canvas tunic bordered with a satin fold and Sicilienne at the sides; long back draperies bordered with satin in wide folds. Bodice with revers. Closely pleated satin waistcoat with revers of Sicilienne.'

'*Day Dress* (Dickins & Jones) of surah with narrow stripes of bronze and crimson on a white ground. The skirt set into the waist in full gathers, edged at the hem with double row of white lace flouncing over a deep band of bronze velvet; full bodice with velvet stomacher and full chemisette. Puffings of white net over green velvet trims the border of bodice and sleeves. Velvet bows catch back the drapery of the skirt.'

'*Indoor Costume* of green cashmere, velvet and Pompadour foulard. The velvet skirt is trimmed with perpendicular bands of foulard. A cashmere tunic open on the right is draped high on the left, the back long and puffed. Bodice full in front with plastron and revers of foulard; small red velvet bow at the throat; pointed basques; elbow sleeves.'

'Costume of pink surah trimmed with moss-green velvet. Surah skirt with plain tablier trimmed with fancy ornaments. Surah tunic open in front and puffed above; surah bodice edged with velvet forming a point below; a deep "V" above, front and back. Velvet bretelles. Rosette on the left shoulder. Sleeves puffed to the elbow and close to the wrist.'

'*Summer Woollen Costume*, the striped velvet skirt with panel of beaded embroidery on the left where the blue woollen tunic is draped high with a long point in front. Long pointed bodice with embroidered waistcoat; striped velvet yoke, collar and cuffs.'

'*Seaside Costume* of striped and plain flannel. The skirt of striped cream and blue flannel; also the bodice which is open in front to a point at the waist over a cream silk chemisette, and with postillions behind. Sailor collar; sleeves full to the elbow. The tunic of plain flannel is drawn up on both sides nearly to the waist, draped as panniers on the hips, and hanging in folds behind.'

'*Summer Costume* of cream and violet striped silk studded with embroidered pansies, and pale pansy-coloured foulard with white spots. The striped skirt is bordered with rows of em-broidered pansies. Foulard tunic draped on the hips, and forming a tablier in front. Basque bodice edged with a frill of striped embroidery, open in front over a foulard plastron and embroidered chemisette. Folds of material from the shoulders meet at the waist. Waistband with ribbon loops and ends hang down over the front of the skirt. Elbow sleeves with ruffles.'

'*Tennis Costumes*, of striped and plain flannel, mixed. Bodice cut in a wide "V" with full front or a waistcoat. Often round waist with folded velvet band; or with scarf drapery. Either double skirt with side panel on the underskirt, or a plain skirt buttoned down the left side. These skirts have alpaca foundations, $2\frac{3}{4}$ to 3 yards round.'

'*Bathing Costumes*, some of stockingette in one piece with detachable short skirt, or tunic over knickerbockers.' (Care should be taken lest they reveal the figure when wet.)

Materials: Striped materials are a feature of the year. The morning dress is made of two woollen materials, the afternoon dress of a woollen and a silk.

Colours: In the summer white dresses are specially notable. Otherwise heliotrope and eucalyptus green are the popular colours.

Evening

These are frequently without trains except for mature matrons when the train is fastened round the hips instead of to the back. The general style is the open robe ('Louis XV') with tablier and side panels, the bodices being semi-high with a waistcoat or plastron, the sleeves short ('mere draperies of lace') fastened high up on the shoulders with a ribbon bow. The draped tunic skirt is also used. There is a tendency to use the low bodice for dinner dress. For ball dresses the cuirasse bodice laced behind, with a deep point and a wide 'V' opening in front and behind bordered with tulle, is a common type. A velvet throat band is commonly worn.

Examples

'*Dinner Gown* of cream satin and plush. The front of the skirt with two panels embroidered with flowers in gold and pearls, with grapes in filigree hanging from the material. Train attached to the waist and turned back to show the lining.'

'Dinner gown, the tablier and train in satin broché, side panels of pleated satin, train lined with satin. Full satin bodice pointed with jetted waistband and bertha; the top in a wide "V". Tight shoulder sleeves edged with velvet balls which also ornament the top of the bodice.'

'Dinner gown of Pompadour silk and cream lace, trimming of velvet. The front of the skirt in silk organ pleats; bows of velvet mark the left side of the tunic. Cream lace is draped diagonally across the front. Lace plastron with silk bodice having small basques and revers. High velvet collar; elbow sleeves edged with velvet band and bows. At the back a draped lace tunic with ribbon bows of velvet.'

'Summer dinner dress of prune surah, Pompadour surah and cream lace. Plain surah skirt mounted in pleats; lace tablier; Pompadour panniers and drapery at the back ornamented with ribbon rosettes. Lace elbow sleeves. Square Pompadour bodice with ribbon rosettes down the front; lace chemisette.'

'*Ball dress*, a foundation of pink satin with panel on the right side of embroidery with pearls; the back of the dress which is veiled in the style now so prevalent, has over a waterfall of pink tulle masses of bronze tulle studded with pink pearls. The drapery on the left side is caught up and tied with a bronze sash; pink satin bodice with pointed waistcoat.'

'Ball dress, the skirt of white tulle with pointed tulle tunic having a design of briar roses in satin. In the corner the outline of a bird's nest with pearl eggs and butterflies. Low satin bodice with tulle bertha ornamented with a spray of wild roses.'

Materials: these tend to be less heavy; surah and crepe de chine are much used.

Colours: for ball dresses, a delicate shade of pink, daffodil yellow, blue and green and—for young ladies—white.

OUTDOOR GARMENTS

The short loose-fronted Battenburg jacket with large buttons and turned-back collar, and the Bernhardt mantle (a short cape with collar and sling sleeves, the back being shaped and the front loose) are the chief novelties. The sling sleeve remains the fashion for mantles, which are generally black, close-fitting behind and short with long side panels, and trimmed on the shoulders and edges with jetted lace. Some long mantles trimmed with astrachan (real and imitation).

ACCESSORIES

High buttoned *Boots* and laced *Shoes*, for day; shoes with patent leather toes are becoming more fashionable than boots.

Stockings. Day, black thread or cotton, and 'ribbed stockings in every imaginable shade'. Evening, plain coloured openwork.

Gloves

Day, grey and tan suede; evening, long white kid or suede with long lace arms with bracelet worn over.

Jewellery. Fancy brooches (*e.g.* 'a miniature pair of tongs in diamonds holding a ruby to represent a redhot coal'), moonstones in necklaces and bangles; Indian silver ornaments. *Pocket Handkerchiefs* with coloured borders, and coloured centres with white borders. Long round *Boas*, of fur in winter and lace in summer. Buttons, often large, of smoked pearl and of the kernel of the corozo nut. 'Rosary beads' are much used for trimming bodices, plastrons, etc. Very small fur *Muffs* with pocket. Large *Parasols*, with bows near the point and at the handle; red parasols fashionable. Fancy headed bonnet pins.

'Notwithstanding the efforts for the preservation of small birds the market is flooded with all kinds to be used on ball gowns, hats and bonnets.'

Prices

Striped tweeds (25 in.) 1/7. Bouclé cloth (42 in.) 2/11. All wool canvas (42 in.) 2/4. Satin merv, 1/11½ to 2/11. French faille, 3/6; satin duchesse 3/6; plush, 3/6 to 6/11; brocaded surah, 1/11; coloured satin surah, 1/3½.

1887

'The increasing spread of outdoor amusements and games is an incentive to simpler dressing.' But simplicity is never much favoured by 'the trade', and Paris, where 'young ladies do not play games', found itself in the mortifying position of accepting new fashions from England, especially in tailor-made costumes. A retrospect of the year's fashions, given in December, summarised the situation: 'The multiplicity of folds which were the chief features of skirt draperies two years back

1883
Promenade dress of terracotta silk powdered with wafers of wallflower-
red plush, and of plain faille
Promenade dress of rifle-green vicuna trimmed with plush, with silk skirt;
waterfall back

1881

1884

1887

1887

have almost entirely disappeared for walking gowns, and were replaced during the summer by the gracefully and slightly draped skirts. Jerseys and Garibaldis have retained their hold. Long mantles have reappeared. In spite of the struggle to revive the Directoire modes Englishwomen show small inclination to adopt them. The Louis XV style is still adhered to by many, but the Louis XIII is distinctly the coming fashion for evening dress gowns.'

The day dress was getting into the hands of the English designer while the evening dress was still in the hands of the French. But the Gothic taste of this country was reviving; even the tailor-mades 'are less severe and more womanly', and 'there is certainly a revulsion against the sombre tints so universally worn in recent years; never was more art displayed in the amalgamation of colours; they are faint in tone though strong contrasts are allowed'. The effect of the Jubilee this year was partly responsible for both the improvement in trade and the more cheerful outlook, which were reflected in the current fashions. 'The chief feature of our present style of dress is that the skirts are all arranged with long straight draperies, most of them with panels of distinctive colouring or material. Bodices have all either revers or full fronts and often both; some with a full drapery brought from the left shoulder across the bodice; 20% of the gowns are white (in summer), or combine two colours such as yellow and smoke-blue, light blue and pink, dark blue and cardinal.'

More attention was being drawn to the bodice with its 'romantic' features, and in the evening 'bodices are decidedly low'; while the skirt, with its shrinking bustle, no longer wholly dominates the picture. Romance is once more in the ascendant.

DRESSES

Day

Tailor-mades; some habit-bodices with revers; others with loose fronts and jabot backs, velvet collars and cuffs; or short tabbed bodice with loose drapery caught up on the left side with a clasp; or made as a covert coat, close fitting behind with loose front showing a fancy coloured shirt kept in place by a broad band, with long ribbons attached to side seams and tied in front hanging down nearly to the ground. The skirt is plain in front and full behind with long square tablier and side panels. Other day dresses with sateen or alpaca foundation 2½ yards wide (back 26 in., front 26 to 14; gores 20 to 13); underskirt plain or in 10 in. wide box-pleats, and side panels. Often of silk. Woollen overskirt, a square piece falling straight to a point on one side and draped up nearly to the waist on the other; or a short drapery about the hips. Or a polonaise.

Bodice. Always with revers, often with side fastening; high collar. Pointed in front and with basques behind, but in the summer many are blouse-shaped with round waist and a broad sash. Waistcoats, like a man's dress waistcoat, worn with a shirt front and collar and narrow necktie, and a jacket bodice with loose fronts. Or plastrons, especially embroidered.

Sleeves, either tight coat-sleeve or fulled on the shoulder, or a loose bishop sleeve with close cuff. Occasionally the sleeve is of different material from the bodice. For dressy occasions puffs, stuffed epaulettes and embroidery on the outer side; butterfly bows on the sleeve are fashionable.

In the summer polonaises and redingotes are popular. Summer washing dresses, of striped or white materials, have plain skirts draped to simulate a tunic or with a straight tunic over a plain full skirt, with bodice banded and made full, gathered on the shoulders and at the waist; or a loose-fronted bodice with full waistcoat or soft silk handkerchief crossing the bust, the ends tucked in at the sides or drawn down to a point.

'The summer cotton dress has a plain foundation of alpaca or sateen bordered by 6 in. pleating;

the tunic, 2 yards long, is caught up in pleats at each side far back and the back gathered at the waist, the back being ½ a yard longer and caught up ("pushed up") so that the fullness overlaps. In front the horizontal folds only reach to the knees so that the material hangs plain beneath just sufficient to reveal the pleating round the hem.'

Lawn tennis dress (Peter Robinson). 1887

The Norfolk blouse and Garibaldis are worn with a variety of skirts, and also jerseys, the front pleated or with revers and shirt front.

Teagowns often with smocked yokes; some with Watteau pleats; others as long open redingotes over fully draped under-dresses. They are often replaced by the tea-jacket, elaborately trimmed with lace, and as they may be worn at dinner they tend to merge into the dinner dress. 'The present tendency is to adjust clothing by folds instead of fitting it to the figure.' Most cloths are now made in double widths to permit draping. In place of kiltings pinked silk flounces at the hem are much used.

The steels, now placed in the back of the underskirt, are smaller, and the bustle, a crescentic pad, 6 in. wide. The bustle is often omitted. Braiding on the skirt is the typical trimming for plain dresses, and silk and velvet ribbon loops on the front and sides of the skirt for dressy toilettes.

Examples

'*Tailor-Made* of grey and white livery cloth; skirt in plain white cloth, the long draperies of the grey cloth; bodice trimmed with broad gold and silver galon going in a straight line down the front; bodice with invisible fastenings.'

'Jacket bodice and skirt in beige cloth striped with blue and white; navy blue velvet on the bodice as collar, tabs, plastron and as a panel in front of the tunic which is of the plain material; underskirt of wide box-pleating.'

'*Afternoon Dress*, the high bodice, back of the tunic and cuffs in mauve Sicilienne; the straight attached collar fastens on one side. Braces, full sleeves and pannier drapery in tileul Surah; sash in shot moiré; pleated skirt in china crepe embroidered in mauve silk.'

'*Indoor Costume*, the skirt of dark beige silk, open on the left over a kilted panel of seal-brown velvet with a large bow in the centre; draped tunic of beige silk to a point in front below knee level. Velvet bodice, with round basque cut out in points, with silk revers opening over a Garibaldi silk front; silk cuffs; high collar.'

'*Luncheon Dress* of tan-coloured nun's veiling striped with brown and gold fancy lines; a yoke gathered horizontally in silk muslin; shoulder knots and bracelets in chestnut-brown velvet faced with tan satin; at the waist and on the right hip droop bow and streamers of corded silk brown ribbon.'

'*Ascot Gown* of black silk; the front of the skirt is a trellis-work of chenille and jet over rose du Barri silk; side panels with large chenille and jet ornaments; pointed bodice with revers and a waistcoat of chenille trellis-work.'

'*Summer Dress* of pink-cream cotton printed with old-rose design; bodice and skirt in one in front, the sides opening to show panels on the underskirt, the one on the right of white embroidery, that on the left three flounces of dress material. The fullness at the back gathered on to the bodice so as to fall in double festoons.'

'*Boating Costume*, of cotton, a loose shirt with sailor collar or a yoke, plain or pointed, worn with plain full skirt with no drapery or foundation.'

340

'*Garden Party Dress*; blouse polonaise embroidered with flowers; a smocked yoke; full sleeves to the elbow with gauged cuff; ribbon bow at the waist; under-dress of buttercup yellow bengaline; the polonaise is caught up at one side with pink and yellow ribbon bow.'

'Costume in faille and striped velvet; the shirt of velvet; faille tunic pointed in front reaching nearly to the hem and puffed behind; it extends up the front over the velvet bodice to the left shoulder forming a blouse front; sleeves and high collar of velvet.'

'*Tea-Jacket* of dark blue velvet close-fitting behind; tight sleeves; in front a loose white silk plastron in pleats.'

'*Wedding Dresses*: afternoon weddings have caused a great reform; a bride is often married in her going-away dress, and a bridal dress is always high to the throat with elbow sleeves.'

Bathing Costumes: 'it is becoming the custom to wear shoes with straw soles and embroidered linen uppers, kept on by sandals. The trousers are now seldom made as knickerbockers.'

'It is to Madame Bernhardt that we owe the graceful loose-fronted gown which has now taken a firm hold on the fashions of the day. The same actress invented the long "sling-sleeve" cloak which for some time was called the "Bernhardt mantle".'

Materials: 'Lighter, brighter and smoother'; woollen above silk or plain woollen above striped woollen, for winter; cottons, light silks and embroidered muslins for summer.

Colours: soft faded tints, two in a dress. White and grey in summer. In winter 'red jerseys, red coats and cloaks, red hose, petticoats, hats, bonnets and muffs, conduce to brighten up the winter sombreness'.

Evening

The bodice tends to be lower, either in a 'V' or round. The dinner gown varies between the low neck, no sleeves, and the teagown. The chief features are 'the rich and glittering effect now aimed at' by beading, sequins, transparent dewdrops and metal moonlight drops; and the use of drooping ribbon bows on the shoulders and skirt. The full evening dress is trained, the train being plain and often gathered to the back of the bodice. 'A butterfly pouf is made by

dividing the back breadth into three, the centre one gathered into the waistband, the side ones tacked to the side of the breadth forming a point which makes a butterfly bow.' The skirt is $3\frac{1}{2}$ yards wide. The front breadth 22 in. sloping up to 14 in., the front gores 20 to 12; back gores, 15 to 12, the two back breadths 22 in. The foundation has a 4 to 6 in. kilting or a pinked flounce which is invisible but keeps the

Jubilee Ball dresses. 1887

skirt out. Bretelles of lace or velvet may be used to form a 'V' in front and behind. The over-dress is usually lace or transparent material, such as grenadine or Algerienne.
A velvet necklet is usually worn.

Ball dresses: low bodices brought up high on the shoulders with bows or epaulettes; bodices of silk, moiré, plush or velvet, and made with short points, front and back, with a wide sash behind. The skirt may be plain (such as one full skirt of tulle over another) with silk or satin foundation. Tulle draped in panniers and loose diagonal folds is usual.

341

'Dinner Dress of pale pink foulard with nine flounces graduated up to the waist, scalloped and pinked; the upper dress of silver-grey corded silk open at the left side and draped on the right; grey silk bodice with revers opening to within 3 in. of the waist, with a pink silk kerchief-fichu. Short sleeves of grey and pink and a long spray of red roses on the left shoulder.'

'Dinner Dress in striped jonquil moiré; the train turned back in revers. Panel on the left side, of cream lace caught together with satin bows; "V" opening to pointed bodice with gauze fichu crossing on the chest.'

'Dinner dress in moiré and lace, the skirt covered with lace flounces; train of moiré in folds from the waist; moiré bodice, a deep "V" front and back, trimmed with lace folds; shoulder straps.'

'Dinner gown, the skirt in blue poult de soie with a tablier of maize coloured grenadine flowered with chestnut brown. Low "V" bodice with kerchief folds over blue silk. Sash ribbon and throat ribbon in watered velvet with pearl buckles.'

'Evening dress in pink satin merveilleux with lace insertion. Tablier consists of alternate lines of the two materials, with a lace cascade on either side. Full pleated back. Pointed bodice with a "V" opening, trimmed with lace on the right side. Sleeves made of folds of the material.' (Dickins & Jones).

'Evening dress: a green satin skirt covered with white lace, a plain satin panel on each side of the tablier. The satin train is surrounded by lace which is looped up at intervals by pink satin bows. Half-high bodice with "V" opening. Lace collarette and full plastron. Round waist with sash; elbow sleeves.'

Materials: moiré is again in fashion while satin has largely gone out.

Colours: peach, old rose and sea green are fashionable.

OUTDOOR GARMENTS

Long Cloaks reaching the ground, fur-edged, in winter. Mantles with hanging sleeve-piece and short at the back. Double-breasted sealskin jackets with short basques. Many mantles have plastrons forming a collar behind and tapering to the waist in front; high in the neck with 'plenty of lace and jet fringe'.

Short Hussar jackets, or of red cloth trimmed with astrachan, with one rever crossing diagonally, and crescentic side-pockets.

Covert coats, fastened at the throat and flying open below.

ACCESSORIES

Evening *Shoes* match the dress and are embroidered, with rosette and Louis heel.

'Red silk *Stockings* studded with swallows' are seen.

Jewellery. Pearls, moonstones; stiff flowers, crosses, rosettes. Ear-rings not worn.

French kid *Gloves*, in beige tones, are now more popular than suede.

Feather or painted gauze *Fans*.

Long *Boas* of mouflon fur.

'Officers' collar'—mere band of fur round the throat.

1888

The outdoor activity of Englishwomen had produced the tailor-made dress which threatened to destroy the voluminously draped skirt and long pointed corsage with its armour-plated stays; the moment was ripe for a freer style permitting more movement. The old domination of Paris had lost some of its hold. 'It is satisfactory to know that smart Americans are beginning to prefer the make of London tailors to that of Parisian modistes for their morning costume.'

Chance, however, in the Spring of this year, supplied the French designers with means for a counter-attack which enabled them to recover much of the lost ground because the new mode exactly fitted the requirements of the day. In Sardou's play 'La Tosca' Sarah Bernhardt, with her stayless figure, astonished the fashionable world in a series of Directoire and Empire costumes. The charm of those simple undraped skirts swept over Europe. She had abolished the overskirt and threatened the long waist. The new French style outbid the English tailor-made. An English comment at the close of this year summed up the change: 'The draped skirts of a year back have entirely disappeared and day by day the modes of the Directoire, Consulate and Empire are gaining ground. We disliked them at first but we have reconciled ourselves by degrees to the long redingotes with their huge revers and pockets, the skimpy perfectly plain skirts, the somewhat eccentric air of the whole toilet. What we cannot bring ourselves to is the high waist, and the various dodges to solve this are amusing. Sashes swathed round the figure or very long waisted waistcoats are the familiar devices for avoiding the dread short waists.' The Englishwoman was attracted by the greater freedom but repelled by the Classical hard lines, so she accepted the former and concealed the latter by Gothic devices.

The new style was by no means universally accepted; it hardly reached the middle class. In Du Maurier's pictures in *Punch* for '88 it seldom appeared. But its influence in leading to the simplification of the skirt must be acknowledged. Sarah Bernhardt had shown how to get rid of a superfluous garment. It also encouraged the open bodice and the loose-fitting blouse, and it gave the bustle its death-blow. Moreover it shortened the day skirt almost to the ankle.

Such changes in any case were no doubt imminent; the impulse in that direction came from the Englishwoman's growing activity but the French actress supplied the model at 'the psychological moment'. It is therefore one of those interesting cases where an eminent person seems to have started a new fashion which would, however, have inevitably arrived at another moment, in some other form. It should be noted that there was also a growing tendency among the cultured towards individualism in dress. 'For a long time the so-called artistic dressmakers have been introducing unconventional models; these are now adopted by others.' Dresses designed and made by Mrs. Nettleship, for example, were often original in a real sense; if any specimens survive they would be difficult to date exactly.

DRESSES

Day

The Directoire Coat: generally of smooth cloth, often black; the wide lapels at the neck extend almost to the shoulders and form a turn-down collar behind; the straight front is cut square above the waist line and extends down the back forming an incomplete overskirt, gathered at the waist behind, and falling in straight lines at the sides to the ankles. It is, in fact, a sort of redingote of which the skirt portion in front is absent. Large buttons down the sides of the body, with flap pockets; close sleeves with turned back cuffs, buttoned.

The body may be closed (*e.g.* double-breasted) with a habit-shirt, or open with a shirt-blouse, in which case a wide folded sash is worn.

The Directoire Jacket is similar except that there is no skirt portion behind. The sash frequently has long purse-ends, ending in tassels (the 'Recamier sash'), or in place of it a long waistcoat, or even a short waistcoat above the sash. The sash is frequently incomplete being merely a piece sewn in across the front to resemble one. The term 'waistcoat' is vaguely used to denote either a separate garment or merely a 'fill-in' which crosses the chest and disappears in the folds of the sash.

The habit-shirts ('silken habits') fasten round the throat with a folded band or small tie.

The skirt; gathered at the waist, and on a foundation. It is made either with a front breadth, four side gores and a narrow back, or with a front breadth, two side gores and a wide back breadth. It is trimmed with braiding or thick ruching or narrow tucks, and is generally of striped silk.

The Empire style. The resemblance to the original is slight but the principle of a full bodice, front and back, a sleeve puffed over the upper arm, and a wide folded sash, and a skirt gathered at the waist is preserved. It is frequently blended with the Directoire features. It is often combined with the old style to the extent of having a plain overskirt added.

The blouse appears in various forms; a tight jersey, a Garibaldi, or with a yoke, plain, embroidered or smocked; worn with a sash or belt and buckle. It is unlined except in the sleeves, which are puffed to the elbow. The collar is upright. Some blouses are sleeveless and worn over a sleeved camisole.

The bodice may be in the form of a blouse, extending over the hips outside the skirt. Or the open bodice as a jacket with revers and plastron, or with fichu folds and a waistcoat. Bodice fronts, when closed, are fastened with hooks and eyes in place of buttons. The attached bodice has varieties: the 'Fanfreluche bodice', the front from the shoulders and throat gathered into a point in the centre just above the top of the corset; the 'statue dress' with drapery falling in folds from the left shoulder down to the hem of a trained skirt.

The sash is worn over a coat-bodice and under a coat, over a full bodice.

The influence of the new styles affects dresses made in the old, especially tending to make bodices open in front, simplifying the skirt and removing or reducing the bustle so that the back falls as a waterfall; the back of the skirt is gathered to the basque of the bodice 'in the new style'. The foundation skirt has three large kilted skirt folds at the back, requiring six or seven yards of material, and retains two steels. The Empire skirt has none.

Examples

'*Walking Dress*: jacket bodice, short square side lapels and redingote skirt in red cloth striped with black and white, and ornamented with silver buttons; the front of the skirt, draped from the waist, and the plastron in red cloth.'

'Walking dress, the kilted skirt of shot silk, the cashmere polonaise fastening slantwise with folds across the bodice to the waist, open over the side of the skirt; high silk collar.' (The box-pleated flounce on underskirt is now invisible.)

'*Visiting Dress*: the skirt of shot silk, reseda and old rose, with a fine white stripe; a deep kilted flounce sewn halfway down and then left to fly out; draped with a soft fawn cloth open at the sides in folds; sleeves puffed at the shoulder and elbow with pleating between; bodice full in front and pointed, with some of the drapery hooked on to one side of it; deep guipure on the bodice and border of the skirt.'

'*Tailor-made* in black cloth; skirt plain in front, cut up each side to the knee and filled in with pleated folds and braided up on each side; the back falls in loose folds; habit bodice with braiding on cuffs, shoulders, and as braces down the front and back.'

'*Empire Dress*: the skirt of shot green and red silk with a full gathered flounce and full horizontally gathered waistcoat to the throat. Over this a string-coloured woollen skirt and bodice in one, the bodice crossing diagonally with but one rever. Sash of shot ribbon coming from beneath the armpits and crossing the bodice apparently twice, falling in a long looped bow on the skirt; silk sleeves wrinkled on the arm with a short woollen oversleeve.'

'*Directoire Coat*, of striped black moiré and satin, the sleeves high on the shoulders, lined with shot duck's-egg satin which appears on the wide revers in front of the bodice of the short coat front; this comes to the waist over a full satin waistcoat covered with black lace ending in a pleated belt; satin rosette on left side; satin skirt covered with lace.'

'*Directoire Gown*, the coat front ending at the waist with three large buttons at each side; revers at the neck reaching almost to the shoulders; long skirt made as a coat, and a crossing waistcoat which disappears in a broad sash belt; cuffs in gauntlet style.'

'*Ascot*: the most marked feature was the Directoire coat, coupled with the general display of green; Directoire jackets are as fashionable as the coats. An Empire dress, plain foulard skirt with cream ground and design of rosebuds; the edge a thick silk ruche pinked in long points; bodice crossed in front with a green Empire sash and puffed sleeves.'

'*Ascot Dress* in steel-grey foulard; Directoire jacket with wide lapels open in front over a white crepe de Chine shirt with wide moiré sash crossing slantwise; coat sleeves to wrist with crepe de Chine turned-back cuffs; draped overskirt with side panels.'

'*Carriage Dress*, a pleated skirt of beige bengaline, with short train attached at the back of the
waist; pinafore drapery in beige silk canvas

*Teagown in black velvet and crepe de chine
(Peter Robinson)*. 1888

striped in Pompadour design, and caught up at
the waist with a belt and clasp; jet yoke with
collar and oversleeves; undersleeves in white
linen.'

'*Teagown*, of grey Indian cashmere with embroidery in silk and silver tinsel round the
bottom; Medici collar lined with moiré;
smocking on the shoulders forming a yoke. A
cross-over of grey muslin is confined by broad
pink Surah sash; full cashmere sleeves with
velvet cuffs; cashmere skirt with tucks round
the bottom.'

(Some teagowns are open robes with loose
flowing fronts of light material and open sleeves;
some with a Swiss belt; some as directoire
redingotes over an under-dress.)

'Teagowns have spoilt the sale of dinner gowns.'

'*Tennis Costumes*: a blouse-shirt (2½ to 3 yards of
flannel, cambric or surah, the shirt below the
waistband being outside the skirt; full sleeves;
deep cuff; the shirt gauged, smocked or full;
any skirt may be worn with it, usually one like
a full round petticoat with gathers or pleats into
a waistband, and reaching just below the

ankles, 3 to 3½ yards round, often with a concealed muslin balayeuse. Black stockings;
black canvas or leather shoes; jockey cap.'

Materials: smooth cloth for Directoire coats; soft
pongees and foulards. Silk more used than formerly. Shot silk; chine silks. Striped materials.

Colours: green, grey, 'the new blotting-paper
pink.' 'This is a year of demi-shades. Every
tone is used in combination with another; red
and blue; brown and green; brown and red; Nil
and orange; smoke and beige,' etc.

NOTE: Owing to the deaths of the two German
Emperors in the Spring the 'London season'
was one of subdued colours; while the un-
usually wet summer encouraged the widespread
use of green.

Evening

'The excessive nakedness of modern full dress is
sometimes a pain and more often an embarrass-
ment to those who only observe. The lowness
of the bodice and the total absence of sleeves
leaves an impression of general nakedness.'

*Greek costume embroidered in gold
(Peter Robinson)*. 1888

The tendency is to low square bodices, short
puffed sleeves and higher or at least round
waists; 'laced up the back so that additional

345

fullness is given to the bust and the waist is seen at its smallest'. Sleeves short, often with bead epaulettes shading the arm. Dinner dresses are either in the form of low jackets with revers; or in a deep 'V', or a low heart-shaped opening; or some with classic drapery from the left shoulder. The Empire style prevails in various modifications, as in bodices arranged like fichus, carried just over the shoulders and confined round the waist by broad bands of soft

Dinner dress in pearl grey satin with appli-qués of plush (Peter Robinson). 1888

silk, folded, worn with a draped skirt and wide sash. 'Evening dresses are rapidly exchanging their close fitting point for the more graceful folds of Empire fashion.' The skirts are narrow, close fitting on the hips and worn without bustles. Long side panels with 'purse ends' are a feature.

Examples
'Directoire *Dinner Gown*, the front of white

moiré slightly open to show a plastron of silver brocade; bodice and narrow train of black moiré with revers of white; a waistcoat, cut in a low square, of silver brocade with a deep lace tucker as a cravat; collar lined with black velvet and a wide sash of the same.'

'Directoire dinner dress (Debenham & Freebody) the bodice and train of grey brocatelle; the Directoire coat-bodice is in the form of a short open jacket with revers and elbow sleeves; to the back is attached the train in gathered folds; a draped tunic of crepe de Chine which also forms the under-bodice, in pleats with a broad sash of pale pink satin across the front of the waist.'

'Empire Dress of cream voile embroidered in the Empire style; the overdress is bordered with this work and draped with a hollow pleat at the side; gathered bodice trimmed with silver.'

'Home Dinner Dress of plain green silk; the skirt, pleated above, is bordered with a full ruche; bodice, sewn to the skirt, is gathered at the shoulders and open over a chemisette collar with a coquille in white batiste; sleeves with large puffs at the shoulders, are trimmed with batiste at the elbow; black silk Empire sash.'

'White Evening Dress: a long surah tunic, trimmed with lace, is draped in front on the cross, and behind is draped at the top to the point of the bodice, the back of which is in folds forming a "V"; underskirt in wide pleats on a silk foundation; front of bodice open heartshaped with folds from the shoulders to the waist; satin bows on shoulders and the half-length sleeves.'

'*Ball Dress* in bronze tulle ornamented with tufts of water grasses, irises and bulrushes; pointed bodice with oval opening, of bronze green velvet with tufts on the shoulders; no sleeves.'

'Ball dress in yellow surah with blue silk ruche across the front which is of silk embroidered tulle; it falls as a straight apron; the straight back is attached to the short-waisted Empire bodice which ends in a wide blue sash; bodice draped with embroidered tulle; sleeves open like a "V".' (Ball dress bodices usually of velvet, faille or moiré with tulle skirts).

'Never was the art of clothing the female form so thoroughly studied and so brilliantly carried out as in the present day; but women cling to their under-petticoats, and petticoats beneath an Empire gown are an impossibility' (Helen Mathers).

OUTDOOR GARMENTS

Long Mantles, completely hiding the dress, high in the throat and fitting the back, the skirt behind being gathered or pleated at the waist. The sleeve, cut from the shoulder and often of a different material, hangs in a long point or square, often with an invisible sleeve beneath. Of matelassé or brocatelle, or plush. Short mantles, short behind with long front ends. Short jackets, double-breasted, opening diagonally. Or open in front, in the Directoire style, with outside flap pockets.

A border of fur is a noticeable feature in winter. Ulsters with capes reaching to the waist.

Cloaks, full, yoked or gathered round the shoulders, or with a shaped neck-piece to which the rest is attached in wide pleats.

ACCESSORIES

Day *Shoes*, magpie, of black patent leather and white buckskin. Day 'Cromwell shoes' with high cut fronts and large bows. Evening shoes, pointed, small bows, medium heels; bronze or black.

Black *Stockings* for day and evening.

Gauze *Fans* painted with large flowers. 'Fans with cats' heads of every kind nestled close together all over the gauze, the heads being the size of furry toy cats; the effect is extremely quaint.' *Muffs*: Christmas cracker shaped with frilled ends, and suspended from the neck by a cord. *Wrist Watches*, worn in leather wristlets, 'very useful but extremely ugly.' *Parasols* with 'sticks as long as alpenstocks', and ball knobs 'as large as billiard balls'. Some sticks 'with insects of repulsive appearance crawling up, cut out of the wood'. Large *Aprons* of spotted muslin, trimmed with lace and a sash ribbon, worn in the morning and at teatime. Long lace *Scarves* tied round the neck and allowed to drop long in front; and fichus with jetted yoke and high collar and long lace ends in front (day).

Prices

French moiré, 5/6; herring-bone cloth, 44 in. 2/6; all wool beige, 44 in. 2/3. Black French faille, 3/11; satin merv, 2/6¾; velveteen, 1/11½ a yard.

(D. H. Evans) Pongee silk, 1/11¾; Lister's silk plush, 2/11¾; surahs, 1/6½; Cheviot tailor-made costume, 15/11; of estamine serge, 27/6, with bodice material. Double-breasted beaver cloth jacket, 27/6. Handmade knickers, lace trimmed, 5/11; cambric chemise, Valenciennes front, 9/11. Lisle thread stockings, 1/6¾; silk (white feet) 2/4½ a pair.

(Jays) Evening dress of Chantilly lace on satin foundation with jetted panel, 5½ guineas. Tea-gown in China silk, 5½ guineas.

1889

'The season of 1889 will long be memorable for its brilliancy and the general prosperity which characterised it.' The fine summer, and the French Exhibition both stimulated fashions. The latter 'has given an immense impetus to the silk trade'. The growing individualism in taste was producing a wide diversity in styles worn, at least by people of culture; here it is only possible to discuss the modes of the majority. At the close of the year a contemporary observed: 'this season there have been more radical changes in Fashion than in any other for the past twenty years. We have given up dress improvers, steels, most skirt draperies and have almost completely altered the cut of dress bodices.' While another remarks: 'The styles of 1828 are much to the fore, only that fashions never do quite reproduce themselves, and if the dresses actually worn in the past could be resuscitated they would lack some of the becomingness of the present revival.' (Such is the confident taste of those who prefer reproductions to originals.)

The Gothic influence was growing and the centre of attraction was becoming the bodice in spite of so-called 'Directoire' and 'Empire' styles which were now mere travesties of the originals. The taste of the day expressed itself as in the later '20's but with less exuberance; the cross-over bodice and the large sleeve, for example, appeared in a subdued form, inspired by a romantic impulse denied the prospect of a natural fulfilment.

DRESSES

Day

Walking dresses are nearly two inches off the ground. The bodice is generally full and crossed in front. In the directoire style the bodice-front is open with a lapel showing a bright lining, and a vest above the waist, buttoned with three buttons. A folded sash on the vest continues below the buttons. The skirt is plain and tight-fitting, and more cut away from the front and hips than in the previous year, so that the underskirt is more exposed; it is becoming almost a single skirt itself, for the redingote supplies only an overskirt behind, re-inforced by side panels. The underskirt is very slightly draped so that the front is almost without the creased effect which had been previously so noticeable. Its plainness is relieved by elaborate embroidery of gold or bronze braid.

The redingote and underskirt are of different materials or at least of different shades of colour.

Variations of the directoire style are numerous; the Incroyable coat with long coat-tails, wide lapels, lace frill and waistcoat; the Eton jacket bodice, with double-breasted fancy waistcoat having revers, collar and tie; and the bodice shaped as a paletot with large revers, flap side pockets, upright collar and huge directoire cravat, are common. In fact, the 'Directoire' is less a style than an influence affecting other styles in varying degrees. Its influence is mainly seen in day dresses, producing forms of open bodice with lapels. With such a waistcoat and high collar, a striped linen shirt front or pleated 'front' is worn according to the degree of opening shown. The older type of pointed bodice, tight-fitting and basqued, has the front embroidered and braided and is either open over a 'vest' or with trimmings simulating an opening. ('Vest' is becoming a synonym for 'waistcoat' and materials for it are known as 'vestings' in the trade.)

The newer type of bodice is full, having folds of the dress material brought from each shoulder to the waist, crossing each other and fastened on the left side; or there may be only one such fold brought from one shoulder. This style, obviously inspired by the modes of the '30's, has full bishop sleeves to below the elbow with a close cuff; those inspired by the directoire have close sleeves with a turned-back cuff. But in both the sleeve is cut extremely high and accentuated by pleating at the shoulder, causing a characteristic 'kick-up' which became a marked feature by the middle of the year.

An incongruous mixing of styles is seen in the fashion for the high Medici collar, common with tailor-made jackets, teagowns and cloaks. In dressy costumes the skirt, in place of drapery, frequently has the sides open to display the under panels on the foundation.

Summer dresses: 'The skirt foundation has a front breadth of 9 in. above, 29 in. below; one gore at each side, 16 above, 24 below; back breadth 37 and quite straight; a small pad bustle may be used with one steel, 12 in. long, placed about 10 in. below the waist.' These are always absent in the directoire style. Two gathered and pinked flounces take the place of a balayeuse with thin materials. A small dress hook on the back of the stays fastens to an eye on the skirt to prevent a side-slip.

Dresses of light materials are now known as 'frocks'. The use of ribbons is a notable feature. These, 3 or 4 inches wide, hang from the waist nearly to the ground, in free ends or loops, and ribbon epaulettes are common.

Examples

'*Teagown* for young lady, of cream Liberty silk with Watteau pleat; tight under-bodice of flannel lined with swansdown; round the hem of the demi-train a thick double ruching of pale blue silk; a loose front of the same falling in graceful folds from the throat to the feet.'

'Empire teagown with rounded yoke and sash, the sleeves hanging in points nearly to the hem.'

'Teagown in heliotrope bengaline with panels of peach and white broché satin; cascade of lace down the front.'

'*Indoor Dress* of brick-coloured cloth and white cloth; a Princess redingote of the former with added basque, opening over a bodice and skirt in white cloth; trimmings of gold braid; the back of the redingote slightly draped from the waist to show the pleating which borders the edge.'

'*Carriage Dress*: a Directoire coat in copper-coloured tweed with brown velvet collar and lapels; sash and kerchief folds in gold-coloured

Costume in navy tweed studded with red and white checks. Waistcoat, collar and cuffs of red silk. 1889

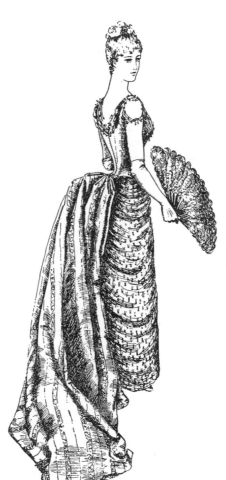

Dinner dress with demi-train in buttercup coloured brocade, front of gold coloured net and pearls. 1889

Directoire costume in reseda cloth with black appliqué trimming. 1889

Costume in lettuce green cashmere trimmed with velvet and gold braid. 1889

Costume in celadon green striped with ribbon of different widths. 1889

surah under waistcoat and cuffs in tan galon.'
(A Directoire coat of dark cloth, and red, embroidered vest and skirt, or a poplin skirt, with silk foundation, are a usual combination.)

'*Afternoon Dress* of absinthe-green Liberty silk, trimmed with galons of opalescent beads; similar panel on the left side; bodice with Medici collar is folded and crossed in front; sleeves puffed at the shoulder.'

'Afternoon dress; a redingote in blotting-paper pink cloth opening on an under-skirt of parchment-coloured crepe embroidered in red; broad belt; chemisette and underskirt in embroidered muslin.'

'Afternoon dress: redingote in electric-blue faille trimmed with broad bands of white cloth embroidered in gold; puffed sleeve to the elbow of veloutine; bodice of crossed folds of China crepe; front of the skirt draped by a button on the left hip.'

'*Ascot Gown* of parchment-coloured bengaline with pale blue cornflowers scattered over it; the skirt made in accordion pleats, the bodice with cross-way pleats of soft blue silk; Medici collar lined with blue; leg of mutton sleeves, tight from the elbow to the wrist, slashed and puffed with silk.'

'*Park Costume* of China silk, blue flowers on primrose ground; bodice with crossed folds on the right and cream embroidery on the left, the former terminating in a sash with long ribbon ends; high collar, epaulettes and plain skirt.'
NOTE: In order to make the bodice more conspicuous it is not uncommon to have the two sides of it different.

'*River Dress*: a scanty serge skirt, unlined; cotton or woollen shirt; sailor tie (pinned) with the long ends tucked inside the waistbelt; loose serge jacket; sailor hat.'

Trimmings, etc. Huge Incroyable bows, of mousselaine de soie and lace, worn at the throat with directoire costumes.
'Smart little Sultane jackets (sleeveless Zouaves) scarcely reaching below the shoulder blades' are fashionable in summer.
Deep pointed guipure, as trimming for the throat, waist, cuffs, side seams.
Materials: cashmere, often flecked with white, and the delaines are much used; in the summer (which was very hot) the cottons, 'or zephyrs as they are nearly all called,' with Pompadour or arabesque designs, on alpaca foundations, together with foulards and washing silks.

Broché materials (broché gingham, alpaca, nun's veiling) are much used.
Colours: shades of green, red and grey are the popular colours of the year.

Evening
The Empire style predominates. The bodice is given a short-waisted look by soft silk scarves wrapped round: some are brought from the shoulder crossing the front and tied behind; others are folded and looped at the side. Five yards of scarf are required. Some have the bodice draped on one side and embroidered on the other. The pointed bodice is open over a pleated plastron or waistcoat.
Many dresses are made en princesse with 'V' backs, laced, the skirt being open in front over an underskirt. For young ladies the 'babyish-looking Empire bodice'. The general tendency is for the opening to be a deep oval with folds of lace or material round the top, shoulder straps and no sleeves; or in the Empire style with shoulder puffs.
The skirt is trained only with full evening dress.
The Empire skirt is round with ruching at the hem and floral embroidery; with pointed bodices the skirt is draped, often with a pointed overskirt, or the overskirt, in the style of a redingote, is cut away at the sides with panels enclosing a tablier of some other material or colour, *e.g.* a gown of rose du Barri armure, and tablier of green crepe.

Ball dresses: skirts just rest on the ground; those à l'Empire are shorter in front than behind. A silk, satin or sateen foundation in four pieces; the back piece over a yard wide with two side gores and a front. The hem is lined with stiffening carried up half a yard inside. Small kilting at the edge except in Empire gowns, where there is a ruche on the outside.
Generally no steels but a petticoat with stiff flounces up the back is worn. The dress is at least 2½ yards wide; the back plain with one layer of net over the foundation and two layers of tulle over that. The front is slightly draped with loose side panels and sash. Empire gowns have a plain front with only one layer of tulle over the foundation. Empire bodice folds over, crossing back and front, ending in a wide sash with long ends on the left side, the sash mounting to the bust with a large bow behind. The two halves of the bodice are often of different materials. Pointed bodices lace behind, are high on the shoulders and slightly draped at the

1881

1884

1885

1887

1888

1896

top. They are well shaped with seams and not, as formerly, cut in one piece with darts. It is impossible for the bodice to fit too tightly. Bodices are made of satin, armure, moiré, velvet and striped silk. Sleeves in one short puff. Long wide ribbons hang from the shoulders nearly to the ground.

There is 'a wealth of flowers on the skirt from the waist to the ground'.

Examples

'*Dinner Dress* (Jay's), a train of grey broché satin with side panels and front of plain satin; revers of black velvet dividing the train from the panels; the front embroidered in velvet, beads and silk, bows on the bodice and train of velvet and beads; high bodice with pointed basque of broché satin, with satin vest and fichu of grey crepon; satin winged sleeves ending at the elbow with a velvet band.'

'Dinner gown (Worth) in blue China crepe, draped with figured and spotted crepe. An informal drapery in blue lisse ornaments the opening of the low bodice and finishes on each shoulder as a puff resting on an epaulette of white gauze; semi-short gauze sleeves. The bodice has a rounded basque slightly pointed in front. The front of the overskirt is slightly draped in front, the back hanging in folds.'

'Evening Bodice of cream lace striped with green ribbons; lace flounce at the bottom forming a basque; puffed epaulettes on elbow sleeves; high collar and rosette at the throat.'

'Empire Evening Dress of white figured muslin; plain skirt striped round the edge; low pleated bodice with ribbon run in along the top; short puffed sleeve, wide Empire sash.'

'Evening dress, the skirt of flowered satin with overskirt of large-meshed black silk canvas intersected with stripes of black velvet. Bodice similar with transparent sleeves partly open up the back; skirt only slightly lifted.'

OUTDOOR GARMENTS

'Four-in-hand capes', or 'coachman's capes', triple or quadruple, of cloth, often with Medici collar. 'Ulster with five capes, of rough blue twilled cheviot, lined with blue and gold checked satin; blue bone buttons fasten the double-breasted bodice which is shaped to the figure.'

'Evening cloak in tan cloth with deep frill of cloth pinked out and headed by beaver fur; high collar and yoke of velvet forming a hood.'

Mantles. 1. Long 'Limousines' in the form of a large circular cloak gauged round the throat; waistband; the fullness falls in folds over the arms as sleeves; or with guipure yoke and gathered heading at the edge. 2. Short, as a

Evening dress in eau de nil broché satin. 1889

cape with long ends; or as a directoire scarf fichu with deep point behind and points hanging over the shoulders.

Many mantles have long square panels known as 'Angel sleeves' reaching nearly to the ground.

351

'A cloak in shrimp-pink armure stamped with foliage; the Princess front fastens diagonally and has a deep fur collar extending in a single band to the waist; muff to match; Angel sleeves of ruby velvet enriched with lines of gimp.'

'Mantle (Peter Robinson) of broché armure with panels to the ground, ornamented with jet; high collar and cape trimmed with jet fringe; full loose sleeve to the elbow.'

'Spring mantle (Peter Robinson) in rich crimson broché satin, the sleeves slit open in front with long hanging panels to the ground.'

NOTE: The high kick-up shoulder frequently appears in the outer garment.

ACCESSORIES

Directoire *Shoes*, with high instep flaps and large buckles.

Evening *Gloves* do not reach above the elbow.

Parasols with Japanese cloisonné or carved ivory knobs.

HEADGEAR OF THE '80's

The singular use of dead animals, whole or in part, as trimmings was perhaps the most noticeable feature during this decade. The head became a mausoleum or even an entomological museum. During most of those years the extreme height obtained by the trimmings helped to produce a generation of tall women. The increasing outdoor exercise, together with less time expended in the malaise of recurrent maternity, was undoubtedly adding to the stature of the new generation.

The social significance of the bonnet was losing its old importance, and the hat was rapidly displacing it. The credit of this change must be attributed to the English 'and American young women who regarded the hat almost as symbolic of emancipation'. This may explain why the bonnet has never recovered its old popularity.

1880

HAIR

'At present the hair is dressed very simply and close to the head showing all its outlines; false hair is not now patronised.' Either in large coils worn low, the front waved, or a large knot on the crown, the front combed back.

COIFFURE

Day. 'Young women no longer wear caps.' Matrons' caps resemble capotes. With tea-gowns mere circles of lace pinned close to the head.

Evening. Dinner caps of marabout feathers, pinned on, or silk caps either turban-shaped or covered with beads, pearls, etc. For balls, three bands of beads, ribbon or velvet over the front, or a floral wreath at the back.

OUTDOORS

Bonnets

1. Small Capotes for dressy occasions of various shapes. 2. Large Directoire bonnets, of many forms. Of straw with high poke brim lined beneath with flowers; a medley of lace, feathers, flowers, etc., on the crown and falling over the back. 'Nothing can be uglier but they are the fashion.' Pinned to the hair on each side, and with or without strings. 3. Foundling bonnet, with stiff front and soft crown, generally of plush and tied under the chin. 'Like the Quaker headgear.' 4. Sunbonnet. Of drawn cotton, for country or seaside.

Bonnet strings usually very wide.

Hats

Generally much larger. Large Gainsboroughs of shaggy felt or beaver, pinched into all forms. Tam-o'Shanters, of silk, velvet, plush, etc.

Toques, of every material; small size; for morning, travelling, etc. 'From being termed fast, as it once was, it is now considered to be the most modest hat that can be worn by a gentlewoman.'

'Velvet toque, trimmed with feathers, on plush, 19/6; Tam-o'Shanter, in black or coloured velvet or plush, 21/-.'

Veils. Slowly passing out of favour.

1880

1. *Visiting Dress.* Bonnet covered with old gold satin, under a design of fancy straw braid, sewn in loops and one rosette in centre of crown; brim slightly raised in front, lined with close pleats of pale blue surah. Round crown, écharpes of blue surah are crossed, below three pale blue ostrich feathers and a heron's aigrette, pleated on each side of the brim and continued to form the strings.

2. *Walking Dress.* Mandarin toque in plush, with a band of Chinese pheasants and head.

3. *Walking Dress.* Niniche bonnet of steel blue felt; brim turned down in front and raised behind, and bound with puffing of steel blue plush; round the crown, a twisted fold of the plush, with a bright coloured bird on the right side.

4. *Walking Dress.* Black straw hat, trimmed with old gold braid, gold satin and black feathers.

5. *Walking Dress.* Black or black and white straw hat, with fancy straw edge; lined with red satin; a bouquet of flowers on left side, and a black and red bow on right.

6. *Walking or Visiting Dress.* Black straw hat trimmed with old gold satin, fastened down by a gold headed bar, and red and green feathers.

1881

1. *Visiting Dress.* Brown straw bonnet, with steel lace at edge of brim; lined with gathered red satin; brown and shaded red feathers; brown satin strings.

2. *Winter Costume.* Dolly Varden bonnet of grey shaggy beaver, tied down with strings of hairy plush ribbon; lophophore's tail in front, and crystal and silver bird at the side.

3. *Winter Costume.* Henri II toque of black satin; plush and satin torsade fastened on right side with jet buckle; three black ostrich tips on left side.

4. *Theatre Headdress.* Toque cap of shot plush; three shaded feathers at the back, and an agraffe of diamonds in front.

5. *Fashionable Bonnet.* (The Russian bonnet.) Crown covered with steel embroidery; brim with steel lace; feathers and satin strings of dark green.

6. *Morning Cap.* Of dark plush, with chenille flowers; edged with Alençon lace.

1. *Walking Dress.* Coarse brown straw hat, trimmed with a garland of roses, and large bow of velvet and faille to match the straw.

2. *Carriage Dress.* A trellis work of pearls mounted on a satin foundation; white pouf of feathers and aigrette; loose embroidered strings.

3. *Walking Dress.* Claret felt hat with band of claret velvet round the crown, and a tuft of feathers with aigrette at the side.

4. *Promenade Costume.* Straw bonnet, lined with red satin; bronze and red strings and feather.

5. *Evening Headdress.*

6. *Walking Dress.* Black beaver hat, with Amazon shaded feather; knot of plaid velvet at back of crown.

1883

1. *Evening Dress.* Slightly curled fringe; back hair in a loose coil towards the crown; comb of amber coloured tortoiseshell.

2. *Morning Cap.* Figured foulard crown, with lace borders and dark velvet ribbon.

3. *Costume for Spa or Seaside.* Fancy straw of red and green; trimmings and strings of red velvet, with paste buckle.

4. *Spa or Visiting Costume.* Pale green straw bonnet, trimmed wheatears and fir cones; straw buckle and green velvet ribbon.

5. *Walking Dress.* Olive green velvet hat, gathered and bouillonné; trimmings of olive velvet and shaded olive feathers.

6. *Garden Party Toilette.* Bonnet of Leghorn straw and gold braid; Olivia brim veiled with lace; flowers and ribbon to correspond.

354

1884

1. *Promenade Dress.* Satin straw hat of champignon (or mushroom); trimmed with velvet of a darker shade, five shaded feathers and pale brown aigrette.

2. *Walking Dress.* Grey hat, of coarse or rustic straw; brim lined with dark red velvet; high tuft of red poppies in front.

3. *Matron's Bonnet.* Crown and fluted brim in gold net and gilt spangles. Loops, ends and strings of chestnut terry velvet on ottoman ribbon.

4. *Capote for Married Woman.* Marie Stuart style, grey straw bonnet, trimmed with emerald green velvet; the edge a trellis of gold braid. Velvet bow and gold feathers.

5. *Fête and Seaside Dress.* 'Gable' bonnet of Italian straw, pointed brim edged inside with a ruche of white net and Mechlin lace; trimmed with two parroquets.

6. *Seaside Hat.* Coarse fancy straw, trimmed with red satin, intermingled with white lace.

1885

1. *Day Headdress.*

2. *Spring Hat.* Postboy shape, in sage green straw, bordered with fawn velvet, studded with gold. Crown has scarf in dark green surah, figured with gold trefoils. Tuft of shaded and gilded feathers.

3. *Walking Dress.* Plain brown felt hat with lined brim; large ostrich feather at the back; small tips among loops of brown terry ribbon.

4. *Visiting or Matron's Costume.* Jet bonnet made in all colours; small bouillonnés of velvet, divided by rows of beads; aigrette of wired and beaded lace; velvet bow in front.

5. *Matron's Costume.* Stockingette bonnet in two shades of green; marron plush bouillonné at edge; front trimmed with high loops and green feathers.

6. *Ball Headdress.* Hair slightly waved and combed back from the forehead; fringe all round the head, curled with irons. Ornaments, a band of pale blue pearls, pouf of feathers, velvet bow and diamond agraffe.

1. *Visiting Costume*. Pale yellow straw lace bonnet, seal brown, trimmed with cordon of wood violets. Straw pearl edged ribbon.

2. *Visiting Costume*. Fancy straw bonnet, seal brown, trimmed with coquillés of faille Française. Half wreath of yellow roses and aigrette of buds.

3. *Walking Dress*. Almond coloured straw hat, trimmed with lace and brown gauze ribbon.

4. *Walking Dress*. Pale yellow straw hat, trimmed with brown velvet and brown and yellow ribbon. Spray of buttercups and fancy grasses at the side.

5. *Walking or Country Dress*. Cap of black and white striped worsted cloth to match costume.

6. *Seaside Costume*. Sailor hat.

1887

1. *Dress Bonnet*. Stringless, covered with folds of sprigged and spangled gold net; coronet front of admiral blue velvet, rosette of Argentan lace, and blue and gold bird.

2. *Directoire Bonnet* in black velvet, with black plumes. Small yellow roses and white hyacinths under the brim.

3. *Walking Dress*. Coarse straw toque, trimmed with lace and velvet.

4. *Travelling Hat*. Fine dark straw, lined with velvet to match; pouf of brown and cream ribbon.

5. *Black Felt Hat*, crown encircled with black velvet; trimming of black faille ribbon.

6. *Country Costume*. Leghorn straw hat; large bow of maize ribbon, fastened with tuft of snowballs; black velvet bow at the back.

1888

1. *Summer Dress Hat* in fawn fancy straw, trimmed with wide fawn and white ribbon.

2. *Carriage Bonnet.* Covered with torsade of cowslip coloured China crepe, entwined with strings of gold beads, and edged with ruching of tinsel lace. Aigrette of tinted yellow roses with filigree buds, and winglike pleating of gilt lace. Shaded ribbon strings.

3. *Young Lady's Hat.* Black felt, brim quilled or organ pleated; bow in striped black ribbon and smaller bow beneath the brim. Note the hair.

4. *Morning Costume.* Black felt hat; brim lined with moss green felt. Black moiré bow and black feather; a narrow feather round crown, which does not show in illustration.

5. *Carriage Costume.* Black velvet bonnet, decorated with chandron coloured beads; ostrich feather to correspond, fastened on left side with horseshoe in cut jet or coloured stones. Short strings of shot corded silk.

6. *Costume Hat.* (Toque.) Soft folded crown of material, encircled with band of feather trimming; cluster of ombré ribbon loops and bird.

1889

1. *The Catagan Headdress.* 'Special design arranged to suit an English head.' Hair plaited behind and turned up with ribbon bow. 'A neat youthful style.'

2. *Toque* in black felt with Spanish feather pompoms and an aigrette. Black velvet bow at the back.

3. *Bonnet of violets* with Alsatian bow of velvet and strings to match.

4. *Bonnet* without strings in the shape of a scallop shell, made of tulle and trimmed with white feather.

5. *Straw Hat* with flat crown and projecting brim; trimmed with roses and lace; deep frill of black lace round the brim.

6. *Mushroom Hat.* In fancy straw, with broché ribbon; natural bird. Worn with new veil of thin net, with drawing-string to tie round the neck.

357

1881

HAIR

Unchanged.

COIFFURE

Day. Plush breakfast caps, edged with lace and fixed with large gold pins; trimming of jet fringes 'which chink like castanets'.

Evening. Wide scarves of net edged with lace worn over the head and round the throat, as a theatre wrap.

OUTDOORS

Bonnets
Capotes larger and slightly raised in front, or imitating turbans. Pokes are much larger and most fashionable.

Hats
Larger than last year's but similar. 'All straw hats and bonnets are lined.'
The novelty of the season is coloured straw lace with silk lining, for hats and bonnets. Trimmings of shaded surah, gauze ribbons, bead fringe, jetted lace, gold or steel lace.

Veils. Spotted veils again in favour.

1882

HAIR

A fringe, plain or frizzed, low on the forehead. Large knot on the back of the head. Sometimes a comb. For evening, similar, with a large flower at the side of the chignon.

COIFFURE

Caps unchanged. For *Evening* 'the newest are covered with maidenhair ferns'.

OUTDOORS

Bonnets
'There are two styles, French and English . . . most are small and close but those sent from Paris are large.' 'Everyone should have a black and a white, the latter for all occasions of etiquette.'
1. Small close-fitting bebe bonnet. 2. Langtry bonnet 'suggested by the one worn by that lady as Miss Hardcastle'.

Hats
1. Toques, made of a pouf to match the dress,

for homely wear. 2. Rustic hat, a kind of gipsy hat, of coarse straw with large front bending over the face and scarcely any brim behind. 3. The Marlborough, large and flat, worn slightly on one side; of lace and Tuscan straw, trimmed with long shaded feathers. Bead trimming very fashionable and 'one milliner has ordered 30,000 pigeons from Germany to trim hats and bonnets'.

Veils. 'Short tulle veils reaching to the tip of the nose are worn over capotes and small hats and under large hats.' Coloured spotted veils worn.

1883

HAIR

Worn higher with plaits winding round and round and loose twists coiled high up.

COIFFURE

Day caps of small bonnet shape, or mob caps.

Evening. Gold nets, caps, flowers, fruit and jewels. For young ladies a tiny wreath worn like a bandeau.

OUTDOORS

Bonnets
'English ladies wear hats better than bonnets.' (French prefer bonnets.) 1. Small close-fitting capotes, for married ladies' visiting and town wear. 2. Large Directoire bonnets. These of gold and silver straw laden with feathers, the brim lined to shade the eyes. Large fancy headed pins thrust through the back.

Hats
'Growing larger and more fanciful.' Leghorns turned up on one side with gathered lining of cream lace, and long drooping feather on the other. 'Others of lace and muslin, gathered and ruched and trimmed with roses in every conceivable shape'; some short behind with high crown; some large garden hats of basket straw, for country wear.

1884

HAIR

Parted across from ear to ear; the front with rolls or curls on the forehead; behind, a knot on the crown with the back hair turned up and twisted round it and pinned.

358

COIFFURE

Evening, a flower or aigrette on the side. Caps worn by the elderly. These are small, trimmed with narrow ribbon for day and flowers or marabout for evening.

OUTDOORS

Bonnets
1. Small with high crown (often transparent). 2. Large. 'The most fashionable is the large gold basket.' 3. The Gable bonnet 'like the angle of a thatched roof forming a point over the face'.
Trimmings of flowers, feathers, ribbons, butterflies, humming-birds, beetles and dragon flies.

Veils, of spotted tulle and gauze, matching the colour of the bonnet.

Hats
1. Toques, for country. 2. Sailor hat, the crown covered with white muslin or silk; a white ribbon round the crown. 3. 'For lawn tennis many girls wear the counterpart of their brothers' cricketing caps with a flap.' Jockey caps 'for toxophilites'. Tam-o'Shanters. 4. Large hats with stiff hard high crowns and broad brims displaying innumerable feathers.

1885

HAIR

For day, either high or low on the neck. For evening very high with combs, fancy-headed pins, jewelled butterflies or a tuft of flowers almost on the top. Or with a catagan worn close to the head where the queue is plaited.

COIFFURE

'Caps now worn by married women with tea and breakfast gowns only.' They resemble the Charlotte Corday full in the crown with lace and a velvet band.

OUTDOORS

Bonnets
Small, set close at the sides but raised high in front, with flowers and feathers 'high and jauntily above the face'. Of thin gauze. 'They do not hide the hair, much less protect the face.'

Hats
1. Dressy hats with high crowns (sometimes nine inches high). Brims generally narrow and tapering behind. 2. Broad-brimmed sailors, of

straw. 3. Sports hats, for tennis and boating, like a jockey's or coalheaver's. 4. Cloth or velvet tam-o'Shanters. Toques worn with tailor-mades.

Veils. The same colour as the hat or costume; pinned at the back of the neck.
Trimmings. 'Of hats and bonnets include not only those insects and birds which appeal to our sense of beauty but those which cause a revulsion of feeling such as spiders, water-beetles, caterpillars and even lizards and toads.' (See a specimen, covered with cockchafers, in the Exeter museum.) 'It is impossible to raise the bows of velvet, flowers or feathers too high in the immediate front.' 'Which are the most hideous, the bonnets or hats, is an unanswerable question.'

1886

HAIR

Worn low in the neck; very small fringe. Basket plaits 'still in vogue'. For evening, usually worn high. Ornaments and caps as in '85.

OUTDOORS

Bonnets
'Growing steadily in height.' But some, of black lace, are of the fanchon shape cut away behind to show the whole of the back of the head.

Hats
1. Toques, Spanish boleros and Gainsborough hats, all with very high crowns. Popularly known as 'three storeys and a basement'. 2. Sailor hats with large bow carried on to the crown in front; the brim inside often covered with tulle. Sports and country hats and caps are a marked feature of the year.

Veils. Tulle, plain or spotted, the same colour as the hat or bonnet. Hats and bonnets secured by large pins, of tortoiseshell, gold or silver, in the shape of a cross, rake, shovel, hatchet, sword, dagger, etc.

1887

HAIR

As in '86, but the fringe tends to be less crimped.

COIFFURE

Day caps only worn by old ladies. For evening, aigrette of ribbon and ostrich feathers, but often no ornament is worn.

OUTDOORS

Bonnets

High in front tapering to a point 'which is higher above the head than the face of the wearer is long'. Two new types: 1. The Poke or Directoire with brim spreading forward over the face. 2. The wreath-shape with no crown but 'cloven in two down the centre of the head'. The pointed arch thus formed behind gives them the name of 'church door crowns'.

Hats

'Age is now no barrier to the adoption of a hat.' 'A perfect war has begun between high and flat crowns.' Large Rembrandt (or Gainsborough) hats with one side of the wide brim turned up and the other bent low over one eye, and literally covered with large rich feathers, for carriage wear. Small toques, called Boleros, of velvet, astrachan, sealskin or dress material, with the back trimming rising over the crown. Sailor hats are turned up behind with much trimming. Fancy straws trimmed with 'mushrooms, bull-rushes, birds, boughs of foliage, bundles of grass, rushes and mignonette erected well in the air.'

1888

HAIR

Front hair always waved, curled or frizzed or the fringe turned back over a cushion. The hair either worn low on the neck in loops or plaits tied with a ribbon, or in high top knots with fancy pins fastening them together.

COIFFURE

Evening, a tiny wreath of flowers round the top knot, fastened by metal butterfly pins. Or feathery aigrettes or fruit and flowers placed high on one side. 'Blackberries for fair and little oranges for dark hair would not look amiss.' Dolly Varden caps (worn with tea-gowns) made of 'a little bit of gathered lace with puckered up crown and a few short lengths of ribbon.' The Dorothy cap, for matrons, of lace and bright-coloured ribbons, *e.g.* 'orange and red judiciously combined, for brunettes.'

OUTDOORS

Bonnets

'Young girls hardly sport anything else but hats and some married women only put on a bonnet when the occasion absolutely demands it.' Many bonnets are stringless. These are either the directoire or the small capote (with lower brim, but high trimming).

Hats

Low crown but high trimming. 'As if a gigantic eagle had perched on it.' Wide brims turned up at the sides, front or back. Some with straight flat prominent brim in front, flat crown with trimming on it and no brim to speak of behind. Or directoire hats, similar to, but larger than the bonnets. Also toques and sport hats.

Veils. Short; with bonnets, just cover the upper half of the face.

1889

HAIR

Worn somewhat lower, the head to look small and compact. The Catagan style for young women.

COIFFURE

Small wreaths on the side of the head may replace the aigrette.

OUTDOORS

Bonnets

1. Large directoire. 2. Small, shallow, flat at the sides and low in the crown. The Corday bonnet is a small plate-like shape of kilted velvet with a full torsade. Flower bonnets, of violets, marsh mallow, lilac, kingcups, etc., on a wired net foundation. The scallop-shell shape and the Alsatian bow (with wide ribbon loops flattened to the sides and narrow strings coming from the back over a wire shape) are very fashionable. Collapsible bonnets, folding flat, for travelling, made with a spring.

Hats

Worn by all in the morning and by the unmarried all day long. Small toque-shaped for morning; large Gainsborough and Rubens hats for afternoon. Some of the large hats are 'like an inverted soup-plate smothered with flowers'. Sailor hats are 'ever popular; women of all ages appear in them.'

Veils. Large directoire veils entirely covering the face and pulled in under the chin by a string 'rather like a nose-bag'. Some, three yards long, cross behind and are brought to the front where they are loosely tied on the chest.

UNDERCLOTHING IN THE '80's

The uses of underclothing had hitherto been to support the dress, to protect from cold, and as a discreet weapon of sex-attraction. During this decade its function was entirely prosaic. 'Wool next the skin', in the form of combinations became, for the average woman, a kind of creed. She was instructed that its use was essential 'to absorb perspiration'. 'But surely', replied a correspondent in '85, 'a gentlewoman rarely does anything to cause such an unpleasant thing!' The dread of a chill still survived with those to whom the notion of violent exercise was abhorrent, and as late as '85 the significant remark is made: 'Many people think it advisable to change the underclothing at night; if this is done great care is needed to prevent a chill.' The tight-fitting tie-back dresses had necessitated a great reduction in the bulk of underclothing and growing popularity of outdoor exercise maintained this. Thus, for day two petticoats, or combinations and one petticoat, were by most of the modern generation considered ample. Hence the warning ('87) 'One of the great mistakes of the present day is the paucity of underclothing that women of fashion indulge in; some have doffed petticoats and are content with combinations only; it is neither seemly nor healthy.' The introduction of Dr. Jaeger's woollen material provided excessively hygienic garments for those whose underclothing ran no risk of being seen; the more fashionable woman, on the other hand, was beginning to experiment with fancy materials, colours and trimmings so that towards the end of the decade she was turning all to favour and to prettiness with baby-ribbons, surah, insertion and lace. But for the majority of women underclothing in the '80's was inspired by practical prudery.

The Chemise

Still reaching below the knees this was generally shaped to the figure, and progressively more and more ornamented with embroidery, insertion or lace down the front. The opening square or 'V' shaped; the sleeves often cut in one with the bodice and buttoned on the top of the shoulder band ('81). Cambric, nainsook and batiste, edged with lace were fashionable as early as '82 (when the chemise was generally gathered at the waist and made with shoulder straps instead of sleeves) and surah and foulard followed. The sleeveless garment in the Princess shape also appeared in '82, two yards wide, with a flounce at the hem and deep pointed stomacher of perpendicular rows of embroidery and lace.

The yoked neck and gauging of the dress appeared also in the chemise, and at the close of the decade there were 'Empire chemises', of nainsook, cambric, insertions and lace, with a high waist and puffed shoulder sleeve.

Combinations

These were usually of wool, especially Dr. Jaeger's variety, while a more intriguing sort were of rich crimson silk and cream, pink or ruby surah' ('81). In '87 combinations of China silk or nainsook trimmed with square lace insertion in front or drawn down from the shoulders in a 'V', with coloured baby ribbon, were fashionable. Being thus trimmed 'no chemise is needed but a short white petticoat is buttoned round the stays and worn under the flannel one'. 'The new cellular cloth for underclothing, of cotton, wool or silk,' appeared in '88.

Drawers

These, worn over the combinations, were frilled at the knees with frilling carried up the sides. Drawers with narrow or deep waistband and edges trimmed with lace and insertion, or knickerbockers with knee bands are described in '86, while as an eccentricity in '89 we are offered complete sets of underclothing in black surah. Equally remarkable must have been 'plush drawers, quite tight with a deep frill of lace at the knee' ('81).

Garters

'These are almost things of the past, suspenders having superseded them; the suspender is made in satin and elastic with gilt mounts and clips, with a shaped belt fitting the corset' ('82); or simply buttoned on the corset. The less fashionable woman continued to embrace her knees as of old with an elastic band.

Petticoats

At the beginning of the decade these were close-fitting, the evening petticoat being flounced up the back, or with detachable flounces put on for evening use. By '82 the day petticoat has back flounces and steels inserted, and to reduce the size of the waist the petticoat buttons on to the stays, the band being omitted. The Princess petticoat, becoming general in this year, had a 'V' neck behind and square opening in front, buttoning down the front, with box-pleating round the hem. Five box-pleats at the back of the waist form a bustle; from the side seams, inside, two pieces of longcloth tie or button across causing the box-pleats to stand out. The quilted petticoat (pale blue, pink or red) usually had two narrow flounces. The evening petticoat, untrained, had five stiff flounces at the back, each with a drawstring. The crinolette-petticoat reappeared in '83. This was made with plain front breadths which buttoned to the corset, the flounced back-breadth being tied round the waist above the stays. The length of the crinolette was 19 to 39 inches and 'is worn when dresses are wider at the hips than at the hem'. Steels were often inserted round the lower part, especially for matrons for whom this arrangement (we read) 'gives a judicious amplitude to the bottom of the skirts making the undue prominence of the upper part of the figure less observable'. The fashion for crinolettes passed by '85 when white petticoats, of cambric, foulard and corah silk, returned to favour. Two petticoats were usually worn, or one with combinations. Many clung to the flannel variety (red, pink, blue or white, with embroidered flounces), while the more fashionable used quilted satin petticoats edged with lace, in winter, the evening garment being of silk lined with flannel. At the close of the decade shot silk with pinked flounces, of various colours, displaced the white once again, at least in the fashionable world.

Bust Bodice

An invention of '89 'of white coutil, laced front and back with bones on each side of the lacing, and worn above the corset,' was a device to support the breasts.

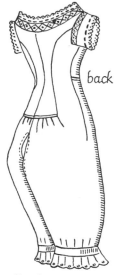

back

Combination garment
1878

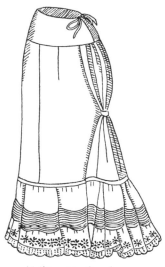

White Under-skirt
1880

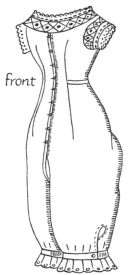

front

1878

Evening Petticoat
of muslin
1879

Train for Under-skirt
1880

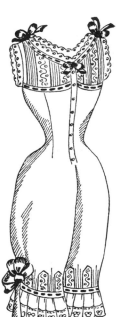

Combinations
1898

Fine woollen Knickers
1896

White nainsook Petticoat
1887

Bustles

It was reported, in '81, that 'tournures are coming back with a vengeance'. 'In addition to stiff muslin flounces under the dress there are now loops of the dress material, 10 to 12 in. in size, and lined with different colours, over the back width.' Others are of crinoline and red Turkey cotton, 5 inches above and 9 inches below, made of a series of small flounces with runners of whalebone. These buttoned on the skirt at the edge of the corset. They grew steadily larger so that in '83 'tournures are very much more modest in Paris than in England where they sometimes approach the ridiculous, not to say the indecent.' A long narrow and pleated bustle, under a petticoat flounced behind, was worn with a ball dress; a short bustle with a walking dress. By '84 the bustle was attached either to the petticoat or to the bodice, when a separate article, or else was introduced into the dress itself so as to hold up the puff at the back in the form of half-circles of steel. Next year the two steels (20 inches long with elastics sewn to each end by which they were drawn into a semi-circle) was supplemented by a horsehair pad, some 6 in. square worn above. The horsehair pad, often called a mattress, or its substitute the American wire bustle ('which answers the purpose far better'), declined in size in '88 and disappeared in the following year, being killed by the Empire style of dress.

Corsets

The long-waisted dress required, of course, a long corset, generally with some form of spoon-shaped basque and coming well down over the hips. 'These are now worn with the old-fashioned flexible steel busks in front and laced at the back because the front fastenings interfere with the set of the tight-fitting plain bodices' ('81). Early in the decade a high degree of elegance was obtained by the use of satin, silk and even brocade, in various colours; for example, a corset 'in apricot and peacock-blue satin', for evening ('86). For recalcitrant figures a leather-covered pattern or one with a leather band round the middle was obtainable which, we are assured, 'while rendering the waist perfectly unstretchable imparts a charming sense of comfort to the wearer.'

Nightgowns

'The latest idea in nightgowns is to carry the trimming entirely down the front to the hem' ('80). Gauging and frilling round the neck and lace ruffles and jabots were features of refinement, while in '83 'white silk is used for nightdresses and pajamas suits'. In '86 the latter is described as 'The combination nightgown or lady's Pyjama', requiring some four and a half yards of material, such as calico or flannel, and made in one in the form of combinations; these are to be frilled below the knee and at the wrists, with a high collar and buttoning down the front. In '87 nightgowns are described as: 'No longer simple garments but pretty and becoming; for example, made of soft pink silk with a Watteau pleat, a tucked yoke trimmed with lace, lace frill down the front and lace ruffles.' Or another 'of cream and pink washing silk with tucks down the front of the bodice, a sailor collar and open sleeves gathered up with ribbons. Coloured zephyr nightgowns (blue and pink

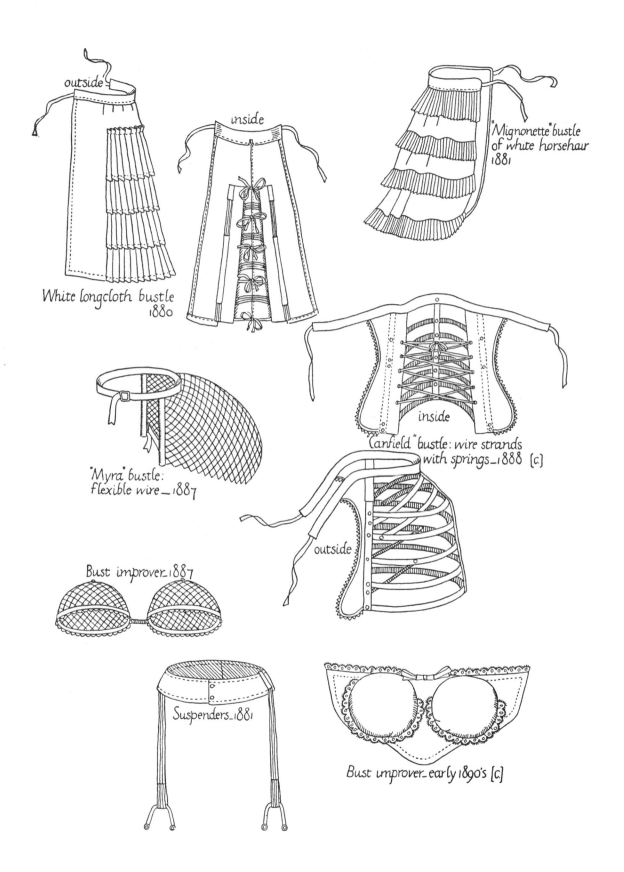

outside

inside

White longcloth bustle
1880

"Mignonette" bustle
of white horsehair
1881

"Myra" bustle:
flexible wire _ 1887

inside

"Canfield" bustle: wire strands
with springs _ 1888 [c]

outside

Bust improver _ 1887

Suspenders _ 1881

Bust improver _ early 1890's [c]

principally) are superseding white ones.' The high collar in '88 with pagoda sleeves and cascades of lace, and slight gathering at the waist to define, or rather suggest, a figure, were characteristic features; and 'delightfully cosy winter night-gowns of cream and pink flannel trimmed with lace and ribbons' ('89), together with sleeping jackets of the Nightingale form, in white or scarlet flannel which 'are a necessity when the chest is delicate', seem to imply a progressive advance in luxury. The Empire nightgown, in pink nun's veiling, gathered at the waist, and trimmed all down the front, with puffed shoulder sleeves and abundance of baby ribbons, the neck being quite low, was an innovation of '89.

The Camisole

This was high and close-fitting, for day, and with a 'V' opening for evening. Plain or edged with lace; at the close of the decade the inevitable baby-ribbon ornaments the top. Materials: calico, silk, wool.

Prices

('80) Merino vests, 1/6; scarlet flannel drawers, 3/11; scarlet flannel under-bodice, 2/11; combinations, longcloth, lawn or batiste, 10/6 to 25/-; merino combinations, 14/6. Princess petticoat, longcloth or cambric, trimmed with embroidery, for day use, 13/6; for evening, 25/-.

('81) Swanbill corsets, 14/6 to 21/-. Stocking suspenders, cotton, 2/9; silk, 4/3.

('85) Merino combinations, the luxury of the age, 18/9; of lamb's wool, 21/6; of silk, 33/6. Crinolette-petticoat, with 2 steels and cushion-bustle, 15/-.

('87) Collapsible spring bustle, 2/6.

('88) Handmade knickers, trimmed with lace, 5/11. Cambric chemise, Valencienne front, 9/11. Trousseau (Addley Bourne): 1884, costing £46, includes: 6 longcloth chemises, trimmed with embroidery, at 6/6; 6 ditto trimmed with insertion, at 10/6; 6 longcloth nightdresses at 10/6; 6 ditto, finer quality, trimmed, at 12/6; 6 longcloth combinations, trimmed, at 12/6; 6 pairs tucked drawers, at 4/6; 6 pairs trimmed drawers, at 7/6; 3 longcloth tucked petticoats, at 5/6; ditto, trimmed, at 12/6; 1 French petticoat, 21/-; 9 nainsook camisoles at 7/6 and 10/6; 6 merino vests at 4/6; 3 plain flannel petticoats at 10/6; 2 ditto embroidered in silk at 21/-; 1 white dressing-gown at 21/-; 1 flannel ditto at 31/6; 1 white flannel toilet jacket and 2 cambric ditto, at 12/6. Stockings, 12 pairs Lisle thread at 2/6; 3 pairs ditto, silk at 10/6. 1 doz. hemstitched handkerchiefs, at 2/-; 1 doz. ditto, coloured borders at 1/0½. 2 pairs French corsets, at 14/6; 1 crinolette, 10/6; 1 white satin nightdress satchet, lace trimmed, 21/-.

CHAPTER X
THE '90's

———

THE depression of trade which had overshadowed most of the previous decade now gave place to a revival, due in part to the mining industry of South Africa and the quick fortunes obtained there, and in a measure to more sentimental causes. The interest in Royalty, stirred by the death of the Duke of Clarence and by the marriage of the Duke of York, was roused to a high pitch of enthusiasm at the Diamond Jubilee which seemed to symbolise, in the minds of the nation, the very apex of commercial success and the leadership of civilisation. As so much of the nation's recently acquired wealth had come out of the soil of South Africa it was a just stroke of fate that it should have been poured out again on the same soil in the War which was to mark the end of the century. The economic effects of it, however, were hardly felt until the new century had begun.

The effects of such influences on English women were indirect; a more direct stimulus on their lives was the introduction of the safety bicycle which not only added enormously to their physical activities but helped very markedly to break down the conventional restrictions. The young woman on a bicycle perforce left her panting chaperon behind as she pedalled gaily towards the new century. She began to explore Man's world and to discover that the ferocity of the animal had been exaggerated; it was even possible to hold her own against his enormous intellect and to earn a living as his rival. The 'New Woman', who figured so largely during this decade, influenced, among other things, the current fashions, partly by her demand for physical freedom and partly by setting up a reaction, in the fashionable world, in the opposite direction. The movement, in which she figured so prominently, produced during most of the decade a style of dress at once aggressive and guarded—pugnacious in a prudish fashion. This spirit was grafted on to modes alleged to be 'Early Victorian'. The huge sleeves of 1830, deprived of their romantic effusion, became in the '90's side-arms defending the female who marched between. The distracting colours of the bodice, the vast revers that guarded the secrets of her shape, the inscrutable gored skirt, composed a sphinx-like figure of petrified virtue. It was a style essentially English; did it not solve the problem by the English device of denying its existence?

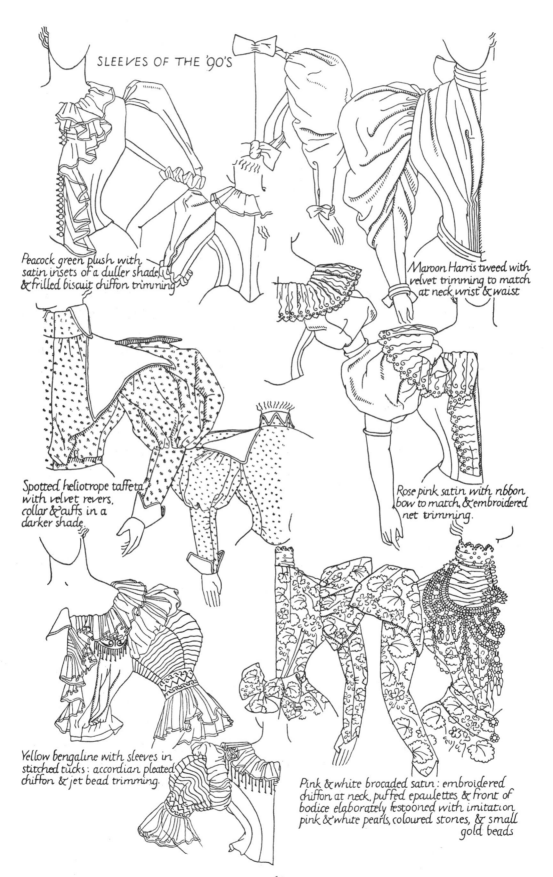

SLEEVES OF THE '90'S

Peacock green plush with
satin insets of a duller shade,
& frilled biscuit chiffon trimming

Maroon Harris tweed with
velvet trimming to match
at neck, wrist & waist

Spotted heliotrope taffeta
with velvet revers,
collar & cuffs in a
darker shade.

Rose pink satin with ribbon
bow to match, & embroidered
net trimming.

Yellow bengaline with sleeves in
stitched tucks: accordian pleated
chiffon & jet bead trimming.

Pink & white brocaded satin: embroidered
chiffon at neck, puffed epaulettes & front of
bodice elaborately festooned with imitation
pink & white pearls, coloured stones, & small
gold beads

It is the custom that whenever woman has made some notable advance into man's domain she will reassure him by adopting, for a spell, an ultra-feminine style of dress, and accordingly she marked the year of the Diamond Jubilee by reverting to the 'clinging' mode. The change was abrupt and complete. It was as though she wished to show that when woman is tired of climbing she clings. . . . While the discordant colours and extraordinary yoked bodices of this decade are the features which most readily catch the eye, it was in reality the skirt which displayed the greatest originality. The gored skirt, in its many varieties, together with the 'flare' and the stitched pleats, was a technical triumph which the '90's may rightly claim to have discovered. For goring was carried to a point never hitherto attempted; even more original was the device of cutting a skirt without seams and also the yoked skirt which gave a new shape to the lower half of the body.

On the other hand we find that there was a decline in quality of workmanship (except in specimens of the more expensive sort), with cheap substitutes in the less conspicuous parts and a singular indifference to the use of an inferior lace on costly materials. The best fabrics were remarkably good, especially the satins. It was a period when silk was revived for dressy occasions, while new woollens such as crepon, were largely employed for all the new outdoor activities. For such use the 'blouse and skirt' reigned supreme and became almost the hall-mark of the typical open-air Englishwoman.

Colours, until the change in '97, were violently discordant, especially in the upper half of the dress. Huge sleeves of one colour against a bodice of another surely indicated some hidden disharmony in the mental outlook. The hats, no longer zoological gardens, were now flower-shows mixed with museums where botany and geology fought for the mastery. If there was one colour which dominated this decade it was yellow, especially in the evening. It is not a colour which usually becomes blonde races but its use, in the brilliance of the new electric light, seemed to turn those tall smooth satin figures into pillars of gold, chaste caryatides in the temple of Mammon. . . .

Meanwhile an extraordinary revolution was going on beneath the surface, rumours of which—coupled with occasional glimpses—were all that was vouchsafed to man. For the first time in history underclothing became artistic, or at least costly without suggesting a moral stigma on the wearer. The use of lace was no longer confined to those bits which might be visible while the fashion for silk underclothing implied a breaking away from the Victorian creed that beautiful garments are a snare and have no other function.

This decade is also notable for the extreme degree of tight-lacing which flourished until near its close. Its purpose was somewhat different from that of former epochs; it aimed less at displaying the smallness of the waist than the size of the hips which became a leading feature of sex-attraction, only rivalled by the solid charms displayed by the extreme decolletage of evening dress. It is noteworthy that so eminent a physiologist as Professor Huxley believed that women, unlike men, did not use the diaphragm in breathing. In his day they could not.

The introduction, from America, of the long pointed shoe met the needs of the walkers but permitted the foot to enlarge far beyond the limits of the ladylike Victorian standard. It is significant that henceforth a small foot ceased to be a prominent feature of feminine attraction. Similarly the hand was expanding and the stock size of gloves grew accordingly. In fact, the rising generation of young women was definitely taller, and the fashions were now designed to accentuate height.

1890

'There is a marked difference between dress in England and Paris.' This was particularly noticeable in the day costume, the Englishwoman demanding a degree of simplicity which the Parisian regarded as evidence of bad taste. 'Simplicity should rule in the daytime, elaboration in the evening, and picturesqueness at all times. Perhaps never in the history of costume was there a wider latitude for the development of individual taste . . . we may adopt the Cavalier style with its deep full-skirted coats, long brocaded waistcoats and ruffles, or the Tudor with tight bodices, exaggerated hips and muslin ruffs; or the simplicity of the Empire period with its high waisted gowns and flowing drapery confined by jewelled girdles, or we may emulate our immediate ancestors in their flounced frocks and corselet bodices lacing down the back.'

Increasing activity in the day necessitated a more practical skirt and therefore a less ornamental one; consequently 'skirts are really so much alike today that they are scarcely worth describing'. The bodice was the region, all through the decade, wherein the emotions found a field for expression. Nevertheless the double skirt (in the form of an open Princess robe over an underskirt) retained its functions as a more dressy costume than the plain 'English skirt'. And imported specimens from Paris may be found which show the old elaboration of excessive trimming, etc., very unlike the native specimens. But in the main 'the enthusiasm with which the perfectly plain skirts were welcomed shows clearly which way English tastes lie'.

DRESSES

Day

Except in the summer the tailor-made dress, or at least its style, reigned supreme.

The 'straight English skirt', ankle-length, the fullness at the back either by gathering or flat pleats, the front and sides gored or shaped by darted seams 4 in. deep at the waist; thus the front breadth 22 in. at hem, 11 in. at waist with three darts, one in the centre, and one at each side, 3 in. apart; the back breadth 26 in. wide and gathered into some 4 in. at the waist; the side breadth 18 in. gored or darted at the waist. The front of the skirt may be perfectly flat or slightly draped above. To prevent clinging the skirt is lined with stiff material for 12 in. up. Often a pleated muslin balayeuse is inserted for the same purpose. In tailor-mades the bodice is usually a double-breasted jacket either open over a white or checked waistcoat or closed to the throat, with a collar and tie. Other bodices are the close-fitting, the cross-over and the yoked blouse. In these dresses the skirt and bodice are separate.

The 'seamless dress' is an innovation, for morning use; made of woollen material, the bodice having seams under the arms only and fastening on the left shoulder and side, the front slightly full at the waist, over a tight boned lining; the skirt with one seam down the centre behind.

The bodice and skirt in one: (1) A plain overskirt turned back to reveal an underskirt of rich material; the jacket and overskirt of one material; the underskirt and sleeves of another.

(2) The cuirasse style: the underskirt and sleeves of velvet, silk or cashmere, an overdress of different material open in front from waist to hem. The bodice fastened on the shoulders, the armholes trimmed with passementerie with flat points projecting towards the front. (3) The pinafore style (in striped woollens or silk): the back of the skirt, sleeves and bodice of striped material; the overskirt in plain, resembling in front an apron joined to the bodice, full at the waist and the upper part cut in a crescent back and front; a girdle worn round the waist.

Sleeves. (1) The gigot, either cut on the cross, gathered on the shoulder and buttoned from the elbow to the wrist; or cut on the straight, gathered on the shoulder and on to a wristband which reaches nearly to the elbow. (2) The accordion-pleated, from the shoulder to the elbow where the fullness is gathered into a close long cuff. (3) Plain sleeve with a wide over-sleeve often of different material, resembling an elongated puff to the elbow.

The French gigot sleeve is often pointed on the back of the hand (a style started by Sarah Bernhardt).

Sleeves are usually very high on the shoulder and mounted on a lining, but tend to come down during the year; likewise the fashion for sleeves of different material from the dress (e.g. of velvet) tends to go out.

The Zouave jacket, actual or simulated by trimming, the Toby ruff, of chiffon or lisse and made of two or three gatherings tied at the throat with ribbon, the linen collar and cuffs, are fashionable items of the year.

Reefer blue serge jackets with starched shirt fronts are much worn, owing to Royal patronage. 'Since the Princess of Wales condescends to wear this costume I suppose I must not say what is in my mind, but I will utter one protest by saying they are unbecoming and unseemly, as any imitation of man's attire must be for a woman.'

The tea jacket (replacing the tailor-made bodice at tea time) trimmed with lace, generally with Medici collar and Zouave front filled in with a waistcoat, is also worn.

Examples

'*Day Gown* of pale beaver cloth with Zouave jacket of a deeper shade of velvet, cloth gigot sleeves, deep velvet cuffs buttoned to the elbow; plain skirt with deep hem piped with velvet.'

'Day dress of black surah spotted with heliotrope; plain skirt, corselet edged top and bottom with jet passementerie pointed in the centre; sleeves plain heliotrope covered with black net and fully gathered at the shoulders' (Jay's).

'Tailor-made (Redfern's) of drab corduroy; the long bodice cut in square tabs with revers and tight vest buttoning down the centre; skirt boxpleated all round, the centre pleat being overlapped by the side ones.'

'Walking Dress of checked cheviot; plain skirt; $\frac{3}{4}$ length bodice with a seam round the hips and

A Liberty 'Empire' costume. 1890

square pockets; double-breasted with revers and plain tight sleeve gathered high into the shoulders.'

'Walking costume of printed pongee silk, ivory ground with heliotrope design. Sleeves and panel of a darker shade of velvet; the panel is partly formed also of pleated silk. Vest of another shade of heliotrope silk, outlined by tiny ivory buttons.'

'*Visiting Dress* of flowered bengaline trimmed with a Swiss belt in jetted gimp and deep lace cuffs. Bodice draped slantwise and adorned with lace frillings; similar lace edges the straight panel of the skirt in front. Between the square train and the side panels slashing displays the gauze underskirt.'

'*Afternoon Dress*, the full bodice and skirt of white silk gauze in fine accordion-pleating divided by embroidered insertions; the foundation of sulphur-yellow taffeta; sash and bracelets round the semi-short sleeve in Ophelia bengaline; pleated neck band in gauze.'

Another in soft China silk (black ground covered with chintz pattern) the bodice in green velvet covered with fine jet; green velvet sleeves high on the shoulders; high collar; pointed basque ending in a fringe.'

'*Teagown* of apple-green cashmere faced with white silk, cut en princesse with a yoke and front panel in one of black guipure on white silk; fastens invisibly on one shoulder and under the arm beneath the drapery. Pointed yoke behind into which a Watteau pleat is inserted. Full sleeve gathered into a deep cuff. The material of the dress is gathered into the yoke and confined below the waist by a girdle with long tassel ends. High collar rolled back in front.'

'*A Polonaise Costume* in mushroom-coloured foulé spotted with white; fastens on the shoulder and under the arm and is fully draped on the hips and across the chest. The full sleeves are gathered at the elbows into turned-back cuffs on white silk; high collar lined with white silk.'

'*Seaside Frock* of white foulard with white and pink marguerites and trimmed with laurel-green ribbons. Tight bodice lacing behind; sleeves gathered into double puffs by ribbons. Hips and edge of the skirt with a fine kilting 3 in. deep. High collar of kilting. Loose ribbon sash with long ends in front.'

'*Summer Dress* of washing material, the bodice full back and front, ending at the waist with skirt sewn on, the union concealed by a narrow band of velvet; no side seams. Lining fitting closely and boned. Pleated chiffon frill round the neck forming a cascade down the front; sleeves in five puffs divided by bands of velvet. The skirt, on a foundation which is bordered with a thick ruche, has a velvet band above the hem, and is caught up at either side into the waistband.'

'Summer dress of fawn cloth, the skirt opening over a front breadth of cream cloth embroidered in fawn and gold at the hem. Large sprays of embroidery start at the waist diminishing to a point. The full fawn cloth back is edged with three narrow rows of gold galon;

gigot sleeve full and high, trimmed with cuffs and ruffles. Behind, the bodice and skirt are cut in one; in front the bodice ends at the waist, the fullness drawn in through a buckle 7 in. long. Detachable cape with straight all-round collar and a frill, wide on the shoulders and narrow in front.'

'*Tennis Costume*, worn by a champion player; a black merino skirt with kilted flounce and insufficient drapery reaching three inches above the ankles; a grey jersey bodice with stiff collar band, the shoulder seam reaching almost to the elbow, and a blue flannel cricketing cap pierced with black-headed pins. What a strangely incongruous figure!'

'A few months ago a lady, wearing trousers, was seen riding at Bournemouth.'

Materials: cloth, tweeds and cheviots for tailor-mades; voiles, mohairs, fancy grenadines, surahs, foulards, mousseline de laine. Furs: Canadian beaver, Persian lamb, astrachan, moleskin, sealskin, blue fox.

Colours: 'A happy medium between art colours and the old standard colours.' Red fashionable in the winter; heliotrope of a pink shade, lichen green, blotting-paper pink, fawn; tartans and checks.

Evening
The bodice is staylike, ending straight across the front and under the arms, the puffed sleeve being added without apparently any connecting armhole. Bodice and train often in one, with a scarf of crepe de Chine from the right shoulder forming half of the bodice and tied on the left hip with a long end reaching the ground; the rest of the bodice of velvet or satin; much lace trimming. All bodices are trimmed on the shoulders with ribbon bows; or arches or jet work; or puffs of material; the sleeves often a series of puffs or as a handkerchief knotted on the shoulder, falling loose on the inner side of the arm, and then knotted on the outer side above the elbow. Frilled chiffon is much used as trimming. The low 'Empire' bodice with a broad sash and muslin bertha is also common. The Princess dress with Medici collar is fashionable. Ruffs are frequently worn.

Ball dresses: Made as flat as possible and with long waist; low bodice. Types of bodice: (1) The Court bodice, well off the shoulders, pointed back and front and laced up behind. (2) Empire bodice.

Sashes with fringed ends or wide ribbon belt with short ends. The skirts are diminishing in

1898

1891

1892. Ball dresses (Dickins and Jones)

Pale blue silk open over underskirt striped with satin and silk, and embroidered with pearls and sequins

Sea-green mirror velvet with velvet under-dress; sable edging

Empire style, of yellow crepe

size; no steels or bustles; generally accordion-pleated.

Dolman mantle of black velvet trimmed with passementerie. 1890

Ball dresses made of crepe de Chine, chiffon, satin, brocade or silk. Two colours are common, one over the other, *e.g.* pink tulle over green; red over grey. 'Sanitary ball dresses', with underbodice of cream or pink kid and a chemisette, to protect the chest, in convalescents from the influenza epidemic.

Examples
'*A Princess Dress* fitting the figure and falling

behind as a slight train; drawn slightly upon the hips into a pannier; open in a "V" to the waist, the opening trimmed with wired lace forming a Medici collar, filled in with a low under bodice of brocade matching the front breadth of the underskirt which is bordered by two lace flounces; sleeves puffed to the elbow with lace gauntlet pieces.'

'*A Tudor Gown* in chiné brocade, the bodice with small round velvet yoke edged with

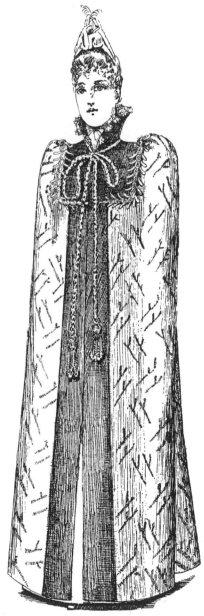

Circular mantle of grey blanket cloth. 1890

beaded passementerie into which the velvet is pleated. A velvet corselet pointed below to which the skirt is pleated. Sleeves puffed above and below the elbow with deep velvet bands.'

'*A Tudor Dress* of bengaline, the back en princesse, the bodice gathered on the shoulders, fitting tightly at the waist with kilted frills on the hips round which is a girdle of jet; the front panel and small waistcoat of brocaded velvet; sleeves with slashed puffs at the shoulders.'

'*An Empire Dress* of spotted white net draped over white satin. The bodice cut low front and back and edged with two deep frills of net with scalloped border, and crossed over to fasten under the arm. A deep flounce round the skirt with a pleated heading. Full sleeve edged down the front with frills.'

'*Dinner Gown*, a low Princess dress in pale green bengaline embossed with gold; open all down the front over a draped under-dress in rose du Barri crepe de Chine with lace flounces. This material also forms a kerchief edged with lace round the neck and the elbow sleeves. Pink satin bows at the elbows; the under-dress reveals a foot kilting of pink surah.'

'*Evening Dress*, the front of the skirt in accordion-pleated pale pink crepe de Chine; three rows of corded ribbon round the hem; bodice and back of pink corded silk with satin stripe; crepe kiltings edging the basque neck and full elbow sleeves.'

'Another of rich yellow satin with a white stripe, brocaded with floral pattern in silver thread; the front of the skirt covered with beaded white lisse bordered with embroidered flowers; full sleeves of beaded lisse drawn into the elbow; bodice draped with the embroidery on one side and lisse on the other.'

'Black evening dress in rich broché. Low square bodice with pointed basque, revers of white satin and front of black with design in silver veiled with tulle; tulle shoulder sleeve draped with a bird in silver on the shoulder. Trained skirt with tablier slightly draped. Side panel of black satin with design of silver birds under tulle drapery between revers of white satin.'

OUTDOOR GARMENTS

Visites with high collar, epaulettes and jet fringe. Long cloaks with high collars, often of velvet, and concealed arm slits. Many have yokes of embroidery or velvet and Tudor collars. Mantles elaborately embroidered, and often trimmed with ostrich feathers. All wraps except mantles are made to fit the figure. Waterproofs of shot silk, with or without capes, and arm slits. Winter cloaks, double-breasted, with crossing rolled fur collar, high shouldered sleeves with bell-opening.

Three-quarter length jackets with pointed flap pocket and crescentic upstanding collar.

ACCESSORIES

Shoes
With higher heels.
Black *Stockings* for day.

Gloves
two and four button, for day; twelve button for evening. Mousquetaire gloves, embroidered and scalloped, for walking.
Fur and feather *Boas*, especially white, short and long.

Gaiters much worn with walking dress.
Very small *Muffs*.

Parasols of chiffon or crepe de Chine, either puffed all over or kilted in two deep flounces. Handles of natural wood.

Jewellery. Ornamental pins, of moonstones and paste, instead of brooches. Moonstones very fashionable. Pendant watches set in crystal balls, hanging from the bodice.
'Buttons out of fashion; dresses are hooked, capes are clasped, jackets are frogged.'
Sleeve-tongs for drawing down the sleeve through the jacket arm.

Prices
Bengaline, 22 in. 2/-. Zephyrs, 9d. to 1/6 a yard. Cocks' feather boas, curled, 3 to 4 guineas; uncurled, 2½ guineas.
Diagonal serge (42 in.) 1/9; fine serge (46 in.) 2/6. Brocade, mother-of-pearl coloured, tinted with lace patterned wreaths of pink and black, 35/- a yard.

1891

'Hitherto Frenchwomen have set the fashion for Englishwomen as well as the women of the rest of the world; to-day all this leading by the Frenchwoman seems changed and all the fashionable world attire themselves à l'Anglaise.' The divergence of taste seems to have cut the dress in two; while the top half accepted the elaborate dictates of Paris ('all our bodices are very full in front and fussily draped and frilled') the skirt developed a plainness that was purely English in spirit. As a result, while the bodice caught the eye, and perhaps the man, it was the skirt in which the fin de siècle woman marched forward to emancipation, a progress in which the English and American woman led the rest of the world.

'Women's morning and country gowns are developing a distinct and separate type, the individuality of which is little affected by the whims of prevailing fashion'; in effect, while the evening dress was designed to charm, the day dress was designed for convenience. It is in the latter that we can detect the English influence which can claim, therefore, to be introducing an original feature in women's dress. It is the day skirt which makes the year 1891 a milestone of importance.

DRESSES

Day

'The greatest change of the year is the abolition, during the latter part of it, of the foundation skirt which has been worn for at least twenty years'; in other words, the underskirt is now replaced by a lined skirt 'which is easier to hold up, and more comfortable and sits better'. The linings may be of silk, alpaca or linen. Some are lined throughout; some with each breadth lined separately; some only lined for 10 to 15 inches above the hem, while with thick materials there may be no lining at all. The feature common to all is that they must not cling. For this purpose a balayeuse is generally used, together with a ruching or narrow flounce. All are plain in front and sometimes buttoned up on each side below the waist in place of a placket hole. The new types are: (1) The gored skirt, requiring $3\frac{1}{2}$ yards of material. Four to six gores may be used; dimensions, front 26 in. gored to $12\frac{1}{2}$ in.; sides, 15 in. gored to 10 in.; back $27\frac{1}{2}$ in. Ankle length for walking. (2) Umbrella skirt made of double-width material on the cross; by the best dressmakers this was made with one seam only down the centre of the back, concealed under a quadruple box-pleat, the skirt fitting tight round the hips by means of a few darts in front and at the sides. Less skilful makers used gores having lap-seams. The front should be 42 in. and the back 46 in. Usually no foundation but a silk lining. The slight train is fan-shaped, and the skirt is tied back inside. (3) The bell skirt, the front breadth fitted by darts, the others gored at the top only, the foot of the skirt stiffened by muslin lining. In addition to these new types the skirt with a 'foundation skirt' survived during most of the year as a more dressy mode, either with square

side panels or as a tight-fitting Princess dress open in front or at the sides. With this exception the bodice is always separate from the skirt.

Bodices with diagonal trimmings; draped; folded; with a yoke; with a corselet. These are usually with added basques of lace or material, some 10 to 20 inches deep, with the waist line defined by a band slightly pointed in front. Many bodices are 'seamless', fastening under the arm; those with only one dart-seam in front, but six seams behind and two either side of the front are most usual. The blouse with round waistband (especially in summer). The blouse (or 'Shirt') becomes very popular in the summer; some with lace cascades down the front, or with collar and Oxford tie. It comes down below the waistband outside the skirt, and is usually made of silk or lawn. Over it a corselet, boned, with attached braces is often worn. Corselets are round, square or in a 'V' at the top with the braces beginning at the waist; made of same material as the skirt and joined to it by a seam round the waist. By the end of the year the blouse does not show below the waistband, which is then slightly pointed. The jacket bodice with basques is also worn; this does not match the skirt, has flap pockets, gauntlets cuffs and is generally trimmed with metal galon. There are three forms of basques: (1) Louis XIV, long, cut in one with the jacket. (2) Louis XV basques gathered on at the waist (French rather than English mode). (3) Louis XVI basques added with plain seam at the hips. 'For wearing with open jackets, fronts made of chiffon gathered and attached to a high collar and falling in a deep plissé frill wide enough to cover the bust; the collar formed of bias folds of some thin material and worn over the ordinary dress collar.'

Sleeves: demi-gigot or close-fitting; with or without a high shoulder; the Italian sleeve, a full puff above the shoulder, thence tight to the wrist, often with a long gauntlet cuff, buttoned; the double sleeve (summer) a loose over sleeve half way down to the elbow over a long tight sleeve to the wrist.

'Jerseys are as popular as ever', many with Newmarket basques added.

Summer dress of rose pink foulard with broad stripe of white. 1891

The Princess dress is more dressy than the coat and skirt, although the tailor-made 'holds its own in spite of the machinations of the crafty Frenchwoman'. The Princess is close-fitting, either with draped bodice and tunic open in one side over a panel, or as a polonaise with coat revers, fastened across on one hip, the skirt open on that side revealing a panel. Some are made with small panniers, and waterfall drapery behind, or a fan-pleated train. The Princess is the principal form of double skirt which survives.

Examples

'*Costume* in black silk; Newmarket jacket piped with velvet; double-breasted with revers and flap pockets; plain skirt' (Redfern's).

'Costume in black and white striped vigogne; gored skirt edged with black ostrich feather trimming; Louis XV coat bodice edged with feathers; high shoulder sleeves; mousquetaire cuffs; high collar; cascade of lace' (Jay's).

'Costume in brown Bedford cloth; trimmings of beaver; cut diagonally in the new style, the left front being cut long en princesse partly overlapping the right, whence it is draped round almost to the back and carried into the side back seam of the skirt which is gored and slightly trained. The back of the bodice is sufficiently deep to join into the basque with which the sides are trimmed. Italian sleeves; turned down collar. Fur heads the top of the deep hem, the basque and the diagonal front of the bodice. Seven yards of material required.'

'Costume in drab material with fancy design in silk; bodice with draped silk vest edged from the shoulders to below the waist with a full lace frill; silk sleeves; lace flounce edges the basque and the bottom of the skirt' (Redfern's).

'*Visiting Dress* in turquoise blue pongee silk; skirt slightly draped in front and arranged in fan-pleats behind; gathered to a pointed bodice; sleeves and epaulettes of a similar silk; square yoke with straight collar and upper part of sleeve in guipure over blue silk; bows on shoulders.'

'Visiting dress of amethyst satin merveilleux trimmed with three folds of mauve bengaline displayed on each side of the cuirasse bodice and extending on the fourreau skirt as two straight panels, slashed and richly embroidered with gold and amethyst beads; front belt to match; feather trimming round the neck, armholes and wrists.'

'Visiting dress of pale blue de laine opening at the side of the skirt to show a panel of spotted surah; waistband, slightly pointed, of green velvet. Italian sleeves with velvet band at the elbows and surah cuffs. Surah chemisette above a drapery of delaine which is drawn into the point of the waist; velvet shoulder straps.'

'*Travelling Dress*, a pale reseda surah skirt bordered with a ruche of ostrich feathers, long coat bodice cut in tabs; vest of pale rose chiffon lined with silk; Medici collar trimmed with ostrich feathers.'

'*Afternoon Dress* is violet diagonal cloth; plain

gored skirt slightly trained; corselet of black satin with tie bows down the centre; full puffed sleeves of pale violet satin banded with jet passementerie.' (Jay's).

'Day Bodice of light woollen worn with plain costume skirt; the back of the bodice with a single pleat in the centre; the front with three pleats from each shoulder to the waist; small velvet vest almost hidden by gathered frills of surah; upper part of sleeve gathered very full and puffed upon the lower portion; straight collar faced with surah.'

'*Summer Dress* in cornflower blue foulard printed with half moons; the new polonaise fashion, the fullness of the bodice drawn in at the waist and descending thence in a double box-pleat to the hem; undersleeves of dark blue velvet apparently drawn over the silk sleeves and slit up to disclose a shoulder puff of foulard; a "V" shaped vest of velvet.'

Evening dress of striped pekin, black and coral. 1891

'*Seaside Costume* of rough diagonal serge; the plain skirt cut on the cross at the back. Semifitting jacket ¾ length, with rounded collar diminishing to the waist and edged with narrow gilt braid. Full blouse tucked under the waistband, of heliotrope surah shot with blue, which material lines the jacket. Oxford tie.'

'Dress of thick olive green armure; the tight bodice, swathed at the waist, fastens down the back and is cut slightly low round the throat: outlined with a band embroidered in gold silk displaying an inner chemisette of gathered silk in pale gold. Skirt, full round the hips, with a rope girdle of green and gold. Long oversleeves of the monk shape with knotted ends; the inner sleeves, gathered to the waist, corresponding with the chemisette.' (Liberty's).

'Liberty *Teagowns*, the backs with double box-pleats and very high collars; the skirts frequently caught up at the side to show the underskirt.'

'The *House Dress* (developed from the teagown) is trained; brighter in colour and richer in material than the ordinary day dress; and closer fitting than the teagown; teagowns can be worn without stays but not the house dress.'

'*Bathing Dresses*, of serge, the bodice and short trousers in one with tunic attached to a belt.'

Materials: The fashion is for rough materials, bouclé cloths and corduroy, together with broad chevron stripes; trimmings of braid, embroidery or ruching at the hem, long fringes from the waist coming to a point in front. Summer materials, especially printed delaines, cottons, with Pompadour sprigs. More silk is used, such as bengaline and surah (with spotted and Japanese patterns) and shot silks.

Colours: a noticeable fashion for semi-mourning colours (black, grey, heliotrope) during the first half of the year, following the winter epidemic of influenza.

Evening

'Corselets and Swiss belts are one of the dominating features, and they are sometimes replaced by bands of ribbon coming from under the arms. Long trains generally distinct from the gowns usually accord with the bodice or corselet. Full puffed sleeve or draped with ribbon bows on top.' A common feature of the bodice is the fullness in front drawn over to one side. It is usually laced behind and either in the form of a long-waisted Medici bodice or round Empire shape. Huge fichus and jabots are worn with high-necked evening dress, and often tuckers with low. A lace flounce round the bottom of the bodice is a feature. The skirt, of the bell or umbrella shape, is trimmed at the

A gown of foulard with festooned flounce of lace. 1891

bottom with embroidery, ruching or a flounce and frequently covered with spangled net. The Empire style of evening dress has a tunic with square opening above and open below over an underskirt. 'The new Mitten sleeve, of lace, etc., fitting the arm closely and reaching the knuckles, for dinner and theatre dresses.'

Examples

'Evening Dress of white satin shot with peach.

A plain gored skirt embroidered in design of peach blossom, the design carried halfway up the right side of the skirt. On the left a panel of peach-coloured velvet. Bodice in folds of velvet and bands of embroidery. Deep basque cut square and embroidered sleeves moderately high.'

'Evening dress of black silk gauze embroidered in heliotrope with lovers' knots, mounted over heliotrope satin and trimmed with gauze edged with narrow fringe; bodice, ornamented with black and heliotrope twisted ribbons, is drawn in to a point at the waist, being cut low above; sleeves a full puff on the shoulders.' (Peter Robinson).

'Cuirasse Bodices or Swiss belts made of jewels, with long glittering fringes, worn with tulle or lace skirts over soft silk underskirts.'

'*Dinner Dress* of heliotrope bengaline striped diagonally in front with jewelled insertions. The right side of the low bodice, with epaulette sleeves, is in white chiffon set off with velvet bows; the left side is in heliotrope bengaline.'

'Dinner dress in rich crimson and black broché, trained; low bodice, the deep "V" draped with folds; epaulettes; skirt with side panels.'

'Dinner gown, the train of yellow satin with pale green and pink true-lovers' knots with very long ends. Long ribbons from the shoulders. The front of bodice and skirt of yellow satin trimmed with jewelled embroidery mixed with topaz and pink opals; bodice draped with tulle.'

'Dinner dress, the underskirt of apricot bengaline brocaded with heliotrope pansies; the slightly trained overskirt, open in front revealing a tablier, is of heliotrope silk. Sleeves, partly of the brocade with the upper portion of velvet, are elbow-length with ruffles. Bodice and high collar trimmed with heliotrope guipure; bodice and tablier edged with cord or velvet; round the waist a folded scarf of silk tied on the right with long ends.'

'*Ball Dress* in white broché with train. Pointed bodice, cut very low, is trimmed with passementerie of silver spangles, pearls and beads. Puffed shoulder sleeves of chiffon. A tablier of net embroidered with silver beads, pearls and spangles; skirt festooned with chiffon at the bottom, caught up with pink roses and foliage.'

OUTDOOR GARMENTS

The Tudor cape, 'a circular pelerine in embroidered cloth lined with plaid surah; pointed yoke front and back, with Medici collar in velvet; upright pleated epaulettes in bengaline.' These high shouldered, high collared short cloaks, often in colours and studded with jet or jewellery, are immensely popular. A variety, the Henri II cape, has unlined sleeves the fronts of which hang loose; in another a loose oblong piece hangs between the shoulders.

The three-quarter length cloak and mantle with high collar and frill; the Henrietta jacket, three-quarter length, lined with quilted satin or merv, the deep collar extending down the loose fronts, are also fashionable.

ACCESSORIES

Gloves

Day. Of suede, shorter to suit the long sleeves; 4 button. White gauntlets for garden parties. Evening. Very long, even 20 buttons.

Shoes

Day. Laced boots, of kid or grey tweed with patent leather caps. Or shoes. Evening. Gilt leather; black satin with jewelled toe caps; butterfly bows.

Stockings. Day. Generally black, but sometimes striped in colours.

Large ostrich feather *Fans*.

Much *Jewellery*, especially turquoises, worn.

Prices

French beiges (44 in.) 1/4½ to 1/11½; Bedford cord (44 in.) 2/6½.

Teagown of brown vigogne with salmon silk sleeves and front, 3 guineas. Teagown in plum plush, the front of pink silk, lace collars and cuffs, 7 guineas. 'It is possible to spend as much as 80 guineas on a teagown without wasting money.'

English chevrette gloves, 3/6 a pair.

Cheap silks (24 in.) 2/6 to 3/-, for dress linings, some made to rustle to suggest a silk foundation. 'Modern fashions show more taste, tact and exquisite elegance than they ever displayed at any former period.'

1892

'Last year the picturesque crept into our raiment; this year it dominates it. Hats, cloaks, dresses, are all picturesque, and if sometimes, in our desire for the picturesque, we overstep the narrow line which borders the sublime from the ridiculous, we are, after all, quite unconscious of the fact. We flatter ourselves that in no period of history was ever costume so beautiful and more reasonable than it is now.'

The year was spent in a contest of styles. In Paris, we read, 'the struggle between the costumiers and the fashionable ladies continues; the former wish to impose the Empire style on their customers who refuse to adopt them'—preferring the modes of 1830. The English genius for compromise devised a combination of the two. Messrs. Worth, in Paris, and Liberty & Co., in London, were the champions of the Empire style, each claiming to have evolved it in its modern form. But the general inclination was towards broadening the shoulder line by huge sleeves and pelerine lapels of 1828–30 in order to suggest a small waist. 'The average waist is now 22 in.' but tight-lacing, producing waists of under 16 inches, was not uncommon. Indeed, the essential feature of the current modes was the small waist, making a revival of the true 'Empire style' with its high waist impracticable. Picturesqueness seems to have been synonymous with a pinched-in middle. The English yearning for the fashions of 1828–30 was stimulated by the Guelph Exhibition held this year. The strong Russian influence, imported from France, may be ascribed to the Entente between France and Russia.

The technical features of the year are principally a lengthening and enlargement of the skirt with more trimmings, to impart a more feminine appearance, and the huge sleeves, generally of startling coloured velvet, on the evening bodice. It may be noted how the strong Gothic influence overcame the Classical even in the so-called 'Empire' dress. And that while borrowing the sleeves of 1828 there was no attempt to cut the bodice off the shoulders. 'Picturesque Prudery' was the result. There was a constant dread of displaying the body; the gored skirt rigidly concealed the shape of 'the limbs'; the frills and yokes disguised the shape of the bosom; the startling sleeves served as red herrings. It was, in effect, a revival of the structure but not of the spirit of 1828. There was no Romance.

DRESSES

Day

Types of bodice: (1) Shaped as a corselet with full top. (2) With long basque behind (the coat-tail back) which is rounded off at the side seams. (3) With a blunt point in front and moderate basque behind, the front being in full

Cambric shirt. 1892

folds. (4) Slightly pointed back and front, finished by a folded sash with bow on one side; the shaped band of the skirt may be trimmed instead of the edge of the bodice, and hooked over it. (5) 'Empire' bodice, with wide revers of different material and Empire sash and round waist. The frilled revers (a revival of the 'pelerine lapels' of 1828-30) expand over the top of the shoulder. These kinds of bodice, being in

part at least of the same material as the skirt, may be classified as 'Costume bodices'.

The 'Blouse and Skirt' dress also has varieties: (1) Blouse with single or double frill down the front; often with simulated Swiss belt composed of close-set upright tucks. (2) Blouse fronts with deep waist and neck-band of chiné silk. (3) Cotton blouses, some with separate basques attached to a band, for wearing outside the skirt; these basques may be knee-length and so resemble a short overskirt. When worn with a coat the short blouse is inside the skirt band. (4) The Russian blouse, full front and back with long round basque added; opening on one side; worn with a belt. Often with large revers. The sleeve, a full puff to the elbow with gauntlet undersleeve. Frequently the gigot undersleeve is used instead.

The 'leg-of-mutton' sleeve now coming in for day use, is usually made with one seam on the inner side; measuring 8 inches round the wrist and 20 inches at the armhole, the fullness being gathered in a space of 5 inches beginning in the front, 7 inches above the seam under the arm. Some are box-pleated into the armhole, the effect being to produce great width at the shoulders without extra height. The purpose was to diminish the apparent size of the waist. 'Nothing could be more becoming to the figure; the waist looked infinitesimal.' To sustain the illusion the waist frill has now disappeared.

Skirts. Except the short skirt for walking, which may be 2 inches off the ground, the day skirt is now semi-trained, fuller and longer. The umbrella skirt is seldom less than $4\frac{1}{2}$–5 yards at the hem; generally lined with silk and stiffened at the bottom with horsehair lining for some 10 inches to keep it out. The 'Empire' skirt, for wearing with short round bodice, required four yards of 48 in. material; composed of two straight pieces for front and back without seams, the back piece being 3 inches longer. Two triangular gores for the sides. The 'Cornet' or 'French' skirt has a seam on each

1893. Costumes
Of dark petunia ondine silk; green velvet epaulettes
Of black ondine silk; vest of pink shot velvet covered with chenille network

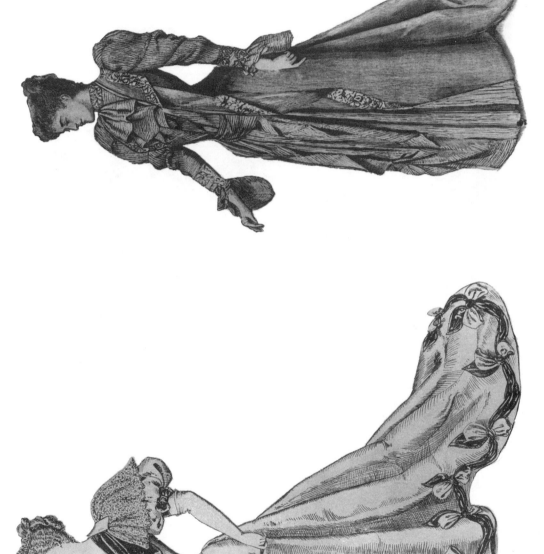

1891. Teagown (Dickins & Jones) of pink silk with chiffon draperies; the revers embroidered in mauve, green, and pink

1893. Dinner dress of pale mauve duchesse satin; fichu folds of Eminence mirror velvet

side and is generally slightly trained. The front piece is slightly gored (40 in. diminishing to 20 in.) with darts at the waist; the back piece, cut on the cross, is in one piece, gored (20 in. diminishing to 10 in.) the train being a segment of a circle. No foundation skirts are used. Some skirts go over the short bodice and are cut up into a point front and back. Others are trimmed with hanging bands ending in tassels. Ruching round the bottom, or two or three bands of narrow velvet above the hem, recall the modes of 1828–30. A tendency to draping of the front is seen towards the end of the year when also the train is found intolerable in muddy weather and is given up for walking skirts.

The tailor-made costume tends to be less masculine in cut. Thus, with a plain skirt, a deep pointed Swiss belt and braces, with open coat showing a fancy shirt and tie. Or with an Eton jacket. 'When the future historian writes of the fashions of the 19th century it is to be hoped he will award a due measure of prominence to the open coat style for surely no other mode of the time has proved so popular nor enjoyed that popularity so long.'

Visiting dresses are more elaborate, often with side panels, a flounce, or made en princesse with simulated jacket fronts and revers.

The short Zouave or Figaro jacket is a notable feature of the year.

Examples

'*Tailor-made* in dark grey mixed cheviot, the skirt trimmed with rows of black military braid; Eton jacket open over double-breasted waistcoat with revers of navy blue; sleeves demi-gigot; linen collar; Oxford tie.'

'*Travelling Dress* in check Harris tweed; a three-quarter coat opening over a pointed waistcoat of blue and white Tattersall which also forms the narrow cuffs; revers of unspottable velvet; sleeves closed at the wrist by silver mess buttons.'

'Travelling Dress of chestnut serge; the bodice with Zouave outer trimming of damask, the rest of the bodice in full silk folds; gigot sleeves; plain trained skirt with sash belt of wide moiré ribbon' (Lewis & Allenby).

'*Walking Dress* of grey-blue cloth; bell skirt with slight train; cord edging; tight undervest edged with cord and Hussar jacket with high collar and large revers braided Hussar-fashion; close-fitting sleeve.'

'Russian Blouse of shot wool poplin lined with rose shot silk; nearly three-quarter length, with cuffs, collar and belt edged with stamped gilt leather.'

'Costume in art muslin with frill round the skirt; full bodice with broad sash of green Surah; sleeve full to the elbow and gauntlet cuff; frilled wide fichu of India muslin' (Liberty & Co.).

'*Morning Costume* in dark heliotrope shot rep, with yellow, green and pale heliotrope stripes; trimming of Russian embroidery; bodice folding across; a short round basque; sleeves puffed above with gauntlet from the elbow' (D. H. Evans).

'*Riding Costume*, a habit coat with close fitting back like a man's; the front single or double-breasted; over a waistcoat of horsecloth, open above to show collar and tie' (Tautz & Co.).

'Half-Mourning Costume of a woollen velvet; violet ground striped with thick lines of grey, white and black; sleeves of violet looking-glass velvet; the consoling influence of such a costume could not fail to be great.' NOTE: 'There has been a decided stand against wearing crape for some years past, but the Princess of Wales gave it the *coup de grâce* by dispensing with it during her mourning for the Duke of Clarence.'

'*Teagowns* with Princess backs, sleeves high on the shoulders; with yokes and capes of lace which begin and end in an indescribable manner.' Teagowns tend to have Watteau pleats and lace pelerines, full sleeves to the elbow and thinner ones to the wrist.

'Teagown in grey crepon with long Watteau pleat; very full sleeve of ivory Surah tucked to form a deep cuff; full front of Surah tucked closely in the form of a Swiss belt; high collar of tucked Surah' (Pontings). Teagowns tend to be replaced by tea-jackets.

'Tea-Jacket of heliotrope velvet, close fitting, with transparent yoke of jet from which fall deep flounces of black net. Full puffed sleeves with deep frills' (Jay's).

'*Wedding Dress* of ivory Duchesse satin with long train. The skirt edged with ruching; Empire bodice with ceinture of folded satin. Broad fichu of guipure; high satin sleeve with deep lace gauntlets. Tulle veil and orange blossom wreath.' 'Wedding veils should fall in a point over the face and have the fullness drawn back on either side with jewelled pins.'

'*Bridesmaid's Dress* of cream canvas over satin; deep sash of pink moiré. Lace yoke falling over pink chiffon; band of cream ribbon between the

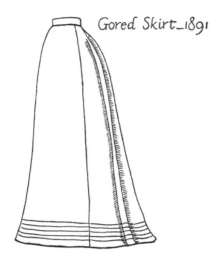

Gored Skirt_1891

Umbrella Skirt_1893

Bell or 1830 Skirt
1893

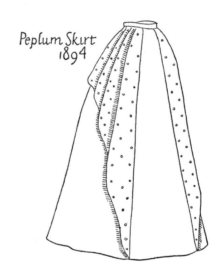

Peplum Skirt
1894

Seven gored Skirt
1895

Flounced Skirt 1898

ruches round the skirt; demi-long and puffed sleeves ending in lace.'

Bathing Dresses. An American lady is surprised that English bathers do not wear black stockings as worn in the U.S.A. for mixed bathing. 'You have no idea how decent they make the whole proceedings.'

Materials: A great revival of silks for day wear, and the popularity of crepons and shot silks were notable; silk increased 12½ per cent. in price. Russian embroidery much used. Grenadine and foulard for light materials. Rough tweeds and cheviots for tailor-mades.

Colours: 'Simplicity as far as colouring is concerned is seldom thought of.' Combinations of brown and petunia with shades of green; Oriental mixtures; blue, green, deep red and yellow are frequently combined. Fawn and green, blue and green, turquoise and mustard, green and pink, violet and red. Magenta is once more fashionable.

Evening

The notable feature is the huge sleeves, generally of velvet differing in colour from the dress. The opposing styles, 'Empire' and '1830', are either distinct or blended. The low bodice is never 'off the shoulders', and is discreetly veiled with lace in bib or fichu fashion or with immense folds resembling the old 'bertha-pelerine' or 'pelerine lapels'. 'No fashionable gown is tolerated without velvet sleeves of preposterous size.' A certain number, however, have very long pendant sleeves of gauze and some low bodies have long close gauze sleeves. The Empire bodices have 'short waists' (simulated at least by the deep sash) and sleeve of one large puff set in a band. The deep waistband is secured by a long narrow gold buckle. The trained skirt has a silk balayeuse. The Princess dress is common with simulated bodice fronts.

'Ball dresses have the skirts severely plain with bodices calculated to display the charms of a good figure to perfection.' The bodice is no longer very long, and the junction of bodice and skirt is hidden by flat trimmings. No waist frills. Skirts, lined with silk, have a silk flounce instead of a balayeuse. Crepon is much used instead of tulle. Sleeves with upright velvet epaulettes over the puff.

Examples

'*Dinner Gown* of dark blue velvet with bodice and sleeves of pale pink satin; Empire belt and panels in gold and Indian embroidery.'

'Dinner gown of green velveteen with short-waisted bodice covered with tracing of yellow silk and laced down the front across a full underbodice of pale yellow silk patterned with green. Round the shoulders a deep frill of velveteen resting on a huge puff of the same which forms the top of the soft silk sleeves. Plain skirt gathered right round the skirt with a Watteau pleat from the shoulders' (Liberty & Co.).

'Dress of heliotrope silk embroidered down the front and left side with pearls and opalescent beads; chiffon flounce; on the right a white lace cascade. Bodice with the new fluted front surmounted by full frill of chiffon. Chiffon knots on the arms, the sleeves being continued on the back of the arms only.'

'A dress in black satin, en princesse, trimmed with spangled tulle festooned round the skirt above the hem. The "V" opening of the bodice is draped with tulle. Large puffed shoulder sleeves of velvet.'

'Dress of old-rose bengaline. Plain skirt with two narrow folds of velvet of a deep rose tint. Bertha of velvet with frills of coffee-coloured guipure and square velvet capes over the full sleeve of bengaline. Guipure tucker. A narrow fold of velvet finishes the short pointed bodice.'

'The skirt of broadly striped pink and white satin interwoven with silver pattern. Round the shoulders a full cape of pink bengaline edged with fringe and drawn into the waist beneath a wide belt of silver passementerie, falling in two long fringed scarves over the skirt' (Howell & James).

'Dress of pearl satin shot apricot. Tight bodice with folds of mushroom coloured velvet brought under the arms to tie in front in a knot, in which is fixed a spray of chrysanthemums. Puffed sleeves of shot velvet with ruffles. Bertha and epaulettes of embroidered net and guipure' (Debenham & Freebody).

'Dress of white brocade patterned with pink roses. The front of the skirt is cut into a pointed corselet with full folds tucked inside it, of pale green satin. Long train of the satin and a short jacket front gathered round the armholes to form a frill on each side. Underbodice of embroidered net run through with green ribbons. The tops of the sleeves of the brocade, with tight transparent sleeves to the wrist' (Debenham & Freebody).

Materials: heavy materials (brocades, satins, bengalines) are preferred.

Colours: 'The mixture of colours now so conspicuous' may be gauged from these instances: 'yellow silk draped with scarlet chiffon and scarlet velvet sleeves. Pink satin with emerald velvet; black and white satin with pink velvet sleeves. Dark red striped velvet with pink yoke.' Peach, straw, turquoise, eau de Nil are commonly used.

'Autumn cape, full gathered, in black velvet shot red, outlined by jet passementerie and edged with Mongolian goat; thick Elizabethan ruff bordered with fur' (Peter Robinson).

OUTDOOR GARMENTS

The large sleeves, as in the early '30's, compel the use of cloaks and capes which are sleeveless. Three tiered capes; three-quarter cloaks with yokes and Watteau pleats. Russian circulars, or 'Talmas', reaching the ground, with deep velvet cape and lace pelerine. Pierrot cape, three-quarter length, with shoulder cape and satin pierrot ruff. Henri II cape, hanging in a loose square from the shoulders.

'Mantles are distinguished by their pronounced ugliness ... these loose-backed atrocities. ...' The use of the pointed Watteau pleat from the shoulders, and a taste for long ribbon streamers from the shoulders are features.

Covert coats with sacque backs and jackets in the style of the Russian blouse are worn with tailor-made costumes.

Examples

'Tailor-made sacque-back coat, three-quarter length, of green cloth, double-breasted and edged with fur; collar, lapels and cuffs faced with drab cloth; sleeves lined with silk.'

ACCESSORIES

Day *Stockings* black, embroidered in colours. *Muffs* small or large. *Parasols* of shot silk and chiffon with frilled edge. Dress fasteners of a metal clasp with cord to the waist.

Jewellery. Chrysoprase fashionable for brooches and cuff links. Necklaces of fringe patterns; dagger brooches; expanding bracelets. *Watch* worn in a pocket in the belt; also sometimes pinned to the front of the bodice.

Plush teagown in myrtle green with canary poplin front trimmed with wool, 3 guineas. Moreen for petticoats guaranteed to produce rustling, 2/9 a yard.

Woollen opera cloak, lined silk, with embroidered cape, 3½ guineas (Peter Robinson). Liberty's velveteens, 3/11.

Corduroy (44 in.) 3/3 a yard. Ribbed corduroy traced with silk lines (52 in.) 7/-. Bouclé cheviot (42 in.) 2/-. Skunk muffs, 15/9. Astrachan muffs, 21/-. Shot surahs, 2/6 to 3/9. Bengaline, 2/9. Moiré, 2/3½.

1893

'There is a struggle for precedence between the Empire and the Victorian eras', but the victory of the latter became obvious during this year. There were several reasons why this should have been so; the innate Gothic taste of the race, the sympathetic interest towards the Royal family evoked by the marriage of the Duke of York to Princess May, and the known affection of the Queen for the modes of her youth, all encouraged an 'early Victorian' revival. In its details the fashions of the year seemed actually to be based on those of 1830–1834 rather than on those of a few years later. From a somewhat aggressive note the mood changed until by the end of the year dress had become distinctly sentimental, softened by feminine frills and furbelow. During the first half of the year (when new modes are 'tried out') the skirts expanded so enormously that the dreadful arrival of the crinoline was hourly expected. But by the summer the alarm had abated. 'The extremely wide bell skirt did not take in England as it did on the Continent as the Princess of Wales declined to have any made for her yachting trip'—or, possibly less exalted women were declining to buy them; and by the autumn the skirt shrank back to its former dimensions. Meanwhile fashionable taste was summarised by contemporary writers thus:

'Women's dress this season is principally remarkable for its exaggerations and aggressiveness in form and colour.' 'It is impossible to look on fashions of the present day with approval; could anything be uglier than the outlines of the woman of to-day with her arms as wide as her waist, her hat as high as her body is long, and her skirt obtrusively disproportionate to any line of nature? Her main object appears to be to look round-about; round and round go the stripes of the skirt, her waist is encircled by hoops, while fullness is everywhere where it should not be. Could any fashion be more hideous than the shaded silks? Why should a woman want to look like a rainbow?' On the other hand while the fuller skirts had their brief reign it was urged that 'nothing could be more ungraceful and almost immodest than the sheath-like skirts we have been wearing until the last few years'.

Fashion could not arrive at the ideal skirt, one which would permit of physical activity while concealing physical structure. The voluminous but flimsy 'early Victorian' skirt did neither; how to adapt it to a more refined utility was the perplexing problem. 'The fin de siècle women do not look well in the fashions of their grandmothers, and the sooner they drop them the better.' But, in fact, they did not; they simply stiffened them. The gored skirt, lined with crinoline material nearly up to the knee was far removed in spirit from that of the early '30's, while the bodice with its startling contrasts of colours drew attention away from the nether regions.

DRESSES

Day

There are many varieties of skirt but they comprise two main types in construction: (1) gored, the front seamless and slightly gored, with three to five side gores, the seamless back breadth cut on the cross and the hem 3½ to 4 yards round. A footing of stiff muslin or crinoline some 9 inches deep as lining. (2) Of double width material, cut in a circular shape, the hem 5½ to 6 yards round. The former is often called the 'gored bell skirt' and the latter the 'Victoria' or the 'Grannie' or the '1830' skirt. In both the fullness is at the back. The 'Victoria' skirt has the new feature that the material stands away from the knee level. During the first half of the year this expansion leads to a fear of the crinoline's being introduced. This kind of skirt is much more trimmed than formerly, and flounces, tucks and bands are much used.

In the shaped flounced skirt there is no foundation, but canvas stiffens the footing under the flounce, which is cut on the cross.

By the autumn the double-skirt dress appears, the overskirt reaching just below the knee. This may be simulated by the deep basques of the coat-bodice, or be an actual overskirt made in one piece cut in a circle.

The single skirt has circular trimmings, such as bands and galons, round the lower part, with perhaps ruching at the hem—reminiscent of

the modes of the early '30's, and the seams are often defined by narrow trimmings. The hem is often faced with a velvet band instead of braid. The effect of these various devices is to keep the bottom of the skirt well away from the feet. The pocket, when present, is behind, by the placket hole. The bodice tends to be basqued, the basque being gored and made separately so as to flare. The principal feature of the bodice is, of course, the sleeves which resemble, in varying degrees, the many forms seen in the early '30's. The general tendency, however, is for the huge puff now to fall more limply over the upper arm. The original 'leg-of-mutton' shape is modified as in a puff ending abruptly at the elbow with a close sleeve to the wrist (known as the Victoria sleeve); or by slashing, gauging at the shoulder, modifications of the bishop sleeve, Garibaldi sleeve, etc. The fullness, in fact, is nearer the elbow (imitating the style of 1835 rather than 1830).

The fashion for the bodice to contrast with the skirt encouraged the use of the blouse. This, usually made over a tight-fitting lining which often was boned, had many forms, *e.g.* 'the new crossing blouse, the skirt fastening over it. The back is cut in one and slightly full with gigot sleeve, the under and upper portion of which are cut in one, very full on the shoulder and tight at the wrist. Front of bodice, fully gathered on the shoulders and at the neck, cut on the cross with a long pointed end like a half-handkerchief crossing in front, passing to the centre of the back where the ends are tied. Three yards of material needed.'

Other blouses with frilled fronts or fronts drawn and fastening on one side; or accordion-pleated, and many with short basques worn outside the skirt, the waistband of folded material with a bow in front or behind.

The sleeves are always full, frequently of the same colour as the skirt; some ballooned at the elbow with a deep frill above and another below.

The pelerine appears as a flat cape on the shoulders and many blouses have 'the new sleeve capes', while costume bodices have wide revers extending like pelerines over the shoulders, or Zouave fronts with wide revers. The corselet front is also used.

The huge sleeves require as much as $3\frac{1}{2}$ yards of material for a pair, and we are told that 'they must be pulled *out*, not *up*'.

'Trim built tailor-mades are quite out'; these are now tempered by trimmings; the skirt may have a few bands above the hem, the bodice with a trimmed front, a crossed vest or a Figaro jacket, the waist-line marked by trimming. The tailor-made is now, in London, only worn in the morning.

Summer dresses, of thin materials, have frequently double or treble skirts or have flounces up to the waist. Owing to the fine summer there was an outburst of flimsy dresses and light colours. The gayer note seemed to begin early in the year. 'When Spring comes women begin to exercise their minds as to what they are to wear to be in the fashion and show off their charms', and the royal wedding in June ensured a brilliant Season.

'Everyone may wear garments of any period or none provided they have big sleeves and revers or frills on their bodices. One of the ambitions of dress just now is the rustle. Nowadays it is not sufficient that all our clothes, meriting the least consideration, are lined with silk, they should also be *stitched* with silk.'

Examples

'*Walking Costume*, the skirt of dark blue velvet with two cloth panels edged with gold canvas worked in coloured wools; short bodice turned back with revers to show a tight cloth vest; over this a Zouave; puffed velvet sleeves to elbow with cloth gauntlets to wrist.'

'Walking dress, a purple velvet blouse over-hanging a wide belt, skirt of chestnut brown cloth trimmed with black gimp; this combination of colours is very successful.'

'Walking Costume in golden-brown camel's hair cloth; double-breasted coat-bodice with deep added basques. Envelope revers of black moiré. Vest of old rose; gigot sleeves; plain skirt.'

'Tailor-made in brown ribbed cloth with square tablier draped over brown velvet panel. Cloth bodice with full basques and revers; brown velvet vest; high collar; cloth sleeves' (Nicholl's).

'Spring Costume in fawn vicuna; skirt in three divisions each edged with dark fawn velvet; bodice with deep revers extending in a point over the shoulders; full gigot sleeves with gauntlet cuffs; cream satin jabot with large bow; velvet waistband' (Peter Robinson). (The revers may be 'in the form of the Victorian bertha with vest and stomacher'.)

'Costume in glacé hopsack; bell skirt with galons at the knee; Zouave with shoulder cape combined; full vest; gigot sleeve in fancy shot silk, peach and green; collar and waistband in Oriental galon' (Dickins & Jones).

'Costume in fancy grey crepon flecked with turquoise blue; double skirt each trimmed with two bands of dark blue velvet; bodice of turquoise surah covered with guipure and bands of velvet outlining a Swiss belt; full sleeve in looking-glass blue velvet with lace gauntlet' (Dickins & Jones).

'Dress in navy-blue hopsack, the skirt trimmed with tucks to above the knee each bordered with pipings of buff velvet. Bodice of yellow and blue fancy foulard turned back at the throat to show a jabot of blue chiffon; the drapery is crossed at the back over small basque ends and fastened at the side of the front with a fancy button' (Swan & Edgar).

'Noah's Ark gown for girls; of cloth, the bodice without darts; gathers of skirt drawn to the back as much as possible; back of bodice seamless and the front gathered and cross-over with velvet revers. Large puffed sleeve to elbow thence tight to wrist. Trimming of several bands of velvet above the hem; two rows round the waist and round the wrist and collar.'

'Morning Summer Dress of brown Holland, the gored skirt piped up the seams with black moiré; bodice with pointed moiré band and stiff pointed revers of moiré; chiffon bow and jabot; large gigot sleeves of Holland' (Jay's).

'Summer, on the river, serge skirts, open jackets and crossing shirts of every hue.'

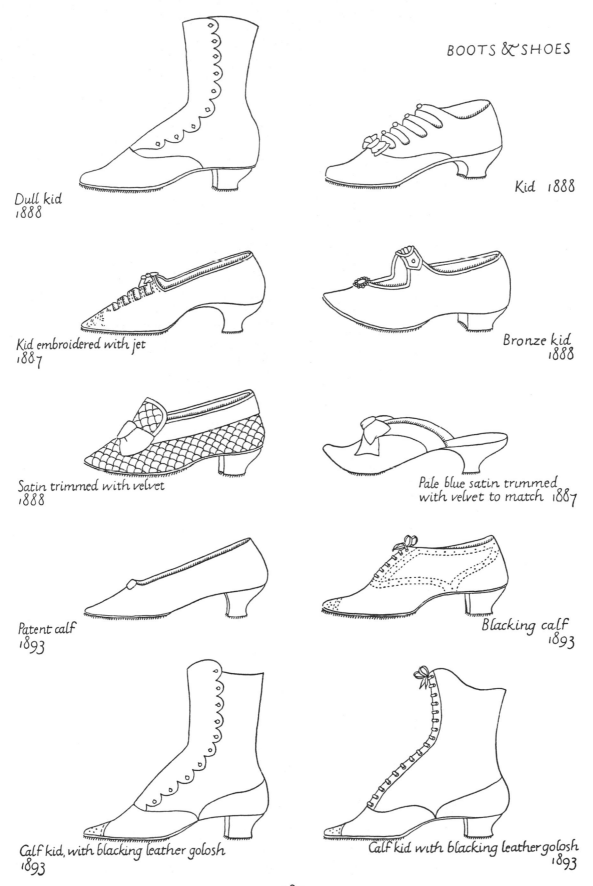

Dull kid
1888

Kid 1888

Kid embroidered with jet
1887

Bronze kid
1888

Satin trimmed with velvet
1888

Pale blue satin trimmed
with velvet to match 1887

Patent calf
1893

Blacking calf
1893

Calf kid, with blacking leather golosh
1893

Calf kid with blacking leather golosh
1893

'*Race Dress* in fawn cloth; coat bodice with strapped seams; deep collar and revers faced with velvet. Double-breasted waistcoat of butcher-blue drill. Large pearl buttons; bell skirt trimmed with two straps of the cloth.'

'Ascot Dress of pale butter-coloured canvas with cream satin ribbon; full bodice with écru lace bib falling from the bust and caught on the shoulders with rosettes. Full loose Garibaldi sleeves. Skirt with five flounces to the waist.'

'*Garden Party Dress* in foulard striped with pale green fading into heliotrope and flecked with black. A deep and narrow flounce; bodice with cross-over fichu in chiffon and lace, fastening at the side with buckle. Full sleeve with double puff; large epaulettes and deep gauntlets' (Derry & Toms).

'Garden Party Dress of soft white silk with heliotrope pin-point spots; double skirt, both accordion pleated and edged with numerous rows of heliotrope baby ribbon. Accordion-pleated bodice, sleeves being large puffs of accordion-pleating to the elbow where they were confined by baby ribbon and thence close-fitting to the wrist.'

'*Golf Suit* of drab covert cloth; bodice a belted Norfolk jacket with deep yoke; full sleeves with wristbands. Plain skirt just covering the ankles. Tam-o'Shanter' (Redfern's).

'*Teagown* of white Liberty silk in accordion pleats from a deep yoke of pale blue broché, broché sleeves to elbow and thence in finely gathered cream silk. Embroidered hem.'

'*Going-away Dress*, the skirt of prune-coloured cloth trimmed nearly to the knees with graduated frills of velvet. Velvet bodice with wide revers and vest of pale blue silk; cream lace jabot. Large bishop sleeves of velvet.'

'Going-away Dress, en princesse, in pale blue cloth; sleeves and under revers in castor velvet; upper revers in castor satin. Blue chiffon vest puffed through jet bands. Jet trimming down the front of the skirt, which is edged with sable tail' (Russell & Allen).

Materials: hopsack, shot materials especially shot crepon with silk warp, matelassé, delaines, delaine sateens, brown Holland, white muslin and cottons, foulards, were specially fashionable. Moiré is much used for facings, etc.

Colours: 'Bright colours in vivid contrast signalise the dress of to-day.' Thus, almond green and peach pink; blouse, lilac with green frill, or green with black, lemon with blue and pink, navy serge skirt and gold and red blouse; the new colour Eminence is very fashionable.

Evening

Bodice usually round-waisted with large sleeves. Skirts stiffened from the knee by a lining and about $5\frac{1}{2}$ yards round. 'Seven yards of material is not too much for a dinner gown.' The feature of the bodice is the lace fall, some three yards gathered round the shoulders and standing out over the sleeves. Or the front may be covered with accordion-pleated chiffon or with net falling from the bust to the ground. The neck opening is usually square cut, with shoulder straps. The large puffed sleeves tend to be replaced by deep full frills. Dress fastenings are concealed, either back lacing or bodice

Dinner dress of pale mauve duchess satin. 1893

1893

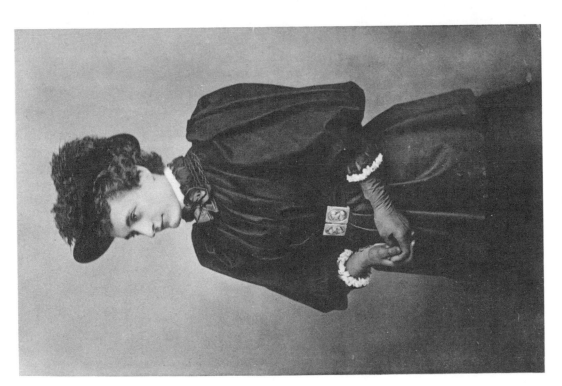

1891

1894

Coat and skirt of summer tweed lined with scarlet silk; revers faced with
black moiré

Short mantle of net covered with jet and steel beads

Costume of navy blue serge; trimmed with wide black braid edged with scarlet

Golf cape with straps, lined with plaid

and skirt attached, the bodice having side fastenings. The fashion for accordion-pleating may be ascribed to the craze for skirt-dancing, established by Loie Fuller.

Examples

'Gown in apricot satin brocade; skirt open in front over embroidered white satin; tabbed basqued bodice with sash and vest of cream satin; muslin fichu; full sleeve tied with ribbon bow at the elbow' (Liberty & Co.).

'Dress of white satin with tunic of pale pink chiffon, accordion-pleated, cut into deep vandykes; bodice covered with the chiffon, the square opening edged with falling lace; white satin shoulder sleeves in loose folds under chiffon. Bunch of roses on the left shoulder' (Jay's).

'*Dinner Gown*, the train of heliotrope shot grey bengaline with turned-back panels edged with jet. Tablier of straw-coloured moiré and scalloped black lace flounce. Straw-coloured jetted vest and heliotrope revers edged with jet and black lace. Puffed sleeves of the moiré with jet bands at the elbows' (Shoolbred's).

'Dinner dress in rose-pink figured moiré. Skirt edged with fur and slightly draped at the waist. Bodice with revers of reseda velvet covered with cream lace. Rose-pink chiffon vest drawn down in the centre by a rosette. Velvet sleeves in a double puff to the elbow' (Dickins & Jones).

'*Ball Dress* of pale blue silk over yellow silk; full skirt with three little ruches of blue silk over frills of guipure. Full bodice cut square and low with bands of guipure; puffed shoulder sleeves' (D. H. Evans).

'Dress for Skirt Dancing, the skirt of accordion pleated chiffon with rows of narrow satin ribbons between the pleats.'

Materials: The return to favour of black satin (known as 'sticking-plaster dresses') and of moiré are features. Soft gauzes, crepon with floral patterns, brocades and a lavish use of lace and chiffon.

Colours: brilliant mixtures, such as yellow and blue or cherry; yellow and Eminence; mauve and light green; steel blue and pink; pink and cerise; burnt sienna and emerald, the bodice contrasting with the skirt.

OUTDOOR GARMENTS

Mantles with wide shoulder capes and huge elbow sleeves. Some with loose Empire fronts attached to yokes and puffed elbow sleeves.

Short jackets with fully pleated capes starting below the revers.

Golfing circular capes with two straps buttoning across the front. Waterproofs of Burberry's waterproof material (the outer surface gabardine, and the inner a soft woollen tweed).

Autumn three-quarter jackets with capes reaching nearly to the knee, sloped full sleeves or bishop sleeves. Autumn pelisses, completely enveloping the figure, fitting round the hips without creases; wide revers and a prominent fur collar; shoulder cape; full sleeves.

ACCESSORIES

Jewellery. 'Hearts are very popular at present.' Narrow bangles and chain bracelets. Safety pin brooches. Single stone rings. French jet. Bracelet and safety-pin watches. 'Nearly every smartly dressed woman wears a lorgnette.'

Flat *Boas*. *Muffs*, some large and flat ('granny muffs'), some small with frilled ends.

1894

Fashions change but do not always progress; the attempt, on the part of Parisian designers, to regain their old ascendancy inspired the double-skirt, while the English taste inclined towards the single. 'Nine women out of ten cling tenaciously to the plain skirt', at least for ordinary use, while the more elaborate form was confined to 'dressy' occasions and the ultra-fashionable. Both types were increasing in size, and panels and trimmings were common features in smart costumes. Far more interest was being paid to the upper half of the dress; here again we can detect a struggle between the designer and the customer. The ready-made blouse, which could be worn with a variety of skirts, was the dressmaker's anathema. 'All the dressmakers are crying out against the continued popularity of the blouse', which was used in a host of forms both for day and evening.

A retrospect at the end of the year states: 'We cannot say that anything new or original marks the year. Bell-shaped skirts, Valois capes, Eton jackets, gigot sleeves, Greek coiffure surmounted by Rembrandt or sailor hats, form a heterogeneous but not unpleasing mixture. Lace is much used and sleeves have increased during the year so that a well-dressed woman can scarcely enter straight through a doorway.'

The spirit of the day is expressed by the remark: 'To be tall and thin seems to be the aim of every woman', and high heels and tight-lacing were useful allies. For desperate cases a 'skin-tight seamless bodice of black kid' is recommended. 'Women of ample proportions have accepted this new bodice with avidity.' The enormous sleeves, creating the illusion of a small waist, the gored skirt restraining the generous impulse of the hips, the bodice of distinct material and poster-like colouring, all helped.

DRESSES

Day

The blouse, worn with a plain skirt, has innumerable forms, generally worn over the skirt with a short basque over the hips. Some have gathered yokes and shoulder frills; others as an

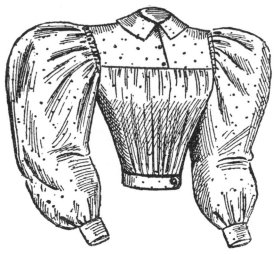

Morning blouse. 1894

open coat bodice showing a shirt front; or with simulated Zouave fronts; others trimmed with lace insertion across the front; others with draped, gauged or loose fronts. Many have the fronts almost hanging over the belt. All have close-fitting linings, often boned. The sleeves are huge, either of the gigot type or with elongated puff to the elbow and thence close to the wrist, or immense bishop sleeves, or double puffs. A large butterfly bow at the throat or at the back of the neck, and ribbon streamers from the shoulders or waist, are common features. The smartest have bodice and basque

of guipure with large silk sleeves, and, in fact, become indistinguishable from bodices. A belt and buckle is worn, and a gold safety pin at the back of the waist to keep the blouse and skirt together.

The costume has sleeves and skirt of one material and bodice of another. The bodice, often resembling a blouse, has wide shoulder capes or frills; frequently with back or underarm fastenings, and is lavishly trimmed with lace, jet, etc. Many are of chiffon, accordion-pleated; others with drapery across the bust, confined in the centre by a rosette or with a fichu or Zouave front. The huge sleeves, which now droop from the shoulders, are 'twice as large as those worn last year', and, like those of the blouse, have a multitude of varieties; ribbons round the elbows, or dividing the puff into two; box-pleating machined down from the elbow to the wrist; some gathered down the front seam and pleated into the armhole. In place of a blouse a shirt of muslin or linen with lace insertion, or with box-pleated front or tucks and linen turndown collar and cuffs, is worn under an Eton jacket, close fitting to the waist with inside belt and moiré revers.

The skirt: The single form: the back breadth organ-pleated at the waist; the front breadth with a ripple frill along the hem; two seams, one on each side, requiring $5\frac{1}{2}$ yards of double width material. Or with plain front, two side gores, full back and 'falling in graceful folds'. Or made to button down the sides. Or with front and sides gored and back plain, mounted on a band, with three box-pleats at the back lined with muslin. Or set in pleats all round, from just above the knee to the hem, tight round the hips; the hem, which may be 5 yards round, is bordered with fur, treble piping or passementerie.

Summer skirts, full at the back with a little fullness across the front and hips, are greatly expanded at the hem; some cut with front breadth on the cross and back breadth straight; others vice versa; or with gores; or 'cut out of two circles one joined to the bottom of the other . . . the lower circle is set on without fullness.'

Double skirt: The underskirt in box-pleats set on to a top portion of silk lining, which is concealed by the upper skirt: the 'yoke underskirt'. Or a short upper skirt cut in a perfect circle with a hole in the centre the size of the waist. 'Being in one piece it does not increase the size of the waist.' (Popular with tailor-mades.) The 'Angel overskirt', with two deep points on each side. The Panel skirt, the upper skirt two inches shorter than the lower and open on a full length panel (*e.g.* of velvet) on the left side.

The Peplum overskirt, a drapery of fancy material, pleated from the back and carried in graceful ripples to the hem along the seam of the front breadth. The underskirt, with narrow gored front breadth, side gores and back; lined. Requires 4½ yards of plain and 2½ yards of fancy material (double width).

Others have simply an overskirt two inches shorter than the underskirt, the former slightly draped at the side. The double skirt style tends to disappear by the autumn.

Examples

'Tailor-made Eton jacket of black cloth with black moiré revers and close-fitting vest of hopsack; check tweed skirt buttoning down one side; draped belt.'

'*Day Dress*, the skirt of purple zibeline; bodice of dahlia satin; turquoise blue ribbon round the neck; hat two shades of purple with pink flowers and black wings; sealskin coat lined with pink; a brilliant success!'

'Blouse in pale pink surah; yoke of cream insertion surrounded by deep frill trimmed with insertion; deep basque' (D. H. Evans).

'Lilac moiré skirt; pale blue chiffon bodice; cream embroidery vest.'

'Costume of myrtle-green hopsack shot with black; cerise velvet yoke; guipure panel; deep folded sash; huge sleeve to elbow, thence close gauntlets. High collar' (Swan & Edgar).

'Costume of bright blue cloth, the skirt with panels of orange satin covered with jet and black chenille; bodice covered with the same. Blue velvet sleeves' (Peter Robinson).

'Smart *Visiting Costume* in rich crimson satin striped with black moiré, bodice of accordion chiffon of same shade with back of black guipure; embroidered in jet and steel sequins. Similar embroidery in draped blouse-fashion in front. Elbow sleeve, sash, cuffs and collar of the chiffon.' (Barker's).

'Dress of Tuscan silk crepon, the overskirt caught up to show underskirt of green brocade strewn with pink marguerites; the draperies

Princess teagown for a matron, of crepon and lace. 1894

piped with black. Back of bodice close fitting; the front as a Zouave showing green brocade waistcoat and large lapels of black satin.'

'Elegant dress in black and pink fancy check very small. Skirt cut round in vandykes, edged with ball gimp and jet, over moiré flounce with moiré bows. Pointed panels of black moiré. Bodice (round waist, no belt) with moiré braces and epaulettes over very large sleeves.'

'Smart Frock of spotted black crepon; the bodice trimmed with jet and open over petunia velvet. Collar also of folded velvet. Moiré waistband with butterfly bow behind. The new gigot sleeve caught in the centre with jet, opening over velvet at the wrist. Long overskirt edged with jet and slightly caught up on both sides at the back with moiré rosettes and long ends to show the velvet and jet-trimmed skirt' (Derry & Toms).

Lace trimmed crepon teagown (Messrs. Harrods). 1894

'*Afternoon Gown*, the accordion-pleated bodice of sea-green crepon with slanting straps of écru insertion edged with black satin. Small cape edged with écru; skirt slightly draped showing underskirt with rows of trimming.'

'*Teagown* of blue satin covered with large bunches of yellow roses; sleeves in two puffs;

back en princesse with large butterfly bow at the waist.'

'*Garden Party Dress* of shot chiné silk; square overskirt of heliotrope faille bordered with lace and black satin rouleaux, a corner of the overskirt being in front. Bodice of chiné with yoke and revers of lace and rouleaux. Sleeves closely gathered to the wrist, slightly puffed over the shoulder. Epaulettes of faille in folds; belt to match' (Peter Robinson).

'Garden party dress of pale rose crepe de Chine; skirt with cascades of black lace down each seam; flounce of crepe de Chine with narrow ruching of black lace. Full bodice with lace Zouave. Large gigot sleeve ruched down the outer side. Folded collar with bow behind' (Woolland Bros.).

'*Ascot Dress* in eau de Nil crepon; plain skirt full and fluted behind, with three large bows and ends of cream ribbon halfway up the seams in front; bodice covered with cream lace and puckered velvet.'

'Goodwood Dress in maize crepon with small green spots; plain gored skirt; bodice in accordion-pleated crepon; deep folded waistband in green Surah, drawn from under the arms. Full kilted sleeves; green silk waistband' (Redfern).

'*Tennis Costume*, two inches off the ground, of serge lined with check silk (glimpses of which would be revealed as she trips hither and thither), cut in one with the corselet which has narrow shoulder straps and laces down the back, thus precluding all possibility of a glimpse of petticoat or staylace—secrets which are frequently seen revealed—check silk shirt; large turndown collar and turnback cuffs.'

'*Golf Suit*, the skirt of tweed buttoning down each side with three buttons; sleeveless coat cut away in front and lined with scarlet silk; scarlet shirt with white spots; large turn-down collar.'

'*Bicycling Costume*, knickerbockers so full that they lack all indecorous suggestion, pleated round the waist and gathered into a band below the knee; long gaiters; Norfolk bodice ending at the waist with belt, revealing a shirt and tie at the neck.'

Materials: cloth, crepon, hopsack and a marked increase in the use of silk, especially moiré (for details such as revers) and chiné silks. Chiffon much used, and Courtauld's new silk crepe.

Colours. 'Every lady nowadays can be seen afar off.' 'The loud and gaudy mixtures of bright colours are disappearing. What lovely colours we use now!' Black and white is fashionable.

Evening

'In fashionable theatres low gowns are generally seen in the stalls but many of the best dressed women in winter wear high dresses.' The waist is round, generally with square opening. 'A low dress which is too low is as unbecoming as it is vulgar; to bring the neck and shoulders into an obvious prominence is not only to overstep the borderland of good taste but to bound into the plains of indecorum.'

The swathed bodice (reminiscent of the former 'Empire sash') is common. Some have the 'full baby bodice'; a lace fall across the bust is often used. A noticeable feature is the evening blouse, with low square neck, shoulder straps, wide lace fall reaching over the shoulders, short basque and belt with bow. A certain number of Princess dresses are seen. Large bows are frequently attached to the bust. The sleeve is smaller than formerly; sometimes a series of wide frills instead of a puff or in the shape of a large bow (a puff caught up with a strap inside and out), or the 'mushroom sleeve' (the material cut down the centre of the width and pleated round the armhole in a deep frill with lace frill below), or a large gathered puff.

The trained skirt has the seams outlined by trimming or with a lace peplum, or side panels outlined by cascades of lace and similar devices to increase the apparent height of the wearer.

Examples

'*Dinner Dress* of pale heliotrope silk with tablier of canary satin, each side of which is an undulation of white lace. Bodice of heliotrope silk over one of heliotrope velvet, the latter forming a corselet; the silk bodice is drawn across the bust from each side seam and fastened in the centre; sleeves of canary satin puffed to the elbow, with vandyked wings.'

'Dinner dress, the bodice in cornflower blue velvet covered with eyelet holes the size of sixpence and threepence pieces edged with jet through which the yellow satin foundation clearly shows; yoke of puffed yellow chiffon and lace insertion. Huge sleeves with chiffon rosettes; satin sash; full skirt of black satin' (Barker's).

'Dress of pale blue spotted chiné silk, patterned in mauve, pink and green; bodice, dragged in the front, fits without seam behind, the decolletage outlined with cream lace drapery tied in a bow in front with a falling end under the belt of heliotrope velvet. Plain skirt set out into three mounted pleats from the waist behind. Sleeves large puffs to the elbow, thence tight to the wrist.'

'*Ball Dress* of satin or moiré; embroideries on satin or velvet outlined with pearls or spangles; pendant fringe; chiffon bodice with small sequins; sleeve a huge bow round the armhole or drapery of chiffon.'

Some ball dresses of net with small kilted flounces to the waist.

Golf cape. 1894

'Ball dress in very pale pink grosgrain edged with small pattern in cerise; skirt with draped panels edged with pink chiffon ruching and cerise satin rosettes. Swathed bodice of electric blue velvet ornamented with cerise bows. Square neck of drawn pink chiffon; sleeve a puffed frill of chiffon under vandykes of grosgrain; throatlet of cerise velvet' (Barker's).

Materials: chiffon, grenadine, chiné silks, moiré, velvet, satin and brocades, are the principal.

Colours. The courageous mixtures may be seen in the following: pale pink satin with red and pink ribbons and blue, mauve and pink hyacinths. Peach moiré with orange puffed sleeves;

pink and blue; green and pink; two vivid tones of heliotrope; black and white; lilac and pale blue, etc.

OUTDOOR GARMENTS

The long pelisse with full skirt, close fitting at the waist and with cape or wide revers and epaulettes; the visite with double capes, short pleated skirt and long ends in front; the jacket with turndown collar and long basques; cape mantles cut on the round, 'decidedly fussy on the shoulders' with frills and double ruffs; cloth travelling coats strapped at the waist. There is little change from existing modes except for the increased size of the sleeves, and the taste for huge butterfly bows on the shoulders.

Materials: caracule is a fashionable fur; Burberry's gabardine, moiré silks, faced cloth and velvet.

ACCESSORIES

Jewellery. The Peridot comes into fashion.
Painted gauze *Fans*, frames of pearl, ivory or tortoiseshell. Feather fans of uncurled ostrich feathers still used. Also black satin. Large *Muffs* with neck chains. Ostrich feather *Boas*, three yards long; fur boas.
'Fashion has decided that the poor little birds are still to be sacrificed for our hats and bonnets.'

1895

Pursuing the desire to exploit the small waist to the uttermost Fashion continued to expand the sleeve and now was driven to preserve some sort of balance by expanding the skirt. This had been the logical sequence in the '30's and was repeated in '95. It was an attempt to recapture the Gothic charm but it lacked the essential ingredient of harmony. The modern woman, physically active, mentally prudish, now displayed in her raiment a nervous lack of assurance, shown especially in her colour sense. 'The vivid colours worn by fashionable people are startling.' By less fashionable folk the colours worn were garish mixtures obeying no rule. A contemporary laments 'the mad folly of present fashions. The majority are uncomfortable, unserviceable, inartistic and unbecoming. The fashionable skirt seems to be made of a series of gores like an umbrella half open and wired at the edge to form a series of folds. Sleeves become larger and larger and are stuffed out with eiderdown or stiffened muslin or small steels. Our skirts are entirely dissimilar to the large full bulging bodices which resemble pouter pigeons . . . we are wearing extensive collars which closely approach to capes; they reach to the arms and in front are often cut up into sections. Scintillating buttons and tawdry finery of unreal stones seems to appertain more to the final scene of a Christmas pantomime than to the habiliments of a modest English lady.'

The prudish dread of anatomical features, balanced by the natural desire to use the bicycle produced a problem which exercised the minds as much as the fashionable machine exercised the limbs. The great question of the day was, in a word, had women legs? The Frenchwoman in huge Zouave knickerbockers emphatically demonstrated that her limbs were unrecognisable as such, while the Englishwoman still clung to the illusion that she was formed like a tree. Innumerable designs of bicycling costumes were put on the market, the principle underlying them all being indicated by the advice: 'the amplitude of the skirt is all important; if it is too scanty then the ankle is unduly exposed and the rider loses some of her femininity.' Another laments the new craze: 'It is a pity that women insist on bicycling; it is not an exercise intended by nature to exploit to the best the outlines

394

of the feminine form divine.' Such quotations are very significant; they reveal the doubt distracting her mind and betrayed in the disharmony of her fashions: should the 'New woman' break away from the traditional pose—a 'divine illusion'—and become a two-legged creature with all its advantages and disadvantages?

DRESSES

Day

1. The Tailor-made coat and skirt. The short coat is basqued in undulating fashion (the basque usually cut in one with the bodice and often absent in front), with accentuated lapels and revers. Some fasten with a single button; others are double-breasted. 'Strapped seams are done to death.' The skirt is wider but 'not in the French fashion of widening at the feet'.

blue; eau de Nil and grass green; blue and pink on heliotrope. 'The mixture of colours is most marked.'

The skirt. There are many variations, all gored, lined and stiffened with horsehair; from 4½ to 6 yards round.

(i) The Marie Antoinette skirt; seven gores; one in front; two at each side, and two at the back in box-pleats; requiring 5½ yards of 44 inch material.

Afternoon blouse. 1895

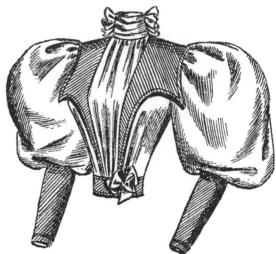

Blouse. 1895

From four to six yards round. Navy and butcher-blue, green, brown and fawn are the fashionable colours.

2. The Blouse and Skirt. The varieties of blouses are enormous, one shop advertising fifty. The front is usually full and somewhat pouched so as to hang over the belt. An innovation is the front box-pleat. The frilled front is becoming less used. All are made over a tight lining; worn inside the skirt, with a belt (often spangled). The size of the sleeve is 'monstrous', requiring 2½ yards of material; the huge puff is often double, or gathered in bands, or gauffred; either close-fitting from the elbow or as a wide bishop sleeve to the wrist.

Materials: Any light material, especially silk; embroidery insertion is much used.

Colours: Frequently a mixture, such as black and light yellow on pink; pink and brown or

(ii) The eleven gore ripple skirt, all gores very narrow at the top, hanging in flutes. Hem 6½ yards round.

(iii) Circular skirt with back gore and upright tuck pleats at the hips and back. Hem 6 yards round.

(iv) Directoire skirt, seven gores, the four at the back fluted.

(v) Tucked skirt; a large box-pleat in front with the side fullness tucked on the hips. Requires 5 yards of double-width material. The back pleats stiffened to the waist with horsehair.

Godet pleats at the back and sides, often with a fine steel in the hem, give the requisite fluting effect to the fashionable skirt. Inside the fluted skirt is 'a labyrinth of black elastic to keep the flutes in place'.

3. The Costume. The bodice may resemble the blouse, or is made as a short jacket. The jacket

may be open over a waistcoat. The blouse-bodice may be slightly draped on the bust, buttoned down the front with 'the everlasting three buttons', and slightly pointed at the

Garden-party dress (Peter Robinson). 1895

waist. Or with an open 'V' neck and a fichu. Wide embroidered collars reaching out over the shoulders, the size of large lampshades, together with collars with high neck; yokes, and lace edgings across the bust are usual.

The skirt in its various forms has already been described, as worn with the blouse; dressy skirts are usually lined with silk of a contrasting colour. Wide sash ends depend from the waist, and wide bows are worn at the back of the neck

and waist. Trimmings tend to be vertical to increase the apparent height. Thus, stole ends may hang from the bust to the knee level; or velvet or satin bands trim the seams of the skirt. For winter, trimmings of narrow bands of fur.

Examples
'Costume of cloth with velvet bands from the waist to the knees ending in rosettes.'
'Costume: blue silk skirt, the front gores flowing open at the feet forming inverted box-pleats, and closed at the hips with jet passementerie. Blue silk blouse-bodice covered with black net striped with fine beads. Sash of violet velvet with large bow in front. Sleeves of blue silk with oversleeves of violet velvet; velvet collar.'
'Costume in blue cloth with gold embroidery marking the seams of the skirt, which hangs in fluted folds. Bodice with pointed vest of green velvet; deep velvet revers under the sleeves which are puffed to the elbow and tight to the wrist with fur cuff. Epaulettes of embroidered velvet edged with fur. High collar of the same' (Redfern).
'Costume, the skirt in tweed checked in copper and black; bodice and basque of olive green cloth edged with sable; deep yoke and sleeves of shot purple and green glacé; belt of perforated leather. The colouring and style are quite remarkable.'
'Day Blouse in palest primrose silk with fine satin stripes in black and pale magenta; vest, belt and cuffs of pale magenta velvet and ruchings of black chiffon. The blouse and balloon sleeves gauged into puffings at the waist and shoulders. Chiffon necklet with wide bow behind.'

'*Princess Day Gown* of corrugated cloth in black and white, opening over a simulated under-bodice of peach-mauve velvet on which is a jet galon. Sleeves very large at the top and tapering to the wrist. Bow at the throat.'

'*Afternoon Dress*, the skirt and sleeves of mignonette-green alpaca; bodice of white silk muslin embroidered in black sprigs. Muslin bows as epaulettes; petunia velvet neckband and belt.'
'Dress with plain skirt of seagreen honeycomb silk crepon; bodice of black accordion-pleated chiffon over green silk; neck band with bow behind. Huge bishop sleeves with black satin wristbands.'

'*Summer Dress* of figured muslin trimmed with black velvet and Swiss embroidery. Square

1896
Princess gown trimmed with velvet bands

1896
Tea jacket (Woolland Bros.)

1896. Evening dress of white satin and black velvet

1896. Evening dress of black accordion-pleated
tulle over pink (Peter Robinson)

tucked yoke; bodice gathered at the waist; velvet sash band and high collar. Full sleeves with elbow frill. Narrow flounce to wide skirt.'
'Summer washing dress with full skirt, unlined, blouse-bodice, lined and full, with large sailor collar; belt; bishop sleeves.'

'*Ascot Dress*, white looking-glass moiré skirt; white chiffon sleeves and bodice; stole of white net embroidered in sequins.'
'Goodwood Dress of green and white striped glacé. Plain skirt. Blouse formed of broad bands of white satin ribbon and écru insertion overlapping each other loosely. High collar with bow at the back.'

'*Golf Costume*, a black serge skirt edged with scarlet leather, 6 inches off the ground. Scarlet blouse with bishop sleeves. Black cloth knickerbockers and gaiters.'
'*Bicycling Costume*, divided skirt, satin breeches, short coat and grebe waistcoat. Bicycling skirt should measure only 2 to 2½ yards round, buttoned up either side; buttons to be left undone while riding, from the knee, the skirt having a very wide wrap so that no possible peep at the knickerbockers can be obtained. Black satin or alpaca knickerbockers; Norfolk jacket.'
Materials: crepon remains the fabric of the year, especially in fancy forms, such as raised in alternate squares, or with alternate bands of silk, etc. Silk, especially chiné, and glacé for the 'fashionable distinct bodices'. Caracule material, bouclé cloth, materials with perpendicular stripes, alpaca and chiffon, grenadine, shot silks, mohair and nacré moiré.
Colours: cornflower-blue, green, grey-blue and brown are fashionable. 'The garish colours of this season' may be gathered from examples.

Evening
The evening blouse and skirt is less dressy than the more formal complete dress. The blouses, full in front and behind with back fastening and elbow sleeves, are mostly worn under the skirt and are generally of two colours.
The dress bodice is usually square cut at the neck or with a slight 'V' opening; or with a pouched front. A short basque or a folded waistband. Trimmed across the bust with a lace fall or open to a point with lace revers and a full vest. A bow on each shoulder and at the neck are common. There are many forms of sleeve:
(1) Satin shoulder strap with bow on the top.
(2) Butterfly bow, pleated on the outside of the

arm to form wings. (3) Puffed elbow sleeve with deep vandyked lace above and below. (4) Triangle sleeve of ribbon tied in bows, forming a band round the armhole and another above it. (5) The 1830 sleeve, a knotted velvet band round the armhole with gauze caught up in the centre a little below it. (6) Gathered full into the armhole and finished off there by a ribbon tied into loops and ends on the shoulder. (7) Gathered into a band above the elbow and trimmed with ribbon band and a bow. (8) Lace

Evening blouse. 1895

flounces falling over the upper arm. (9) A huge puffed sleeve with lace epaulette and frill.
Large lace fichus of the Marie Antoinette type are frequently worn.
The skirt is fluted and excessively full and trained. Vertical trimmings such as long stole ends from the waist, and the lavish use of sequins and coloured stones on the bodice are features. 'The more jet you introduce on a dinner gown the more fashionable' (especially jet cut in cabochon).

Examples
'Evening Dress of pale peach satin brocaded with light green leaves; bodice with loose eau de Nil chiffon vest, transparent shoulder straps

of gold and pearl passementerie. Chiffon frills between the shoulders. Huge puffed sleeve' (Dickins & Jones).

'Evening dress of cream satin brocaded in pink and maize. Full plain skirt. Full bodice with box-pleat in front. Deep lace flounce falling from the neck. Lace sleeves caught up with pink roses. Bodice back-fastening concealed by lace scarf; waistband of light green velvet with large bow behind.'

Dinner gown in pink broché (*Peter Robinson*). 1895

'Evening dress of yellow satin; plain skirt with velvet bow in front above the hem; another at the waist. Square cut bodice, round at the waist and embroidered with pearls and turquoises. Double puffed sleeve of purple chiffon. Ribbon bow on one shoulder and bunch of flowers on the other.'

'Dress in pink chiné silk. Full plain skirt. White ribbon belt with a bow at each side. Fullness of the bodice divided by bands of embroidery on white guipure, mixed with coloured stones.

Sleeves composed of large fluted flounce from the shoulders. Back of bodice similar but with the full popular basque in pleats.'

'Evening Blouse of yellow satin cut slightly square at the neck, and forming a pouch at the waist; tucked at the top, meeting a turned down lace frill. Open sleeve through which appears gatherings of chiffon.'

'Full Plain Skirt of pink poult de soie; bodice of black velvet outlined with white satin medallions studded with crystal sequins. The front of the bodice open to a point over white satin under lace. Lace basques at the sides in points, and on the shoulders' (Debenham & Freebody).

OUTDOOR GARMENTS

The enormous sleeves of the dress compel any garment worn over them to be either in the form of a cape, or with still larger and looser sleeves into which the wearer must struggle as best she may.

The 'Policeman's cape' cut in one on the round; short capes with side shoulders; large cloaks reaching the feet; long voluminous mantles richly trimmed with fur and wadded, and short Bolero mantles are the chief types.

'Tremendous collars' are a feature, which seems to have had one attraction: 'The throat should be well hidden which is to the advantage of the weak-minded as the chin discovers this defect more surely than any other feature.' We are also told that 'chins are worn high this season'. Any outer garment was inconvenient, but 'you can go out in London without any mantle'.

The use of Burberry's gabardine for sports and raincoats is fashionable.

ACCESSORIES

Shoes

Day. With large flaps and prominent buckles. Evening, in black brocade satin with paste buckles.

Jewellery. Turquoises, and paste ornaments. Watches worn from a metal bow on the left side of the bodice.

Fans, 10 inch, painted and spangled.

The death of M. Worth recalls the fact that his usual charge for ordinary silk evening dresses was £50 to £70.

'Some twenty to thirty million dead birds are imported to this country annually to supply the demand of murderous millinery.'

The event of the year was the collapse of the sleeve. A similar event had occurred exactly sixty years before, but in 1836 the puff in a shrunken form seemed to slide down to the elbow; now in 1896 the shrunken puff retreated to the shoulder, leaving the whole arm in a close-fitting sleeve. The bicycling vogue may have been responsible; it is significant that whereas on the former occasion the change originated in Paris, this time it started in England. At the same time the day skirt grew less voluminous at the sides and shorter. 'Many are three or four inches off the ground.' The top-heaviness of the dress is now being rectified and Gothic angles revive together with a more feminine air of trimmings and frillings and the foam of flounced petticoats. We are assured that: 'If a girl wants to remain an old maid all her life she can dress as she pleases, for she is certain never to have a proposal from a good man.' The good man will, presumably, succumb to devices which the bad man will resist. 'The blouse with its loose front is most opportune to correct angularities or hide abundancies.' Celluloid or hair cloth bust improvers are widely advertised and 'girls pull themselves in while they pad their hips and the side lines of the bust to make themselves look as much like an hourglass as possible'. The shortened skirt permits visions of frillies, and 'there is a decidedly fussy element in all good underclothing'. What good man could resist these chiffon and celluloid charms?

There is a corresponding change of materials used; the softer outlines are obtained by silky alpacas, chiné silks, mohairs and grass lawn, with the lavish use of lace. 'It is almost impossible to wear too much lace on the fronts of dresses.'

Meanwhile the costume for bicycling is still a distracting problem. 'Those horrible knickerbockers should be tabooed!' cries one. 'If I meet a girl dressed in that loud style I feel pleased when she is out of sight; not till then do the modest wildflowers seem to look skywards.' But the short bicycling skirt had a dreadful habit of blowing up . . . all sorts of expedients were employed. 'Princess Maud is having her skirts weighted with shot.'

The aim of fashion is now to accentuate height. The average height of girls is said to have rapidly increased (as the result of sports, etc.), and the object of all is to look tall.

DRESSES

Day

1. The Blouse and Skirt. The blouse is now a generic name for any bodice differing in material from the skirt, *e.g.* velvet blouse and cloth skirt.

'Blouses may be counted by tens of thousands.' Some with wide pleated fronts; or vertical trimmings; the fronts full with yokes or designs simulating Zouaves or corselets; or with jabots; or accordion pleated; or tucked, with bands of narrow lace, etc. High collars with bow at the back of the neck. Six yards of material is required. Worn with a folded sash band and bow in front. 'Blouses are worn even on Sundays.'

2. Coat and skirt worn with a shirt with linen collar and tie. The long Louis XV coat, of velvet or plush, worn with blouse front, is known as a 'Prince Rupert'.

3. Costume. The bodice may be open in front to a point with revers, with a soft chiffon front edged with cascades of lace; or with a detachable front. The 'bodice fronts' may be of soft material, or satin, with attached collars. A common form is the bolero bodice, actual or

simulated, rounded in front; or as a Zouave, square in front (worn with loose-fronted bodice); or as an Eton jacket which is somewhat longer at the waist (and worn with a waistcoat). Another variation is made with wide box-pleats on each side descending below the waist. Boleros, of silk, velvet or moiré, may be united to the vest (made of frills of lace from the neck to the waist); some are without backs, the end of the bolero at the waist forming deep sash-ends. Lace boleros are worn over silk blouses. With the short bolero a deep Empire sash is often worn. The bodice tends to have the basque in narrow godet pleats behind, and a blunt point in front develops during the year.

The Sleeve. The new forms are: (1) Plain close-fitting and shaped over the hand; open puff draped to the shoulder and edged with chiffon. (2) Close-fitting, with shoulder puff cut on the cross and stiffly lined. (3) With a large puff to the elbow tied in the centre with ribbon. (4) Puffed to the elbow with gatherings on the shoulder and frill at the wrist. (5) Close sleeve gauged on the outer side, with epaulette.

NOTE: The object of the sleeve is to give the appearance of length.

The Skirt. This is somewhat narrower, often of two pieces only, the back in two box-pleats or big flutes. Four yards of cloth is sufficient. It is often trimmed; the tailor-made with bands of stitching above the hem; the costume skirt often with narrow side panels. Many have narrow ruching round the hem. On the whole the skirt absorbs little attention, all of which is drawn to the bodice. Tailor-mades tend to merge into the dressmakers' styles. For dressy costumes the foundation skirt returns to favour, and, with the decline of the big sleeve, the dress en princesse for smart occasions.

'The godet skirt is doomed but not yet defunct.' There is a general use of fichus, jabots and steinkirks which help to brighten up a prosaic bodice.

Examples

'Blouse of glacé chiné silk of two colours; velvet let in the front each side of a centre box-pleat; sleeves formed of pleats starting from the shoulders and puffed to the forearm; thence pleated.'

'Blouse in grass lawn embroidered with iridescent beads and sequins. Collar, sash, and bow in front, of shot glacé ribbon. Basque. Drooping puffed sleeves.'

'*Morning Dress* in mohair shot green and red.

Sleeve gathered on the shoulder in three or five runners which are a marked feature in to-day's fashions. Bodice opens in front with a straight Eton cut and is faced with velvet over a shirt; short habit basque behind.'

'Day Gown of grey mohair over plain silk-line skirt; bodice opening over white satin waistcoat. Embroidered satin collar. Flap pockets and cuffs, embroidered. The front trimmed with falling lace.'

'Tailor-made Costume in faced cloth with revers, cuffs and sailor collar of white embroidered satin. Skirt with strapped seams.'

'*Walking Dress* in green canvas. Bolero bodice edged with white lace and jet; revers of white satin covered with appliqué. Vest of chiné silk and chiffon with white satin hanging band "in a box-pleat down the front".'

'Gown in blue mohair spotted with black. Bodice with plastron "V" shaped in front and cross-folded behind in blue bengaline. Slightly pointed waist with folded belt. Close fitting sleeve with gathered fullness over the hand. Divided puff on the shoulder under a stiff epaulette; high collar with bow behind' (Dickins & Jones).

'Alpaca Costume in pale grey; plain skirt; full bodice with pouch front of white satin and black satin bows. High ruff; wide collar of embroidered lawn over the shoulders' (Redfern).

'Summer Costume of blush-pink foulard spotted with rosebuds. Skirt gathered into a band of muslin guipure which descends on each side of the skirt. Bodice with corselet of folded foulard which is formed into a fichu. Full sleeves with ruffles. Spotted net chemisette' (Peter Robinson).

'*Goodwood Dress* of embroidered grass lawn over rose silk. Black Swiss belt with two frills as basque. Rucked sleeve falling over the hands with small double shoulder puffs; tulle bow at the throat.'

'*Teagown*, the back of pink brocade; the front of lettuce-green satin with gold-embroidered lisse and lace; cascade of soft lace round the throat forming a jabot; high collar.'

Materials: alpaca, mohair, chiné silk, figured grenadine, foulard taffeta and grass lawn (especially in the hot summer). Crepon declined in favour. Bouclé woollens in the autumn.

Colours: grey, periwinkle and softer tones. Red fashionable in the autumn. The striking colours were reserved for the upper half (*e.g.* moss-green skirt with plum-coloured bodice; red bolero over black bodice). Blouse fronts of strongly contrasting colours were popular.

Evening

The bodice, generally distinct from the skirt and laced at the back; usually pointed slightly front and back; or with a corselet of black satin high under the arms and diminishing to a point in front. Square neck opening cut lower than formerly. Some with a fold of the same material carried slightly over the hips, and continued to the back where there is a battlement basque; or the full bodice in which the centre seam opens some two inches above the waist and soft material in folds is let in up to the neck. Or a long stiff bodice with a Louis XV stomacher of different colour. Others are swathed or drawn across the figure, and the Princess style also appears.

For less dressy occasions the evening blouse, similar in make to the day, but of more elaborate materials, is worn. Some are low off the shoulders with straps. The sleeve is in the form of a single puff, draped with thin material; or of tulle as a succession of double flounces standing out; or as a small Empire puff with close fitting band underneath; while some dinner dresses have long transparent sleeves with epaulettes.

Evening boleros and fichus are common.

Skirts, untrained, or very slightly trained, have frequently embroidered breadths, and some have narrow side panels of different material. They are generally plain or with slight perpendicular trimmings down the seams. A certain number have a transparent net overdress. But it was the petticoats which provided the thrills.

Examples

Blouses. 'White crimped mousselaine de soie with centre box-pleat, bow at the back of the neck; balloon sleeves; sashband with bow.' 'Blouse of sequined lisse over satin with transparent square yoke.' 'Blouse of green striped chiffon; low square neck; velvet bows on shoulders and at the waist.' 'Blouse in peach-coloured satin and purple velvet.'

'*Dinner Gown* in ivory poult de soie with demitrain. Panels embroidered in dull gold beads and tinsel. Bodice embroidered in pearls, gold and tinsel. Peacock green sash. Large lace epaulettes. Basque of lace at the back and sides which descends down the front outlining the front breadth. Flowers on one shoulder, ribbon bow on the other' (Jay's).

'*Evening Dress*, the skirt, bow and sleeves of white satin. Slightly pointed bodice of gold cloth draped across the top with green tulle. Bouquet of cornflowers and wild roses on one shoulder. Point of the bodice outlined with jet. A marvellous effect.'

'Dress of black accordion-pleated net over pink silk with bands of black satin. Square neck edged with ruching. Round waist. Sash band and bow in front; balloon sleeves' (Peter Robinson).

'Dress of cream satin; skirt edged with sable. Lace scarves hang on each side of the front panel. Bodice dragged across the figure to a rosette on the left side. Inner chemisette of muslin and lace insertion forming a square opening. Sleeves a loose puffing of lace on the outer side of the arm, open on the inner. The top portion of the bodice has the appearance of lingerie.' (The slightly undressed appearance would be, of course, alluring.)

'Dress of pale rose duchesse satin; panel on the left side of spangled pink chiffon over white satin, edged with pink chiffon ruche. Pink chiffon bodice with satin swathing across diagonally. Square top. Chiffon short puffed sleeve; roses and lace on the shoulders.'

'Dress of yellow and white brocade with openings in the skirt to show pleatings of tulle. Bodice with wired bolero of écru embroidered with pearls. Slightly pointed bodice.'

'Princess Gown of puce satin fastens under one of the spangled strips which extend on either side from the shoulder straps in black net strewn with emerald green spangles. Bertha flounce across the top extending over the short balloon sleeves in white lace over silk of contrasting colour.'

'Princess dress of nacré mirror velvet. Down each side of the bodice bands of green and pink embroidery. Pink tulle sleeves under capes of the same with narrow bands of pink velvet let in. Lace epaulettes; two velvet rosettes at the top of the bodice which is edged with tulle.'

'Princess dress in lily-of-the-valley and green mirror-velvet. Draped bertha with huge bow in front and wreath of loops forming sleeves, in Pompadour ribbons edged with dark velvet. Floral epaulettes. Bodice low in front and behind.'

'*Ball Dresses* of tulle over satin or lisse, with deep ruche at the hem. Slightly shaped basque;

bodice square cut on the shoulders. Battlement basque. The only stiffness allowed is the wired bows in front and the epaulettes. Some with full bebé front or embroidered stomacher.'

Ball dresses of figured gauzes, tulle, tarlatan.

Materials: silks, satin, velvet, brocades, and for the bodice tulle, chiffon and soft materials mixed.

Colours: 'Colours are curiously blended, such as dahlia and black, arsenic green and black, and "brilliant tints of doubtful taste". Royal blue and reed green are acceptable together.'

OUTDOOR GARMENTS

With smaller sleeves the jacket became possible, especially the sac-back. Short capes, excessively wide with high collars; pelisses with wide revers; mantles with huge winged sleeves. All with full ruffles of chiffon and lace round the neck. The high collar, wired to shape, clear of the back of the head, and frequently lined with bright velvet or satin, was a notable feature. Huge bows under the chin served at least to keep the head high while bows on the shoulders also accentuated the apparent height of the wearer.

Mandelburg's waterproofs in silk stripe proofing.

Example

'Cape in shot green and terra-cotta glacé, with lattice work of narrow black velvet and jet. Borders of thick black lace and fringed silk ruching.'

ACCESSORIES

Shoes

White doeskin in summer. Tan or patent leather with buckle. Often a pointed flap. No fastenings.

Day *Stockings* in black lisle thread, some with fronts worked in dazzling colours.

Jewellery. Bangles. Pearls, diamonds.

Small Empire *Fans*. Satin fan bag, hung on the arm. Velvet *Muffs* with frilled ends, on chains. Also monster muffs. Day elastic *Belts* embroidered with coloured stones.

Parasols of plain satin chiné with ornamental Dresden handles.

NOTE: Artificial silk, from wood, made at Besançon from an invention in '93; a factory is now to be started in England. 'Last year we imported 17 million pounds worth of silk.'

1897

This year introduced a change of style so complete as almost to amount to a new conception. The notion, which had prevailed for some years, seemed to have been that the dress should have a clean cut outline, a hard surface, and a distracting colour scheme, conveying a sense of harsh resistance and solidity. The new conception was that the dress should be fluffy and frilly, undulating in movement with ripples of soft foam appearing at the feet; colours harmonising with each other, surfaces broken with flimsy trimmings and revealing submerged depths of tone. The softened outlines, willowy and slender, created the illusion that these aery habitations must be occupied by beings composed of stuff less solid than flesh and blood. It was the old 'feminine mystery' but in a new setting. This style survived well into the present century and during the last three years of the nineteenth century it did not arrive at its maturity.

The change may be attributed to a number of causes. The emancipatory movement associated with the nickname 'the New Woman', together with the widespread use of the bicycle which was upsetting conventional restrictions—it was suggested that young ladies on bicycles should at least be followed by chaperons in motor-cars—the alarm created by such innovations produced, as it usually does, an apparent swing-back to the ultra-feminine in fashions. By such devices the pace of progress is seemingly checked and the male sex reassured. After a stride forward woman will affect to mark time by a return to fluffiness. The year of the Diamond

Jubilee encouraged a revival of Early Victorian modes; 'but these are so modified as to be scarcely recognisable'. Increasing national prosperity had the usual effect of increasing luxury in clothes and 'l'homme moyen sensuel' could afford to pay the bill. Fluffiness is, no doubt, expensive but irresistible to the old Adam grown a little weary of the new Eve.

The new style was very suitable to the French designers who wished to recapture the English market, and consequently such modes resembled the Parisian more closely than they had for some years. At the same time the purely English tailor-mades and sports' costumes were themselves affected by the wave of frilliness, at least as regards the top half where the blouse, in a thousand forms, concealed the shape of nature. The froth on the surface of the dress was even exceeded by the foam beneath. 'The petticoat', we are told, 'is now at the zenith of its glory, an ever-present enemy to the New Woman.' Fluffed out with flounces and accordion-pleating with lace trimmings and made of the most diaphanous materials, together with wide flimsy drawers similarly decorated, the woman of fashion seemed to have plunged up to the knees in an enormous meringue, inspiring a writer to describe her as 'that soft, sweet and tender bit of humanity which Heaven distinctly intended her to be'. The significance of the new tactics is sufficiently betrayed by the exclamation of a woman writer of the day: 'The petticoat, foamingly soft, adored by man; while the clinging folds and soft outlines of the Tea Gown add a subtle attraction and dignity, varying and dangerous, and treble the fascinations of her slender Form. . . . In a teagown a woman will appear just "adorable", and what more can a woman want to be?' It was the question which the Victorian man had been asking for sixty years.

Technically the shrunken sleeves removed that top-heaviness which had threatened to disturb the balance. 'The prevailing fashions all keep pace with the increased height of Englishwomen.'

DRESSES

Day

The ubiquitous blouse appeared in all forms, materials and colours. 'Some of the blouses are in atrocious taste, scrappy indefinite arrangements, as though people had shied bits of ribbon, brocade and lace on to a foundation.' Most of them had pouched fronts and the Russian blouses with jewelled belts were prominent in the later part of the year. The broad front box-pleat with fancy buttons down it, often of tartan patterns on blouses and shirts (the latter worn with cambric frill and stock or linen collar and tie) was a usual type. Many had a frill down the left side of the front. With these a short Bolero 'worn on nearly every dress, morning and evening'. The Bolero, cut very short, was sometimes curved in front, sometimes cut square and hanging with loose front pleats of embroidery, or of some contrasting colour. A modified form was a short sacque jacket.

The sleeve was close fitting to the arm with a much diminished puff, often frilled, either single or double, or an epaulette on the shoulder. The surface of the sleeve commonly ruched, or tucked throughout and extending over the hand. The puff was often of the same material as the trimming.

The skirt usually with wide front breadth, narrow side gore and back with sharply sloped seam up the centre, requiring $5\frac{1}{2}$ yards of double-width material. The fullness is all at the back; some with double box-pleats behind. The craze for accordion-pleating extended to the skirt and produced the 'sun ray skirt'; this was made either from two lengths of 52 inch material joined together to form a square, then cut in a circle with a hole in the centre for the waist; or by a shaped front width with two joins running from this round the back, for silk widths, and requiring 9 yards. Such a skirt had

Coat in black velours du Nord, lined with green satin. 1897

a separate foundation. This was, in fact, the first form of the *yoke skirt*. This method of construction was then applied to other materials, stuffs, etc., the back pleats being laid over the yoke behind, so that the skirt would fit closely

over the hips and down to near the knee and then spread outwards. (The fore-runner of the 'flared skirt'.)

A good many plain skirts were seen. For dressy occasions narrow tucks in groups, or lace flounces festooned in vandykes, or rows of insertion striping the skirt downwards, both on the skirt and the bodice. The coat and skirt appeared 'of every variety, long, double-breasted, single, Eton jacket, or mess jacket with Hussar braidings'. Trimmed largely with braiding extending upwards or with two frills or ruches round at intervals not far from the waist.

The Costume bodice is commonly open down the front, the sides being embroidered, with a full vest, often pouched; and the skirt may be slashed up the sides, or slightly lifted on one side, to show the gay colour of the underskirt.

'The present mania for braided dresses' called for the use of military braid, cords and galons of metals on white cloth and in winter narrow trimmings of fur.

Summer dresses, in consequence of the wonderful 'Queen's weather', were of 'the airy materials now so popular, gauzes, grenadines, chiffon, grass lawn, muslins'.

Generally with tucked bodice flopping over, front and back; wide satin sash; skirt tucked in three rows at the top, at the knees and at the hem; sleeves puffed and divided in the middle by a band, or ruched all the way up. Fichus were often worn with them. The 'baby bodice' with threaded ribbons and wide sash with long ends at the side, is common. Accordion-pleating is extremely popular especially with blouses and teagowns. All thin transparent materials were worn over coloured glacé foundations; while thick skirts had silk or a material guaranteed to rustle as a foundation.

Examples

'*Walking Toilette* of pale pink muslin embroidered with flowers, with vandyked lace insertion bands. Lined with pink glacé. Double flounce of lace at the foot. Lace beneath puffs at the neck and wrists. Tight sleeve with shoulder puff. Full fronted bodice with cascade of lace from the left shoulder to the waist. Sash of checked silk; high collar splayed open at the sides and back.'

'*Day Dress* of black and white check canvas over a pink foundation. Full front of cream lace over white. Braided black velvet Zouave. Sleeves of the check tucked. Revers of tomato-

404

1897. Evening dress of spotted net,
flounced

1897. Gown of grey cloth with sac
jacket and tucked skirt

1898. Pelisse of black velvet with
chinchilla and lace

coloured mirror velvet embroidered in silk; collar to correspond' (Peter Robinson).

'Blouse of pale blue chiffon pouching over the waistband, and trimmed with two deep frills of lace across the bust. Ruched sleeve with frills.'

'Afternoon Blouse; a loose vest of white crepe de Chine with worked silk stripes; Zouave with shoulder straps of orange-coloured silk, arranged in a series of tiny tucks; black velvet waistband; black chiffon at the neck.'

'*Afternoon Dress* of pearl grey foulard trimmed with narrow tucks and tiny frills of black chiffon. Square yoke of white chiffon. Collar and belt of silver sequins. Close sleeve with tucks and epaulette. Frilled collar.'

'Afternoon dress of accordion-pleated silk. Pinafore bodice of black lace; overskirt of black lace open at the sides to show silk skirt. Sash ends of black velvet. Epaulettes.'

'Afternoon dress with plain skirt of mauve cloth. Short jacket of cream guipure; vest of blue and mauve shot chiffon; high collar.'

'Summer Dress of grass green muslin; bodice with double revers of white satin; jabot of fluffy frills of white chiffon. Sash edged with chiffon frills.'

'*Garden Party Dress* of emerald green corded silk; plain skirt; over the corsage a loose Zouave, square at the neck both in front and behind, of cream net embroidered with beads and pearls. Sleeves with frill over the hands. Small shoulder puff.'

Evening

The chief features were the widespread use of transparent over-dresses, the lavish use of sequins and beads—'spangles galore and yards of satin ribbon'—and the use of flounces, festoons and tucks on the skirt, with lace and passementerie on the bodice. Chiffon bodices with broad lace frill round the shoulders, and sleeves short and puffed, or long to the hand, of wrinkled transparent material, worn with silk skirts, often black, were common for dinner dress; the evening blouse served the same purpose.

For full dress the bodice was cut low and square, generally the front draped, with a round waist and sash; Empire styles were not uncommon.

The use of the bolero in a great variety of forms was a feature.

Ball dresses were often accordion-pleated, the skirt nine yards at the hem and only one yard at the waist; others had multiple skirts of alternate white and coloured gauze, and others were tucked from hem to waist; or with rows of tulle ruching across, widely spaced. Very wide sashes were worn with them.

Bodices were swathed, or as a corselet with soft folds of material above or draped across the figure.

Flowers were worn on the shoulders; sleeves often long, of transparent gauze, etc. Dresses of transparent materials had satin foundations.

Liberty teagown in satin and soft silk. 1897

Examples

'*Dinner Dress*, a turquoise blue satin bodice with high Medici collar; bolero of black spangled gauze; black satin skirt; long wrinkled sleeve of turquoise chiffon; pointed epaulettes; cuffs of black gauze.'

'Dinner dress of pale blue satin brocaded with white flowers; plain skirt; low square bodice with shoulder straps and lace epaulettes over elbow sleeves frilled at the ends. Pointed basques of lace in front. Folded sashband and skirt of blue satin.'

'Evening dress of pale pink moiré; skirt with front and back panels of white satin covered

405

with white net sprinkled with crystal drops. Corsage of embroidered moiré open over full front of pink velvet. Square low neck; shoulder sleeve of white satin and velvet bows.'

'Evening dress of white mirror velvet with pink satin stripes; plain skirt. Corsage of folded velvet with narrow bands of silver and pearl embroidery. Square opening; band of white moiré at the neck. White lace sleeve; a frill of white moiré descends on the right of the bodice

Mantle in velours du Nord, lined with quilted satin. 1897

and a trail of pink roses on the belt; a single rose on the right hip.'

'Evening dress of pale mauve chiffon, accordion-pleated. Overskirt of pale green embroidery studded with steel beads. Hanging angel sleeves of both materials. Square neck.'

'Evening dress of black net over black satin, embroidered with sequins and trimmed with chiffon, satin ribbon and shaded orchids; trained' (Peter Robinson).

'Evening dress in eau de Nil soft silk; skirt draped up on the right hip; bodice crossing in folds over under-bodice of cream net, the top of which has a band of pink roses.

Folded corselet of faded pink velvet. Sleeve draped in a short puff on the outer side of the shoulder.'

'Accordion-pleated Opera Cloak with chiffon Medici collar and cape.'

OUTDOOR GARMENTS

Short sacque-backed jackets, edged with fur; jackets with cape sleeves. Capes full and half-fitting, high 'storm collars', usually braided.

The outer garments of previous years have now modified sleeves, but the square-shoulder effect is preserved. Coats tend to be pouched in front and many fasten across on the left side. The basques are now short.

ACCESSORIES

Jewellery. Ear-rings ('always worn by the Duchess of York') are returning to favour. Waist buckles of paste are large and often worn at the back. Small fur *Necklets.*

Mourning
Widow: A year and a day, the dress entirely covered with crepe; then nine months trimmed with crepe.
Daughter: Crepe for one year; black for three months; half mourning for three months.
Sister: Crepe three months; black three months.
Mother: Crepe six months; black three months; half mourning three months.
Niece: Black two months; half mourning one month.
Cousin: Black three months; half mourning three months.

Prices
Blouse and skirt in white piqué, 21/6 (Pontings). Accordion-pleated mousselaine de soie (46 in.) 3/11. (Dickins & Jones).
Blouse of pale blue silk veiled with white muslin in fine tucks and frilled with lace slantwise across; a foam of lace and muslin down the left side where it fastens, 65/-. Tartan silk shirts, 25/6; of French cambric, 5/11; of white crepon, 15/6½. Courtauld's pure silk crepes (29 in.) 1/11¾ to 5/11; (40 in.) 8/11 to 10/9. Hopsack, all wool, 2/6 to 3/-. Silk warped alpacas (42 in.) 3/6. Pale pink lustrous alpaca (42 in.) 2/6½. Striped ottomans (27 in.) 2/-. Bright glacés (22 in.) 1/4¾. Watered moirette for rustling foundations (24 in.) 2/3. Crepe de Chine (22 in.) 2/6½. Pongee (22 in.) 8d. Satin merveilleux, 2/9. All silk duchesse satin (22 in.)

4/-; black skirts of ditto, lined and stiffened with elastic canvas, 31/6.
Four-button kid gloves, day, all colours, 2/8 per pr. Evening kid, with lace arms, 6/10; 12-button kid, 4/6; 20-button, 7/6.

White buckskin laced shoes, 16/9. Glacé kid Cromwell shoes, 18/9.
Tea-jacket in black satin with revers of myrtle green velvet, the front of white silk, £3. 8. 6.
Bust bodice in white coutille, 3/6.

1898

As commonly happens when the preceding year has introduced a profound change in style the subsequent year is occupied mainly in consolidating the advance. 1898, therefore, produced only modifications of 1897. 'The real novelties in dress are not many this year. . . . Dresses are long and trailing, and unless for a bicycle the short dress is not seen. Even the tailor-made more than touches the ground; for these the gored skirt or narrow front gore and two or more at the side is preferred.' As for materials 'everything that is clinging and soft' was the vogue. The general effect is thus described: 'This season we are all to be willowy trailing creatures, slim and slight.' The new pose encouraged the use of the Princess dress, but the tight-fitting bodice revealing the shape of the figure is extinct, together with the Victorian bosom. The centre of attraction is henceforth to be the hips, emphasised by undulating movements as the graceful creature manages to display her frillies as she walks. The hair, mounting upwards, increases her height; the growing taste for monochrome colouring, or at least for cloudy evasive tones which blend into a whole, leaves nothing to distract the eye from the sinuous lines.

DRESSES

Day

The bodice of different colour from the skirt may be worn, in simple costumes, under a jacket, but not for dressy occasions.

The bodice may be blouse-shaped, generally fastening on the left side, and slightly pouched; or with a yoke, often pointed in a reversed 'V'; or sailor collar; or open down the front with revers over a vest; or open from the waist to the bust; or open in the form of a bolero, Eton jacket or Figaro. In these the sides are rounded below. The bolero comes just to the waist, crossing over the chest in two narrow revers peaked up over the shoulders and fastened with a double row of buttons. With such the neck opening is filled in with an enormous bow of chiffon or tulle cravat tied under a high collar. Frillings simulating a bolero, or a low bodice with high chemisette are common. The Eton jacket is braided and frogged across. Three-quarter length coat bodices with rounded basques, or Directoire swallow-tailed coats are also worn.

Blouses are often open in front with revers and short basque, worn with a gathered chemisette; or with lace yokes which may be pointed upwards at the back. The Russian blouse, without pouching, has basques sewn on the band so that the blouse can be worn with or without them.

The high collar is splayed out and known as the 'saucer collar'. 'High collars are the craze of the season.' Sleeves are close-fitting throughout with a small single or double epaulette. They reach down over the hand, and may be square or pointed at the ends.

The Skirt. Some with two box-pleats behind; others without pleats or gathers. Walking skirts with pointed yoke with a lower part attached which is cut from a circle; or with narrow front breadth and two side pieces joining behind, the front outlined by machine-stitched straps; the hem faced up four to six inches. Sateen or moirette lining. Or tucked at regular intervals all the way up, with narrow panel of braid or broché on the left.

Dressy skirts are trimmed with a flounce, one deep flounce for woollens, or several small superimposed flounces for light materials, forming the 'feather-brush' skirt; or the flounce may slope from the middle of the back downwards to the front, or be 'V' shaped in front and behind. Or the whole dress may be trimmed with a succession of piped tucks, or with trimmings of braid or passementerie descending down the front and continued round the hem at the sides and back. With such skirts the foundation is separate but attached to the band, often with an accordion-pleated flounce, and made of a different coloured material from the dress. Where no foundation is used an underskirt of taffeta is usual. The feature of all skirts is that they should fit closely round the hips and flare outwards from the knee, touching the ground.

A certain number of double skirts or tunics are seen; also skirts cut up from the bottom halfway to show the underskirt and caught by tiny straps.

Teagowns are usually made en princesse, with frills, flounces, fichus, and large collars; often with an inside bodice boned and laced, dispensing with a corset. 'Without accordion-pleating and chiffon we should have to give up the teagown.'

Waistbands have the buckle at the back, or a ribbon sash with buckle and long ends (no bow) behind.

Buckles of paste or steel.

Examples

'*Walking Costume* of pearl-grey cloth with pipings up to the knee. Open bodice over soft cream vest. Collar, cuffs and belt of green velvet.'

'Walking dress of violet woollen rep. Plain skirt. Blouse-bodice, double-breasted, with pointed revers of velvet.'

'Walking dress, the skirt of grey woollen broché simulating a double one; a gored foundation covered for 10 inches deep at the foot with the material, with the material skirt over it and five inches shorter. Jacket of plain grey cloth, with three-quarter basque rounded off in front. High collar, cuffs and revers faced with broché. Full vest of old rose broché gauze over silk. Grey velvet collar and waistband.'

'*Afternoon Dress* of embroidered net over black taffeta, the former with ruched hem. Bodice covered with gathered net and trimmed with rows of narrow ribbon-velvet of lettuce green. Collar, waistband, and bows on the shoulders of the same. Sleeves of quilled net.'

'Afternoon dress of violet cashmere cloth. Front of the bodice covered with a pinafore arrangement in mauve glacé, embroidered in white silk, edged with black lace over white, and covering the shoulders. Plain tight sleeves with wide cuffs over the hand. Plain skirt edged with ruching.'

'Afternoon dress of green cloth with short points from the waist of brown and green broché edged with fur. Bodice with deep velvet corselet. Short Zouave-trimming of broché. Lace ruffles and cravat. Tight sleeves with two scalloped frills on the shoulder. High saucer collar.'

'Tunic dress, the tunic reaching just below the knees and slashed up at the sides. Bodice open in front over coloured vest. Collar high at the back.'

'Princess Dress, all in one behind but with blouse front, finished with a corselet. The apron width in front defined by pleated panels let in on each side, the apron width being carried on round the hem as a flounce.'

'Princess home dress of fawn faille, slightly trained. Panel of willow-green brocade slightly on the left side, twelve inches wide at the hem, diminishing to a point on the left shoulder. Buttons down the left side. Front of bodice cut into a scalloped point, the opening filled in with brocade. Rose velvet collar and cream lace ruffle. Coat-shaped sleeves with brocade epaulettes.'

'Muslin Gown; the skirt with vertical tucks from the middle of the bodice to the knees; thence a full flounce trimmed with narrow horizontal ruches of black gauze; yoke and sleeves of black figured lace over muslin foundation. Bodice ornamented with black velvet bands. Black velvet sash and buckle behind.'

'*Summer Dress* of fine cloth; basqued bodice and narrow revers; waistcoat of white satin with cream lace over it. Lace and chiffon bow at the back. Short overskirt pointed in front, edged with velvet bands.'

'Summer dress of muslin over silk underskirt. The muslin skirt with Spanish flounce which is edged with a narrow flounce at the hem and headed. A triple cape worn over the bodice.'

'Summer dress of silver-grey cloth. Skirt with piped tucks nearly to the waist; on a foundation of brown silk trimmed at the foot with three small gathered frills. Blouse bodice with a tabbed basque embroidered in beads and silk. Open front with white silk vest and full ruffle of white lace and double waterfall to the waist. Piped sleeves with small embroidered epaulettes.'

Materials: faced cloth; all soft clinging materials. Silky crepons; striped taffeta replacing foulard. Glacé and shot silks. Chiffon ruching (as trimming for summer).

Colours: soft tints, cloudy or monochrome

Grey-brown Alpaca:
red braid trimming
1867

Pink Flannel with
fine white stripe.
red braid trimming
1870's

Waterproof bag
1870's

Blue waterproof
Satin cap
1870's

White Canvas shoe.
rope sole, red braid trimming
& red wool stitching — 1870's

Red Serge:
white braid
trimming_
1880's

Waterproof cap:
blue with white
spots — 1890's

Navy blue
Serge: white braid trimming — 1890's

powdered with white. The exception is in the silk linings of dressy skirts; violet lined with heliotrope; red with pink; sapphire with pale blue, in order to attract the eye.

Evening
The bodice, laced behind, may be high, slightly pouched and often fastening on the left, with long sleeves to the hand. Or low, usually with square opening, and shoulder straps or transparent long sleeves. Never plain, but either draped across or folded so as to come over the band, or trimmed with chiffon, etc., either as a bertha or with a waterfall often on one side. Or the evening blouse may be worn with separate skirt.

The skirts are trained; thin materials with a deep flounce shaped into a point in front or at the back from the waistline. A feature is the transparent overdress of net elaborately embroidered with sequins; a glittering effect is the desideratum.

The Princess dress is common, in which the front breadth may be detached from the side breadths to which it is loosely fastened by velvet straps; revealing the elaborate underdress (*e.g.* of chiffon and lace). Trails of chiffon and chenille, raised flowers, or lace foliage outlined with tinsel decorate the surface. Flowers are much worn on evening dresses; also large old paste buckles clasping at the back the sash-scarves. A pearl dog-collar or velvet band with diamond clasp or band of quilled muslin is worn round the neck.

Ball dresses frequently have low bodices pointed front and back, with bertha frill forming sleeves. The skirts trail slightly on the ground and are often made with a yoke of trellised net forming a heading to rows of flounces.

Examples
'Evening Blouse in mauve jetted chiffon and green velvet straps in vertical bands; large velvet pansies on the shoulders.'

'Dress of cornflower chiffon entirely covered with steel sequins; full skirt; bodice cut low front and back, pouching slightly over a girdle; forming a waterfall of glittering steel. Sleeves with three straps of turquoise velvet at the top.'

'Dress of white muslin over gored foundation of white glacé with two pinked frills on the outer side of the hem. Skirt with short gathered flounce on the cross with a piped heading. Bodice with tight-fitting silk lining. The muslin is tucked twice across the bust and twice below. The front and back full, the sides plain. Back

lacing. Low square cut above with a puffing of silk muslin. Shoulder straps with ribbon bows. Sash at the back.'

'A gored skirt of pale yellow silk lined with sateen; three shaped flounces of white tulle, the edge of each with narrow moiré ribbon run on. The top flounce slopes up from a narrow point in front. Bodice, laced behind, is covered with white chiffon full all round, with double pleatings round the square cut top. A double waterfall of chiffon descends on the left side. Silk shoulder straps with bunches of roses; yellow chiné silk sash.'

'Princess Dress in maize satin, slightly trained, with two narrow flounces headed by chiffon ruching; overdress, open in front from the waist, of white lace with fichu and sleeve frills in white chiffon.'

'*Ball Dress* of pale pink over mauve chiffon. Triple flounced skirt, each flounce edged with ruche of mixed tulle deepening to violet from the palest mauve and pink. Long scarf-sash of chiffon trimmed with tulle ruches. Sleeve of "cock's comb" frills of chiffon and tulle put on to the shoulder straps of violets and small roses which form "V" shaped bretelles front and back.'

'Ball dress, the skirt of three billowy flounces of white gauze edged with brilliants. Bebé bodice with let-in front of brilliants. Small sleeve of three frills of gauze edged with brilliants. Folded belt of white satin with cluster of pink roses on one side.'

Materials: chiffon; hand-painted muslin, muslin with silk crewel work patterns, or with lace insertions; tulle sparkling with cobweb pattern in silver and gold; dewdrop tulle; coloured net, crepe de Chine, are the usual for full evening or ball dresses; light Pompadour chiné, glacé, and satins for others. Painted satin and moiré, and chiné flowers outlined in spangles.

Colours: flamingo, coral, red, yellow and chiné effects.

OUTDOOR GARMENTS

Short jackets with semi-tight sleeves, slightly puffed at the top, some shaped as blouse-bodices with yoke and fur collar; others sacque-shaped.

Redingotes with fitting back and semi-fitting front.

Summer mantles with deep frills of accordion-pleated uncrushable chiffon and Medici collars; often with double frills simulating capes.

Three-quarter coats, tight-fitting, without revers, invisibly fastened under fur trimming. Rounded three-quarter capes. Capes pointed front and back. A feature of the outdoor garment is the tendency to have the corners rounded; long coats nearly to the ground, in winter, with fur trimming, help to emphasise the height. The excessive breadth of the shoulder line is diminished and the narrow sleeves admit the more general use of coats rather than capes.

ACCESSORIES

Shoes and Boots
American Boots and Shoes with long pointed toes. White shoes and stockings with white summer dresses. Evening shoes with red Louis heels and paste buckles. Tan or patent leather shoes with two straps (Day).
'It is rare to see *Gloves* worn except out walking, while in the country many ladies never wear gloves at all.' Evening mittens often worn in place of gloves; or gloves with attached mitten.

Jewellery much worn, especially chains 'with or without the everlasting heart'. 'Bracelets with all sorts of things hanging from them.' Many rings. Feather *Boas*.
Stock with bow, for morning or cycling, worn with white tabbed collar.

1899

The approaching close of the Nineteenth Century suggesting the end of an epoch, inspired a number of contemporary reflections on the changes of feminine fashion. Thus one remarks: 'The costume of a period unfailingly reflects its spirit and its aims. The universal adoption of the coat and skirt bespeaks the fin de siècle woman, energetic, spirited and sensible . . . adopting the simpler costume that is akin, though even remotely, to the costume of man, she insists the more upon sex in the chapeau and the dainty trivialities of the blouse.' M. Jean Worth (who had succeeded to his father's business) expressed the view: 'The love of the modern woman for athletics, though perhaps to be deplored from the aesthetic point of view, has made any revival of the crinoline impossible; besides, latter-day modes have a tendency to become more and more utilitarian, while at the same time those women who live for dress no longer slavishly follow the fashion; the lady of the twentieth century will realise that it is her duty to look her best under all circumstances and not to follow the blind dictates of fashion.'

Meanwhile, we learn, 'everything is reaching the highest stage of perfection in dress . . . that the graceful outlines of to-day may not perish from over-popularity is the prayer of everyone blessed with the really artistic instinct.' A more cautious observer admits that: 'It is a merciful provision of nature that whatever is the mode of the present we all declare it to be prettier than that of the past.'

The mode of 1899 was to feature the hips in the popular 'eel skirt' (sometimes with the added charms of artificial hips, as advertised). 'Every month skirts grow tighter round the hips; walking has become an impossibility and a sort of gliding motion has become the fashionable gait.' (The provocative pelvic roll was borrowed from professional ladies of easy virtue.) On the other hand the upper half of the body remained swathed in obscurity. 'There is a prejudice in the minds of many against showing the figure.' The overskirt ('tunic') and the Princess dress increase in popularity, while towards the end of the year a new form of skirt (with pleats stitched down to the knee) appears. Colours become more harmonised. Clinging soft femininity is to be the note on which the new century is to open.

DRESSES

Day

The bodice is often replaced by a tight-fitting small coat with short basque all round, the fronts covered with lace, or with revers; or in the form of a bolero over a shirt; these bolero-coats are without basques except for slight points in front. The Eton jacket with rounded fronts is also common. Such open bodices are worn over vests or shirts, the fronts of which are draped, pouched or drawn across the bust with abundance of lace trimmings and have frequently yoked tops. The tailor-mades have double revers, one usually of velvet, and may be in the form of short coats, double-breasted reefers, or coatlets with long rounded fronts. Blouses, mounted over fitted linings, except in summer, may have left-sided fastenings or centre fastenings and revers (over a vest). Heart-shaped yokes or tucked fronts are usual. The blouse must now harmonise in colour with the skirt; light colours with a black skirt are not permissible, but the blouse itself may be of two colours (green and pink; blue and pink; violet and lemon). Sleeves of blouses may be ruched or somewhat full; frills or folds across the yoke falling over the top of the sleeve. Otherwise sleeves are close-fitting, and all extend over the hand. Lace ties and silk scarves replace linen collars with summer blouses. The embroidered collar of the vest or shirt is excessively high and generally pointed at the sides. 'A fashionable beauty can hardly turn her head in the prison of whalebone and wire that holds her head as in a vice.'

The skirt: always excessively tight over the hips and long, touching the ground all round; from below the knee there is a slight flare but less than formerly. The popular form is the 'eel skirt', cut on the cross, consisting of a front piece, two side gores and two back gores, all except the front having a circular hem. Other forms are the umbrella skirt, cut on the cross without seams, the skirt with a single seam behind, and the skirt composed of a narrow front and two wide side pieces which also form the back. These skirts are plain, being trimmed in front only with machine-stitching. In the autumn a skirt with pleats stitched down to just below the knee and thence free to expand, is an important innovation.

The yoked skirt with a shaped flounce below the knee simulating a tunic is also seen.

Skirts fasten up at the side or in front or sometimes behind, but there is no open placket hole or inside pocket. Occasionally a pocket in the hem is found. Skirts in thin summer materials fasten up the front and may have bias folds of satin or velvet on either side in straight or wavy lines, or may have three bias flounces mounted on cotton or silk foundation.

The tunic dress: The upper skirt may be pointed front and back, the points reaching nearly to the ground; or with scalloped edge; or as part of a polonaise closed at the waist in front and sloped off at the knees, the underskirt having a plain or accordion-pleated flounce, or flounces edged with frills. Such flounces are sewn on to the foundation. Tunics are frequently fringed or simulated by trimming.

As rustling is no longer fashionable and a silent gliding walk preferred, the underskirt should be of satin or cashmere or soft silk. 'We have long passed the day when to wear pretty underskirts is to be demi-monde.'

Examples

'*Walking Dress* of green cloth with tucked vest. Bodice mounted on a fitted lining fastens towards the left, the shoulder outlined with lie-over collar. Double skirt, the upper lined with silk, fastens in front, the bottom sloping off to the back. Waistband of satin ribbon. Tight sleeves pleated into the armholes; flared cuffs. Requires nine yards of material.'

'Outdoor Dress of pastel blue cloth trimmed with stitched strappings and buttons. Long skirt lying on the ground, front and back, lined throughout and stiffened at the hem. Buttons behind with two rows of buttons joined together with cords ... Jacket, tight-fitting behind, the front loose but shaped in at the sides. The fronts fasten to the left. Flat stiffened collar. Fitting sleeves gathered into the armholes and very long at the wrists. Jacket lined with silk. Seven yards of double-width cloth required.'

'*Afternoon Dress*, a green moiré skirt; Princess polonaise in green cloth cut into two long points in front and behind; fastening across on the left side at the waist. Double revers of velvet and satin; lace vest and high saucer collar.'

'Princess Home Dress in blue-grey cashmere with velvet yoke and flat epaulettes over tight sleeves. Yoke trimmed with appliqué design in lace; back fastening.'

'Princess dress in blue cloth, shaped tunic-fashion and fastening down the left side, revealing the underskirt in front only. Upper part of the bodice with revers trimmed with embroidery over a chemisette of lace insertion.

1898. Dinner dress of white glacé; overskirt of
spangled net, flounced and ruched

1899. Dinner gown (Peter Robinson); four skirts (pink peau de soie under accordion-pleated chiffon under plain chiffon and lace); swathed bodice

1899. Cloth gown (Lewis and Allenby) of pale grey with black velvet

Velvet scarf across the bust tied in a bow on the left.'

'Summer Gown in pale grey voile spotted with white, with cross-over bodice; revers and flat collar trimmed with lace appliqué. Tight sleeves expanding over the hand. Tucked white chiffon chemisette and neck-band. Deep folded waist-band, with three buttons at the side. Skirt with straight lines of insertion carried round the top of the flared flounce.'

'*Teagown* in black satin merveilleux with pleated frills across the top; loose hanging front in black spotted mousseline de soie, the front coat-shaped; the back en princesse' (Swan & Edgar).

'Empire Teagowns, short-waisted, with yoke on a sort of little bolero meeting in two points at the centre of the bust, the back of the bolero forming an inverted "V". Often with transparent overdress pleated from a short yoke.'

'*Wedding Dress* with polonaise and Princess front draped and crossing over embroidered yoke.'

Materials: cloth, soft material, voile, crepe de Chine, satin de laine, wool poplin. A great deal of lace and guipure is used. (Summer), white piqué and checked muslins. Transparent dresses mounted on matching coloured underdresses; lace over white. Barège revived.

Colours: soft pastel colours, especially blue-grey. 'Pale colours with a vivid touch at the neck or in the hat.' With tunics, one colour and material over another, such as heliotrope canvas over white silk; grey alpaca over crimson poplin.

Evening

'The Victorian decolletée is reaching such a pitch that the bodice hangs on the shoulders by a miracle.' For full dress a very low 'Victorian' bodice cut square or round with trimmings of frills and ruches of tulle. For semi-evening the high neck and chemisette of transparent material.

The evening dress may be vaguely 'Empire' in shape, or a Princess, or an evening blouse. A principal feature is some kind of transparent overdress hanging over a coloured underdress; net or chiffon over coloured silk, or open lace tunic over chiffon. Net trimmed with sequins to weigh it down produces the desired 'clinging effect'. Many are draped en princesse across the decolletage to the left hip, fastening there with a buckle. Or the Princess dress may be swathed

from decolletage to knee. Other Princess dresses, buttoning down the back, have panels rounded off in front to show a front breadth of the underdress, of guipure, lace or satin. Others are plain, being embroidered or hand-painted in spiral lines winding round and ascending to the bodice.

The Empire dresses display Greek key patterns, laurel leaves or pineapple designs.

The skirt is plain, slightly trimmed and clings round the hips. Many have spoon-shaped trains.

Trimmings in relief (lace, flowers, butterflies) are common. It is a feature for the sides of a low bodice to be different, *e.g.* a shoulder strap on one, feathers with bow or buckle on the other. Somewhere there will be a bold splash of colour, such as a large black bow; or a wide bow of turquoise velvet across the bust of a flesh-coloured satin dress; or a ball dress of amber velvet with wide corselet-sash of rose and pink. Many low bodices have lace berthas.

The low 'Victorian bodice' has only a shoulder strap; the 'Empire' bodice with small square decolletage has an elbow sleeve 'draped to show the arm in a sort of Greek fashion'.

Evening blouses, known as 'fancy bodices', of lace with basque behind, often have velvet straps forming a sort of Zouave; blouse-jackets with painted or embroidered revers are worn over accordion-pleated vests. Blouses draped from one shoulder and slightly pouching, others with transparent yokes, form various degrees of evening or semi-evening dress.

The use of fichu-fronts with straps and bows of velvet give an 'evening effect'. The use of hand-painted materials is noteworthy.

The new material Panne is fashionable.

Examples

'Evening Blouse of pale blue satin, the low square top draped across with folds of heliotrope velvet in two shades; velvet bows on the shoulder. The front embroidered with gilt sequins and long hanging fringe of beads. White chiffon round the shoulders. Round belt of velvet' (Peter Robinson).

'A Princess Dress of pink moiré trimmed with jet and chiffon; back fastening. The lower edge trimmed with band of satin ribbon embroidered in jet. Low square decolletage trimmed with passementerie edged with fringe. Shoulder straps of satin ribbon; chiffon rosettes with hanging ends on the front of the shoulders. Requires 14 yards of moiré; 3 of chiffon.'

413

'Dress of black brocade; the bodice open to a point at the waist with revers of salmon-pink satin covered with cream lace. Gathered vest of pink gauze; elbow sleeves with ruffles.'

'Dress of silk with two frills round the bottom; upper skirt of lace edged with chiffon ruche; silk bodice, with low square decolletage, has rounded revers across the front covered with lace; the rest of the bodice is draped slantwise. Round velvet waistband. Elbow sleeves with ruffles.'

'Silk dress, the bodice of tucked silk mounted on silk lining and fastening behind. Broad ribbon scarves are banded from the right shoulder to the left side of the waist with ribbon rosettes on the right shoulder. Skirt with three tunics, each descending to a blunt point in front and edged with lace.'

'Dress of black satin, the bodice gathered over a fitted lining and trimmed with bands of white lace en Zouave; back fastening. Shoulder straps of velvet which also edges the decolletage from which hangs a white lace frill.'

'Dress of lettuce-green satin veiled with a pale grey mousseline de soie embroidered in silver and jet and jewelled with large turquoises.'

'Dress of black accordion-pleated net over apple-green silk. Bodice, with square opening trimmed with jet and having in the centre a choux of velvet with long hanging ends; spray of poppies on the right shoulder. Elbow sleeves in transparent net with folds and bows of chiffon.'

OUTDOOR GARMENTS

Winter capes, plain over the shoulders, slightly moulded to the figure and fluting out below, 27″ long; many with high collars.

Winter. Long three-quarter coats, loose backs and fronts, trimmed with tabs of the material diminishing up to a point in front. Large roll-over collars; invisible fastenings.

Semi-fitting long coats, the fronts cut in sharp points. Semi-fitting sacques, with wide capes. Mantles, like circulars, one end flung over the shoulder, of coloured cloth. Mantles lined with white glacé and profusely frilled inside with lace or chiffon.

Coatlets, of velvet or fur, with fan-shaped collars and large revers of fur. Frogged and braided cloth coatlets.

'Outdoor three-quarter coat with rounded basque, fur edged; flat square revers and storm collar.'

Long circular cloaks, of brocade, coming from a short yoke and collar of fur, in one; the cloak frilled on to the yoke which forms a point in front and double box-pleat behind.

Victorines, with high fluted collars and edged with frill of shaped flounce of fur; some short to the waist; others reaching nearly to the ground.

ACCESSORIES

Shoes excessively pointed, so that a small foot is no longer to be seen.

Day *Stockings*, black or brown; occasionally scarlet with scarlet shoes.

Day *Gloves*, pearl grey suede and pale tan. Evening gloves, suede, often with lace tops. Occasionally mittens.

Jewellery. Very high pearl collars are worn with evening dress. Diamonds much worn. Screw-on ear-rings (diamonds or turquoises) are a novelty. Bright *Sunshades* striped with wide bands of fancy silk, or plain. Flat feather *Boas*. Tulle boas in several shades of a colour. Fur *Muffs* with removable linings projecting beyond each end.

HEADGEAR IN THE '90's

From '94 onwards the principle was to emphasise the height, while the growing taste for outdoor pursuits, especially cycling, was incompatible with the use of false hair. Unlike the '70's, therefore, adventitious aids were abandoned (returning, however, in the next century). The bicycle also helped to destroy the bonnet which was becoming more and more the headgear of the elderly. The hat has always been the insignia of emancipation. The astonishing blend of colours and materials which decorated the hats served to draw attention to the increased height and to compel man to look up to woman with increased respect, or at least attention.

1890

1. *Red Velvet Hat*, lined with black velvet; bunches of feathers and ospreys.

2. *Costume for Races*. Hat in fancy straw, with tufts of beige ostrich feathers and a clump of roses.

3. *Evening Dress*. Large twist of hair turned round and round with a Galatea comb.

4. *Morning Costume*. Brown felt toque, trimmed with brown velvet and fancy bird; coral pink velvet bow at the back.

5. *Driving, Racing or Sports Costume*. Small hat to match coat.

6. *At Home Costume*. Floral and crownless capote.

NOTE: Both 4 and 6, with strings, would be known as bonnets.

1891

1. *Black Velvet Toque*, trimmed with feathers and spider's web veil.

2. *Demi-Saison Millinery*. Grey felt hat, trimmed with green ribbon and grey wing; similar bow and green and grey wing under brim behind; green velvet bandeau on brim.

3. *Travelling or Yachting Costume*. Sailor's hat, in mixed straw, bound and encircled with waterproof ribbon.

4. *Afternoon Costume*. Bonnet of lace leaves, veined with jet; crown of large bows of old rose satin ribbon; lace aigrette.

5. *Headdress for middle-aged lady*. Plain bandeaux in front, marteaux at the back, and a tortoiseshell comb.

6. *Winter Hat*, in black velvet, with garland of small curled ostrich feathers; tuft of feathers at the side.

1. *Afternoon Costume.* Grey silk bonnet, the soft crown covered with jet circles; trimmed with dark grey feather pipings and picquet of shaded pink ostrich tips. Velvet ribbon strings and upright bows.

2. *Visiting Toilette.* Hat of white straw, with black lace frill and high plumes; strings of coral ribbon.

3. *High-Crowned Hat* of fine black straw, with lace insertion round brim; pottle crown; fancy green ribbon bows in front and three black plumes at the back.

4. *Papillon Black Straw Hat* with coral bow and jet butterfly; roses veiled with lace under the brim.

5. *Morning Dress.* Brown felt hat, the edge raw; trimmed with several yellow wings 'in the butterfly style, extending sideways and giving breadth'. Brim caught up at the back with rouleau of velvet.

Note the hair done in the new style.

6. *Afternoon Dress.* Red velvet bonnet, trimmed with black tips; black ribbon strings.

1893

1. *Visiting Toilette.* '1830' bonnet in sage green chip, with bands of black velvet and paste buckle. High ostrich plumes, one green and one pink, grey osprey (Debenham and Freebody).

2. *Visiting Toilette.* Hat in Eminence chip, trimmed with black satin rosettes and black tips; crown with open-work jet top; cluster of Eminence roses on the hair behind (Debenham and Freebody).

3. *Hat in Brown Rock Straw,* with witches' (or sugar-loaf) crown of brown velvet trimmed with violets, cowslips and fancy quills. Small green rosette on the hair.

4. *Summer Hat,* in buttercup straw with scroll front, trimmed with black lace, black satin rosettes and shaded crimson roses (Peter Robinson).

5. *Bonnet,* with fashionable Mercury wings at the back, and bow in front; elongated at the ears.

6. *Sailor Hat,* with Mercury wings.

416

1894

1. *Dutch Bonnet*, trimmed with white violets; the front formed of flowers resting on the hair.

2. *Toque*, in fancy straw and guipure; lace wings, green velvet bow with paste buckle; bouquets of black violets.

3. *Picture Hat*, in black nutmeg straw, trimmed with shaded roses and bows of apricot velvet.

4. *Boat-Shaped Hat*, in fawn felt, trimmed with Argos quills and bows of brown ribbon.

5. *Hat in Brown Straw*, with brown lisse bows and cornflower rosettes, and bands of green velvet.

6. *Brown Felt Toreador Hat*, with natural feather pompoms and wings.

1895

1. *Toque*, of bright apricot straw, turned up with jet; Paradise plume of shaded yellows in front; large bunches of yellow and white daisies at the back and sides.

2. *Nelson Hat*, in straw, trimmed with quills.

3. *Straw Hat*, covered with marguerites, the crown somewhat high and widening towards the top; trimmed with green velvet bows, spray of flowers and double set of white wings.

4. *Hat*, in black accordion chiffon with black crown, and rays of white guipure lace; plume of black ostrich feathers and white osprey at one side; pink roses under the brim.

5. *Jet Toque*, with flat crown, trimmed with lemon coloured velvet ribbon, looped up with studs, upright feather aigrette on left side, and drooping bunch of yellow flowers on the right.

6. *Hat of Brown Straw*, with white velvet crown; bunch of Parma violets on each side, and brown emu aigrette on the left.

417

1896

1. *Toque*, with new hour-glass crown, in light straw, trimmed with red velvet, feathers and poppies.

2. *Hat of Castor Felt*, trimmed with folds and double loops of pervenche velvet and cluster of shaded plumes (Redfern of Cowes).

3. *Fawn Felt Hat*, with black velvet and paste buckles; black coque plumes.

4. *Pale Grey Felt Hat*, with red velvet band and coque plumes. Worn for riding or bicycling.

5. *Coiffure*, with waved hair loosely turned back from the forehead, 'arranged in the graceful handle coil (or door knocker) now so fashionable.'

6. *Black Straw Hat*, with frills of tulle, bordered with pale green baby ribbon; bouquet of cerise double poppies (Peter Robinson).

1897

1. *Hat for the Country*, of scarlet felt outline, row of velvet, and bow of scarlet, finished with white coque's feathers.

2. *Hat in Fawn Velvet*, bordered with brown feather trimming; flame coloured velvet roses round the sides and back of brim; owl with large wings transfixed with a diamond arrow.

3. *Ball Coiffure*. 'Victorian style of three stiff, smooth bows; these can only be made to retain their position and looped appearance by the application of specially prepared pomade.'

4. *Middle-Aged Lady's Bonnet*. Front of black roses and sequin wing; cluster of pink roses at the side, with fan of cream lace; black velvet ribbon bows at the back, black osprey, black lace and pink roses. Strings of black velvet ribbon. Price 12/11d.

5. *Toque of Green Straw*, front of pink and black roses, with foliage; new bow and rosettes of pale blue ribbon; fans of black kilted lisse. Price 8/11¾d.

6. *Large Straw Sailor Hat*, trimmed with roses and black ribbon; worn well tilted forwards.

418

1898

1. *Grey Felt Hat*, trimmed with grey feathers and bow in cream velvet, clasped in the centre with ornamental paste buckle.

2. *Blue Felt Hat*, in the new shape, turned back from the face. Black ostrich feathers round the brim, and wired velvet bow in the centre.

3. *Toque*, in écru guipure, with bunch of shaded crimson and pink roses and two tips at the left side, one black and one white. Price 1 guinea.

4. *Dark Blue Straw Hat*, trimmed with pink ribbon, striped with black, 'suitable for a young married woman.'

5. *Rice Straw Hat*, trimmed with roses and red ribbon.

6. *Evening Headdress*. Hair dressed high, with black aigrette and diamond star.

1899

1. *Toque*, of pink fancy straw, brim consisting of two wreaths of roses, without foliage, placed side by side all round. Wired rosette in shaded pink silk at left side.

2. *Halo Hat*, with large feather; bandeau under the brim all round, covered with velvet or chiffon, and ornamented in front with large buckle.

3. *Grey Chip Hat*, with grey feathers; black velvet trimming and strings.

4. *Fancy Straw Hat*, trimmed with black ospreys and velvet.

5. *Marquis Hat*, trimmed with black feather.

6. *Red Velvet Hat*, trimmed with red velvet in two shades, twisted together round crown, finished in front with two velvet loops.

419

1890

HAIR

worn a little fuller but always off the ears; the knot frequently high on the head, or a coil above the nape of the neck.

COIFFURE

The catagan less popular. Evening combs and aigrettes worn. Day caps now only worn by the elderly.

OUTDOORS

Bonnets. 'It would seem hardly possible to have a bonnet too infinitesimal, and the most quaint and curious flowers have been introduced, especially dandelions; still roses are the universal flower.' French crownless bonnets and toques 'do not meet with much approval. . . . What will not women venture at the bidding of fashion, even though neuralgia and rheumatism be the penalty.'

Hats. Large, with low crowns and flat brims, either pointed or round but always turned up at the back, with a bow of ribbon, a bird or feathers. Open crowns and crumpled crowns in white horsehair also worn.

Veils as before.

1891

HAIR

as in '90, or in the Greek style.

COIFFURE

unchanged, for day and evening.

OUTDOORS

Bonnets. Still very small—'composed of two moss roses and a toothpick'. 'A bonnet of colours may be worn without reference to the colour of the dress.'

Hats. Small or large; some flat on the top with the front brim low on the forehead; or with brim upstanding, the space between it and the forehead filled in with a bow or gauze puff. Crinoline, fancy straw and latticed hats popular. Upright trimmings of feathers, ribbons, flowers and birds. 'Crayfish are seen to be crawling up the back of some of the fashionable head-

gears and serpents in various forms adorn hats and bonnets.'

Veils. 'The spider's web of a new and realistic kind.'

1892

HAIR

Either in the Greek style, or with a flat twist on the top and a smooth parting, or with a 'bun' at the nape of the neck. The knot at the back 'is sometimes irreverently called a bird's nest'. The hair is more smooth and tidy than it was.

COIFFURE

Evening aigrettes generally worn.

OUTDOORS

Bonnets. 'Dwindling into a stiff fan of lace and a few roses, or to an ethereal cap encircled by a coronet of jet and worn far back.' Also 'miniature bonnets looking as if they were originally intended for big dolls'.

Hats. (1). Large, some flat with flat crowns, others with flat or waved brims and small high crowns.
(2). Small, either toques, or with small crowns and turned-up brims.
Some hats are worn with sideways tilt.
'The crowns of the new hats and bonnets present quite a novelty. They are very tiny and high and go under various names: Steeple, Welsh, Swiss, Pottle, Jampot and Pickle-jar.' Generally have velvet strings, one inch wide, tied under the chin.

Trimmings. Always upstanding, even lace; a Prince of Wales plume is common. Black common. Felt hats no longer bound but the cut edge is left raw.

Veils. Some very deep with figured border and plain centre.

1893

HAIR

The 'bun or tea-cake coiffure' persists, with invisible net. Hair frames are used to increase the size of the 'bun', and are secured by two hair-pins.

COIFFURE

Day caps still worn by the elderly. Evening unchanged.

420

OUTDOORS

Bonnets. (1). Very small and flat without crowns, known as 'Puritans' or 'Buy a brooms'. Consist of 'mere triangles, point in front, or ovals, forming a base for lace, lisse, aigrettes, etc.'. 'Some have long ear-pieces forming a horse-shoe edge behind; these have strings.' 'Some look like spikey tiaras of jet.'

(2). Large, known as 'Granny' or 'poke' or '1830' bonnets. 'A huge erection with wide and flaring brim and potlike crown and decorated with feathers.'

Toques. 'Such a convenient fashion for they can be adapted to young and old and by the addition of strings can take the place of bonnets.'

Hats. Large and small; crowns low or sugar-loaf shaped. Brims waved or cleft in front. 'Straw hats in two colours are very popular.' The Homburg shape fashionable.

Trimming. Upright flowers; small Mercury wings in front.

Veils. Of thin spotted tulle in various colours. Bridal veils have one corner falling over the face to the knee level.

1894

HAIR

Dressed much higher with a knob standing out behind. Often over a cage. The front in fluffy curls or waved and combed up high over the forehead or with centre parting.

COIFFURE

Evening, unchanged.

OUTDOORS

Bonnets very small, and almost invisible from in front. The 'Dutch' bonnet resembles a close nurse's cap. The small capote, favoured by the Princess of Wales, is fashionable.

Hats. (1). Large, with wide brim and known as the 'picture hat'; of thin materials or straw of vivid colours, and trimmed with violent contrasts of colours, *e.g.* green with heliotrope, orange with pink, pink with blue. Very wide hat ribbons, the bows set up on edge with wings, flowers and accordion-pleated chiffon.

(2). Medium sized 'Toreador hats'.

(3). Small boat-shaped hats with sides rolled upwards.

Toques like stringless bonnets.

1895

HAIR

'It is impossible to wear the hats of the day unless the hair takes wide outlines.' 'There is no practice more general than the waving of the hair', which is brushed back from the forehead. The ears are partly or completely covered.

OUTDOORS

Bonnets. Slightly larger, with 'squareness across the brows'.

Hats and Toques. The latter, being 'more youthful than the bonnet', are taking its place. Hats with brim of one colour and crown of another, and trimming of upright bows and lace. Masses of flowers in summer. Pleated brims popular. Often of shot straw.

Veils. Large spotted veils.

1896

HAIR

Dressed still higher, with outstanding centre and coils round it; the front parted and slightly waved, the sides somewhat loose. Often in large undulating waves with 'door-knocker coil' standing out behind.

COIFFURE

A fancy tortoiseshell comb or aigrette placed far back, for evening wear.

OUTDOORS

Bonnets. Hardly any change except for a tendency to be raised in front.

Hats. Larger and wider in the brim, which is much bent about and often turned up behind, with drooping flowers at the back. Hats are worn tipped over the forehead. 'Our millinery is the brightest part of our apparel and the quietest of women seem to select the most vivid hues.' Floral toques are popular. Many hat brims are bound with black velvet.

New crowns: The Yeoman crown, widening at the top. The hour-glass, a variety of the yeoman but smaller and diminishing in size towards the middle.

Bicycling hats: Sailor, boat-shaped and toques. 'A small felt hat with black ribbon and three groups of green cock's feathers, with white lining bearing the time-table to instruct the cyclist when she should light her lamp' (Marshall & Snelgrove).

Veils. Large spotted veils much worn.

1897
HAIR

Increasing in height with loops and bows. The waving becoming more fuzzy, and the hair brushed off the face.

COIFFURE

for evening, combs, daggers and aigrettes general.

OUTDOORS

Bonnets and Hats. 'All millinery may be described as rather gorgeous in colour and exuberant in decoration. The toque is everywhere and is worn, like the straight-brimmed sailor-hat, straight over the forehead, while the large hat and the toreador are much slanted on one side.' Bonnets are smaller. 'Strings are reserved entirely for the middle-aged; girls will have none of them.' 'Straws in brilliantly vivid colours'; leghorns trimmed with 'a perfect avalanche of black ostrich feathers'.

Veils, of black spotted chenille.

1898
HAIR
No change.

Bonnets and Hats. As in '97, except for a droop-ing, rather turned-down brim; or with a turned-up brim (the 'Polichinelle') under which is a bandeau of feathers, flowers or ribbon. 'A great deal of trimming is used on all our hats.'

'Where is the once popular bonnet? It seems to have fallen into the limbo of forgotten things in spite of the patronage of Royalty.'

1899
HAIR

Dressed high and loosely brushed back from the forehead.

OUTDOORS

Hats. (1) Large with brim turned down in front and behind or on one side, and worn tilted. (2) 'Halo hats' with upturned brim. (3) Wide toques and turban-toques. (4) Marquise or three-cornered shape. (5) Sailor hats.

Colours very varied. 'I have never seen such a range of colours in straw, the Jacqueminot and pickled cabbage being quite the best.'

Trimmings. Fancy cock feathers, cherries, currants, hazel nuts and mountain ash, flowers, tulle, lace and ribbon. 'Hats are more poetical than ever. We have entered into the era of fancy and rustic straws covered with honeysuckle, eglantine or morning glories. Tulle hats and others of gathered chiffon blend hyacinth shades with rose, pink and petunia in every possible tint.'

UNDERCLOTHING IN THE '90's

During this decade a new conception as to the functions of underclothing developed. No longer merely utilitarian it was to be primarily beautiful. But it must also serve as a weapon of sex-attraction. That this was a purpose never to be forgotten is constantly implied in such phrases as: 'There is a decidedly fussy element in all good underclothing' ('96). 'Bewitching silk petticoats' ('95). Equally significant was the slightly old-fashioned warning that no nice-minded girl would wish to wear beautiful underclothing. The singular fashion, so noticeable during most of the decade, for petticoats which would emit a mysterious rustle also implied a desire to remind the audience of their existence, and the art of displaying frillies was carefully studied.

At the same time it was being realised that these once mundane garments were a possible medium for artistic expression so that one and all received an intense amount of interest and attention. Owing to the amount of lace employed as well as silk that portion of the wardrobe became extremely expensive as compared to the modern woman's. A large number of women, of course, were content to continue with the more homely garments, combinations and serge knickerbockers, etc., especially those who bicycled and took active exercise.

The Chemise

The Princess shape, of cambric, batiste or linen, or surah. Longcloth had become very old-fashioned. Many were made in the Empire shape with belt and fitting bodice, and skirt frilled at the edge with lace. The chemise was largely displaced by combinations. Chemises with bishop sleeves. ('92). Chemise with full front shaped by graduated tucks, deep cambric frill round the neck. ('92).

Combinations

Of natural wool, 7/- to 12/6. ('90). Many of silk and wool mixture 'fitting like a glove'. Or of surah edged with lace. 'New undergarment of fine muslin edged with lace, combining low bodice, petticoat and drawers, worn over the corset which is worn over the vest.' (Introduced by Marshall & Snelgrove, 1892.) Combinations in accordion-pleated surah or shot silk. ('92). Bands of lace and insertion threaded with coloured ribbon decorate the garment which is no longer a close-fitting affair but resembles a chemise with loose drawers attached. Thus, in '95, 'charming pale pink llama combinations with frills of torchon lace at the knee and neck.' Others in nainsook or ribbed silk with shoulder straps and low square opening.

Petticoats

'Coloured flannel petticoats are things of the past' ('90). Accordion-pleated or with scalloped edge trimmed with lace, or fine materials including shot silk, appear at the beginning of the decade. In '91 petticoats 'are 2½ yards wide at the hem, close gored at the top, with a drawing-string behind; trimmed with one or two scanty frills of scalloped embroidery with insertion'. Bright coloured silk or satin petticoats with a slightly gathered flounce (in winter often lined with flannel), while moreen, at 2/9 a yard, is much used to produce a rustling effect ('92). The more dressy article, often in coloured stripes, may have vandyked frills or bands of lace insertion as well as lace trimming. To increase the apparent number of frills a white petticoat with a deep lace flounce may be worn over a muslin petticoat having a double flounced edge producing the effect of three petticoats. Quilted satin petticoats edged with rows of baby ribbon loops ('93) for winter.

To match the shape of the dress the bell-shaped petticoat at this time had two gores on each side and was gathered at the back of the waist and again further down.

The white petticoat which had for a few years been somewhat displaced by the coloured, returned to favour in '94, now with accordion-pleated frills or beadings run through with coloured ribbons or with chiffon frills. 'The ordinary woman will wear only combinations and a silk petticoat lined with flannel, or if a cambric petticoat an underpetticoat of silk with woollen lining.' ('94). The garment 'now at the zenith of its glory' ('95) may be 'of spotted net with endless rows of tucks, lace insertions, frillings and puffings', and edged with ruching, etc. It is cut wide and much gored at the top.

The rustling garment is replaced by softer materials in '98 when it is cut tight to the knee level, thence with a series of tiny flounces edged with lace and often baby ribbon or chiffon ruches.

Drawers

These are cut extremely wide in the leg and elaborately trimmed with lace flounces and insertion. Prosaic serge knickers, gathered at the knee or below, are commonly worn by those who disapprove of a garment 'twenty inches round at the knee with a ten inch lace frill', and its moral significance. 'Coloured silk knickerbockers of enormous dimensions, some two yards wide, often lined with flannel' suggest a broader outlook. By '95 the fashionable garment had become as wide as the petticoat itself.

Stays

For the greater part of the decade excessive tight-lacing was the mode. It was the ambition of every young lady to have a waist measurement not exceeding 21 inches if she made any claim to be fashionable. Stays were beautified by being made of brocade, satin and silk coutil and 'the corset is now always worn over the petti-coat' ('91). A number were constructed with attached 'bust-improvers'. The more elaborate were trimmed with lace frills and coloured ribbon rosettes ('94). The stays were somewhat shorter than in the previous decade. By '99 we read 'corsets are fast disappearing'. Certainly a number were wearing 'the new skeleton corset of a few crossed straps worn under a belt-corset of fine batiste'. Tight-lacing had begun to decline.

Bust Improvers

These were frequently employed. Some in flexible celluloid were advertised in '96. A simpler type—but no doubt effective—consisted of an embroidered band into which could be inserted pads of various sizes, an example of which (worn in 1892) is in my collection. The original owner explained that the size of pad to be worn at a dance would depend on 'who her partner was likely to be'.

Nightdresses

These became more and more elaborate, generally with yoked necks and frills, and made of silk, surah and nainsook. Even the flannel variety was often trimmed with lace. Accordion-pleating or wide frills down the front and round the wide sleeves (which imitated the gigot sleeves of the day dress during the middle of the decade) were usual features. Some in the 'Empire style' had the upper part re-sembling an Empire bodice with bands of puffing and insertion and a lace yoke and Toby frill, with full bishop sleeves and ruffles; or with a cape-like collar. Baby ribbons run in and out at the elbow and wrist ('93); or a frilled plastron and tucked front ('94) were varieties. The 'copious use of pink ribbons' is noted in '95. In '94 are described: 'Lady's pyjamas in pale blue and white silk and wool mixture; tied round the waist with an encased ribbon and finished at the wrist, ankles and throat

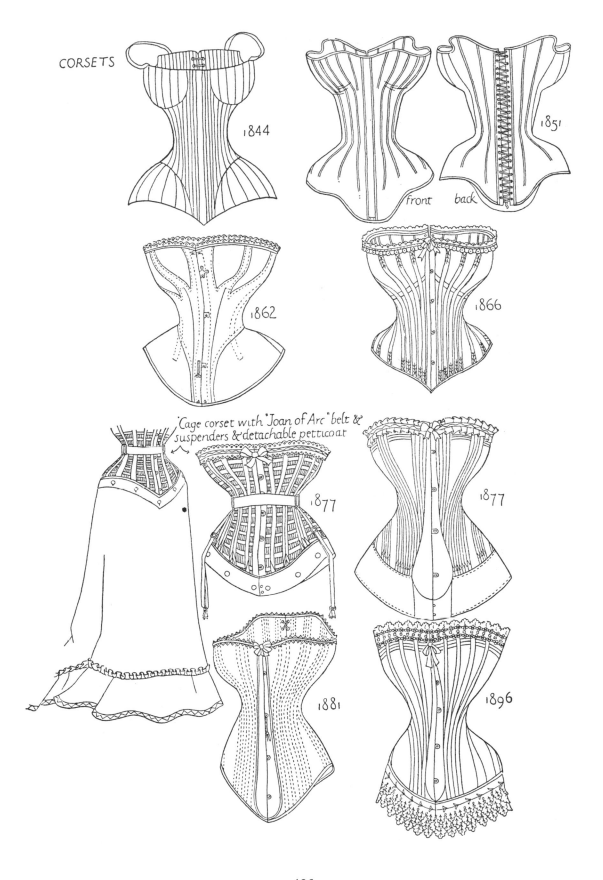

CORSETS

1844

1851

front   back

1862

1866

'Cage corset with "Joan of Arc" belt &
suspenders & detachable petticoat

1877

1877

1881

1896

with lace; large bishop sleeves; cascade of lace down the bodice.' Towards the end of the decade the sleeves were often wide at the wrist in the pagoda shape.

The Petticoat Bodice and Camisole

This is described (in '91) as being made without any fastenings, the front cut on the cross, the fronts crossing over and disappearing under the petticoat band.

RETROSPECT

A survey of women's clothing in the nineteenth century reveals two chief features; the most obvious is the technical improvements, due to science and machinery, whereby materials were multiplied and cheapened enabling an ever increasing number to indulge in the luxury of following the fashions. That this was, on the whole, beneficial to the wearers is, I think, unquestionable. Although the Upper Class perpetually complained of the encroachment of the Lower Orders who would persist in aping their betters by copying their clothes, they overlooked the fact that better clothes induce better conduct which is the first step towards a higher standard of thinking and feeling. Clothing has gradually become almost an integral part of the personality and shabby clothing in itself creates a sense of degradation. The Victorian lady, very conscious of this as regards herself, was unwilling to recognise it as regards her inferiors. As an elevating force silk is perhaps more potent even than sermons.

Less obvious but even more profound in its effects was the introduction of the 'tailor-made' and 'sports' costume, that is to say, a type of dress designed for purposes other than that of being 'attractive'. For the first time in the history of costume it was being recognised that a woman's life might have other aspects than those based upon her sex. Hitherto a sexual career was the only honourable, lady-like and respectable one open to her, and an early marriage entailed a quarter of a century to be spent with perpetual reminders of the fact. It would have been strange if this preoccupation were not reflected in her conduct, manners and clothing. It may not have been a mere chance that the taste for huge distended skirts, which reigned during the middle of the century, coincided with the super-fertility epoch of the '40's, '50's and '60's. But the new idea, becoming noticeable in the last quarter of the century and now a commonplace to the modern generation, was the beginning of a psychological revolution, the first traces of which can be detected in that unprepossessing garb, the 'tailor-made' of sixty years ago. Similarly the double-skirted, aproned tennis costume of the early '80's was the progenitor of the modern 'sports dress', representing an attire designed ad hoc in which the possible effect on the male was scarcely considered. England can claim the credit of this revolutionary idea, the most significant in the history of women's dress.

A study of the nineteenth century destroys the illusion that feminine fashions always originate in Paris. During the whole century the Parisian designers were essentially conservative in their ideas, relying on recurrent revivals of modes borrowed from the eighteenth and earlier centuries. Even the high-waisted dress associated with the First Empire had originated in England a few years before 1800. Paris led the world of fashion from after Waterloo until the middle of the '60's when the emancipatory movement began in this country and in America, and English fashions started to deviate along their own lines. The United States, in the person of Mrs. Bloomer, may, if they choose, claim to have driven the first wedge splitting the monolith in two from which the modern biped eventually emerged; but we look in vain to France for any fundamentally new idea in dress. The '80's may claim to have introduced, among cultured people, a degree of individualism in styles of dress, in opposition to the rigid decrees of fashion, an enterprise mainly of English origin, and traceable to the English Aesthetic movement. The Pre-Raphaelite movement, on the other hand, seemed hardly to have affected women's fashions perhaps because they were then so dominated by Paris.

The tendency of fashion to exaggerate a feature can only be explained on the ground that it attempts to excite emotion in the observer or the wearer, and it is well recognised that to sustain the same intensity of feeling a stimulus must be progressively increased until, at last, exhaustion is arrived at. The kind of appeal must then change, the most effective being in the opposite direction. Change, indeed, is essential. 'Quel est le plus grand ennemi de l'amour? C'est l'habitude.' That such was the prime function of fashion in the last century is, I think, sufficiently demonstrated. That it will always remain so, however, is doubtful. We are arriving at the notion that woman's dress should express not so much her social rank or physical charm as her competence. The changes and the progress made since 1900 I hope to describe in a subsequent volume.

1892
Dinner dress of brocaded satin and faille; chiffon drapery

GLOSSARY OF MATERIALS

(The bracket figures indicate the year when a material is first mentioned in contemporary books.)

ADRIANOPLE. ('76). An unglazed cotton lining; in '80, a red calico printed with arabesques.

AEROPHANE. (about '20). A fine crimped crepe.

ALBERT CRAPE ('62). A superior quality of black silk crape, for mourning.

ALEPINE. ('32). Resembles bombazine.

ALGERINE. ('40). A twilled shot silk, green and poppy, or blue and gold.

ALLIBALLI. An Indian muslin.

ALPACA. ('41). A springy, shiny textile, of the wool of the Alpaca goat and silk: later, cotton. Invented by Sir Titus Salt, 1838.

ALPAGO. ('43). 'A stout satin delaine.'

AMY ROBSART SATIN. ('36). 'White ground with white flowers traced in gold thread, or pale-coloured ones in silver.'

ANDALUSIAN. ('25). A fine open washing silk with broché pattern.

ANGLO-MERINO. (about '09). A textile, nearly as fine as muslin, made from George III's merino flock. Manufactured at Norwich.

ANGOLA. ('15). 'The new lama cloth.' Made from the hair of the llama goat.

ARIEL. ('37). A woollen gauze quadrilled in white on light coloured ground.

ARMOIRE. ('80). A very thick corded silk.

ARMOZEAU. ('20's). 'A silk similar to lutestring but not so thick.'

ARMOZEEN. 'A stout silk almost invariably black.'

ARMURE. ('50). A rich silk and wool textile with an almost invisible design, such as a twill, a triangle or a chain on the surface.

ARMURETTE. ('74). A fancy silk and wool textile.

BAGDAD. ('72). An Eastern silk, striped like Algerienne but with wider lines and of thicker material.

BALERNOS. ('74). A very soft and silky mohair.

BALZARINE. ('30's). A cotton and worsted textile similar to barège.

BALZERINE. ('89). A sort of narrow striped grenadine with broad silk crepe stripes.

BAMBULO. ('85). A coarsely woven, slightly transparent shot canvas cloth.

BARATHEA. ('40's). A silk and worsted mixture, black; used for mourning.

BARÈGE. ('19). A semi-transparent textile of silk and wool, the former thrown up on the surface; open mesh. Sometimes of all wool.

BARÈGE DE PYRENEES. ('50). A barège printed with delicate foliage and brilliant flowers.

BARÈGE-GRENADINE. ('77). A cotton and jute barège.

BARPOUR. ('47). A twilled wool and silk mixture.

BASIN DE LAINE. ('55). A thick woollen dimity, the right side ribbed, the other with a long soft nap.

BATISTE. ('20's). A dressed cotton muslin with a wiry finish.

BAYADÈRE. ('69). A striped silk and wool textile, the stripes being alternately plain and satiny.

BECHE-CASHMERE. ('48). A woollen textile 'thicker than flannel and as soft as silk'.

BEIGE. ('74). A woollen Vicuna cloth usually coffee-coloured; a firm, thin worsted with a smooth twill.

BELGIAN LINEN. ('79). A thick damask-like linen with coloured pattern on cream ground.

BENGALINE. ('69). A very light mohair, self-coloured or brocaded with very small flowers.

('80). Similar to a silk barège.

('84). 'A new name for Sicilienne; a corded silk and wool textile, the weft of wool.'

BENGALINE POPLIN. ('65). A Poplin with a thick cord.

BENGALINE RUSSE. ('92). A shot wool and silk, flecked in contrasting colours.

BOMBAZET. A plain twilled worsted, used for mourning.

429

BOMBAZINE. A textile, the warp of silk, the weft of worsted, and having a twilled appearance.

BONÉETTE. ('77). A wool and silk mixture having a damask pattern over it.

BOURACAN. ('67). A kind of ribbed poplin.

BOURRETTE. ('77). A twilled woollen ground with multi-coloured knots and threads of spun silk on it.

BRAZILIAN CORDED SARCENET. ('20). A thick white satin cord running through a coloured sarcenet.

BRILLIANTINE. ('36). A very light textile of cashmere wool and silk.

BRILLIANTS. ('63). A silk textile, the white ground with small damask pattern.

BROCADE. A silk or stuff of which the pattern is formed by extra weft.

BROCANTINE. ('98). A fine woollen brocaded with silk in monochrome.

BROCHÉ. A velvet or silk with a satin figure on the face.

BULGARIAN CLOTH. ('83). A cream coloured cotton, plain or striped, worked in tinsel and coloured silk.

BUNTING. ('81). A coarse kind of nun's cloth.

BURE. ('74). A coarse woollen stuff with broad diagonal rib.

BURIDAN. ('36). A wide horizontally striped silk of two tones of one colour.

BYZANTINE. ('81). A dull semi-transparent textile of silk and wool, closely woven; used for mourning.

BYZANTINE GRANITÉ. ('69). A dark brown woollen material enlivened by a few threads of gold.

CACHEMIRE. ('76). A textile of fine wool and silk, the patterns usually of Eastern shades.

CACHEMIRE ROYAL. ('89). Resembles a rich cashmere with a silk back.

CALAMANCO. A cotton and worsted textile, highly glazed, plain or twilled.

CALEDONIAN SILK. ('10–'20). Similar to poplin but with a more silky surface, and having a chequered pattern on white ground.

CAMAYEUX SILK. ('50). Chiné silk with colour on colour.

CAMELEON. ('30). A silk figured in large bouquets on the outside and stripes inside. In the '40's a silk shot in three colours; in the '50's a shot poplin.

CAMLET. Originally a textile of the hair of the camel or of the Angora goat; later, of wool and hair, silk and hair, plain or twilled.

CARACULE. ('92). Astrachan with a wide curl in the hair.

CARACULE MATERIAL. ('94). A crocodile mohair surface over a sort of flannel lining, giving the effect of black shot with colour.

CARMELINE. ('70). A fine cloth.

CARMELITE. ('90's). Similar to thin beige but more open.

CASHMERE. A twilled worsted made of the wool of the Tibet goat; European imitations in sheep's wool.

CASHMERE SYRIEN. ('40). A very fine twilled cashmere, more substantial than mousselaine de laine but very soft and without a wrong side.

CASHMERIENNE. ('80). A fine woollen with a twill on both sides.

CASHMERE TWILL. ('90). A cotton imitation of French cashmere.

CASIMIR. ('77). A thin twilled woollen textile.

CASIMIR DE SOIE. ('53). A silk and wool textile having the effect of shot silk.

CHALEY OR CHALLIS. ('32). A thin textile, twilled, of silk and wool, originally of camel's hair; printed in colours, usually floral patterns.

CHAMBERTINE. ('72). A mixture of linen and wool, for light costumes.

CHAMBRAY. ('80's). A thick, strong, coarse zephyr.

CHATOYANTE. ('47). A thin woollen, grey ground covered with broad satin check.

CHEVIOT. ('80). A soft woollen textile made in tiny hair stripes and checks.

CHEVRON DE LAINE. ('78). A fine diagonally woven cloth, of German make, each horizontal line being reversely twilled.

CHIFFON. ('90). A delicate silk barège or grenadine.

CHINA CREPE. Made of raw silk, gummed and twisted. Thicker than ordinary crepe.

CHINA DAMASK. ('79). A cotton damask in two shades, with palm pattern.

CHINA GAUZE. ('78). A gauze in light colours sprinkled with tufts of floss silk.

CHINÉ SILK. ('20's). A silk, the pattern having the appearance of having 'run'.

CISELÉ VELVET. ('76). A satin ground with raised pattern in velvet.

CLEMENTINE. ('34). A rich thick silk gauze, used for lining bonnets, etc.

CLOTIDIENNE. ('33). A ribbon-striped satin.

COBURG. ('40's). A wool and cotton twilled stuff resembling French merino.

CONCERTINA CLOTH. ('92). A corded cloth with silk lines running through it.

CORDELIÈRE. ('46). A silk and wool mixture.

CORINNA. ('37). A richly flowered silk resembling embroidery.

COTELÉ. ('65). A thick ribbed silk.

COTELETTE. ('81). A stocking-woven woollen which does not stretch.

COTELINE. ('92). A striped woollen corduroy.

COTOLINE. ('86). A mixture of faille and wool, black, resembling Ottoman but softer.

COURTAULD'S NEW SILK CREPE. ('94). 'Almost as thin and soft as chiffon.'

COUTIL. ('40's). A French species of jean but lighter in weight; a twilled cotton cloth.

CRAPE OR CREPE. A transparent crimped silk gauze.

CREPE DE CHINE. A very soft China crepe.

CREPE-LISSE. See Lisse.

CREPELINE. ('70's). A cheap substitute for crepe de Chine.

CREPE POPLIN. ('71). A silk and wool textile, slightly repped, but crinkly, like crepe.

CREPE ROYAL. ('89). A transparent kind of crepe de Chine.

CREPON. ('66). A China crepe with a silky lustre and soft feel.
('82). A wool or silk or mixed fabric with silky surface resembling crepe but thicker.
('90's). A woollen creped to look puffed between stripes or squares of plain weave. Often with a slight admixture of silk in it.

CRETONNE. ('67). A twilled unglazed cotton fabric printed in colours.

DAMASK. A figured fabric of silk or linen, the pattern of which appears reversed on the back.

DIEPPE SERGE. ('72). A serge with a coarse diagonal twill.

DIMITY. A stout cotton fabric, plain or twilled, with a raised pattern on one side, sometimes printed.

DIPHERA. ('52). A fine soft kid leather, used for bonnets.

DJEDDA. ('66). A poil de chevre with silk spots.

DRAP DE FRANCE. ('71). A double-twilled cashmere.

DRAP DE PARIS. ('60). A very fine soft cloth.

DRAP DE SOIE. Synonymous with poplin.

DRAP DE VELOURS. ('61). A thick soft velvety cloth.

DRAP DE VENISE. ('66). A ribbed poplin.

DRAP FOURREAU. ('67). A thick smooth cloth with a plush surface on the inner side.

ECCELIDE. ('37). A cashmere and silk material, chiné and striped.

EGYPTIAN CLOTH. ('66). A fabric of silk with some wool; soft in substance.

ELEPHANT CLOTH. ('69). Of twisted flax-cord, having a basket-like appearance.

EPANGELINE. ('68). A rep-like material, entirely of wool.

EPANGLINE. ('90's). A woollen sateen with a slight cord.

ESMERALDA. ('31). A white crepe or gauze embroidered in black and gold.

ESTAMINE. ('76). A somewhat thick serge, firm in texture.

ETRUSCAN CLOTH. ('73). A cloth with a rough surface like bath-towelling.

FAILLE. ('63). 'An unwatered moiré', softer and brighter than gros grain.

FAILLETTE. ('98). A soft ribbed woollen fabric with a gloss like silk.

FLANNELETTE. ('76). An American cloth fabric, one side twilled, the other with a plush-like surface.

FLORENCE. ('40's). A kind of corded barège or grenadine. Also used for a thin kind of taffeta used for lining.

FOULARD. A soft, light, washing silk, twilled. Originally, in the '20's, of Indian manufacture; later of French.

FOULARD POILE DE CHEVRE. ('70). A foulard-like fabric of goat's hair 'with the brilliance of Jap silk'.

FOULÉ. ('82). 'A material resembling casimir with a silky look', soft and velvety.

FRENCH JET. ('93). Jet facets applied to metal.

FRISÉ BROCADE. ('85). A brocade with the pattern upstanding like terry.

FROU-FROU. ('70). A satin-like washing cloth.

FUSTIAN. A coarse, stout, twilled cotton; many varieties, including jean.

GABARDINE. ('79). Patented by Burberry. A waterproof cloth of Egyptian cotton proofed before weaving.

GALATEA. A strong, firm, striped cotton fabric woven in imitation of linen.

GAUZE. A delicate transparent textile woven of silk, or silk and flax, or cotton; the holes made by twisting the threads round each other.
Of Indian, Chinese, French, English and Scotch manufacture.

GAUZE ILLUSION. ('31). A fine, close gauze.

GAUZE SYLPHIDE. ('32). Of alternate stripes of gauze and satin ribbon, the latter brocaded with bouquets of flowers.

GAZE PERLÉE. ('33). Semi-transparent gauze with small silk squares figured on it.

GAZELINE BARÈGE. ('77). A half-transparent textile of pure llama wool, resembling barège.

GENAPPE CLOTH. ('63). Of wool and cotton, generally striped in two shades of the same colour.

GENOA PLUSH. ('87). A plush with a very short thick pile, resembling velvet.

GENOA VELVET. ('76). 'A term now applied when the ground is satin and the arabesque figures are velvet.'

GINGHAM. A stout chequered cloth made of linen; later of cotton.

GLACÉ SILK. A plain silk with a peculiar lustrous quality.

GOALY. ('74). A kind of écru silk, the texture like fine canvas.

GRANITE. ('20). A stuff made of chenille and used for headdresses.
('65). A sort of chiné woollen textile in two shades of one colour.

GRENADINE. An open silk, or silk and wool, gauze resembling barège but with a more open mesh. Many varieties both plain and figured.

GROGRAM. An old name for gros grain.

GROS OR GROS GRAIN. A stout silk of rich quality showing a cord from selvedge to selvedge.

GROS DE LONDRES. ('83). Similar to Ottoman but with a much finer cord, comprising 'two small grains between two large'.

GROS DE NAPLES. ('15). A corded Italian silk similar to Irish poplin; 'lutestring, now termed gros de Naples.' (Mrs. Papendiek, 1837.)

GROS DE ROME. ('71). A crinkled silk between a China crepe and a foulard.

GROS DE SUEZ. ('67). A silk with 'three small grains between two larger'.

GROS DE TOURS. ('33). A rich corded silk, resembling terry velvet; practically identical with rep Imperial.

GROS DES INDES. ('27). A heavy silk with narrow transverse stripes.

GROS D'HIVER. A silk between a tabby and a paduasoy.

HENRIETTA CLOTH. ('90's). Resembles fine cashmere, but with silk warp or weft.

HOPSACK. ('93). A coarsely woven woollen serge-canvas.

IMPERIAL GAUZE. 'An open gauze, having a white warp with a coloured weft.'

IMPERIAL VELVET. ('70). A textile composed of alternate stripes of corded silk and velvet, the latter double the width of the former.

IPSIBOE. ('21). A yellow crepe.

JACCONET. A thin cotton textile, between muslin and cambric. Nainsook is the modern equivalent.

JANUS CORD. ('67). A black rep of wool and cotton, the fine cord showing equally on both sides; used for mourning.

JAPANESE PONGEE. ('70). A silk of the same texture as a crepe, but with a smooth surface.

JAPANESE SILK. ('67). A silk textile, hard and springy resembling alpaca.

JARDINIÈRE. ('41). A striped and gauffred crepe strewn with small flowers.

JEAN. A twilled cotton cloth, thick and strong; later a twilled sateen.

JERSEY. ('79). An elastic woollen material resembling fine knitting.

KARAMINI. ('78). A light woollen fabric with slightly fleecy surface.

KERSEYMERE. 'A twilled fine woollen cloth of a peculiar texture, one-third of the warp being always above and two-thirds below each shoot of weft.'

KINGKOB. An Indian muslin, gauze or silk, sometimes embroidered with gold or silver.

KLUTEEN. ('15). A striped French figured silk for Spencers and Pelisses.

KNICKERBOCKER. ('67). A thick, coarse woollen stuff, self-coloured or speckled.

LAINE FOULARD. ('61). A silk and wool washing silk.

LENO. A transparent muslin-like textile of linen thread.

LEVANTINE. ('15). A twilled sarcenet.
('40's). A rich faced, stout twilled silk, similar to the surah of the '70's and '80's.

LEVANTINE FOLICÉ. ('37). A soft rich silk in arabesque patterns.

LIMOUSINE. ('74). A thick rough woollen, coarser than cheviot, and hairy.

LINSEY. A coarse mixed material of wool and flax, the warp of thread, the woof of worsted.

LISSE. A silk uncrimped gauze.
('94). 'The new name for improved, uncrushable Chiffon.'

LOOKING-GLASS SILK. ('92). 'A glacé with a suspicion of moiré on its shining surface.'

LOVE. A thin silk, used for ribbons, with narrow satin stripes in it.

LUISINE. ('34). A heavy rep silk.

LUSTRE. A thin kind of poplin, of silk and worsted.
('90's). A variety of mohair with shiny surface.

LUTESTRING. A very fine corded glossy silk fabric.

MACABRE. ('32). A light silk and wool textile figured in small designs and edged with a Gothic border.

MADRAS. ('25). See Muslins.

MALINES. ('85). A fancy canvas closely woven, having the appearance of being inter-woven.

MARABOUT. Feathers from a species of stork. Also ('77) a woollen soft to the touch but looking rough and mossy on the surface.

MARCELINE. ('33). 'A brilliant but slight kind of sarcenet.'

MARCELLA. A cotton quilting or coarse pique with a diaper pattern in relief.

MARIPOSA. ('72). A washing sateen with stripes alternately plain and dotted.

MATELASSÉ. ('74). A firm substantial silk woven to resemble quilting.

MECCA. ('77). A gauze of the thinnest texture with dashes of silk in the wool.

MEMPHIS. ('36). A semi-transparent textile of very fine cashmere wool.

MERINO. A thin woollen twilled cloth, of the wool of the Spanish merino sheep; sometimes a mixture of wool and silk. The French merino is equally good on both sides.

MERINO CREPE. A mixture of silk and worsted producing a shot effect.

MIKADO. ('75). A silk alpaca imitating Jap silk (made by Lister of Bradford).

MILANESE TAFFETA. ('80). A semi-transparent silk textile woven on the cross.

MIRROR VELVET. ('90's). A watered velvet having the appearance of reflections in it.

MISTAKE. ('06). A shaded silk used for ribbons.

MOHAIR. A fabric made of the hair of the Angora goat, woven with silk, wool, or cotton warps; resembles coarse alpaca.

MOIRÉ ANTIQUE. A heavy stout watered gros grain, the watering being in irregular waves.

MOIRÉ VELOURS. ('97). A silk and wool watered velvet with a large irregular design.

MOLLETON. ('65). A sort of thick smooth flannel.

MONTPENSIER CLOTH. ('71). A smooth soft cloth twilled on the wrong side.

MORAVIAN WORK. ('12). Cut work with button-holing at the edges; a fore-runner of broderie anglaise.

MOSS CLOTH. ('78). A soft rich mixture of silk and wool with a mossy texture.

MOUSSELAINE DE LAINE. ('33). A fine light woollen cloth, of a muslin-like texture, and often 'figured in gay patterns like a calico print'.

MOUSSELAINE DE LAINE CHINÉ. ('41). A similar fabric with chiné patterns.

MOUSSELAINE DE SOIE. A very fine soft silk textile with a mesh like muslin.

MOUSSELAINE THIBET. ('32). A silk and wool textile, watered and semi-transparent.

MOUSSELAINE VELOURS. ('32). Mousselaine de laine figured with cut velvet stripes.

MOZAMBIQUE. ('65). A silk broché wool grenadine.

MULL. See Muslin.

MUSCOVITE. ('84). 'A handsome thick corded silk.'

MUSCOVITE VELVET. ('83). A velvet brocade on a ribbed silk ground.

MUSLIN. A fine thin semi-transparent cotton textile.

Many varieties:

1. *Book.* Similar to Swiss but coarser.
2. *Indian.* Soft, thin, opaque and silky.
3. *Leno.* Very open and stiff.
4. *Madras.* Transparent ground with a pattern in thick soft thread apparently darned upon it.
5. *Mull.* Similar to Indian but not silky; finer than Nainsook.
6. *Organdy.* Soft opaque muslin with a raised spot worked in it.
7. *Swiss.* Has a hard finish and is nearly transparent.

NAINSOOK. A delicate muslin.

NANKEEN. A yellowish cotton cloth.

NATTÉ. ('74). A firm substantial silk woven to resemble cane-platting.

NEIGEUSE. ('77). A soft twilled woollen textile with a surface speckled or 'clotted', and rough-faced.

NET. An open fabric, the holes made by knotting.

NORWICH CREPE. A textile with a silk warp and worsted weft, of two shades of a colour; resembles bombazine but is not twilled.

NUN'S CLOTH. ('81). 'A fine thin untwilled woollen fabric formerly called mousselaine de laine; it is a kind of bunting.'

NUN'S VEILING. ('79). Synonymous with Voile, a kind of thin woollen barège; later, used as a synonym for Nun's Cloth.

ONDINE. ('71). A very soft and brilliant silk and wool mixture.
('93). A corded silk crepon.

ORIENTAL SATIN. ('69). An all-wool or wool and silk textile, soft and thick; woven in two colours, one brilliant, the other dark.

ORLEANS CLOTH. ('37). Resembles an untwilled Coburg; the warp of thin cotton, the weft of worsted.

OTTOMAN PLUSH. ('82). A silk textile, having a broad corded ground with plush figures of close thick pile.

OTTOMAN REP. ('82). A repped lustrous satin woven on both sides with flat cording.

OTTOMAN SATIN. ('32). A rich shaded satin brocaded with flowers.

OTTOMAN SILK. ('82). 'A term loosely applied to every kind of silk with a horizontal thick cord and two or three cords between.'

OTTOMAN VELVET. ('69). A velvet with coloured patterns brocaded over it.

('79). A richly repped uncut velvet.

PADUASOY. A smooth strong rich silk textile.

PALMYRENE. ('27). Between a poplin and a barège; embroidered in silk.

PALMYRIENNE. ('31). A wool and silk textile, shot; resembles mousselaine de soie.

PANNE. ('99). A soft silk material between velvet and satin.

PARAMATTA. A kind of Bombazine, the weft of worsted, the warp of cotton; originally with silk warp. Used for mourning.

PEAU DE SOIE. ('80's). A dull, sateen-finished silk.

PEKIN. ('30's). A silk textile woven in stripes; the term was used loosely for any light striped silk.

('79). A term for any textile with alternate dull and lustrous stripes.

PEKIN LABRADOR. ('37). A Pekin flowered in wreaths.

PEKIN POINT. ('40). A very rich white silk painted with flowers or bouquets with foliage, with a light mixture of gold in the pattern.

PEKIN VICTORIA. ('42). A silk with a satiné ground, shot in white and cherry or blue, with patterns in white.

PERCALE. A fine calico cloth, slightly glazed, often having a small printed design.

('63). 'A fine glazed linen.'

PERCALINE. ('48). A textile between a gingham and a muslin, striped or quadrilled and printed in flowers.

PERKALE. ('18). The French term for cambric muslin.

PERSIAN. A very thin silk textile, almost transparent.

PERSIAN THIBET. ('32). A woollen textile with embroidered design similar to shawls.

PLUSH. A shaggy, hairy kind of silk or cotton velvet, with a long, soft nap, resembling fur.

POILE DE CHEVRE. ('61). A textile of goat's hair with a shiny satin-like surface.

POMPADOUR CHINÉ. ('40). A woollen twilled textile with small chiné pattern and striped horizontally in minute thread-like stripes.

POMPADOUR DUCHESSE. ('50). A satin with broad stripes divided by other stripes sprinkled with tiny flowers.

POMPADOUR SILK. ('32). A silk fabric with black ground and a highly raised pattern in detached sprigs, in lemon, rose and green.

POMPADOUR SHANTUNG. ('80). A thick washing silk like foulard, covered with Pompadour designs on a brilliant ground.

PONGEE. ('70's). Synonymous with Shantung.

POPLIN. A kind of rep made of a silk warp and wool or worsted weft, having a fine cord on the surface and produced in several varieties, brocaded, watered and plain. There are three classes, the single, the double and the terry; the last is richly corded and unlike terry velvet is the same on both sides.

POPLINETTE. ('59). 'Sometimes known as Norwich Lustre, and occasionally as Japanese silk.' Is made with a glazed thread and silk.

POPLIN LACTÉE. ('37). A poplin shot with white.

POPLIN LAMA. ('64). Similar to mousselaine de laine, but softer and thicker.

POULT DE SOIE. A pure corded silk of a rich quality.

('63). 'A mixture of silk and alpaca with a shiny surface.'

PULLCAT. (Eighteenth and early nineteenth century). A printed muslin or cotton. (From Pulicat, a town near Madras.)

RADZIMIR. ('49). A black silk, deeper than bombazine, and used for mourning.

REGENCE. ('89). A rich silk textile with a ribbed satin face.

REP. A textile composed of silk, or silk and wool, or wool only, having a thick cord and resembling poplin, the ribs running horizontally.

REP-BLUET. A dark blue silk figured with cornflowers in black satin.

REP IMPERIAL. ('35). A rich silk imitating terry velvet.

REP SARCENET. A textile between gros de Naples and a fine cut French velvet.

RHADAMES. ('83). A soft satin with a diagonal grain.

ROSADIMOI. ('20). A corruption of the name 'Ras de St. Maur', and later called Radzimir.

ROSILLE DE SOIE. ('40). A dead silk with pattern in network strewed with flowers in monochrome.

RUM-SWIZZLE. ('50). An Irish frieze made of undyed wool.

RUSSELL CORD. ('90's). Resembling a coarse corded alpaca; used for linings.

RUSSIAN CREPE. ('81). A species of mat cloth coarsely interwoven.

RUSSIAN VELVET. ('92). A light woollen of even grain and checked, the stripes being small round raised twists of a different colour from the foundation.

SARCENET. A thin kind of silk textile, plain or twilled.

SATEEN. ('78). A cotton textile with satin face.

SATIN. A silk twill of very glossy appearance on the face and dull at the back. Usually seven out of every eight threads of the warp are visible, whereas in other silk stuffs each half of the warp is raised alternately. Its brilliancy is augmented by dressing.

SATIN ANTOINETTE. ('34). Satin with white ground and satin-shaded rays, and small detached bouquets of flowers.

SATIN BLONDE. ('33). Satin flowered in white on coloured ground, resembling blonde lace upon satin.

SATIN CASHMERE. ('93). An all-wool fabric with soft silky surface, and uncrushable.

SATIN DE CHINE. ('50). A satin of silk and worsted.

SATIN DU BARRY. ('32). A satin with alternate stripes of black and figuring.

SATIN DUCHESSE. ('70). A thick plain satin, very durable.

SATIN ESMERALDA. ('37). A rich satin of various colours, with applications of velvet of a darker shade.

SATIN FONTANGE. ('41). A satin with broad stripes, alternately white and coloured.

SATIN FOULARD. ('48). A silk stuff satined either in stripes or spots.

SATIN JEAN. ('70). A finely twilled cotton textile with a satiny gloss.

SATIN MERINO. ('46). A textile, the right side of which is finer and more silky than cashmere; the wrong side resembles plush.

SATIN MERV. ('86). A broad-ribbed satin.

SATIN MERVEILLEUX. ('81). A soft twilled satin resembling thick rich surah, but with a brighter face and duller back.

SATIN MONTESPAN. ('33). A rich silk of a dead white ground, striped in large squares.

SATIN POMPADOUR. ('35). A satin with white ground embroidered in coloured flowers.

SATIN TURC. ('68). A soft and very brilliant woollen textile.

SATIN VELOUTÉ. ('37). A satin 'as rich as velvet and as supple as muslin'.

SATIN VICTORIA. ('54). A woollen material resembling silk, with narrow stripes.

SATINÉ PLAYÉ. ('73). A striped cotton and wool mixture, the face very satiny and the stripes twilled.

SATINET. ('16). A textile of silk and wool with a satin stripe.

SCOTIA SILK. ('09). A textile of cotton and silk, resembling broché.

SERGE. A loosely woven twilled material, the warp of worsted, the woof of wool.

SERGE ROYALE. ('71). Of flax and wool, with bright silky appearance.

SHAGREEN. A silk with a grained ground.

SHALLOON. A loosely woven worsted stuff, twilled on both sides.

SHANTUNG. ('70's). A thin soft China silk, undyed.

SICILIENNE. A fine quality of poplin, the warp of silk, the woof of cashmere wool.

SILESIA. A fine brown glazed linen, used for linings.

SILISTRIENNE. ('68). A wool and silk textile of firm texture.

SILK DAMASCENE. ('76). A silk and wool textile with fine stripes of wool and satin alternating.

SOYEUX LINSEY. ('69). A light and brilliant woollen poplin.

STRASBURG CLOTH. ('81). Resembles corduroy without the plush surface.

SULTANE. ('66). A fabric of silk and mohair, resembling fine alpaca, in alternate stripes of clear or satin (or chiné).

SURAH. ('73). A soft and brilliant Indian silk, twilled on both sides, more substantial than foulard.

SYLVESTRINE. ('31). A material imitating silk, manufactured from wood.

TABBINET. A watered poplin.

TABBY. A coarse kind of silk taffeta, thick, glossy and watered. Moiré antique is a tabby.

TAFFETA. A thin glossy silk of a wavy lustre.

TAFFETA COUTIL. ('47). A mixture of silk and cotton, in blue or lilac stripes on white ground.

TAFFETALINE. ('76). Mohair.

TAMATIVE. ('63). A light material resembling grenadine, but thicker.

TAMISE. ('76). A soft woollen textile with a little silk in it.

TARLATAN. ('30's). A thin, gauze-like muslin, much stiffened.

TATTERSALL. ('91). A cloth in vivid checks resembling a horse cloth.

TERRENDAM ('06). An Indian muslin.

TERRY VELVET. A silk textile having a fine corded surface on the face. It has no resemblance to velvet. The Terry Velvet of the first quarter of the century appears to have been an uncut velvet.

THE UNION. ('15). A mixture of silk and cotton, shot.

THIBET CLOTH. ('74). A soft, thick, flannel-like cloth with long goat's hair on the surface.

TIFFANY. A thin, semi-transparent silk, resembling gauze.

TIGRINE. ('34). A mixture of silk and cashmere resembling twilled satin, very soft and supple.

TOILE DE SOIE. ('98). A thick silk and cotton fabric shot of two colours, having a thick rib.

TOILONETTE. ('10). A fine woollen material somewhat like merino.

TRIPOLINE. ('74). A twilled satin Turc.

TULLE. A fine silk net.

TULLE ARACHNÉ. ('31). A very clear tulle embroidered in light patterns with a mixture of gold and silk.

TURCO POPLINNES. ('67). A woollen fabric with a soft silky sheen.

TURIN GAUZE. A gauze woven of raw silk.

TURIN VELVET. ('60). A textile of silk and wool, imitating terry.

TUSSORE. ('69). A textile, half wool, half cotton, looking like poplin. Later the name invariably indicated tussore silk.

TUSSORE SILK. A soft raw Indian silk textile.

UMRITZUR. ('80). A rough-surfaced material of camel's hair, soft and light, in art colours; introduced by Liberty & Co.

UNION. A stout material, being a mixture of linen and cotton much dressed and stiffened.

VALENCIA. ('50). A cloth used for riding habits.

VALENTINE. ('33). A slight, shaded silk material.

VELETINE. ('12). A small figured silk textile.

VELLUTO. ('83). A cloth imitating Genoa velvet.

VELOURS BROCHÉ. A satin pattern on velvet ground.

VELOURS DE LAINE. ('94). Velvet stripes or checks on a woollen ground.

VELOURS DU NORD. ('81). A black satin ground shot with a colour, and covered with velvet flowers stamped in relief.

VELOURS EPINGLÉ. Terry velvet.

VELVET IMPERATRICE. ('60). A kind of dark terry velvet.

VELVETEEN. ('80's). An imitation of silk velvet, the pile being silk on a cotton back.

VERANO CLOTH. ('80). A kind of ribbed cretonne.

VERGLAS. ('94). A moiré with a peculiar watering resembling reflections on water.

VICTORIA CREPE. A crepe made entirely of cotton.

VICTORIA SILK. ('93). A silk and wool mixture for petticoats, 'guaranteed to rustle.'

VICUGNA. ('77). A very soft textile, generally plain, of llama wool.

VIGOGNE. An all-wool cloth, twilled, in neutral colours.

VOILE. ('85). A very thin woollen stuff; see Nun's veiling.

WINSEY. A cotton and wool mixture resembling linsey.

YEDDO CREPE. ('80). A cotton textile, thick as linen but soft; printed in Chinese designs.

YOKOHAMA CREPE. ('80). A cotton textile printed in stripes with Japanese floral designs.

ZEPHYR. ('80's). A light, fine gingham, thin and silky, often with coloured warp and finer weft.

ZIBELLINE. ('56). Between a barège and a paramatta; used for mourning.

GLOSSARY OF CERTAIN TECHNICAL TERMS

AGRAFE. An ornamental clasp on hook.

BASQUE. The prolongation of a corsage below the waist-line. In the second half of the century it is loosely used as a synonym for Basquine.

BASQUINE. The extension below the waist-line of the material forming the corsage, either cut in one with it, or applied as separate pieces.

BERET. A flat hat, usually made entirely of velvet, with wide overhanging brim; also used to describe a sleeve which has a somewhat similar shape, being very short and excessively wide in diameter.

BIAS. Material cut on the cross.

BOUFFANT. A puffed-out part of a dress.

BOUILLON. A puffed-out applied trimming.

BOURRELET. A pad inserted into a dress.

BRANDEBOURG. A braid trimming consisting of a transverse cord with acorn tassels; anglicé, 'frog'.

BRETELLE. A strap-shaped trimming.

BUGLES. A trimming of cylindrical glass beads.

CHICORÉE. Material cut with its edge unhemmed.

JOCKEY. A flat trimming applied over the outer part of the shoulder, having its lower border free.

LANGUETTE. A flat applied trimming shaped like a tongue.

MANCHERON. A short, flat oversleeve.

MATILDAS. The velvet ornaments round the hem of a dress. Also applied (in the '40's) to a bunch of flowers worn in the hair.

PASSEMENTERIE. Flat trimmings of braid.

PINKING. The unhemmed edge of material cut in a series of minute 'V's.

QUILLING. Small round pleatings used as trimming.

ROLLIO. A trimming of material rolled lengthwise into a narrow tubular shape.

ROULEAU. A trimming of material loosely puffed into tubular shape.

ROBIN. A kind of trimming on the front of a dress (vide description of stomacher front dresses, Chapter 2).

VOLAN. A flounce; especially used for small flounce-like trimmings applied elsewhere than on the skirt (e.g. at the shoulder or wrist).

NOTE:

HIGH DRESS indicates a dress reaching up to the throat.

HALF-HIGH DRESS reaches nearly to the base of the neck.

LOW DRESS exposes the upper part of the bosom.

EN COEUR. A dress with a heart-shaped front opening; that is, the sides of the opening curve inwards as they descend.

HALF DRESS ('demi-toilette'). The nearest modern equivalent would be a dress for an afternoon social function.

DINNER DRESS. The dinner hour, during the first part of the century, was an afternoon rather than an evening function, five or six o'clock, at which a hat was worn with low dress; by the '40's the hour was becoming steadily later, and a 'dinner dress' was a semi-evening costume, with an evening headdress.

FULL DRESS was reserved for evening functions and was always 'low neck' except perhaps in 'out of the Season'.

It was not uncommon for the names of persons, either historical or from fiction, to be attached to passing fashions. Usually there was some sort of justification; the mode copies a style made familiar by well-known portraits or some fashionable actress of the day.

A list of such names with their dates will enable the reader to see what historical periods were in vogue as revivals in the first half of the nineteenth century, while the names of contemporaries indicate the source of other fashions.

Agnes Sorel, 1409–1450. Mistress of Charles VII.

Ann Boleyn, 1507–1536. Second wife of Henry VIII.

Catherine de Medici, 1519–1589.

Marie Stuart, Queen of Scots, 1542–1587.

Gabrielle d'Estrées, 1517–1599. Mistress of Henri IV.

Marquise de Sevigné, 1626–1696.

Madame de Maintenon. Wife of Louis XIV, 1635–1719.

Madame de Montespan, 1641–1707. Mistress of Louis XIV.

Duchesse de Fontanges, 1680.

Marie Camargo, 1710–1770.

Madame de Pompadour, 1721–1764. Mistress of Louis XV.

Madame du Barry, 1746–1793. Mistress of Louis XV.

Empress Josephine, 1763–1814.

Charlotte Corday, 1768–1793.

General Bolivar, 1783–1830.

Empress Marie Louise, 1791–1847.

Princess Charlotte, 1796–1817.

Taglioni, 1804–1884. A famous dancer.

'Clarissa Harlowe' and 'Pamela' (from Richardson's novels). 1740 and 1748.

'Crispin'. A character from an Italian comedy, 1654, with traditional dress.

'Roxalane'. A character from *The Sultan*, an eighteenth century farce revived in 1806 and subsequently.

Marino Falièro, by Lord Byron, 1820.

Ipsiboe. A romance by Vicomte d'Arlincourt, 1821.

Amy Robsart, by Victor Hugo, 1828.

Hernani by Victor Hugo, 1830.

Esmeralda, by Victor Hugo, 1838.

Norma, opera by Bellini, 1831.

GLOSSARY OF OBSOLETE COLOUR NAMES

(The bracketed numbers indicate the approximate years when such terms were first used. The second column indicates the corresponding modern colour-number in the Dictionary of Colours, issued by the British Colour Council.)

Obsolete Name and Date.	Modern Name and British Colour Council Number.
APOLLO. (1823).	A BRIGHT GOLD.
AUBERGINE. (1892).	'A RICH REDDISH BROWN.'
AURORA. (1809).	CHILLI. 98.
AURORA. (1829).	SHELL-PINK. 206.
AVENTURINE. (1831).	MURREY. 135.
BAGDAD. (1886).	'A PINKISH BRICK-DUST.'
BALTIC. (1887).	Identical with EAU DE NIL.
BIRD OF PARADISE. (1830).	STRAW. 51.
BLÉ TURC. (1866).	A VERY DEEP MAIZE.
BLUE:	
Adelaide. (1831).	STEEL BLUE. 44.
Amelie. (1832).	BUNTING AZURE. 131.
Azure, Aetherial or Celestial. ('20's)	SKY BLUE. 162.
Barbel. (1818).	POMPADOUR. 194.
Clarence. (1811).	SAXE. 45.
Corinth. (1833).	CALAMINE. 167.
de Berri. (1831).	FORGET-ME-NOT. 184.
de France. (1840).	ADONIS BLUE. 85.
De Roi. (1835).	DELPHINIUM. 195.
Eugenie. (1860).	PALE CORNFLOWER. 217.
Gobelin or Goblin. (1887).	'A SHADE OF GREY-BLUE.'
Marie Louise. (1812).	CALAMINE. 167.
Mexican. (1817).	STEEL BLUE. 44.
Mexico. (1868).	LARKSPUR. 196.
Napoleon. (1853).	LARKSPUR. 196.
Niagara. (1887).	'Between PEACOCK and TURQUOISE.'
Porcelain. (1840).	WEDGWOOD. 215.
Raymond. (1834).	POWDER BLUE. 193.
Victoria. (1840).	ALICE BLUE. 43.

Obsolete Name and Date.	Modern Name and British Colour Council Number.
BOUFFON. (1893).	'A SHADE DARKER THAN EAU DE NIL.'
BROWN:	
Alma. (1854).	COPPER-BROWN.
Bismarck. (1867).	NUTMEG. 168.
Bois de Rose. (1866).	LIGHT REDDISH BROWN.
Devonshire Brown. (1812).	MASTIC. 167.
Egyptian Brown. (1809).	MACE. 73.
Orleans Brown. (1832).	ROSE BEIGE. 18.
CAMELEON. (1843).	RASPBERRY, 155, shot with BLUE.
CAMELOPARD. (1828).	FRENCH BEIGE. 166.
CARMELITE. (1872).	A REDDISH PLUM.
CASTOR. (1872).	A BROWNISH GREY.
CENDRE DE ROSE. (1872).	'GREY WITH A PINK SHADE.'
CLEOPATRA. (1893).	'THE NEW NAME FOR MAGENTA.'
CONGO. (1883).	'A RICH BURNISHED COPPERY GOLD.'
CREMORNE. (1872).	'A FAINT REDDISH BROWN.'
DUST OF PARIS. (1851).	ECRU. 63.
DUST OF RUINS. (1822).	SQUIRREL.
EAU DE GANGES. (1846).	GAULT G. 18771.
EMINENCE. (1829).	CRUSHED STRAWBERRY. 158.
EMINENCE. (1893).	'VIOLET WITH A DASH OF DEP RED.'
ESTERHAZY. (1822).	SILVER GREY. 153.
FLEXINE. (1892).	REDDISH SLATE.
FLORENTINE. (1867).	'YELLOW WITH A BRONZE TINT.'

439

Obsolete Name and Date.	Modern Name and British Colour Council Number.	Obsolete Name and Date.	Modern Name and British Colour Council Number.
FLY'S WING. (1843).	GRAPHITE. 155.	MODENA RED. (1828).	FUCHSIA. 199.
GREEN:		MONTEBELLO. (1872).	A DARK GARNET.
Adriatic. (1873).	'A BLUISH GREEN.'	MORONE. (1811).	PEONY RED. 37.
American. (1830).	MISTLETOE. 9.	NACCARAT. (1800).	TANGERINE. 55.
Azoff. (1857).	BETWEEN MISTLETOE, 9, and ALMOND, 10.	NARCORAT. (1854).	DARK CLARET.
		NAVARINO SMOKE. (1828).	'A SHADE LIGHTER THAN LONDON SMOKE.'
Bosphore. (1854).	SEA GREEN.		
Chinese. (1830).	MALACHITE. 23.		
Corinthe. (1854).	LIGHT GREEN.	OISEAU. (1837).	CHARTREUSE YELLOW 75.
Gas-Green. (1868).	DIOPTASE. 203.		
Indian. (1831).	OPALINE. 201.	OPHELIA. (1868).	A RED VIOLET.
Metternich. (1868).	Between BEETLE, 24 and BOTTLE-GREEN 25.	ORPHELIAN. (1862).	CLARET. 36.
		OXFORD AND CAMBRIDGE MIXTURE. (1885).	'TWO SHADES OF IRON GREY.'
Pomona. (1811).	SEA GREEN. 102.	PALESTINE. (1883).	A PINK MAUVE.
Spring. (1810).	COSSACK GREEN. 105.	PALISANDRE. (1835).	PURPLE BROWN. 136.
GRENAT. (1868).	BURGUNDY. 40.	PENSEE. (1829).	A DARK PURPLE.
HAVANNAH. (1860).	Between CINNAMON, 204, and OLIVE-BROWN, 205.	PRUNE DE MONSIEUR. (1871).	PANSY. 180.
ISABELLA. (1821).	CREAM.	PRUNE DUMAS. (1883).	A DARK-BLUE VIOLET.
JAPANESE ROSE. (1826).	CRUSHED STRAWBERRY. 158.	PUCE. (1830).	AMETHYST. 28.
		PUNCH. (1884).	A SHADE OF BLUE-GREY SMOKE.
JAQUEMAR. (1898).	'A RICH SHADE OF RED.'		
		RAMONEUR. (1833).	BRAZIL NUT. 128.
JOSIE. (1872).	'A LIGHT YELLOWISH OLIVE.'	RED: CAROUBIER. (1869).	PEONY. 37.
LAVENDER. (1824).	Between HELIOTROPE 178 and PARMA VIOLET, 216.	RESEDA. (1872).	A GREYER TINT THAN MODERN RESEDA.
		ROSANILINE. (1859).	The first ANILINE DYE.
LAVINIA. (1830).	WEDGWOOD. 215.	ROSE DE PARNASSE. (1830).	CYCLAMEN PINK. 33.
LILAC:		RUSSIAN FLAME. (1811).	PALE MASTIC. 167.
Grey Lilac. (1836).	VIOLET GREY. 41.		
Princess Elizabeth Lilac. (1812).	ALICE BLUE. 43.	SAMSON. (1893).	GRASS GREEN.
Red Lilac. (1832).		SOLFERINO. (1860).	FUCHSIA. 199.
LONDON DUST. (1830)	HELIOTROPE, 178.	TERRE DE CUBA. (1833).	ROSE BEIGE. 18.
LONDON MUD. (1827).	FRENCH GREY. 188.	TERRE D'EGYPTE. (1824).	BRICK RED. 125.
	'A DULL DARK BROWN.'	TERRE DE POLOGNE. (1831).	RUST. 58. 'A DEEP SHADE OF YELLOW BORDERING ON BROWN.'
LONDON SMOKE. (1836).	SQUIRREL. 187.		
LUCIFER. (1880).		TILLEUL. (1877).	SKY GREEN. 101.
MAGENTA. (1859).	BRICK DUST.	TOURTERELLE. (1829).	MUSHROOM. 181.
	Nearer RASPBERRY, 159, than the modern Magenta.	TROCADERO. (1824).	Between SPECTRUM ORANGE, 57, and FLAME, 95.
MANDARIN. (1877).	BRIGHT ORANGE.		
MARRON. (1873).	CHESTNUT. 60.	VIOLET. (prior to aniline dyes).	PARMA VIOLET. 216.
MARSH MALLOW. (1829).	CROCUS, 177, or OLD ROSE, 167.		
MARYLAND. (1873).	NUTRIA. 139.		

AUTHORITIES

PERIODICALS:

The Lady's Magazine. 1800–1839.
The Gallery of Fashion. 1800–1802.
The Ladies' Monthly Museum. 1800–1831.
Le Beau Monde. 1806.
La Belle Assembleé. (Monthly). 1806–1863.
Ackerman's Repository. 1809–1829.
The British Lady's Magazine. 1815.
Le Journal des Modes. 1819.
The Ladies' Pocket Magazine. 1828–1838.
The World of Fashion. 1828–1871.
The Court Magazine. 1832–1836.
The Royal Lady's Magazine. 1832.
The Ladies' Cabinet. 1832–1855.
The Maids', Wives', & Widows' Magazine. 1832–1833.
The Weekly Belle Assembleé. 1833–1835.
Punch. 1841–1899.
Mrs. Leslie's Magazine. 1843.
Illustrated London News. 1844–1899.
Nouveau Beau Monde. 1845–1846.
The Pictorial Times. 1846.
London & Paris Ladies' Magazine of Fashion. 1847, 1866–1871.
The Lady's Newspaper. 1847–1852.
Ladies' Gazette of Fashion. 1847–1848.
Graham's Magazine. 1849.
Godey's Lady's Book. 1849, 1850, 1865, 1870, 1876.
The Ladies' Companion. 1850–1859.
The Illustrated Times. 1854–1857.
Englishwoman's Domestic Magazine. 1854–1879.
Magazin des Demoiselles. 1856–1858.
The Ladies' Treasury. 1858–1894.
La Mode Illustré. 1862–1872.
The Queen. 1863–1897.
The Young Englishwoman, 1864–1876.
Fun. 1866–1876.
The Young Ladies' Journal. 1867–1898.
Tinsley's Magazine. 1867–1869.
Young Ladies of Great Britain. 1869.
London Journal. 1869.
The Graphic. 1869–1899.
Journal des Demoiselles. 1870.

Bow Bells. 1870–1873.
Journal des Modes. 1874–1875.
Judy. 1874–1876.
The Milliners' & Dressmakers' Gazette. 1874–1875.
Cassell's Family Magazine. 1876–1897.
Sylvia's Home Journal. 1878, 1880, 1882, 1883, 1893.
Ladies' Gazette of Fashion. 1879.
Le Follet. 1879.
Girls' Own Paper. 1880–1899.
Burlington Magazine. 1881.
Letts' Magazine. 1883–1885.
The Lady. 1885–1894.
The Woman's World. 1887–1888. 1889.
The Gentlewoman. 1890–1894.
Fashions of To-day. 1892–1898.
Home Notes. 1894–1896.
Home Chat. 1895.
Woman at Home. 1895–1899.
Woman's Life. 1896.
The Ladies' Realm. 1897–1899.

ILLUSTRATIONS WITHOUT TEXT:

The Fashions of London & Paris (R. Phillips). 1800–1810. (The descriptive text of many of these occurs in the corresponding volumes of *The Lady's Magazine.*)
Townsend's Monthly Selection of Parisian Costumes. 1826–1833. (With brief description).

BOOKS OF THE TOILET AND DRESSMAKING.

The Elegance of Fashion & the Mirror de la Mode. 1803.
Records of Fashion & Court Elegance. Mrs. Fiske. 1807.
The Lady's Economical Assistant, or the Art of Cutting Out. 1808.
The Mirror of the Graces or the English Lady's Costume. 1811.
A Picture of the Changes of Fashion. D. S. Mackie. 1818.
The Art of Beauty. 1825.
The Young Lady's Book. (Vizatelly, Branston & Co.), 1829.

Female Beauty. Mrs. Walker. 1837.
Exercises for Ladies. Donald Walker. 1837.
The Young Lady's Friend. 1837.
The Ladies' Pocket Book of Etiquette. 1838.
The Art of Dress or Guide to the Toilette. Chas. Tilt. 1839.
The Female Instructor. Esther Copley. 1840.
Handbook of the Toilet. 1841.
Hints on Etiquette, by a Lady of Rank. 1843.
Handbook of Millinery. Mrs. Howell (London). 1847.
Journal of Design & Manufactures. 1849–1851.
Dress as a Fine Art. Mrs. Merrifield. 1854.
The Corset & the Crinoline. 1867.
How to Dress on £15 a Year, as a Lady, by a Lady. 1873.
How to Dress Well on a Shilling a Day, by Sylvia. 1876.
Art & Ornament in Dress. Charles Blanc. 1877.
The Dictionary of Needlework. Caulfield & Saward. 1882.
The Science of Dress. Ada Ballin. 1885.
The Elements of Modern Dressmaking. Miss Davis. 1896.
Practical Dress Cutting. E. M. F. Carlisle. 1899.

PRINTS:
by Gilray, G. Cruikshank, Woodward, Heath, etc.

PHOTOGRAPHS:
A collection of about 3000 contemporary photographs from the late '50's to the end of the century.
Cartoons of notable contemporaries from the *Whitehall Review*. 1876–1884.

MEMOIRS AND JOURNALS:
Mrs. Calvert, Susan Sibbald, Mary Frampton, Gronow, Creevey, etc.

CONTEMPORARY NOVELS AND MAGAZINES, ILLUSTRATED.

TRADE PUBLICATIONS:
Open Spaces (Messrs. Burberry, Ltd.).
Catalogues by Liberty & Co., etc.

SECONDARY AUTHORITIES:
The Dawn of the 19th Century. Ashton, 5th. ed. 1806.
Social Life under the Regency. Ashton. 1899.
The History of Fashion in France. Challamel. 1882.
Fashion in Paris in the 19th Century. O. Uzanne. 1901.
Modes & Manners of the 19th Century. Fischel & von Beohn. 1927.
Le Costume. Hottenroth. N.D.
Le Pantalon feminin. P. Dufay. 1906.
Spencer Walpole's History of England. 1878.

CHRONOLOGICAL TABLE

1800. Value of the £—£3 17 0. Income Tax, 2/-.

1801. Jacquard loom invented.

1802. (March). Peace with France. Duty on imported wool, 5/3 a cwt.

1803. War resumed.

1805. Trafalgar.

1808. Peninsular War.

1810. George III's Jubilee.

1811. Regency of the Prince of Wales.

1813. Import duty on wool, 6/8 a cwt.

1814. Peace celebrations.

1815. Waterloo.

1816. Income Tax abolished. Marriage of Princess Charlotte.

1817. Death of Princess Charlotte.

1819. Birth of Princess Victoria. Duty on imported wool, 56/- a cwt.

1820. Accession of George IV.

1822. King's visit to Scotland. Duty on imported wool reduced to 8/6 a cwt.

1824. Trade revival; reduction of silk duties.

1825. Value of the £—£2 16 4.

1830. Accession of William IV.

1831. Tax on printed calicoes repealed.

1832. The Reform Act. 'The income of the upper and middle class have increased since 1815 by 50 per cent. and purchasing power by 80 per cent.'

1837. Accession of Queen Victoria.

1839. The Eglington Tournament.

1840. Queen Victoria's marriage.

1841. *Punch* started. Price of cotton cloth fallen 50 per cent. in 12 years.

1843. Income Tax 7d.

1845. Duty on cotton repealed.

1846. Corn Laws repealed.

1848. Pre-Raphaelite Brotherhood started.

1850. Value of the £—£1 15 2.

1851. Great Exhibition. Visit of Mrs. Bloomer to England.

1853. Marriage of Napolcon III to the Empress Eugenie.

1854. Crimean War started. Income Tax 1/2.

1856. War ended. Income Tax 1/4.

1860. Aniline dyes (Magenta and Solferino) introduced. French treaty removing duty on foreign silk goods.

1861. Death of the Prince Consort.

1862–4. Lancashire cotton famine owing to American Civil War.

1863. Marriage of the Prince of Wales to Princess Alexandra.

1864. Garibaldi's visit to London. Income Tax 7d.

1870–1. Franco-Prussian War. End of the Second Empire. Death of Charles Dickens (July '70).

1872. Income Tax 4d.

1875. Value of the £—£2 1 10.

1878. The 'Aesthetic Movement'.

1880. Income Tax 5d.

1881. Gilbert & Sullivan's Opera *Patience*.

1882. Egyptian War.

1887. The first Jubilee.

1892. Death of the Duke of Clarence. Guelph Exhibition in London.

1893. Marriage of the Duke of York (afterwards George V) to Princess May.

1894. Lehner's invention of artificial silk. Du Maurier's *Trilby*.

1895. Death of M. Worth, the dress designer.

1897. The Diamond Jubilee.

1899. (Oct.). South African War started.

1900. Value of the £—£1 13 0.

NOTE ON ENGLISH MUSEUMS CONTAINING NINETEENTH-CENTURY COSTUMES

ALTHOUGH Costume is the oldest of the Arts and evokes a far wider interest than any other, it is not as yet considered of sufficient importance in this country to have a museum dedicated solely to its study. Such museums as devote space to exhibiting old dresses do so often with obvious reluctance and display only those which may attract a cursory glance on account of their being pretty or quaint, or because they once adorned some notable person. Yet one does not find, say, a geological museum exhibiting fossils for their prettiness or because they were picked up by a duchess.

A costume museum, if it is to be something better than a mere mausoleum for old clothes, needs to be organised scientifically. Each specimen should be there for some purpose, illustrating either social or technical change. It should, in a word, be typical. The ordinary, commonplace dress is therefore of greater scientific value than one which is 'almost unique' or atypical. Technical features should be adequately displayed. Groups illustrating aspects of social life should be assembled. Costumes distinctive of social classes and occupations are also important. The guiding principle should be to collect those specimens which will interest posterity and faithfully portray the past.

It is perhaps necessary to add that modern methods of illumination would improve existing conditions in our museums, and specimens need sufficient and accurate labelling. The description 'Silk dress, mid-Victorian' would correspond to marking a neolithic arrow-head 'Stone implement, prehistoric'. It lacks precision.

The existing museums in this country labour under difficulties not of their own making and attempts are being made, in many cases, to overcome them. The only solution is, of course, a national museum dedicated solely to Costumes and adequately supplied with funds: but it seems that only nations poorer than England can afford that luxury.

A list of those museums which I have visited may be of use to others. I have, I think, explored every cupboard in them, sometimes discovering very important specimens, and sometimes moths. A note of the chief items contained in each (at the time of my visit) is given. I have only to add that in all cases the various curators have been most obliging in allowing me to examine their charges.

1. *The Victoria and Albert Museum, South Kensington.*

The nucleus of the nineteenth century section is the Talbot Hughes collection presented by Messrs. Harrods in 1913. About 70 dresses of the period 1795-1925 are shown on dummies; some thousands of items and accessories are stored but can be seen on request.

The specimens displayed are now accurately dated but the descriptions of materials are slight. There are many gaps, especially in headgear; the commonplace dress is hardly represented; few accessories or underclothing are shown.

2. *The Bethnal Green Museum.*

A collection supplementary to the above and of about the same size. Many of the specimens are in poor condition and badly set out. In both these 'national' museums the illumination is deplorable (a fault with most of our museums); it is astonishing that no catalogue is obtainable.

3. *The London Museum, Lancaster House, St. James'.*

About 100 dresses of the nineteenth century are displayed and a large number are in store. The last quarter of the century is well represented and special costumes with historical associations form a feature. A catalogue is available.

444

4. *Norwich. Strangers Hall.*

20 dresses, 10 bonnets. A mourning dress of 1817; a pink satin dress hat (about 1810); a Dolly Varden hat (1871); a whip parasol and two 'uglies' are specially interesting.

Norwich. Bridewell.

An important collection of Norwich shawls.

5. *Birmingham. Museum and Art Gallery.*

About 30 dresses; 10 bonnets.

A printed cotton dress (1805-1809) with narrow pleating over the breast; a white spotted muslin (1800-1803) with a boned front lining to the bodice; and a fine collection of Empire combs.

6. *Leicester.*

About six dresses, especially a red silk and wool gauze evening dress (1816); two early child's hats (1807); a child's 'bibi' bonnet (1834); a Nankin spencer (1809).

7. *Colchester.*

About ten good dresses of the '70's.

8. *Halifax. Bankfield Museum.*

Some six dresses, including a claret coloured crape (1824); a few bonnets and hats of the '70's and '80's. An interesting dyer's pattern book.

9. *Leeds.*

A pelisse (1824).

10. *Manchester. Platt Hall.*

An excellent collection, admirably displayed, of some 90 dresses, including types not to be seen elsewhere, such as a blouse dress and a dress en blouse of 1822; a Japanese printed cotton of 1835; a yellow cotton embroidered in chain-stitch worsted (1825). A number of bonnets, including one of 1820, two bibi bonnets and a capote of the early '30's, two hair nets (1803) and two superb berets of 1827 and 1829. I have only seen one other, at Exeter. This collection is rapidly increasing and now rivals any in the country.

11. *Cardiff Museum.*

About a dozen dresses, mostly country made printed cotton, of the end of the '20's. A cerise velvet evening dress (1837), some six bonnets of the '50's and '60's, and two crinolines.

12. *Cheltenham. Municipal Museum.*

Ten dresses of the '70's and '80's. Five crinolines and four bustles and a number of parasols.

13. *Hereford Museum.*

Some 60 dresses of which a remarkable specimen in printed velvet (1835) is noteworthy. A good many accessories including shawls and corsets. This collection has recently been much enlarged and rivals the Manchester collection in interest.

14. *Northampton.*

About a dozen dresses; 8 hats and bonnets, including a circular Leghorn hat embroidered with chip and straw (1810); a flat 'saucer hat' (1867). An excellent collection of shoes and boots, mainly of the second half of the century.

15. *Exeter. Royal Albert Memorial Museum.*

14 dresses, notably one of the '20's in cashmere trimmed with ostrich feathers together with muff and pelerine; a silk chintz-pattern dress ('20's); a green satin day dress with cape ('30's); a red silk dress (1835); a dozen bonnets, especially a superb green velvet (1835); a black velvet beret (1828); and a bonnet trimmed with cockchafers ('80's). An early pair of pantaloons is a rare specimen.

16. *Hull. The Municipal Museum.*

About a dozen dresses, mostly on loan.

17. *Bristol. Museum and Art Gallery.*
      A collection is now in process of formation.

18. *The Abbey Folk Museum. New Barnet.*
      Contains a considerable number of dresses but at present space does not permit of their being displayed.

19. *Blackmore Museum, Salisbury.*
      Contains a number of examples of dated wedding dresses, and other items.

INDEX

456